Synthesizes and integrates rigorous and relevant strategy material

The book offers a mix of classic and contemporary content—strategy material that has stood the test of time (e.g., Porter's five forces model, the resource-based view) as well as up-to-date strategy material and current research (e.g., dynamic capabilities, the triple bottom line). It also includes student-accessible coverage of strategic management research drawn from both academic journals and best-selling business books. In every chapter, one section provides a critical evaluation, based on empirical research, of a specific theory or concept as it relates to competitive advantage.

 Uses up-to-date examples and discusses current topics within a global context

The book's current examples illustrate how companies apply strategy concepts in today's business world. Examples throughout the book and in the boxed Strategy Highlights reflect the global nature of competition and the importance of emerging economies. Additionally, a number of the in-text examples relate to sustainable strategy with a focus on "green" products and issues.

 Presents core concepts, frameworks, and techniques in a comprehensive yet concise way

While not compromising on the quality and grounding expected by instructors, the text is written in a student-friendly and engaging manner. This textbook will be an *enjoyable read* for students—clear, concise, and filled with examples from companies students know—while also providing the content and value-add that instructors expect.

 Offers high-quality cases, well integrated with textbook chapters

Instructors have varying needs for top-notch, up-to-date cases that are well-integrated with textbook content. This book offers three types of cases, to suit diverse needs. The **ChapterCases** (which begin and end each chapter) frame chapter content, and 12 **MiniCases** (following Chapter 12) present short case scenarios. Both types of case materials were researched and written by Frank T. Rothaermel. In addition, the book offers 30 **full-length Cases** (available through McGraw-Hill's custom-publishing *Create™* program). Half of these cases were researched and written by Frank Rothaermel specifically for the book, and half were selected from high-quality sources such as HBS Premier Cases, Darden, and Ivey. The full-length cases are supported with Case Teaching Notes, Case PowerPoints, and video cases, all developed by Professors Marne L. Arthaud-Day (Kansas State University) and Robert Porter (University of Central Florida), in close collaboration with Frank Rothaermel. All three types of case materials are **closely connected to chapter content**, for optimal teaching and learning, and all cases come with a set of questions.

FOR THE LATEST INFORMATION AND CURRENT UPDATES TO THE TEXTBOOK AND CASES, PLEASE VISIT THE AUTHOR AT:

www.ftrStrategy.com

McGraw-Hill *Connect® Management* is the **leading online assignment and assessment system for business courses**. This web-based solution enhances your efforts to make your classroom a place for **meaningful, engaging learning**. With *Connect Management*, you can track student progress with just a few clicks of the mouse, save time through automatic grading, and generate an unparalleled array of reports.

For students, *Connect* improves learning and retention by helping students prepare for class, master concepts, and review for exams.

The Instructor's site in Connect:

- Houses **powerful tools and features** that facilitate development and grading of assignments.

- Generates an unparalleled array of reports that enable instructors to **assess learning outcomes** for accreditation purposes.

- Offers **teaching notes**, including lecture outlines and exams, PPT slide guidance, small-group exercises, suggestions for end-of-chapter answers and discussion points, and notes on topic extensions in Connect interactive applications.

- Includes a rich online **Test Bank**, with 100–150 test questions per chapter, including both **multiple-choice** and **short-answer** questions.

- Provides **PowerPoint® slides** that build upon and extend coverage from the book, with **embedded video links**, optional small-group exercise slides, and notes on topics covered in *Connect* Interactive Applications.

And, to save you time, assessment of student responses **flows easily into your grade book.**

The Student's site in Connect:

- Includes a minimum of three unique **instantly graded *Interactive Applications*** per chapter that ask students to apply strategic management concepts to real-world scenarios.

Included in the Interactive Applications are:

- An **interactive video case** in every chapter, covering a key chapter learning objective. Contemporary video topics include business in China, pricing of water, use of solar energy, and global forces affecting the future of business.

- **Drag-and-drop interactive assignments** that allow students to actively engage the material for deeper understanding of key tools and applications presented in the chapters.

- **Chapter quizzes** for student review in preparation for course exams.

- **Templates for strategic financial analysis** and a "How to do a case analysis" guide, complete with financial ratios used to compare performance between firms.

- A **financial review activity**—for students who wish to *refresh* or *extend* their working knowledge of major financial measures in a strategic framework.

All ancillary content in **Connect Management** was developed by Professor Anne W. Fuller, from California State University, Sacramento, in close collaboration with Frank T. Rothaermel.

Strategic Management

CONCEPTS

McGraw-Hill
Irwin

Strategic Management

CONCEPTS

FRANK T. ROTHAERMEL

Georgia Institute of Technology

Mc
Graw
Hill **McGraw-Hill**
Irwin

McGraw-Hill
Irwin

STRATEGIC MANAGEMENT, CONCEPTS

Published by McGraw-Hill/Irwin, a business unit of The McGraw-Hill Companies, Inc., 1221 Avenue of the Americas, New York, NY, 10020. Copyright © 2013 by The McGraw-Hill Companies, Inc. All rights reserved. Printed in the United States of America. No part of this publication may be reproduced or distributed in any form or by any means, or stored in a database or retrieval system, without the prior written consent of The McGraw-Hill Companies, Inc., including, but not limited to, in any network or other electronic storage or transmission, or broadcast for distance learning.

Some ancillaries, including electronic and print components, may not be available to customers outside the United States.

This book is printed on acid-free paper.

1 2 3 4 5 6 7 8 9 0 DOW/DOW 1 0 9 8 7 6 5 4 3 2

ISBN   978-0-07-732445-2
MHID   0-07-732445-5

Vice president and editor-in-chief: *Brent Gordon*
Editorial director: *Paul Ducham*
Executive editor: *Michael Ablassmeir*
Executive director of development: *Ann Torbert*
Development editor II: *Laura Griffin*
Editorial coordinator: *Andrea Heirendt*
Vice president and director of marketing: *Robin J. Zwettler*
Marketing director: *Amee Mosley*
Senior marketing manager: *Michelle Heaster*
Vice president of editing, design, and production: *Sesha Bolisetty*
Lead project manager: *Harvey Yep*
Buyer II: *Debra R. Sylvester*
Designer: *Matt Diamond*
Senior photo research coordinator: *Jeremy Cheshareck*
Photo researcher: *Allison Grimes*
Senior media project manager: *Bruce Gin*
Cover design: *MicroArts Pvt Limited (http://microarts.biz/)*
Interior design: *Matt Diamond*
Typeface: *10/12 Times Roman*
Compositor: *Laserwords Private Limited*
Printer: *R. R. Donnelley*

Library of Congress Cataloging-in-Publication Data

Rothaermel, Frank T.
    Strategic management : concepts / Frank T. Rothaermel.
      p. cm.
    Includes index.
    ISBN-13: 978-0-07-732445-2 (alk. paper)
    ISBN-10: 0-07-732445-5 (alk. paper)
    1. Strategic planning. I. Title.
HD30.28.R6646 2013
658.4'012--dc23

2011045042

www.mhhe.com

Dedication

To my eternal family for their love, support, and sacrifice:
Kelleyn, Harris, Winston, Roman, and Adelaide

—Frank T. Rothaermel

FRANK T. ROTHAERMEL
Georgia Institute of Technology

Frank T. Rothaermel (PhD) is the Angel and Stephen M. Deedy Professor in the College of Management at the Georgia Institute of Technology. He is an Alfred P. Sloan Industry Studies Fellow, and also holds a National Science Foundation (NSF) CAREER award, which "is a Foundation-wide activity that offers the National Science Foundation's most prestigious awards in support of . . . those teacher-scholars who most effectively integrate research and education . . ." (NSF CAREER Award description).

Frank's research interests lie in the areas of strategy, innovation, and entrepreneurship. To inform his research he has conducted extensive field work and executive training with leading corporations such as Amgen, Daimler, Eli Lilly, GE Energy, GE Healthcare, Kimberly-Clark, Microsoft, McKesson, and NCR, among others. *Bloomberg Businessweek* named Frank one of Georgia Tech's Prominent Faculty in its national survey of business schools. The Kauffman Foundation views Frank as one of the world's 75 thought leaders in strategic entrepreneurship and innovation.

Frank has published over 25 articles in leading academic journals such as the *Academy of Management Journal, Academy of Management Review, Organization Science, Strategic Management Journal,* and others. Some of his academic articles are highly cited. Frank currently serves (or has served) on the editorial boards of the *Academy of Management Journal, Academy of Management Review, Strategic Management Journal,* and *Strategic Organization.* He regularly translates his research findings for practitioner audiences in articles in *Forbes, MIT Sloan Management Review, The Wall Street Journal,* and elsewhere.

He has received several recognitions for his research, including the Sloan Industry Studies Best Paper Award, the Academy of Management Newman Award, the Strategic Management Society Conference Best Paper Prize, the DRUID Conference Best Paper Award, and the Israel Strategy Conference Best Paper Prize, and he is the inaugural recipient of the Byars Faculty Excellence Award. Frank has extensive teaching experience at a number of institutions and programs, including Georgia Tech, Georgetown University, Michigan State University, and the University of Washington. He has received multiple teaching awards at the undergraduate and MBA levels.

Frank holds a PhD degree in strategic management from the University of Washington, an MBA from the Marriott School of Management at Brigham Young University, and an MA in economics from the University of Duisburg, Germany. He was a visiting professor at the University of St. Gallen, Switzerland, and an Erasmus Scholar at Sheffield Hallam University, UK. Professor Rothaermel is a member of the Academy of Management, the Industry Studies Association (Founding Member), and the Strategic Management Society.

PREFACE

The vision for this book is to provide students with core concepts, frameworks, and analysis techniques in strategy that will not only integrate their functional course offerings but also help them to become managers who make better strategic decisions. It is a research-based strategy text for the issues that managers face in a globalized and turbulent 21st century, blending theory, empirical research, and practical applications in a student-accessible form.

The competition in the strategy textbook market can be separated into two overarching categories: traditional strategy textbooks, which are the first-generation books (from the 1980s), and more recent, research-based strategy textbooks, which are the second-generation books (from the 1990s). This new textbook aims to be different—a third-generation strategy textbook, positioned to compete successfully with the primary first- and second-generation incumbents. The third-generation approach you will find in this book combines the student accessibility and application-oriented frameworks found in first-generation books with the strategy research in the second-generation books.

In this book, I synthesize and integrate theory, empirical research, and practical applications in a unique combination of rigor and relevance. With a single strong voice, the book weaves together classic and cutting-edge theory with in-chapter cases and strategy highlights, to demonstrate how companies gain and sustain competitive advantage. The strategic intent for the book is to combine quality and value with user-friendliness. The mental model I used throughout the process of writing and developing the project is Apple Inc.'s innovation approach, which tightly integrates different competencies to launch novel, but highly user-friendly products. I view this book, the different options for accompanying cases, and the additional instructor and student resources in much the same way.

In particular, this book is based on the following principles, each of which provides a value-added dimension for instructors or students, or both:

- *Synthesis and integration of rigorous and relevant strategy material.* For example, the book includes strategy material that has stood the test of time (such as the resource-based view and Porter's five forces model) as well as up-to-date strategy material and current research (such as the dynamic capabilities perspective and the triple bottom line).

    The book also includes *student-accessible coverage* of strategic management research. It draws on articles published in the leading academic journals (for instance, *Strategic Management Journal, Academy of Management Journal/Review, Organization Science, Management Science, Journal of Management,* and so on). Although academic theory and empirical research form the foundation of the text, I also have integrated insights from leading practitioner outlets (such as *Harvard Business Review, Sloan Management Review, California Management Review*) to enhance the application of concepts. To weave in current examples and developments, I draw on *The Wall Street Journal, The Economist, Bloomberg Businessweek, Fortune, Forbes,* and others. In sum, theory is brought to life via the embedded examples within each framework and concept.

- *The comprehensive yet concise presentation of core concepts, frameworks, and techniques.* Although comprehensive, the book does not include every single idea ever introduced to the strategy field. Many students don't read the assigned readings in their strategy textbooks because the books contain too much information, presented in a disjointed fashion. Many strategy books read more like a literature review, without addressing *what* the research findings mean and *why* they are important for managers. This jumble prevents students from seeing the bigger strategic picture. They may see the trees, but they fail to see the forest. In contrast, this textbook will be an *enjoyable read* for students—clear, concise, and filled with examples from companies today's students know—while at the same time providing the content and value-add that instructors expect. *It's one book with one voice!*

■ ***Combination of traditional and contemporary chapters.*** As a review of the chapter-contents listing will demonstrate (see the contents listing on pages xli–xlvi), the book includes the traditional chapters needed in the core strategy course. In addition, it includes three contemporary *standalone chapters* that reviewers have identified as providing additional value: Chapter 2 offers an overview of the strategic management process and the importance of vision, mission, and values, before the book addresses the topics of external and internal analysis. Chapter 5 neatly ends the analysis section of the book by providing five approaches to measuring firm performance and assessing competitive advantage. Chapter 7 addresses the important topics of innovation and strategic entrepreneurship as aspects of business strategy. For more information about those chapters, see the discussion in the upcoming "Unique Features and Pedagogy" section.

■ ***Up-to-date examples and discussion of current topics within a global context.*** The book has been written for today's students to reflect the turbulence and dynamism that they will face as managers. I have drawn on up-to-date examples to illustrate how companies apply strategy concepts in today's business world. Although this text contains a standalone chapter on *Global Strategy,* examples throughout the book reflect the global nature of competition and the importance of emerging economies such as the BRIC countries. Additionally, a number of the examples relate to sustainable strategy with a focus on "green" products and issues.

I also have drawn topics and examples from recent and current bestsellers, such as *Co-opetition; Hypercompetition; Innovator's Dilemma (and Solution); Predictably Irrational; The Long Tail; Wisdom of the Crowds; Built to Last; How the Mighty Fall; Why Smart Executives Fail;* and *The World Is Flat,* among others. I have included these ideas to expose students to topics that today's managers talk about. Being conversant with these concepts from business bestsellers will help today's students interview better and effortlessly join the discourse in the corporate world.

Having spoken to hundreds of students across the world, I want to minimize the frustration they express in seeing the same, out-of-date examples in so many of their (generic and boiler-plate) business-school textbooks.

■ ***Use of the AFI strategy framework.*** The book demonstrates that "less is more" through a focused presentation of the relevant strategy content using *A*nalysis, *F*ormulation, and *I*mplementation as a guiding framework. This model (see Exhibit 1.9 on page 20) integrates process schools of strategy (based on organization theory, psychology, and sociology) with content schools of strategy (based on economics). Process and content can be viewed as the "yin and yang" of strategy. Current strategy textbooks typically favor one or the other but do not integrate them, which leads to an unbalanced and incomplete treatment of strategic management. The AFI strategy strives for beauty through balance, which is lacking in most current strategy texts on the market. The model also emphasizes that gaining and sustaining competitive advantage is accomplished in an iterative and recursive fashion. The framework offers a repository for theoretical strategy knowledge that is well translated for student consumption, and it provides a toolkit for practicing managers.

■ ***High-quality cases, well integrated with textbook chapters.*** We all know that cases are a fundamental ingredient in teaching strategy. My interactions with colleagues, reviewers, and focus group participants in the course of writing and developing this book indicate varying instructor needs for top-notch, up-to-date cases that are well-integrated with the content presented. Within this book itself are two types of cases: **ChapterCases,** which begin and end each chapter, and an additional 12 **MiniCases** (following Chapter 12), all based on original research. The ChapterCases frame the chapter topic and content, while the MiniCases provide a decision scenario that a company's manager might face, and offer dynamic opportunities to apply strategy concepts in one or two class sessions. The case materials come with a set of questions to stimulate class discussion or provide guidance for written assignments. The instructor resources offer sample answers that apply chapter content to the cases.

I have taken pride in authoring *all* of the ChapterCases and MiniCases. This additional touch not only allows quality control but also ensures that chapter content and cases use one voice and are closely interconnected. For more description of the in-book cases, see the upcoming "Unique Features and Pedagogy" section. (In addition, full-length cases are available through McGraw-Hill's custom-publishing *Create*™ program. Among these are 15 full-length cases I authored or co-authored specifically to accompany this textbook.)

- *Direct applications of strategy to students' careers and lives.* The examples in the book discuss products and services from companies with which students are familiar. Use of such examples aids in making strategy relevant to students' lives and helps them internalize strategy concepts and frameworks.

  In addition, at the end of each chapter's homework materials is an innovative text feature, titled *my*Strategy, which personalizes strategy concepts through direct application of the chapter topic to students' lives. For example, questions asked in these sections include: *What is your positioning strategy in the job market? How will you differentiate yourself, and at what cost?* and *How much is an MBA worth to you?* These and similar questions are intended to help students think through strategic issues related to their budding careers.

UNIQUE FEATURES AND PEDAGOGY

As mentioned, the book contains three standalone chapters that set it apart from the competition. While some competitors may highlight one or the other topic, none has these three standalone chapters:

- **Chapter 2,** *The Strategic Management Process*—This chapter allows for a thorough discussion of the strategic management process, including the role of vision, mission, and values; strategic intent; customer versus product-oriented missions; the combination of intended and emergent strategies; and the importance of long-term success in anchoring a firm in ethical values.

- **Chapter 5,** *Competitive Advantage and Firm Performance*—This chapter looks at three traditional approaches to measure performance: economic value creation, accounting profitability, and shareholder value creation. It also looks at two holistic approaches: the balanced scorecard and the triple bottom line. Each of the five approaches is linked to a separate learning objective, enabling instructors to easily cover as many of the approaches as desired for their course and its goals. As the concluding chapter in Part 1, this chapter helps anchor the analysis content and prepares students with tools for the formulation chapters that follow.

- **Chapter 7,** *Business Strategy: Innovation and Strategic Entrepreneurship*—Driven by Schumpeter's "perennial gale of creative destruction," competition seems more heated than ever, with innovation playing a key role in gaining and sustaining competitive advantage. This chapter addresses various aspects of innovation, beginning with the industry life cycle and the modes of competition and business-level strategies at various stages in the life cycle. Using tools and concepts of strategic management, it explores four types of innovation, as well as the Internet as a disruptive force, paradigm changes, and hypercompetition. This chapter especially will engage students and provide much food for thought in their jobs and careers.

ChapterCases

Each chapter opens with a short case highlighting a strategic issue that a well-known company faced and relates that company to a concept to be taught in the chapter:

- The Premature Death of a Google Forerunner at Microsoft (Chapter 1, p. 3)
- Teach For America: Inspiring Future Leaders (Chapter 2, p. 31)
- Build Your Dreams (BYD) to Sidestep Entry Barriers (Chapter 3, p. 55)
- From Good to Great to Gone: The Rise and Fall of Circuit City (Chapter 4, p. 85)
- Assessing Competitive Advantage: Google vs. Microsoft (Chapter 5, p. 113)
- Trimming Fat at Whole Foods Market (Chapter 6, p. 139)
- From Encyclopedia Britannica to Encarta to Wikipedia (Chapter 7, p. 171)
- Refocusing GE: A Future of Clean-Tech and Health Care? (Chapter 8, p. 201)
- Facebook: From Dorm Room to Dominant Social Network (Chapter 9, p. 237)
- Hollywood Goes Global (Chapter 10, p. 269)
- Zappos: An Organization Designed to Deliver Happiness (Chapter 11, p. 301)
- HP's CEO Mark Hurd Resigns amid Ethics Scandal (Chapter 12, p. 333)

The end of each chapter returns to the ChapterCase. Here, we ask students to reconsider the case, applying concepts and information presented in the chapter, along with additional information about the focus company. Questions in the *"Consider This . . ."* section serve as good jumping-off points for class discussion.

Gaining & Sustaining Competitive Advantage Critical Analyses

Each chapter contains a section that puts one specific theory or concept "under the magnifying glass." The purpose is to critically evaluate if and how the theory or concept is linked to competitive advantage, the overarching goal in strategic management. In these sections, marked with a magnifying glass icon, we combine strategic management research with real-world observations. The list:

- Stakeholders (Chapter 1, p. 18)
- Mission Statements and Competitive Advantage (Chapter 2, p. 36)
- Five Forces in Airlines vs. Soft Drinks (Chapter 3, p. 68)
- How to Protect a Competitive Advantage (Chapter 4, p. 102)
- Assessing Competitive Advantage: Google vs. Microsoft, Continued (Chapter 5, p. 123)
- The Dynamics of Competitive Positioning (Chapter 6, p. 161)
- Hypercompetition (Chapter 7, p. 191)
- Corporate Diversification (Chapter 8, p. 221)
- Mergers and Acquisitions (Chapter 9, p. 241)
- Regional Clusters (Chapter 10, p. 289)
- Organizational Culture and Competitive Advantage (Chapter 11, p. 319)
- Corporate Social Responsibility (Chapter 12, p. 341)

Strategy Highlight Boxes

Every chapter contains between one and four *Strategy Highlight* boxes. These in-chapter examples apply a specific concept to a specific company. They are right-sized for maximum student appeal—long enough to contain valuable insights, and short enough to encourage student reading. Examples:

- Threadless: Leveraging Crowdsourcing to Design Cool T-Shirts (Chapter 1, p. 17)
- Starbucks's CEO: "It's Not What We Do!" (Chapter 2, p. 44)
- UBS Relents to Pressure by U.S. Government (Chapter 3, p. 57)
- How Nintendo Focused on the Casual Gamer (Chapter 4, p. 95)
- Interface: The World's First Sustainable Company (Chapter 5, p. 128)
- Ryanair: Lower Cost than the Low-Cost Leader! (Chapter 6, p. 148)
- GE's Reverse Innovation: Disrupt Yourself! (Chapter 7, p. 186)
- ExxonMobil Diversifies into Natural Gas (Chapter 8, p. 218)
- Pixar and Disney: From Alliance to Acquisition (Chapter 9, p. 247)
- Does GM's Future Lie in China? (Chapter 10, p. 275)
- *USA Today:* Leveraging Ambidextrous Organizational Design (Chapter 11, p. 312)
- GE's Board of Directors (Chapter 12, p. 346)

To see all of the Strategy Highlight boxes, by chapter, go to the detailed Contents list beginning on page xlii.

*my*Strategy Applications

Near the end of the chapter, immediately before the chapter endnotes, is a feature titled *my*Strategy, which applies strategy concepts from the chapter to students' lives. You may choose to make this feature a regular part of the course, or you may prefer to let students explore these items outside of the regular coursework. In whatever way they are used, the *my*Strategy features demonstrate opportunities to personalize strategy as students plan or enhance careers following completion of the strategy course and their degrees. Examples:

- How to Position Yourself for Career Advantage? (Chapter 1, p. 25)
- How Much Are Your Values Worth to You? (Chapter 2, p. 51)
- Is My Job the Next One Being Outsourced? (Chapter 3, p. 80)
- Looking Inside Yourself: What Is My Competitive Advantage? (Chapter 4, p. 110)
- How Much Is an MBA Worth to You? (Chapter 5, p. 134)
- Different Value and Cost Drivers—What Determines *Your* Buying Decisions? (Chapter 6, p. 166)
- Do You Want to Be an Entrepreneur? (Chapter 7, p. 196)
- How Diversified Are You? (Chapter 8, p. 230)
- What Is Your Network Strategy? (Chapter 9, p. 262)
- Should There Be More H1-B Visas? (Chapter 10, p. 295)
- For What Type of Organization Are *You* Best-Suited? (Chapter 11, p. 328)
- Are You Part of Gen-Y, or Will You Manage Gen-Y Workers? (Chapter 12, p. 362)

MiniCases

Following the book's final chapter are an additional 12 original MiniCases; most are one or two pages in length. With suggested links to related chapters, the MiniCases include a handful of attached discussion questions (with suggested responses available to instructors in the online instructor's resources). These MiniCases are short enough to be assigned as add-ons to chapters, either as individual assignments or as group work, or to be used for class discussion. They are:

- Michael Phelps: Strategizing for Gold (MiniCase 1, p. 367)
- Strategy and Serendipity: A Billion-Dollar Bonanza (MiniCase 2, p. 369)
- The Home Depot's Eco Options Boost Profit Margins (MiniCase 3, p. 370)
- Starbucks: Re-creating its Uniqueness (MiniCase 4, p. 371)
- GE under Jack Welch vs. Jeffrey Immelt (MiniCase 5, p. 372)
- JetBlue: Losing the Magic Touch? (MiniCase 6, p. 374)
- Which Automotive Technology Will Win? (MiniCase 7, p. 375)
- Core Competencies From Circuit City to CarMax (MiniCase 8, p. 377)
- P&G's New Corporate Strategy: "Connect+Develop" (MiniCase 9, p. 379)
- The Wonder from Sweden: Is IKEA's Success Sustainable? (MiniCase 10, p. 383)
- Sony's Silos Prevent Collaboration Across Divisions (MiniCase 11, p. 385)
- PepsiCo's Indra Nooyi: "Performance with a Purpose" (MiniCase 12, p. 387)

For further information about the book's features, see the **Features Walkthrough,** beginning on page xvii.

ACKNOWLEDGMENTS

Any list of acknowledgements will almost always be incomplete, but I would like to thank some special people without whom this book would not have been possible. First and foremost, my wife Kelleyn, and our children: Harris, Winston, Roman, and Adelaide. Over the last few years, I have worked longer hours than when I was a graduate student to conduct the research and writing necessary for this text and accompanying case studies and other materials. I sincerely appreciate the sacrifice this has meant for my family.

I was also fortunate to work with McGraw-Hill, and the best editorial and marketing team that one can imagine: Michael Ablassmeir (Executive Editor), Paul Ducham (Editorial Director), Ann Torbert (Executive Director of Development), Laura Griffin (Development Editor II), Anke Weekes-Braun (Executive Marketing Manager), Michelle Heaster (Senior Marketing Manager), and Harvey Yep (Lead Project Manager, EDP). This book was created through a parallel new product development process: All functions from basic research to marketing were involved from the start, including top management support, which made all the difference. Mike's vision to create a third-generation strategy text drove this project. It felt like an entrepreneurial venture, given that all parameters were up for discussion. Paul's support and candid input from the get-go made this a better book. Ann is the best content development editor one can imagine; her dedication to this project and her unwavering drive for quality made this book what it is today. Laura made sure that all of the many pieces would fall into place, and Harvey made the impossible possible: meeting our publication date! Anke has a keen understanding of market needs, and her ability to effectively communicate with customers (and authors), and to make complex events such as focus groups successful, is clearly unique—so much so that she was promoted to a new role. Michelle Heaster smoothly picked up the marketing reins and has ably guided the project as it goes to market. Thank you to senior management at McGraw-Hill/Irwin B&E who assembled this fine team.

I was fortunate to work with Anne W. Fuller (Georgia Tech PhD, and assistant professor at California State University, Sacramento) on the end-of-chapter material, the instructor resource manual, the *Connect Management* material (on which Anne is a digital co-author), the PowerPoint presentations that accompany the textbook, chapter videos, and the Test Bank. Anne has been a terrific contributor from the very beginning, combining strong academic training with more than 20 years of professional management experience at Motorola in the United States and China.

I was also fortunate to work with Marne L. Arthaud-Day (Indiana University PhD, and associate professor at Kansas State University) on the "How to Conduct a Case Analysis" section (page 389) and the many other case materials. Thanks, too, to Robert Porter (PhD University of Central Florida) for his fine work.

Over the years, I have been privileged to work with Karyn Lu, a superb copyeditor, on my scholarly research papers and on this project. Karyn has been much more than a copyeditor, she has been a sounding board for ideas and has helped to make the delivery of the content as user-friendly as possible. Karyn was also instrumental in launching the social media support for professors and students on www.ftrStrategy, Facebook, and Twitter for this book, a novel addition in the strategy textbook market.

I would also like to thank Carol Jacobson (of Purdue University) for providing solid content and editorial suggestions on numerous chapters.

The Georgia Institute of Technology provided a conducive intellectual environment and superb institutional support to make this project possible. I thank Angel and Stephen M. Deedy for generously funding the professorship that I am honored to hold. I'm grateful for

Dean Salbu and Senior Associate Dean Narasimhan for providing the exceptional leadership that allows faculty to fully focus on research, teaching, and service. I have been at Georgia Tech for now more than eight years, and could not have had better colleagues—all of whom are not only great scholars but also fine individuals whom I'm fortunate to have as friends: Dan Breznitz, Marco Ceccagnoli, Annamaria Conti, Stuart Graham, Matt Higgins, David Ku, Jay Lee, John McIntyre, Alex Oettl, Henry Sauermann, and Jerry Thursby and Marie Thursby. At Georgia Tech, we have a terrific group of current and former PhD students, many of whom had a positive influence on this project, including: Shanti Agung, Drew Hess (University of Virginia), Kostas Grigoriou, Nicola McCarthy, German Retana, Jose Urbina, and Wei Zhang.

I'd also like to thank my students at Georgia Tech, both in the full-time day MBA and the executive MBA programs, as well as the executive MBA students from the ICN Business School in Nancy, France, on whom I beta-tested the materials. Their feedback helped fine-tune the content and delivery. I'm also grateful for professors and students at the undergraduate level who beta-tested various materials: Joshua Aaron at East Carolina University; Brent Allred at The University of William & Mary; Melissa Appleyard at Portland State University; Marne Arthaud-Day at Kansas State University; Bindu Arya at the University of Missouri-St. Louis; Danielle Dunne, formerly at Binghamton University, SUNY, now at Fordham University; Anne Fuller at California State University, Sacramento; Elouise Mintz at Saint Louis University; Chandran Mylvaganam at Northwood University; Louise Nemanich at Arizona State University; Frank Novakowski at Davenport University; Richard Quinn at The University of Central Florida; Beverly B. Tyler at North Carolina State University; and Joel West, formerly at San Jose State University, now at Claremont Graduate University. Their willingness to use the materials as they were being developed, and to gather student opinions, provided lots of useful feedback.

Last, but certainly not least, I wish to thank the reviewers and focus group attendees who shared their expertise with us, from the very beginning when we developed the prospectus to the final text and cases that you hold in your hands. The reviewers have given us the greatest gift of all—the gift of time! These very special people are listed starting on page xxxiv.

I have long yearned to write a textbook that shows students and managers how exciting strategic management can be but that at the same time presents the recent developments in the field, including the rigor upon which concepts and frameworks are now built, to make better strategic decisions in a turbulent and dynamic world. I'm fortunate that I had the support of many people to make this vision become a reality, and I'm truly grateful.

Frank T. Rothaermel
Georgia Institute of Technology

Web: http://ftrStrategy.com
Twitter: @ftrStrategy
Facebook: http://on.fb.me/r8kczS

In addition to the traditional chapters needed in the strategy course, *Strategic Management* includes three separate, standalone chapters (Chapters 2, 5, and 7) that address topics that add value for your course and your students. Following the final chapter is a set of 12 author-written MiniCases.

"... includes relevant, current examples from the business world while taking a focused approach in introducing and discussing the concept of strategy."

CH 1

Bindu Arya, University of Missouri–St. Louis

"The approach is fresh, direct, and serious. . . it did not dilute the theoretical base of the information. The inclusion of the discussion of 'what strategy is not' helps frame the course from the start."

Isaiah O. Ugboro,
North Carolina A&T State University

"Rothaermel's coverage of scenario planning is probably the best I have seen."

CH 2

James W. Bronson,
University of Wisconsin-Whitewater

"This is a terrific chapter: well-integrated, proceeding from the 'outside' in PESTEL to the 'inside.' The use of frameworks is exceptionally strong; they are developed well and applied well."

CH 3

Melissa M. Appleyard, Portland State University

"I found this chapter riveting, and one of the most comprehensive and clear textbook explanations of the resource-based view I have seen. It does an outstanding job of explaining the RBV in a very practical way."

CH 4

Stephen V. Horner, Arkansas State University

PART 2
Strategy Formulation

« **CH 5**

"This is an excellent chapter to discuss competitive advantage both conceptually and operationally. . . . Outstanding."

Chris Papenhausen,
University of Massachusetts, Dartmouth

  CH 6

"The value-cost figures and accompanying discussions are very good, whereas other textbooks have often overlooked and underemphasized these points."

Carol Jacobson, Purdue University

  CH 7

"This chapter is a great addition! The examples are extremely current and relevant to the student population. . . . If we as strategy professors can do something

valuable for our students, it is to show them the power of innovation and try to get them to think about future possibilities and strategic directions."

Tammy G. Hunt,
University of North Carolina, Wilmington

« **CH 8**

"All theoretical notions are illustrated with real-world examples of domestic and international firms, which the students would find particularly helpful. . . . The real-world examples and corresponding theoretical concepts are in lock-step and well integrated, which is its key strength."

Deepak Sethi, Old Dominion University

"This chapter provides one of clearest and most easily comprehended discussions of alliances, mergers and networks that I have read in the past 12 years."

 CH 9

Richard A. Quinn, University of Central Florida

"Great chapter. Would not change a thing. Gives content regarding why international context is becoming more important."

 CH10

Linda F. Tegarden, Virginia Tech

"This is one of the best organizational design chapters that I have read. It provides more integration between strategy and structure than I have seen in other texts. The chapter's exhibits are

CH11

integral to the value-added for this chapter—and truly exceptional. I feel like the students will greatly benefit from this understanding and it provides a more holistic approach to the concept of fitting structure to strategy under strategic management."

Jill A. Brown, Lehigh University

"This chapter did a great job covering all three topics of governance, ethics, and leadership. Many texts have these concepts in different chapters, which is too much. This chapter combines them in a logical manner that makes sense, provides the appropriate attention to each, and ties them all together."

 CH12

Brent B. Allred, The College of William & Mary

Unparalleled Integration

>>

The author's **AFI framework** (*A*nalysis, *F*ormulation, *I*mplementation) focuses content and organizes the book's "less is more" approach. The framework's unique integration of the *process* schools of strategy (based on organization theory, psychology, and sociology) with the *content* schools of strategy (based on economics) provides students with a balanced and complete treatment of strategy not found in other books for the course.

EXHIBIT 1.9
The AFI Strategy Framework and Text Outline

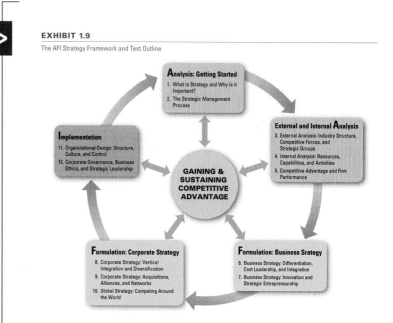

> ". . . has a well-conceived **textbook structure**, and also it has a **well balanced approach** among theories, practices, and applications."
>
> *Seung Bach, California State University, Sacramento*

<<

Cohesive and Interconnected

With a single strong voice, the author weaves together classic and cutting-edge theory with in-chapter cases and strategy examples. Unlike other texts that often outsource cases, Rothaermel took pride in authoring *all* of the *ChapterCases* and *MiniCases*, and in authoring or co-authoring half of the full-length *Cases* (available through *Create*™).

"The cases, written to align with the text's vocabulary, are a definite plus. . . . The book offers a **new, refreshing approach to the field of strategic management.** Its presentation stays true to important strategic concepts and related topics while providing contemporary explanations, examples and relevant illustrations of them."

Frank Novakowski, Davenport University

"The author packs in a lot of information relative to the amount of text. The charts are useful rather than just filler to achieve a predetermined ratio of text to graphics."

Added Value for Instructors and Students

In a presentation that is comprehensive yet concise, rigorous yet relevant, the author includes classic and cutting-edge strategy material in a student-accessible format. By addressing *what* the research findings mean and *why* they are important for managers and by eliminating excess detail and outdated examples, the book helps students see the bigger strategic picture.

In addition, a key aspect of the author's vision is to provide value-added dimensions for both instructors and students, including:

FLEXIBILITY FOR INSTRUCTORS: The author has crafted the book to provide maximum teaching flexibility. Each chapter is sufficiently self-contained that it can be taught in any order. This flexibility supports teaching the content of the course in modules and other high-flex delivery approaches.

AN ENJOYABLE READ FOR STUDENTS: Filled with examples from companies today's students know, the book conveys to students how exciting strategic management can be and prepares them for the realities of strategic management in the turbulent 21st century.

"The examples were relatable to everyday life, and the **read was 'easy'** compared to my other [strategy] textbook. No filler info . . . straightforward."

"[This text] does an outstanding job framing the **pivotal strategic management theories,** capturing their essence and translating them into practice."

"I really like how the author has brought in so many **current stories involving major companies** and how those firms have struggled to develop and implement strategies to gain a sustainable competitive advantage. **This brings the concepts to life**."

A "Good Read" That Is Both Rigorous and Relevant

Rigorous, Relevant, and Balanced

A MIX OF CLASSIC AND CONTEMPORARY CONTENT: The book includes strategy material that has stood the test of time (the resource-based view, Porter's five forces model, etc.), as well as up-to-date strategy material and current research (dynamic capabilities perspective, and the triple bottom line, etc.). The book also includes student-accessible coverage of strategic management research drawn from both academic journals and best-selling business books.

UNDER THE MAGNIFYING GLASS SECTIONS: Each chapter contains a section that puts one specific theory or concept **"under the magnifying glass."** Combining strategic management research with real-world observations, these sections critically evaluate if and how the theory or concept is linked to competitive advantage.

Corporate Diversification

Corporate managers pursue diversification to gain and sustain competitive advantage. But does corporate diversification indeed lead to superior performance? To answer this question, we can evaluate the performance of diversified companies. The critical question to ask when doing so is whether the individual businesses are worth more under the company's management than if each were managed individually.

Research shows that the diversification-performance relationship is a function of the underlying type of diversification. A cumulative body of research indicates an inverted U-shaped relationship between the type of diversification and overall firm performance, as depicted in Exhibit 8.9.[59] High and low levels of diversification are generally associated with lower overall performance, while moderate levels of diversification are associated with higher firm performance. This implies that companies that focus on a single business, as well as companies that pursue unrelated diversification, often fail to achieve additional value creation. Firms that compete in single markets could potentially benefit from economies of scope by leveraging their core competencies into adjacent markets.

Firms that pursue unrelated diversification are often unable to create additional value, and thus experience a *diversification discount* in the stock market: the stock price of such highly diversified firms is valued at less than the sum of their individual business units.[60] In contrast, companies that pursue related diversification are more likely to improve their performance, and thus create a *diversification premium*: the stock price of related-diversification firms is valued at greater than the sum of their individual business units.[61]

Why is this so? At the most basic level, a corporate diversification strategy enhances firm performance when its value creation is greater than the costs it incurs. Exhibit 8.10 (next page) lists the sources of value creation and costs for different corporate strategies, for vertical integration as well as related and unrelated diversification. For diversification to enhance firm performance, it must do at least one of the following:

- Provide economies of scale, and thus reduce costs.
- Exploit economies of scope, and thus increase value.
- Reduce costs *and* increase value.

GAINING & SUSTAINING COMPETITIVE ADVANTAGE

>> LO 8-8
Explain when a diversification strategy creates a competitive advantage, and when it does not.

EXHIBIT 8.9
The Diversification-Performance Relationship

[Graph: Performance (vertical axis) vs Level of Diversification (horizontal axis), showing an inverted U-shaped curve. Horizontal axis labels: Single Business, Dominant Business, Related Diversification (Related-Constrained, Related-Linked), Unrelated Diversification]

Source: Adapted from L. E. Palich, L. B. Cardinal, and C. C. Miller (2000), "Curvilinearity in the diversification-performance linkage: An examination of over three decades of research," *Strategic Management Journal* 21: 155–174.

"The writing style is considerably 'down-to-earth' in terms of **meeting students where they are intellectually and bringing them along into more complex understanding** of competitive advantage and firm performance."

Stephen V. Horner, Arkansas State University

"The writing style . . . is a tonic for the strategic management student and faculty member. My [current] text takes a blunderbuss and shoots it against the barn wall, listing and covering everything the authors can think of; Rothaermel uses a competition grade rifle to pinpoint and logically focus the given area of concern."

Dr. Gene Simko, Leon Hess Business School, Monmouth University

 **Relevant**

Written to meet the needs of today's students, the book prepares them for the turbulence and dynamism that they will face as managers in the 21st century. *Strategic Management* consistently:

ENGAGES AND INTERESTS GEN-Y STUDENTS through use of up-to-date examples.

BRINGS THEORY TO LIFE THROUGH EMBEDDED EXAMPLES within each framework and concept.

INCLUDES TOPICS FROM RECENT AND CURRENT BESTSELLERS, exposing students to topics that today's managers talk about.

"**Excellent examples**—e.g., Facebook/Myspace; Amazon/Apple; Pixar/Disney, and **interesting discussion** [in Chapter 9] of why M&A may not increase value. . . . The content is **rich, and easy to read.**"

Dorothy Brawley, Kennesaw State University

"[My favorite aspects of this text are the] **more in-depth examples** of more **modern companies**. There was more **application to balance the theory** than in the traditional text used—and more recent examples."

Stacy Litchford, MBA student at The College of William & Mary

Fascinating Cases and Engaging Features
That Get Students Thinking . . .

CHAPTERCASES frame the chapter topic and content and focus on **companies and industries of interest to students**, such as Google, Microsoft, Teach for America, GE, Whole Foods, Wikipedia, Facebook, Hollywood movies, and Zappos.

>>

"Timely/relevant info about an interesting problem at an interesting company."

K. Matis, student at The College of William and Mary

CHAPTERCASE 3

Build Your Dreams (BYD) to Sidestep Entry Barriers

THE BIG THREE—GM, Ford, and Chrysler—dominated the U.S. car market throughout most of the 20th century. As the competition in the industry became increasingly global, foreign car makers entered the U.S. market mainly by importing vehicles from overseas plants. Among the first were German carmakers Volkswagen, Daimler, and BMW as well as Japanese carmakers Honda, Toyota, and Nissan. The foreign entrants intensified competition, threatened the market share of the Big Three, and led to political pressure to impose import restrictions in the 1980s. The new players responded by building U.S. plants in order to avoid import restrictions. More recently, Korean car makers Hyundai and Kia have begun making and selling cars in the United States.

Although globalization and deregulation paved the way for significant new entry into the U.S. auto market, the worldwide car manufacturing industry has been exposed to few new entrants. In fact, no new major car manufacturers have emerged in the last couple of decades in part because automobiles powered by internal combustion engines are made out of thousands of precisely engineered parts; few industrial products, excluding commercial airplanes, are as complex as cars. Car manufacturers also require large-scale production in order to be cost-competitive. These facts create seemingly insurmountable barriers to entry into car manufacturing.

Thus, it would seem that an unknown startup from an emerging economy, attempting to enter the car industry during the deepest economic recession since the Great Depression, would surely be a fool's errand.

Yet Wang Chuanfu, founder and chairman of the Chinese technology startup Build Your Dreams (BYD) begs to differ. His strategy is to use new technology to sidestep entry barriers. BYD began its life as a battery company in 1995 and is now leveraging this expertise into electric vehicles. Unlike complex gasoline engines, electric cars are powered by simple motors and gearboxes that have very few parts. Electric vehicles are therefore much cheaper and more straightforward to build.

BYD's claim to fame is a lithium ferrous phosphate battery on which cars can run 250 miles on a single three-hour charge. Already one of the fastest growing independent automakers, BYD is selling plug-in hybrids and all-electric vehicles in China, Africa, the Middle East, and South America. It plans to sell cars in the U.S. and other Western countries in the near future.

Legendary investor Warren Buffett found BYD interesting enough to put in some $230 million for a 10 percent equity stake. Consumers may flock to BYD cars as well. Not only are they "green" cars, but their sticker price is anticipated to be about half that of the Chevy Volt (whose starting price is $40,000). Other companies entering the car industry by leveraging new battery technology include Tesla Motors and Fisker Automotive, both in California, as well as Think Global in Norway and Lightning Car in the United Kingdom. Sparks are sure to fly as the car industry becomes more competitive in the 21st century.[1]

After reading the chapter, you will find more about this case, with related questions, on page 77.

55

CHAPTERCASE 3 | *Consider This . . .*

CHAPTERCASE 3, about BYD, notes that the firm entered the electric-vehicle market from a strong base in designing and building batteries. This expertise permitted BYD to circumvent some historically strong barriers to entry in the automotive industry. While the success of BYD in automobiles is still far from assured, it was the fastest-growing carmaker in China in 2009, selling more than 500,000 vehicles in 2010. In part, these strong sales may be due to some government incentives for electric vehicles in China, which will encourage the development and sale of electric cars. For example, in some major cities such as Shanghai, the Chinese government will pay 60,000 yuan (approximately $9,000) toward purchase of an electric vehicle.[52]

Thinking about the chapter-opening case, answer the following questions.

1. Which PESTEL factors are the most salient for the electric-vehicle industry of the 21st century?

2. Think about the structure of the automotive industry in your home country. Is it structured more like an oligopoly or monopolistic competition?

3. Using the industry-attractiveness model (see Exhibit 3.5), explain the overall automotive industry. How would it change for the electric-vehicle industry?

>>

"Consider This . . . " sections
use additional information, plus concepts and information from the chapter, to extend and complete the ChapterCase example.

Questions in the "Consider This . . ." section are good **jumping-off points for class discussion.**

"The 'Strategy Highlights' are interesting."

Matthew DeRemer, student at University of Central Florida

Strategy Highlight Boxes

These engaging boxes apply a specific concept to a specific company. Each box is:

RIGHT-SIZED FOR MAXIMUM STUDENT APPEAL—long enough to contain valuable insights, yet short enough to encourage student reading.

FOCUSED ON COMPANIES THAT STUDENTS KNOW—Threadless, Sony, Starbucks, Nintendo, Toyota, Apple, GE, ExxonMobil, Pixar, GM, Walmart, W.L. Gore, USA Today, among others.

Forming Strategic Intent

Strategic intent is the staking out of a desired leadership position in the long term that far exceeds a company's current resources and capabilities.[4] Challenging goals that stretch an individual or an organization can lead to higher performance.[5] Many Japanese competitors set ambitious stretch goals of global leadership (reflected in their missions) and made them a reality: Canon "beat Xerox," Komatsu "encircled Caterpillar," and Honda became "a second Ford." (Today this may not sound like a desirable goal, but it was in the 1970s when Honda began its quest for global leadership.) Currently, Chinese companies such as Baidu, BYD, and Lenovo aspire to world leadership. These companies set their ambitious goals when they were only a fraction the size of the companies they were chasing. Indeed, they were so small that initially the market leaders did not even recognize them as potential competitors; many had never competed outside their domestic markets. Yet all made global leadership their mission, with goals so ambitious they exceeded the firms' existing resources and capabilities by a large margin. Effective use of stretch goals created at all levels of the organization an obsession with winning that is sustained over several decades.[6]

STRATEGY HIGHLIGHT 5.1

Interface: The World's First Sustainable Company

Interface, Inc. is a leader in modular carpeting, with annual sales of roughly $1 billion. What makes the company unique is its strategic intent to become the world's first *fully sustainable* company. In 1994, founder Ray Anderson set a goal for the company to be "off oil" entirely by 2020. That included not using any petroleum-based raw materials or oil-related energy to fuel the manufacturing plants.

According to Collins and Porras in *Built to Last*, their classic study of high-performing companies over long periods of time, this is a "BHAG"—*a big hairy audacious goal*. BHAGs are bold missions declared by visionary companies and are a "powerful mechanism to stimulate progress."[28] Weaning Interface off oil by 2020 is indeed a BHAG. Many see the carpet industry as an extension of the petrochemical industry, given its heavy reliance on

fossil fuels and chemicals in the manufacturing, shipping, and installation of its products.

Today, Interface is a leader in both modular carpet and sustainability. The company estimates that between 1996 and 2008, it saved over $400 million due to its energy efficiency and use of recycled materials. Its business model is changing the carpet industry. Speaking of sustainability as a business model, Mr. Anderson stated in 2009:

> Sustainability has given my company a competitive edge in more ways than one. It has proven to be the most powerful marketplace differentiator I have known in my long career. Our costs are down, our profits are up, and our products are the best they have ever been. Sustainable design has provided an unexpected wellspring of innovation, people are galvanized around a shared higher purpose, better people are applying, the best people are staying and working with a purpose, the goodwill in the marketplace generated by our focus on sustainability far exceeds that which any amount of advertising or marketing expenditure could have generated—this company believes it has found a better way to a bigger and more legitimate profit—a better business model.[29]

STRATEGY HIGHLIGHT 7.3

From King Gillette to King of Incremental Innovation

In 1903, entrepreneur Mr. King C. Gillette invented and began selling the safety razor with a disposable blade. This radical innovation launched the Gillette company (now a brand of Procter & Gamble). To sustain its competitive advantage, Gillette not only made sure that its razors were inexpensive and widely available (thus introducing the "razor and razor blade" business model),[31] but it continuously improved its razor blades. In a classic example of incremental innovation, Gillette kept adding an additional blade with each new version of its razor until the number had gone from one to six![32] Though this innovation strategy seems predictable, it worked: Gillette's top-selling razor today, the Fusion, holds about 45 percent market share and brings in annual revenues of more than $1 billion. Moreover, with each new razor introduction, Gillette is able to push up its per-unit cartridge price. A four-pack of razors for the new Fusion Proglide retailed for $17.99 when introduced in 2010.[33]

A Global Context

 In addition to the standalone chapter on global strategy, examples throughout the book reflect the **global nature of competition** and the importance of emerging economies such as the BRIC countries.

 Additionally, a number of the examples relate to sustainable strategy with a **focus on "green" products and issues**.

A Variety of End-of-Chapter Features Meet Varying Course Needs

Chapter summaries link key chapter content to the chapter's learning objectives.

End-of-chapter materials also include a list of **key terms** introduced in the chapter.

Take-Away Concepts

This chapter defined corporate-level strategy and then looked at two fundamental corporate-level strategy topics, vertical integration and diversification, as summarized by the following learning objectives and related take-away concepts.

LO 8-1 Define corporate-level strategy, and describe the three dimensions along which it is assessed.

>> While business strategy addresses "how to compete," corporate strategy addresses "where to compete."

>> Corporate strategy concerns the scope of the firm along three dimensions: (1) vertical integration (along the industry value chain); (2) horizontal integration (diversification); and (3) geographic scope (global strategy).

>> To gain and sustain competitive advantage, any corporate strategy must support and strengthen a firm's strategic position regardless of whether it is a differentiation, cost leadership, or integration strategy.

LO 8-2 Describe and evaluate different options firms have to organize economic activity.

>> Transaction cost economics help managers decide what activities to do in-house ("make") versus what services and products to obtain from the external market ("buy").

> "I do not typically use the end-of-chapter material for the textbooks I use, but I got excited about the **excellent material provided** and believe I would use this material in my class."
>
> *Brent B. Allred, The College of William & Mary*

Discussion Questions offer broad scope for classroom settings and uses.

Social/Ethical Issues and Questions enliven class discussion.

Small Group Exercises allow for different pedagogical approaches and offer opportunities to break up long class periods or promote group work outside of class.

All end-of-chapter features have been **beta-tested** in various classroom settings and different levels (undergraduate, MBA, and executive MBA).

Discussion Questions

1. Assume you work for a small firm that developed a better and faster operating system for netbooks than Microsoft Windows. What strategy might the firm use to unseat Windows in this market?

2. How does the industry life cycle affect business strategy? Detail your answer based on each stage: introduction, growth, maturity, and decline.

3. Describe a firm you think has been highly innovative. Which of the four types of innovation—radical, incremental, disruptive, or architectural—did it use? Did the firm use different types over time?

4. Why are standards important in many industries? As standards get adapted and become dominant, how does this process influence the competitive nature of the industry?

Ethical/Social Issues

1. You are a co-founder of a startup firm making electronic sensors. After a year of sales your business is not growing rapidly, but you have some steady customers keeping the business afloat. A major supplier has informed you it can no longer supply your firm because it is moving to serve large customers only, and your volume does not qualify. Though you have no current orders to support an increased commitment to this supplier, you do have a new version of your sensor coming out that you hope will increase the purchase volume by over 75 percent and qualify you for continued supply. This supplier is important to your plans. What do you do?

2. Making innovations successful often relies on being the first to commercialize a technology. What are some practices a firm could use to enhance its first-mover advantage? Does the stage of the industry life cycle affect the available practices? Are there long-term consequences for the firm from these practices?

Small Group Exercises

SMALL GROUP EXERCISE 1

Your group works for Warner Music Group (www.wmg.com), a large music record label whose sales are declining largely due to piracy. Your supervisor assigns you the task of developing a strategy for improving this situation.

1. What are the key issues you must grapple with to improve the position of Warner Music Group (WMG)?

2. In what phase of the life cycle is the record-label industry?

3. How does this life-cycle phase affect the types of innovation that should be considered to help WMG be successful?

SMALL GROUP EXERCISE 2

Strategy Highlight 7.4 outlines GE's development of the Vscan, which will likely cannibalize the sales of its existing ultrasound machines. Part of the difficult decision to reverse-innovate is the prospect of losing not just sales revenue but also jobs. In 2010, GE Healthcare employed over 45,000 people. Assume 10,000 jobs strongly connected to supporting GE's high-end imaging systems are in imminent jeopardy if sales of the systems drop off. Put yourself in the role of GE Healthcare managers.

1. Pull together a memo of talking points for the managers of the new Vscan that may put many other men and women at GE out of work.

2. How do you explain the societal benefits of lower-cost medical scanning equipment yet address real job security concerns among the employees?

> "The chapter review questions are good, and the project ideas are good especially for those who are relatively new to the course."
>
> *Isaiah O. Ugboro, North Carolina A&T State University*

Strategy Term Project >>

Breaks a long-term project into a series of **focused, targeted tasks**.

Requires **data collection and analysis**, using the tools and concepts from each chapter.

Provides an extended, "hands-on" project, ideal for use by **individual students or small groups**.

Fulfills the **AACSB requirement** for an integrative management exercise.

Strategy Term Project

MODULE 2: MISSION, GOALS, AND THE STRATEGIC MANAGEMENT PROCESS

1. Search for a mission statement for the firm. Not all organizations publish such a statement, so alternatively you can look for enduring principles and values upon which the firm seems to be anchored. This information is often available at the firm's website (though it may take some searching) or is contained in its annual reports. You may also interview a manager of the firm or contact "investor relations."

2. Identify the major goals of the company.
3. Does the firm seem to have any longer-term challenging or stretch goals that would serve as its strategic intent?
4. Trace any changes in strategy that you can identify over time. Try to determine whether the strategic changes of your selected firm are a result of intended strategies, emergent strategies, or some combination of both.

Strategy Term Project

MODULE 4: INTERNAL ANALYSIS
In this section, you will study the internal resources, capabilities, core competencies, and value chain of your selected firm.

1. A good place to start with an internal firm analysis is to catalog the assets a firm has. Make a list of the firm's tangible assets in the firm. Then, make a separate list of the intangible assets you can identify.

3. Identify the core competencies that are at the heart of the firm's competitive advantage. (Remember, a firm will have only one, or at most a few, core competencies, by definition.)
4. Use the strategic activity system framework to diagram the important and supportive activities the firm has that are key to delivering and sustaining the firm's value proposition. (For an example, refer to Exhibits 4.7 and 4.8 showing the activity system of the Vanguard Group.)

"The *my*Strategy module is a very cool feature, and the questions used to develop this are excellent."

Parthiban David, Kogood School of Business, American University

*my*Strategy

FOR WHAT TYPE OF ORGANIZATION ARE *YOU* BEST-SUITED?

A s noted in the chapter, firms can have very distinctive cultures. Recall that Zappos has a standing offer to pay any new hire $2,000 to quit the company during the first month. Zappos makes this offer to help ensure that those who stay with the company are comfortable in its "create fun and a little weirdness" environment.

You may have taken a personality test such as Myers-Briggs or The Big Five. These tests may be useful in gauging compatibility of career and personality types. They are often available for both graduate and undergraduate students a...

the following questions, think about your next job and your longer-term career plans.

1. Review Exhibit 11.3 and circle the organizational characteristics you find appealing. Cross out those factors you think you would not like. Do you find a trend toward either the mechanistic or organic organization?

2. Have you been in school or work situations in which your values did not align with those of your peers or colleagues? How did you handle the situation? Are there certain values or norms important enough for you to consider as you look for a new job?

3. As you consider your career after graduation, which control and rewards system discussed in the concluding section of the chapter would you find most motivating? Is this different from the controls used at...

*my*Strategy

LOOKING INSIDE YOURSELF: WHAT IS MY COMPETITIVE ADVANTAGE?

H ere, we encourage you to take what you have learned about competitive advantage and apply it to your personal career. Spend a few minutes looking at yourself to discover *your own* competitive advantage.

1. Write down your own personal strengths and weaknesses. What sort of organization will permit you to really leverage your strengths and keep you highly engaged in your work (person–organization fit)? Do some of your weaknesses need to be mitigated through additional training or mentoring from a more seasoned professional?

2. Personal capabilities also need to be evaluated over time. Are your strengths and weaknesses different

today from what they were five years ago? What are you doing to make sure your capabilities are dynamic? Are you upgrading skills, modifying behaviors, or otherwise seeking to change your future strengths and weaknesses?

3. Are some of your strengths valuable, rare, and costly to imitate? How can you organize your work to help capture the value of your key strengths (or mitigate your weaknesses)?

4. In this chapter, we discussed that the strategic activity system happening inside the firm can be a vital source of sustainable competitive advantage. If you are currently or previously employed, consider how your professional activities can help reinforce the key value-added activities in your department or organization.

*my*Strategy Boxes

Apply strategy concepts to students' lives.

Show students **how to internalize** strategy as they plan or enhance their careers.

Setting a "Gold Standard" for High-Quality Cases

Three Types of Cases—*ChapterCases*, *MiniCases*, and *Cases*—inform, instruct, and inspire students and meet varying classroom needs:

 CHAPTERCASES (all written by the author) begin and end each chapter, framing chapter content and bringing concepts to life.

 Twelve original, Author-Written MINICASES

- Provide a decision scenario that a company's manager might face.

- Include discussion questions and are linked to specific chapters.

- Are short enough to be assigned as add-ons to chapters as individual assignments or group work and can also be used for discussion.

 30 Full-Length CASES

Cases are available through McGraw-Hill's custom-publishing *Create™* program.

Half of the book's Cases were written or co-written by the author specifically for use with the book, ensuring that chapter content and cases are closely interconnected.

The full-length Cases:

- Are preceded by "How to Conduct a Case Analysis," including a full set of financial ratios.

- Can be used for longer, more in-depth class discussion, case analysis, or term case papers.

- Are accompanied by a full set of *Case Teaching Notes*, written by Professors Marne L. Arthaud-Day of Kansas State University and Robert Porter of the University of Central Florida, in collaboration with Frank T. Rothaermel. Cases are also accompanied by **high-quality videos**.

"This type of mini-case, with the kinds of questions added at the bottom, is exactly what I like to use. I find these types of cases, in addition to opening vignettes, are right on especially for undergrads . . . they want to get to the heart of the matter rather quickly."

Michael D. Santoro, College of Business and Economics, Lehigh University

---

MICHAEL PHELPS, nicknamed MP, won an unprecedented eight gold medals at the Beijing Summer Olympics, and while doing so set seven new world records. Eight short days in August 2008 changed Olympic history and Michael Phelps's life forever, making MP one of the greatest athletes of all time. Immediately after the event, *The Wall Street Journal* reported that Phelps would be likely to turn the eight gold medals into a cash-flow stream of more than $100 million through a vari-

... activities.[1] The ... nes were product ... dorsements: His ... s included AT&T ...gg's, Omega, ...ta Stone, Speedo, ...port. Other offers ...tic and the mun- ...d movies, sculp- ...g his muscled ...aintings, dog food (given Michael's ...sh bulldog, Herman), commemorative ...ar rims, and even bobblehead dolls.

...MP was diagnosed with attention defi- ...disorder (ADHD). Doctors prescribed ...lp him release his energy. It worked! ...nd 2008, Michael Phelps attended the ...ichigan, studying marketing and man- ...d already competed quite successfully ...ns Summer Olympics, where he won ...o gold and two bronze. Right after the ...he then-19-year-old sat down with his ...arlisle, and his long-time swim coach, ...o map out a detailed strategy for the ...The explicit goal was to win nothing ...medal in each of the events in which ...te in Beijing, thus preparing the launch ...stardom.[2]

...n was responsible for getting MP into ...ysical shape he needed for Beijing and ...ntal toughness required to break Mark ...ecord of seven gold medals won in the ...lympic Games. Peter Carlisle, mean- ...d of a detailed strategy to launch MP

as a world superstar during the Beijing Games. While MP spent six hours a day in the pool, Carlisle focused on exposing MP to the Asian market, the largest consumer market in the world, with a special emphasis on the Chinese consumer. The earliest tie-in was with a Hong Kong–based manufacturer of MP3 players and other consumer electronics, Matsunichi, with whom MP became affiliated right after the 2004 Athens Games. MP made several other visits to China during the 2005–2007 period, among them the "Visa Friendship Lanes Tour" to promote the Special Olympics.

MP's wide-ranging presence in the real world was combined with a huge exposure in the virtual world. Phelps posts and maintains his own Facebook page, with millions of "phans" whose click-through rivaled the site of President Barack Obama in popularity. MP is also a favorite of YouTube and other online blogs (e.g., Swimroom.com), garnering worldwide exposure to an extent never before achieved by an Olympian.[3] The gradual buildup of Phelps over a number of years enabled manager Peter Carlisle to launch MP as a superstar right after he won his eighth gold medal at the Beijing Games. By then, MP had become a worldwide brand.

Clearly, a successful strategy rests on leveraging unique resources and capabilities. Accordingly, some suggest that MP's success can be explained by his unique physical endowments: his long thin torso, which reduces drag; his arm span of 6 feet 7 inches (204 cm), which is disproportionate to his 6-foot-4-inch (193 cm) height; his relatively short legs for a person of his height; and his size-14 feet which work like flippers due to hypermobile ankles.[4] While MP's physical attributes are a *necessary* condition for winning, they are not *sufficient*. Many other swimmers, like the Australian Ian Thorpe (who has size-17 feet) or the German "albatross" Michael Gross (with an arm span of 7 feet or 213 cm), also brought extraordinary resource endowments to the swim meet. Yet neither of them won eight gold medals in a single Olympics.

367

JETBLUE AIRWAYS was founded by former Southwest Airlines (SWA) employee David Neeleman in 1998. Mr. Neeleman became part of SWA in 1992, when SWA acquired Morris Air, an airline he founded in 1984 at the age of 25. Morris Air was a low-fare airline that pioneered many of the activities, such as e-ticketing, that later became standard in the industry.

When Neeleman designed JetBlue, he improved upon the SWA business model to enable his new company to provide tickets at even lower costs than SWA. JetBlue reproduces many of SWA's cost-reducing activities such as flying point-to-point to directly connect city pairs. It also predominantly uses one type of airplane, the Airbus A320, to lower its maintenance costs. In addition, JetBlue flies longer distances and transports more passengers per flight than SWA, further driving down its costs. Initially, JetBlue enjoyed the lowest cost per available seat-mile in the United States.

JetBlue also attempts to enhance its differential appeal, thus driving up its perceived value. JetBlue founder Neeleman argues that the airline combines high-tech to drive down costs with "high-touch" to enhance the customer experience. Some of JetBlue's value-enhancing features include high-end 100-seat Embraer regional jets with leather seats, individual TV screens (with 20th Century Fox movies, LiveTV, Fox TV, and DirectTV programming), 100 channels of XM Satellite Radio, and free in-flight Wi-Fi capabilities (offered in partnership with BlackBerry and Yahoo), along with friendly and attentive on-board service and other amenities. (JetBlue ads invite customers to hit the in-cabin "call button.") While JetBlue offers a highly functional website for reservations and other travel-related services, some customers (about 30 percent) prefer speaking to a live agent. Rather than outsourcing its reservation system to India, JetBlue employs stay-at-home parents in the Rocky Mountain states. The company suggests this "home sourcing" is

at least 30 percent more productive than outsourcing. More importantly, customers value their reservation experience much more, which the carrier believes more than makes up for the wage differential between the U.S. and India.

In early 2007, however, JetBlue's reputation for outstanding customer service ("we bring humanity back to air travel") took a major hit when several flights were delayed due to a snowstorm in which the airline kept passengers on board the aircraft, some sitting on the tarmac for up to nine hours. Many wondered whether JetBlue was losing its magic touch. In May 2007, David Neeleman left JetBlue. He founded Azul (which means "blue" in Portuguese), a Brazilian airline in 2008.[1]

DISCUSSION QUESTIONS

Review Chapter 6: Business Strategy: Differentiation, Cost Leadership, and Integration.

1. What type of generic business strategy is JetBlue pursuing: cost leadership, differentiation, or integration?

2. What challenges is JetBlue facing with its chosen business strategy? What is the cause of these challenges? How should they be addressed?

3. What do you recommend JetBlue's top management should do to improve the airline's competitiveness?

Endnotes

1. This MiniCase is based on: Neeleman, D. (2003), *Entrepreneurial Thought Leaders Lecture*, Stanford Technology Ventures Program, April 30; Friedman, T. (2005), *The World Is Flat: A Brief History of the Twenty-First Century* (New York: Farrar, Straus and Giroux); Bryce, D. J., and J. H. Dyer (2007), "Strategies to crack well-guarded markets," *Harvard Business Review*, May; "Held hostage on the tarmac: Time for a passenger bill of rights?" *The New York Times*, February 16, 2007; and "Can JetBlue weather the storm?" *Time*, February 21, 2007.

374

McGraw-Hill *Connect® Management*:
Today's Leading Online Assignment and Assessment System for Business Courses

No other web-based solution gives you the power to make your classroom a place for meaningful, engaging learning like **Connect Management**. With Connect, you can save time through automatic grading, track student progress with just a few clicks of the mouse, and generate an unparalleled array of reports.

For students, Connect improves learning and retention by helping students prepare for class, master concepts, and review for exams.

The Instructor site in Connect:

- Houses **powerful tools and features** that facilitate development and grading of assignments.

- Generates an unparalleled array of reports that enable instructors to **assess learning outcomes** for accreditation purposes.

- Offers **teaching notes**, including lecture outlines and exams, PPT slide guidance, small-group exercises, suggestions for end-of-chapter answers and discussion points, and notes on topic extensions in Connect interactive applications.

- Includes a rich online **Test Bank**, with 100–150 test questions per chapter, including both **multiple-choice** and **short-answer** questions.

- Provides **PowerPoint® slides** that build upon and extend coverage from the book, with **embedded video links**, optional small-group exercise slides, and notes on topics covered in Connect Interactive Applications.

And, to save you time, assessment of student responses flows easily into your grade book.

All ancillary content in **Connect® Management** was developed by Dr. Anne Fuller, from California State University, Sacramento, in close collaboration with Frank Rothaermel.

For more information, contact your local McGraw-Hill sales rep or visit www.mcgrawhillconnect.com.

The Student site in Connect:

- Includes a minimum of three unique instantly graded Interactive Applications per chapter that ask students to apply strategic management concepts to real-world scenarios.

Included in the Interactive Applications are:

- An interactive video case in every chapter, covering a key chapter learning objective. Contemporary video topics include business in China, pricing of water, use of solar energy, and global forces affecting the future of business.

- Drag-and-drop interactive assignments that allow students to actively engage the material for deeper understanding of key tools and applications presented in the chapters.

- Chapter quizzes for student review in preparation for course exams.

- Templates for strategic financial analysis and a "How to do a case analysis" guide, complete with financial ratios used to compare performance between firms.

- A financial review activity—for students who wish to refresh or extend their working knowledge of major financial measures in a strategic framework.

All ancillaries have the same look and feel, the same voice, and the same high quality as the book itself.

McGraw-Hill *Create*™

With McGraw-Hill's state-of-the art *Create*™ search engine, it is easy to find, arrange, and **personalize content**—whether from this textbook and its resources or from different sources—to create a customized book, perfect for your course, and at an affordable price.

For more information, contact your local McGraw-Hill sales rep or visit www.mcgrawhillcreate.com.

Blackboard® integration . . . Your life, simplified

Now you and your students can access McGraw-Hill's Connect® and Create™ right from within your Blackboard course—all with **one single sign-on**.

Not only do you get single sign-on with Connect and Create, you also get **deep integration of McGraw-Hill content and content engines** right in Blackboard.

When a student completes an integrated Connect assignment, the grade for that assignment automatically (and instantly) feeds your Blackboard grade center.

A solution for everyone—whether your institution is already using Blackboard or you just want to try Blackboard on your own, we have a solution for you. McGraw-Hill and Blackboard can now offer you easy access to industry leading technology and content, whether your campus hosts it, or we do.

The **Best** of **Both Worlds**

www.domorenow.com

Instructor Resources

Multiple resources, authored by Professor Anne W. Fuller, California State University, Sacramento, are available to make your teaching life easier:

- The **Instructors Manual (IM)** includes thorough coverage of each chapter as well as time-saving features such as a chapter outline including hyperlinks to later content in the chapter, a suggested lecture outline, teaching tips, PowerPoint references, video links and references, and answers to all end-of-chapter exercises.
- The **PowerPoint (PPT)** slides provide comprehensive lecture notes, video links, and company examples not found in the textbook, in an animated format for greater classroom interest.
- The **Test Bank** includes 100–150 questions per chapter, in a range of formats and with a greater-than-usual number of comprehension and application (or scenario-based) questions. It's tagged by learning objective, Bloom's Taxonomy levels, and AACSB requirements.

All of these instructors' resources have been copyedited and accuracy-checked to ensure a good fit with the textbook.

The **DVD** that accompanies the text includes videos that cover concepts from chapters. It offers video clips from sources such as Big Think, Stanford University's Entrepreneurship Corner, *The Economist, The* McKinsey *Quarterly,* MSNBC, NBC, and PBS. Videos are also conveniently referenced in the Instructor's Manual and Case Teaching Notes.

The **Online Learning Center (OLC)** is located at www.mhhe.com/ftrstrategy.

- At the **instructors' portion** of the OLC, which is password-protected, instructors can access all of the teaching resources described above, a Case Matrix relating cases back to concepts within the chapters, and comprehensive Case Teaching Notes, including case financial analysis.
- At the **students' portion** of the OLC, students can take chapter quizzes to review concepts, review chapter PowerPoint slides, and watch videos that relate back to concepts covered in this chapter and/or cases. Students can easily upgrade to a richer set of Premium Online Resources right on this site.

Tegrity Campus

Tegrity Campus makes class time available 24/7 by automatically capturing every lecture in a searchable format for students to review when they study and complete assignments. With a simple one-click start-and-stop process, you capture all computer screens and corresponding audio. Students can replay any part of any class with easy-to-use browser-based viewing on a PC or Mac.

Tegrity Campus's unique search feature helps students efficiently find what they need, when they need it, across an entire semester of class recordings. Help turn all your students' study time into learning moments immediately supported by your lecture.

To learn more about Tegrity, watch a two-minute Flash demo at http://tegritycampus.mhhe.com.

Simulations

- McGraw-Hill has two current strategy simulations—Business Strategy Game and GLO-BUS—that can be used with the textbook.
- For more information, contact your local McGraw-Hill sales representative.

McGraw-Hill Customer Care Contact Information

At McGraw-Hill, we understand that getting the most from new technology can be challenging. That's why our services don't stop after you purchase our products. You can e-mail our Product Specialists 24 hours a day to get product-training online. Or you can search our knowledge bank of Frequently Asked Questions on our support website. For Customer Support, call **800-331-5094,** e-mail **hmsupport@mcgraw-hill.com,** or visit **www.mhhe. com/support.** One of our Technical Support Analysts will be able to assist you in a timely fashion.

Assurance of Learning Ready

Many educational institutions today are focused on the notion of *assurance of learning,* an important element of many accreditation standards. *Strategic Management* is designed specifically to support your assurance of learning initiatives with a simple yet powerful solution.

Each chapter in the book begins with a list of numbered learning objectives, which appear throughout the chapter as well as in the end-of-chapter assignments. Every Test Bank question for *Strategic Management* maps to a specific chapter learning objective in the textbook. Each Test Bank question also identifies topic area, level of difficulty, Bloom's Taxonomy level, and AACSB skill area. You can use our Test Bank software, *EZ Test* and *EZ Test Online*, or *Connect Management* to easily search for learning objectives that directly relate to the learning objectives for your course. You can then use the reporting features of *EZ Test* to aggregate student results in a similar fashion, making the collection and presentation of Assurance of Learning data simple and easy.

AACSB Statement

McGraw-Hill/Irwin is a proud corporate member of AACSB International. Understanding the importance and value of AACSB accreditation, *Strategic Management* recognizes the curricula guidelines detailed in the AACSB standards for business accreditation by connecting selected questions in the Test Bank to the general knowledge and skill guidelines in the AACSB standards.

The statements contained in *Strategic Management* are provided only as a guide for the users of this textbook. The AACSB leaves content coverage and assessment within the purview of individual schools, the mission of the school, and the faculty. While *Strategic Management* and the teaching package make no claim of any specific AACSB qualification or evaluation, we have within *Strategic Management* labeled selected questions according to the six general knowledge and skills areas.

This book has gone through McGraw-Hill/Irwin's thorough development process. Over the course of several years, it has benefited from numerous developmental focus groups and hundreds of reviews by hundreds of reviewers across the country. The author and publisher wish to thank the following people who shared their insights, constructive criticisms, and valuable suggestions throughout the development of this project. Your contributions have improved this product.

Product-Development Focus Groups

Fall 2009

Melissa M. Appleyard
Portland State University

Marne Arthaud-Day
Kansas State University

Bindu Arya
University of Missouri, St. Louis

Tim Blumentritt
Kennesaw State University

Jill A. Brown
Lehigh University

Anne W. Fuller
California State University, Sacramento

Devi R. Gnyawali
Virginia Tech

Steve Gove
Virginia Tech

Stephen F. Hallam
The University of Akron

Duane Helleloid
University of North Dakota

George Hruby
Cleveland State University

John G. Irwin
Troy University

Jerry Kopf
Radford University

Bruce C. Kusch
Brigham Young University, Idaho

K. Blaine Lawlor
University of West Florida

Marty Lawlor
Rochester Institute of Technology

John Lawrence
University of Idaho

David Leibsohn
California State University, Fullerton

Richard T. Mpoyi
Middle Tennessee State University

Chandran Mylvaganam
Northwood University, Michigan

Chris Papenhausen
University of Massachusetts, Dartmouth

Luis A. Perez-Batres
Central Michigan University

JoDee Phillips
Kaplan University

Jim Sena
California Polytechnic State University, San Luis Obispo

Anju Seth
Virginia Tech

Lise Anne D. Slatten
University of Louisiana at Lafayette

Thuhang Tran
Middle Tennessee State University

Beverly B. Tyler
North Carolina State University

Arvids A. Ziedonis
University of Oregon

Fall 2010

Seung Bach
California State University, Sacramento

Dorothy Brawley
Kennesaw State University

Anne W. Fuller
California State University, Sacramento

Tim Heames
West Virginia University

Grant Miles
University of North Texas

Elouise Mintz
Saint Louis University

Frank Novakowski
Davenport University

Srikanth Paruchuri
*The Pennsylvania State
University*

Richard A. Quinn
*The University of Central
Florida*

Simon Rodan
San Jose State University

Michael D. Santoro
Lehigh University

Deepak Sethi
*Old Dominion
University*

Eugene S. Simko
Monmouth University

Linda F. Tegarden
Virginia Tech

Isaiah O. Ugboro
*North Carolina A&T State
University*

Joel West
*Claremont Graduate
University*

Marta Szabo White
Georgia State University

Market-Development Focus Groups
Summer 2011

Brent B. Allred
*The College of William
& Mary*

Betty S. Coffey
Appalachian State University

Anne Cohen
*University of Minnesota,
Twin Cities*

Darla Domke-Damonte
Coastal Carolina University

Stephen Drew
*Florida Gulf Coast
University*

David Duhon
*The University of Southern
Mississippi*

J. Michael Geringer
*California Polytechnic
State University, San Luis
Obispo*

Mahesh P. Joshi
George Mason University

Paul Mallette
Colorado State University

Michael Merenda
*University of New
Hampshire*

Michael Pitts
*Virginia Commonwealth
University*

Robert Porter
*The University of Central
Florida*

Deepak Sethi
Old Dominion University

Fall 2011

Moses Acquaah
*University of North
Carolina at Greensboro*

Garry Adams
Auburn University

David Baker
Kent State University

Geoff Bell
*University of Minnesota
Duluth*

Heidi Bertels
University of Pittsburgh

David Epstein
*University of Houston
Downtown*

Kevin Fertig
*University of Illinois at
Urbana-Champaign*

Susan Fox-Wolfgramm
Hawaii Pacific University

Tammy Hunt
*University of North
Carolina Wilmington*

Syeda Inamdar
San Jose State University

Jon Lehman
Vanderbilt University

David Leibsohn
*California State University,
Fullerton*

David Major
Indiana University

Michael Miller
*University of Illinois at
Chicago*

Chandran Mylvaganam
Northwood University

Louise Nemanich
Arizona State University

Ronaldo Parente
Florida International University

Keith Perry
San Jose State University

Vasudevan Ramanujam
Case Western Reserve University

Gary Scudder
Vanderbilt University

Thomas Shirley
San Jose State University

Eugene Simko
Monmouth University

Jing'an Tang
Sacred Heart University

Kim K. J. Tullis
University of Central Oklahoma

Isaiah Ugboro
North Carolina A&T State University

Jia Wang
California State University, Fresno

Margaret White
Oklahoma State University

Marta White
Georgia State University

Zhe Zhang
Eastern Kentucky University

Reviewers

Joshua R. Aaron
East Carolina University

Todd M. Alessandri
Northeastern University

Brent B. Allred
The College of William & Mary

Semiramis Amirpour
University of Texas at El Paso

Melissa M. Appleyard
Portland State University

Marne Arthaud-Day
Kansas State University

Bindu Arya
University of Missouri, St. Louis

Seung Bach
California State University, Sacramento

Dennis R. Balch
University of North Alabama

Edward R. Balotsky
Saint Joseph's University

Kevin Banning
Auburn University

Tim Blumentritt
Kennesaw State University

William C. Bogner
Georgia State University

Dorothy Brawley
Kennesaw State University

Michael G. Brizek
South Carolina State University

James W. Bronson
University of Wisconsin, Whitewater

Jill A. Brown
Lehigh University

Kenneth H. Chadwick
Nicholls State University

Clint Chadwick
The University of Alabama in Huntsville

Betty S. Coffey
Appalachian State University

Susan K. Cohen
University of Pittsburgh

Parthiban David
American University

Arthur J. Duhaime III
Nichols College

Danielle Dunne
Fordham University

Alan Ellstrand
University of Arkansas

Michael M. Fathi
Georgia Southwestern State University

Kevin Fertig
University of Illinois at Urbana-Champaign

Robert S. Fleming
Rowan University

Daniel Forbes
University of Minnesota

Isaac Fox
University of Minnesota

Steven A. Frankforter
Winthrop University

Anne W. Fuller
California State University, Sacramento

Venessa Funches
Auburn University at Montgomery

Jeffrey Furman
Boston University

J. Michael Geringer
*California Polytechnic State
University, San Luis Obispo*

Debbie Gilliard
*Metropolitan State College
of Denver*

Michelle Gittelman
Rutgers University

Devi R. Gnyawali
Virginia Tech

Sanjay Goel
*University of Minnesota
Duluth*

Steve Gove
Virginia Tech

Michael Gunderson
University of Florida

Craig M. Gustin
*American InterContinental
University*

Stephen F. Hallam
The University of Akron

Jon Timothy Heames
West Virginia University

Richard A. Heiens
*University of South
Carolina Aiken*

Duane Helleloid
University of North Dakota

Andrew M. Hess
University of Virginia

Ken Hess
*Metropolitan State
University*

Phyllis Holland
Valdosta State University

Stephen V. Horner
Arkansas State University

George Hruby
Cleveland State University

Tammy G. Hunt
*University of North
Carolina Wilmington*

John G. Irwin
Troy University

Carol K. Jacobson
Purdue University

Scott Johnson
Oklahoma State University

Necmi Karagozoglu
*California State University,
Sacramento*

J. Kay Keels
*Coastal Carolina
University*

Franz Kellermanns
*The University of
Tennessee*

Jerry Kopf
Radford University

Bruce C. Kusch
*Brigham Young University,
Idaho*

K. Blaine Lawlor
University of West Florida

Marty Lawlor
*Rochester Institute of
Technology*

John Lawrence
University of Idaho

Jun Lin
*State University of New
York (SUNY), New Paltz*

Joseph Mahoney
*University of Illinois at
Urbana-Champaign*

Paul Mallette
Colorado State University

Daniel B. Marin
Louisiana State University

Louis Martinette
*University of Mary
Washington*

Anthony U. Martinez
*San Francisco State
University*

David McCalman
*University of Central
Arkansas*

Jeffrey McGee
*The University of Texas
at Arlington*

Grant Miles
University of North Texas

Elouise Mintz
Saint Louis University

Gwen Moore
*University of Missouri,
St. Louis*

James P. Morgan
*Webster University, Fort
Leonard Wood Campus*

Richard T. Mpoyi
*Middle Tennessee State
University*

Chandran Mylvaganam
*Northwood University,
Michigan*

Louise Nemanich
Arizona State University

Frank Novakowski
Davenport University

Kevin O'Mara
Elon University

Chris Papenhausen
*University of
Massachusetts, Dartmouth*

James M. Pappas
Oklahoma State University

Srikanth Paruchuri
The Pennsylvania State University

Christine Cope Pence
University of California, Riverside

Luis A. Perez-Batres
Central Michigan University

JoDee Phillips
Kaplan University

Michael W. Pitts
Virginia Commonwealth University

Richard A. Quinn
The University of Central Florida

Annette L. Ranft
The University at Tennessee

Gary B. Roberts
Kennesaw State University

Simon Rodan
San Jose State University

Yassir M. Samra
Manhattan College

Michael D. Santoro
Lehigh University

Jim Sena
California Polytechnic State University, San Luis Obispo

Deepak Sethi
Old Dominion University

Mark Sharfman
University of Oklahoma

Eugene S. Simko
Monmouth University

Faye A. Sisk
Mercer University, Atlanta

Lise Anne D. Slatten
University of Louisiana at Lafayette

Garry D. Smith
Mississippi State University

James D. Spina
University of Maryland

Linda F. Tegarden
Virginia Tech

Thuhang Tran
Middle Tennessee State University

Isaiah O. Ugboro
North Carolina A&T State University

Bruce Walters
Louisiana Tech University

Andrew Ward
Lehigh University

Vincent Weaver
Greenville Technical College

Laura Whitcomb
California State University, Los Angeles

Marta Szabo White
Georgia State University

Ross A. Wirth
Franklin University

Michael J. Zhang
Sacred Heart University

Yanfeng Zheng
The University of Hong Kong

Arvids A. Ziedonis
University of Oregon

Beta Testers

Instructors

Joshua R. Aaron
East Carolina University

Brent B. Allred
The College of William & Mary

Melissa M. Appleyard
Portland State University

Marne Arthaud-Day
Kansas State University

Bindu Arya
University of Missouri, St. Louis

Danielle Dunne
formerly Binghampton University, SUNY (now at Fordham University)

Anne W. Fuller
California State University, Sacramento

Elouise Mintz
Saint Louis University

Chandran Mylvaganam
Northwood University, Michigan

Louise Nemanich
Arizona State University

Frank Novakowski
Davenport University

Richard A. Quinn
The University of Central Florida

Beverly B. Tyler
North Carolina State University, Raleigh

Joel West
formerly San Jose State University (now at Claremont Graduate University)

Students

Over 400 students at various colleges and universities beta-tested parts of this textbook and shared their feedback. Special thanks to the following, who gave permission to include their names in the book.

Chelsea Aaberg
University of Missouri, St. Louis

Erin Allan
University of Missouri, St. Louis

Nolan Andelin
Arizona State University

Amy L. Ariss
Arizona State University

Christopher Bain
The University of Central Florida

Patrick Battillo
Arizona State University

Neha Bhatnagar
The College of William & Mary

Collin Breuhaus
Saint Louis University

Jennifer Brinkerhoff
The College of William & Mary

Chelsea Brooks
The University of Central Florida

Bethany Brown
Binghamton University

Michael Camey
The University of Central Florida

Gonzalo Carrillo
North Carolina State University

Tania Chackumkal
Saint Louis University

Meredith Chalk
Saint Louis University

Kerry Conaty
Saint Louis University

Zachary Davis
The University of Central Florida

Matthew DeRemer
The University of Central Florida

Lauren Dickerson
The University of Central Florida

Leah Ducey
Saint Louis University

Sumair Dugan
The University of Central Florida

Patrick Earley
Saint Louis University

Tony Fantozzi
University of Missouri, St. Louis

John Frankenhoff
The College of William & Mary

Nicole Friedman
Binghamton University

Jacob Galper
The University of Central Florida

Talia Gholson
University of Missouri, St. Louis

Tyler Greer
North Carolina State University

Scott Gumieny
Davenport University

Nicole Hansen
Portland State University

Lindsey Helgeson
Saint Louis University

David Herendeen
University of Missouri, St. Louis

Ashly Hughes
Arizona State University

David Hurdle
Arizona State University

Sodeth Im
Arizona State University

Stephen Kincaid
Saint Louis University

Juliya Korenchenkova
The University of Central Florida

Robert Lancaster
The College of William & Mary

Shawn Larson
Northwood University

Iris Lau
Binghamton University

Tak Lay
Arizona State University

Sanggyu Lee
Binghamton University

Angela Licata
University of Missouri, St. Louis

Laura Linton
The University of Central Florida

Stacy Litchford
*The College of William &
Mary*

Ashley Marlow
*The University of Central
Florida*

Blaire Martin
*The University of Central
Florida*

Jonathan Martin
Saint Louis University

Joshua Martinez
*The University of Central
Florida*

K. Matis
*The College of William &
Mary*

Jennifer Maxson
Saint Louis University

Jill Mazur
*The College of William &
Mary*

Lindsay McClure
*The University of Central
Florida*

Stephen McGillivray
*The College of William &
Mary*

Jonathan McGovern
*The University of Central
Florida*

Bryan Mecklenburg
Davenport University

Steven Miller
*The University of Central
Florida*

Aretia Dian Moir
*Portland State
University*

Sudha Movva
*The College of William &
Mary*

Eric Murray
Arizona State University

Alejandra M. Nauman
*North Carolina State
University*

Dmitriy Ostrobrod
Binghamton University

Joseph Owen
Binghamton University

Timi Oyeleke
*The University of Central
Florida*

Richard Ratkai
*The University of Central
Florida*

Kirthi Ravi
*The College of William &
Mary*

Rebecca Reibel
Northwood University

Amanda Rodriguez
*The University of Central
Florida*

Suela Shaho
*The University of Central
Florida*

Zachary Shapiro
Binghamton University

Amit Sharma
*The College of William &
Mary*

Greg Smith
Arizona State University

Matthew Smith
*The University of Central
Florida*

Andrea Smith
Binghamton University

Darshini Swamy
*The College of William &
Mary*

Mariela Tchobanova
Arizona State University

David Tepper
Davenport University

C. Thornton
*The College of William &
Mary*

Osman Alican Turhan
Binghamton University

James A. Unti
Arizona State University

Rachel Wheeler
*North Carolina State
University*

Caroline Williams
*North Carolina State
University*

Cho Ting Wong
Binghamton University

Anda Wood
*The College of William &
Mary*

David Wright
*North Carolina State
University*

Yiming Xu
Binghamton University

Linfeng Zhang
Northwood University

PART 1
Analysis: Getting Started
1. What Is Strategy and Why Is It Important?
2. The Strategic Management Process

Implementation
11. Organizational Design: Structure, Culture, and Control
12. Corporate Governance, Business Ethics, and Strategic Leadership

PART 1
External and Internal Analysis
3. External Analysis: Industry Structure, Competitive Forces, and Strategic Groups
4. Internal Analysis: Resources, Capabilities, and Activities
5. Competitive Advantage and Firm Performance

GAINING & SUSTAINING COMPETITIVE ADVANTAGE

Formulation: Corporate Strategy
8. Corporate Strategy: Vertical Integration and Diversification
9. Corporate Strategy: Acquisitions, Alliances, and Networks
10. Global Strategy: Competing Around the World

Formulation: Business Strategy
6. Business Strategy: Differentiation, Cost Leadership, and Integration
7. Business Strategy: Innovation and Strategic Entrepreneurship

PART 1
Strategy Analysis

CHAPTER 1

What Is Strategy and Why Is It Important?

LEARNING OBJECTIVES

After studying this chapter, you should be able to:

LO 1-1   Define competitive advantage, sustainable competitive advantage, competitive disadvantage, and competitive parity.

LO 1-2   Define strategy and explain its role in a firm's quest for competitive advantage.

LO 1-3   Explain the role of firm effects and industry effects in determining firm performance.

LO 1-4   Describe the role of corporate, business, and functional managers in strategy formulation and implementation.

LO 1-5   Outline how business models put strategy into action.

LO 1-6   Describe and assess the opportunities and challenges managers face in the 21st century.

LO 1-7   Critically evaluate the role that different stakeholders play in the firm's quest for competitive advantage.

The Premature Death of a Google Forerunner at Microsoft

IN 1998, 24-year-old Sergey Brin and 25-year-old Larry Page founded Google. They met as graduate students in computer science at Stanford University, where they began working together on a web crawler, with the goal of improving online searches. What they developed was the PageRank algorithm, which returns the most relevant web pages more or less instantaneously and ranks them by how often they are referenced on other important web pages. A clear improvement over early search engines such as AltaVista, Overture, and Yahoo, all of which indexed by keywords, the PageRank algorithm is able to consider 500 million variables and 3 billion terms. What started as a homework assignment launched the two into an entrepreneurial venture when they set up shop in a garage in Menlo Park, California.

Today, Google is the world's leading online search and advertising company, with some 70 percent market share of an industry estimated to be worth more than $25 billion a year, and that is growing quickly. Though Yahoo is a distant second with less than 20 percent share, in 2008 Microsoft's CEO Steve Ballmer offered to buy the runner-up for close to $50 billion to help his company gain a foothold in the paid-search business where Google rules. Yahoo turned down the offer.

What haunts Ballmer is that Microsoft actually had its own working prototype of a Google forerunner, called Keywords, more than a decade earlier.

Scott Banister, then a student at the University of Illinois, had come up with the idea of adding paid advertisements to Internet searches. He quit college and drove his Geo hatchback to the San Francisco Bay Area to start Keywords, later joining an online ad company called LinkExchange. In 1998, Microsoft bought LinkExchange for some $265 million (about one two-hundredth the price it would later offer for Yahoo). LinkExchange's managers urged Microsoft to invest in Keywords. Instead, Microsoft executives shut down LinkExchange in 2000 because they did not see a viable business model in it. One LinkExchange manager actually approached Ballmer himself and explained that he thought Microsoft was making a mistake. But Ballmer said he wanted to manage through delegation and would not reverse a decision made by managers three levels below him. Thus ended Microsoft's first online advertising venture.

In 2003, Microsoft got a second chance to enter the online advertising business when some of its mid-level managers proposed buying Overture Services, an innovator in combining Internet searches with advertisements. This time, Ballmer, joined by Microsoft's co-founder Bill Gates, decided not to pursue the idea because they thought Overture was overpriced. Shortly thereafter, Yahoo bought Overture for $1.6 billion.

Having missed two huge opportunities to pursue promising strategic initiatives that emerged from lower levels within the firm, Microsoft has been playing catch-up in the paid-search business ever since. In the summer of 2009, it launched its own search engine, Bing. Microsoft's new search engine will also power Yahoo searches, after the two announced a strategic alliance. These two strategic moves helped Microsoft increase its share in the lucrative online search business to roughly

25 percent, up from just over 8 percent. It remains an open question whether this is sufficient, however, to challenge Google's dominance. In particular, Bing's increase in market share of online searches is obtained at the expense of Yahoo's, and not Google's, market share.[1]

After reading the chapter, you will find more about this case, with related questions, on page 21.

▲ **HOW DID A STARTUP** by two college students outperform Microsoft, one of the world's leading technology companies, in online search and advertising? Why is Google successful in the online search business while Yahoo is struggling? For that matter, why is any company successful? What enables some firms to gain and then sustain their competitive advantage over time? Why do once-great firms fail? How can a firm's managers influence performance?

Answering these questions requires integrating the knowledge you've obtained in your studies of different business disciplines (such as accounting, finance, economics, marketing, operations, IT management, organizational behavior, and human resource management) to understand what leads to superior performance. Strategic management, the topic of this course and this book, is the integrative management field that combines analysis, formulation, and implementation in the quest for competitive advantage. The AFI strategy framework shown on the part-opening page (page 1) embodies this view of strategic management. In this chapter, we lay the groundwork for the study of strategic management by introducing some foundational ideas about strategy and competitive advantage, and by looking at the components of the AFI framework.

WHAT STRATEGY IS: GAINING & SUSTAINING COMPETITIVE ADVANTAGE

>> **LO 1-1**
Define competitive advantage, sustainable competitive advantage, competitive disadvantage, and competitive parity.

The desire to perform better than our competitors applies to nearly every area of our lives. Universities compete for the best students and professors. Startup firms compete for financial and human capital. Existing companies compete for future growth, and employees compete for raises and promotions. University professors compete for research grants, and college students for jobs and graduate school admission. Political candidates compete for votes, and charities for contributions.

In every competitive situation, the winners are generally those with the better strategy. In general terms, *strategy* is the planned and realized set of actions a firm takes to achieve its goals. For instance, the general manager of the Oakland A's, Billy Beane, applied a sophisticated analysis to formulate and implement a new strategy.[2] Beane began by devising new metrics to assess a player's potential and performance more accurately. These metrics, in turn, allowed the Oakland A's to field a low-cost team that could compete against much richer rivals in Major League Baseball. Taken together, strategy governs the ubiquitous quest for superior performance.

What Is Competitive Advantage?

A firm that formulates and implements a strategy that leads to superior performance relative to other competitors in the same industry or the industry average has a competitive advantage. Google has a competitive advantage over Microsoft, Yahoo, and others competing in the online search and advertising business. A firm that is able to outperform its competitors or the industry average over a prolonged period of time has a sustainable competitive advantage.[3] It appears that Google has a sustainable competitive advantage, because it has outperformed its rivals consistently over time. Yet, past performance is no guarantee of future performance. Microsoft, Yahoo, and others are working hard to neutralize Google's competitive advantage.

In both business and sports, strategy is about outperforming one's rivals. Identifying the winner in a sporting event, however, is relatively easy. In 2011, the University of Connecticut Huskies won the NCAA basketball championship, beating the Butler University Bulldogs 54-41 in the title game. We could say that the UConn Huskies gained a temporary competitive advantage. To answer the question of who has a *sustainable* competitive advantage, however, is a bit trickier. Here, we need to look at the recent history of tournaments. If we say, for example, that 10 years is an appropriate time period over which to assess the sustainability of competitive advantage (2002–2011), then we find that seven teams were victorious: the University of Connecticut, the University of Florida (Gators), and the University of North Carolina at Chapel Hill (Tar Heels) each two times; and Duke University, the University of Kansas, Syracuse University, and the University of Maryland each one time. We could argue that over this 10-year period the Huskies, the Gators, and the Tar Heels enjoyed a sustainable competitive advantage over other NCAA teams. Since competitive advantage needs to be assessed relative to other competitors, we can only say that the Huskies, Gators, and Tar Heels, although outperforming the other contenders, performed at a similarly high level. This example shows that assessing competitive advantage, let alone sustainable competitive advantage, is not an easy task.

In business, we have no *absolute* measure of performance for competitive advantage as we do for height or weight or NCAA tournament victories. Rather, we compare performance to a benchmark, either the performance of other firms in the same industry or an industry average. If a firm underperforms its rivals or the industry average, for instance, it has a competitive disadvantage. A 15 percent return on invested capital (RoIC) may sound like superior firm performance, but in the energy industry where the average RoIC has been above 20 percent the last few years, it is actually a competitive disadvantage. In contrast, if a firm's RoIC is 5 percent in a commodity industry like steel, where the industry average is 1–2 percent, then the firm has a competitive advantage. Should two or more firms perform at the same level, they have competitive parity.

If other companies can easily imitate a firm's source of competitive advantage, then any edge the firm gains is short-lived. But if the advantage is difficult to understand or imitate, the firm can sustain it over time. Patents, for example,

---

strategic management An integrative management field that combines analysis, formulation, and implementation in the quest for competitive advantage.

competitive disadvantage Underperformance relative to other competitors in the same industry or the industry average.

competitive advantage Superior performance relative to other competitors in the same industry or the industry average.

competitive parity Performance of two or more firms at the same level.

sustainable competitive advantage Outperforming competitors or the industry average over a prolonged period of time.

often protect certain products from direct imitation for a period. Pfizer's Lipitor, a patent-protected cholesterol-lowering drug, is the best-selling prescription drug ever, grossing some $14 billion dollars in revenues each year between 2006 and 2009.[4] This highly successful product contributed to a competitive advantage for Pfizer, accounting for roughly one-third of its total annual revenues.[5] The patent on Lipitor expired in 2010, however, allowing generic drug makers to copy the drug and offer it at much lower prices, eroding Pfizer's competitive advantage.

What Is Strategy?

Strategy describes the goal-directed actions a firm intends to take in its quest to gain and sustain competitive advantage.[6] The firm that possesses competitive advantage provides superior value to customers at a competitive price or acceptable value at a lower price. Profitability and market share are the consequences of superior value creation. Henry Ford was driven by his ambition to mass-produce a reliable car at a low cost. Larry Page and Sergey Brin were motivated to create a better search engine. For Ford, Page, and Brin, and numerous other businesspeople, making money was the *consequence* of providing a product or service consumers wanted. The important point here is that strategy is about creating superior value, while containing the cost to create it. The greater the difference between value creation and cost, the greater the economic contribution the firm makes, and thus the greater the likelihood for competitive advantage.

Strategy is not, however, a zero-sum game—it's not always the case that one party wins while all others lose. Many strategic successes are accomplished when firms or individuals cooperate with one another.[7] Even direct competitors cooperate occasionally, to create win–win scenarios. When competitors cooperate with one another to achieve strategic objectives, we call this co-opetition.[8] The new Cell microprocessor, which powers the PlayStation 3 game console, was the result of a collaborative effort among IBM, Toshiba, and Sony—companies that directly compete with one another in other markets.

We've noted that to gain a competitive advantage, a firm needs to provide either goods or services consumers value more highly than those of its competitors, or goods or services similar to the competitors' but at a lower price. The essence of strategy, therefore, is being different from rivals and thus unique. Managers accomplish this difference through *strategic positioning,* staking out a unique position in an industry that allows the firm to provide value to customers, while controlling costs.

Strategic positioning requires trade-offs, however. As a low-cost retailer, JCPenney has a clear strategic profile and serves a specific market segment. Upscale retailer Neiman Marcus also has built a clear strategic profile by providing superior customer service to a specific (luxury) market segment. While the companies are in the same industry, their respective customer segments overlap very little, if at all, and thus they are not direct competitors. To keep it that way, their managers must make conscious trade-offs that enable both to strive for competitive advantage in the same industry.

As emphasized by Michael Porter of Harvard Business School, strategy is as much about deciding what *not* to do, as it is about deciding what to do. Because the supply of resources is not unlimited, managers must carefully consider their business strategy choices in their quest for competitive advantage. Trying to be everything to everybody would be a recipe for inferior performance. For example, to ward off successful low-cost entrants like Southwest Airlines (SWA), Continental and Delta added low-cost Continental

Lite and Delta's Song to their core hub-and-spoke businesses. Their managers fell prey to the illusion that they could straddle a low-cost leadership position (already well-executed by SWA) and their existing differentiation strategy of serving a large number of destinations. Both new ventures failed because they left Continental and Delta *stuck in the middle*, leading to inferior performance in both markets. (We'll consider different business strategies in more depth in Chapter 6.)

Strategy as a Theory of How to Compete

A firm's strategy can be seen as its managers' theory about how to gain and sustain competitive advantage. A *theory* answers the questions, what causes what and why?[9] It's a contingent statement based on assumptions about how the world works. Based on the law of gravity, for example, we can predict what will happen if you drop something out the window—without your having to do it to find out. As the old adage goes, nothing is more practical than a good theory. Based on their assumptions about competitive conditions— that is, the relative value of their firm's resources and capabilities as compared to those of their collaborators and competitors, predictions about the actions that competitors may initiate, and the development of trends in the external environment—managers express their theory of how to gain and sustain competitive advantage in the strategy they set for the firm.[10] As we will see in Chapters 3 and 4, a firm can gain competitive advantage by leveraging its internal resources, capabilities, and relationships to exploit opportunities in its external environment.

Strategy as a *theory of how to compete* provides managers with a roadmap to navigate the competitive territory. The more accurate the map, the better strategic decisions managers can make. In the competitive world, managers test their theories in the marketplace. Positive feedback validates managers' strategic assumptions: "iPhone sales vastly exceeded expectations, so it must have been the right product at the right time." Negative feedback allows managers to adjust their assumptions: "The Apple Newton flopped [in 1993], so its price—over $1,000 in today's dollars—and bulkiness weren't right for the PDA market at that time." The Newton's failure, however, laid the foundation for later successes such as Apple's iPhone and the iPad. Competitors also learned from the Newton debacle: They subsequently introduced improved products, including Palm's Pilot, Handspring's Visor, and RIM's BlackBerry, at a lower price. A firm's relative performance in the competitive marketplace provides managers with the necessary feedback to assess how well their strategy works in their quest for competitive advantage. *The strategic management process, therefore, is a never-ending cycle of analysis, formulation, implementation, and feedback.*

Walmart became the world's largest retailer in part due to founder Sam Walton's accurate assumptions about the connection between low retail prices in underserved rural and suburban areas and high volume, thus generating the ability to be the low-price leader in mass-merchandising.[11] His insight of how to do things differently in the retail industry created a competitive advantage for his firm. Later, Walmart reinforced its competitive advantage with a revolutionary IT system that tracks sales in real time and allows just-in-time deliveries. For the year 2008, one of the worst stock performance years on record, the Dow Jones Industrial Average fell 34 percent, yet Walmart's shares actually rose 18 percent, outperforming the average of the 30 blue-chip firms by 52 percentage points. The reason? When managers align their assumptions closely with competitive realities, they can draft and implement a successful strategy that yields superior firm performance. Walmart's cost leadership strategy became even more valuable in a time of economic hardship.

In contrast, when managers' theories of how to gain and sustain competitive advantage do not reflect reality, their firm's strategy will destroy rather than create value and will lead to inferior performance. The U.S. auto manufacturers Chrysler, Ford, and GM have fallen on hard times partly because their managers built their strategies around the flawed assumptions that gasoline prices would remain low and U.S. drivers would continue to want big trucks and sport utility vehicles. These were also the only vehicles that U.S. car manufacturers, given their inflated cost structure, could sell at a profit. The Ford F-150 pickup truck is the most-sold vehicle of all time in the United States, and the Hummer (about 8 miles per gallon) was once one of GM's most profitable vehicles. When gas prices rose above $4 per gallon in the summer of 2008 (up from less than $2.50 a gallon just a year earlier), consumer preferences for more fuel-efficient and "green" cars increased.

Meanwhile, in Japan where gas prices have always been high, Toyota's managers had begun to think as early as the 1990s about how fuel efficiency and possible regulation would influence consumer behavior. So while Toyota provided large SUVs and pickup trucks to meet U.S. market demand, it also developed hybrid vehicles to compete in an environment of increased regulation, higher gas prices, and heightened consumer concerns about the ecological impact of gas-guzzling cars. In 1997, Toyota launched the Prius (60 miles per gallon), which has since sold more than 2 million units. Because the strategies of U.S. car manufacturers were based on flawed assumptions and each manufacturer had long-term resource commitments that were not easily reversible, U.S. car manufacturers did not have a competitive fuel-efficient (or hybrid) vehicle.[12] The poor financial performance that followed was the logical consequence of a strategy that no longer fit the competitive realities. In 2009, both GM and Chrysler filed for bankruptcy. Engineering a shrewd strategic turnaround, Ford (which, by the way, did not receive a government bailout) is experiencing a resurgence.[13]

Industry vs. Firm Effects in Determining Performance

firm effects The results of managers' actions to influence firm performance.

industry effects The results attributed to the choice of industry in which to compete.

Managers' actions tend to be more important in determining firm performance than the forces exerted upon the firm by its external environment. Thus, firm effects—the results of managers' actions to influence firm performance—tend to have more impact than industry effects—the results attributed to the choice of industry in which to compete.[14] Based on a number of empirical studies, academic researchers found that the industry a firm is in determines about 20 percent of a firm's profitability, while the firm's strategy within a given industry explains between 30–45 percent of its performance.[15] These findings are depicted in Exhibit 1.1. Although a firm's industry environment is not quite as important as the firm's strategy within its industry, they jointly determine the firm's overall performance.

Astute managers create superior performance through strategy.

EXHIBIT 1.1

Industry, Firm, and Other Effects Explaining Superior Firm Performance

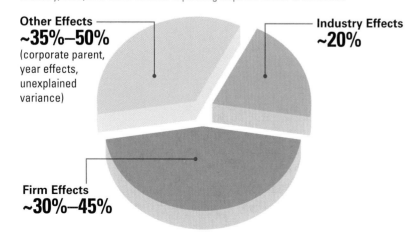

Other Effects
~35%–50%
(corporate parent, year effects, unexplained variance)

Industry Effects
~20%

Firm Effects
~30%–45%

They leverage a company's strengths while mitigating its weaknesses. They turn external threats into opportunities. Strategy generally requires making important trade-offs (think low-cost Kia versus luxury Ferrari in the car industry). Indeed, some of the biggest advances in competitive positioning have been accomplished when managers resolved apparent trade-offs. Toyota introduced lean manufacturing to resolve the trade-off between quality and cost. This process innovation allowed Toyota to produce higher-quality cars at a lower unit cost, and to perfect the mass customization of cars. Lean manufacturing, over time, has become a necessary but not sufficient condition for competitive advantage in the auto industry. Today, if a carmaker can't produce high-quality, mass-customized cars at low cost, it is not even in the game. More recently, Toyota stumbled as questions arose whether the company could maintain its stellar quality record while growing so fast. Korea's Hyundai stepped into this void, offering cars that surpass Toyota in quality while attempting to provide luxury similar to Lexus vehicles.[16] Hyundai's managers carved out a strong strategic position for the company by focusing on resolving the trade-offs between luxury, quality, and cost. The ups and downs in the car industry clearly show that competitive advantage is transitory. It is a difficult quest to gain competitive advantage; it is even more difficult to sustain it. The tools of strategic management aid managers in this important challenge.

>> **LO 1-3**
Explain the role of firm effects and industry effects in determining firm performance.

What Strategy Is *Not*

To gain a deeper understanding of what strategy is, it is helpful to know what strategy is *not*.[17] You will hear many people today refer to a host of different plans and activities as pricing strategy, Internet strategy, alliance strategy, operations strategy, IT strategy, brand strategy, marketing strategy, HR strategy, and so on. While all these elements may be *part* of a firm's functional strategy to support its business model (see the next section), we will reserve the term *strategy* for describing the firm's overall efforts to *gain and sustain competitive advantage.*

Nor is competitive benchmarking "strategy." Best-in-class practices such as just-in-time inventory, enterprise resource planning (ERP) systems, and Six Sigma quality initiatives all fall under the umbrella of *tools* for operational effectiveness. Being best-in-class is a sufficient but not a necessary condition for competitive advantage. Take this idea to its extreme in a quick thought experiment: If all firms in the same industry pursued Six Sigma in the same fashion, all would have identical cost structures and none could gain a competitive advantage. Indeed, competition would be cut-throat because all firms would be more or less the same, but very efficient. Everyone would be running faster, but nothing would have changed in relative strategic positions.

Rather than focusing on copying a competitor, the key to successful strategy is to combine a set of activities to stake out a unique position in an industry. Competitive advantage has to come from performing activities differently than rivals do. Operational effectiveness, marketing skills, and other functional expertise, along with best practices, contribute to a unique strategic position, but by themselves they are not a substitute for strategy. Exhibit 1.2 summarizes the concept of strategy.

EXHIBIT 1.2

What Is Strategy?

Definition: *Strategy is the quest to gain and sustain competitive advantage.*

- It is the managers' theories about how to gain and sustain competitive advantage.
- It is about being different from your rivals.
- It is about creating value while containing cost.
- It is about deciding what to do, and what *not* to do.
- It combines a set of activities to stake out a unique position.
- It requires long-term commitments that are often not easily reversible.

FORMULATING STRATEGY ACROSS LEVELS: CORPORATE, BUSINESS, AND FUNCTIONAL MANAGERS

>> LO 1-4
Describe the role of corporate, business, and functional managers in strategy formulation and implementation.

Strategy formulation concerns the choice of strategy in terms of *where* and *how* to compete. To understand the interdependencies across different levels, it is helpful to break down strategy formulation into three distinct levels: corporate, business, and functional.

Corporate strategy involves decisions made at the highest level of the firm about *where* to compete. *Corporate executives* need to decide in which industries, markets, and geographies their company should compete, as well as how they can create synergies across business units that may be quite different. They are responsible for setting overarching strategic goals and allocating scarce resources, among the different business divisions, monitoring performance, and making adjustments to the overall portfolio of businesses when needed. Corporate executives determine the scope of the business, deciding whether to enter certain industries and markets and whether to sell certain divisions. The objective of corporate-level strategy is to increase overall corporate value. Over the last 20 years, due to a new corporate-level strategy, IBM's CEO Sam Palmisano and his predecessors have transformed IBM from a hardware company to a global IT services firm. It even sold its PC unit to Lenovo, a Chinese high-tech company as part of the transformation process.

Exhibit 1.3 shows that corporate strategy is formulated at headquarters, and that *business strategy* occurs within strategic business units, the standalone divisions of a larger conglomerate, each with its own profit-and-loss responsibility. *General managers* in strategic business units (SBUs) must answer the strategic question of *how* to compete in order to achieve superior performance within the business unit. Currently, for example, IBM has four strategic business units or divisions: hardware, software, technology services, and financing. General managers are responsible for formulating a strategic position for their business unit. The technology services SBU at IBM is led by a senior vice president, who has profit-and-loss responsibility for IBM's technology services worldwide. The same goes for the heads of the other three SBUs at IBM.

strategic business unit (SBU) A standalone division of a larger conglomerate, with its own profit-and-loss responsibility.

EXHIBIT 1.3

Strategy Formulation and Implementation Across Levels: Corporate, Business, and Functional Strategy

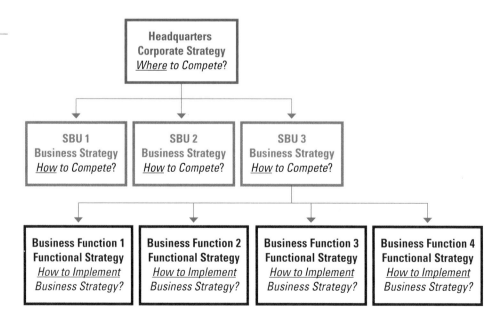

Within each SBU are various business *functions* such as accounting, finance, human resources, information technology, product development, operations, marketing, and customer service. Each *functional manager* is responsible for decisions and actions within a single functional area that aid in the implementation of the business-level strategy. A manager in IBM's product-development function, for example, may be responsible for encouraging new product offerings. The set of functional strategies enables the general managers of the SBUs to pursue their respective business-level strategy, which in turn needs to be in line with the overall corporate-level strategy.

Functional managers, who are closer to the final products, services, and customers than managers at higher levels, may sometimes be able to come up with strategic initiatives that may influence the direction of the company. One functional manager at IBM, for instance, suggested entry into the life sciences field.[18] In 2000, she saw a business opportunity for IBM, in which application of high-performance computing and information technology could solve thorny problems that accompanied data-intensive work such as decoding human genomes and furthering personalized medicine. IBM's general and corporate managers supported this strategic initiative, dubbed "information-based medicine."[19] This new business opportunity generated more than $5 billion in revenue by 2006.

BUSINESS MODELS: PUTTING STRATEGY INTO ACTION

We've said that strategy denotes the managers' theories of how to compete, but theory alone is useless if it is not put into action. The translation of strategy into action takes place in the firm's business model, which details the firm's competitive tactics and initiatives. Simply put, the firm's business model explains how the firm intends to make money. If it fails to translate a strategy into a profitable business model, the firm will cease to exist. To come up with a business model, the firm first transforms its theory of how to compete into a blueprint of actions and initiatives that support the overarching strategy. In a second step, the organization implements this blueprint through structures, processes, culture, and procedures.

>> **LO 1-5**
Outline how business models put strategy into action.

The so-called *razor–razor-blade business model* is a famous example. The idea is to give away or sell for a small fee the product and make money on the replacement part needed. As the name indicates, it was invented by Gillette, which gave away its razors and sold the replacement cartridges for relatively high prices. The razor–razor-blade model is found in many business applications today. For example, HP charges very little for its laser printers but imposes high prices for its replacement cartridges.

Similarly, telecommunications companies provide a basic cell phone at no charge or significantly subsidize high-end smartphones when you sign up for a two-year wireless service plan. They combine the razor–razor-blade model with the *subscription-based business model,* which was first introduced by magazines and newspapers. They recoup the subsidy provided for the smartphone by requiring customers to sign up for lengthy service plans. The leading provider of audio books, Audible, a subsidiary of Amazon, also uses a subscription-based business model.

The opening case foreshadows the up-and-coming battle between Google and Microsoft as each moves progressively on to the other's turf. Although Google started out as an online search and advertising company, it now offers software applications (Google Docs, word processing, spreadsheet, e-mail, interactive calendar, and presentation software) and operating systems (Chrome OS for the web and Android for mobile applications), among many other online products and services. In contrast, Microsoft began its life by offering an operating system (since 1985, called Windows), then moved into software applications with its

business model
Organizational plan that details the firm's competitive tactics and initiatives; in short, how the firm intends to make money.

EXHIBIT 1.4

Competing Business
Models: Google vs.
Microsoft

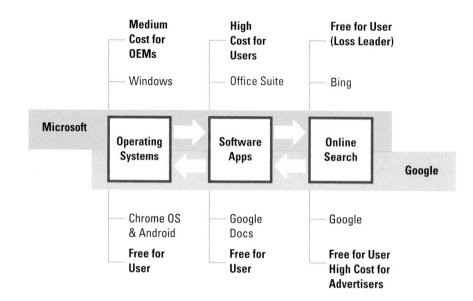

Office Suite, and now into online search and advertising with Bing. Thus, the stage is set for a clash of the technology titans.

In fighting this battle, Google and Microsoft pursue very different business models, as shown in Exhibit 1.4.[20] Google offers its applications software Google Docs for free to induce and retain as many users as possible for its search engine. Although Google's flagship search engine is free for the end user, Google makes money from sponsored links by advertisers. The advertisers pay for the placement of their ad on the results pages and every time a user clicks through an ad (which Google calls a "sponsored link"). Thus, many billion mini-transactions add up to a substantial business. As indicated in Exhibit 1.4, Google uses part of the profits earned from its lucrative online advertising business to subsidize Google Docs. Giving away products and services to induce widespread use allows Google to benefit from *network effects*—the increase in the value of a product or service as more people use it. Thus, Google can charge advertisers for highly targeted and effective ads, allowing it to subsidize other product offerings that compete directly with Microsoft.

Microsoft's business model is almost the reverse of Google's. Initially, Microsoft focused on creating a large installed base of users for its PC operating system (Windows). It now holds some 90 percent market share in operating system software worldwide. Once the users are locked into a Microsoft operating system (which generally comes preloaded with the computer they purchased), they then want to buy applications that run seamlessly with the operating system. The obvious choice for most users is Microsoft's Office Suite (containing Word, Excel, PowerPoint, Outlook, and Access), but they need to pay several hundred dollars for the latest version. As shown in Exhibit 1.4, Microsoft uses the profits from its application software business to subsidize its search engine Bing, which is—just like Google's—a free product offering for the end user. Given Bing's relatively small market share, however, and the tremendous cost in developing the search engine, Microsoft, unlike Google, does not make any money from its online search offering; rather, it is a big money loser. The logic behind Bing is to provide a countervailing power to Google's dominant position in online search. The logic behind Google Docs is to create a threat to Microsoft's dominant position in application software. These strategies create *multi-point competition* between the two technology firms.[21] Taken together, Google and Microsoft compete with one another for market share in several different product categories through quite different business models.

STRATEGY IN THE 21ST CENTURY

As the adage goes, change is the only constant—and the rate of change appears to be increasing.[22] Changing technologies spawn new industries, while others die out. Managers today face an increasingly competitive world and a truly global marketplace. These trends, rapid technological change and increasing globalization, dramatically affect how to formulate and implement an effective strategy in the 21st century. Here we expand on the impact of key trends (accelerating technological change, a truly global world, and future industries) that will affect strategy making in the 21st century.

Accelerating Technological Change

The rate of technological change has accelerated drastically over the last hundred years. Exhibit 1.5 shows how many years it took for different technological innovations to reach 50 percent of the U.S. population (either through ownership or usage). As an example, it took 84 years for half of the U.S. population to own a car, but only 28 years for half the population to own a TV. The pace of the adoption rate of recent innovations continues to accelerate. It took 19 years for the PC to reach 50 percent ownership, but only 6 years for MP3 players to accomplish the same diffusion rate.

What factors explain rapid technological diffusion and adoption? One factor is that initial innovations like the car, airplane, telephone, and use of electricity provided the necessary infrastructure for newer innovations to diffuse more rapidly. Another reason is the emergence of new business models that make innovations more accessible. For example, Dell's direct-to-consumer distribution system improved access to low-cost PCs, and Walmart's low-price, high-volume model utilized its sophisticated IT logistics system to fuel explosive growth. In addition, satellite and cable distribution systems facilitated the ability of mass media such as radio and TV to deliver advertising and information to a wider audience. The speed of technology diffusion has accelerated further with the emergence of the Internet, social networking sites, and viral messaging.

The life experience of the Gen-Y population reflects the accelerated pace of technology diffusion. New technologies are a natural part of their lives, like eating and breathing. The

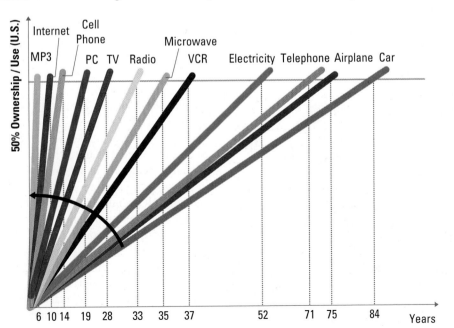

EXHIBIT 1.5

Accelerating Speed of Technological Change

Source: Data from U.S. Census Bureau; Consumer Electronics Association; *Forbes;* and National Cable and Telecommunications Association.

Gen-Y cohort came of age during the boom of the Internet; its members are accustomed to constant connectivity and to rapid technological change. By the time they graduate from college, the average Gen-Y student has spent over 10,000 hours playing video games and over 20,000 hours watching TV.[23] The Gen-Y cohort is sometimes called *digital natives*—people who grew up with the Internet and other advanced technologies and who need no help to adapt to new technologies.[24] Those who did not grow up with the Internet and other advanced technologies, and so have taken longer to adapt to them, are called *digital immigrants.* We discuss the strategic implications of innovation and technological change in Chapter 7.

A Truly Global World

New York Times columnist and author Thomas Friedman used his book title, *The World Is Flat,*[25] to describe a truly global marketplace in which goods, services, capital, knowledge, ideas, and people move freely across geographic boundaries in search of greater opportunities. Advances in information technology and transportation have led to the "death of distance."[26]

Due to falling trade and investment barriers, companies are now part of a global economy made up of several key markets. Combining 27 member states and more than 500 million people, the European Union (EU) is the world's largest economy.[27] Sixteen EU countries are almost a fully integrated bloc with unified economic and monetary policies, using the euro as a common currency.[28] China, with more than 1.4 billion people, is the most populous country in the world, and India, with 1.2 billion people, is the world's largest democracy. Together with Brazil and Russia, they make up the *BRIC countries,* which have more than 40 percent of the world's population and occupy more than a quarter of the world's landmass. This group of fast-growing, emerging economies could one day eclipse the richest countries in the world.

Many U.S. companies have become global players. The technology giant IBM employs 425,000 people and has revenues of roughly $100 billion. Although IBM's headquarters is in Armonk, NY, the vast majority of its employees (more than 70 percent) actually work outside the United States. IBM, like many other U.S.-based multinationals, now earns the majority of its revenues (roughly two-thirds) outside the United States (as shown in Exhibit 1.6).[29] IBM's revenues in the BRIC countries have been growing at between 20 and 40 percent per year, while they have grown by only about 1 to 3 percent in developed markets such as the United States. IBM's goal is to obtain 35 percent of its total revenue from fast-growing emerging economies such as the BRIC countries by 2015. To capture these opportunities, IBM (along with many other multinational companies) has been reducing the U.S. headcount while increasing employment in emerging economies such as India.[30]

While many multinational companies like Coca-Cola, Procter & Gamble, and

EXHIBIT 1.6

Geographic Sources of IBM Revenues, 2010

Source: 2010 IBM Annual Report.

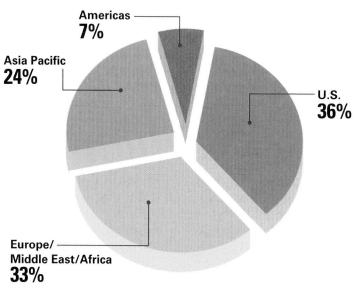

Americas
7%

Asia Pacific
24%

U.S.
36%

Europe/
Middle East/Africa
33%

Sony tend to focus on more affluent customers, some 4 billion people on the planet live on less than $2,000 a year (or $5.50 a day).[31] Recently, scholars have shown that this so-called bottom of the pyramid of the global economy—the largest but poorest socioeconomic group of the world's population—can yield significant business opportunities, which—if satisfied—could improve the living standard of the world's poorest.[32] Muhammad Yunus, winner of the 2006 Nobel Peace Prize, founded Grameen Bank in Bangladesh to provide small loans (so-called *microcredit*) to impoverished villagers. Loans provided funding for their entrepreneurial ventures so that villagers could help themselves climb out of poverty. As a follow-up business, Grameen Telecom now offers a microloan combined with a cell phone for local entrepreneurs. Other businesses have also found profitable business opportunities at the bottom of the pyramid. In India, Arvind Mills offers jeans in a ready-to-make kit that costs only a fraction of the high-end Levi's. The Tata Group, a widely diversified multinational conglomerate headquartered in Mumbai, India, in 2009 introduced its Nano car, the lowest-priced car in the world.[33] Although the Nano sells for less than $2,500 ("one lakh" rupees), sales of hundreds of millions of them can add up to a substantial business. Given its importance, we take up global strategy in Chapter 10.

Future Industries

Tomorrow's winners are the ones that focus today on making investments to build a position in up-and-coming industries. Given current trends, several industries promise significant potential for value creation (and thus career opportunities), among them health care, the green economy, and Web 2.0.[34]

HEALTH CARE. In 2010, U.S. health care spending reached $2.5 trillion, or 16 percent of total economic activity, making it the largest industry in the country.[35] With aging baby boomers making up the largest age demographic in the United States, the growth of the health care industry, estimated at 7 percent annually, will far outstrip the growth rate of the overall economy. As a consequence, by 2019 the health care sector is estimated to be 20 percent of total U.S. economic activity.

Not only are baby boomers a large part of the U.S. population, most of the wealth is also concentrated in this group. As baby boomers age, they will demand more professional health care, wellness and enhancement services such as Botox treatments, liposuction, and laser eye surgery. Important medical breakthroughs in biotechnology, nanotechnology, and genomics will allow health care providers to offer individualized medicine to support longer and healthier living. For example, 23andMe, an entrepreneurial venture founded by Anne Wojcicki and Linda Avey, leverages the convergence of IT, genomics, and biotechnology to allow customers to understand their own unique genetic makeup in terms of health, traits, and ancestry. After having one's personal DNA tested, 23andMe will provide an individualized profile of how that genetic makeup is related to the probability of developing any of over 100 different diseases and conditions.

Given the opportunities in the health care industry, GE announced its *healthymagination* initiative, in which it will invest $6 billion to attempt to solve strategic trade-offs in health care by increasing access, improving quality, and lowering costs.[36] Patterned after its successful *ecomagination* program, this initiative allows GE to draw on the expertise of its various business units. It is intended to refocus GE on its industrial strength, but in a way that looks to emerging opportunities.

Although the health care sector of the economy seems to provide significant business opportunities in the future due to favorable demographics in the U.S. and most developed economies, managers must also consider impending threats such as more government regulation. While more Americans will be required to have health insurance, the

bottom of the pyramid The largest but poorest socioeconomic group of the world's population.

reimbursements for specific procedures are likely to go down. This will decrease the incentives for firms to make investments in this industry and for students to become nurses or medical doctors. Health care providers, moreover, face the challenge of squaring a circle when required by law to provide more access, equal- or higher-quality care, and lower cost. One possible way to resolve this trade-off is innovation in products and processes, a topic that we will take up in Chapter 7.

GREEN ECONOMY. The vast majority of today's economic activity around the globe is powered by carbon-based sources of energy such as oil, coal, and natural gas. Yet, these carbon-based energy sources are finite, and they come with a cost that businesses and consumers do not bear. Such a cost, which economists call externalities, represents the side-effects of production and consumption that are not reflected in the price of the product. The externalities of carbon-based energy are CO_2 emissions, which some researchers suggest are linked to air pollution and global warming,[37] and ecological disasters such as the BP oil spill in the Gulf of Mexico.[38]

Moreover, fossil fuels are a finite, non-renewable resource. Oil prices spiked to almost $150 a barrel in the summer of 2008, pushing up gas prices in the U.S. to over $4 a gallon from $1.25 (inflation-adjusted) in the late 1990s. The increase in oil prices over time occurred in a roller coaster fashion as shown in Exhibit 1.7. The global trend line of oil prices, however, is pointing upwards as supplies dwindle and energy demand increases, especially in the rapidly developing countries. Higher oil prices and increasing public awareness of the externalities produced by the burning of fossil fuels have led to a search for renewable energy sources that are more ecologically friendly.

The *green and clean-tech economy* describes future business opportunities in renewable energy, energy conservation, efficient energy use, and energy technology.[39] The goal is to develop a sustainable global economy that the earth can support indefinitely.[40] Several governments across the world such as Germany, Denmark, Israel, and Spain provide incentives to induce businesses to invest in the green economy, and thus create sustainable jobs. The U.S.

externalities Side-effects of production and consumption that are not reflected in the price of a product.

EXHIBIT 1.7

Conceptual Depiction of Oil Prices and Predicted Trend

Source: Adapted from Shai Agassi's presentation at TED, February 2009, www.ted.com/talks/lang/eng/shai_agassi_on_electric_cars.html.

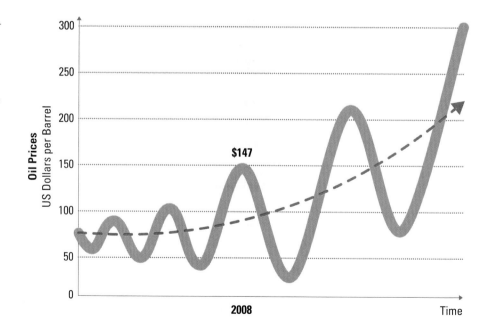

plans to invest $150 billion over the next decade to help jump-start a green economy. It hopes to create five million new jobs that pay well, can't be outsourced, and reduce America's dependence on middle-eastern oil.[41] In the meantime, China is fast becoming the world's leading producer of solar panels, having driven the prices for such panels down by almost 50 percent within just a year.[42] If the size of the current energy industry is any indication, the green and clean-tech economy is likely to be a multi-trillion dollar business. This of course creates opportunities for existing companies such as ABB, GE Energy, Philips, and Siemens, as well as entrepreneurs, in their quest to make an ecosystem of energy innovation become a reality.[43]

Again, a note of caution is in order: Although the green economy receives significant media attention, most green energy sources are not yet cost-competitive with old-line coal and oil. This is partly due to the fact that market prices do not include externalities. Some studies also indicate that world oil reserves will be sufficient for another 100 years or more.[44] Moreover, the U.S. has the largest proven coal reserves worldwide (roughly 30 percent), and is most likely to use those to provide the base load for its energy consumption. Famed investor Warren Buffett shares this perspective: his Berkshire Hathaway company acquired Burlington Northern railroads for over $26 billion.[45] Railroads are the most cost-effective way of transporting commodities such as coal, steel, wheat, lumber, and consumer goods over long distances. Burlington Northern moves coal from where it is mined to population-rich states that receive much of their power from coal-fired plants. As in any business situation, managers must carefully consider both opportunities and threats when making strategic decisions.

STRATEGY HIGHLIGHT 1.1

Threadless: Leveraging Crowdsourcing to Design Cool T-Shirts

Threadless, a community-centered online apparel store (www.threadless.com), was founded in 2000 by Jake Nickell, then a student at the Illinois Institute of Art, and Jacob DeHart, then a student at Purdue University, with $1,000 as startup capital. After Jake had won an online T-shirt design contest, the two entrepreneurs came up with a business model to leverage user-generated content. The idea is to let consumers "work for you" and thus turn consumers into *prosumers,* a hybrid between producers and consumers.

Members of the Threadless "community" do most of the work, which they consider fun: They submit T-shirt designs online, and community members vote on which designs they like best. The designs receiving the most votes are put in production, printed, and sold online. Threadless leverages crowdsourcing, a process in which a group of people voluntarily perform tasks that were traditionally being completed by a firm's employees. Rather than outsourcing its work to other companies, Threadless outsources its T-shirt design to its website community. The Web 2.0 concept of leveraging a firm's own customers to help produce better products is explicitly included in Threadless's business model.

WEB 2.0. In the early days of the Internet, websites more or less passively displayed information. Examples of the "old" WWW (World Wide Web) are initial versions of companies' websites that merely displayed information such as their logo, hours, phone numbers, address, and a brief overview of the company. The term *Web 2.0* was coined to denote interactivity, with the goal of harnessing the collective intelligence of web users.[46] The idea was that the more people participate, the better the resulting websites and in turn the better the resulting products and services. Web 2.0, therefore, relies on network effects.[47] As an example, the more people use Google's search engine, the better the search engine gets as it continuously fine-tunes its PageRank algorithm. Many companies are devising ways to utilize social networking to strengthen customer relationships and thus the basis for competitive advantage. Amazon, Netflix, YouTube, Facebook, Flickr, and Threadless are but a few examples of Web 2.0 applications that benefit from network effects. Strategy Highlight 1.1 shows how the online startup Threadless uses Web 2.0 technology to craft an innovative business model.

crowdsourcing A process in which a group of people voluntarily performs tasks that were traditionally completed by a firm's employees.

Threadless's business model translates real-time market research and design contests into quick sales. Threadless produces only T-shirts that were approved by its community. Moreover, it has a very good understanding of market demand because it knows the number of people who participated in each design contest. In addition, when scoring each T-shirt design in a contest, Threadless users have the option to check "I'd buy it." These features give the Threadless community a voice in T-shirt design and also coax community members into making a pre-purchasing commitment. Threadless does not make any significant investments until the design and market size are determined, thus basically minimizing its downside. Not surprisingly, Threadless has sold every T-shirt that it has printed. Moreover, it has a cult-like following and is outperforming established companies such as Old Navy and Urban Outfitters with their more formulaic T-shirt designs.[48]

GAINING & SUSTAINING COMPETITIVE ADVANTAGE

>> LO 1-7
Critically evaluate the role that different stakeholders play in the firm's quest for competitive advantage.

STAKEHOLDERS

Each chapter contains a section entitled *Gaining & Sustaining Competitive Advantage,* in which we put one specific theory or concept under the magnifying glass to critically evaluate if and how it is linked to competitive advantage, the overarching goal in strategic management. To accomplish this, we combine strategic management research with real-world observations. We conclude this chapter by looking at stakeholders and their relationship to competitive advantage.

Successful business strategies generate value for society. When firms or individuals compete in their own self-interest while obeying the law and acting ethically, they ultimately create value. In so doing, they make society better.[49] Value creation lays the foundation for all the important benefits successful economies can provide: education, public safety, and health care, among others. Superior performance allows a firm to reinvest some of its profits to accrue more resources and thus to grow. This in turn provides more opportunities for employment and fulfilling careers. In the chapter opener, we saw that Google created tremendous value, and with it career opportunities. In contrast, strategic mistakes can be expensive. Conservative estimates of the ill-fated AOL TimeWarner merger suggest it destroyed about $100 billion of shareholder value and with it many employment and career opportunities.

Competitive advantage, therefore, not only is of interest to the CEO or shareholders, but also directly affects every person who has an interest in a company. These persons are stakeholders—individuals or groups who can affect or are affected by the actions of a firm.[50] They have a claim or interest in the performance and continued survival of the firm. As shown in Exhibit 1.8, *internal stakeholders* include stockholders, employees (including executives, managers, and workers), and board members. *External stakeholders* include customers, suppliers, alliance partners, creditors, unions, communities, and governments at various levels (local, state, federal, and supranational in the case of the European Union). As Exhibit 1.8 indicates, all stakeholders make specific contributions to the firm, which in turn provides different types of inducements to different stakeholders. The firm, therefore, has a multifaceted exchange relationship with a number of diverse internal and external stakeholders. (Given the importance of stakeholders to firm performance, we take up this topic again in Chapter 12 when studying strategy implementation.)

Some stakeholders can exert a powerful influence on firms. In some instances, firms are able to *create* a competitive advantage but fail to *capture* it because of actions of their stakeholders.[51] This sounds like a contradiction, doesn't it? It is not. Consider this: Once a firm has created a competitive advantage, a battle can ensue over how the spoils of that competitive advantage are split among the firm's different stakeholders.[52] In the U.S. car industry, the United Auto Workers (UAW) had such a stronghold on GM, Chrysler, and Ford that some argue they were a major factor in creating a competitive disadvantage

stakeholders
Individuals or groups who can affect or are affected by the actions of a firm.

EXHIBIT 1.8

Internal and External
Stakeholders in an
Exchange Relationship
with the Firm

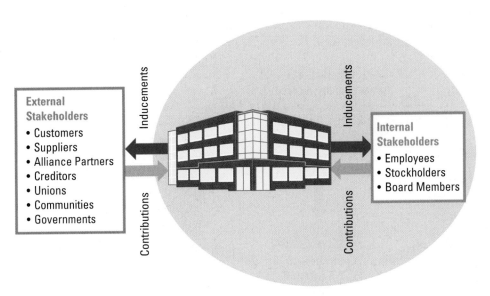

(although management signed the labor contracts with the unions).[53] In the investment banking industry, employees are powerful stakeholders. Skilled human capital is one of the most important resources in investment banking (as in other professional services such as management consulting and law firms). As a consequence of their strong position, the combined annual bonuses of investment banks' employees frequently exceed the bank's net income. In 2007, the year before the financial meltdown, the net income of the big-five U.S. investment banks combined (Bear Sterns, Goldman Sachs, Lehman Brothers, Merrill Lynch, and Morgan Stanley) was a little over $10 billion, and the total of the bonuses paid to the employees was close to $40 billion.[54] During 2008, the worst year in terms of stock performance since the Great Depression, the big-five investment banks lost $25 billion, but still paid bonuses that exceeded $25 billion.[55] These data show that although investment banks clearly have valuable resources (namely, employees) that can create competitive advantage, those same resources are powerful stakeholders that can capture the value they create. By capturing that value, the employee stakeholders left less value for other stakeholders, such as stockholders or customers.

These examples show that although some stakeholders have a strong influence in helping a firm gain and sustain competitive advantage, they also capture much of the value created because these key employees realize how critical they are in creating the value in the first place. Not all stakeholder groups are created equal, and their differential power influences how the economic value created is distributed among different stakeholder groups. If some stakeholders are able to extract significant value, the firm's competitive advantage may not be realized when comparing overall firm performance to that of competitors. 🔍

THE AFI STRATEGY FRAMEWORK

A successful strategy details a set of goal-directed actions that managers intend to take to improve or maintain overall firm performance. Building strategy is the result of three broad management tasks:

1. Analyze (A)
2. Formulate (F)
3. Implement (I)

EXHIBIT 1.9

The AFI Strategy Framework and Text Outline

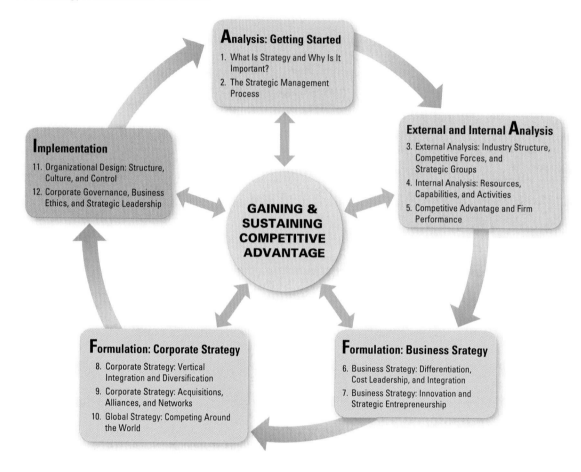

These are the pillars of research and knowledge about strategic management. Although we will study each task one at a time, they are highly interdependent and frequently happen simultaneously. A firm cannot really formulate a strategy without thinking about how to implement it, for instance, and while implementing a strategy, managers are constantly analyzing the need to adjust to changing circumstances. We've captured those relationships in the AFI strategy framework, shown in Exhibit 1.9. This model links the three interdependent management tasks—analyze, formulate, and implement. What we want our model to do is explain and predict differences in firm performance. This information will allow managers to conceive of and implement a strategy that can improve its performance and result in competitive advantage.

In each of the three broad management tasks, managers focus on specific *questions*, listed next. (We address those questions in specific chapters, as indicated.)

AFI strategy framework A model that links three interdependent strategic management tasks—analyze, formulate, and implement—that, together, help firms conceive of and implement a strategy that can improve performance and result in competitive advantage.

Strategy analysis (*A*):

- The strategic management process: *What are our vision, mission, and values? What is our process for "making" strategy (how does strategy come about)?* (Chapter 2)
- External analysis: *What effects do forces in the external environment have on strategy and competitive advantage?* (Chapter 3)

- Internal analysis: *What effects do our internal resources and capabilities have on strategy and competitive advantage?* (Chapter 4)
- Firm performance: *How can we measure competitive advantage?* (Chapter 5)

Strategy formulation (*F*):

- Business strategy: *How should we compete?* (Chapters 6 and 7)
- Corporate strategy: *Where should we compete?* (Chapters 8 and 9)
- Global strategy: *Where and how should we compete around the world?* (Chapter 10)

Strategy implementation (*I*):

- Organizational design: *How should we organize to put the formulated strategy into practice?* (Chapter 11)
- Corporate governance, business ethics, and strategic leadership: *What type of strategic leadership and corporate governance do we need? How do we anchor our decision in business ethics?* (Chapter 12)

The AFI strategy framework shown in Exhibit 1.9 will be repeated at the beginning of each of the book's parts, to help show where we are in our study of the firm's quest to gain and sustain competitive advantage.

CHAPTERCASE 1 | *Consider This . . .*

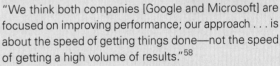

ON THE OPENING PAGE of the chapter, ChapterCase 1 provides background information about a quest for competitive advantage taking place in the Internet-search market. Microsoft's Bing picked up a new partner—Facebook—in its continuing journey to unseat Google from the top of the search engine business. In terms usually reserved for a hot new Silicon Valley startup, Facebook's CEO, Mark Zuckerberg, announced the company's surprising decision to partner with the "really scrappy . . . underdog" Bing, rather than the incumbent Google. Zuckerberg stated, "When you're an incumbent in an area . . . there is a tension between innovating and trying new things versus what you already have."[56] Perhaps the announcement shouldn't have been such a surprise. After all, in 2007 Microsoft did invest $240 million, for an ownership share of less than 2 percent, in privately held Facebook.[57]

Microsoft and Facebook are rolling out a variety of features to make "search more social." If, say, you are looking for a new restaurant in your area, Bing searches can include data on what your Facebook friends have "liked." A view of Microsoft's attempt to unseat Google

can be found from Bing director Lisa Gurry, who notes, "We think both companies [Google and Microsoft] are focused on improving performance; our approach . . . is about the speed of getting things done—not the speed of getting a high volume of results."[58]

Thinking about this chapter's opening case, answer the following questions.

1. Google was not the first search engine on the Internet, but it has been the most successful for a decade. What is Google's competitive advantage?

2. LinkExchange was created in 1996 by Sanjay Madan and Tony Hsieh (more recently with Zappos) and, as noted in the case, was purchased by Microsoft in 1998. Why was Microsoft not interested in keeping the Keywords project in 2000?

3. What strategy and business model is Microsoft using today with Bing to try to succeed in the Internet-search business?

Take-Away Concepts

This chapter defined strategy and competitive advantage and set the stage for further study of strategic management, as summarized by the following learning objectives and related take-away concepts.

LO 1-1 Define competitive advantage, sustainable competitive advantage, competitive disadvantage, and competitive parity.

>> Competitive advantage is always judged relative to other competitors or the industry average.

>> To obtain a competitive advantage, a firm must either create more value for customers while keeping its cost comparable to competitors, or it must provide value equivalent to competitors but at lower cost.

>> A firm able to dominate competitors for prolonged periods of time has a sustained competitive advantage.

>> A firm that continuously underperforms its rivals or the industry average has a competitive disadvantage.

>> Two or more firms that perform at the same level have competitive parity.

LO 1-2 Define strategy and explain its role in a firm's quest for competitive advantage.

>> Strategy is the set of goal-directed actions a firm intends to take in its quest to gain and sustain competitive advantage.

>> An effective strategy requires that strategic trade-offs be recognized and addressed—e.g., between value creation and the costs to create the value.

>> Managers' strategic assumptions are an outflow of their theory of how to compete. Successful strategy requires three integrative management tasks—analysis, formulation, and implementation.

>> When managers align their assumptions closely with competitive realities, they can create and implement successful strategies, resulting in value creation and superior firm performance.

>> When managers' theories about how to gain and sustain competitive advantage do not reflect reality, their firm's strategy will destroy rather than create value, leading to inferior firm performance.

LO 1-3 Explain the role of firm effects and industry effects in determining firm performance.

>> A firm's performance is more closely related to its managers' actions (firm effects) than to the external circumstances surrounding it (industry effects).

>> Firm and industry effects, however, *are interdependent and thus both are relevant in determining firm performance.*

LO 1-4 Describe the role of corporate, business, and functional managers in strategy formulation and implementation.

>> Corporate executives must provide answers to the question of *where* to compete (in industries, markets, and geographies), and *how to create synergies* among different business units.

>> General (or business) managers must answer the strategic question of *how to compete* in order to achieve superior performance. They must manage and align all value-chain activities for competitive advantage.

>> Functional managers are responsible for *implementing business strategy* within a single functional area.

LO 1-5 Outline how business models put strategy into action.

>> To put a firm's strategy into action, a business model must: (1) translate the firm's strategy into competitive tactics and initiatives, and (2) implement the strategy through effective structures, processes, culture, and procedures.

LO 1-6 Describe and assess the opportunities and challenges managers face in the 21st century.

>> The competitive landscape of the 21st century is characterized by ever-faster technological change in a truly global marketplace.

>> Examples of industries that seem likely to provide good future opportunities are health care, the green economy, and Web 2.0.

LO 1-7 Critically evaluate the role that different stakeholders play in the firm's quest for competitive advantage.

>> Stakeholders are individuals or groups that have a claim or interest in the performance and continued survival of the firm; they make specific contributions for which they expect rewards in return.

>> Internal stakeholders include stockholders, employees (including executives, managers, and workers), and board members.

>> External stakeholders include customers, suppliers, alliance partners, creditors, unions, communities, and governments at various levels.

>> Some stakeholders are more powerful than others, and may extract significant rewards from a firm, so much that any firm-level competitive advantage may be negated.

Key Terms

AFI strategy framework *(p. 20)*

Bottom of the pyramid *(p. 15)*

Business model *(p. 11)*

Competitive advantage *(p. 4)*

Competitive disadvantage *(p. 5)*

Competitive parity *(p. 5)*

Co-opetition *(p. 6)*

Crowdsourcing *(p. 17)*

Externalities *(p. 16)*

Firm effects *(p. 8)*

Industry effects *(p. 8)*

Stakeholders *(p. 18)*

Strategic business unit (SBU) *(p. 10)*

Strategic management *(p. 4)*

Strategy *(p. 6)*

Sustainable competitive advantage *(p. 5)*

Discussion Questions

1. How is a strategy different from a business model? How is it similar?

2. Threadless (in Strategy Highlight 1.1) is an example of a firm building on its customer base to use new products and also to participate in the design and vetting of popular designs. In the summer of 2010, Dell Computer announced a partnership with Threadless for designs on its laptop computers. For a small additional fee (and an extra day's delay in shipping), you can get a Threadless design etched on your new Dell laptop.[59] Why do you think Dell is keen on offering this service? What other firms use this crowdsourcing technique? Where else might this type of business model show up in the future?

3. As noted in the chapter, research found that firm effects are more important than industry effects. What does this mean? Can you think of situations where this might not be true?

4. This chapter introduces three different levels appropriate for strategic considerations (see Exhibit 1.3). In what situations would some of these levels be more important than others? How should the organization ensure the proper attention to each level of strategy as needed?

Ethical/Social Issues

1. Given that traditional U.S. firms such as IBM have over 70 percent of their employees and almost two-thirds of revenues come from outside the United States, what is an appropriate definition of a "U.S. firm"? Is there any special consideration a firm should have for its "home country"?

2. Corporate leaders are responsible for guiding the firm's strategies. Their goal is to help the firm gain and sustain a competitive advantage and thus

a profit for the shareholders. What responsibility do company managers have for other consequences of their strategies? For example, should Walmart try to mitigate the negative impact its arrival in communities can have on small locally owned stores? Why or why not? Explain.

Small Group Exercises

SMALL GROUP EXERCISE 1

The chapter argues that Microsoft and Google have quite different business models. In 2009, Microsoft revenues were $58.4 billion, an amount that was down 3 percent from 2008 levels (the first annual decline in Microsoft's history). Google had sales of $23.6 billion—an increase of 9 percent over its 2008 levels.[60]

Form a group of three or four students and spend 5 to 10 minutes discussing one of the following questions. (Your instructor may assign the question.)

1. Is this revenue downturn a sign that Microsoft is in trouble or just a result of the recession over the period? Should Microsoft change any of its strategies based on this information?

2. While Google increased sales, 97 percent of its revenues came from advertising. Is this a problem going forward? Should it change any of its strategies?

3. Apple and IBM are two firms in the competitive landscape. Should Microsoft (Google) be more proactive in addressing these competitors?

SMALL GROUP EXERCISE 2

Corporations are starting to become more aware of blogging on the Internet. Blogging can be a factor that can increase buyers' ability to have either positive or negative effects on a firm.

In one well-publicized case, journalist/blogger Jeff Jarvis of www.buzzmachine.com blogged about problems with a Dell computer he purchased. His site was inundated with others who also had poor experiences with Dell. The "Dell hell" uproar resulted in Dell not only calling Mr. Jarvis and resolving his problem but opening its own blog www.dell.com/blogs. Additionally, some time later Mr. Jarvis visited Dell's headquarters and wrote an article for *BusinessWeek* entitled "Dell Learns to Listen."[61]

1. Use a search engine to find large companies that include a blog on their official website. (Keywords "fortune 500 blogs" will steer you to many lists of such companies.)

2. What seems to be the primary purpose of most of the blogs you found?

3. Does the blog seem to be updated regularly?

4. Does the blog allow users to post comments or questions to the firm? If so, do any of the questions get answered by the company?

Strategy Term Project

PROJECT OVERVIEW

The goal of the strategy term project is to give you practical experience with the elements of strategic management. Each end-of-chapter assignment requires data collection and analysis relating the material discussed in the chapter to the firm you select here for study throughout the course. At the end of each chapter, we make additional stages of a strategic analysis available. The goal of this term-long project is to give you a tangible application of many of the concepts discussed in the text. By the end of the project, you will not only have practice in using key strategic management components and processes to increase your understanding of the material, but you also will be able to conduct a complete strategic management analysis of any company.

MODULE 1: INITIAL FIRM SELECTION AND REVIEW

In this first module, you will identify a firm to study for this project. We suggest you select one company and use it for each module in this term project. Choose a firm that you find interesting or one that is part of an industry you would like to know more about. Throughout the modules, you will be required to obtain and analyze a significant amount of data about the firm. Therefore, a key criterion is also to choose a firm that has data available for you to gather.

The primary approach to this project is to select a publicly held firm. Many large firms such as Apple, Coca-Cola, and GE have been widely reported on in the business and popular press, and a wealth of information is available on them. Other medium-sized public firms such as GameStop, Netflix, and Under Armour can be used as example firms for this project. One cautionary note: For firms that are less than three years public or in industries that are not well-defined, it will take some additional reflection to properly identify such items as competitors and suppliers. But if it is a firm you are truly motivated to study, the effort can be quite rewarding.

Relevant data on all public firms can be freely obtained using web services such as Edgar (www.sec .gov/edgar.shtml). Annual reports for firms also are a treasure-trove of information. These reports and other quarterly update materials are often available from the firm's own website (look for "about us" or "investor relations" tabs, often located at the bottom of the company's website). Additionally, most university and public libraries have access to large databases of articles from many trade publications. (Factiva and ABI/ Proquest are two examples.) Company profiles of a variety of publicly listed firms are available at reliable websites such as Hoovers.com and finance.yahoo.com. Also, many industries have quite active trade associations that will have websites and publications that can also be useful in this process. Your local librarian can likely provide you some additional resources that may be licensed for library use or otherwise not available online. Examples of these are Value Line Ratings & Reports and Datamonitor.

A second approach to this project is to select a smaller firm in your area. These firms may have coverage in the local press. However, if the firm is not public, you will need to ensure you have access to a wide variety of data from the firm. If this is a firm for which you have worked or where you know people, please check ahead of time to be sure the firm is willing to share its information with you. This approach can work well, especially if the firm is interested in a detailed analysis of its strategic position. But to be successful with this project, be sure you will have access to a broad range of data and information (perhaps including interviews of key managers at the firm).

If you are in doubt on how to select a firm, check with your instructor before proceeding. In some instances, your instructor will assign firms to the study groups.

For this module, answer the following questions:

1. Provide a brief history of the company.

2. List the top management of the firm and note what experience and leadership skills they bring to the firm. If a larger conglomerate, list both corporate and business managers.

3. What is the principal business model of the firm? (How does the firm make most of its profits?)

*my*Strategy

HOW TO POSITION YOURSELF FOR CAREER ADVANTAGE

As the chapter discussed, firm-level decisions have a significant impact on the success or failure of organizations. Industry-level effects, however, can also play a role. Many considerations go into deciding what career choices you make during your working life. The chapter notes that some sectors (such as health care, the green economy, and Web 2.0) are expected to grow faster than others.

At the top of the next page is a sample of revenue growth rates in various industries for a recent five-year period.

Sample Five-Year Growth Rates (2005–2009)[62]

Industry Name	Change in Sales	Industry Name	Change in Sales
Power	54.51%	Medical supplies	12.87%
Petroleum (production)	44.64%	**Total market average**	**12.79%**
Pharmacy services	43.68%	Apparel	0.50%
Insurance (property/casualty)	37.60%	Retail stores	0.49%
Advertising	35.99%	Banking	0.00%
Biotechnology	35.06%	Semiconductor equipment	−16.66%
Pharmaceuticals	24.88%	Homebuilding	−30.52%
Natural gas (diversified)	24.54%	Public/private equity	−32.41%
E-commerce	20.32%	Insurance (life)	−71.81%
Securities brokerage	16.20%		
Telecommunication services	16.05%		
Entertainment technology	15.99%		
Computer software/services	15.26%		
Internet	13.71%		
Chemical (diversified)	13.52%		

1. If you are about to embark on a new career, what effect should the likelihood of industry growth play in your decision?

2. Why could growth rates be an important consideration? Why not?

Endnotes

1. This ChapterCase is based on the following sources: "Yahoo to buy Overture for $1.63 billion," CNET News, July 14, 2003; "Microsoft bid to beat Google builds on a history of misses," *The Wall Street Journal,* January 16, 2009; "Yahoo tie-up is latest sign tide turning for Microsoft's Ballmer," *The Wall Street Journal,* July 30, 2009; "Bingo! A deal between Microsoft and Yahoo!" *The Economist,* July 30, 2009; and "Google, Microsoft spar on antitrust," *The Wall Street Journal,* March 1, 2010.

2. For an in-depth discussion, see Lewis, M. (2003), *Moneyball: The Art of Winning an Unfair Game* (New York: Norton).

3. Porter, M. E. (1980), *Competitive Strategy: Techniques for Analyzing Competitors* (New York: The Free Press).

4. Top 15 Global Products (2009), *IMS Health,* www.imshealth.com.

5. Ibid.

6. This section draws on: Porter, M. E. (1996), "What is strategy?" *Harvard Business Review,* November–December: 61–78; and Porter, M. E. (1980), *Competitive Strategy.*

7. Dyer, J. H., and H. Singh (1998), "The relational view: Cooperative strategy and sources of interorganizational competitive advantage," *Academy of Management Review* 23: 660–679; and Rothaermel, F. T., and A. Hess (2010), "Innovation strategies combined," *MIT Sloan Management Review,* Spring: 12–15.

8. Brandenburger, A. M., and B. J. Nalebuff (1996), *Co-opetition* (New York: Currency Doubleday); and Gnyawali, D., J. He, and R. Madhavan, (2006), "Impact of co-opetition on firm competitive behavior: An empirical examination," *Journal of Management* 32: 507–530.

9. Christensen, C. M., and M. E. Raynor (2003), "Why hard-nosed executives should care about management theory," *Harvard Business Review,* September: 1–10.

10. Drucker, P. (1994), "The theory of business," *Harvard Business Review,* September–October: 95–105.

11. Duke, M. T. (2010), presentation at the Georgia Institute of Technology, April 1, 2010.

12. For more details, see Rothaermel, Frank T., with V. P. Singh (2013), "Tesla Motors and U.S. Auto Industry," case study, in Rothaermel, F. T., *Strategic Management* (Burr Ridge, IL: McGraw-Hill).

13. "Ford touts its small-car resurgence," *The Wall Street Journal,* January 11, 2010; and "Epiphany in Dearborn. How Ford turned a crash into a profit—without a government bail-out," *The Economist,* December 9, 2010.

14. Hansen, G. S., and B. Wernerfelt (1989), "Determinants of firm performance: The relative importance of economic and organizational factors," *Strategic Management Journal* 10: 399–411; and McGahan, A. M., and M. E. Porter (1997), "How much does industry matter, really?" *Strategic Management Journal* 18: 15–30.

15. The remaining 35–50 percent of variance in a firm's profitability is due to corporate-parent effects, year effects, and unexplained variation. This interesting debate unfolds in the following articles, among others: Rumelt, R. P. (1991), "How much does industry matter?" *Strategic Management Journal* 12: 167–185; and McGahan, A. M., and M. E. Porter (1997), "How much does industry matter, really?" *Strategic Management Journal* 18: 15–30.

16. See recent J.D. Power's quality reports, for example, as presented in "Ford touts its small-car resurgence," *The Wall Street Journal,* January 11, 2010.

17. This discussion is based on Porter, M. E. (1996), "What is strategy?" *Harvard Business Review,* November–December: 61–78.

18. This example is drawn from O'Reilly, C. A., B. Harreld, and M. Tushman (2009), "Organizational ambidexterity: IBM and emerging business opportunities," *California Management Review* 51: 75–99.

19. This is a play on the acronym IBM, which stands for International Business Machines.

20. This discussion is based on Anderson, C. (2009), *Free: The Future of a Radical Price* (New York: Hyperion).

21. Chen, M. J. (1996), "Competitor analysis and interfirm rivalry: Toward a theoretical integration," *Academy of Management Review* 21: 100–134; Gimeno, J. (1999), "Reciprocal threats in multimarket rivalry: Staking out 'spheres of influence' in the U.S. airline industry," *Strategic Management Journal* 20: 101–128; and Gimeno, J., and C. Y. Woo (1999), "Multimarket competition, economies of scale, and firm performance," *Academy of Management Journal* 42: 239–259.

22. Drucker, P. (1992), *The Age of Discontinuity: Guidelines to Our Changing Society* (New York: Transaction Publishers); D'Aveni, R. (1994), *Hypercompetition. Managing the Dynamics of Strategic Maneuvering* (New York: The Free Press); Friedman, T. L. (2005), *The World Is Flat. A Brief History of the Twenty-first Century* (New York: Farrar, Straus and Giroux); Esty, D. C., and A. S. Winston (2006), *Green to Gold. How Smart Companies Use Environmental Strategy to Innovate, Create Value, and Build Competitive Advantage* (Hoboken, NJ: Wiley); and Friedman, T. (2008), *Hot, Flat, and Crowded: Why We Need a Green Revolution—and How It Can Renew America* (New York: Farrar, Straus, and Giroux).

23. Prensky, M. (2001), "Digital natives, digital immigrants." From *On the Horizon,* Vol. 9, No. 5, October, MCB University Press.

24. Ibid.

25. Friedman, T. L. (2005), *The World Is Flat.*

26. Cairncross, F. (1997), *The Death of Distance: How the Communications Revolution Will Change Our Lives* (London, U.K.: Orion Business Books); and Kotha, S., V. Rindova, and F. T. Rothaermel (2001), "Assets and actions: Firm-specific factors in the internationalization of U.S. internet firms," *Journal of International Business Studies* 32: 769–791.

27. The 27 EU member states are Austria, Belgium, Bulgaria, Czech Republic, Cyprus, Denmark, Estonia, Finland, France, Germany, Greece, Italy, Ireland, Latvia, Lithuania, Luxembourg, Hungary, Malta, the Netherlands, Poland, Portugal, Romania, Slovakia, Slovenia, Spain, Sweden, and the United Kingdom. (Source: www.europa.eu.)

28. The Eurozone countries are Austria, Belgium, Finland, France, Germany, Greece, Italy, Luxembourg, Malta, the Netherlands, Portugal, Slovakia, Slovenia, and Spain. The euro is used by five other European countries that are not part of the Eurozone. In total, some 327 million Europeans are using the euro. Another 175 million people worldwide use currencies that are pegged to the euro, making it the second largest reserve currency in the world after the U.S. dollar. (Source: www.europa.eu.)

29. IBM annual reports. Various years.

30. "IBM to cut U.S. jobs, expand in India," *The Wall Street Journal,* March 26, 2009.

31. Peng, M. (2009), *Global Strategy,* 2nd ed. (Mason, OH: South-Western Cengage).

32. Prahalad, C. K., and S. Hart (2002), "The future at the bottom of the pyramid," *Strategy+Business* 26: 54–67; Prahalad, C. K. (2004), *The Future at the Bottom of the Pyramid* (Upper Saddle River, NJ: Wharton School Publishing); and Hart, S. (2005), *Capitalism at the Crossroads* (Upper Saddle River, NJ: Wharton School Publishing).

33. "The new people's car," *The Economist,* March 26, 2009.

34. For an in-depth discussion of future industries and its strategic as well as career implications, see: Reich, R. (2000), *The Future of Success. Working and Living in the New Economy* (New York: Knopf); Canton, J. (2006), *The Extreme Future. The Top Trends that Will Reshape the World in the Next 20 Years* (New York: Penguin); and Shuen, A. (2008), *Web 2.0: A Strategy Guide* (Sebastopol, CA: O'Reilly Media).

35. "Health-care providers pledge to try to curb costs," *The Wall Street Journal,* May 11, 2009.

36. "GE launches 'healthymagination'; Will commit $6 billion to enable better health focusing on cost, access and quality," *GE Press Release,* May 7, 2009. See also: www.healthymagination.com.

37. See data compiled by NASA's Goddard Institute for Space Studies and reports by the Intergovernmental Panel on Climate Change (IPCC).

38. "BP hit by doubts over ability to pay for costs of oil spill," *The Wall Street Journal,* June 9, 2010.

39. King, A., and M. Lenox (2002), "Does it really pay to be green?" *Journal of Industrial Ecology* 5: 105–117.

40. Hart, S. (1997), "Beyond greening: Strategies for a sustainable world," *Harvard Business Review,* January–February.

41. "The change we need," *The Wall Street Journal,* November 3, 2008.

42. "China races ahead of U.S. in drive to go solar," *The New York Times,* August 25, 2009.

43. Esty, D. C., and A. S. Winston (2006), *Green to Gold;* and Friedman, T. (2008), *Hot, Flat, and Crowded.*

44. "Another century of oil? Getting more from current reserves," *Scientific American,* October 2009.

45. "Buffett bets big on railroads," *The Wall Street Journal,* November 4, 2009.

46. Shuen, A. (2008), *Web 2.0.*

47. For an in-depth discussion on network effects see: Arthur, W. B. (1989), "Competing technologies, increasing returns, and lock-in by historical events," *Economic Journal* 99: 116–131; Arthur, W. B. (1990), "Positive feedbacks in the economy," *Scientific American* 262: 92–99; Arthur, W. B. (1996), "Increasing returns and the new world of business," *Harvard Business Review:* 100–109; and Shuen, A. (2008), *Web 2.0.*

48. This Strategy Highlight is based on: Rothaermel, F. T., and S. Sugiyama (2001), "Virtual Internet communities and commercial success: Individual and community-level theory grounded in the atypical case of TimeZone.com," *Journal of Management* 27: 297–312; Hippel, E. von (2005), *Democratizing Innovation* (Cambridge, MA: MIT Press); Howe, J. (2008), *Crowdsourcing. Why the Power of the Crowd Is Driving the Future of Business* (New York: Crown); Ogawa, S., and F. T. Piller (2006), "Collective Customer Commitment: Reducing the risks of new product development," *MIT Sloan Management Review* 47 (Winter): 65–72; Shuen, A. (2008), *Web 2.0*; and Surowiecki, J. (2004), *The Wisdom of Crowds. Why the Many Are Smarter than the Few and How Collective Wisdom Shapes Business, Economies, Societies, and Nations* (New York: Doubleday).

49. Smith, A. (1776), *An Inquiry into the Nature and Causes of the Wealth of Nations,* 5th ed. (published 1904) (London: Methuen and Co.).

50. Freeman, E. R. (1984), *Strategic Management: A Stakeholder Approach* (Boston, MA: Pitman); Freeman, E. R., and J. McVea (2001), "A stakeholder approach to strategic management," in Hitt, M. A., E. R. Freeman, and J. S. Harrison (eds.), *The Handbook of Strategic Management* (Oxford, U.K.: Blackwell), pp. 189–207; and Phillips, R. (2003), *Stakeholder Theory and Organizational Ethics* (San Francisco, CA: Berrett-Koehler).

51. Coff, R. (1999), "When competitive advantage doesn't lead to performance: Resource-based theory and stakeholder bargaining power," *Organization Science* 10: 119–133.

52. Freeman, E. R. (1984), *Strategic Management;* and Phillips, R. (2003). *Stakeholder Theory and Organizational Ethics.*

53. Lieberman, M., and R. Dhawan (2005), "Assessing the resource base of Japanese and U.S. auto producers: A stochastic frontier production function approach," working paper, UCLA Anderson School of Management.

54. "On street, new reality on pay sets in," *The Wall Street Journal,* January 31, 2009.

55. "Goldman Sachs staff set for bumper bonuses as bank earns $38 million per day," *The Guardian,* July 31, 2009.

56. Carr, A., "Facebook friends an 'underdog,' Microsoft," *Fast Company,* October 13, 2010.

57. "Bing upgrades draw upon Facebook, other partners," Associated Press, San Francisco, December 15, 2010.

58. Carr, A., "'Underdog' Bing talks Facebook partnership, Google rivalry," *Fast Company,* December 17, 2010.

59. Saadi, S., "Crowdsourcer Threadless' life beyond T-shirts," *Bloomberg BusinessWeek*, September 16, 2010.

60. Data compiled from company annual reports 2009.

61. Jeff, J. (2009), *What Would Google Do?* (New York: Collins Business); and "Dell learns to listen: The computer maker takes to the blogosphere to repair its tarnished image," *BusinessWeek,* October 29, 2007.

62. Compiled from Value Line Data by Dr. A. Damodaran, NYU, http://pages .stern.nyu.edu/~adamodar/.

CHAPTER 2

The Strategic Management Process

LEARNING OBJECTIVES

After studying this chapter, you should be able to:

LO 2-1   Explain the role of vision, mission, and values in the strategic management process.

LO 2-2   Describe and evaluate the role of strategic intent in achieving long-term goals.

LO 2-3   Distinguish between customer-oriented and product-oriented missions and identify strategic implications.

LO 2-4   Critically evaluate the relationship between mission statements and competitive advantage.

LO 2-5   Explain why anchoring a firm in ethical values is essential for long-term success.

LO 2-6   Compare and contrast strategic planning, scenario planning, and strategy as planned emergence, and discuss strategic implications.

CHAPTERCASE 2

Teach For America: Inspiring Future Leaders

TEACH FOR AMERICA is a nonprofit organization that recruits college graduates and professionals to teach for two years in socially and economically disadvantaged communities in the United States. The idea behind Teach For America was developed by then 21-year-old Wendy Kopp as her senior thesis at Princeton. Kopp was convinced young people today are searching for meaning in their lives by making a positive contribution to society.

The genius of Kopp's idea was to turn on its head the social perception of teaching—to make what appeared to be an unattractive, low-status job into a high-prestige professional opportunity. Kopp established a mission for the organization she had in mind: to *eliminate educational inequality by enlisting our nation's most promising future leaders in the effort.* Her underlying assumption was that significant numbers of young people have a desire to take on meaningful responsibility in order to have a positive impact on the lives of others. To be chosen for TFA is a badge of honor. In 2010, TFA received some 46,000 applications for only about 4,500 positions across the country (paying the same as all other first-year teachers, ranging from $30,000 to $51,500 a year). This translates to a mere 12 percent acceptance rate, comparable to being accepted to study at Harvard (a little less than 10 percent), Stanford (12 percent), or MIT (14 percent).[1]

After reading the chapter, you will find more about this case, with related questions, on page 47.

▲ **PERSUADING** highly qualified teachers to take up jobs in inner-city Detroit or Los Angeles and some rural areas in West Virginia or the Mississippi Delta region has been an elusive goal for many decades. How did an undergraduate student accomplish what the Department of Education, state and local school boards, and the national Parent-Teacher Association could not accomplish, despite trying for decades and spending billions of dollars in the process? First, Kopp established a clear mission that appealed to a large number of young people. Second, she made the hiring process highly selective and turned down many who might easily qualify for teaching jobs. Making TFA highly selective changed the social perception of teaching in underprivileged areas. Suddenly, it was an honor (and great résumé builder) to be chosen for TFA. In Chapter 2, we move from thinking about why strategy is important to considerations of how firms and other organizations define their vision, mission, and values and then translate them into strategic intent and plans.

VISION, MISSION, AND VALUES

>> **LO 2-1**
Explain the role of vision, mission, and values in the strategic management process.

In this chapter, we study the strategic management process, which describes the method by which managers conceive of and implement a strategy that can lead to a sustainable competitive advantage. The strategic management process follows the analyze-formulate-implement (AFI) strategy framework introduced in Chapter 1.

Discovering a firm's vision and mission and defining its values are the first steps in the strategic management process. For new organizations, like TFA, the founders usually begin with a driving vision that they must further shape into statements about what they want to accomplish and how they will do so. For existing firms, this step is about fine-tuning their vision and mission as well as reaffirming their values. To begin the strategic management process, managers ask the following questions:

■ What do we want to accomplish ultimately? What is our *vision?*
■ What are we about? What is our *mission?*
■ How do we accomplish our goals? What are our *values?*

To answer questions about vision, mission, and values, managers need to *begin with the end in mind.* Think of building a house. The future owner must communicate her vision to the architect, who draws up a blueprint of the home. The process is iterated a couple of times until all the homeowner's ideas have been translated into the blueprint. Only then does the building of the house begin. The same holds for strategic success. Thus, success is created twice: first by creating, through strategic analysis, a clear mental model of what the firm wants to accomplish, and second by formulating and implementing a strategy that makes this vision a reality. An effectively communicated strategy should guide everyone in the organization.

Visionary Organizations

A vision is a statement about what an organization ultimately wants to accomplish. It captures the company's aspiration. An effective vision pervades the organization with a sense of winning and motivates employees at all levels to aim for the target, while leaving room for individual and team contributions. Employees in visionary companies tend to feel like part of something bigger than themselves. An inspiring vision helps employees find meaning in their work. Monetary rewards form only one part of what motivates people. An effective vision allows employees to reap intrinsic rewards by making the world a better place through their work activities.[2] This in turn is highly motivating for employees, leading to higher organizational performance.[3] Basing actions on its vision, a firm will build the necessary resources and capabilities through continuous organizational learning, including learning from failure, to translate into reality what begins as a "stretch goal."

Vision statements should be forward-looking and inspiring to provide meaning for employees when pursuing the organization's ultimate goals. Take Teach For America (TFA), whose vision is that *"one day, all children in this nation will have the opportunity to attain an excellent education."* It effectively and clearly communicates what TFA ultimately wants to accomplish; it provides an inspiring target to aim for. Exhibit 2.1 contains TFA's vision, mission, and values.

It's not surprising that vision statements can be inspiring and motivating in the not-for-profit sector. Many people would find meaning in wanting to help children attain an excellent education (TFA) or wanting to be "always there," touching the lives of people in need (American Red Cross). But what about for-profit firms? The main difference is the metric by which we assess successful performance. TFA measures its organizational success by the effects its teachers have on student performance. In the for-profit sector,

EXHIBIT 2.1

Teach For America: Vision, Mission, and Values

Vision	One day, all children in this nation will have the opportunity to attain an excellent education.
Mission	Eliminate educational inequality by enlisting our nation's most promising future leaders in the effort.
Values	**Relentless Pursuit of Results:** We assume personal responsibility for achieving ambitious, measurable results in pursuit of our vision. We persevere in the face of challenges, seek resources to ensure the best outcomes, and work toward our goals with a sense of purpose and urgency.
	Sense of Possibility: We approach our work with optimism, think boldly, and greet new ideas openly.
	Disciplined Thought: We think critically and strategically in search of the best answers and approaches, reflect on past experiences and data to draw lessons for the future, and make choices that are deeply rooted in our mission.
	Respect and Humility: We value all who are engaged in this challenging work. We keep in mind the limitations of our own experiences and actively seek out diverse perspectives.
	Integrity: We ensure alignment between our actions and our beliefs, engage in honest self-scrutiny, and do what is right for the broader good.

Source: www.teachforamerica.org

companies typically measure financial performance. Chapter 5 explores the various perspectives by which to measure performance and capture the multifaceted nature of competitive advantage.

Forming Strategic Intent

Strategic intent is the staking out of a desired leadership position in the long term that far exceeds a company's current resources and capabilities.[4] Challenging goals that stretch an individual or an organization can lead to higher performance.[5] Many Japanese competitors set ambitious stretch goals of global leadership (reflected in their missions) and made them a reality: Canon "beat Xerox," Komatsu "encircled Caterpillar," and Honda became "a second Ford." (Today the latter may not sound like a desirable goal, but it was in the 1970s when Honda began its quest for global leadership.) Currently, Chinese companies such as Baidu, BYD, and Lenovo aspire to world leadership. These companies set their ambitious goals when they were only a fraction the size of the companies they were chasing. Indeed, they were so small that initially the market leaders did not even recognize them as potential competitors; many had never competed outside their domestic markets. Yet all made global leadership their mission, with goals so ambitious they exceeded the firms' existing resources and capabilities by a large margin. Effective use of stretch goals created at all levels of the organization an obsession with winning that has been sustained over several decades.[6]

Strategic intent allows managers to operationalize their vision because it is not only forward-looking and future-oriented but also helps in identifying steps that need to be taken to make a vision become reality. Creating and executing strategy to achieve a strategic fit with *today's* environment is like driving a car while looking only in the rearview mirror. The focus should be how to create competitive advantage *tomorrow*. In fact, rather than

>> **LO 2-2**
Describe and evaluate the role of strategic intent in achieving long-term goals.

---

strategic management process
Method by which managers conceive of and implement a strategy that can lead to a sustainable competitive advantage.

vision A statement about what an organization ultimately wants to accomplish; it captures the company's aspiration.

strategic intent The staking out of a desired leadership position that far exceeds a company's current resources and capabilities.

Winning Through Strategic Intent

In the aftermath of World War II, an obscure Japanese technology startup firm named Tokyo Tsushin Kogyo K.K. began its life by repairing shortwave radios and inventing an electric rice cooker. Its lead scientist, Masaru Ibuka, thought a portable radio based on transistors might be possible. He conferred with scientists from Bell Labs, the U.S. firm that invented the transistor. They told him a transistor radio was not technologically feasible. Undeterred, Ibuka asked Japan's Ministry of International Trade and Industry (MITI) to obtain a license for the transistor from Bell Labs so he could build the portable radio. MITI turned him down, believing the fledgling firm could not commercialize such cutting-edge technology given its lack of track record and resources.

Ibuka persisted, however. Finally, in 1953 he secured permission to license the transistor. He then created an explicit strategic intent for his firm, focusing on being first to market with an innovative portable transistor radio of the highest possible quality.

Ibuka faced long odds: Radios then were enclosed in large pieces of decorative furniture; at that time, "Made in Japan" was synonymous with poor quality; and by the mid-1950s, Bell Labs scientists had already won two Nobel Prizes for physics. The idea that a Japanese startup working out of makeshift quarters in Tokyo could beat Bell Labs in commercializing the transistor radio seemed preposterous. But Ibuka inspired his hungry engineers to pursue their strategic intent. In 1957, they introduced the world's first pocket transistor radio, the TR-55. It sold 1.5 million units and catapulted the firm to leadership in consumer electronics. In 1958, the company changed its Japanese name to Sony Corporation.

Over time, Sony continually honed its core competency in miniaturization, which allowed it to create the Walkman, Discman, and MP3 players. More recently, though, Sony has fallen on hard times. Blamed on a silo mentality, it was not able to capitalize on its MP3 player or its electronic readers and has lost market share to Apple.[7]

attempting a strategic fit between a firm's resources and capabilities and today's external industry environment, strategic intent creates an extreme misfit by setting ambitious goals and then challenging managers and employees across all organizational levels to close the gap by building the resources and capabilities necessary to accomplish these goals. It does matter where you are today, but more importantly, it matters where you want to go tomorrow. Strategy Highlight 2.1 illustrates the powerful effects that strategic intent can have. It also demonstrates, however, what can happen when a firm accomplishes its strategic intent but then fails to set new stretch goals.

Mission Statements

Building on the vision, organizations establish a mission, which describes what an organization actually does—the products and services it plans to provide and the markets in which it will compete. Effective mission statements work through metaphors that help employees make appropriate decisions when faced with day-to-day situations, which sometimes can be novel or stressful.

Let's look at Disney's mission, which is *to make people happy.*[8] Disney's translation of this mission to employees who work at a Disney theme park is that they are not mere employees, they are cast members. Similarly, visitors to the park are not customers, they are audience members, there to enjoy a show. This metaphor has important implications for employees' behavior, beginning before they are even hired. Rather than interviewing for a job, for instance, they audition for a role, like cast members in a play. Thus any time a Disney park employee is in uniform, he or she is actually "on stage," delivering a performance. Even street sweepers (often college students on break) are part of the cast. Because they have the closest contact with guests, they are trained in great detail and are evaluated not only on personal neatness and job performance, but also on their knowledge about rides, parades, and restaurant and restroom locations. Like cast members in the theater, Disney employees pull off daily "the show must go on" performances that allow them to fulfill Disney's mission to make people happy.

CUSTOMER-ORIENTED MISSIONS. Disney's mission is aimed at its customers. *A customer-oriented mission* defines a business in terms of providing solutions to customer needs. Companies that have customer-oriented missions ("We are in the business of providing

the firm's revenues to various non-governmental organizations (NGOs) that promote literacy. After a while, the founders realized that the way they operationalized their mission was threatening the future viability of the venture. They decided they had to reduce their donation commitment from 50 percent of revenues to between 7 and 10 percent. BWB provides an example in which a firm's mission and competitive advantage can be negatively associated, especially when competitive advantage is understood more narrowly as superior financial performance. (We will explore more about the triple-bottom line concept and competitive advantage in Chapter 5.)

No Association Between Mission Statements and Competitive Advantage. In some cases, mission statements have little or no effect on performance and competitive advantage. Intel Corporation, one of the world's leading silicon innovators, provides an illustrative case. Intel's early mission was to be *the pre-eminent building-block supplier of the PC industry*. Intel designed the first commercial microprocessor chip in 1971 and set the standard for microprocessors in 1978; during the personal computer (PC) revolution in the 1980s, microprocessors became Intel's main line of business. Intel's customers were OEMs (original equipment manufacturers) that produce consumer end-products, such as computer manufacturers HP, IBM, Dell, and Compaq.

In the Internet age, however, the standalone PC as the end-product has become less important. Customers now want to stream video and share photos online. Such activities consume a tremendous amount of computing power. To reflect this shift, Intel in 1999 changed its mission to focus on being *the preeminent building-block supplier to the Internet economy*. Later, in 2008, Intel fully made the shift to a customer-oriented mission: Its current mission statement is to *delight our customers, employees, and shareholders by relentlessly delivering the platform and technology advancements that become essential to the way we work and live.* Part of this shift can be explained by a hugely successful "Intel Inside" advertising campaign in the 1990s that made Intel a household name worldwide.

Intel accomplished superior firm performance over decades through *continuous adaptation* to changing market realities. Yet its formal mission statement lagged the firm's transformations. Intel regularly changed its mission statement *after* it had accomplished successful transformation.[15] In such a case, mission statements and firm performance are clearly not related to one another.

Taken together, what empirical research shows is that sometimes mission statements and firm performance are *associated* with one another. What is less clear, however, is whether these relationships are *causal*—whether an effective mission statement *leads* to competitive advantage. The upshot is that an effective mission statement can lay the foundation upon which to craft a strategy that creates economic value, leading to competitive advantage. (You will learn more about *economic value creation* in Chapter 5, when studying competitive advantage in more depth.)

To be effective, firms do need to back up their mission statements with strategic commitments, actions that are costly, long-term oriented, and difficult to reverse. Boeing's decision to develop the 787 Dreamliner, for example, is a multibillion-dollar, multidecade strategic commitment.[16] Without such commitments, the firm's mission statement is just words. Eventually, both employees and external stakeholders may perceive the hollowness of the mission statement and realize that, however good the statement, it will not result in competitive

strategic commitments
Actions that are costly, long-term oriented, and difficult to reverse.

advantage without strategic actions to back it up. Moreover, if the vision-mission-values are not in coherence with each other, then a firm's strategy will necessarily be compromised. Effective alignment is key when translating a mission statement into strategic actions.

Living the Values

Organizational values are the ethical standards and norms that govern the behavior of individuals within a firm or organization (and within society). Strong ethical values, in turn, have two important functions: First, they form a solid foundation on which a firm can build its mission and long-term success. They also are the guardrails put in place so the company can stay on track when pursuing its mission in its quest for competitive advantage.

Employees tend to follow values practiced by strategic leaders. Without commitment and involvement from top managers, any statement of values remains a meaningless public relations exercise. Employees find out very quickly by observing executives' day-to-day decisions whether they are guided by an unchangeable and ethical core that is reflected in the company's mission, or whether they merely pay lip service to its values. True values must be lived with integrity, especially by the top management team. Unethical behavior by top managers is like a virus that spreads quickly throughout the entire organization.

The values espoused by a company provide answers to the question, *How do we accomplish our goals?* They help individuals make choices that are both ethical and effective in advancing the company's goals. For instance, John Hammergren, Chairman and CEO of McKesson, a $110 billion health care company, sees a direct relationship between the company's performance and its values: "At McKesson, we are guided by a common set of values: integrity, customer-first, accountability, respect, and excellence. We call them our ICARE Shared Principles, and they serve as the framework for who we are and how we interact with each other and our customers. These ethics and behavior models are the cornerstones on which we have built our business and our culture."[17] The key issue is the extent to which these ICARE Shared Principles are used in everyday business situations. Do they really guide employee behavior, or are they just a part of public relations?

At McKesson, employees incorporate the ICARE Shared Values into their daily activities. For example, the employees of McKesson's U.S. Pharmaceutical Distribution center worked long overtime hours after the tragedies of hurricanes Katrina and Rita when assisting the Federal Emergency Management Agency (FEMA). One functional-level manager, credits this experience for helping workers to gain a deeper appreciation of the impact their work has on the well-being of thousands of people in need. It also helped families understand the importance of what McKesson's employees do for a living.[18]

Google's values also guided some tough strategic decisions.[19] In 2006, Google entered the Chinese market with a customized search engine (google.cn) to service some 400 million new online customers. This was a self-censored version of its regular search engine (google.com) to comply with China's restrictions on free speech. At that time, Google felt the good that access to its searches, albeit censored, would bring to the Chinese people would outweigh its discomfort with censorship. By 2010, Google felt it could no longer continue to provide self-censored searches; it alleged that the firm was the target of sophisticated hacker attacks, accessing some of its users' Gmail accounts, including those of Chinese human rights activists. Google decided it would no longer censor its searches in China, thus risking having its search engine shut down by the Chinese government. Google's strong values—such as "democracy on the web works," "you can make money without doing evil," and "the need for information crosses all borders"—guided this decision, which had potentially far-reaching strategic consequences.[20] Google now runs its China website on a server in Hong Kong. After several months of negotiations, the Chinese government renewed Google's

LO 2-5
Explain why anchoring a firm in ethical values is essential for long-term success.

organizational values Ethical standards and norms that govern the behavior of individuals within a firm or organization.

license to do business in China.[21] Yet, Google's exit from mainland China further strengthened Baidu's lead with an almost 75 percent share of one of the fastest-growing online markets worldwide.[22] Baidu is a domestic Chinese company founded by Robin Li.

In contrast, when a firm does not have strong organizational values to inform the behavior of its top managers or other employees, major stakeholder value destruction is likely to follow. In the following examples, managers acted unethically and illegally:

- Using a giant Ponzi scheme, Bernie Madoff, with the help of several employees in his investment securities firm, defrauded high-profile institutional and individual investors such as bank HSBC, Banco Santander, Human Rights First, the International Olympic Committee, film producer and CEO of DreamWorks Animation Jeffrey Katzenberg, actor Kevin Bacon, and Nobel Peace Prize winner Elie Wiesel. Madoff's fraud totaled an estimated $65 billion. He was sentenced to 150 years imprisonment and fines of more than $170 billion.[23]

- At one time, it was hailed as one of "America's Best Companies to Work For," with more than 22,000 employees and over $100 billion in annual revenues. Enron's mission statement touted integrity as one of its key values. Yet, Enron's top-level executives were systematically defrauding investors, employees, customers, and other stakeholders. Enron's collapse in 2001 remains one of the biggest bankruptcies in U.S. history. Former Enron president Jeffrey Skilling was convicted of fraud and insider trading and is currently serving a 25-year term in a federal prison. The Enron shockwaves also sank Arthur Andersen, formerly the largest of the big five accounting firms, because of its role as an accomplice in the accounting scandal. Some 30,000 Andersen accountants and consultants lost their livelihoods.[24]

STRATEGIZING FOR COMPETITIVE ADVANTAGE: HOW IS STRATEGY "MADE"?

Since we now have a basic understanding of what strategy is and why it is important (discussed in Chapter 1) as well as vision, mission, and values, we can think about how strategy is made. How does strategy come about? When strategizing for competitive advantage, managers rely on three different approaches that can complement one another: (1) strategic planning, (2) scenario planning, and (3) strategy as planned emergence.

Strategic Planning

With the tremendous growth of corporations in the prosperous decades following World War II, corporate executives began to use strategic (or long-range) planning to manage firms more effectively and enhance their performance. Top executives and scholars alike understood strategic planning to be a rational, top-down process through which they could program future success.[25] One scholar wrote during this time: "Long-range planning is one of the really new techniques left to management that can give a company a major competitive advantage."[26]

With strategic planning, all strategic intelligence and decision-making responsibilities are concentrated in the office of the CEO who, much like a military general, leads the company strategically through competitive battles. Five-year plans, revisited regularly, predict future sales based on anticipated future growth. Strategic planners provide careful analyses of internal and external data and apply it to all quantifiable areas: prices, costs, margins, market demand, head count, and production runs. Top executives tie the allocation of the annual corporate budget to the strategic plan and monitor ongoing performance accordingly. In this process, the formulation of strategy is separate from implementation, and thinking about strategy is separate from doing it.

>> **LO 2-6**
Compare and contrast strategic planning, scenario planning, and strategy as planned emergence, and discuss strategic implications.

strategic (long-range) planning
A rational, top-down process through which management can program future success; typically concentrates strategic intelligence and decision-making responsibilities in the office of the CEO.

Shell's Future Scenarios

Shell predicts that in 2025 most of our energy will continue to be generated from fossil fuels but 20 percent will come from alternative energy sources like wind, solar, and hydro power. Shell managers thus focus more on fossil fuels in their scenario analysis than on renewable technologies.

Given Shell's past success in using scenario planning, one ought to pay attention to its predictions. Shell can claim a number of accurate predictions to its credit. In the 1960s, with the price of a barrel of crude oil around $10 (compared to a record high of close to $150 in the summer of 2008), managers at Shell began to formulate strategic plans for a future with a strong OPEC (the cartel of oil-exporting countries) and an accompanying drastic rise in oil prices. When the price of crude oil suddenly surged to over $80 a barrel in the late 1970s, Shell was well-positioned to take advantage of this new situation; other oil companies were scrambling to adjust. Shell activated one of its alternative strategic plans that detailed how to obtain crude oil from North Sea drilling, to which the firm had already secured the rights.

In the early 1980s, Shell made strategic preparations to take advantage of another apparently far-fetched scenario when it speculated that communism might fail, bringing down the powerful Soviet Union and ending Soviet artificial restrictions on the supply of natural gas. As a consequence of these strategies, Shell moved from eighth place to become the second-largest oil company in the world.[30]

Top-down strategic planning works reasonably well when the environment does not change very much, because it rests on the assumption that we can predict the future from the past. One major shortcoming of the strategic planning approach is that we cannot know the future. Unforeseen events can make even the most scientifically developed and best formalized plans obsolete. Moreover, as seen in Chapter 1, the rate of change appears to be increasing, which further undercuts the effectiveness of strategic planning.

Scenario Planning

Given that the only constant is change, should managers even use strategic planning? The answer is yes, but they also need to expect that unpredictable events will happen. We can compare strategic planning in a fast-changing environment to the operations of a fire department.[27] There is no way to know where and when the next emergency will arise, nor can we know its magnitude beforehand. Nonetheless, fire chiefs put contingency plans in place to address a wide range of emergencies along different dimensions. In the same way, scenario planning asks the "what if" questions. It is a strategy-planning activity in which managers envision different scenarios to anticipate plausible futures. As General (and later President) Eisenhower wisely said, "In preparing for battle, I have always found that plans are useless, but planning is indispensable."[28]

In scenario planning, managers envision different what-if scenarios: New laws might restrict carbon emissions or expand employee health care. Demographic shifts may alter the ethnic diversity of a nation, while changing tastes or economic conditions will affect consumer behavior. How would those changes affect a firm and how should it respond? Typical scenario planning addresses both optimistic and pessimistic futures. For instance, strategy executives at UPS recently identified six issues as critical to shaping its future competitive scenarios: (1) the price of oil; (2) climate change; (3) trade barriers (such as "buy American" or "buy Chinese" clauses in new laws around the world); (4) the emerging BRIC (Brazil, Russia, India, and China) economies; (5) political instability; and (6) online commerce worldwide.[29] Managers then formulated strategies they can activate and implement should one of the envisioned scenarios play a more significant role. Strategy Highlight 2.2 shows how the energy company Shell has used scenario planning to significantly improve its performance.

Exhibit 2.2 shows how to use the AFI strategy framework for scenario planning, to create strategic plans that are more flexible, and thus more effective, than the more static strategic planning approach.

In the *analysis stage,* managers brainstorm to identify possible future scenarios. Input from several different hierarchies within the organization and from different functional areas such as R&D, manufacturing, and marketing and sales is critical. UPS executives

scenario planning Strategy-planning activity in which managers envision different what-if scenarios to anticipate plausible futures.

EXHIBIT 2.2

Scenario Planning
in the AFI Strategy
Framework

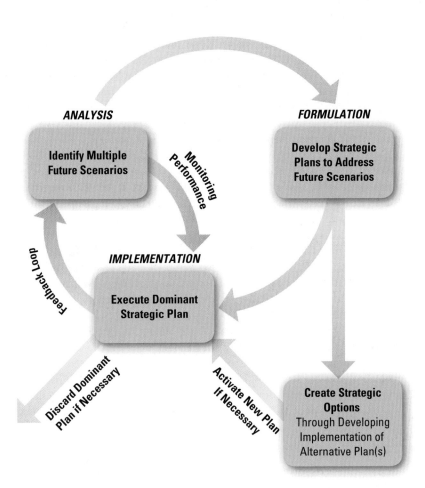

considered how they would compete if the price of a barrel of oil was $35, or $125, or even $200. Managers may also attach probabilities (highly likely vs. unlikely, or 85 percent likely vs. 2 percent likely) to different future states.

Managers often overlook pessimistic future scenarios. For example, many were caught off-guard by the recent economic downturn. Managers should consider negative scenarios more carefully, for example, how to obtain liquidity when credit and equity markets are tight. This was a serious problem during the 2008–2009 world financial crisis. An exporter like Boeing or Harley-Davidson would want to analyze the impact of shifts in exchange rates on sales and production costs—what if the euro depreciated to $1 per euro, or the Chinese yuan depreciated rather than appreciated?

In the *formulation stage,* management teams develop different strategic plans to address possible future scenarios. This kind of what-if exercise forces managers to consider contingency plans in the formulation stage, before events occur. Each plan relies on the entire set of analytical tools (which will be introduced in upcoming chapters) to capture the firm's internal and external environments and to answer several key questions:

- What resources and capabilities do we need to compete successfully in each future scenario?
- Which strategic initiatives should we put in place to respond to each?
- How can we shape our expected future environment?

By formulating responses to the scenario analysis stage, managers achieve strategic flexibility by building a portfolio of future options. They continue integrating additional information over time, which in turn influences future decisions. Finally, they transform the most viable options into full-fledged strategic plans to be activated when needed.

In the *implementation stage,* managers activate the dominant strategic plan, the option they think most closely matches reality. If reality changes, managers can quickly retrieve and implement any of the alternate plans developed in the formulation stage. The firm's performance in the marketplace provides feedback to the managers concerning the viability of the dominant strategic plan. If the performance feedback is positive, managers continue to pursue the dominant strategic plan, while fine-tuning it in the process. If the performance feedback is negative, managers consider whether modifying the dominant strategic option will enhance firm performance or whether they are better off activating one of the alternative strategic plans.

To conduct successful scenario planning, managers need current information. The network-equipment giant Cisco Systems has invested huge sums in technology to generate just this kind of data.[31] Cisco's senior executives can track daily customer order data from its sales teams around the globe with up-to-the-minute accuracy. Walmart's CEO Mike Duke indicates that he too is using real-time sales data tracking, enabling top executives to monitor daily sales of each of the over 8,500 Walmart stores worldwide in real time.[32] With these real-time data systems, managers can identify emerging trends in each region and market segment long before they materialize in financial data. This in turn allows them to fine-tune their functional strategy with unprecedented accuracy and speed.

The circular nature of the scenario-planning model in Exhibit 2.2 highlights the continuous interaction between analysis, formulation, and implementation. Through this interactive process, managers can adjust and modify their actions as new realities emerge. The interdependence among analysis, formulation, and implementation also enhances organizational learning and flexibility.

"DON'T SEPARATE STRATEGIC ANALYSIS FROM STRATEGIC ACTION!" Critics of strategic planning and scenario planning, most notably Henry Mintzberg of McGill University, argue that strategic *planning* is not the same as strategic *thinking.*[33] In fact, Mintzberg suggests the strategic planning process often is too regimented and confining and does not allow for strategic thinking. Managers doing strategic planning may fall prey to an *illusion of control*—the hard numbers in a strategic plan can convey a false sense of security. To be successful, say these critics, a strategy should be based on an inspiring mission, and not on hard data alone. They advise that managers should focus on all types of information sources, including "soft" sources that can generate new insights, such as personal experience or the experience of front-line employees. The important work, say the critics of strategic planning, is to synthesize *all available input* into an overall strategic mission, which should then guide the firm's strategy.

Indeed, some companies *choose* not to articulate a corporate or business strategy. Rather, they focus on consistency in strategic actions across all levels of the organization.[34] For example, Nucor Corporation had 2010 sales of $16 billion and employed 22,500 people (fewer than 100 of them in its corporate headquarters), making it the largest steel maker in the United States.[35] Nucor has been profitable for several *decades* and has never laid off an employee for lack of work. Its employees are among the highest paid in the industry (two-thirds of their compensation is performance-related), and it has the lowest labor cost per ton of steel produced. Yet Nucor has no written strategic plan, no written mission statement, and no written goals and objectives. It does, however, have a strong organizational culture based on peer control combined with a set of clear operational rules supporting its functional-level strategy.[36]

How can a company like Nucor be so successful without an overarching strategic plan? Because lack of a *written strategic plan* does not indicate lack of a strategy. We can deduce a firm's strategy from the pattern of its actions.[37] Indeed, everything Nucor's managers and employees do across all levels of the organization indicate its strategy of cost leadership (providing an acceptable standard of product quality or value to the customer at the lowest cost to produce it). The absence of an explicitly formulated plan may give Nucor flexibility to more quickly react to changes in the marketplace. In addition, it may make Nucor's strategy less transparent and its future strategic moves less obvious to competitors. All this contributes to protecting and sustaining Nucor's competitive advantage.

Strategy as Planned Emergence: Top-Down *and* Bottom-Up

We now come to the third approach to strategizing for competitive advantage. In contrast to the two rational planning approaches just discussed, another view considers less formal and less stylized approaches to the development of strategy.

A strategic initiative is any activity a firm pursues to explore and develop new products and processes, new markets, or new ventures. Strategic initiatives can come from anywhere. They could be the result of top-down planning by executives, and they also can emerge through a bottom-up process. Strategic initiatives can emerge from deep within a firm through *autonomous actions* by lower-level employees, from random events, and maybe even luck.[38] Consider the following examples, in which the impulse for strategic initiatives emerged from the bottom up.

- Google's Vice President Marissa Mayer reports that 50 percent of the firm's new products come from the *20 percent rule,* which allows all employees to spend one day a week (20 percent of the workweek) on ideas of their own choosing. Examples of innovations that resulted from the 20 percent rule include Gmail, Google News, and Orkut.[39]
- A mid-level engineer at General Electric in 2001 proposed buying Enron Wind, a division that was up for sale as part of Enron's bankruptcy proceedings. CEO Jack Welch's response was that GE wouldn't touch anything with the name Enron on it, given its large-scale accounting fraud. When the mid-level engineer kept insisting, after being rejected several times, GE's leadership relented and bought Enron Wind for $200 million. It turned out to be a huge success, with revenues over $6 billion in 2009, and it opened up other significant opportunities for GE in the alternative-energy industry such as its *ecomagination* initiative. GE's shift from a product-oriented company ("*We bring good things to life*") to a more consumer-oriented one ("*Imagination at work*") was part of the leadership change from Jack Welch to Jeffrey Immelt, who approved the investment in Enron Wind.[40]

A firm's actual strategy, therefore, is often a combination of its top-down strategic intentions (which typically are expressed in written strategic plans) and bottom-up emergent strategy.[41] An emergent strategy describes any unplanned strategic initiative undertaken by mid-level

---

dominant strategic plan The strategic option that managers think most closely matches reality at a given point in time.

strategic initiative Any activity a firm pursues to explore and develop new products and processes, new markets, or new ventures.

emergent strategy Any unplanned strategic initiative undertaken by mid-level employees of their own volition.

Starbucks's CEO: "It's Not What We Do!"

Diana, a Starbucks store manager in southern California, received several requests a day for an iced beverage offered by a local competitor. After she received more than 30 requests one day, she tried the beverage herself. Thinking it might be a good idea for Starbucks to offer a similar iced beverage, she requested that headquarters consider adding it to the product lineup. Diana had an internal champion in Howard Behar, then one of Starbucks's top executives. Mr. Behar presented this strategic initiative to the Starbucks executive committee on which he sat, but it was voted down in a 7:1 vote. Starbucks's CEO Howard Schultz commented, "We do coffee, we don't do iced drinks."

Diana, however, was undeterred. She started experimenting with a blender to re-create this specific drink. Satisfied with her results, she began to offer the drink in her store. When Howard Behar visited Diana's store, he was shocked to see this new drink on the menu—all Starbucks stores were supposed to offer only company-approved drinks. But Diana told him the new drink was selling well.

Howard Behar flew Diana's team (and her blender) to Starbucks headquarters in Seattle, to serve this new drink to the executive committee. They liked the drink, but still said no. Then Behar pulled out the sales numbers that Diana had carefully kept. The drink was selling like crazy: 40 drinks a day the first week, 50 drinks a day the next week, and then 70 drinks in the third week after introduction. They had never seen such growth numbers. These results persuaded the executive team to give reluctant approval to introduce the drink in all Starbucks stores. You've probably by now guessed the drink—Starbucks's Frappuccino. Frappuccino is now a billion-dollar business for Starbucks, and at one point brought in more than 20 percent of Starbucks's total revenues (which were $11 billion in 2010).[43]

As the Starbucks example shows, companies can benefit from an attitude of "expect the unexpected, and react to it strategically"! Strategy can be planned, but sometimes important strategic initiatives simply emerge from the bottom up.

employees of their own volition.[42] If successful, emergent strategies have the potential to influence and shape a firm's strategy. Strategy Highlight 2.3 provides further evidence for the notion that successful emergent strategies are sometimes the result of *serendipity* combined with the tenacity of lower-level employees.

MINTZBERG'S PLANNING FRAMEWORK. To reflect the reality that strategy can be planned *or* can emerge from the bottom up, Mintzberg developed a more integrative and complete framework for strategy-making, shown in Exhibit 2.3.

According to this more holistic model, the strategy process may begin with a top-down strategic plan. Based on external and internal analyses, top-level executives design an intended strategy—the outcome of a rational and structured, top-down strategic plan. This is the first important step in strategy-making. However, in today's complex and uncertain world, unpredicted events can have huge effects. Very few people predicted, for example, that easy credit would lead to a housing bubble. The bursting of that bubble in 2008 rendered obsolete the best-laid strategic plans of financial, mortgage and insurance companies like Bank of America, Citigroup, Fannie Mae, Freddy Mac, and AIG. Indeed, most of these venerable institutions and many other firms would have faced bankruptcy were it not for a government bailout of $10 trillion.[44]

Unpredicted changes don't have to be cataclysmic, however, to be disruptive. Apple's hugely popular iPod and iPhone upset the strategic plans of a number of companies including Nokia, Sony, and RIM (the maker of the BlackBerry), forcing them to respond. Apple is trying to repeat this feat with its iPad, which could lead to industry convergence in computing, telecommunications, and media.[45] When unexpected events have dramatic strategic implications, part (or all) of a firm's strategic plan becomes an unrealized strategy and falls by the wayside.

Sometimes new ideas for strategic initiatives pop up in unusual ways. In these instances, astute managers combine serendipity and bottom-up emergent strategy into a successfully realized strategy. An unexpected event at the largest rail carrier in the world, Japan Railways, led to diversification from railroads into bottled water.[46] This may sound far-fetched, but here is how it happened: Japan Railways was constructing a new bullet train through the mountains north of Tokyo, requiring many tunnels. In one

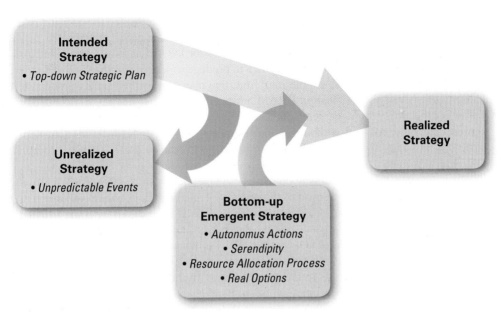

EXHIBIT 2.3

Realized Strategy
Is a Combination of
Top-down Intended
Strategy and
Bottom-up Emergent
Strategy

Source: Adapted from
H. Mintzberg and A. McHugh
(1985), "Strategy formation in
an adhocracy," *Administrative
Science Quarterly* 30: 162.

of the mountains, persistent flooding caused huge problems. Engineers responded by drawing up complex plans to drain the water. Meanwhile, workers inside the tunnel were making good use of the water—they were drinking it. A maintenance worker suggested the water should not be pumped away but rather bottled and sold as premium drinking water because it tasted so fresh. Its source was snow pack, purified and filtered in the slow percolation process through the mountain's geological layers and enhanced on the way with healthy amounts of calcium, potassium, and magnesium. Eventually, Japan Railways set up vending machines on 1,000 railroad platforms in and around Tokyo, and home delivery of water, juices, and coffee followed. The employee's proposal had turned an expensive engineering problem into a multimillion-dollar business. Because Japan Railways was willing to define its business as broader than just being in railroads, it was able to capture the emergent strategy and diversify into drinking water.

Bottom-up strategies can also emerge as a consequence of the firm's *resource allocation process (RAP).*[47] The core argument linking the RAP and strategy is that the way a firm allocates its resources can be critical in shaping its realized strategy.[48] Intel Corp.'s famous rule to "maximize margin-per-wafer-start" illustrates this concept.[49] Intel was founded in 1968 to produce DRAM (dynamic random-access memory) chips. From the start, producing these chips was the firm's top-down strategic plan, and initially it worked well. However, in the 1980s, Japanese competitors brought better-quality chips to the market at lower cost, threatening Intel's position and strategic plan. Intel was able, however, to pursue a strategic transformation due to the way it set up its RAP. In a sense, Intel was using functional-level strategies to drive business and corporate strategies. In particular, during this time Intel had only a few "fabs" (fabrication plants to produce silicon-based products). It would have taken several years and billions of dollars to build additional fabs.

---

intended strategy The outcome of a rational and structured top-down strategic plan.

unrealized strategy Part or all of a firm's strategic plan that falls by the wayside due to unexpected events.

realized strategy Combination of intended and emergent strategy.

Since Intel's production capacity was constrained, it had implemented the decision rule to "maximize margin-per-wafer-start." Each time functional managers initiated a new production run, they were to consider the profit margins for DRAM and for semiconductors (the "brains" of personal computers), and then to produce *whichever product* delivered the higher margin. Following this simple rule, front-line managers shifted Intel's production capacity away from the low-margin DRAM business to the higher-margin semiconductor business. The firm's focus on semiconductors thus emerged from the bottom up, based on resource allocation and without top-management planning. Indeed, by the time top-management finally approved the de facto strategic switch, the company's market share in DRAM had dwindled to less than 3 percent.[50]

Taken together, the Japan Railways and Intel examples demonstrate that a firm's realized strategy is frequently a combination of top-down strategic intent and bottom-up emergent strategies, as Exhibit 2.3 shows. Strategy-making has thus been called by some *planned emergence,* in which organizational structure and systems allow bottom-up strategic initiatives to emerge and be evaluated and coordinated by top management.[51]

A word of caution is in order: Not all emergent strategies are successful. As the story of Microsoft's Keywords in Chapter 1 shows, promising strategic initiatives can emerge from deep within the company, but top managers must have a system in place that allows them to judge whether to support those initiatives and allow them to influence and shape the firm's overall strategy. Although Microsoft missed the opportunity to lead in online search and advertising, it has a history of adapting successfully to quickly evolving environments. Mid-level Microsoft employees envisioned and developed both Internet Explorer (the leading web browser with more than two-thirds market share) and the Xbox videogame system to address threats posed by Netscape and Sony's PlayStation.

Implications for the Strategist

What approach can managers take to ensure that potentially high-impact strategic initiatives receive due consideration? When new ideas emerge, managers can go beyond standard evaluation metrics like net present value (NPV) and apply a *real options perspective.*[52] Both NPV and real options are tools taught in corporate finance. They provide critical information when a firm is making strategic decisions.

Though widely used, the net present value calculation is often inappropriate to assess the potential of highly uncertain strategic initiatives: It applies a high discount rate on the net present value of future cash flows, to reflect the high risk of these initiatives. At the same time, it ignores the potentially huge upside of such strategic initiatives. Applying net present value calculations, therefore, frequently leads to a premature death of strategic initiatives such as the Keywords project within Microsoft. Since there was no viable business model for it, shutting it down—based on an NPV calculation—was a rational decision.

In contrast, applying a real-options perspective to strategic decision making would break down a large investment decision into a set of smaller decisions that are staged sequentially over time. This approach allows the firm to obtain additional information in planned stages. At each stage, the firm evaluates a *real option,* which is the right, but not the obligation, to make a business decision. (Real options are sometimes called *strategic options,* to differentiate them from *financial options.*) Unlike the final "go or no-go" decision that an NPV calculation requires, applying a real-options framework allows managers to break down a big decision into smaller, stepped decisions based on a sequence of option payments over time. The idea is to keep the firm's alternatives open so that more information can reveal itself. Basically, managers are keeping open the possibility of changing the scope or timing of projects and other strategic initiatives, or even abandoning them altogether, as new information emerges.

Some cost is always involved in a real-options approach, but it's often less cost than a full-bore investment in a project that will not pan out. This approach reduces the uncertainty that surrounds the value of a bottom-up strategic initiative. Moreover, it prevents prematurely closing down a strategic initiative that is of high potential, but whose potential is revealed only at a later date. For example, rather than shutting down the Keywords initiative, Microsoft could have invested some money in it, to see if a business opportunity would arise.

A profitable business model in online search was demonstrated by Yahoo and later by Google. Microsoft's CEO Ballmer now attempts to apply a real-options perspective to emerging strategic initiatives: "The biggest mistakes I claim I've been involved with is where I was impatient—because we didn't have a business yet in something, we should have stayed patient. If we'd kept consistent with some of the ideas, we might have been in paid search. We are letting more flowers bloom."[53] Basically, the idea is not to shut down strategic experiments prematurely to foreclose future options. This approach requires not only application of a real-options perspective, but also recognition of strategy as planned emergence.

Here, we conclude our discussion of the strategic management process, which marks the end of the "getting started" portion of the AFI framework. The next chapter moves us into the analysis part of the framework—where we begin by studying the important topics of external and internal analysis, followed by consideration of how competitive advantage can be measured.

CHAPTERCASE 2 | *Consider This . . .*

IN FEBRUARY 2011, Teach For America (TFA) celebrated its 20th anniversary. In those 20 years, it has grown into a $212 million organization that attracted 12 percent of all Ivy League seniors in its 2010 application pool.[54] Studies show that TFA teachers have a stronger positive effect on high-school students' test scores than regular certified teachers—and that the performance difference was especially pronounced in math and science.[55]

A recent publication by TFA notes that teacher effectiveness is improved when teachers have course objectives that are "student-achievement based, measureable, and rigorous." Such course objectives are, in effect, mission statements. According to TFA, a poorly worded objective might be "The teacher will present a lesson on ordering fractions with different denominators." An improved objective would be "The student will be able to order fractions with different denominators."[56]

1. What role (if any) do you think TFA's vision statement may have had in the success of the organization?

2. How has TFA succeeded in recruiting so many Ivy League students into teaching in the lowest-performing regions of the United States?

3. Do you think TFA could have been just as successful if it had been structured as a traditional for-profit company?

Take-Away Concepts

This chapter explained the role of vision, mission, and values in the strategic management process and gave an overview of how strategy is made, as summarized by the following learning objectives and related take-away concepts.

LO 2-1 Explain the role of vision, mission, and values in the strategic management process.

>> A vision captures an organization's aspirations. An effective vision inspires members of the organization.

>> A mission statement describes what an organization actually does—what its business is—and why it does it.

>> Values define the ethical standards and norms that should govern the behavior of individuals within the firm.

>> Success is created twice: first by creating a mental model of what the firm wants to accomplish, and second by formulating and implementing a strategy that makes this vision a reality.

LO 2-2 Describe and evaluate the role of strategic intent in achieving long-term goals.

>> Strategic intent finds its expression in stretch goals that exceed the firms' existing resources and capabilities by a large margin.

>> Effective use of strategic intent creates at all levels of the organization an obsession with winning that can help companies ascend to global leadership.

LO 2-3 Distinguish between customer-oriented and product-oriented missions and identify strategic implications.

>> Customer-oriented missions define business in terms of providing solutions to customer needs.

>> Product-oriented missions define a business in terms of a good or service provided.

>> Customer-oriented missions provide managers with more strategic flexibility than product-oriented missions.

LO 2-4 Critically evaluate the relationship between mission statements and competitive advantage.

>> Mission statements can help a firm achieve superior performance, but mission statements by themselves do not directly affect firm performance.

>> To be effective, mission statements need to be backed up by hard-to-reverse commitments.

LO 2-5 Explain why anchoring a firm in ethical values is essential for long-term success.

>> Ethical core values enable employees to make day-to-day decisions that are guided by correct principles.

>> Strong ethical values are the guardrails that help keep the company on track when pursuing its mission and its quest for competitive advantage.

LO 2-6   Compare and contrast strategic planning, scenario planning, and strategy as planned emergence, and discuss strategic implications.

>> Top-down strategic (long-range) planning works reasonably well when the environment does not change much.

>> In scenario planning, managers envision different what-if scenarios and prepare contingency plans that can be called upon when necessary.

>> Strategic initiatives can be the result of top-down planning by executives or can emerge through a bottom-up process from deep within the organization.

>> A firm's realized strategy is generally a combination of its top-down intended strategy and bottom-up emergent strategy, resulting in planned emergence.

Key Terms

Dominant strategic plan *(p. 42)*

Emergent strategy *(p. 43)*

Intended strategy *(p. 44)*

Mission *(p. 34)*

Organizational values *(p. 38)*

Realized strategy *(p. 44)*

Scenario planning *(p. 40)*

Strategic commitments *(p. 37)*

Strategic initiative *(p. 43)*

Strategic intent *(p. 33)*

Strategic management process *(p. 32)*

Strategic (long-range) planning *(p. 39)*

Unrealized strategy *(p. 44)*

Vision *(p. 32)*

Discussion Questions

1. What characteristics does an effective mission statement have?

2. What is strategic intent? How can it be useful for goal setting and achievement?

3. In what situations is top-down planning likely to be superior to bottom-up emergent strategy development?

4. Based on discussions in this chapter, which railroad firm seems more prepared to use planned emergence, CSX or Japan Railways? Why?

5. Discuss how scenario planning can be used to prepare a firm for future events. Can some industries benefit more than others from this type of process?

Ethical/Social Issues

1. As noted in the "Living the Values" section, over 50,000 people lost their jobs and many their life savings in the Enron debacle. Some of those at Enron who were closely involved in the scandal, such as Jeffrey Skilling (CEO) and Andrew Fastow (CFO), are serving significant prison sentences. What responsibility do lower-level executives bear for not reporting such questionable practices by the firm's leadership? Why do you think only one employee initially came forward to report the irregularities and help with the investigation?

2. In the circumstance when an emergent idea arises that appears to mid-level managers to have strong merits yet conflicts with an existing intended strategy from the top managers, how would you suggest the organization decide which idea to push forward into a plan of action and thus contribute to a realized strategy? What would you do in this situation if you were (a) a mid-level manager or (b) an executive?

Small Group Exercises

SMALL GROUP EXERCISE 1

The National Aeronautics and Space Administration (NASA) is leading the public space program in the United States. Its vision is "to advance U.S. scientific, security, and economic interests through a robust space exploration program." Its mission is "to pioneer the future in space exploration, scientific discovery, and aeronautics research." To accomplish its vision and mission, in 2006 NASA specified a set of six strategic goals to be accomplished over the next 10 years:

1. Fly the Shuttle as safely as possible until its retirement, not later than 2010.

2. Complete the International Space Station in a manner consistent with NASA's International Partner commitments and the needs of human exploration.

3. Develop a balanced overall program of science, exploration, and aeronautics consistent with the redirection of the human spaceflight program to focus on exploration.

4. Bring a new Crew Exploration Vehicle into service as soon as possible after Shuttle retirement.

5. Encourage the pursuit of appropriate partnerships with the emerging commercial space sector.

6. Establish a lunar return program having the maximum possible utility for later missions to Mars and other destinations.

NASA's quest to accomplish these goals is grounded in its values of (1) safety, (2) teamwork, (3) integrity, and (4) mission success. In NASA's strategic plan, each of the six strategic goals is broken down into a number of detailed sub-goals. These goals are accompanied by a detailed list of expected outcomes that enables NASA to measure its progress and report its accomplishments back to its stakeholders. Michael Griffin, the NASA Administrator when the strategic plan was devised, said that "By pursuing the goals of the Vision for Space Exploration, NASA will contribute to American leadership in defining and pursuing the frontiers that expand humankind's reach, and we will help keep our nation at the cutting edge of science and technology. We also will work with other nations to do those things that fulfill the dreams of humankind, dreams that always have included the desire to see what lies beyond the known world."[57]

1. How is NASA including its mission and values in its strategic planning to make its goals become reality?

2. Do you think a 10-year planning horizon is realistic? Why or why not?

3. Do you agree with Michael Griffin's interpretation of the expected results of pursuing NASA's mission? Discuss why or why not.

SMALL GROUP EXERCISE 2

In many situations, promising ideas emerge from the lower levels of an organization only to be discarded before they can be tested and implemented. It was only due to extraordinary tenacity (and indeed disregard) for the policy of selling only corporate-approved drinks that permitted the Frappuccino to "bloom" within Starbucks (see Strategy Highlight 2.3). Some scholars have suggested that companies should set aside up to 2 percent of their budgets for *any* manager with budget control to be able to invest in new ideas within the company.[58] (Someone with a $100,000 annual budget to manage would be able to invest $2,000 in cash or staff time toward such a project. Multiple managers could go in together for somewhat larger funds or time amounts.)

Through such a process, the organization can generate a network of "angel investors." Small funds or staff time can be invested into a variety of projects. Approval mechanisms would be easier for these small "seed stock" ideas, to give them a chance to develop before going for bigger funding at the top levels of the organization.

What would be some problems that would need to be addressed to introduce this "angel network" idea into a firm? Use a firm someone in your group has worked for or knows well to discuss possible issues of widely distributing small funding level approvals across the firm.

Strategy Term Project

MODULE 2: MISSION, GOALS, AND THE STRATEGIC MANAGEMENT PROCESS

1. Search for a mission statement for the firm. Not all organizations publish such a statement, so alternatively you can look for enduring principles and values upon which the firm seems to be anchored. This information is often available at the firm's website (though it may take some searching) or is contained in its annual reports. You may also interview a manager of the firm or contact "investor relations."

2. Identify the major goals of the company.

3. Does the firm seem to have any longer-term challenging or stretch goals that would serve as its strategic intent?

4. Trace any changes in strategy that you can identify over time. Try to determine whether the strategic changes of your selected firm are a result of intended strategies, emergent strategies, or some combination of both.

*my*Strategy

HOW MUCH ARE YOUR VALUES WORTH TO YOU?

How much are you willing to pay for the job you want? This may sound like a strange question, since your employer will pay you to work, but think again. Consider how much you value a specific type of work, or how much you would want to work for a specific organization because of its values.

A recent study shows scientists who want to continue engaging in research will accept some $14,000 less in annual salary to work at an organization that permits them to publish their findings in academic journals, implying that some scientists will "pay to be scientists." This finding appears to hold in the general business world, too. In a recent survey, 97 percent of Stanford MBA students indicated they would forgo some 14 percent of their expected salary, or about $11,480 a year, to work for a company that matches their own values with concern for stakeholders and sustainability. According

to Monster.com, an online career service, about 92 percent of all undergraduates want to work for a "green" company. These diverse examples demonstrate that people put a real dollar amount on pursuing careers in sync with their values.

On the other hand, certain high-powered jobs such as management consulting or investment banking pay very well, but their high salaries come with strings attached. Professionals in these jobs work very long hours, including weekends, and often take little or no vacation time. These workers "pay for pay" in that they are often unable to form stable relationships, have little or no leisure time, and sometimes even sacrifice their health. People "pay for"—make certain sacrifices for—what they value, because strategic decisions require important trade-offs.[59]

1. What values are (were) most important to you in your career choice?

2. How much less salary would (did) you accept to find employment with a company that is in line with your values?

Endnotes

1. This ChapterCase is based on the following sources: Frankl, V. E. (1984), *Man's Search for Meaning* (New York: Washington Square Press); Kopp, W. (2001), *One Day, All Children…: The Unlikely Triumph of Teach For America and What I Learned Along the Way* (Cambridge, MA: Perseus Book Group); Xu, Z., J. Hannaway, and C. Taylor (2008), "Making a difference? The effect of Teach For America on student performance in high school," *Urban Institute,* March 27; and data from the U.S. Census Bureau, www.hernandezcollegeconsulting.com/ivy-league-admission-statistics-2009/.

2. Frankl, V. E. (1984), *Man's Search for Meaning.*

3. Xu, Z., J. Hannaway, and C. Taylor (2008), "Making a difference? The effect of Teach For America on student performance in high school."

4. This section is based on: Hamel, G., and C. K. Prahalad (1989), "Strategic intent," *Harvard Business Review* (May–June): 64–65; and Hamel, G., and

C. K. Prahalad (1994), *Competing for the Future* (Boston, MA: Harvard Business School Press).

5. Locke, E. A., and G. P. Latham (1990), *A Theory of Goal Setting and Task Performance* (Englewood Cliffs, NJ: Prentice Hall).

6. Hamel, G., and C. K. Prahalad (1989), "Strategic intent," *Harvard Business Review*; and Hamel, G., and C. K. Prahalad (1994), *Competing for the Future.*

7. This Strategy Highlight is based on: Heath, C., and D. Heath (2007), *Made to Stick. Why Some Ideas Survive and Others Die* (New York, NY: Random House), pp. 93–95; and www.sony.net/SonyInfo/CorporateInfo/History/history.html.

8. The Disney and Subway discussion is based on: Heath, C., and D. Heath (2007), *Made to Stick,* pp. 60–61.

9. "The three habits…of highly irritating management gurus," *The Economist,* October 22, 2009.

10. Author's interviews with Blaine Lawlor, former staff analyst at Shell Canada, and now a strategic management professor at the University of West Florida, November 6–7, 2009.

11. Collins, J. C., and J. I. Porras (1994), *Built to Last: Successful Habits of Visionary Companies* (New York: Harper Collins). Collins and Porras define visionary companies as follows: "Visionary companies are premier institutions—the crown jewels—in their industries, widely admired by their peers and having a long track record of making a significant impact on the world around them" (p. 1).

12. www.merck.com.

13. George W. Merck, address to the Medical College of Virginia, Richmond, VA (December 1, 1950), quoted in Collins, J. C., and J. I. Porras (1994), *Built to Last,* p. 48.

14. Rothaermel, F. T., K. Grigoriou, and V. Eberhardt (2013), "Better World Books: Social Entrepreneurship and the Triple Bottom Line," case study, in Rothaermel, F. T., *Strategic Management* (Burr Ridge, IL: McGraw-Hill).

15. Burgelman, R. A., and A. S. Grove (1996), "Strategic dissonance," *California Management Review* 38: 8–28; and Grove, A. S. (1996), *Only the Paranoid Survive: How to Exploit the Crisis Points that Challenge Every Company* (New York: Currency Doubleday).

16. Dixit, A., and B. Nalebuff (1991), *Thinking Strategically: The Competitive Edge in Business, Politics, and Everyday Life* (New York: Norton); and Brandenburger, A. M., and B. J. Nalebuff (1996), *Co-opetition* (New York: Currency Doubleday).

17. www.mckesson.com.

18. Ibid.

19. The original statement about Google's new approach to China is at http://googleblog.blogspot.com/2010/01/new-approach-to-china.html. Other sources: "Google threat jolts China web users," *The Wall Street Journal,* January 13, 2010; and "Flowers for a funeral," *The Economist,* January 14, 2010.

20. Google's values are at www.google.com/corporate/tenthings.html.

21. "China renews Google's license," *The Wall Street Journal,* July 11, 2010.

22. "How Baidu won China," *Bloomberg BusinessWeek,* November 11, 2010.

23. "Q&A on Madoff case," *The Wall Street Journal,* March 12, 2009.

24. "Watch out! If your mission statement is a joke, Enron may be the punchline," *Entrepreneur Magazine,* May 2002; and McLean, B., and P. Elkind (2003), *The Smartest Guys in the Room. The Amazing Rise and Scandalous Fall of Enron* (New York: Portfolio).

25. This discussion is based on: Mintzberg, H. (1993), *The Rise and Fall of Strategic Planning: Reconceiving Roles for Planning, Plans, and Planners* (New York: Simon & Schuster); and Mintzberg, H. (1994), "The fall and rise of strategic planning," *Harvard Business Review* (January–February): 107–114.

26. Payne, B. (1956), "Steps in long-range planning," *Harvard Business Review* (March–April): 97–106.

27. Grove, A. S. (1996), *Only the Paranoid Survive.*

28. As quoted in Rothaermel, F. T. (2008), "Competitive advantage in technology intensive industries," *Advances in the Study of Entrepreneurship, Innovation, and Economic Growth* 18: 203–226.

29. Personal communication with UPS strategy executives during onsite visit in corporate headquarters, June 17, 2009.

30. This Strategy Highlight is based on: deGeus, A. P. (1988), "Planning as learning," *Harvard Business Review* (March–April); Grant, R. M. (2003), "Strategic planning in a turbulent environment: Evidence from the oil majors," *Strategic Management Journal* 24: 491–517; Willmore, J. (2001), "Scenario planning: Creating strategy for uncertain times," *Information Outlook* (September); and "Shell dumps wind, solar, and hydro power in favour of biofuels," *The Guardian,* March 17, 2009.

31. "Managing in the fog," *The Economist,* February 26, 2009.

32. Duke, M. T. (CEO of Walmart) (2010), presentation at Georgia Institute of Technology, April 1; and Walmart–Corporate Fact Sheet (walmartstores.com).

33. Mintzberg, H. (1993), *The Rise and Fall of Strategic Planning;* and Mintzberg, H. (1994), "The fall and rise of strategic planning."

34. Inkpen, A., and N. Choudhury (1995), "The seeking of strategy where it is not: Toward a theory of strategy absence," *Strategic Management Journal* 16: 313–323.

35. www.nucor.com.

36. See discussion on Nucor in Chapter 11, "Organizational Design: Structure, Culture, and Control."

37. Mintzberg, H., and J. A. Waters (1985), "Of strategies, deliberate and emergent," *Strategic Management Journal* 6: 257–272.

38. Arthur, B. W. (1989), "Competing technologies, increasing returns, and lock-in by historical events," *Economic Journal* 99: 116–131; and Brown, S. L., and K. M. Eisenhardt (1998), *Competing on the Edge. Strategy as Structured Chaos* (Boston, MA: Harvard Business School Press).

39. Mayer, M. (2006), "Nine lessons learned about creativity at Google," presentation at Stanford Technology Ventures Program, May 17.

40. John Rice (GE Vice Chairman, President & CEO, GE Technology Infrastructure) (2009), presentation at Georgia Institute of Technology, May 11.

41. Mintzberg, H., and A. McHugh (1985), "Strategy formation in an adhocracy," *Administrative Science Quarterly* 30: 160–197.

42. Ibid.; and Hill, C. W. L., and F. T. Rothaermel (2003), "The performance of incumbent firms in the face of radical technological innovation," *Academy of Management Review* 28: 257–274.

43. Based on Howard Behar (retired President, Starbucks North America and Starbucks International) (2009), Impact Speaker Series Presentation, College of Management, Georgia Institute of Technology, October 14. See also Behar, H. (2007), *It's Not About the Coffee: Leadership Principles from a Life at Starbucks* (New York: Portfolio).

44. "U.S. taxpayers risk $9.7 trillion on bailout programs," *Bloomberg News,* February 9, 2009.

45. "The book of Jobs," *The Economist,* January 28, 2010.

46. This example is based on Robinson, A. G., and S. Stern (1997), *Corporate Creativity: How Innovation and Improvement Actually Happen* (San Francisco, CA: Berret-Koehler Publishers).

47. Bower, J. L. (1970), *Managing the Resource Allocation Process* (Boston, MA: Harvard Business School Press); Bower, J. L., and C. G. Gilbert (2005), *From Resource Allocation to Strategy* (Oxford, UK: Oxford University Press); Burgelman, R. A. (1983), "A model of the interaction of strategic behavior, corporate context, and the concept of strategy," *Academy of Management Review* 8: 61–71; and Burgelman, R. A. (1983), "A process model of internal corporate venturing in a major diversified firm," *Administrative Science Quarterly* 28: 223–244.

48. Bower, J. L., and C. G. Gilbert (2005), *From Resource Allocation to Strategy.*

49. Burgelman, R. A. (1994), "Fading memories: A process theory of strategic business exit in dynamic environments," *Administrative Science Quarterly,* 39: 24–56.

50. Burgelman, R. A., and A. S. Grove (1996), "Strategic dissonance," *California Management Review* 38: 8–28.

51. Grant, R. M. (2003), "Strategic planning in a turbulent environment: Evidence from the oil majors," *Strategic Management Journal* 24: 491–517; Brown, S. L., and K. M. Eisenhardt (1997), "The art of continuous change: Linking complexity theory and time-based evolution in relentlessly shifting organizations," *Administrative Science Quarterly* 42: 1–34; Farjourn, M. (2002), "Towards an organic perspective on strategy," *Strategic Management Journal* 23: 561–594; Mahoney, J. (2005), *Economic Foundation of Strategy* (Thousand Oaks, CA: Sage); and Burgelman, R. A., and A. S. Grove (2007), "Let chaos reign, then rein in chaos – repeatedly: Managing strategic dynamics for corporate longevity," *Strategic Management Journal* 28: 965–979.

52. Dixit, A. K. S., and R. Pindyck (1994), *Investment Under Uncertainty* (Princeton, NJ: Princeton University Press); Amram, M., and N. Kulatilaka (1998), *Real Options: Managing Strategic Investment in an Uncertain World* (Boston, MA: Harvard Business School Press); McGrath, R. G., and I. C. MacMillan (2000), "Assessing technology projects using real options reasoning," *Research Technology Management* 43: 35–49; Hill, C. W. L., and F. T. Rothaermel (2003), "The performance of incumbent firms in the face of radical technological innovation"; and Adner, R., and D. A. Levinthal (2004), "What is not a real option: Considering boundaries for the application of real options to business strategy," *Academy of Management Review* 29: 74–85.

53. "Microsoft bid to beat Google builds on a history of misses," *The Wall Street Journal,* January 16, 2009.

54. "What They're Doing After Harvard," *The Wall Street Journal,* July 10, 2010.

55. Xu, Z., J. Hannaway, and C. Taylor (2008), "Making a difference? The effect of Teach For America on student performance in high school."

56. "Teaching as leadership: The highly effective teachers' guide to closing the achievement gap," Jossey-Bass, February 3, 2010.

57. "2006 NASA Strategic Plan," NASA (www.nasa.gov).

58. Hamel, G. (2007), *The Future of Management* (Boston, MA: Harvard Business School Publishing).

59. This *my*Strategy vignette is based on Stern, S. (2004), "Do scientists pay to be scientists?" *Management Science* 50(6): 835–853; and Esty, D. C., and A. S. Winston (2009), *Green to Gold: How Smart Companies Use Environmental Strategy to Innovate, Create Value, and Build Competitive Advantage,* revised and updated (Hoboken, NJ: John Wiley).

CHAPTER 3

External Analysis: Industry Structure, Competitive Forces, and Strategic Groups

LEARNING OBJECTIVES

After studying this chapter, you should be able to:

LO 3-1   Apply the PESTEL model to organize and assess the impact of external forces on the firm.

LO 3-2   Apply the structure-conduct-performance (SCP) model to explain the effect of industry structure on firm profitability.

LO 3-3   Apply the five forces model to understand the profit potential of the firm's industry.

LO 3-4   Describe the strategic role of complements in creating positive-sum co-opetition.

LO 3-5   Understand the role of industry dynamics and industry convergence in shaping the firm's external environment.

LO 3-6   Apply the strategic group model to reveal performance differences between clusters of firms in the same industry.

Build Your Dreams (BYD) to Sidestep Entry Barriers

THE BIG THREE—GM, Ford, and Chrysler—dominated the U.S. car market throughout most of the 20th century. As the competition in the industry became increasingly global, foreign car makers entered the U.S. market mainly by importing vehicles from overseas plants. Among the first were German carmakers Volkswagen, Daimler, and BMW as well as Japanese carmakers Honda, Toyota, and Nissan. The foreign entrants intensified competition, threatened the market share of the Big Three, and led to political pressure to impose import restrictions in the 1980s. The new players responded by building U.S. plants in order to avoid import restrictions. More recently, Korean car makers Hyundai and Kia have begun making and selling cars in the United States.

Although globalization and deregulation paved the way for significant new entry into the U.S. auto market, the worldwide car manufacturing industry has been exposed to few new entrants. In fact, no new major car manufacturers have emerged in the last couple of decades in part because automobiles powered by internal combustion engines are made out of thousands of precisely engineered parts; few industrial products, excluding commercial airplanes, are as complex as cars. Car manufacturers also require large-scale production in order to be cost-competitive. These facts create seemingly insurmountable barriers to entry into car manufacturing.

Thus, it would seem that an unknown startup from an emerging economy, attempting to enter the car industry during the deepest economic recession since the Great Depression, would surely be a fool's errand.

Yet Wang Chuanfu, founder and chairman of the Chinese technology startup Build Your Dreams (BYD) begs to differ. His strategy is to use new technology to sidestep entry barriers. BYD began its life as a battery company in 1995 and is now leveraging this expertise into electric vehicles. Unlike complex gasoline engines, electric cars are powered by simple motors and gearboxes that have very few parts. Electric vehicles are therefore much cheaper and more straightforward to build. BYD's claim to fame is a lithium ferrous phosphate battery on which cars can run 250 miles on a single three-hour charge. Already one of the fastest growing independent automakers, BYD is selling plug-in hybrids and all-electric vehicles in China, Africa, the Middle East, and South America. It plans to sell cars in the U.S. and other Western countries in the near future.

Legendary investor Warren Buffett found BYD interesting enough to put in some $230 million for a 10 percent equity stake. Consumers may flock to BYD cars as well. Not only are they "green" cars, but their sticker price is anticipated to be about half that of the Chevy Volt (whose starting price is $40,000). Other companies entering the car industry by leveraging new battery technology include Tesla Motors and Fisker Automotive, both in California, as well as Think Global in Norway and Lightning Car in the United Kingdom. Sparks are sure to fly as the car industry becomes more competitive in the 21st century.[1]

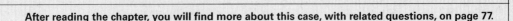

After reading the chapter, you will find more about this case, with related questions, on page 77.

▲ **THE BYD STORY** illustrates that the structure of an industry has a direct bearing on a firm's performance. Industry structure captures important economic characteristics such as the number and size of competitors, whether the offering is an undifferentiated commodity like steel or a highly differentiated service like management consulting, and the height of entry and exit barriers. Having been protected by high entry barriers for a long time, GM, for example, once held more than a 50 percent U.S. market share; it was highly profitable for many decades, until about 1980. Ford and Chrysler also did well during this period.

The BYD ChapterCase also illustrates that competitive forces in an industry have an impact on firm performance. Globalization led to extensive entry by foreign car manufacturers, increasing the number of competitors in the U.S. auto industry, and with it, competitive rivalry. The Japanese automakers, for example, were successful in the U.S. market because their cars were generally of better quality, their production systems were more efficient, and they were more responsive to changes in customer preferences. Today, advances in battery technology allow startups like BYD to enter the electric car segment (or strategic group), thereby circumventing high entry barriers into the broad automotive market. With more firms vying for a smaller pie in the U.S. auto market, competitive intensity is sure to increase.

In this chapter, we turn our attention to what is considered the firm's *external environment:* the industry in which the firm operates and the competitive forces that surround the firm from the outside.

THE PESTEL FRAMEWORK

>> LO 3-1
Apply the PESTEL
model to organize and
assess the impact of
external forces on the
firm.

We now take a first look at the firm's external environment. Understanding the forces in the external environment allows managers to mitigate threats and leverage opportunities.

As Exhibit 3.1 shows, a firm is embedded in different layers in its environment. The firm falls into a *strategic group,* the set of companies that pursue a similar strategy within a specific industry. The strategic group, in essence, consists of the firm's closest competitors. Just outside the strategic group is the industry in which the company operates. Industries differ along important structural dimensions such as the number and size of competitors in an industry and the type of products or services offered. Industries, in turn, are embedded in the larger macro environment, in which a wide variety of forces exert their influence

EXHIBIT 3.1

The Firm Embedded in Its External Environment: Global World, PESTEL Forces, Industry, and Strategic Group

on industries, strategic groups, and firms. Depending on the firm's strategy, these forces can affect its performance in a positive or negative fashion. We now turn to studying each of these environmental layers in detail, moving from a firm's general environment to its task environment. That is, we will work from the outer to the inner ring in Exhibit 3.1.

For purposes of discussion, we can group the forces at the most macro level into six segments—*political, economic, sociocultural, technological, ecological,* and *legal,* which form the acronym PESTEL. Although many of the PESTEL factors are interdependent, the PESTEL model provides a relatively straightforward way to categorize and analyze the important external forces that might impinge upon a firm. As markets have opened up and international trade has increased exponentially in recent decades, the PESTEL forces have become more global. These forces are embedded in the global environment and can create both opportunities and threats, so it pays to monitor them closely.

Political Factors

The political environment describes the processes and actions of government bodies that can influence the decisions and behavior of firms.[2] Governments, for example, can affect firm performance by exerting political pressure on companies, as described in Strategy Highlight 3.1.

Economic Factors

The economic factors in the external environment are largely macroeconomic, affecting economy-wide phenomena. Managers need to consider how the following five macroeconomic factors can affect firm strategy:

- Growth rates
- Interest rates
- Levels of employment
- Price stability (inflation and deflation)
- Currency exchange rates.

GROWTH RATES. The overall economic *growth rate* is a measure of the change in the amount of goods and services produced by a nation's economy. It indicates what stage of the business cycle the economy is in—that is, whether business activity is expanding (boom) or contracting (recession). In periods of economic expansion, consumer and business demand are rising, and competition among firms frequently decreases. Basically, the rising tide of economic growth "lifts all boats." During these economic boom cycles, businesses expand operations to satisfy demand and are more likely to be profitable.

STRATEGY HIGHLIGHT 3.1

UBS Relents to Pressure by U.S. Government

UBS, a venerable Swiss banking institution with global business activities, experienced the significant implications that political factors can have on the bottom line. The U.S. government alleged that by advertising its "tax savings" advantages to U.S. clients, UBS aided wealthy Americans in siphoning off billions of dollars to a safe haven that the IRS cannot touch. The government requested from UBS the names of 52,000 U.S. citizens who it suspected were tax evaders.

Initially, UBS declined to release names, citing Swiss banking laws and regulations that guarantee privacy of customers. However, UBS was in a lose–lose situation: If it resisted the IRS, it risked losing its U.S. banking license. If it disclosed names of its customers, it would break the traditional Swiss banking secrecy and potentially violate Swiss law, which makes it a felony to improperly disclose client information. In 2009, after multiple rounds of intense negotiations, UBS finally relented to significant pressure by the U.S. government and released the names of 4,450 U.S. citizens who are suspected to have evaded taxes.

This incident marks a watershed for UBS and the entire Swiss banking system. Banking secrecy has formed the basis for a sustained competitive advantage in the financial industry for over 75 years. Estimates suggest that foreigners hold assets worth some $2 trillion in Switzerland, which could be withdrawn if banking secrecy is not guaranteed.[3]

PESTEL model
A framework that categorizes and analyzes an important set of external forces (political, economic, technological, ecological, and legal) that might impinge upon a firm. These forces are embedded in the global environment and can create both opportunities and threats for the firm.

Occasionally, boom periods can overheat and lead to speculative bubbles. Between 1995 and 2000, for example, the United States witnessed such a bubble, propelled by new companies seeking to capture business opportunities on the Internet. The market for dot-com companies was characterized by "irrational exuberance,"[4] with the NASDAQ stock index peaking at its all-time high of 5,132 points on March 10, 2000. Hundreds of dot-com businesses were founded during this time, but very few survived the burst of the bubble. Among the survivors are today's powerhouses of the Internet economy including Google, Amazon, and eBay.

In the early 2000s, the United States saw yet another bubble—this time in housing.[5] Easy credit, made possible by the availability of subprime mortgages and other financial innovations, fueled an unprecedented demand in housing. Real estate, rather than stocks, became the investment vehicle of choice for many Americans, in the common belief that house prices could only go up. The housing bubble burst in the fall of 2008. Many financial institutions had to write off billions of dollars in toxic or worthless mortgage assets. All of the large U.S. financial institutions, including Bank of America, Citigroup, Wells Fargo, and insurance giant AIG, ended up being bailed out by taxpayers. With the bursting of the housing bubble, the economic recession of 2008–2009 began, affecting in some way nearly all businesses in the United States and worldwide.

Periods of economic boom and bust are natural occurrences in free-market systems. Austrian economist Joseph Schumpeter argued that such uproar is the "music of capitalism"[6]—a healthy and normal thing to expect in free-market economies. Indeed, shrewd managers *initiate* strategic successes during periods of economic downturn. During a recessionary period in 2001, Apple boosted spending on research and development to design and develop the iPod. When the economy picked up again, Apple was ready to launch the iPod combined with iTunes services, a highly profitable strategic move.[7] More recently, Apple launched the iPad in early 2010, following the severe 2008–2009 recession.

INTEREST RATES. Another key macroeconomic variable for managers to track is *interest rates*—the amount that savers are paid for use of their money and the amount that borrowers pay for that use. The economic boom during the early years in the 21st century, for example, was fueled by cheap credit. Low interest rates have a direct bearing on consumer demand. When credit is cheap (because interest rates are low), consumers buy homes, automobiles, computers, and even vacations on credit. All this demand fuels economic growth. During periods of low interest rates, firms can easily borrow money to finance future growth. Borrowing at lower rates lowers their cost of capital, enhancing their competitiveness. These effects reverse, however, when interest rates are high. Consumer demand slows down; credit is harder to come by, and firms thus find it more difficult to borrow money to support operations and might defer expansions.

LEVELS OF EMPLOYMENT. The state of the economy directly affects the *level of employment.* In boom times, unemployment is low, and skilled human capital becomes a scarce and thus more expensive resource. In economic downturns, unemployment rises. As more people search for employment, skilled human capital is abundant and wages usually fall.

A period of high unemployment could be a good time for firms to expand or upgrade their human capital base. Although U.S. companies generally lay off people during recessions, some Japanese companies, such as Toyota, prefer to use the downturn to train their workers on the latest manufacturing techniques.[8] Clearly, this strategy is a short-term expense for Toyota, yet it positions the company well when the economy picks up again.

PRICE STABILITY. *Price stability*—the lack of change in price levels of goods and services—is rare. Therefore, companies will often have to deal with changing price levels. The price level is a direct function of the amount of money in any economy. When there is too much money in an economy, we tend to see rising prices—*inflation.* Indeed, a popular economic definition of inflation is "too much money chasing too few goods and services."[9] Inflation tends to go along with higher interest rates and lower economic growth.

Deflation describes a decrease in the overall price level. A sudden and pronounced drop in demand generally causes deflation, which in turn forces sellers to lower prices to motivate buyers. Because many people automatically think of lower prices from the buyer's point of view, a decreasing price level seems at first glance to be attractive. However, deflation is actually a serious threat to economic growth because it distorts expectations about the future.[10] For example, once price levels start falling, companies will not invest in new production capacity or innovation because they expect a further decline in prices. Deflation also cools demand: "Why should I purchase something today if it is likely to cost less tomorrow?" Both lower demand and lower investment in turn will deepen any recession. If an economic downturn is especially severe and prolonged, a recession may turn into a *depression.*

CURRENCY EXCHANGE RATES. The *currency exchange rate* determines how many dollars one must pay for a unit of foreign currency. It is a critical variable for any company that either buys or sells products and services across national borders. If the U.S. dollar is weak, for example, it takes more dollars to buy one euro. This in turn makes U.S. exports like Boeing aircraft or John Deere tractors cheaper in Europe. By the same token, European imports like BMW automobiles become more expensive for U.S. buyers. This process reverses when the dollar appreciates against the euro.

The important point here is that the currency exchange rate is partly a function of the interest rates in the United States versus the European Union, with higher interest rates leading to stronger currencies. The *balance of trade,* which is the difference between a nation's exports and imports, is an even more important factor in determining foreign exchange rates. For example, Americans consume a lot more Chinese goods than Chinese consume American products. This imbalance implies that the U.S. runs a huge balance of trade deficit with China, which in turn puts downward pressure on the U.S. dollar.

In summary, economic factors affecting business are ever-present and rarely static. Managers need to fully appreciate the power of these factors, in both domestic and global markets, in order to assess their effects on firm performance.

Sociocultural Factors

Sociocultural factors capture a society's cultures, norms, and values. Because sociocultural forces not only are constantly in flux but also differ across groups, managers need to closely monitor such trends and consider the implications for firm strategy. Changing sociocultural factors create opportunities as well as threats. In recent years, for example, a growing number of U.S. consumers have become more health-conscious about what they eat. This trend led to a boom for the sandwich store Subway and the organic grocery store Whole Foods. At the same time, traditional fast-food companies like McDonald's and Burger King and grocery chains like Albertsons and Publix all had to scramble to provide healthier choices in their product offerings. Similarly, Coca-Cola was slow in spotting the trend toward noncarbonated and healthier drinks, like bottled water and natural juices. In contrast, long-time rival Pepsi seized upon this opportunity more quickly, capturing market share from Coca-Cola.[11]

Demographic trends are also important sociocultural forces. They capture characteristics in a population related to age, gender, family size, ethnicity, sexual orientation, religion, and socioeconomic class. Like other sociocultural factors, demographic trends present opportunities but can also pose threats. For example, as baby boomers begin to retire in larger numbers, business may see opportunities from an increased demand for health care and wellness services. To finance their retirement, however, baby boomers will begin to drain their retirement savings accounts, which may cause a decline in demand for investment services.

Technological Factors

Technological factors capture the application of knowledge to create new processes and products. Recent innovations in process technology include lean manufacturing, Six Sigma quality, and biotechnology. Recent product innovations are the electric vehicle and the iPad.

Technological progress is relentless and seems to be picking up speed over time.[12] Think about the Internet or advancements in biotechnology and nanotechnology. Shopping online has radically altered business and consumer behavior. U.S. online retail sales accounted for 6 percent of total retail sales or $140 billion in 2008, and are expected to reach 8 percent by 2013.[13] The largest U.S. online retailers (or *e-tailers*) are Amazon, Staples, Office Depot, Dell, and Hewlett-Packard (HP).[14] Leveraging the biotechnology revolution, newcomers like Genzyme or Biogen are now full-fledged pharmaceutical companies.[15] The revolution in nanotechnology is just beginning, but promises major upheaval in a vast array of industries ranging from tiny medical devices to new-age materials for earthquake-resistant buildings.[16]

Given the importance of a firm's innovation strategy to competitive advantage, we discuss the effect of technological factors in detail in Chapter 7.

Ecological Factors

Ecological factors concern broad environmental issues such as the natural environment, global warming and sustainable economic growth. Managers can no longer separate the natural and the business worlds; they are inextricably linked.[17] BP's infamous oil spill in the Gulf of Mexico following the explosion on the Deepwater Horizon drilling rig may cost the company an estimated $40 billion.[18] Moreover, the perceived failure of BP's CEO Tony Hayward to manage the crisis cost him the CEO position, and he was replaced by Bob Dudley. Ecological factors also highlight the importance of a triple-bottom-line approach to a sustainable competitive advantage as discussed in Chapter 5.

Legal Factors

The *legal environment* captures the official outcomes of the political processes as manifested in laws, mandates, regulations, and court decisions. These in turn can have a direct bearing on a firm's bottom line. In 2009, for example, U.S. chipmaker Intel was found not to comply with the antitrust regulations of the European Union, which levied a $1.45 billion fine against Intel for alleged abuse of monopoly power.[19] Intel holds some 80 percent market share in semiconductors worldwide.[20] Its primary rival, U.S. chipmaker AMD, alleged that Intel leveraged its position as the largest supplier in the market to provide deep discounts to large computer manufacturers, to keep them from using AMD chips. EU regulators concluded that Intel's actions harmed millions of consumers by keeping the price of computer chips above competitive levels.

Regulatory changes tend to affect entire industries. The California Air Resource Board (CARB) in 1990 passed a mandate for introducing zero-emissions cars, which stipulated that 10 percent of new vehicles sold by car makers must be zero-emissions by 2003.[21] This mandate not only accelerated research in alternative energy sources for cars, but also led to the development of the first fully electric production car, GM's EV1. GM launched the car in California and Arizona in 1996. Competitive models followed, with the Toyota RAV EV and the Honda EV. In this case, regulations in the legal environment fostered innovation in the automobile industry.

Companies are not only influenced by forces in their environment but can also influence the development of those forces. The California mandate on zero-emissions, for example, did not stand. Several stakeholders, including the car and oil companies, fought it through lawsuits and other actions. CARB ultimately relented to the pressure and abandoned its zero-emissions mandate. When the mandate was revoked, GM recalled and destroyed its EV1 electric vehicles and terminated its electric-vehicle program. This decision turned out to be a strategic error that would haunt GM a decade or so later. Although GM was the leader among car companies in electric vehicles in the mid-1990s, it did not have a competitive model to counter the Toyota Prius or the Honda Insight when their sales took off in the early 2000s. The Chevy Volt (a plug-in hybrid), GM's first major competition to the Prius and the Insight, was delayed by several years because GM had to start its electric-vehicle program basically from scratch. Not having an adequate product lineup during the early 2000s, GM's U.S. market share dropped below 20 percent in 2009 (from over 50 percent a few decades earlier), the year it filed for bankruptcy.

This example demonstrates that it may be possible to influence the development of forces but it may not be the best use of management time and resources. GM's strategic decision to fight the regulatory outcome rather than change the product lineup also ignored changing trends in the sociocultural environment (a growing number of customers wanted low-emission cars) and the importance of the ecological environment. This goes to show that strategic decisions have long-term consequences that are not easily reversible.

UNDERSTANDING DIFFERENCES IN INDUSTRY PERFORMANCE: THE STRUCTURE-CONDUCT-PERFORMANCE MODEL

From the external PESTEL forces, we move one step closer to the firm and come to the industry in which a firm functions. An industry makes up the supply side of the market, while customers make up the demand side. An industry, therefore, is a group of companies offering similar products or services. In the $300 billion management-consulting industry, each of the major competitors such as Accenture, Boston Consulting Group, and McKinsey offers similar consulting services.[22] Our purpose in looking at the firm's industry is to understand differences in industry performance.

The structure-conduct-performance (SCP) model is a theoretical framework, developed in industrial-organization economics, that explains differences in industry

>> **LO 3-2**
Apply the structure-conduct-performance (SCP) model to explain the effect of industry structure on firm profitability.

---

industry A group of companies offering similar products or services. It makes up the supply side of the market, while customers make up the demand side.

structure-conduct-performance (SCP) model A framework that explains differences in industry performance. It identifies four different industry types:

(1) perfect competition, (2) monopolistic competition, (3) oligopoly, and (4) monopoly. Fragmented industries tend be less profitable than consolidated ones.

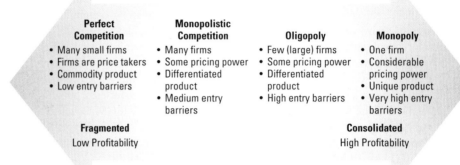

performance.[23] According to the SCP model, the underlying *industry structure* determines *firm conduct,* which concerns the firm's ability to differentiate its goods and services and thus to influence the price it can charge. Industry structure and firm conduct combine to determine firm performance.

Exhibit 3.2 shows different industry types along a continuum from fragmented to consolidated structures. At one extreme, *fragmented industry structures* consist of many small firms and tend to generate low profitability. At the other end of the continuum, *consolidated industry structures* are dominated by a few firms, or even just one firm, and tend to be highly profitable. The SCP model categorizes industry structure into four main industry types: (1) perfect competition, (2) monopolistic competition, (3) oligopoly, and (4) monopoly. Here, we discuss each of the four different industry types and describe the differences.

Perfect Competition

A *perfectly competitive* industry is characterized as fragmented and has many small firms, a commodity product, ease of entry, and little or no ability for each individual firm to raise its prices. The firms competing in this type of industry are approximately similar in size and resources. Consumers make purchasing decisions solely on price, because the commodity product offerings are more or less identical. The resulting performance of the industry shows low profitability. Under these conditions, firms in perfect competition have difficulty achieving even a temporary competitive advantage and can achieve only competitive parity. While perfect competition is a rare industry structure in its pure form, markets for commodities such as natural gas, copper, and iron tend to approach this structure.

Many Internet entrepreneurs learned the hard way that it is difficult to beat the forces of perfect competition. Fueled by eager venture capitalists, about 100 e-tailers such as *pets. com, petopia.com,* and *pet-store.com* had sprung up by 1999, at the height of the Internet bubble.[24] Cut-throat competition ensued, with online retailers selling products below cost. To make matters worse, at the same time category-killers like PetSmart and PetCo expanded rapidly, opening some 2,000 brick-and-mortar stores in the United States and Canada. As a consequence, most e-tailers of pet supplies went out of business. Applying the SCP model could have predicted that online pet supply stores are unlikely to be profitable: Many small firms offering a commodity product in an industry that is easy to enter would be unable to increase prices and generate profits. The ensuing price competition led to an industry shakeout, with online retailers exiting the industry and the large brick-and-mortar retailers still standing.

Monopolistic Competition

A *monopolistically competitive* industry is characterized by many firms, a differentiated product, some obstacles to entry, and the basis for raising prices for a relatively unique product while retaining customers. The key to understanding this industry structure is that the firms now offer products or services that have unique features.

The computer hardware industry is one example. Many firms compete in this industry, and even the largest firms like Apple, Dell, or HP have less than 20 percent market share. Moreover, while products of one competitor tend to be similar to products of a rival, they are not identical. As a consequence, managers selling a product with unique features tend to have some ability to raise prices. When a firm is able to differentiate its product or service offerings, it carves out a niche in the market in which it has some degree of monopoly power over pricing, thus the name "monopolistic competition." Firms frequently communicate the degree of product differentiation through advertising.

Although undifferentiated agricultural products are commodities leading to a perfect competitive market structure, some farmers have noted the demographic trend toward organic food and recognized the opportunity to respond by differentiating their products. The demand for organic milk far outstrips supply, and allows dairy companies to command a 50–100 percent price premium over non-organic milk. The dairy producers now enjoy some pricing power as a result of their differentiated, rather than commodity, product.

Oligopoly

The term *oligopoly* comes from the Greeks and means "few sellers." An *oligopolistic* industry is becoming more consolidated with few (large) firms, differentiated products, high barriers to entry, and some degree of pricing power. The degree of pricing power depends, just as in monopolistic competition, on the degree of product differentiation.

One of the key features of an oligopoly is that the competing firms are *interdependent.* With only a few competitors, the actions of one competitor influence the behavior of the other competitors. Each competitor in an oligopoly, therefore, must consider the strategic actions of the other competitors. This type of industry structure is often analyzed using *game theory,* which attempts to predict strategic behaviors by assuming that the moves and reactions of competitors can be anticipated.[25] Due to their strategic interdependence, companies in oligopolies have an incentive to coordinate their strategic actions to maximize their joint performance. Although explicit coordination such as price fixing is illegal in the United States, tacit coordination such as "an unspoken understanding" is not.

The express-delivery industry is an example of an oligopoly. The main competitors in this space are FedEx and UPS. Any strategic decision made by FedEx (e.g., to expand delivery services to ground delivery of larger-size packages) directly affects UPS; likewise, any decision made by UPS (e.g., to guarantee next-day delivery before 8:00 a.m.) directly affects FedEx. Other examples of oligopolies include the soft drink industry (Coca-Cola vs. Pepsi), airframe manufacturing business (Boeing vs. Airbus), home-improvement retailing (The Home Depot vs. Lowe's), toys and games (Hasbro vs. Mattel), and detergents (P&G vs. Unilever).

Companies in an oligopoly tend to have some pricing power if they are able to differentiate their product or service offerings from those of competitors. *Non-price competition* is the preferred mode of competition. What does that mean? It means competing by offering unique product features or services rather than competing on price. When one firm in an oligopoly cuts prices to gain market share from its competitor, the competitor typically will respond in kind and also cut prices. This process initiates a price war, which can be especially detrimental to firm performance if the products are close rivals.

In the early years of the soft drink industry, for example, whenever Pepsi was lowering prices, Coca-Cola followed suit. These actions resulted only in reduced profitability for both competitors. In recent decades, the managers of Coca-Cola and Pepsi have repeatedly demonstrated that they learned this lesson. They shifted the basis of competition from price cutting to new-product introductions, product innovation, and lifestyle advertising. Any price adjustments are short-term promotions. By leveraging innovation and advertising, managers from Coca-Cola and Pepsi have moved to non-price competition, which in turn allows them to charge higher prices and to improve industry and company profitability.[26]

Monopoly

An industry is a *monopoly* when there is only one (large) firm supplying the market. "Mono" means *one,* and thus a monopolist is the only seller in a market. The firm may offer a unique product, and the challenges to moving into the industry tend to be high. The monopolist has considerable pricing power. As a consequence, firm (and thus industry) profitability tends to be high.

In some instances, the government will grant one firm the right to be the sole supplier of a product or service. This is often done to incentivize a company to engage in a venture that would not be profitable if there was more than one supplier. For example, public utilities incur huge fixed costs to build plants and to supply a certain geographic area. Public utilities supplying water, gas, and electricity to businesses and homes are frequently monopolists. Georgia Power is the only supplier of electricity for over 2 million customers in the Southeastern United States. Philadelphia Gas Works is the only supplier of natural gas in the city of Philadelphia, PA, serving some 500,000 customers. These are so-called *natural monopolies,* for which the governments involved believe the product or service would not be supplied by the market if there were not a monopoly. In the past few decades, however, more and more of these natural monopolies have been deregulated in the United States, including airlines, telecommunications, railroads, trucking, and ocean transportation. This deregulation allowed competition to emerge, which theoretically should lead to lower prices, better service, and more innovation.

While natural monopolies appear to be disappearing from the competitive landscape, so-called *near monopolies* are of much greater interest to strategists. These are firms that have accrued significant market power. In the process, they are changing the industry structure in their favor, generally from monopolistic competition or oligopolies to near monopolies. These near monopolies are firms that have accomplished product differentiation to such a degree that they are in a class by themselves, just like a monopolist. As highlighted in the legal ruling discussed earlier, the European Union views Intel, with its 80 percent market share in semiconductors, as a near monopoly. This is an enviable position in terms of the ability to extract profits, although a monopoly position may attract the anti-trust regulators and lead to legal repercussions.

COMPETITIVE FORCES AND FIRM STRATEGY: THE FIVE FORCES MODEL

>> LO 3-3
Apply the five forces model to understand the profit potential of the firm's industry.

Building on the SCP model, Michael Porter developed the highly influential five forces model.[27] As Exhibit 3.3 shows, Porter's model identifies five key competitive forces that managers need to consider when analyzing the industry environment and formulating strategy:

1. Threat of entry
2. Power of suppliers
3. Power of buyers
4. Threat of substitutes
5. Rivalry among existing competitors

Porter's model aims to enable managers not only to understand their industry environment but also to shape their firm's strategy. As a rule of thumb, the stronger the five forces, the lower the industry's profit potential—making the industry less attractive to competitors. The reverse also is true: The weaker the five forces, the greater the industry's profit potential—making the industry more attractive. The model's perspective is that of the manager of an existing (incumbent) firm competing for advantage in an established industry. Managers need to position their company in an industry in a way that relaxes the constraints of strong forces and leverages weak forces. We next discuss each of the five competitive forces in detail, and will take up the topic of competitive positioning in Chapter 6 when studying business-level strategy.

EXHIBIT 3.3

Porter's Five Forces Model

Source: Michael E. Porter, "The five competitive forces that shape strategy," *Harvard Business Review,* January 2008.

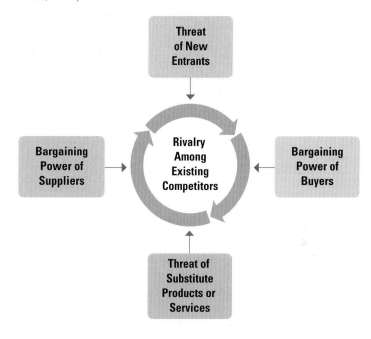

Threat of Entry

Entry barriers are obstacles that determine how easily a firm can enter an industry. High entry barriers can correspond to high industry profitability, assuming there is no excess capacity in the industry. Take the example of BYD in the ChapterCase. Entry barriers into the broad automobile industry seem almost insurmountable because of the engineering competence needed for manufacturing gasoline-powered engines and the need for large-scale production. Many industry analysts argue that to be viable, a car company must be able to produce and sell some 5 million cars per year.[28] This fact explains in part why Chrysler, selling less than 2 million vehicles per year, was bought out in part by Fiat, an Italian carmaker, itself a small company selling an estimated 2.5 million vehicles per year.

Given the industry structure in the automobile business and the economic downturn of 2008–2009, entering the auto manufacturing industry right now doesn't seem advisable. Yet BYD is joining the fray. How can it sidestep such insurmountable entry barriers? The answer: Technology is leveling the playing field. Mr. Wang, founder and chairman of BYD, explains his strategic intent: "It's almost hopeless for a latecomer like us to compete with GM and other established automakers with a century of experience in gasoline engines. With electric vehicles, we're all at the same starting line."[29] Actually, BYD may even have a head start because of its deep experience in batteries, selling them to technology giants like Motorola, Nokia, and Samsung. This example shows how managers can use technological innovation to avoid entry barriers into the broad industry and build a position in a smaller strategic group.

This shift in the external environment, in turn, has significant competitive implications for the existing firms in the automobile industry. Having new firms such as BYD and Tesla

five forces model
A framework proposed by Michael Porter that identifies five forces that determine the profit potential of an industry and shape a firm's competitive strategy.

entry barriers
Obstacles that determine how easily a firm can enter an industry. Entry barriers are often one of the most significant predictors of industry profitability.

Motors enter the industry leads to higher competitive intensity. Incumbent firms such as GM and Nissan are responding to the new entrants by introducing innovations of their own such as the Chevy Volt and the Nissan Leaf. Consumers are likely to benefit from an increase in competitive intensity if more innovative and efficient products are introduced with lower prices. Only time will tell if the new entrants will mature to be full-fledged industrial enterprises and become strong enough to push some incumbents out of the industry.

The height of entry barriers is also relevant to *potential competitors*—those that are not yet competing in the industry but have the capability to do so if they choose. The likelihood of entry is determined by the level of capital investment required to enter the industry and the expected return on investment. For example, in the Southeastern United States, TV cable company Comcast has entered the business for residential and commercial telephone services and Internet connectivity (as an ISP, Internet service provider), thus emerging as a direct competitor for AT&T and Bell South, who merged. The new AT&T responded to Comcast's threat by introducing U-verse, a product combining high-speed Internet access with cable TV and telephone service, all provided over its super-fast fiber-optic network. In turn, Comcast acquired a majority stake in NBC Universal, combining delivery and content.[30]

The Power of Suppliers

The bargaining power of suppliers captures pressures that industry suppliers can exert on an industry's, and therefore a company's, profitability. Inputs into the production process include raw materials and components, labor (may be individuals or labor unions, when the industry faces collective bargaining), and services. Powerful suppliers can raise the cost of production by demanding higher prices or delivering lower-quality products. As an example, the United Autoworkers (UAW) union is a powerful stakeholder that extracts significant profits from competitors in the auto industry like GM, Ford, and Chrysler by successfully demanding restrictive work rules and generous health care and retiree benefits. As an indication of UAW power, it owned the majority of Chrysler and almost one half of GM following their bankruptcy reorganizations.[31]

Suppliers are powerful relative to the firms in the industry if there are only few substitutes available for the products and services supplied. For example, crude oil is still a critical input in many industries, and oil suppliers are fairly powerful in raising prices and squeezing industry profitability where products and services rely heavily on oil inputs such as fertilizers or plastics. Suppliers are also in a more powerful position when the extent of competition among suppliers is low, which often goes along with a small number of large suppliers. Supplier power is further enhanced when the supplied product is unique and differentiated or when the companies in the industry face significant switching costs. Supplier power is also strengthened when suppliers provide a credible threat of *forwardly integrating* into the industry (i.e., moving into their buyers' market), or when the companies in the industry buy only small quantities from the suppliers.

Power of Buyers

The bargaining power of buyers concerns the pressure buyers can put on the margins of producers in the industry, by demanding a lower price or higher product quality. When buyers successfully obtain price discounts, it reduces a firm's top line (revenue). When buyers demand higher quality and more service, it generally raises production costs. Strong buyers can therefore reduce industry profitability and with it, a firm's profitability.

The buyers of an industry's product or service may be individual consumers—like you or me when we decide which provider we want to use for our wireless devices. In many areas, you can choose between several providers—AT&T, Sprint, or Verizon. Although we might be able to play different providers against one another when carefully comparing their individual service plans, as individual consumers we generally do not have significant buyer power. On the other hand, large institutions like businesses or universities have significant buyer power when deciding which provider to use for their wireless services, because they are able to sign up or move several thousand employees at once.

Buyers have strong bargaining power when they purchase in large quantities and control many access points to the final customer. Walmart, for example, can exert tremendous pressure on its suppliers to lower prices and to increase quality—or it will choose to not place the suppliers' products on its shelves. Walmart's buyer power is so strong that many suppliers co-locate offices directly next to Walmart's headquarters in Bentonville, Arkansas; such proximity enables Walmart's managers to test the supplier's latest products and negotiate prices.

Buyer power also increases when the buyer's switching costs are low. Having multiple suppliers of a product category located close to its headquarters helps Walmart demand further price cuts and quality improvements. Walmart can easily switch from one supplier to the next. This threat is even more pronounced if the products sold to buyers are non-differentiated commodities in the perception of the end consumer; for example, Walmart can easily switch from one producer of plastic containers (e.g., Rubbermaid) to another (e.g., Sterlite) by offering more shelf space to the producer that offers the greatest price cut or quality improvement.

Buyers also tend to be quite powerful when they are the only customer buying a certain product. Many modern defense technologies rely on the latest innovations, but frequently these products are bought by only one buyer, the U.S. Department of Defense (DoD).[32] Being the sole buyer implies that the DoD has considerable bargaining power to demand lower prices and higher quality. In many cases, however, this is balanced by the fact that there is only one supplier, like Lockheed Martin, of a type of specialized military equipment.

Buyers are also powerful when they can credibly threaten backward integration. *Backward integration* occurs when a buyer moves upstream in the industry value chain, into the seller's business. This situation is commonly observed in the auto-component supply industry, in which car manufacturers like GM, Ford, or BMW have the capability to backward-integrate in order to produce their components in-house if their demands for lower prices and higher product quality are not met by their suppliers.

In sum, powerful buyers have the ability to extract a significant amount of the value created in the industry, leaving little or nothing for producers.

Threat of Substitutes

The threat of substitutes is the idea that products or services available from *outside the given industry* will come close to meeting the needs of current customers. The existence of substitutes that have attractive price and performance characteristics results in low switching costs, increasing the strength of this threat. For example, if the price of coffee increased significantly, customers might switch to tea or other caffeinated beverages to meet their needs.[33] Other examples of substitutes are: video conferencing vs. business travel; e-mail vs. express mail; plastic vs. aluminum containers; gasoline vs. biofuel; and landline telephone services vs. Voice over Internet Protocol (VoIP, offered by Skype or Vonage).

Rivalry among Existing Competitors

Rivalry among existing competitors describes the intensity with which companies in an industry jockey for market share and profitability. It can range from genteel to cut-throat. As shown in Exhibit 3.3, the forces discussed earlier—threat of entry, power of buyers and suppliers, and the threat of substitutes—all put pressure on the rivalry among existing competitors. The stronger the forces, the stronger the expected competitive intensity, which in turn limits the industry's profit potential. When intense rivalry among existing competitors brings about price discounting, industry profitability clearly tends to erode. When non-price competition such as pressure to innovate, increased advertising, and improved service is the primary basis of competition, costs will increase, which may have some impact on industry profitability. However, when these moves create products that respond closely to customer needs and willingness to pay, then average industry profitability tends to increase because producers are able to raise prices and thus increase revenues.

The rivalry among existing competitors is also a function of industry's exit barriers, the obstacles that determine how easily a firm can leave an industry. An industry with low exit barriers is more attractive, because underperforming firms can exit more easily, reducing the competitive pressure on the existing firms as excess capacity is removed.

Exit barriers are comprised of both economic and social factors. They include costs that must be paid regardless of whether the company is operating in the industry or not (fixed costs). A company exiting an industry may still have contractual obligations to suppliers, such as an obligation to the suppliers of labor that could include health care and retirement benefits as well as severance pay. GM's health care and retirement costs are contractual obligations that would accrue regardless of whether GM produces and sells any vehicles. Some of these costs were restructured during GM's time in Chapter 11 bankruptcy (which allows companies to continue to operate while providing temporary relief from its creditors). Although GM's healthcare cost per vehicle sold remains above that of its foreign competitors, it is now reduced to about $330 per vehicle instead of $1,500 pre-bankruptcy.[34]

Social factors include things like emotional attachments to certain geographic locations. In Michigan, entire communities depend on GM, Ford, and Chrysler. If any of those carmakers were to exit the industry, communities would suffer. During the 1980s and 1990s, massive layoffs at GM factories devastated the economy of Flint, Michigan. Many more communities were affected during GM's 2009 bankruptcy, which resulted in the closing of more than a dozen manufacturing plants and thousands of dealerships.[35] Other social and economic factors include ripple effects through the supply chain. When one major player in an industry shuts down, its suppliers are affected adversely, potentially leading to further layoffs.

When managers understand the strength or weakness of the five forces that affect the competition in an industry, they are better able to position the company in a way that protects it from the strong forces and exploits the weak forces. The goal is of course to improve the firm's ability to achieve a competitive advantage. To summarize our discussion of the five forces, Exhibit 3.4 provides you with a checklist that you can apply to any industry when assessing the underlying five competitive forces. The key take-away from the five forces model is that *the stronger (weaker) the forces, the lower (greater) the industry's ability to earn above-average profits, and correspondingly, the lower (greater) the firm's ability to gain and sustain a competitive advantage.* The airline and soft drink industries provide illustrative examples.[36]

exit barriers Obstacles that determine how easily a firm can leave an industry.

GAINING & SUSTAINING COMPETITIVE ADVANTAGE

Five Forces in Airlines vs. Soft Drinks

Let's put the five forces model under the magnifying glass, to critically evaluate what it can tell us about how companies gain and sustain competitive advantage. To do so, we will contrast two industries—airlines and soft drinks.[37]

Airlines have been one of the least profitable industries for decades, with an average return on invested capital (ROIC) of 5.9 percent between 1992 and 2006. Michael Porter

EXHIBIT 3.4

The Five Forces
Competitive Analysis
Checklist

THE THREAT OF ENTRY IS HIGH WHEN:

>> Customer switching costs are low.

>> Capital requirements are low.

>> Incumbents do not possess:

   ■ Proprietary technology

   ■ Established brand equity

>> New entrants expect that incumbents will not or cannot retaliate.

THE POWER OF SUPPLIERS IS HIGH WHEN:

>> Incumbent firms face significant switching costs when changing suppliers.

>> Suppliers offer products that are differentiated.

>> There are no readily available substitutes for the products or services that the suppliers offer.

>> Suppliers can credibly threaten to forward-integrate into the industry.

THE POWER OF BUYERS IS HIGH WHEN:

>> There are a few large buyers.

>> Each buyer purchases large quantities relative to the size of a single seller.

>> The industry's products are standardized or undifferentiated commodities.

>> Buyers face little or no switching costs.

>> Buyers can credibly threaten to backward-integrate into the industry.

THE THREAT OF SUBSTITUTES IS HIGH WHEN:

>> The substitute offers an attractive price–performance trade-off.

>> The buyer's cost of switching to the substitute is low.

THE RIVALRY AMONG EXISTING COMPETITORS IS HIGH WHEN:

>> There are many competitors in the industry.

>> The competitors are roughly of equal size.

>> Industry growth is slow, zero, or even negative.

>> Exit barriers are high.

>> Products and services are direct substitutes.

---

calls airlines a "zero star" industry, because each of the five forces is strong, leading to inferior industry performance. The nature of rivalry among airlines is incredibly intense, because the consumer views each airline's service to be undifferentiated and makes decisions mainly based on price. Thanks to Internet travel sites such as Orbitz and Travelocity, real-time price comparisons are effortless. Low switching costs and nearly perfect information combine to strengthen buyer power. Entry barriers are relatively low, resulting in a number of new airlines popping up. To enter the industry (in a small way, serving a few select cities), a prospective new entrant needs only a couple of airplanes (which can be rented), a few pilots and crew members, some routes connecting city pairs, and gate access in those cities. The supplier power is strong, with providers of aircraft engines such as GE, Rolls-Royce, or Pratt & Whitney, aircraft maintenance companies such as Goodrich, labor unions, and airports controlling gate access—all bargaining away the profitability of airlines. To make matters worse, substitutes are also readily available: If prices are seen as too high, customers can drive their cars or use the train or bus. As an example, the route between Atlanta and Orlando (roughly 400 miles) used to be one of the busiest and most profitable ones for Delta. Given the increasing security delays at airports, more and more people now prefer to drive. Taken together, the competitive forces are quite unfavorable for generating a profit potential in the airline industry: low entry barriers; high supplier power; high buyer power due to instant price information provided by websites, combined with low customer switching costs; and the availability of low-cost substitutes. This unfavorable environment leads to intense rivalry among existing firms and low industry profitability.

In contrast, soft drinks have been one of the most profitable industries for decades, with an average ROIC of 37.6 percent between 1992 and 2006. Michael Porter calls soft drinks a "five star" industry; by that, he means that each of the five forces is weak, leading to superior industry performance. The nature of competition between Pepsi and Coke is benign for the most part, focusing on non-price factors such as lifestyle advertising and product innovation rather than on price. The barriers to entry are high, because of the strong brand equity enjoyed by Coke and Pepsi, which has been built up over many decades. In addition, bottling is a capital-intensive activity. Consumers tend to be loyal to "their" cola, identifying themselves as Coke or Pepsi drinkers. The power of suppliers is quite limited: Arguably the most valuable input (e.g., Coke's secret formula) is provided by the soft drink companies, while the other inputs are commodities (e.g., water, aluminum cans, plastic bottles, and others). Likewise, the power of buyers is weak, because intermediate customers like bottling franchises and distributors are locked into long-term exclusive contracts with the soft drink companies, and the final end consumer market is extremely fragmented. Not even Walmart is able to force significant price discounts from Coca-Cola or Pepsi, focusing instead on offering its private-label cola Sam's Choice. Favorable competitive forces indicate a significant profit potential in the soft drink industry that the dominant players Coke and Pepsi are well positioned to capture.

Applying the five forces to the airline and soft drink industries shows the model's usefulness in evaluating the effects the industry environment can have on a firm's ability to gain and sustain competitive advantage.

ADDING A SIXTH FORCE: THE STRATEGIC ROLE OF COMPLEMENTS

>> LO 3-4
Describe the strategic role of complements in creating positive-sum co-opetition.

complement
A product, service, or competency that adds value to the original product offering when the two are used in tandem.

complementor
A company that provides a good or service that leads customers to value your firm's offering more when the two are combined.

As valuable as the five forces model is for explaining the profitability and attractiveness of industries, some have suggested extensions of it. Intel's former chairman and CEO, Andy Grove, as well as strategy scholars, suggested that the value of the Porter's five forces model could be further enhanced if one also considers the availability of complements.[38]

A complement is a product, service, or competency that adds value to the original product offering when the two are used in tandem.[39] Complements increase demand for the primary product, thereby enhancing the profit potential for the industry and the firm. A company is a complementor to your company if customers value your product or service offering more when they are able to combine it with the other company's product or service.[40]

Firms may choose to provide the complements themselves or work with another company to accomplish this. Several examples illustrate this point:

■ The French tire company Michelin and car manufacturers such as Ford and GM are complementors. Of course, people need tires for their cars, but more importantly, people who drive more need to replace their tires more often. Thus, Michelin has been publishing (since the early 1900s) the highly acclaimed Michelin guidebooks for travel and tourism, which encourage people to drive more and hopefully buy more Michelin tires.

- Claiming that Xerox office paper is specially designed to work best with its complex copying machines, and thus reducing downtime caused by jamming and other problems, Xerox is now one of the leading suppliers of office paper.

- Illegal music downloads created a powerful substitute for CD record sales, which plummeted with the availability of file-sharing software to facilitate illegal downloads. Seeing a strategic opportunity, Apple established the iTunes music store to complement its iPod music player. Apple makes money by selling the hardware (iPods), while providing the complement (iTune software) for free. That combination allows you to load your iPod with thousands of songs that can be selected from more than 14 million offered at the iTunes music store at a reasonable price (beginning at $0.69 each). Similarly, when Apple launched the iPad, it had already established relationships with several major publishing houses as complementors to fill its iBook online store with millions of e-books. Moreover, since the iPad runs on the same operating system as the iPhone, the over 400,000 apps for the iPhone are also available for the iPad through Apple's iTunes online store.

EXHIBIT 3.5

Determining Industry Attractiveness

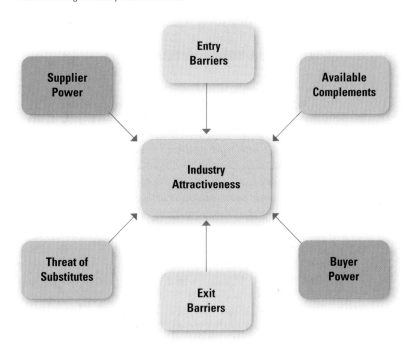

Industry attractiveness, in terms of profit potential, is therefore determined by *three distinct pairs of two forces* (as shown in Exhibit 3.5): (1) supplier and buyer power, (2) entry and exit barriers,[41] and (3) available complements and the threat of substitutes. A complete competitive analysis needs to consider not only Porter's five forces, but also the availability of complements. A successful manager, therefore, should search out complementors and encourage collaboration with them. Rather than seeing competition as a zero-sum game, those who prefer the five-forces-plus-complements model suggest that industry competition can be a positive-sum game. They use the term *co-opetition* to describe cooperative interactions among competitors, which results in success for each of the players—a larger pie for everyone involved.[42]

Strategy Highlight 3.2 (next page) shows how Microsoft—with Intel as complementor—was able to dominate the personal computer software industry for several decades.

CHANGES OVER TIME: INDUSTRY DYNAMICS

Although the five-forces-plus-complements model is useful in understanding an industry's profit potential, it provides only a point-in-time snapshot of a moving target. With it (and other static models), one cannot determine the speed of the change in an industry or the

>> **LO 3-5**
Understand the role of industry dynamics and industry convergence in shaping the firm's external environment.

Microsoft's Attractive OS Software Business: How Much Longer?

Microsoft dominates the industry for PC operating system (OS) software with a 90 percent market share. How can this be? Microsoft's strategy shaped the industry structure in its favor. Its installed base of Windows operating systems on existing computers and its long-term relationships with original equipment manufacturers (OEMs) like Dell and Lenovo create tremendous entry barriers for newcomers. The buyer power of OEMs in turn is low, given the fact that the successful combination of Microsoft's Windows and Intel's processors has produced the *Wintel standard* in the PC industry.

Perhaps most important, consumer switching costs are high. Once users have learned a specific software application program such as MS Word, they are much less likely to use a product from a different vendor. Supplier power is also low, because writing computer code has become a commodity. The threat of comparable substitutes that deliver similar or higher performance benefits, including compatibility among different software programs, is low.

Finally, Intel's semiconductor chips are the perfect complement to Microsoft's operating system. Every time Microsoft releases a new operating system, demand for Intel's latest processor goes up, because new operating systems require more computing power. Due to the complementary nature of their products, Microsoft's and Intel's alternating advances have created a *virtuous cycle*. The competitive forces of the PC operating system software industry and Microsoft's positioning in the industry combine to make the PC-OS software industry very attractive for Microsoft.

Yet, the Wintel standard is not without competition. Linux provides a free, open-source alternative. Red Hat, a software company, has created an $800 million business by distributing and servicing customized Linux versions for many major corporations. In addition, *cloud computing*—the move to distributed computing over the Internet—is also gaining momentum. All these forces threaten the dominance of the Wintel standard in certain segments of the industry and thus undermine the value of Microsoft's dominance in the PC-OS software industry.

rate of innovation. This drawback implies that managers need to repeat their analysis over time, to create a more accurate picture of their industry. It is therefore important that managers consider industry dynamics.

Different conditions prevail in different industries at different times, directly affecting the firms competing in these industries and their profitability. Exhibit 3.6 depicts industry performance as measured by average annual growth in profitability over the five-year time period between 2003 and 2008.[43] It is immediately apparent that industries differ widely in their average profitability. The average annual growth in profitability for metals such as aluminum and steel was almost 58 percent. How can this be? The 2003–2008 period was a boom period, characterized by high demand for metals in fast-growing economies such as China and India, to keep up with new construction and infrastructure projects. In second place were Internet service providers and online retailers with about 55 percent growth in average annual profitability. During this period, many people shifted purchases online, patronizing companies such as Amazon, eBay, and Zappos. On the other hand, the average growth in profitability of general merchandisers like Target, Sears, Macy's, and Kohl's was barely above 1 percent, coming in last.[44] As could be predicted by applying the SCP and five-forces-plus-complements models, significant differences exist in industry performance.

Industry structures, moreover, are not stable over time. Rather, they are dynamic. Since a consolidated industry tends to be more profitable than a fragmented one, firms have a tendency to change the industry structure in their favor, making it more consolidated through (horizontal) mergers and acquisitions. Having fewer competitors generally equates to higher industry profitability. Thus, industry incumbents have an incentive to reduce the number of competitors in the industry. For example, the U.S. banking industry has experienced major consolidation, and banking giants like Citigroup, Bank of America, and Wells Fargo have emerged. In a similar fashion, there used to be the Big Eight in the accounting and professional services industry, handling the audits of publicly traded and well-to-do private companies. Today, only the Big Four remain: PricewaterhouseCoopers, Deloitte, Ernst & Young, and KPMG.

Sometimes oligopolistic industry structures break up and become more fragmented. This generally happens when there are external shocks to an industry such as deregulation, new legislation, technological innovation, or globalization. The emergence of the Internet moved the stock brokerage business from an

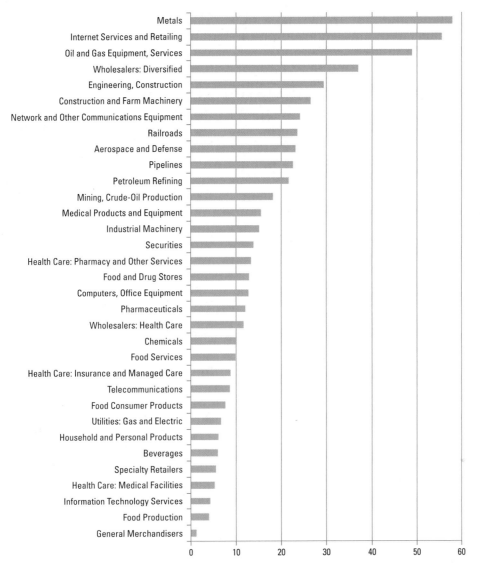

EXHIBIT 3.6

Average Annual
Growth in Industry
Profitability, 2003–2008

Source: Data from *Fortune,*
May 4, 2009.

oligopoly controlled by full-service firms like Merrill Lynch and Morgan Stanley to monopolistic competition with many generic online brokers such as Ameritrade, E*TRADE, and Scottrade that offer trades at low prices.

Another dynamic to be considered is industry convergence, a process whereby formerly unrelated industries begin to satisfy the same customer need. Industry convergence is often brought on by technological advances. For years, the many players in media industries have been converging due to technological progress in IT, telecommunications, and digital media. Media convergence unites computing, communications, and content, thereby causing significant upheaval across previously distinct industries. Content providers in industries such as newspapers, magazines, TV, movies, radio, and music are all scrambling to adapt. Many standalone print newspapers are closing up shop, while others try to figure out how to offer online news content for which consumers are willing to pay.[45] As a consequence of media convergence, annual online ad spending is predicted to reach $62 billion in 2011, overtaking print advertising ($60 billion) and closing in fast on TV advertising ($80 billion).[46] Internet companies such as Google, Yahoo, and Twitter are changing the

industry convergence A process whereby formerly unrelated industries begin to satisfy the same customer need.

industry structure by constantly morphing their capabilities and thus forcing old-line media companies like News Corp., Time Warner, and Disney to adapt. For example, Amazon's Kindle e-reader, Apple's iPad, or Sony's e-reader provide a new form of content delivery that has the potential to make print media obsolete.

EXPLAINING PERFORMANCE DIFFERENCES WITHIN THE SAME INDUSTRY: STRATEGIC GROUPS

>> **LO 3-6**
Apply the strategic group model to reveal performance differences between clusters of firms in the same industry

In further analyzing the firm's external environment, we now move to firms *within the same industry,* to explain performance differences. As noted early in the chapter, a firm occupies a place within a strategic group, a set of companies that pursue a similar strategy within a specific industry in their quest for competitive advantage (see Exhibit 3.1).[47] Strategic groups differ from one another along important dimensions such as expenditures on research and development, technology, product differentiation, product and service offerings, pricing, market segments, distribution channels, and customer service. Applying the idea of strategic groups to the automobile industry featured in ChapterCase 3, one could identify (1) an old-line internal-combustion engine strategic group such as GM, Ford, Chrysler, Toyota, and Honda, and (2) an electric-car strategic group composed of new entrants such as BYD and Tesla Motors. The distinction between the two groups would highlight the underlying technology and market segment.

To explain differences in firm performance within the same industry, scholars offer the strategic group model, which clusters different firms into groups based on a few key strategic dimensions.[48] They find that even within the same industry, the performance of firms differs depending on strategic group membership. For example, the two auto-industry strategic groups just mentioned have different performance results. Some strategic groups tend to be more profitable than others. This difference implies that firm performance is determined not only by the industry to which the firm belongs but also by its strategic group membership.

The distinct differences across strategic groups reflect the strategies that firms pursue. Firms in the same strategic group tend to follow a similar strategy, whereas firms in a different strategic group follow a different strategy. Companies in the same strategic group, therefore, are direct competitors. Thus, the rivalry among firms of the same strategic group is generally more intense than the rivalry between strategic groups: *intra-group rivalry exceeds inter-group rivalry.* The number of different business strategies pursued within an industry determines the number of strategic groups in that industry. In most industries, strategic groups can be identified along a fairly small number of dimensions. In many instances, two strategic groups are in an industry: one that pursues a low-cost strategy and a second that pursues a differentiation strategy. (We'll discuss each of these generic business strategies in detail in Chapter 6.)

strategic group The set of companies that pursue a similar strategy within a specific industry.

strategic group model A framework that explains firm differences in performance in the same industry by clustering different firms into groups based on a few key strategic dimensions.

Mapping Strategic Groups

To understand competitive behavior and performance within an industry, we can map the industry competitors into strategic groups. When mapping strategic groups, it is important to focus on several factors:

- Identify the most important strategic dimensions (such as expenditures on research and development, technology, product differentiation, product and service offerings, pricing, market segments, distribution channels, and customer service).

- Choose two key dimensions for the horizontal and vertical axes, which expose important differences among the competitors.

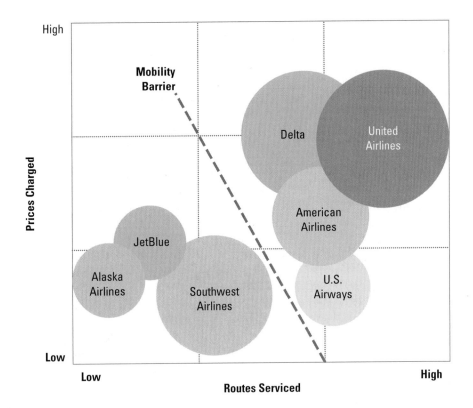

EXHIBIT 3.7

Strategic Groups and the Mobility Barrier in the U.S. Airline Industry

- The dimensions chosen for the axes should not be highly correlated.
- Position on the graph the firms in the strategic group, indicating each firm's market share by the size of the bubble by which it is represented.[49]

The U.S. airline industry provides an illustrative example. Exhibit 3.7 maps the companies active in the industry. The two strategic dimensions are the prices charged and the routes serviced. As a result of this mapping, two strategic groups are apparent: low-cost, point-to-point airlines versus differentiated airlines using a hub-and-spoke system (meaning the airline designates a geographic hub, upon which travelers between airports not connected by direct flights converge to change planes and continue to their final destination). The low-cost, point-to-point airlines are clustered in the lower-left corner; they include Alaska Airlines, JetBlue, and Southwest Airlines (SWA, which bought AirTran Airways in 2010). They cluster together on this plot because they tend to offer low ticket prices but generally service a smaller number of routes.

The differentiated airlines offering full service using a hub-and-spoke route system are the so-called legacy carriers, including American, Delta, United, and U.S. Airways. They tend to cluster in the upper-right corner: Their ticket prices tend to be somewhat higher, and they tend to offer many more routes than the point-to-point low-cost carriers, made possible by use of the hub-and-spoke system. This functional-level strategy allows the legacy airlines to offer many different destinations. For example, Delta's main hub is in Atlanta, GA.[50] If you were to fly from Seattle, Washington, to Miami, Florida, you would stop to change planes in Delta's Atlanta hub on your way.

The strategic-group mapping in Exhibit 3.7 allows some more insights:

- *The competitive rivalry is strongest between firms that are within the same strategic group.* The closer firms are on the strategic-group map, the more directly and intensely they are competing with one another. The mega-airlines Delta (merged with NWA in 2010) and United (merged with Continental, also in 2010) are competing head-to-head not only in the U.S. domestic market but also globally. We would expect strategists at United to monitor closely the actions of Delta, whose strategic decisions have the strongest impact on United's profitability (and vice versa). In contrast, U.S. Airways (which flies mainly on the East Coast, with some international routes) and Alaska Airlines (mainly West Coast and Alaska) are not direct competitors.

■ *Strategic groups are affected differently by the external environment.* During times of economic downturn, for example, the low-cost airlines tend to take market share away from the legacy carriers. Moreover, given their higher cost structure, the legacy carriers are often unable to be profitable during recessions (at least on domestic routes). This implies that external factors like recessions or high oil prices favor the companies in the low-cost strategic group.

■ *Strategic groups are affected differently by the competitive forces.* Let's look at three of the five competitive forces discussed earlier. *Barriers to entry,* for example, are higher into the hub-and-spoke (differentiated) airline group than into the point-to-point (low-cost) airline group. Following deregulation in 1978, many airlines entered the industry, but all of these new players used the point-to-point system. Since hub-and-spoke airlines can offer worldwide service and are protected from foreign competition by regulation, they often face weaker *buyer power,* especially from business travelers. While the hub-and-spoke airlines compete head-on with the point-to-point airlines when they are flying the same or similar routes, the *threat of substitutes* is stronger for the point-to-point airlines. This is because they tend to be regionally focused and thus also compete with car, train, or bus travel, which are viable substitutes.

■ *Some strategic groups are more profitable than others.* Historically, airlines clustered in the lower-left corner tend to be more profitable. Why? Because they create similar, or even higher, value for their customers in terms of on-time departure and arrival, safety, and fewer bags lost while keeping ticket costs below those of the legacy carriers. The point-to-point airlines are able to offer their services at a lower cost and a higher perceived value, thus creating the basis for a competitive advantage.

Mobility Barriers

Although some strategic groups tend to be more profitable and therefore more attractive than others, movement between groups is restricted by mobility barriers. These are industry-specific factors that separate one strategic group from another.[51]

The two groups identified in the U.S. airline industry map in Figure 3.7 are separated by the fact that the group using a hub-and-spoke operational model offers international routes, while the point-to-point airlines do not. Offering international routes necessitates the hub-and-spoke model. Indeed, the international routes tend to be the only remaining profitable routes left for the legacy carriers. This economic reality implies that if carriers in the lower-left cluster, such as SWA or JetBlue, would like to compete globally, they would likely need to change their point-to-point operating model to a hub-and-spoke model. Or, they could select a few profitable international routes and service them with long-range aircraft such as Boeing 787s or Airbus A-380s. To add international service to the low-cost model would require significant capital investments, and a likely departure from a well-functioning business model. Reinforcing the mobility barriers, moreover, are regulatory hurdles such as securing landing slots at international airports around the world. From the perspective of the legacy carriers whose profits tend to be generated

mobility barriers Industry-specific factors that separate one strategic group from another.

primarily from international routes, the mobility barriers protect this profit sanctuary for the time being.

The strategic group model has two important shortcomings. First, just like the five forces model, it is static. It provides a snapshot of what is actually a moving target and thus does not allow for consideration of industry dynamics. Second, it does not help us understand fully *why* there are performance differences among firms in the *same* strategic group. To better understand differences in firm performance, we must look *inside the firm* to study its resources, capabilities, and activities. We do this in the next chapter.

CHAPTERCASE 3 | *Consider This . . .*

CHAPTERCASE 3, about BYD, notes that the firm entered the electric-vehicle market from a strong base in designing and building batteries. This expertise permitted BYD to circumvent some historically strong barriers to entry in the automotive industry. While the success of BYD in automobiles is still far from assured, it was the fastest-growing carmaker in China in 2009, selling more than 500,000 vehicles in 2010. In part, these strong sales may be due to some government incentives for electric vehicles in China, which will encourage the development and sale of electric cars. For example, in some major cities such as Shanghai, the Chinese government will pay 60,000 yuan (approximately $9,000) toward purchase of an electric vehicle.[52]

Thinking about the chapter-opening case, answer the following questions.

1. Which PESTEL factors are the most salient for the electric-vehicle industry of the 21st century?

2. Think about the structure of the automotive industry in your home country. Is it structured more like an oligopoly or monopolistic competition?

3. Using the industry-attractiveness model (see Exhibit 3.5), explain the overall automotive industry. How would it change for the electric-vehicle industry?

Take-Away Concepts

This chapter demonstrated various approaches to analyzing the firm's *external environment,* as summarized by the following learning objectives and related take-away concepts.

LO 3-1 Apply the PESTEL model to organize and assess the impact of external forces on the firm.

>> A firm's macro environment consists of a wide range of political, economic, sociocultural, technological, ecological, and legal (PESTEL) factors that can affect industry and firm performance.

These external forces have both domestic and global aspects.

>> The political environment describes the influence government bodies can have on firms.

>> The economic environment is mainly affected by five factors: growth rates, interest rates, levels of employment, price stability (inflation and deflation), and currency exchange rates.

>> Sociocultural factors capture a society's cultures, norms, and values.

>> Technological factors capture the application of knowledge to create new processes and products.

>> Ecological factors concern a firm's regard for environmental issues such as the natural environment, global warming, and sustainable economic growth.

>> Legal environment factors capture the official outcomes of the political processes that manifest themselves in laws, mandates, regulations, and court decisions.

LO 3-2 Apply the structure-conduct-performance (SCP) model to explain the effect of industry structure on firm profitability.

>> The structure-conduct-performance (SCP) model is a framework that helps to explain differences in industry performance.

>> A perfectly competitive industry is characterized by many small firms, a commodity product, low entry barriers, and no pricing power for individual firms.

>> A monopolistic industry is characterized by many firms, a differentiated product, medium entry barriers, and some pricing power.

>> An oligopolistic industry is characterized by few (large) firms, a differentiated product, high entry barriers, and some degree of pricing power.

>> A monopoly exists when there is only one (large) firm supplying the market. The firm may offer a unique product, the barriers to entry are high, and the monopolist has considerable pricing power.

LO 3-3 Apply the five forces model to understand the profit potential of the firm's industry.

>> Five competitive forces shape an industry's profit potential: (1) threat of entry, (2) power of suppliers, (3) power of buyers, (4) threat of substitutes, and (5) rivalry among existing competitors.

>> The stronger a competitive force, the greater the threat it represents.

>> The weaker the competitive force, the greater the opportunity it presents.

>> A firm can shape an industry's structure in its favor through its strategy.

LO 3-4 Describe the strategic role of complements in creating positive-sum co-opetition.

>> Co-opetition (co-operation among competitors) can create a positive-sum game, resulting in a larger pie for everyone involved.

>> Complements increase demand for the primary product, enhancing the profit potential for the industry and the firm.

>> Industry attractiveness can be determined by three pairs of two forces: (1) supplier and buyer power, (2) entry and exit barriers, and (3) available complements and the threat of substitutes.

>> Attractive industries for co-opetition are characterized by high entry barriers, low exit barriers, low buyer and supplier power, a low threat of substitutes, and the availability of complements.

LO 3-5 Understand the role of industry dynamics and industry convergence in shaping the firm's external environment.

>> Industries are dynamic—they change over time

>> Different conditions prevail in different industries, directly affecting the firms competing in these industries and their profitability.

>> In industry convergence, formerly unrelated industries begin to satisfy the same customer need. It is often brought on by technological advances.

LO 3-6 Apply the strategic group model to reveal performance differences between clusters of firms in the same industry.

>> A strategic group is a set of firms within a specific industry that pursue a similar strategy in their quest for competitive advantage.

>> Rivalry among firms of the same strategic group is more intense than the rivalry between strategic groups: intra-group rivalry exceeds inter-group rivalry.

>> Movement between strategic groups is restricted by mobility barriers—industry-specific factors that separate one strategic group from another.

Key Terms

Complement *(p. 70)*

Complementor *(p. 70)*

Entry barriers *(p. 65)*

Exit barriers *(p. 68)*

Five forces model *(p. 64)*

Industry *(p. 61)*

Industry convergence *(p. 73)*

Mobility barriers *(p. 76)*

PESTEL model *(p. 57)*

SCP (structure-conduct-performance) model *(p. 61)*

Strategic group *(p. 74)*

Strategic group model *(p. 74)*

Discussion Questions

1. Why is it important for an organization to study and understand its external environment?

2. How do the five competitive forces in Porter's model affect the profitability of the overall industry? For example, in what way might weak forces increase industry profits, and in what way do strong forces reduce industry profits?

3. What is a strategic group? How can studying such groups be useful in industry analysis?

4. How do mobility barriers affect the structure of an industry? How do they help us explain firm differences in performance?

Ethical/Social Issues

1. Strategy Highlight 3.1 discussed Swiss bank UBS's release of over 4,000 names of U.S. citizens suspected of not paying U.S. taxes. The government's case was helped immensely by a former employee at UBS who cooperated with prosecutors on details of how such transactions occur. The "whistleblower," a U.S. citizen, has been lauded for his help in the investigation. Yet, in January 2010 he also began serving a 40-month prison sentence for his own guilty plea for helping his clients at UBS evade taxes.[53] Some in the industry believe such a surprisingly long prison term, despite his cooperation with investigators, will dramatically reduce motivation for other potential whistleblowers to come forward.

   a. What is the proper role for a multinational firm in cases where government regulations across countries are in conflict?

   b. What is the responsibility of individual employees to their employers and to their government, when there seems to be a conflict?

Small Group Exercises

SMALL GROUP EXERCISE 1 (ETHICAL/SOCIAL ISSUES)

Your group is a team of Genentech (www.gene.com) sales representatives. You are meeting to discuss methods to promote additional sales of the drug Avastin which has been FDA approved to treat several metastatic cancers. Sales of Avastin were over $4 billion in 2008 in the United States alone, so it is already a market success. However, there is a controversy among doctors and some patient groups surrounding the costs and benefits of the drug. The *New England Journal of Medicine* reported that Avastin could extend the life of colorectal cancer patients by 4.7 months at a cost of nearly $50,000. The annualized cost of treatments for a number of diseases is $100,000 for a delay in the patient's death of several months.

As part of a sales team for one of the most expensive and widely marketed drugs, your task is to consider the approach to take with doctors who may be reluctant to prescribe Avastin due to the high cost of the treatment for the benefits received.[54]

SMALL GROUP EXERCISE 2

One industry with an impact on both undergraduate and MBA students is textbook publishing. Traditional printed textbooks are being challenged by the growing demand for electronic versions of these materials. As noted in the chapter, e-readers such as the Amazon Kindle and Apple iPad are examples of devices that are likely to drive industry convergence. Millions of e-readers are sold each year.[55]

Also, improvements abound in the availability of inexpensive and lightweight "netbooks" as a hardware complement to the demand for e-textbook media with a traditional keyboard. Netbooks, created in 2007, are smaller, lighter, and less-powerful than typical laptop computers. They tend to run reduced-features operating systems and often use applications from the Internet ("cloud computing") rather than hosting all the software on the device itself. In 2010, the price for a netbook was typically under $200 in the United States.

Use the five forces model to think through the various impacts such technology shifts may have on the textbook industry. Include in your response answers to the following questions.

1. How should managers of a textbook-publishing company respond to such changes?

2. Will the shifts in technology be likely to raise or lower the textbook industry-level profits? Explain.

Strategy Term Project

MODULE 3: EXTERNAL ANALYSIS

In this section, you will study the external environment of the firm you have previously selected for this project.

1. Are any changes taking place in the macro environment that might have a positive or negative impact on the industry in which your company is based? Apply the PESTEL framework to identify which factors may be the most important in your industry. What will be the effect on your industry?

2. Apply the five forces model to your industry. What does this model tell you about the nature of competition in the industry?

3. Identify any strategic groups that might exist in the industry. How does the intensity of competition differ across the strategic groups you have identified?

4. How dynamic is the industry in which your company is based? Is there evidence that industry structure is reshaping competition, or has done so in the recent past?

*my*Strategy

IS MY JOB THE NEXT ONE BEING OUTSOURCED?

The outsourcing of IT programming jobs to India is now commonly understood after years of this trend. However, more recently some accounting functions have also begun to flow into India's large technically trained and English-speaking work force. For example, the number of U.S. tax returns completed in India rose a startling 1,600 percent in the three years from 2003 to 2005 (25,000 in 2003 to 400,000 in 2005). Some estimate that millions of U.S. tax returns will be prepared in India within the next few years.

Outsourcing in the accounting functions may affect the job and career prospects for accounting-oriented business school graduates. Tax accountants in Bangalore, India, are much cheaper than those in Boston or Baltimore. Moreover, tax accountants in India often work longer hours and can therefore process many more tax returns than only U.S.-based CPAs and tax accountants during the crunch period of the U.S. tax filing system.[56]

1. Which aspects of accounting do you think are more likely to resist the outsourcing trends just discussed? Think about what aspects of accounting are the high-value activities versus the routine standardized ones. (If it's been a while since you took your accounting courses, reach out for information to someone in your strategy class who is an accounting major.)

2. What industries do you think may offer the best U.S. (or domestic) job opportunities in the future? Which industries do you think may offer the greatest job opportunities in the global market in the future? Use the PESTEL framework and the five forces model to think through a logical set of reasons that some fields will have higher job growth trends than others.

3. Do these types of macro environmental and industry trends affect your thought process about selecting a career field after college? Why or why not? Explain.

Endnotes

1. This ChapterCase is based on: "Technology levels playing field in race to market electric car," *The Wall Street Journal,* January 12, 2009; "Bright sparks: Electric propulsion provides some excitement amid the gloom," *The Economist,* January 15, 2009; and "GM hopes Volt juices its future," *The Wall Street Journal,* August 12, 2009.

2. For a detailed treatise on how institutions shape the economic climate and with it, firm performance, see: North, D. C. (1990), *Institutions, Institutional Change, and Economic Performance* (New York, Random House).

3. "UBS customers shielded by Swiss law, bank says," *The Wall Street Journal,* February 23, 2009; "Swiss to relax bank secrecy laws," *The Wall Street Journal,* March 14, 2009; "Picking on the Swiss," *The Wall Street Journal,* July 15, 2009; and "UBS to give 4,450 names to U.S.," *The Wall Street Journal,* August 20, 2009.

4. This phrase was used in a speech to the American Enterprise Institute on December 5, 1996, by the former Chairman of the Federal Reserve Bank, Alan Greenspan, to describe the mood in the equity markets.

5. Lowenstein, R. (2010), *The End of Wall Street* (New York: Penguin Press).

6. McCraw, T. (2007), *Prophet of Innovation: Joseph Schumpeter and Creative Destruction* (Cambridge, MA: Belknap Press).

7. "R&D spending holds steady in slump," *The Wall Street Journal,* April 6, 2009.

8. "Toyota keeps idled workers busy honing their skills," *The Wall Street Journal,* October 13, 2008.

9. "Professor Emeritus Milton Friedman dies at 94," University of Chicago press release, November 16, 2006.

10. Lucas, R. (1972), "Expectations and the neutrality of money," *Journal of Economic Theory* 4: 103–124.

11. Yoffie, D. B., and Y. Wang (2009), *Cola Wars Continue: Coke and Pepsi in 2006,* Harvard Business School Case Study 9-706-447.

12. Bettis, R., and M. A. Hitt (1995), "The new competitive landscape," *Strategic Management Journal* 16 (Special Issue): 7–19; Hill, C. W. L., and F. T. Rothaermel (2003), "The performance of incumbent firms in the face of radical technological innovation," *Academy of Management Review* 28: 257–274; and Afuah, A. (2009), *Strategic Innovation: New Game Strategies for Competitive Advantage* (New York: Routledge).

13. "Bleak Friday," *The Economist,* November 26, 2009.

14. "E-commerce," *The Economist,* October 8, 2009.

15. Rothaermel, F. T., and C. W. L. Hill (2005), "Technological discontinuities and complementary assets: A longitudinal study of industry and firm performance," *Organization Science* 16: 52–70.

16. Rothaermel, F. T., and M. Thursby (2007), "The nanotech vs. the biotech revolution: Sources of incumbent

productivity in research," *Research Policy* 36: 832–849; and Woolley, J. L., and R. M. Rottner (2008), "Innovation policy and nanotech entrepreneurship," *Entrepreneurship Theory and Practice* 32: 791–811.

17. Anderson, R. C. (2009), *Confessions of a Radical Industrialist: Profits, People, Purpose—Doing Business by Respecting the Earth* (New York: St. Martin's Press); and Esty, D. C., and A. S. Winston (2009), *Green to Gold: How Smart Companies Use Environmental Strategy to Innovate, Create Value, and Build Competitive Advantage,* revised and updated (Hoboken, NJ: John Wiley).

18. "Nine questions (and provisional answers) about the spill," *Bloomberg BusinessWeek,* June 10, 2010; and "Obama v BP," *The Economist,* June 17, 2010.

19. "Intel fine jolts tech sector," *The Wall Street Journal,* May 14, 2009.

20. "Intel's market share rises on AMD problems," *CNET News,* April 24, 2007.

21. The GM example is based on: Rothaermel, F. T., with V. Singh (2009), "Tesla Motors and the U.S. Auto Industry," Georgia Institute of Technology Case Study.

22. "Giving advice in adversity," *The Economist,* September 25, 2008.

23. This discussion is based on: Bain, J. S. (1968), *Industrial Organization* (New York, NY: John Wiley); Scherer, F. M., and D. Ross (1990), *Industrial Market Structure and Economic*

Performance, 3rd ed. (Boston, MA: Houghton-Mifflin); Carlton, D. W., and J. M. Perloff (2000), *Modern Industrial Organization,* 3rd ed. (Reading, MA: Addison-Wesley); and Allen, W. B., K. Weigelt, N. Doherty, and E. Mansfield (2009), *Managerial Economics: Theory, Application, and Cases,* 7th ed. (New York: Norton).

24. Besanko, D., E. Dranove, M. Hanley, and S. Schaefer (2010), *The Economics of Strategy,* 5th ed. (Hoboken, NJ: Wiley).

25. Dixit, A., S. Skeath, and D. H. Reiley (2009), *Games of Strategy,* 3rd ed. (New York: Norton).

26. Yoffie, D. B., and Y. Wang (2009), *Cola Wars Continue.*

27. The discussion in this section is based on: Porter, M. E. (1979), "How competitive forces shape strategy," *Harvard Business Review,* March–April: 137–145; Porter, M. E. (1980), *Competitive Strategy: Techniques for Analyzing Industries and Competitors* (New York: Free Press); and Porter, M. E. (2008), "The five competitive forces that shape strategy," *Harvard Business Review,* January.

28. "Fiat nears stake in Chrysler that could lead to takeover," *The Wall Street Journal,* January 20, 2009.

29. "Technology levels playing field in race to market electric car," *The Wall Street Journal,* January 12, 2009.

30. "Comcast, GE strike deal; Vivendi to sell NBC stake," *The Wall Street Journal,* December 2, 2009.

31. "The UAW in the driver's seat," *The Wall Street Journal,* April 30, 2009.

32. If there is only one buyer in the market, that market organization is a *monopsony.*

33. Whether a product is a substitute (complement) can be estimated by the cross-elasticity of demand. The cross-elasticity estimates the percentage change in the quantity demanded of good X resulting from a 1 percent change in the price of good Y. If the cross-elasticity of demand is greater (less) than zero, the products are substitutes (complements). For a detailed discussion, see: Allen, W. B., K. Weigelt, N. Doherty, and E. Mansfield (2009), *Managerial Economics.*

34. "Detroitosaurus wrecks," *The Economist,* June 6, 2009.

35. Ibid.

36. This discussion is based on: "An Interview with Michael E. Porter: The Five Competitive Forces that Shape Strategy," Harvard Business Publishing video (June 30, 2008).

37. This section is based on: Porter, M. E. (2008), "The five competitive forces that shape strategy"; "An Interview with Michael E. Porter: The Five Competitive Forces that Shape Strategy," Harvard Business Publishing video; author's interviews with Delta executives; and Yoffie, D. B. (2006), *Cola Wars Continue: Coke and Pepsi in 2006,* Harvard Business School Case Study 5-706-514, teaching note.

38. Brandenburger, A. M., and B. Nalebuff (1996), *Co-opetition* (New York: Currency Doubleday); and Grove, A. S. (1999), *Only the Paranoid Survive* (New York: Time Warner).

39. Milgrom, P., and J. Roberts (1995), "Complementarities and fit strategy, structure, and organizational change in manufacturing," *Journal of Accounting and Economics* 19(2-3): 179–208; and Brandenburger, A. M., and B. Nalebuff (1996), *Co-opetition.*

40. In this recent treatise, Porter also highlights positive-sum competition. See Porter, M. E. (2008), "The five competitive forces that shape strategy," *Harvard Business Review,* January.

41. Michael Porter subsumes exit barriers under intensity of rivalry.

42. Porter, M. E. (2008), "The five competitive forces that shape strategy."

43. Profits are shown after taxes; after extraordinary credits or charges, if any, that appear on the income statement; and after cumulative effects of accounting changes. Source: *Fortune,* May 4, 2009.

44. Note that several industries actually had negative profitability over the 2003–2008 time period: Entertainment (–35.1 percent); Wholesalers: Electronics and office equipment (–33.8 percent); Automotive retailing and services (–29.2 percent); Hotels, casinos, and resorts (–20.7 percent); Insurance: Life, health (mutual) (–18.3 percent); Energy (–15.6 percent);

Motor vehicles and parts (–11.8 percent); Home equipment and furnishings (–10 percent); Insurance: Life, health (stock) (–9.3 percent); Insurance: Property and casualty (stock) (–6.2 percent); Commercial banks (–5 percent); Diversified financials (–1.8 percent). Source: *Fortune,* May 4, 2009.

45. "Reading between the lines," *The Economist,* March 26, 2009; and "New York Times is near web charges," *The Wall Street Journal,* January 19, 2010.

46. "Online ads to overtake U.S. newspapers," *Financial Times,* August 7, 2007.

47. Hunt, M. S. (1972). *Competition in the Major Home Appliance Industry, 1960–1970,* Unpublished doctoral dissertation, Harvard University; Hatten, K. J., and D. E. Schendel (1977), "Heterogeneity within an industry: Firm conduct in the U.S. brewing industry," *Journal of Industrial Economics* 26: 97–113; and Porter, M. E. (1980), *Competitive Strategy: Techniques for Analyzing Industries and Competitors* (New York: Free Press).

48. This discussion is based on: Hunt, M. S. (1972), *Competition in the Major Home Appliance Industry, 1960–1970;* Hatten, K. J., and D. E. Schendel (1977), "Heterogeneity within an industry: Firm conduct in the U.S. brewing industry"; Porter, M. E. (1980), *Competitive Strategy;* Cool, K., and D. Schendel (1988), "Performance differences among strategic group members," *Strategic Management Journal* 9: 207–223; Nair, A., and S. Kotha (2001), "Does group membership matter? Evidence from the Japanese steel industry," *Strategic Management Journal* 22: 221–235; and McNamara, G., D. L. Deephouse, and R. Luce (2003), "Competitive positioning within and across a strategic group structure: The performance of core, secondary, and solitary firms," *Strategic Management Journal* 24: 161–181.

49. In Exhibit 3.7 United Airlines is the biggest bubble, because it merged with Continental in 2010, creating the largest airline in the U.S. Delta is the second-biggest airline in the U.S. after merging with Northwest Airlines in 2008.

50. American's hub is at Dallas–Fort Worth; Continental's is at Newark, NJ; United's is at Chicago, IL; and U.S. Airways's is at Charlotte, North Carolina.

51. Caves, R. E., and M. E. Porter (1977), "From entry barriers to mobility barriers," *Quarterly Journal of Economics* 91: 241–262.

52. "Buffett to visit BYD in China amid declining sales, disputes," *Bloomberg BusinessWeek,* September 22, 2010.

53. "Crying foul, ex-UBS banker starts prison term," *The Wall Street Journal,* January 9, 2010.

54. Mayer, R. J. (2004), "Two steps forward in the treatment of colorectal cancer," *New England Journal of Medicine* 350: 2406–2408; "A cancer drug shows promise, at a price that many can't pay," *The New York Times,* February 15, 2006; and Arthaud-Day, M. L., F. T. Rothaermel, and W. Zhang (2013), "Genentech: After the Acquisition by Roche," case study, in Rothaermel, F. T., *Strategic Management* (Burr Ridge, IL: McGraw-Hill).

55. "E-Readers everywhere: The inevitable shakeout," *Bloomberg BusinessWeek,* January 11, 2010.

56. The *my*Strategy exercise is based on: Friedman, T. (2005), *The World Is Flat: A Brief History of the Twenty-first Century* (New York: Farrar, Strauss & Giroux); and ValueNotes (2006), "Offshoring tax return preparations to India," *November,* p. 118.

CHAPTER 4

Internal Analysis: Resources, Capabilities, and Activities

LEARNING OBJECTIVES

After studying this chapter, you should be able to:

LO 4-1 Distinguish among a firm's resources, capabilities, core competencies, and firm activities.

LO 4-2 Differentiate between tangible and intangible resources.

LO 4-3 Describe the critical assumptions behind the resource-based view.

LO 4-4 Apply the VRIO framework to assess the competitive implications of a firm's resources.

LO 4-5 Identify competitive advantage as residing in a network of firm activities.

LO 4-6 Outline how dynamic capabilities can help a firm sustain competitive advantage.

LO 4-7 Identify different conditions that allow firms to sustain their competitive advantage.

LO 4-8 Conduct a SWOT analysis.

From Good to Great to Gone: The Rise and Fall of Circuit City

CIRCUIT CITY WAS at one time the largest and most successful consumer-electronics retailer in the United States. Indeed, Circuit City was so successful that it was included as one of only 11 companies featured in Jim Collins's 2001 bestseller *Good to Great.* To qualify for this august group of high performers, a company had to attain "extraordinary results, averaging cumulative stock returns 6.9 times the general market in the 15 years following their transition points."[1]

Indeed, Circuit City was the best-performing company on Collins's good-to-great list, outperforming the market 18.5 times during the 1982–1997 period.

How did Circuit City become so successful? The company was able to build and refine a set of core competencies (a unique set of activities that the firm excels at) that enabled it to create a higher economic value than its competitors. In particular, Circuit City created world-class competencies in efficient and effective logistics expertise: It deployed sophisticated point-of-sale and inventory-tracking technology, supported by IT investments that enabled the firm to connect the flow of information among geographically dispersed stores. This expertise in turn allowed detailed tracking of customer preferences and thus enabled Circuit City to respond quickly to changing trends. The company also relied on highly motivated, well-trained sales personnel to provide superior service and thus build and maintain customer loyalty. These core competencies enabled Circuit City to implement a "4S business model"—service, selection, savings, and satisfaction—that it applied to big-ticket consumer electronics with an unmatched degree of consistency throughout the United States.

Perhaps even more important during the company's high-performance run, many capable competitors were unable to replicate Circuit City's core competencies. Further underscoring Circuit City's superior performance is the fact, as Jim Collins described it, that "if you had to choose between $1 invested in Circuit City or $1 invested in General Electric on the day that the legendary Jack Welch took over GE in 1981 and held [that investment] to January 1, 2000, you would have been better off with Circuit City—by [a factor of] six times."[2] In the fall of 2008, however, Circuit City filed for bankruptcy. What happened?[3]

After reading the chapter, you will find more about this case, with related questions, on page 106.

▲ **ONE OF THE KEY** messages of this chapter is that a firm's ability to gain and sustain competitive advantage is partly driven by core competencies—unique strengths that are embedded deep within a firm. Circuit City's core competencies lost value because the firm neglected to upgrade and protect them and was thus outflanked by Best Buy and online retailers like Amazon.[4] Moreover, Circuit City's top-management team was also distracted

core competencies
Unique strengths embedded deep within a firm.

by pursuing noncore activities such as the creation of CarMax,[5] a retail chain for used cars, a foray into providing an alternative to video rentals through its proprietary DivX DVD player,[6] and an attempted merger with Blockbuster (which filed for bankruptcy in 2010).

Perhaps the biggest blunder that Circuit City's top-management team committed was to lay off 3,000 of the firm's highest-paid sales personnel. The layoff was done to become more cost-competitive with Best Buy and, in particular, the burgeoning online retailers. The problem was that the highest-paid salespeople were also the most experienced and loyal ones, better able to provide superior customer service. It appears that laying off key human capital—given their valuable, rare, and difficult-to-imitate nature—was a supreme strategic mistake! Not only did Circuit City destroy part of its core competency, it also allowed its main competitor—Best Buy—to recruit Circuit City's top salespeople. With that transfer of personnel to Best Buy went the transfer of important tacit knowledge underlying some of Circuit City's core competencies, which in turn not only mitigated Circuit City's advantage but also allowed Best Buy to upgrade its core competencies. In particular, Best Buy went on to develop its innovative "customer-centricity" model, based on a set of skills that allowed its store employees to identify and more effectively serve specific customer segments.[7] (Best Buy now faces its own challenges competing with online retailers such as Amazon, highlighting the dynamic nature of the competitive process.)

INTERNAL ANALYSIS: LOOKING INSIDE THE FIRM FOR CORE COMPETENCIES

>> **LO 4-1**
Distinguish among a firm's resources, capabilities, core competencies, and firm activities.

In this chapter, we study analytical tools to explain why differences in firm performance exist even within the *same* industry. For example, why did Best Buy outperform Circuit City in the electronics retail industry? Since both companies competed in the same industry and thus faced the same external opportunities and threats, the source for the observable performance difference must be found *inside the firm.*

Exhibit 4.1 depicts how we move from the firm's external environment to its internal environment. To formulate and implement a strategy that enhances the firm's chances of gaining and sustaining competitive advantage, the firm must have certain types of resources and capabilities that combine to form core competencies. These in turn are leveraged through the firm's activities. The goal should be to develop resources, capabilities, and competencies that create a *strategic fit* with the firm's environment. Rather than creating a static fit, the firm's internal strengths should change with its external environment in a *dynamic* fashion. Upon completion of this chapter, you will have a deeper understanding of the sources of competitive advantage that reside within a firm.

It's time to introduce a more formal definition of core competencies. These are unique strengths, embedded deep within a firm, that allow a firm to differentiate its products and services from those of its rivals, creating higher value for the customer or offering products and services of comparable value at lower cost. The important point here is that competitive advantage can be driven by core competencies.[8] Core competencies that are not continuously nourished will eventually lose their ability to yield a competitive advantage, as did Circuit City's. Without upgrading and ongoing improvement to core competencies, competitors are more likely to develop equivalent or superior skills, as did Best Buy. This insight will allow us to explain differences between firms in the same industry. It also will help us identify strategies with which firms gain and sustain a competitive advantage and weather an adverse external environment.

Core competencies are built through the interplay of resources and capabilities. Exhibit 4.2 shows this relationship. *Resources* are assets such as cash, buildings, or intellectual property that a company can draw on when crafting and executing a strategy. Resources

core competencies
Unique strengths, embedded deep within a firm, that allow a firm to differentiate its products and services from those of its rivals, creating higher value for the customer or offering products and services of comparable value at lower cost.

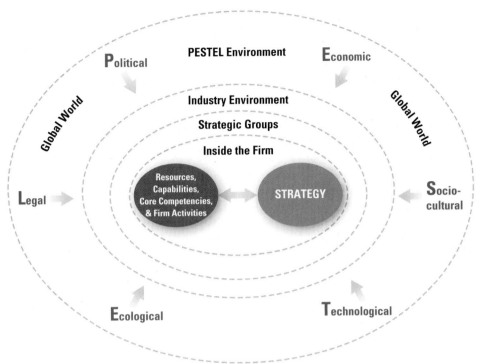

EXHIBIT 4.1

Creating a Strategic Fit to Leverage a Firm's Internal Strengths to Exploit External Opportunities

can be either tangible or intangible. *Capabilities* are the organizational and managerial skills necessary to orchestrate a diverse set of resources and to deploy them strategically. Capabilities are by nature intangible. They find their expression in a company's structure, routines, and processes. *Activities* enable firms to add value by transforming inputs into goods and services. In the interplay of resources and capabilities, resources reinforce core competencies, while capabilities allow managers to orchestrate their core competencies.

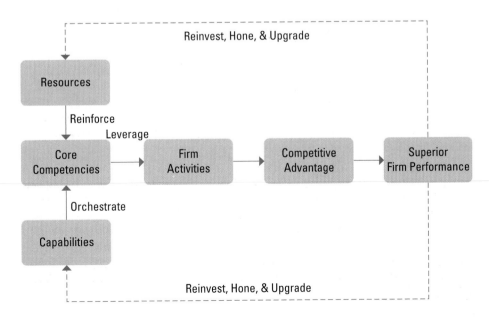

EXHIBIT 4.2

Linking Resources, Capabilities, Core Competencies, and Activities to Competitive Advantage and Superior Firm Performance

Strategic choices find their expression in firm activities, which leverage core competencies for competitive advantage. The arrows leading back from performance to resources and capabilities indicate that superior performance in the marketplace generates profits that can be reinvested into the firm (retained earnings) to further hone and upgrade a firm's resources and capabilities in its pursuit of competitive advantage and improved profitability.

Company examples of core competencies abound: Honda's life began with a small two-cycle motorbike engine. Through continuous learning over several decades, and often from lessons learned from failure, Honda built the core competency to design and manufacture small but powerful and highly reliable engines for which it now is famous. This core competency results from superior engineering know-how and skills carefully nurtured and honed over several decades. Today, Honda engines can be found everywhere: in cars, SUVs, vans, trucks, motorcycles, ATVs, boats, airplanes, generators, snow blowers, lawn mowers and other yard equipment, and so on. Due to their superior performance, Honda engines have been the only ones used in the Indy Racing League (IRL) since 2006. (Not coincidentally, 2006 was also the first year in its long history that the Indy 500 was run without a single engine problem.) One way to look at Honda is to view it as a company with a distinct competency in engines and a business model of finding places to put its engines. That is, underneath the products and services that make up the visible side of competition lies a diverse set of competencies that make this happen. These core competencies reside deep within the firm, implying that companies compete as much in the product and service markets as they do in developing and leveraging core competencies.

In a similar way, Sony's strategy in the consumer electronics industry was to first build the resources and capabilities to successfully commercialize a pocket radio. This success laid the foundation for Sony's core competency in the miniaturization of electronic technology and was subsequently applied to the Sony Walkman, followed by its MP3 Player. In the same industry (mobile devices), Apple has demonstrated core competency in user-friendly product design, which challenges Apple engineers to empathize with customers and deploy engineering knowledge in innovative and category-defining products like the iPod, iPhone, and iPad. Apple products have long been seen as engineered for users' enjoyment, resulting in a "cult-like following" among Apple users. Exhibit 4.3 identifies the core competencies of a number of companies, with application examples.

THE RESOURCE-BASED VIEW

>> **LO 4-2**
Differentiate between tangible and intangible resources.

To gain a deeper understanding of how resources and capabilities can be a source of competitive advantage, we turn to the resource-based view of the firm to provide a model that systematically aids in identifying core competencies.[9] As the name suggests, this model sees resources as key to superior firm performance. It defines resources broadly to include all assets that a firm can draw upon when formulating and implementing strategy. If a resource exhibits certain attributes (which we'll discuss next) that resource enables the firm to gain and sustain a competitive advantage.

As Exhibit 4.4 (page 90) illustrates, resources fall broadly into two categories: tangible and intangible. Tangible resources have physical attributes and are visible. Examples of tangible resources are capital, land, buildings, plant, equipment, and supplies. Intangible resources have no physical attributes and thus are invisible. Examples of intangible resources are a firm's culture, its knowledge, brand equity, reputation, and intellectual property.

Let's take Google as an example. Its tangible resources ("fixed assets"), valued at $5 billion, include its headquarters ("The Googleplex") in Mountain View, California, and numerous server farms (clusters of computer servers) across the globe. The Google brand, an intangible resource, is valued at over $100 billion (#1 worldwide)—which is twenty

EXHIBIT 4.3

Company Examples of Core Competencies and Applications

Company	Core Competencies	Application Examples
Amazon	Providing one of the largest selections of items online, combined with superior IT systems and customer service.	Expansion to cover most electronic media, digital downloads, e-readers as well as apparel, toys, electronics, and tools. Offering cloud computing services.
Apple	Leveraging industrial design to integrate hardware and software in innovative and category-defining mobile devices that take the user's experience to a new level.	iMac, iPhone, iPod, iPad, iTunes, Apple TV.
Coca-Cola	Leveraging one of the world's most recognized brand names (based on its original "secret formula") into a diverse lineup of soft drinks and other beverages.	Coke Zero, Diet Coke, Fanta, Fresca, Sprite, Dasani, Powerade, etc.
ExxonMobil	Discovering and exploring fossil-fuel–based energy sources globally.	Oil and gas.
General Electric	Designing and implementing efficient management processes, training leaders, leveraging industrial engineering.	Energy, health care, airplane jet engines, finance.
Google	Developing proprietary search algorithms.	Gmail, Goog411, Google Maps/Earth, AdWords, AdSense, Google Books, Google Scholar.
IKEA	Designing modern functional home furnishings at low prices offered in a unique retail experience	Fully furnished room setups, practical tools for all rooms, do-it-yourself.
Netflix	Providing Internet subscription services for televised media combined with superior algorithms to track individual customer preferences.	Online subscription, streaming, connection to game consoles.
Nike	Designing and marketing innovative athletic shoes and apparel.	Footwear, clothes, equipment.
Starbucks	Providing high-quality beverages and food, combined with superior customer service in a friendly and welcoming environment.	Customized handcrafted (coffee) beverages; warm/cold, seasonal, and fruit drinks; comfortable and convenient ambience in retail outlets; free Wi-Fi Internet connections (unlimited).
UPS	Providing superior supply chain management services at low cost.	Package tracking and delivery, transportation, ecommerce, consulting services.

resource-based view A model that sees resources as key to superior firm performance. If a resource exhibits VRIO attributes (see the section "The VRIO Framework" on page 91), the resource enables the firm to gain and sustain a competitive advantage.

tangible resources Resources with physical attributes, which thus are visible.

intangible resources Resources that do not have physical attributes and thus are invisible.

Tangible
Physical Attributes, Visible

- Capital
- Land
- Buildings
- Plant
- Equipment
- Supplies

Intangible
No Physical Attributes, Invisible

- Culture
- Knowledge
- Brand Equity
- Reputation
- Intellectual Property
  - Patents
  - Copyrights
  - Trademarks
  - Trade Secrets

EXHIBIT 4.4

Tangible and Intangible
Resources

times higher than the value of its tangible assets.[10] This relationship is even more skewed if we look at Apple. Its brand (#6 worldwide) is valued at over $63 billion, while its tangible assets are valued at a mere $2 billion.[11]

Competitive advantage is more likely to spring from intangible rather than tangible resources. Tangible assets, like buildings or computer servers, can be bought on the open market by any comers who have the necessary cash. However, a brand name must be built, often over long periods of time. Google accomplished its enormous brand valuation fairly quickly due to its ubiquitous Internet presence, while the next four companies on the list of the most valued brands—Microsoft, Coca-Cola, IBM, and McDonald's—took much longer.[12]

Google's headquarters provides examples of both tangible and intangible resources. The Googleplex is a piece of land with a futuristic building, and thus a tangible asset. The *location* of the company in the heart of Silicon Valley is an intangible resource that provides access to a valuable network of contacts and gives the company several benefits. It allows Google to tap into a large and computer-savvy work force and access to graduates and knowledge spillovers from world-class universities such as Stanford and the University of California, Berkeley, which adds to Google's technical capabilities.[13] Another benefit stems from Silicon Valley's designation as having the largest concentration of venture capital in the United States, which is beneficial because venture capitalists tend to look first for local investments.[14] Google received initial funding from the famous venture capital firms Kleiner Perkins Caufield & Byers and Sequoia Capital, both located in Silicon Valley.

Two Critical Assumptions

>> LO 4-3
Describe the critical assumptions behind the resource-based view.

Two assumptions are critical in the resource-based model: (1) *resource heterogeneity* and (2) *resource immobility*.[15] What does this mean? In the resource-based view, a firm is assumed to be a bundle of resources and capabilities. The first critical assumption—resource heterogeneity—is that bundles of resources and capabilities differ across firms. The insight that the resource-based view brings to strategy is that the resource bundles of firms competing in the *same* industry (or even the same strategic group) are unique to some extent and thus differ from one another. For example, although Southwest Airlines (SWA) and Alaska Airlines both compete in the same strategic group, they draw on different resource bundles. SWA's employee productivity tends to be higher than that of Alaska Airlines, because the two companies differ along human and organizational resources. At SWA, job descriptions are informal and employees pitch in to "get the job done." Pilots may help load luggage to ensure an on-time departure; flight attendants clean airplanes to help turn them around at the gate within 15 minutes from arrival to departure. This allows SWA to keep its planes flying for longer and thus lowers its cost structure, savings which SWA passes on to passengers in lower ticket prices.

The second assumption—resource immobility—is that resources tend to be "sticky" and don't move easily from firm to firm. Because of that stickiness, the resource differences that exist between firms are difficult to replicate and, therefore, can last for a long time. For example, SWA has enjoyed a sustained competitive advantage, allowing it to outperform its competitors over several decades. That resource difference is not due to a lack of imitation attempts, though. We mentioned (in Chapter 1) that Continental and

Delta both attempted to copy SWA, with Continental Lite and Song airline offerings, respectively. Neither Continental nor Delta, however, was able to successfully imitate the resource bundles and firm capabilities that make SWA unique. The important point is that resource bundles are different across firms, and these differences can persist for long periods of time. These assumptions are critical to explaining superior firm performance in the resource-based model.

Note, by the way, that the critical assumptions of the resource-based model are fundamentally different from the way in which a firm is viewed in the perfectly competitive model introduced in Chapter 3. In perfect competition, all firms have access to the same resources and capabilities, ensuring that any advantage that one firm has will be short-lived. That is, when resources are freely available and mobile, competitors can move quickly to acquire resources that are utilized by the current market leader. Although some commodity markets approach this situation, most other markets include firms whose resource endowments differ from one another. The resource-based view thus provides useful insights to firms in their quest for competitive advantage.

The VRIO Framework

We are now in a position to evaluate a firm's resource endowments and to answer the question of what resource attributes underpin competitive advantage. In the resource-based model, certain *types of resources* are seen as key to superior firm performance.[16] For a resource to be the basis of a competitive advantage, it must be *valuable (V), rare (R), costly to imitate (I),* and the firm must *organize (O) to capture the value of the resource.* Following the lead of Jay Barney, one of the pioneers of the resource-based view of the firm, we call this model the VRIO framework.[17] A firm can gain and sustain a competitive advantage only when it has resources and capabilities that satisfy the VRIO criteria.

Exhibit 4.5 captures the VRIO framework. You can use this decision tree to decide if the resource or capability under consideration fulfills the VRIO requirements. As you study

>> **LO 4-4**
Apply the VRIO framework to assess the competitive implications of a firm's resources.

EXHIBIT 4.5

Applying the Resource-Based View: A Decision Tree Revealing Competitive Implications

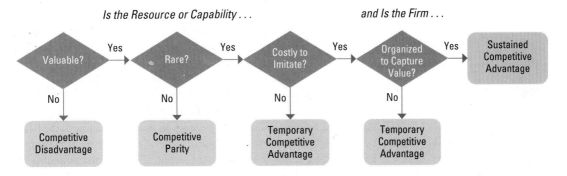

resource heterogeneity
Assumption in the resource-based view that a firm is a bundle of resources and capabilities that differ across firms.

resource immobility
Assumption in the resource-based view that a firm has resources that tend to be "sticky" and that do not move easily from firm to firm.

VRIO framework A theoretical framework that explains and predicts firm-level competitive advantage. A firm can gain a competitive advantage if it has resources that are valuable (V), rare (R), and costly to imitate (I); the firm also must organize (O) to capture the value of the resources.

the following discussion of each of the VRIO attributes, you will see that the attributes accumulate. Only if a firm's managers are able to answer "yes" four times to the attributes listed in the decision tree is the resource in question a core competency that underpins a firm's sustainable competitive advantage.

VALUABLE (V). A resource is valuable if it helps a firm increase the perceived value of its product or service in the eyes of consumers, either by adding attractive features or by lowering price because the resource helps the firm lower its costs. By raising the perceived value of the product, the resource increases the firm's revenues, in turn increasing the firm's profitability (assuming costs are not increasing). If the resource allows the firm to lower its cost, it also increases profitability (assuming perceived value is not decreasing).

Honda's competency in designing and producing efficient engines increases the perceived value of its products for consumers. That competency, supported by its lean manufacturing system, enables quality to be designed and built directly into the product and also helps Honda lower its costs. Thus, Honda's ability in designing and building engines is a valuable resource.

In our quest for competitive advantage, we next need to find out if the resource is also rare.

RARE (R). A resource or capability is rare if only one or a few firms possess the resource or can perform the capability in the same unique way. If the resource or capability is common, it will result in perfect competition where no firm is able to maintain a competitive advantage. A firm is on the path to competitive advantage only if it possesses a valuable resource that is also rare. As Toyota built its initial position as a global auto manufacturer, its lean manufacturing system was a valuable and rare resource. As the leading innovator in developing an efficient and effective approach to manufacturing, Toyota was the first carmaker to resolve a trade-off that had existed for many decades: to lower production costs *and* maintain the high quality of essentially "mass-customized" cars. Looking again at Exhibit 4.5, we can see the result of a resource being both valuable and rare: During the time period when lean manufacturing was a valuable and rare resource, Toyota was able to gain a *temporary competitive advantage.*

Tiffany & Co. has developed a core competency—elegant jewelry design and craftmanship—that is valuable, rare, and costly for competitors to imitate. Since the mid-1800s, its trademarked Tiffany Blue Box® has stood as a symbol of its sustained competitive advantage.

However, as knowledge about lean manufacturing diffused throughout the car industry, Toyota was not able to sustain its competitive advantage. *Knowledge diffusion* can occur through benchmarking studies, new methods taught in college courses, and consultants. After some time, use of lean manufacturing to produce mass-customized cars with high quality and low cost became a necessary but not sufficient condition for competitive advantage. Once lean manufacturing became an industry standard, the best firms could do was to achieve competitive parity. Over time, lean manufacturing had become a valuable but common resource, leading to competitive parity.

COSTLY TO IMITATE (I). A resource is costly to imitate if firms that do not possess the resource are unable to develop or buy the resource at a reasonable price. If the resource in question is valuable, rare, and costly to imitate, then it is an internal strength and a core competency (again, see Exhibit 4.5). If the firm's competitors fail to duplicate the strategy based on the valuable, rare, and costly-to-imitate resource, then the firm can achieve a temporary competitive advantage. Apple's core competencies in user-friendly product design (e.g., iPod, iPhone, and iPad) and complementary and user-friendly services (e.g., Apps, iTunes, and iBooks) are valuable, rare, and costly-to-imitate capabilities. Although Sony clearly has a strength in inventing and developing innovative and high-quality mobile devices (e.g., Walkman, Discman, MP3 player, e-book Reader, portable PlayStation PSP), it lacks Apple's design, integration, and marketing competencies, which are costly and difficult for Sony (and others) to imitate. The combination of the three resource attributes ($V + R + I$) has allowed Apple to enjoy a competitive advantage for many years.

A firm that enjoys a competitive advantage, however, attracts significant attention from its competitors, who will attempt to negate a firm's resource advantage. A competing firm can succeed in this effort through directly imitating the resource in question (*direct imitation*) or through working around it to provide a comparable product or service (*substitution*). Later in this chapter, we will discuss the need to continuously upgrade and reinforce the resources and capabilities that provide the basis for competitive advantage.

Take Crocs Shoes, the maker of a plastic clog, as an example. Launched in 2002 as a spa shoe at the Ft. Lauderdale, Florida, boat show, Crocs experienced explosive growth selling tens of millions of pairs each year and reaching over $650 million in revenue in 2008. Crocs are worn by people in every age group and walk of life, including celebrities such as Heidi Klum, Adam Sandler, Matt Damon, and Brooke Shields. To protect its unique shoe design, the company owns several patents. However, numerous cheap imitators of Crocs have sprung up to copy its colorful and comfortable plastic clog. Despite its patents and celebrity endorsements, other firms were able to more or less directly copy the shoe, taking a big bite into Crocs's profits. Indeed, Crocs's share price plunged from a high of $74.75 on October 31, 2007, to $0.94 on November 20, 2008. This example illustrates that competitive advantage cannot be sustained if the underlying capability (i.e., creating molds to imitate the shape, look, and feel of the original Crocs shoe) can easily be replicated and can thus be directly imitated. Any competitive advantage in a fashion-driven industry, moreover, is notoriously short-lived if the company fails to continuously innovate or build such brand recognition that imitators won't gain a foothold in the market. Crocs Shoes was more or less a "one-trick pony." Nike, on the other hand, was able to do both—continuously innovate *and* build tremendous brand recognition—and thus provides a counter-example of how to avoid losing a competitive advantage through direct imitation.

The second avenue of imitation is through *substitution,* which often entails some kind of work-around. The commercialization of the CAT scanner provides a classic example, in which substitution allowed a second mover not only to mitigate the innovator's advantage but also to gain and even sustain a competitive advantage. Based on internal research, the British conglomerate EMI developed and launched the computed axial tomography (CAT) scanner.[18] This technology, for which EMI received several patents, can take

---

valuable resource One of the four key criteria in the VRIO framework; a resource is valuable if it allows the firm to take advantage of an external opportunity and/or neutralize an external threat.

rare resource One of the four key criteria in the VRIO framework; a resource is rare if the number of firms that possess it is less than the number of firms it would require to reach a state of perfect competition.

costly to imitate resource One of the four key criteria in the VRIO framework; a resource is costly to imitate if firms that do not possess the resource are unable to develop or buy the resource at a comparable cost.

three-dimensional pictures of the human body and is considered to be the most important breakthrough in radiology since the discovery of X-rays. The invention of the CAT scanner also paved the way for follow-up innovations like nuclear magnetic resonance imaging (MRI). Despite its initial success, EMI lost out quickly to GE Medical Systems (GEMS). How can the innovator with a patent-protected technology lose out to a follower? GEMS was able to reverse-engineer EMI's CAT scanner to produce a model that worked around EMI's patents. Moreover, GEMS was able to leverage important complementary resources such as financing, large-scale manufacturing, and a wide distribution and marketing network. While EMI clearly possessed a valuable and rare resource, it was not able to protect itself from GE's substitution attempt.

Substituting for a firm's valuable and rare resource can also be accomplished through *strategic equivalence*. Take the example of Jeff Bezos launching and developing Amazon.com. Prior to inception, the retail book industry was dominated by a few large chains and many independent mom-and-pop bookstores. Bezos realized that he could not compete with the big-box book retailers directly and needed a different business model. The emergence of the Internet allowed him to come up with a new distribution system that negated the need for retail stores (and thus high real-estate costs). Bezos's new business model of ecommerce not only substituted for the traditional (fragmented) supply chain in book retailing, but also allowed Amazon to offer lower prices due to its lower operating costs.

ORGANIZED TO CAPTURE VALUE (O). The final criterion of whether a rare, valuable, and costly-to-imitate resource can form the basis of a sustained competitive advantage depends not on the resource or capability but on the *firm's ability* to capture the resource's value. To fully exploit the competitive potential of its resources and capabilities, a firm must be organized to capture value—that is, it must have in place an effective organizational structure and coordinating systems. (We will study organizational design in detail in Chapter 11.)

Before Apple, Dell, or Microsoft had any significant share of the personal computer market, Xerox PARC invented and developed an early word-processing application, the graphical user interface (GUI), the Ethernet, the mouse as pointing device, and even the first personal computer—all of which laid the foundation of the desktop-computing industry.[19] Due to a lack of appropriate organization, however, Xerox failed to appreciate and exploit the many breakthrough innovations made by its Palo Alto Research Center (PARC) in computing software and hardware. Xerox failed to exploit the value of these important resources because they did not fit within its business focus on photocopiers. Under pressure in its core photocopier business from Japanese low-cost competitors, Xerox's top management was busy looking for innovations in the photocopier business. The organization of the company's innovation system did not allow it to appreciate the competitive potential of the valuable and rare resources generated at PARC. The organizational problems were accentuated by the fact that Xerox headquarters is on the East Coast in Norwalk, Connecticut, while PARC was on the West Coast in Palo Alto, California. Nor did it help that development engineers at Xerox headquarters had a disdain for the scientists engaging in basic research at PARC.

In the resource-based view, for a firm to gain and sustain a competitive advantage, its resources and capabilities need to interact in such a way as to create unique core competencies. Ultimately, though, only a few competencies may turn out to be *core* competencies that fulfill the VRIO requirements.[20] A company cannot do everything equally well and must carve out a unique identity for itself, making necessary trade-offs.[21] Strategy Highlight 4.1 demonstrates application of the VRIO framework.

organized to capture value One of the four key criteria in the VRIO framework; the characteristic of having in place an effective organizational structure and coordinating systems to fully exploit the competitive potential of the firm's resources and capabilities.

value chain The internal activities a firm engages in when transforming inputs into outputs; each activity adds incremental value. Primary activities directly add value; support activities add value indirectly.

How Nintendo Focused on the Casual Gamer

Video gaming is big business—revenues were over $22 billion in 2009 and are expected to grow to more than $60 billion in 2013. The leading game consoles are Sony's PlayStation 3, Microsoft's Xbox 360, and Nintendo's Wii. Sony and Microsoft tend to compete on stronger technological prowess, a larger library of games, and deeper pockets of cash. On the other hand, Nintendo has over the years created and nurtured a valuable, rare, and hard-to-imitate resource: a deep understanding of the casual gamer that has enabled Nintendo to develop products that respond to the casual gamer's preferences.

While early home video games were played by die-hards, mostly teenage and college-age young men who spent hours playing Halo or Grand Theft Auto, Nintendo began courting the casual gamer with the introduction of its Game Boy line of handheld devices in 1990, followed by the Nintendo DS in 2004 and the DS3 in 2011. The line of handheld game consoles expanded the market by appealing to younger players and other customers who were not hard-core video-game aficionados.

With the introduction of its Wii game console, Nintendo's knowledge of the "casual gamer" became a *valuable* resource. The Wii console has the unique feature of a wireless handheld pointing device that can detect movements in three dimensions. The Wii remote allows players to imitate real-life movements like swinging a tennis racket or hurling a bowling ball. This unique feature allows Nintendo to court a broader demographic, thereby continuing to expand Nintendo's knowledge of its customer base and strengthening its basis for competitive advantage. With the introduction of the Wii game console, Nintendo became the market leader in game consoles: It has sold some 52 million Wii consoles worldwide, which equates to some 49 percent market share. As of 2010, Microsoft has sold about 31 million Xbox 360 consoles (29 percent market share), and Sony sold 23 million PlayStation 3 consoles (22 percent market share). (Those sales and market shares will continue to change, of course, as the companies jockey for competitive advantage.)

Nintendo's deep knowledge about the casual gamer is also *rare,* as Sony and Microsoft have largely ignored this market segment. It is *difficult to imitate* as well, since that knowledge has been built over such a long period of time. Similar to Apple, Nintendo tightly integrates hardware and software to enhance the user experience, and thus it is *organized* to exploit its deep knowledge of the casual gamer. That knowledge of its customer is therefore a VRIO resource, allowing it to gain a competitive advantage in the hotly contested video-game market. Yet, the competition is not standing still. In November 2010, Microsoft introduced *Kinect* for its Xbox 360, which—similar to the feature in Wii—allows users to interact without a controller because it responds to voice commands and gestures.[22]

THE VALUE CHAIN AND ACTIVITY SYSTEMS

The value chain describes the internal activities a firm engages in when transforming inputs into outputs.[23] Each activity the firm performs along the chain adds incremental value—raw materials and other inputs are transformed into components that are finally assembled into finished products or services for the end consumer. The value chain concept can be applied to basically any firm, from those in old-line manufacturing industries to those in high-tech ones or even service firms.

Primary and Support Activities

The value chain transformation process is composed of a set of distinct activities, shown in Exhibit 4.6 (next page). The value chain is divided into primary and support activities. The primary activities add value directly as the firm transforms inputs into outputs—from raw materials through production phases to sales and marketing and finally customer service.

>> **LO 4-5**
Identify competitive advantage as residing in a network of firm activities.

primary activities
Firm activities that add value directly by transforming inputs into outputs as the firm moves a product or service horizontally along the internal value chain.

EXHIBIT 4.6

The Value Chain:
Primary and Support
Activities

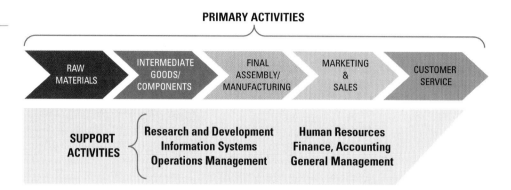

PRIMARY ACTIVITIES

| RAW MATERIALS | INTERMEDIATE GOODS/ COMPONENTS | FINAL ASSEMBLY/ MANUFACTURING | MARKETING & SALES | CUSTOMER SERVICE |

SUPPORT ACTIVITIES

Research and Development
Information Systems
Operations Management

Human Resources
Finance, Accounting
General Management

Other activities, called support activities, add value indirectly. These activities—such as research and development (R&D), information systems, operations management, human resources, finance, accounting, and general management—*support* each of the primary activities.

In the value chain perspective, resources and capabilities are needed to perform the firm's activities. While the RBV model helps to identify the integrated set of resources and capabilities that are the building blocks of core competencies, the value chain perspective helps managers to see how competitive advantage flows from the firm's *system of activities.* In the value chain perspective, the distinct activities a firm engages in are therefore the basic units of competitive advantage. It is important to note, however, that competitive advantage at the firm level is the outcome of the interplay among *all* of the firm's activities, not just a selected few. To create competitive advantage, a firm must be operationally efficient and also able to leverage its unique system of activities. Michael Porter emphasizes that the essence of strategy is to *choose* what activities to engage in and, more importantly, what *not* to do.[24] Companies that attempt to be too many things to too many customers often will be at a competitive disadvantage. The goal is to combine activities into a complex system that creates competitive advantage and also protects from imitation.

As an example, let's again look at the question, "What core competency underlies Southwest Airlines's superior performance?" To answer that question through the lens of the value chain perspective, we need to identify (1) a set of activities and (2) how SWA coordinates and orchestrates them to form a coherent low-cost strategy. SWA uses activities such as frequent and reliable departures, limited in-flight passenger service, low ticket prices, short-haul point-to-point flights using secondary airports, flying only one type of aircraft (which reduces pilot training time and maintenance cost), high aircraft utilization, and a lean, highly productive, and highly motivated ground and gate crew. Each core activity, in turn, is supported by a number of other activities. For example, the core activity of a lean, highly productive, and highly motivated ground and gate crew is supported by stock compensation plans and flexible contracts and work hours. Ideally, the activities pursued are consistent with one another, and complement and reinforce one another. The interconnected system of a firm's activities is more than the sum of its parts. Competitive advantage, therefore, can be embedded in a complex system of value-adding activities.

A strategic activity system conceives of a firm as a network of interconnected activities.[25] Strategic activity systems are socially complex. While one can easily observe several elements of a strategic activity system, the capabilities necessary to orchestrate and manage the network of activities cannot be so easily observed and therefore are difficult to imitate. Let's assume firm A's activity system, which lays the foundation of its competitive advantage, consists of 25 interconnected activities. Attracted by firm A's competitive

support activities
Firm activities that add value indirectly, but are necessary to sustain primary activities.

strategic activity system The conceptualization of a firm as a network of interconnected activities.

advantage, competitor firm B closely monitors this activity system and begins to copy it through direct imitation. Moreover, firm B is very good at copying; it achieves a 90 percent accuracy rate. Will firm B, as the imitator, be able to copy firm A's activity system and negate its competitive advantage? Far from it. Firm A's activity system is based on 25 *interconnected* activities. Because each of firm A's 25 activities is copied with a 90 percent accuracy, firm B's overall copying accuracy of the entire system is $0.9 \times 0.9 \times 0.9 \ldots$, repeated 25 times. The probabilities quickly compound to render copying an entire activity system nearly impossible. In this case, firm B's "success" in copying firm A's activity system is $0.9^{25} = 0.07$, meaning that firm B's resulting activity system will imitate firm A's with only a 7 percent accuracy rate. Thus, the concept of the strategic activity system demonstrates the difficulty of using imitation as a path to competitive advantage.

Dynamic Strategic Activity Systems

In order for a firm to sustain competitive advantage, strategic activity systems need to evolve over time. This is because the external environment changes and also because a firm's competitors get better in developing their own activity systems and capabilities. Managers need to adapt their firm's strategic activity system by upgrading value-creating activities that respond to changing environments. To gain and sustain competitive advantage, managers may add new activities, remove activities that are no longer relevant, and upgrade activities that have become stale or somewhat obsolete. Each of these changes would require changes to the resources and capabilities involved.

For an example, let's look at The Vanguard Group's strategic activity system.[26] Vanguard is one of the world's largest investment companies, with about $1.4 trillion of assets under management. It serves individual investors, financial professionals, and institutional investors such as state retirement funds. Vanguard's mission is "to help clients reach their financial goals by being the world's highest-value provider of investment products and services."[27] Since its founding in 1929, Vanguard has emphasized low-cost investing and quality service for its clients. Vanguard's average expense ratio (as a percentage of total net assets) is 0.20 percent, generally the lowest in the industry.[28]

Vanguard pursued its mission in 1997 through its unique set of interconnected activities depicted in Exhibit 4.7 (next page). The six larger (blue) ovals depict Vanguard's strategic core activities: strict cost control, direct distribution, low expenses with savings passed on to clients, offering of a broad array of mutual funds, efficient investment management approach, and straightforward client communication and education. These six strategic themes were supported by clusters of tightly linked activities (smaller brown circles), further reinforcing the strategic activity network.

The needs of Vanguard's customers, however, have changed since 1997. Exhibit 4.8 shows Vanguard's strategic activity system in 2011. Again, the large ovals symbolize Vanguard's strategic core activities that help it realize its strategic position as the low-cost leader in the industry. However, the system evolved over time as Vanguard's management added a new core activity—customer segmentation—to the six core activities already in place in 1997 (still valid in 2011). Vanguard's managers put in place the customer-segmentation core activity, along with two new support activities, to address a new customer need that could not be met with its older configuration. Its 1997 activity system did not allow Vanguard to continue to provide quality service targeted at different customer segments at the lowest possible cost. The 2011 activity-system configuration allows Vanguard to customize its service offerings: It now separates its more traditional customers, who invest for the long term, from more active investors, who trade more often but are attracted to Vanguard funds by the firm's high performance and low cost.

EXHIBIT 4.7

The Vanguard Group's
Activity System in 1997

Source: Adapted from
N. Siggelkow (2002),
"Evolution toward fit,"
*Administrative Science
Quarterly* 47: 146.

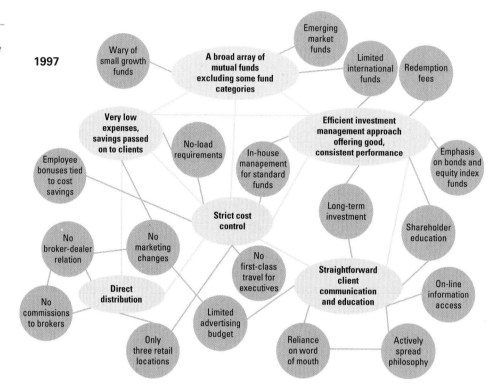

EXHIBIT 4.8

The Vanguard Group's
Activity System in 2011

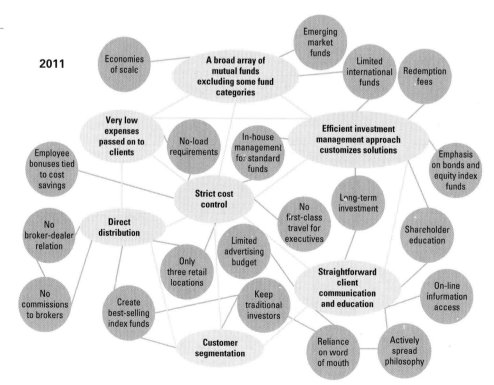

The core activity Vanguard added to its strategic activity system was developed with great care, to ensure that it not only fit well with its existing core activities but also further reinforced its activity network. For example, the new activity of "Create best-selling index funds" also relies on direct distribution; it is consistent with and further reinforces Vanguard's low-cost leadership position. As a result of achieving its "best-selling" goal, Vanguard is now one of the largest investment-management companies. This allows Vanguard to benefit from economies of scale (e.g., cost savings accomplished through a larger number of customers served and a greater amount of assets managed), further driving down cost. In turn, by lowering its cost structure, Vanguard can offer more customized services without raising its overall cost. Despite increased customization, Vanguard still has one of the lowest expense ratios in the industry. Even in a changing environment, the firm continues to pursue its strategy of low-cost investing combined with quality service. If firms add activities that don't fit their strategic positioning (e.g., if Vanguard added local retail offices in shopping malls, thereby increasing operating costs), they create "strategic misfits" that are likely to erode a firm's competitive advantage.

In summary, a firm's competitive advantage can result from its unique network of activities. The important point, however, is that a static fit with the current environment is not sufficient; rather, a firm's unique network of activities must evolve over time to take advantage of new opportunities and mitigate emerging threats. The goal of achieving such a *dynamic* fit lies—as the name suggests—at the heart of the dynamic capabilities perspective, which we'll discuss next.

THE DYNAMIC CAPABILITIES PERSPECTIVE

Dynamic capabilities describe a firm's ability to create, deploy, modify, reconfigure, upgrade, or leverage its resources in its quest for competitive advantage.[29] For a firm to sustain advantage over time, any fit between its internal strengths and the external environment must be dynamic. That is, the firm must be able to change its resource base and activity system as the external environment changes. Dynamic capabilities are essential in order to gain and sustain competitive advantage. Vanguard's dynamic capabilities, for example, helped it to reconfigure and adjust its activity system to sustain its advantage over time.

>> **LO 4-6**
Outline how dynamic capabilities can help a firm sustain competitive advantage.

Not only do dynamic capabilities allow firms to adapt to changing market conditions, they also enable firms to *create market changes* that can strengthen their strategic position. Apple's dynamic capabilities allowed it to redefine the market for portable music through its iPod, generating environmental change to which Sony and others had to respond. With its iPhone, Apple redefined the market for smartphones, again creating environmental change to which competitors like RIM, Nokia, HP, or Motorola must respond. More recently, Apple's introduction of the iPad attempts to redefine the media market, forcing competitors to respond. Dynamic capabilities are especially relevant for surviving and competing in markets that shift quickly and constantly, such as the high-tech space in which firms like Apple compete.

In the dynamic capabilities perspective, competitive advantage is the outflow of a firm's capacity to modify and leverage its resource base in a way that enables it to gain and sustain competitive advantage in a constantly changing environment. The firm may create, deploy, modify, reconfigure, or upgrade resources so as to provide value to customers and/or lower costs in a dynamic environment. The essence of this perspective is that competitive advantage is not derived from static resource or market advantages, but from a dynamic reconfiguration of a firm's resource base. Today, consumers value reliable, gas-powered engines made by Honda. If consumers start to value electric motors more (because they produce zero emissions), the value of Honda's engine competency will decrease. If this

dynamic capabilities perspective A model that emphasizes a firm's ability to modify and leverage its resource base in a way that enables it to gain and sustain competitive advantage in a constantly changing environment.

IBM's Dynamic Strategic Fit

In 2010, IBM generated 80 percent of its $99 billion of revenues from software sales and service. About 150,000 people now work in IBM Global Services, up from a mere 7,600 in 1992. Exhibit 4.9 depicts IBM's product scope in 1993 (the year its transformation began) and in 2010. Revenues from computing hardware declined from 50 percent to 18 percent, while revenues from software and services increased from 33 to 80 percent. Compared with 1993, total revenues are up by almost 70 percent. How did the company transform itself so radically?

IBM—nicknamed Big Blue—helped kick-start the PC revolution in 1981 by setting an open standard in the computer industry with the introduction of the IBM PC running on an Intel 8088 chip and a Microsoft operating system (MS-DOS). Ironically, in the years following, IBM nearly vanished after experiencing the full force of that revolution, because its executives believed that the future of computing lay in mainframe and mini-computers that would be produced by fully integrated companies. However, with an open standard in personal computing, the entire industry value chain disintegrated, and many new firms entered into its different stages. Intel entered as a provider of microprocessors and Microsoft as a provider of operating system and application software. This in turn led to a strategic misfit for IBM, which resulted in a competitive *dis*advantage.

By the early 1990s, the great U.S. computing icon was near bankruptcy. IBM's stock price had dropped to levels not seen in a decade, and more than 60,000 employees were laid off by the firm once known for offering lifetime employment. At the time, it was the biggest layoff in U.S. history. Lou Gerstner, an executive from consumer-products company RJR Nabisco, became IBM's CEO in 1993. Gerstner was not only an industry outsider, he was the first CEO of IBM not promoted from within. At the time, IBM was a stodgy hardware company. Rather than breaking up IBM into independent businesses, Gerstner refocused the company on satisfying market needs, which demanded sophisticated IT *services*.

Keeping IBM together as one entity allowed Gerstner to integrate hardware, software, and services to provide sophisticated solutions to customers' IT challenges. IBM was also quick to capitalize on the emergence of the Internet to add further value to its business solutions. The IBM of today is an agile and nimble global IT-services company.[30]

happens, BYD (the Chinese automaker introduced in Chapter 3), which morphed from a battery maker to a car company, might gain an advantage over Honda. While Honda views itself as an engineering-driven automotive company, startup BYD views its core competency as batteries, which in turn can be leveraged into strong strategic position in electric-power systems for cars, cell phones, laptops, cameras, medical devices, and so on. Imitation by competitors is especially difficult in such a case because it requires hitting a moving target.

Dynamic capabilities are especially relevant in markets that are constantly shifting. Given the accelerated pace of technological change, in combination with deregulation, globalization, and demographic shifts, dynamic markets today are the rule rather than the exception. Strategy Highlight 4.2 shows how IBM developed dynamic capabilities to reposition itself from a hardware company to a global IT-services firm.

IBM's successful turnaround is the result of the dynamic capabilities that its management team built, painstakingly, from its crisis in 1993 on. But how exactly do firms develop dynamic capabilities? Dynamic capabilities describe the firm's ability to reconfigure its resource base and to create external market change for others. Notice that we refer here not to the tangible resources themselves but to the ability to change those resources; thus, dynamic capabilities are an *intangible* resource.

One way to think about developing such intangible resources is to distinguish between resource stocks and resource flows.[31] Resource stocks are the firm's current level of

EXHIBIT 4.9

IBM Product Scope in 1993 and 2010 ($ in billions)

IBM 1993 Product Scope (total revenues $60bn)

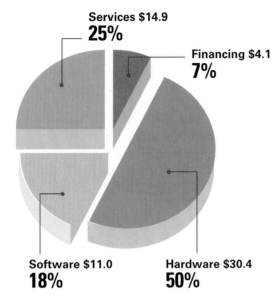

Services $14.9
25%

Financing $4.1
7%

Software $11.0
18%

Hardware $30.4
50%

IBM 2010 Product Scope (total revenues $99bn)

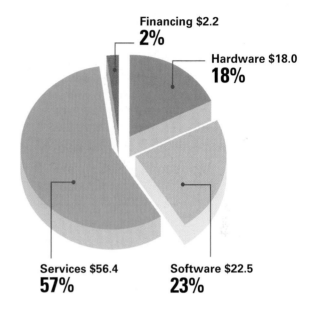

Financing $2.2
2%

Hardware $18.0
18%

Services $56.4
57%

Software $22.5
23%

Source: Data from IBM Annual Reports, 1993 and 2010.

intangible resources. Resource flows are the firm's level of investments to maintain or build a resource. A helpful metaphor to explain the differences between resource stocks and resource flows is a bathtub that is being filled with water (see Exhibit 4.10, next page).[32] The amount of water in the bathtub indicates a company's level of a specific intangible resource stock—such as its dynamic capabilities, new-product development, engineering expertise, innovation capability, reputation for quality, and so on. Intangible-resource stocks are built through investments over time. This is represented in the drawing by the different faucets, from which water flows into the tub. These different faucets indicate investments the firm can make in different intangible resources. Investments in building an innovation capability, for example, differ from investments made in marketing expertise. Each investment flow would be represented by a different faucet. We saw that Vanguard and IBM both made specific investments in their resources over time, such as recruiting and retaining the best human capital and investing in R&D, among other activities.

How fast a tub fills depends on how much water comes out of the faucets and how long the faucets are left open. Intangible resources are built through continuous investments and experience over time. Many intangible resources, such as Hyundai's reputation for quality or Ritz-Carlton's excellence in customer responsiveness, take a long time to build. Organizational learning also fosters the build-up of intangible-resource stocks.

How fast the bathtub fills, however, also depends on how much water leaks out of the tub. The outflows represent a reduction in the firm's intangible-resource stocks. Resource

resource stocks The firm's current level of intangible resources.

resource flows The firm's level of investments to maintain or build a resource.

EXHIBIT 4.10

The Bathtub Metaphor:

The Role of Inflows and Outflows in Building Stocks of Intangible Resources

Source: Figure based on metaphor used in I. Dierickx and K. Cool (1989), "Asset stock accumulation and sustainability of competitive advantage," *Management Science* 35: 1504–1513.

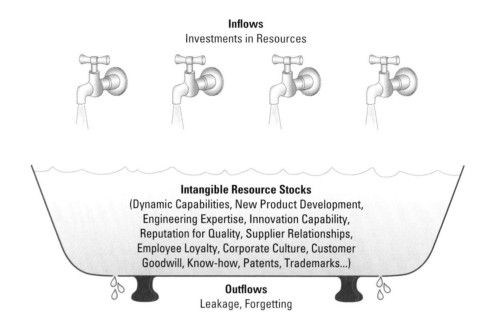

Inflows
Investments in Resources

Intangible Resource Stocks
(Dynamic Capabilities, New Product Development,
Engineering Expertise, Innovation Capability,
Reputation for Quality, Supplier Relationships,
Employee Loyalty, Corporate Culture, Customer
Goodwill, Know-how, Patents, Trademarks...)

Outflows
Leakage, Forgetting

leakage might occur through employee turnover, especially if key employees leave. Significant resource leakage can erode a firm's competitive advantage (as was the case for the Circuit City key employees who were let go and ended up at Best Buy). A reduction in resource stocks can occur if a firm does not engage in a specific activity for some time and forgets how to do this activity well.

GAINING & SUSTAINING COMPETITIVE ADVANTAGE

>> **LO 4-7**
Identify different conditions that allow firms to sustain their competitive advantage.

HOW TO PROTECT A COMPETITIVE ADVANTAGE

We will now consider whether specific internal conditions exist—above and beyond core competencies—that might help a firm protect and sustain its competitive advantage. Although no competitive advantage can be sustained indefinitely, several conditions can offer some protection to a successful firm by making it costly for competitors to imitate the resources or capabilities that underlie its competitive advantage: (1) better expectations of future resource value (or simply luck), (2) path dependence, (3) causal ambiguity, and (4) social complexity.[33] If one, or any combination, of these conditions is present, a firm may strengthen its basis for competitive advantage, increasing its chance to be sustainable over a longer period of time.

Better Expectations of Future Resource Value

Sometimes firms can acquire resources at a low cost, which lays the foundation for a competitive advantage later when expectations about the future of the resource turn out to be more accurate. Take a real estate developer, for example. One important decision she must make is to decide when and where to buy land for future development. Her firm may gain a competitive advantage if she buys a parcel of land for a low cost in an undeveloped rural area 30 miles north of San Antonio, Texas. Several years later, an interstate highway is built right near her firm's land. With the highway, suburban growth explodes as many new neighborhoods and shopping malls are built. Her firm is now able to develop this particular piece

STRATEGY HIGHLIGHT 4.3

Bill "Lucky" Gates

Taking a closer look at the richest man in the world shows that the co-founder of Microsoft, Bill Gates, was lucky on more than one occasion (as he himself freely admits). He was lucky to be born as William H. Gates III, into a well-to-do Seattle family. His father was a prominent attorney and co-founder of what is today the law firm K&L Gates LLC (one of the largest law firms in the world). His mother hailed from a banker's family in Nebraska. As a graduate from the University of Washington, Mrs. Mary Gates worked as a teacher and was active in civic affairs.

Young Bill was lucky to be enrolled in Lakeside School, an exclusive preparatory school in Seattle. In 1968, when Bill was in eighth grade, the Mothers Club at Lakeside School used proceeds of a rummage sale to buy a computer terminal along with time-share programming from GE. Suddenly, Lakeside School had more computer power than many premier research universities at that time. Bill fell in love with programming and spent every free minute he had on the computer, writing software programs. In 1973, he enrolled at Harvard, where he met Steve Ballmer, who later became Microsoft's CEO. The first minicomputer, the MITS Altair 8800, appeared on the cover of *Popular Electronics* magazine in January 1975. Paul Allen and Bill Gates wrote the Altair BASIC program and sold it to MITS of Albuquerque, New Mexico. In the same year, 19-year-old Bill Gates dropped out of Harvard and founded Microsoft with 22-year-old Paul Allen.

Microsoft's biggest break came in 1980 when IBM asked Microsoft to write the operating system for its PC. How did IBM, the world leader in computing, know about a fledgling startup? Here Bill Gates was lucky again. Mary Gates was the first woman to chair the United Way's national executive committee, and IBM's CEO, John Akers, also served on the charity's prestigious board. At one of the board meetings, Mr. Akers shared with Mrs. Gates the fact that IBM was looking for an operating system for its soon-to-be released PC that would set the standard in the industry. Mrs. Gates in turn suggested that her son's company would be the right partner.

The only catch was that Bill Gates didn't have an operating system that would meet IBM's needs, but he knew that a small computer outfit in Seattle had developed an operating system called Q-DOS, short for "quick and dirty operating system." On short notice, Bill Gates borrowed $50,000 (approximately $130,000 in today's value) from his father to buy Q-DOS from Seattle Computer Products, who did not know that IBM was looking for an operating system. Gates then turned around and sold a license of what is now MS-DOS to IBM, but he did not transfer the copyright to the operating system as part of the sale because he correctly believed that other hardware vendors would want to adopt IBM's open standard.[34] As discussed in Chapter 3, Microsoft later leveraged MS-DOS into industry dominance.

of property to build high-end office or apartment buildings. The value creation far exceeds the cost, and her firm gains a competitive advantage. The resource has suddenly become valuable, rare, and costly to imitate, allowing the developer's firm a competitive advantage. Other developers could have bought the land, but once the highway was announced, the cost of the developer's land and that of adjacent land would have risen drastically, reflecting the new reality and thus negating any potential for competitive advantage. In this case, the developer had better expectations than her competitors of the future value of the resource (the land she purchased). If this developer can repeat such "better expectations" over time, she will have a sustained competitive advantage.

Sometimes, better expectations result from luck, at least initially. The role of luck is illustrated in Strategy Highlight 4.3, about Bill Gates and Microsoft.

Path Dependence

Path dependence describes a process in which the options one faces in a current situation are limited by decisions made in the past.[35] Often, early events—sometimes even random ones—have a significant effect on final outcomes. For example, the U.S. customary system

> **path dependence**
> A situation in which the options one faces in the current situation are limited by decisions made in the past.

of measurements using miles, pounds, gallons, and so on was established in the 1820s. Today, the United States is the only industrial nation in the world not using the metric system as the official method of measurement, putting it at a disadvantage in some cross-border transactions and negotiations.

Other examples of path dependence highlight the notion that time cannot be compressed at will. Honda and Sony provide illustrative examples: Both companies took many decades to build their respective core competencies in high-powered efficient engines and electronic miniaturization. A competitor cannot imitate or create these competencies quickly, nor can one go out and buy a reputation for quality or innovation on the open market. These types of valuable, rare, and costly-to-imitate resources must be built and organized effectively over time, often through a painstaking process that may even include learning from failure.

Causal Ambiguity

Causal ambiguity describes a situation in which the cause and effect of a phenomenon are not readily apparent. We've defined strategy as the managers' theory of how to compete for advantage. This definition implies that managers need to have some kind of understanding about causes for superior and inferior performance. Understanding the underlying reasons of observed phenomena is far from trivial, however. Everyone can see that Apple has had several hugely successful innovative products such as the iMac, iPod, and iPhone. These successes stem from Apple's set of *V, R, I, O* core competencies that supports its ability to continue to offer a variety of innovative products.

However, a deep understanding of exactly *why* Apple has been so successful is very difficult. Even Apple's managers themselves may not be able to clearly pinpoint the sources of their success. Is it the visionary role that CEO Steve Jobs played? Is it the rare skills of its uniquely talented design team within Apple? Is it the timing of the company's product introductions? Or is it Apple's Chief Operating Officer who adds superior organizational skills and puts all the pieces together when running the day-to-day operations? If the link between cause and effect is ambiguous for Apple's managers, it is that much more difficult for others seeking to copy this valuable resource.

Social Complexity

Social complexity describes situations in which different social and business systems interact with one another. There is frequently no causal ambiguity as to how the *individual* systems such as supply chain management or new product development work in isolation. They are often managed through standardized business processes such as Six Sigma or ISO 9000. Social complexity, however, emerges when two or more such systems are *combined.* Copying the emerging complex social systems is difficult for competitors because neither direct imitation nor substitution is a valid approach. The interactions between different systems create too many possible permutations for a system to be understood with any accuracy. The resulting social complexity makes copying these systems difficult, if not impossible, resulting in a valuable, rare, and costly-to-imitate resource that the firm is organized to exploit.

A simple thought experiment can illustrate this point. A group with three people has three relationships, connecting every person directly with one another. Adding a fourth person to this group increases the number of direct relationships to six. Just introducing one more person then doubles the number of relationships to 12.[36] This gives you some idea of how complexity might increase when we combine different systems with many different parts.

A firm may be able to protect its competitive advantage (even for long periods of time) when its managers have consistently better expectations about the future value of resources, it has accumulated a resource advantage that can be imitated only over long periods of time, or when the source of its competitive advantage is causally ambiguous or socially complex. It is also important to note that while Bill Gates got a lucky break when starting Microsoft, luck cannot be sustained over time. Microsoft leveraged its initial break into a dominant position for several decades through an effective strategy (see Strategy Highlight 3.2).   🔍

PUTTING TOGETHER INTERNAL AND EXTERNAL ANALYSIS: THE SWOT ANALYSIS

We've now reached a significant point in the book: Combining tools for external analysis from Chapter 3 with the frameworks for internal analysis introduced in this chapter allows you to begin formulating a strategy that matches the firm's internal resources and capabilities to the demands of the external industry environment. Ideally, managers want to leverage a firm's internal strengths to exploit external opportunities, while mitigating internal weaknesses and external threats. This allows them to formulate a strategy that is tailored to their company, creating a unique fit between the company's internal resources and the external environment. If a firm achieves a dynamic fit, it is likely to be able to sustain its advantage over time.

>> **LO 4-8**
Conduct a SWOT analysis.

We synthesize insights from an internal analysis of the company's *strengths* and *weaknesses* with those from an analysis of external *opportunities* and *threats,* using the well-known SWOT analysis. Internal strengths (S) and weaknesses (W) concern resources, capabilities, and competencies. Whether they are strengths or weaknesses can be determined by applying the VRIO framework. External opportunities (O) and threats (T) are in the firm's general environment and can be captured by a PESTEL analysis.

A SWOT analysis allows managers to evaluate a firm's current situation and future prospects by simultaneously considering internal and external factors. It is one of the most popular tools used. The SWOT analysis encourages managers to scan the internal and external environments, looking for any relevant factors that might affect the firm's current or future competitive advantage. The focus is on internal and external factors that can affect—in a positive or negative way—the firm's ability to pursue its strategic goals. Ideally, a shrewd manager solicits input for the SWOT analysis from different perspectives and hierarchal levels within the organization. In Exhibit 4.11 (next page), the vertical axis is divided into factors that are *external to the organization* (the focus of Chapter 3) and the horizontal axis into factors that are *internal to the organization* (the focus of this chapter).

The gathering of information for a SWOT analysis allows managers to link internal factors (strengths and weaknesses) to external factors (opportunities and threats). The principal question to ask (as displayed in the northwest quadrant of Exhibit 4.11) is, "How can the firm use its strengths (the resource base and core competencies) to take advantage of an

---

causal ambiguity A situation in which the cause and effect of a phenomenon are not readily apparent.

social complexity A situation in which different social and business systems interact with one another.

SWOT analysis A framework that allows managers to synthesize insights obtained from an internal analysis of the company's strengths and weaknesses (S and W) with those from an analysis of external opportunities and threats (O and T).

Strategic Questions	Strengths	Weaknesses
Opportunities	How can managers use strengths to take advantage of opportunities?	How can managers overcome weaknesses that prevent the firm from taking advantage of opportunities?
Threats	How can managers use strengths to reduce the likelihood and impact of threats?	How can managers overcome weaknesses that will make threats a reality?

EXHIBIT 4.11

Addressing Strategic Questions within the SWOT Analysis

external opportunity in order to improve the performance of the firm?" Looking further ahead, managers need to consider additional resources and capabilities that may be needed in order to take advantage of external opportunities and mitigate threats. Considering these issues allows managers to match current and future resources and capabilities to the external environment.

You have now acquired the toolkit with which to conduct a complete strategic analysis of a firm's internal and external environments. In the next chapter, we consider various ways to measure competitive advantage. That chapter will complete Part 1, on strategy analysis, in the AFI framework.

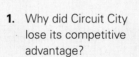

CHAPTERCASE 4 *Consider This . . .*

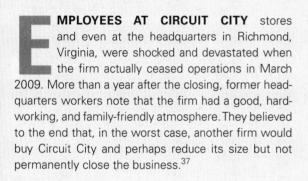

EMPLOYEES AT CIRCUIT CITY stores and even at the headquarters in Richmond, Virginia, were shocked and devastated when the firm actually ceased operations in March 2009. More than a year after the closing, former headquarters workers note that the firm had a good, hardworking, and family-friendly atmosphere. They believed to the end that, in the worst case, another firm would buy Circuit City and perhaps reduce its size but not permanently close the business.[37]

1. Why did Circuit City lose its competitive advantage?

2. What could Circuit City's management have done differently?

3. What is the future of Best Buy as the leader in big-box electronic retailing? What resources and capabilities will positively impact its future?

Take-Away Concepts

This chapter demonstrated various approaches to analyzing the firm's *internal environment,* as summarized by the following learning objectives and related take-away concepts.

LO 4-1 Distinguish among a firm's resources, capabilities, core competencies, and firm activities.

>> Core competencies are unique, deeply embedded, firm-specific strengths that allow firms to

differentiate their products and services to create more value for consumers than their rivals or to offer products and services of acceptable value at lower cost.

>> Resources are assets that a company can draw on when crafting and executing strategy. Capabilities are the organizational skills necessary to orchestrate a diverse set of resources to deploy them strategically. Activities enable firms to add value by transforming inputs into goods and services.

LO 4-2 Differentiate between tangible and intangible resources.

>> Tangible resources have physical attributes and are visible.

>> Intangible resources have no physical attributes and are invisible.

>> Competitive advantage is more likely to be based on intangible resources.

LO 4-3 Describe the critical assumptions behind the resource-based view.

>> The resource-based view makes two critical assumptions: resource heterogeneity (resources differ across firms) and resource immobility (resources are sticky).

LO 4-4 Apply the VRIO framework to assess the competitive implications of a firm's resources.

>> For a firm's resource to be the basis of a competitive advantage, it must have VRIO attributes: valuable (V), rare (R), and costly to imitate (I). The firm must also be able to organize (O) in order to capture the value of the resource.

LO 4-5 Identify competitive advantage as residing in a network of firm activities.

>> Each primary activity the firm performs should add incremental value directly by transforming inputs into outputs. Support activities sustain primary activities.

>> A network of primary and supporting firm activities can create a strategic fit that can lead to competitive advantage.

>> A strategic activity system conceives of a firm as a network of interconnected activities. Firms need to upgrade their value activities over time, in response to changes in the external environment and to moves of competitors.

LO 4-6 Outline how dynamic capabilities can help a firm sustain competitive advantage.

>> To sustain a competitive advantage, any fit between a firm's internal strengths and the external environment must be dynamic. This is accomplished through the ability to create, deploy, modify, reconfigure, or upgrade the resource base.

LO 4-7 Identify different conditions that allow firms to sustain their competitive advantage.

>> Several conditions make it costly for competitors to imitate another firm's resource or capability that underlie its competitive advantage: (1) better expectations of future resource value (or simply luck), (2) path dependence, (3) causal ambiguity, and (4) social complexity.

LO 4-8 Conduct a SWOT analysis.

>> Formulating a strategy that increases the chances of gaining and sustaining a competitive advantage is based on synthesizing insights obtained from an internal analysis of the company's strengths (S) and weaknesses (W) with those from an analysis of external opportunities (O) and threats (T).

>> A SWOT analysis by itself is insufficient to guide strategy formulation.

Key Terms

Causal ambiguity *(p. 104)*
Core competencies *(p. 85, 86)*
Costly to imitate resource *(p. 92)*
Dynamic capabilities perspective *(p. 99)*
Intangible resources *(p. 88)*
Organized to capture value *(p. 94)*

Path dependence *(p. 103)*
Primary activities *(p. 95)*
Rare resource *(p. 92)*
Resource-based view *(p. 88)*
Resource flows *(p. 101)*
Resource heterogeneity *(p. 90)*
Resource immobility *(p. 90)*
Resource stocks *(p. 100)*

Social complexity *(p. 104)*
Strategic activity system *(p. 96)*
Support activities *(p. 96)*
SWOT analysis *(p. 105)*
Tangible resources *(p. 88)*
Valuable resource *(p. 92)*
Value chain *(p. 95)*
VRIO framework *(p. 91)*

Discussion Questions

1. Why is it important to study the internal resources, capabilities, and activities of firms? What insights can be gained?

2. Strategy Highlight 4.2 explains IBM's major transformation from a hardware to a services-oriented company. List the major dynamic capabilities that enabled IBM to make this change. Can you think of other firms that have been successful at a major transition such as this?

3. The resource-based model identifies four criteria that firms can use to evaluate whether particular resources and capabilities are core competencies and can, therefore, provide a basis for competitive advantage. Are these measures independent or interdependent? Explain. If (some of) the measures are interdependent, what implications does that fact have for managers wanting to create and sustain a competitive advantage?

Ethical/Social Issues

1. As discussed in this chapter, resources that are valuable, rare, and costly to imitate help create a competitive advantage. In many cases, firms try to "reverse-engineer" a particular feature from a competitor's product for their own uses. It is commonplace, for example, for cell phone manufacturers to buy the newest phones on the market and take them apart to see what new components/features the new models have implemented.

   However, as the competition between Google (www.google.com) and Baidu (www.ir.baidu.com) over Internet searches in China makes clear, this sort of corporate behavior does not stop with hardware products. Baidu is a 10-year-old firm that has allegedly adapted many of the search tools that Google uses. Baidu however modifies its searches inside China (its major market) to accommodate Chinese-government guidelines. In protest over these same guidelines, in 2010

   Google left the Chinese market and is running its Chinese search operations from Hong Kong.[38]

   It is legal to take apart publicly available products and services and try to replicate them and even develop work-arounds for relevant patents. But is it ethical? If a key capability protected by patents or trademarks in your firm is being reverse-engineered by the competition, what are your options for a response?

2. The chapter mentions that one type of resource flow is the loss of key personnel who move to another firm. Assume that the human resources department of your firm has started running ads and billboards for open positions very near the office of your top competitor. Your firm is also running Google ads on a keyword search for this same competitor. Is there anything unethical about this activity? Would your view change if this key competitor had just announced a major layoff?

Small Group Exercises

SMALL GROUP EXERCISE 1

Brand valuations were mentioned in the chapter as a potential key intangible resource for firms. Some product brands are so well-established the entire category of products (including those made by competitors) may be called by the brand name rather than the product type. In your small group, develop two or three examples of this happening in the marketplace. In any of the cases noted, does such brand valuation give the leading brand a competitive advantage? Or does it produce confusion in the market for all products or services in that category?

SMALL GROUP EXERCISE 2

An enhancement on the basic SWOT analysis is to consider both *current* as well as *potential* conditions.[39] That is, conduct the SWOT in two stages: First, list the elements that are current strengths, weaknesses, opportunities, and threats; then repeat the process with the focus on potential strengths, weaknesses, opportunities, and threats. This two-stage process provides a perspective of the possible dynamic changes facing the organization.

Try this two-step approach on a firm of your group's choice (e.g., the firm that you use for your strategy term project) or use a firm assigned by the instructor.

CURRENT CONDITIONS

Strengths

1. _____
2. _____
3. _____
4. _____

Weaknesses

1. _____
2. _____
3. _____
4. _____

Opportunities

1. _____
2. _____
3. _____
4. _____

Threats

1. _____
2. _____
3. _____
4. _____

POTENTIAL CONDITIONS

Strengths

1. _____
2. _____
3. _____
4. _____

Weaknesses

1. _____
2. _____
3. _____
4. _____

Opportunities

1. _____
2. _____
3. _____
4. _____

Threats

1. _____
2. _____
3. _____
4. _____

Strategy Term Project

MODULE 4: INTERNAL ANALYSIS

In this section, you will study the internal resources, capabilities, core competencies, and value chain of your selected firm.

1. A good place to start with an internal firm analysis is to catalog the assets a firm has. Make a list of the firm's tangible assets in the firm. Then, make a separate list of the intangible assets you can identify.

2. Now extend beyond the asset base and use the VRIO framework to identify the competitive position held by your firm. Which, if any, of these resources are helpful in sustaining the firm's competitive advantage?

3. Identify the core competencies that are at the heart of the firm's competitive advantage. (Remember, a firm will have only one, or at most a few, core competencies, by definition.)

4. Use the strategic activity system framework to diagram the important and supportive activities the firm has that are key to delivering and sustaining the firm's value proposition. (For an example, refer to Exhibits 4.7 and 4.8 showing the activity system of the Vanguard Group.)

5. Perform a SWOT analysis for your firm. Remember that strengths and weaknesses (S, W) are internal to the firm, and opportunities and threats (O, T) are external. Refer to Small Group Exercise 2 earlier for an enhanced version of the SWOT analysis.

*my*Strategy

LOOKING INSIDE YOURSELF: WHAT IS MY COMPETITIVE ADVANTAGE?

Here, we encourage you to take what you have learned about competitive advantage and apply it to your personal career. Spend a few minutes looking at yourself to discover *your own* competitive advantage.

1. Write down your own personal strengths and weaknesses. What sort of organization will permit you to really leverage your strengths and keep you highly engaged in your work (person–organization fit)? Do some of your weaknesses need to be mitigated through additional training or mentoring from a more seasoned professional?

2. Personal capabilities also need to be evaluated over time. Are your strengths and weaknesses different

today from what they were five years ago? What are you doing to make sure your capabilities are dynamic? Are you upgrading skills, modifying behaviors, or otherwise seeking to change your future strengths and weaknesses?

3. Are some of your strengths valuable, rare, and costly to imitate? How can you organize your work to help capture the value of your key strengths (or mitigate your weaknesses)?

4. In this chapter, we discussed that the strategic activity system happening inside the firm can be a vital source of sustainable competitive advantage. If you are currently or previously employed, consider how your professional activities can help reinforce the key value-added activities in your department or organization.

Endnotes

1. Collins, J. (2001), *Good to Great: Why Some Companies Make the Leap . . . and Others Don't* (New York: HarperCollins), p. 3.

2. Ibid., p. 33.

3. This ChapterCase is based on: Collins, J. (2001), *Good to Great;* and Collins, J. (2009), *How the Mighty Fall: And Why Some Companies Never Give In* (New York: HarperCollins).

4. For an insightful discussion of Circuit City's rise and fall, see: Collins, J. (2001), *Good to Great;* and Collins, J. (2009), *How the Mighty Fall.*

5. For a detailed discussion of CarMax, see Mini Case 8.

6. Jim Collins describes the DivX DVD player concept as follows: "Using a special DVD player, customers would be able to 'rent' a DVD for as long as they liked before playing it, using an encryption system to unlock the DVD for viewing. The advantage: not having to return a DVD to the video store before having had a chance to watch it." See J. Collins (2009), *How the Mighty Fall,* pp. 30–31.

7. Rothaermel, F. T., M. L. Arthaud-Day, and N. McCarthy (2013), "Best Buy After Circuit City," case study in Rothaermel, F. T. (2013), *Strategic Management* (Burr Ridge, IL: McGraw-Hill).

8. Prahalad, C. K., and G. Hamel (1990), "The core competence of the corporation," *Harvard Business Review,* May–June.

9. This discussion is based on: Amit, R., and P. J. H. Schoemaker (1993), "Strategic assets and organizational rent," *Strategic Management Journal* 14: 33–46; Barney, J. (1991), "Firm resources and sustained competitive advantage," *Journal of Management* 17: 99–120; Peteraf, M. (1993), "The cornerstones of competitive advantage," *Strategic Management Journal* 14: 179–191; and Wernerfelt, B. (1984), "A resource-based view of the firm," *Strategic Management Journal* 5: 171–180.

10. "Top 100 Most Valuable Global Brands 2009," report by Millward Brown, WPP.

11. Ibid.

12. Ibid.

13. For a discussion on the benefits of being located in a technology cluster, see: Saxenian, A. L. (1994), *Regional Advantage: Culture and Competition in Silicon Valley and Route 128* (Cambridge, MA: Harvard University Press); and Rothaermel, F. T., and D. Ku (2008), "Intercluster innovation differentials: The role of research universities," *IEEE Transactions on Engineering Management* 55: 9–22.

14. Stuart, T., and O. Sorenson (2003), "The geography of opportunity: Spatial heterogeneity in founding rates and the performance of biotechnology firms," *Research Policy* 32: 229–253.

15. This discussion is based on: Amit, R., and P. J. H. Schoemaker (1993), "Strategic assets and organizational rent"; Barney, J. (1991), "Firm resources and sustained competitive advantage"; Peteraf, M. (1993), "The cornerstones of competitive advantage"; and Wernerfelt, B. (1984), "A resource-based view of the firm."

16. This discussion is based on: Amit, R., and P. J. H. Schoemaker (1993), "Strategic assets and organizational rent"; Barney, J. (1991), "Firm resources and sustained competitive advantage"; Barney, J., and W. Hesterly (2009), *Strategic Management and Competitive Advantage,* 3rd ed. (Upper Saddle River, NJ: Pearson Prentice Hall); Peteraf, M. (1993), "The cornerstones of competitive advantage"; and Wernerfelt, B. (1984), "A resource-based view of the firm."

17. Barney, J. (1991), "Firm resources and sustained competitive advantage"; and Barney, J., and W. Hesterly (2009), *Strategic Management and Competitive Advantage,* 3rd ed.

18. Ceccagnoli, M., and F. T. Rothaermel (2008), "Appropriating the returns to innovation," *Advances in Study of Entrepreneurship, Innovation, and Economic Growth* 18: 11–34.

19. Chesbrough, H. (2006), *Open Innovation: The New Imperative for Creating and Profiting from Technology* (Boston, MA: Harvard Business School Press).

20. Prahalad, C. K., and G. Hamel (1990), "The core competence of the corporation."

21. Porter, M. E. (1996), "What is strategy?" *Harvard Business Review,* November–December: 61–78.

22. This Strategy Highlight is based on: Asia Case Research Centre (2009), "Nintendo's disruptive strategy: Implications for the video game industry," *The University of Hong Kong* (HKU814); *Los Angeles Times,* http://latimesblogs.latimes.com/technology/nintendo/; and www.vgchartz.com/.

23. This discussion is based on: Porter, M. E. (1985), *Competitive Advantage: Creating and Sustaining Superior Performance* (New York: Free Press); Porter, M. E. (1996), "What is strategy?"; and Siggelkow, N. (2001), "Change in the presence of fit: The rise, the fall, and the renaissance of Liz Claiborne," *Academy of Management Journal* 44: 838–857.

24. Porter, M. E. (1996), "What is strategy?"; and Porter, M. E. (2008),

"The five competitive forces that shape strategy," *Harvard Business Review,* January.

25. Porter, M. E. (1996), "What is strategy?"

26. This discussion draws on: Porter, M. E. (1996), "What is strategy?"; and Siggelkow, N. (2002), "Evolution toward fit," *Administrative Science Quarterly* 47: 125–159.

27. https://personal.vanguard.com/us/content/Home/WhyVanguard/AboutVanguardWhoWeAreContent.jsp.

28. "Funds: How much you're really paying," *Money,* November 2005; and https://personal.vanguard.com/us/content/Home/WhyVanguard/AboutVanguardWhoWeAreContent.jsp.

29. This discussion is based on: Eisenhardt, K. M., and M. Martin (2000), "Dynamic capabilities: What are they?" *Strategic Management Journal* 21: 1105–1121; and Helfat, C. E., S. Finkelstein, W. Mitchell, M. A. Peteraf, H. Singh, D. J. Teece, and S. G. Winter (2007), *Dynamic Capabilities: Understanding Strategic Change in Organizations* (Malden, MA: Blackwell).

30. This Strategy Highlight is based on: Gerstner, L. V. (2002), *Who Says Elephants Can't Dance?* (New York: HarperBusiness); Grove, A. S. (1996), *Only the Paranoid Survive: How to Exploit the Crisis Points that Challenge Every Company and Every Career* (New York: Currency Doubleday); Harreld, J. B., C. A. O'Reilly, and M. Tushman (2007), "Dynamic capabilities at IBM: Driving strategy into action," *California Management Review* 49: 21–43; and IBM Annual Reports (diverse years).

31. Dierickx, I., and K. Cool (1989), "Asset stock accumulation and sustainability of competitive advantage," *Management Science* 35: 1504–1513.

32. Ibid.

33. This discussion is based on: Barney, J. (1986), "Strategic factor

markets: Expectations, luck, and business strategy," *Management Science* 32: 1231–1241; Barney, J. (1991), "Firm resources and sustained competitive advantage," *Journal of Management* 17: 99–120; Dierickx, I., and K. Cool (1989), "Asset stock accumulation and sustainability of competitive advantage"; and Mahoney, J. T., and J. R. Pandian (1992), "The resource-based view within the conversation of strategic management," *Strategic Management Journal* 13: 363–380.

34. This Strategy Highlight is based on: Manes, S., and P. Andrews (1994), *Gates: How Microsoft's Mogul Reinvented an Industry and Made Himself the Richest Man in America* (New York: Doubleday); and Gladwell, M. (2008), *Outliers. The Story of Success* (New York: Little, Brown, and Company).

35. Arthur, W. B. (1989), "Competing technologies, increasing returns, and lock-in by historical events," *Economics Journal* 99: 116–131; and Dierickx, I., and K. Cool (1989), "Asset stock accumulation and sustainability of competitive advantage."

36. More formally, the number of relationships (r) in a group is a function of its group members (n), with $r = n(n - 1)/2$.

The assumption is that two people, A and B, have only one relationship (A $\longleftrightarrow$ B), rather than two relationships (A $\rightarrow$ B and A $\leftarrow$ B). In the latter case, the number of relationships (r) in a group with n members doubles, where $r = n(n - 1)$.

37. *A Tale of Two Cities: The Circuit City Story*, film documentary by Tom Wulf, released November 2010.

38. "How Baidu won China," *Bloomberg BusinessWeek*, November 11, 2010.

39. This Small Group Exercise is drawn from: Blumentritt, T. (2009), *A Primer on the SWOT Analysis.* Teaching Note, Kennesaw State University.

CHAPTER 5

Competitive Advantage and Firm Performance

LEARNING OBJECTIVES
After studying this chapter, you should be able to:

LO 5-1   Describe and evaluate economic value creation when measuring competitive advantage.

LO 5-2   Describe and evaluate accounting profitability when measuring competitive advantage.

LO 5-3   Describe and evaluate shareholder value creation when measuring competitive advantage.

LO 5-4   Describe and evaluate the balanced-scorecard approach for assessing competitive advantage.

LO 5-5   Describe and evaluate the triple-bottom-line approach when assessing competitive advantage.

LO 5-6   Compare and contrast different approaches to measuring competitive advantage, and derive managerial implications.

Assessing Competitive Advantage: Google vs. Microsoft

WE BEGAN OUR JOURNEY into strategic management (in Chapter 1) by looking at Google's success in online search and advertising and Microsoft's challenges in catching up. Google holds some 70 percent market share and has outperformed its rivals for a number of years. Although it is relatively easy to pick a winner in a narrowly defined market segment, we also saw—when comparing Google's and Microsoft's business models in Chapter 1—that both firms compete with one another in a number of different markets and thus are exposed to multipoint competition. We discussed the quest to gain and sustain competitive advantage as managers' ability to formulate and implement a strategy that leads to superior firm performance.

Competitive advantage thus is defined and assessed at the *firm level*. In order to measure the firm's overall performance, we need tools to assess performance across all of the firm's different business activities. While that idea is straightforward enough, it is far from clear which performance metric is best.

Exhibit 5.1 (next page) compares Google and Microsoft using common performance metrics. Based on *revenues* and *net income*, Microsoft ($66 bn in revenues and $21 bn in net income) outperformed Google ($28 bn and $8 bn, respectively) by a wide margin. In the first quarter of 2011, Microsoft's market value (market capitalization, or "market cap") was $241 billion, while Google's was $196 billion.

But is this a valid comparison? Using *absolute* numbers such as these is like comparing apples and oranges: With 23,331 employees, Google is much smaller than Microsoft, which has 89,000 employees. When we adjust revenues, net income, and market value by the number of employees, so that the measures represent performance *per employee* (see the bottom row in Exhibit 5.1), we see Google outperforming Microsoft by a wide margin on each of the three performance dimensions.

After reading the chapter, you will find more about this case, with related questions, on page 130.

▲ **COMPARING THE PERFORMANCES** of Google and Microsoft makes it clear that understanding and measuring competitive advantage presents some challenges. Looking at *absolute* firm-level measures such as revenues, net income, and market capitalization, we concluded that Microsoft outperformed Google. When we adjusted these measures for size (in this case, size as measured by performance per employee), we saw Google outperforming Microsoft. As you know from your coursework in finance and accounting, it is also possible to use various other measures to analyze firm performance. For example, financial ratios adjust for firm size and thus are often preferred over absolute measures when tracking firm performance.

EXHIBIT 5.1

Comparing Google and Microsoft along Different Performance Dimensions

(Top row: absolute values; bottom row: ratios.)

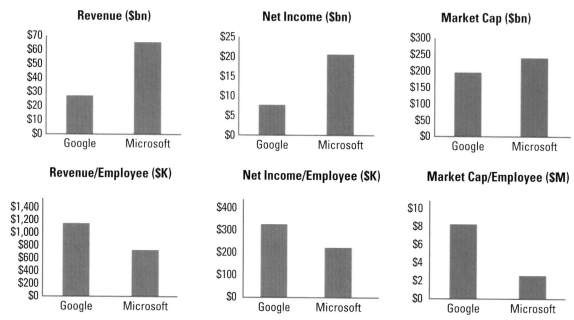

Source: Data gathered from companies' SEC filings. All data are as of December 31, 2010, except market capitalization, which is as of January 2011.

Competitive advantage leads to superior firm performance. Gaining and sustaining competitive advantage is the goal of strategic management. To explain and predict differences in firm performance, therefore, we must think hard about how to best measure it. We devote this chapter to studying how to measure performance. In particular, we introduce different frameworks and a diverse set of measures to capture the multifaceted nature of competitive advantage. These various tools will facilitate a critical evaluation of a firm's performance and help determine whether it has a competitive advantage.

MEASURING COMPETITIVE ADVANTAGE

If competitive advantage is always *relative*—measured in relation to other firms—then how do we know when a firm has competitive advantage? How do we measure competitive advantage? Surprisingly, these apparently simple questions do not have simple answers. Strategic management researchers have debated them intensely for at least 25 years.[1]

To answer these key questions, we will develop a *multidimensional perspective* to measuring competitive advantage. That is, we will apply not only the standard economic, accounting, and financial metrics, but also a wider set of performance metrics, some of which are qualitative rather than quantitative. Let's begin by focusing on the three standard dimensions by asking:[2]

1. How much *economic value* does the firm generate?
2. What is the firm's *accounting profitability?*
3. How much *shareholder value* does the firm create?

These performance dimensions tend to be correlated, particularly when considered over longer time periods. That is, economic value and accounting profitability tend to be reflected in the firm's stock price.

Economic Value Creation

Let's first consider performance through the dimension of *economic value.* Three factors are critical when evaluating any good or service a firm offers in the marketplace: (1) *value (V),* (2) *price (P),* and (3) *cost (C).*

Value denotes the dollar amount (V) a consumer would attach to a good or service. Simply put, how much are you willing to pay for it? Value captures a consumer's willingness to pay. (Economists call this amount the *reservation price.*) If the value you attach to a good or service is greater than the *price* charged (P), you are likely to purchase it. The cost (C) to produce the good or service matters little to the consumer, but it matters a great deal to the producer (supplier) of the good or service. The difference between a buyer's willingness to pay for a product or service and the firm's cost to produce it is the economic value created. A firm has a competitive advantage when it is able to create more economic value than its rivals.

Let's assume, for example, you are hungry and you value (V) a pizza at $12. You thus are willing to pay a price (P) of $10 for the pizza that your local bistro offers, even though you realize it probably costs less than $10 to produce it. Suppose the bistro's total cost (C) is in fact $7. The difference between value (V = $12) and cost (C = $7) is the economic value created by the entrepreneur who runs the bistro, in this case, $V - C = \$12 - \$7$, or $5. The economic value created is sometimes also called the *economic contribution.*

The difference between the price charged (P), and the cost to produce (C), is the entrepreneur's profit or (in economics) producer surplus. In our example, the profit is $P - C = \$10 - \$7 = \$3$. The entrepreneur captures this amount as profit. As the consumer, you capture the difference between what you would have been willing to pay (V) and what you paid (P) as something called consumer surplus. In our example, the consumer surplus is $V - P = \$12 - \$10$, or $2.

As you can see from the pizza example, economic value created therefore also equals the sum of consumer and producer surplus (that is, profit):

$$\text{Economic value created} = \$12 - \$7 = \$5$$
$$\text{Consumer surplus} + \text{Producer surplus} = \$2 + \$3 = \$5$$

The relationship between consumer and producer surplus is the reason trade happens: Both transacting parties capture *some* of the overall value created. (Note, though, that the distribution of the value created between parties need not be equal to make trade worthwhile.) Thus, in an economic context, strategy is about (1) *creating economic value* and (2) *capturing as much of it as possible.*

From an economic point of view, revenues are a function of the value created for customers and the price of the good or service, which together drive the volume of

>> **LO 5-1**

Describe and evaluate economic value creation when measuring competitive advantage.

---

value The dollar amount (V) a consumer would attach to a good or service; the consumer's *maximum willingness to pay;* sometimes also called *reservation price.*

economic value created Difference between value (V) and cost (C), or (V − C); sometimes also called *economic contribution.*

profit (producer surplus) Difference between price charged (P) and the cost to produce (C), or (P − C).

consumer surplus Difference between the value a consumer attaches to a good or service (V) and what he or she paid for it (P), or (V − P).

goods sold. Thus, economists define a firm's profit (Π) as total revenues (TR) minus total costs (TC):

$$\Pi = TR - TC, \text{ where } TR = P \times Q, \text{ or price times quantity sold}$$

Total costs include both fixed and variable costs. *Fixed costs* are independent of consumer demand—e.g., the cost of capital to rent the bistro space and buy the pizza oven and other equipment. *Variable costs* change with the level of consumer demand—e.g., flour, tomato sauce, cheese, and other pizza ingredients as well as labor and utilities. Because the cost of capital and the cost of the bistro are fixed, the bistro becomes more profitable as the bistro entrepreneur sells more pizzas and thus spreads her fixed costs over a larger sales volume.

Also, if the economic value created ($V - C$) by the pizzeria across the street is only $4, then the bistro entrepreneur has a competitive advantage because $5 > $4. (For simplicity, assume there are no other pizza parlors or delivery services nearby.)

Exhibit 5.2 graphically illustrates how these concepts fit together. On the left side of the graph, V represents the value of the product to the consumer, as captured in the consumer's *maximum willingness to pay*. In the center bar, C is the cost to produce the product or service (the unit cost). It follows that the difference between the consumers' maximum willingness to pay and the firm's cost ($V - C$) is the *economic value created*. The price of the product or service (P) is indicated in the dashed line. The economic value created ($V - C$), as shown in Exhibit 5.2, is split between producer and consumer: ($V - P$) is the value the consumer captures (*consumer surplus*), and ($P - C$) is the value the producer captures (*producer surplus*, or *profit*).

Competitive advantage goes to the firm that achieves the largest difference between V, the consumer's willingness to pay, and C, the cost to produce the good or service. The reason is that a large difference between V and C gives the firm two distinct pricing options: (1) It can charge higher prices to reflect the higher product value and thus increase its profitability. Or (2) it can charge the same price as competitors and thus gain market share. Given this, the strategic objective is to maximize ($V - C$), or the economic value created.

opportunity costs The value of the best forgone alternative use of the resources employed.

One last aspect of how to measure economic value merits mention: When economists measure economic value created, they include opportunity costs. Opportunity costs capture the value of the best forgone alternative use of the resources employed. The bistro entrepreneur, for example, faces two types of opportunity costs: (1) forgone wages she could be earning if she was employed elsewhere and (2) the cost of capital she invested in her bistro, which could instead be invested in, say, the stock market or U.S Treasury bonds. At the end of the year, the bistro entrepreneur considers her business over the last 12 months. She made an *accounting profit* of $60,000, calculated as total revenues minus expenses (which include all historical costs but not opportunity costs). But she also realizes she has forgone $40,000 in salary she could have earned at another firm. In addition, she knows she could have earned $25,000 in interest if she had bought U.S. Treasury bills with a 5 percent return instead of investing $500,000 in her business. The opportunity cost of operating the bistro was $65,000 ($40,000 + $25,000). Therefore, when considering all

EXHIBIT 5.2

Competitive Advantage and Economic Value Created: Looking at Different Components

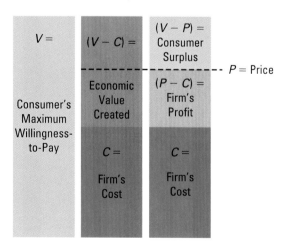

costs, including opportunity costs, she actually experienced an economic loss of $5,000 ($60,000 − $65,000). She should stay in business only if she values her independence more than $5,000 or thinks business will be better next year.

Understanding economic value creation gives us a good start toward measuring competitive advantage, but we must remember the following:

- *Determining the value of a good in the eyes of consumers is not a simple task.* One way to tackle this problem is to look at consumers' purchasing habits for their revealed preferences, which indicate how much each consumer is willing to pay for a product or service. In our pizza example, the value (V) you placed on the pizza—the highest price you were willing to pay, or your reservation price—was $12. If the entrepreneur is able to charge the reservation price ($P = \$12$), she captures all the economic value created ($V − C = \$5$) as producer surplus or profit ($P − C = \$5$).

- *The value of a good in the eyes of consumers changes based on income, preferences, time, and other factors.* If your income is high, you are likely to place a higher value on some goods (e.g., business-class air travel) and a lower value on other goods (e.g., Greyhound bus travel). In regard to preferences, you may place a higher value on a ticket for the final game of the NCAA basketball tournament if your school is playing in it than if it is not. As an example of time value, you place a higher value on an airline ticket that will get you to a business meeting tomorrow than on one for a planned trip to take place eight weeks from now. Airlines know this too, so they tend to charge you a higher price when you book your ticket closer to the departure date. (This pricing strategy again reverses a few short hours before departure if seats are still available: Remaining seats are then often sold at a discount as "stand-by" tickets, to obtain incremental revenues. However, given airlines' use of sophisticated yield-management algorithms in recent years, fewer last-minute stand-by tickets are now offered.)

- *To measure firm-level competitive advantage, we must estimate the economic value created for all products and services offered by the firm.* This estimation may be a relatively easy task if the firm offers only a few products or services. However, it becomes much more complicated for diversified firms like General Electric, Unilever, or the Tata Group (an Indian conglomerate) that may offer hundreds or even thousands of different products and services across many different industries and geographies. While the performance of individual strategic business units (SBUs) can be assessed along the dimensions described here, it becomes more difficult to make this assessment at the corporate level. Yet, assessing corporate-level performance is critical in order to justify the existence of diversified conglomerates (more on this in our discussion on diversification strategy in Chapter 8).

The economic perspective—in particular, the concept of economic value created—gives us one useful way to measure competitive advantage. This approach is conceptually quite powerful, and it lies at the center of many strategic management frameworks (such as the generic business strategies we discuss in the next chapter). However, it falls short when managers are called upon to operationalize competitive advantage. When the need for "hard numbers" arises, managers and analysts frequently rely on accounting data to assess firm performance. We now turn to *accounting profitability*, as a second traditional way to measure competitive advantage.

>> **LO 5-2**
Describe and evaluate accounting profitability when measuring competitive advantage.

Accounting Profitability

When assessing competitive advantage by measuring accounting profitability, we use standard metrics derived from publicly available accounting data such as income statements and balance sheets.[3] Public companies are required by law to release these data, which must comply with the generally accepted accounting principles (GAAP) set by the Financial Accounting Standards Board (FASB) and be audited by certified public accountants.[4] Publicly traded firms are required to file the Form 10-K (or 10-K report) annually with the U.S. Security and Exchange Commission (SEC), a federal regulatory agency.[5] The 10-K reports are the primary source of companies' accounting data. As a result of the Enron scandal, which also led to the collapse of Enron's accounting firm Arthur Andersen, accounting data released to the public in the United States must now comply with more stringent legislation (the Sarbanes-Oxley Act of 2002), which in turn enhances the data's usefulness.

Though not perfect, accounting data enable us to conduct direct performance comparisons between different companies. Some of the profitability metrics most commonly used in strategic management are *return on assets* (*ROA*), *return on equity* (*ROE*), *return on invested capital* (*ROIC*), and *return on revenue* (*ROR*). In Table 1 in the "How to Conduct a Case Analysis" module at the end of the book, you will find a complete presentation of accounting measures (profitability, activity, leverage, liquidity, and market measures), how they are calculated, and their benefits and shortcomings. These will be useful for you when working through your strategy term project or analyzing different case studies and business situations. (You may want to bookmark the table.)

To visualize competitive advantage in accounting terms, let's take a look at the top 10 companies in the *Fortune 500* (based on December 31, 2010, accounting data). The *Fortune 500* is an annual list of the 500 largest U.S. companies by revenues. Exhibit 5.3 shows the top performers in terms of profits (net income). Given this metric, Exxon Mobil, with over $19.3 billion in profits, was the most successful company, followed by Microsoft ($14.6 bn), Walmart ($14.3 bn), and Procter & Gamble ($13.4 bn).

Although the performance of these companies is impressive in absolute terms, things look quite different when we compare their *relative* profitability in terms of return on revenue, which gives us a size-adjusted measure of profitability. Return on revenue (ROR) measures the profit earned per dollar of revenue, expressed in percentages. Exhibit 5.4 shows the top 10 performers in terms of return on revenue. Liberty Media, a multimedia conglomerate, shows by far the highest ROR, at 62.1 percent, followed by pharmaceutical companies, Bristol-Myers Squibb and Merck, with 49.1 percent and 47.0 percent RORs, respectively. Interestingly, when we compare the top 10 companies based on profits in Exhibit 5.3 and the top 10 based on ROR in Exhibit 5.4, only one company (Merck) appears in both rankings.

Although it is useful to see the top performers at any given point in time, we can improve the analysis further on two dimensions: First, since strategy is about gaining *and sustaining* competitive advantage, we need to go beyond a single year, which can at best provide a snapshot. Second, since we need to assess competitive advantage relative to a firm's competitors (or the industry average), we need to look at companies in the same industry. These added dimensions allow us to compare apples to apples.

EXHIBIT 5.3

Top 10 *Fortune 500* Companies by Profits (in $ million)

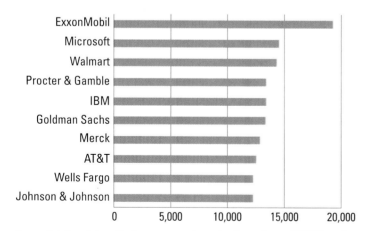

Source: Data from *Fortune,* http://money.cnn.com/magazines/fortune/fortune500/2010/, as of December 31, 2010.

Exhibit 5.5 shows the performance of four large pharmaceutical companies—Abbott, Johnson & Johnson (J&J), Merck—across the 2005–2009 time period based on return on assets (ROA). Over this five-year period, none of the firms was able to sustain a competitive advantage. Pfizer had the lead in 2005 through 2007 but was outperformed by J&J and Merck since 2007. Exhibit 5.5 clearly shows that is it difficult to gain competitive advantage, and even more difficult to sustain it. *Competitive advantage is transitory!*

Although accounting data tend to be readily available and we can easily transform them to assess competitive performance, they also exhibit some important limitations:

- *All accounting data are historical data and thus backward-looking.* Accounting profitability ratios show us only the outcomes from past decisions, and the past is no guarantee of future performance. Dell Computer, for example, clearly outperformed its competition based on accounting data in the first few years of the 21st century, but more recently it has been outperformed by Apple and Hewlett Packard. Also, as you probably already noticed in the earlier exhibits, there is a significant time delay until accounting data become publicly available. Some strategy scholars have even gone so far as to suggest that using accounting data to make strategic decisions is like driving a car by looking in the rearview mirror.[6]

- *Accounting data do not consider off–balance sheet items.* Off–balance sheet items, such as pension obligations (quite large in some U.S. industries) and operating leases in the retail industry, can be significant factors. For example, one retailer may own all its stores, which would properly be included in the firm's assets; a second retailer may lease all its stores, which would *not be* listed as assets. All else being equal, the second retailer's return on assets (ROA) would be higher. We address this shortcoming by adjusting accounting data to obtain an *equivalent* economic capital base, so that we can compare companies with different capital structures.

EXHIBIT 5.4

Top 10 *Fortune 500* Companies by Return on Revenue (ROR)

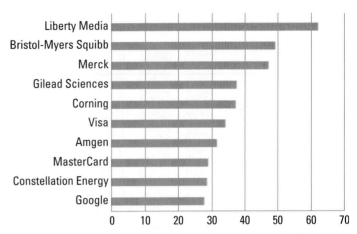

Source: Data from *Fortune*, http://money.cnn.com/magazines/fortune/fortune500/2010/, as of December 31, 2010.

EXHIBIT 5.5

Firm Performance in the Pharmaceutical Industry by Return on Revenue (ROR)

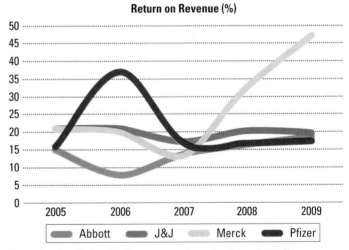

Source: Data from *Fortune*, http://money.cnn.com/magazines/fortune/fortune500.

EXHIBIT 5.6

The Declining Importance of Book Value in a Firm's Stock Market Valuation, 1980–2010

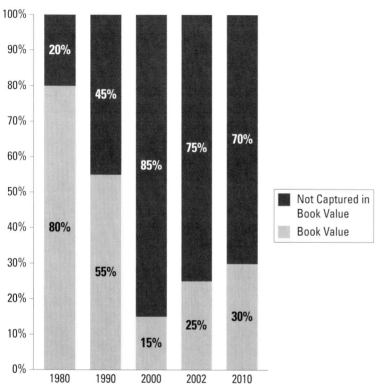

Book Valuation as Part of Total Market Valuation, S&P 500

Source: Data from Compustat, 1980–2010.

■ *Accounting data focus mainly on tangible assets, which are no longer the most important.*[7] Although accounting data capture some intangible assets, such as the value of intellectual property (patents, trademarks, and so on) and customer goodwill, many key intangible assets are not captured. Competitively important assets in the 21st century tend to be intangibles such as innovation and quality, which are not included in a firm's balance sheets. For example, Hyundai's reputation for quality and Honda's core competency in designing highly reliable engines are not balance sheet items.

Indeed, intangibles that are not captured in accounting data such as a firm's reputation for quality and innovation or superior customer service have become much more important in firm stock market valuations over the last few decades. Look at Exhibit 5.6 which shows the firm's book value (accounting data that capture the firm's actual costs of assets minus depreciation) as part of a firm's total stock market valuation (number of outstanding shares times share price). The firm's book value captures the historical cost of a firm's assets, whereas market valuation is based on future expectations for a firm's growth potential and performance. For the firms in the S&P 500, the importance of a firm's book value has declined dramatically over time, while the importance of intangibles that contribute to growth potential and are not captured in a firm's accounting data has increased commensurately (see Exhibit 5.6). In 1980, about 80 percent of a firm's stock market valuation was based on its book value, and 20 percent was based on the market's expectations concerning the firm's future performance. This almost reversed by 2002 (in the aftermath of the Internet bubble), when firm valuations were based only 25 percent on assets captured by accounting data. The important take-away is that intangibles that are not captured in firms' accounting data have become much more important to a firm's competitive advantage (about 70 percent in 2010, for example).

Key financial ratios based on accounting data give us one more tool with which to assess competitive advantage. In particular, they help us measure *relative* profitability, which is useful when comparing firms of different size over time. While not perfect, they are an important starting point when analyzing the competitive performance of firms (and thus are a critical tool for case analysis).

We next turn to *shareholder value creation*, as a third traditional way to measure competitive advantage.

Shareholder Value Creation

Shareholders—individuals or organizations who own one or more shares of stock in a public company—are the legal owners of public companies. From the shareholders' perspective, the measure of competitive advantage that matters most is the return on their risk capital,[8] which is the money they provide in return for an equity share, money that they cannot recover if the firm goes bankrupt. In September 2008, the shareholders of Lehman Brothers, a global financial services firm, lost their entire investment of about $40 billion when the firm declared bankruptcy.

Investors are primarily interested in a company's total return to shareholders, which is the return on risk capital, including stock price appreciation plus dividends received over a specific period. Unlike accounting data, total return to shareholders is an *external* performance metric. It essentially indicates how the stock market views all available information about a firm's past, current state, and expected future performance (with most of the weight on future growth expectations). The idea that all available information about a firm's past, current state, and expected future performance is embedded in the market price of the firm's stock is called the *efficient-market hypothesis*.[9] In this perspective, a firm's share price provides an objective performance indicator.

All public companies in the United States are required to report total return to shareholders annually in the statements they file with the Securities and Exchange Commission (SEC). In addition, companies must also provide benchmarks, usually one comparison to the industry average and another to a broader market index (which is relevant for more diversified firms).[10] Since competitive advantage is defined in relative terms, these benchmarks allow us to assess whether a firm has a competitive advantage. In its annual reports, Microsoft, for example, compares its performance to two stock indices: the NASDAQ computer index and the S&P 500. The computer index includes over 400 high-tech companies traded on the NASDAQ, such as Apple, Dell, Intel, Oracle, and Google. It provides a comparison of Microsoft to the computer industry—broadly defined. The S&P 500 provides a comparison to the wider stock market beyond the computer industry. In its 2010 annual report, Microsoft shows that it *out*performed the S&P 500 over the last five years but *under*performed in comparison to the NASDAQ computer index.[11]

Effective strategies to grow the business can increase a firm's profitability and thus its stock price.[12] Indeed, investors and Wall Street analysts expect continuous growth. A firm's stock price generally increases only if the firm's rate of growth exceeds investors' expectations, because investors discount into the present value of the firm's stock price whatever growth rate they foresee in the future. If a low-growth business like Nucor (in steelmaking) is expected to grow 2 percent each year but realizes 5 percent growth, its stock price will appreciate. In contrast, if a fast-growing business like Dell in the early 2000s is expected to grow by 20 percent annually but delivers "only" 18 percent growth, its stock price will fall.

Investors also adjust their expectations over time. Since the business in the slow-growth industry surprised them by delivering higher than expected growth, they adjust their expectations upward. The next year, they expect this firm to again deliver 5 percent growth. On the other hand, if the industry average is 20 percent a year in the high-tech business, the firm that delivered 18 percent growth will again be expected to deliver at least the industry average growth rate; otherwise, its stock will be further discounted.

In Exhibit 5.5, we compared the performance of four leading pharmaceutical companies (Abbott, Johnson & Johnson, Merck, and Pfizer) based on ROA for the 2004–2009 time period. In Exhibit 5.7 (on next page), we compare the same companies over the same period using as a performance metric *normalized stock returns,* in which we compare the

>> **LO 5-3**
Describe and evaluate shareholder value creation when measuring competitive advantage.

risk capital Capital provided by shareholders in exchange for an equity share in a company; it cannot be recovered if the firm goes bankrupt.

total return to shareholders Return on risk capital that includes stock price appreciation plus dividends received over a specific period.

EXHIBIT 5.7

Normalized Stock
Returns for Abbott,
Johnson & Johnson
(J&J), Merck, and
Pfizer, 2005–2010
(2005 = base year)

Source: Companies' stock
price data.

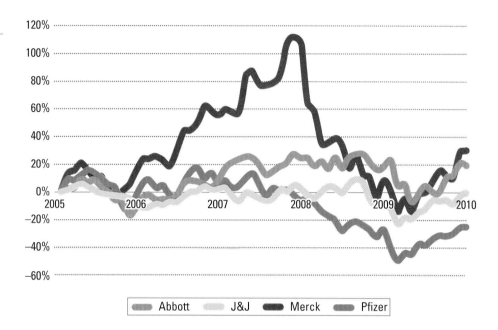

percentage change to a base year. The year 2005 is the base year, and we plot the percentage change in stock appreciation or depreciation over time. The percentages on the vertical axis are percentage changes relative to the 2005 stock price. In contrast to Exhibit 5.5, we now see that Merck had at least a temporary competitive advantage over the other three firms during 2006–2008. Pfizer, on the other hand, appeared to have experienced a competitive disadvantage since 2008, underperforming the other three companies.

Although measuring firm performance through total return to shareholders has many advantages, it is not without problems, as the 2008–2009 global financial crisis made abundantly clear:

■ *Stock prices can be highly volatile, making it difficult to assess firm performance, at least in the short term.* This volatility implies that total return to shareholders is a better measure over the long term due to the "noise" introduced by market volatility, external factors, and investor sentiment.

■ *Overall macroeconomic factors such as the unemployment rate, economic growth or contraction, and interest and exchange rates all have a direct bearing on stock prices.* Thus it can be difficult to ascertain the extent to which a stock price is influenced more by external macroeconomic factors (as discussed in Chapter 3) or the firm's strategy.

■ *Stock prices frequently reflect the psychological mood of investors, which can at times be irrational.* Stock prices can overshoot expectations based on economic fundamentals amidst periods like the Internet boom, during which former Federal Reserve Chairman Alan Greenspan described investors' buoyant sentiments as "irrational exuberance."[13] Similarly, stock prices can undershoot expectations during busts like the 2008–2009 worldwide financial crisis, during which investors' sentiment was described as "irrational gloom."[14]

Assessing Competitive Advantage: Google vs. Microsoft, Continued

GAINING & SUSTAINING COMPETITIVE ADVANTAGE

Using what we've so far learned about measuring competitive advantage, let's continue to look at Google vs. Microsoft, which are becoming more direct competitors (as discussed in ChapterCase 1). Which of the two has competitive advantage? Since we can find good financial data for this purpose, let's focus on assessing the competitive advantage of each in terms of accounting profitability and shareholder value creation.

Since Microsoft is many times larger than Google and thus records a higher net income ($20.6 bn vs. $7.9 bn in 2010) it has a higher ROA and ROE, as shown in Exhibit 5.8. Note, though, that high-tech companies like Google and Microsoft have relatively few tangible assets. This in turn limits the usefulness of accounting profitability when assessing competitive advantage. Key to their performance are intangible assets such as Google's ability to invent proprietary search and data-management algorithms and Microsoft's ability to develop proprietary software code for its Windows operating system. When we compare these two companies on ROA and ROE (as shown in Exhibit 5.8), we can see that Microsoft outperformed Google in 2010. This finding, however, demonstrates the importance of intangible over tangible assets. Both firms rely on intangibles that are not captured in a firm's accounting data for performance.

In ChapterCase 5, we made the argument that Google had at least a temporary competitive advantage over Microsoft, based on the three size-adjusted performance metrics shown in Exhibit 5.1 (revenue per employee; net income per employee; and market cap per employee). Exhibit 5.9 (next page) validates this assessment. It shows the normalized stock price performance of Google, Microsoft, and the NASDAQ-100 index over the 2005–2010 time period. The NASDAQ-100 is an index of the 100 largest nonfinancial companies listed on this U.S. stock exchange. In addition to Google and Microsoft, it includes many other high-tech companies, such as Adobe, Amazon, Apple, Cisco, Dell, Intel, Logitech, and Yahoo. Google outperformed both Microsoft and the NASDAQ-100 by a wide margin, reaching over 250 percent stock price appreciation in 2008 and over 200 percent in 2010 (compared with its 2005 stock price).

Google and Microsoft are direct competitors on only some dimensions, although their competitive overlap in various market segments seems to be increasing. Google is a software company focusing on the information industry; the vast majority of its revenues (approximately 97 percent) stem from online advertising. Microsoft dominates the personal computer world with its Windows operating system and Office application software suite. Google outperformed by a wide margin the NASDAQ-100 (represented by the purple line at the bottom of Exhibit 5.9); Microsoft's stock performance seems to correlate with the NASDAQ-100. When applying shareholder value creation as a yardstick, our conclusion

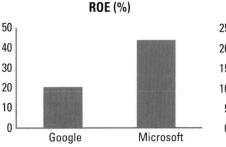

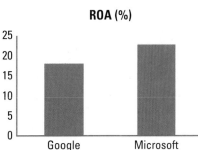

EXHIBIT 5.8

Comparing Google and Microsoft Using Return on Equity (ROE) and Return on Assets (ROA)

Source: Data obtained from companies' SEC filings, as of December 31, 2010.

EXHIBIT 5.9

Normalized Stock
Returns for Google,
Microsoft, and
NASDAQ-100, 2005–
2010 (2005 = Base
Year)

Source: Companies' stock
price data. MSN money,
http://moneycentral.msn.com

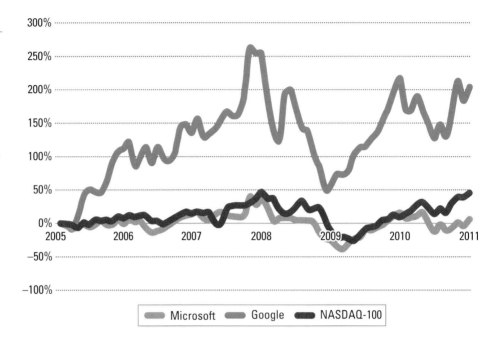

is thus that Google is experiencing a (sustained) competitive advantage, while Microsoft is experiencing a (sustained) competitive disadvantage compared with Google, and competitive parity when compared with the industry average.

You may have noticed that the information/software industry depicted in Exhibit 5.9 appears to be more volatile and to perform at a higher level than the pharmaceutical industry depicted in Exhibit 5.7. At their respective performance peaks, Google reached over 250 percent stock appreciation, while Merck accomplished over 100 percent. As we discussed in Chapters 3 and 4, there are pronounced differences in firm performance not only within the same industry, but also across different industries. 🔍

We've now completed our consideration of the three standard dimensions for measuring competitive advantage—economic value, accounting profitability, and shareholder value. Although each provides unique insights for our assessment of a firm's performance, one drawback is that they are more or less one-dimensional metrics. Focusing on just one performance metric when assessing competitive advantage, however, can lead to significant problems, because each metric has its shortcomings, as listed earlier. We now turn to two conceptual frameworks—the balanced scorecard and the triple bottom line—that attempt to provide a more holistic perspective on firm performance.

THE BALANCED SCORECARD

>> **LO 5-4**

Describe and evaluate
the balanced-scorecard
approach for assessing
competitive advantage.

Just as airplane pilots rely on a number of instruments to provide constant information about key variables such as altitude, airspeed, fuel, position of other airplanes in the vicinity, and destination in order to ensure a safe flight, so should managers rely on multiple yardsticks to more accurately assess company performance in an integrative way. Kaplan and Norton proposed a framework to help managers achieve their strategic objectives more effectively.[15] Called the balanced scorecard, this approach harnesses multiple internal and external performance metrics in order to balance both financial and strategic goals.

Exhibit 5.10 depicts the balanced-scorecard framework. Managers using the balanced scorecard develop strategic objectives and appropriate metrics by answering four key questions that Kaplan and Norton, during a yearlong research project with a number of different companies, identified as the most salient.[16] Brainstorming answers to these questions (ideally) results in a set of measures that give managers a quick but also comprehensive view of the firm's current state. The four key questions are:

EXHIBIT 5.10

A Balanced-Scorecard Approach to Creating and Sustaining Competitive Advantage

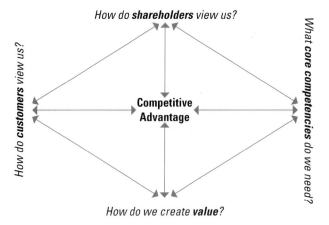

1. *How do customers view us?* The customer's perspective concerning the company's products and services is linked directly to its revenues and profits. The perceived value of a product determines how much the customer is willing to pay for it. The question, "How do customers view us?" is therefore directly linked to how much economic value a firm can create. If the customer views the company favorably, she is willing to pay more for a certain product or service, enhancing its competitive advantage (assuming production costs are well below the asking price).

   To learn how customers view a company's products or services, managers collect data to identify areas to improve, with a focus on speed, quality, service, and cost. In the air-express industry, for example, managers learned from their customers that many don't really need next-day delivery for most of their documents and packages; rather what they really cared about was the ability to track the shipments. This discovery led to the development of steeply discounted 2nd-day delivery by UPS and FedEx, combined with sophisticated online tracking tools.

2. *How do we create value?* Answering this question challenges managers to come up with strategic objectives that ensure future competitiveness, innovation, and organizational learning. It focuses on the business processes and structures that allow a firm to create economic value. One useful metric, for example, is the percentage of revenues obtained from new-product introductions. 3M, for example, requires that 30 percent of revenues must come from products introduced within the last four years.[17] A second metric, aimed at assessing a firm's external learning and collaboration capability, is to stipulate that a certain percentage of new products must originate from outside the firm's boundaries.[18] Through its Connect and Develop program, the consumer products giant Procter & Gamble has raised the percentage of new products that originated (at least partly) from outside P&G, from 15 to 35 percent.[19]

3. *What core competencies do we need?* This question focuses managers internally, to identify the core competencies needed to achieve their objectives, and the accompanying business processes that support, hone, and leverage those competencies. Robert Clarke, former president of performance development at Honda, argues that Honda is at its heart an engine company (not a car company).[20] Beginning with motorcycles in 1948, Honda nurtured this core competency over many decades, and today is leveraging it to reach stretch goals in the design, development, and manufacture of small airplanes.

4. *How do shareholders view us?* The final perspective in the balanced scorecard is the shareholders' view of financial performance. Some of the measures in this area rely on

balanced scorecard Strategy implementation tool that harnesses multiple internal and external performance metrics in order to balance financial and strategic goals.

accounting data such as cash flow, operating income, ROE, and, of course, total returns to shareholders. Understanding the shareholders' view of value creation leads managers to a more future-oriented evaluation.

Taken together, the four balanced-scorecard questions are directly linked to economic value creation: They help managers increase the perceived value of their goods and services in the marketplace. By relying on both an internal and an external view of the firm, the balanced scorecard combines the strengths provided by the individual approaches to assessing competitive advantage discussed earlier: economic value creation, accounting profitability, and shareholder value creation.

Advantages of the Balanced Scorecard

The balanced-scorecard approach is popular in managerial practice because it has several advantages. In particular, the balanced scorecard allows managers to:

- Communicate and link the strategic vision to responsible parties within the organization.
- Translate the vision into measureable operational goals.
- Design and plan business processes.
- Implement feedback and organizational learning in order to modify and adapt strategic goals when indicated.

The balanced scorecard can accommodate both short- and long-term performance metrics. It provides a concise report that tracks chosen metrics and measures and compares them to target values. This approach allows managers to assess past performance, identify areas for improvement, and position the company for future growth. Including a broader perspective than financials allows managers and executives a more balanced view of organizational performance—hence its name. In a sense, the balanced scorecard is a broad diagnostic tool. It complements the common financial metrics with operational measures on customer satisfaction, internal processes, and the company's innovation and improvement activities.

Let's look at FMC Corporation, a chemical manufacturer employing some 5,000 people in different SBUs and earning over $3 billion in annual revenues, as an example of how to implement the balanced-scorecard approach.[21] To achieve its mission of becoming "the customer's most valued supplier," FMC's managers initially had focused solely on financial metrics such as return on capital employed (ROCE) as performance measures. FMC is a multibusiness corporation with several standalone profit-and-loss strategic business units; its overall performance was the result of both over- and underperforming units. FMC's managers had tried several approaches to enhance performance, but they turned out to be more or less ineffective. Perhaps even more significant, short-term thinking by general managers was a major obstacle in the attempt to implement a business strategy.

Searching for improved performance, FMC's CEO decided to adopt a balanced-scorecard approach. It enabled the managers to view FMC's challenges and shortcomings from a holistic, company perspective, which was especially helpful to the general managers of different business units. In particular, the balanced scorecard allowed general managers to focus on market position, customer service, and new-product introductions that could generate long-term value. Using the framework depicted in Exhibit 5.10, general managers had to answer tough follow-up questions such as: How do we become the customer's most valued supplier, and how can my division create this value for the customer? How do we become more externally focused? What are my division's core competencies and contributions to the company goals? What are my division's weaknesses?

Implementing a balanced scorecard allowed FMC's managers to align their different perspective to create a more focused corporation overall. General managers now review progress along the chosen metrics every month, and corporate executives do so on a quarterly basis. Although successful for FMC, implementing a balanced-scorecard approach is not a one-time effort, but requires continuous tracking of metrics and updating of strategic objectives, if needed. It is a continuous process, feeding performance back into the strategy process to assess its effectiveness (see Chapter 2).

Disadvantages of the Balanced Scorecard

Though successfully implemented by many businesses, the balanced scorecard is not without its critics.[22] It is important to note that the balanced scorecard is a tool for *strategy implementation*, and not for *strategy formulation*. It is up to a firm's managers to formulate a strategy that will enhance the chances of gaining and sustaining a competitive advantage. In addition, the balanced-scorecard approach provides only limited guidance about which metrics to choose. Different situations call for different metrics. All of the three approaches to measuring competitive advantage—economic value creation, accounting profitability, and shareholder value creation—in addition to other quantitative and qualitative measures, can be helpful when using a balanced-scorecard approach.

Once the metrics have been selected, the balanced scorecard tracks chosen metrics and measures and compares them to target values. It does not, however, provide much insight into how metrics that deviate from the set goals can be put back on track. Some argue that the balanced scorecard is sometimes seen as not much more than a set of metrics that are tracked over extended periods of time, thus not really providing any new approach.[23]

When implementing a balanced scorecard, managers need to be aware that a failure to achieve competitive advantage is not so much a reflection of a poor framework but of a strategic failure. The balanced scorecard is only as good as the skills of the managers who use it: They first must devise a strategy that enhances the odds of achieving competitive advantage. Second, they must accurately translate the strategy into objectives that they can measure and manage within the balanced-scorecard approach.[24]

THE TRIPLE BOTTOM LINE

In the 21st century, managers are frequently asked to maintain and improve not only the firm's economic performance but also its social and ecological performance. Non-economic factors can have a significant impact on a firm's financial performance, not to mention reputation and goodwill. BP's infamous oil spill in the Gulf of Mexico put the company on the brink of collapse and threatened to destroy fauna and flora along the U.S. shoreline from Texas to Florida, as well as the livelihood of hundreds of thousands of people in the tourism and fishing industries. BP's estimated damages could be as high as $40 billion; the loss of reputation and goodwill is likely to be much higher.[25] Ironically, with an extended moratorium on deepwater drilling and more stringent regulation, the oil industry—especially smaller companies—were also threatened in their survival.

In contrast, being proactive along non-economic dimensions can make good business sense. In anticipation of industry regulation in terms of "extended producer responsibility," which requires the seller of a product to take it back for recycling at the end of the its life, the German carmaker BMW was proactive. It not only lined up the leading car-recycling

>> **LO 5-5**
Describe and evaluate the triple-bottom-line approach when assessing competitive advantage.

EXHIBIT 5.11

The Triple Bottom Line

The simultaneous pursuit of performance along social, economic, and ecological dimensions provides a basis for a sustainable strategy.

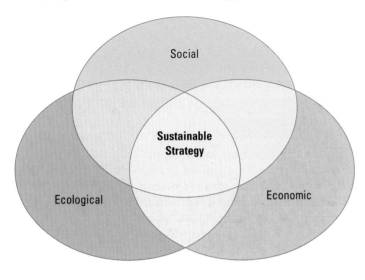

triple bottom line
Combination of economic, social, and ecological concerns that can lead to a sustainable strategy.

companies but also started to redesign its cars using a modular approach. The modular parts allow for quick car disassembly and reuse of components in the after-sales market (so-called "refurbished or rebuilt auto parts").

Three dimensions—*economic, social, and ecological*—make up the triple bottom line. As Exhibit 5.11 suggests, achieving results in all three areas can lead to a sustainable strategy. Like the balanced scorecard, the triple bottom line takes a more integrative and holistic view in assessing a company's performance.[26] Using a triple-bottom-line approach, managers audit their company's fulfillment of its social and ecological obligations to stakeholders such as employees, customers, suppliers, and communities in as serious a way as they track its financial performance.[27] In this sense, the triple-bottom-line framework is related to *stakeholder theory,* an approach to understanding a firm as embedded in a network of internal and external constituencies that each make contributions and expect consideration in return (see discussion in Chapters 1 and 12). For an example of how Interface uses a triple-bottom-line approach to gain and sustain a competitive advantage, read Strategy Highlight 5.1.

Interface: The World's First Sustainable Company

Interface, Inc., is a leader in modular carpeting, with annual sales of roughly $1 billion. What makes the company unique is its strategic intent to become the world's first *fully sustainable* company. In 1994, founder Ray Anderson set a goal for the company to be "off oil" entirely by 2020. That included not using any petroleum-based raw materials or oil-related energy to fuel the manufacturing plants.

According to Collins and Porras in *Built to Last,* their classic study of high-performing companies over long periods of time, this is a "BHAG"—a *big hairy audacious goal.* BHAGs are bold missions declared by visionary companies and are a "powerful mechanism to stimulate progress."[28] Weaning Interface off oil by 2020 is indeed a BHAG. Many see the carpet industry as an extension of the petrochemical industry, given its heavy reliance on

fossil fuels and chemicals in the manufacturing, shipping, and installation of its products.

Today, Interface is a leader in both modular carpet and sustainability. The company estimates that between 1996 and 2008, it saved over $400 million due to its energy efficiency and use of recycled materials. Its business model is changing the carpet industry. Speaking of sustainability as a business model, Mr. Anderson stated in 2009:

> Sustainability has given my company a competitive edge in more ways than one. It has proven to be the most powerful marketplace differentiator I have known in my long career. Our costs are down, our profits are up, and our products are the best they have ever been. Sustainable design has provided an unexpected wellspring of innovation, people are galvanized around a shared higher purpose, better people are applying, the best people are staying and working with a purpose, the goodwill in the marketplace generated by our focus on sustainability far exceeds that which any amount of advertising or marketing expenditure could have generated—this company believes it has found a better way to a bigger and more legitimate profit—a better business model.[29]

IMPLICATIONS FOR THE STRATEGIST

In this chapter, we discussed how to measure competitive advantage using three traditional approaches: economic value creation, accounting profitability, and shareholder value. We then introduced two conceptual frameworks to help us understand competitive advantage in a more holistic fashion: the balanced scorecard and the triple bottom line. Exhibit 5.12 summarizes the concepts we've discussed about how to measure competitive advantage.

>> **LO 5-6**
Compare and contrast different approaches to measuring competitive advantage, and derive managerial implications.

Several managerial implications emerge from our discussion of competitive advantage and firm performance:

■ Both *quantitative and qualitative* performance dimensions matter in judging how effective a firm's strategy is. Those who focus on just one metric risk being blindsided by poor performance on another. Rather, managers need to rely on a more holistic perspective when assessing firm performance, measuring different dimensions over different time periods.

■ Since the goal of strategic management is to integrate and align each business function and activity to obtain superior performance at the company level, competitive advantage is best measured by criteria that reflect *overall company performance* rather than the performance of specific parts. While the functional managers in the marketing department may (and should) care greatly about the success or failure of their recent ad campaign, what the *general* manager cares most about is not specifics at the functional level but performance implications at the firm level. Thus, metrics that aggregate upward and reflect overall firm performance are most useful to assess the effectiveness of a firm's strategy.

■ Since no *best* strategy exists—only *better* ones (better in comparison with others)—we must interpret any performance metric relative to those of competitors and the industry average. True performance can be judged only in comparison to other contenders in the field, not on an absolute basis.

This concludes our discussion of competitive advantage and firm performance and of Part 1 on strategy analysis. In Part 2 of the book, we turn our attention to the topic of strategy formulation. There, in Chapters 6 and 7, we focus on business strategy (*"how to compete"*), and in Chapters 8 and 9 we study corporate strategy (*"where to compete"*). Chapter 10, which concludes Part 2, looks at global strategy (*"where and how to compete around the world"*).

EXHIBIT 5.12

How Do We Measure Competitive Advantage?

Competitive advantage is reflected in superior firm performance.

>> We always assess competitive advantage relative to a benchmark, either using competitors or the industry average.

>> When maintained over time, competitive advantage is *sustainable*.

>> Competitive advantage is a multifaceted concept.

>> We can assess competitive advantage by measuring economic value, accounting profit, or shareholder value.

>> The balanced-scorecard approach harnesses multiple internal and external performance dimensions to balance a firm's financial and strategic goals.

>> More recently, competitive advantage has been linked to a firm's triple bottom line, the ability to maintain performance in the economic, social, and ecological contexts.

CHAPTERCASE 5 | *Consider This . . .*

T WOULD SEEM that Google and Microsoft will be competing in a variety of areas for many years to come. Though they have approached the market from different directions, they are now key competitors in areas such as Internet search, computer applications, and computer operating systems. One particularly interesting area of competition may be in the mobile device operating system. Smartphone shipments, by operating system, for the third quarter of 2010 are shown in the nearby table.[30]

Google's operating system had a strong lead for this time period. However, in November 2010 Microsoft started shipping its Windows Phone 7 operating system. Just 10 weeks later, Microsoft announced it had reached 2 million units. For comparison, when Apple launched the first iPhone in 2007, it sold 1 million units in the first 10 weeks. The Android operating system took six months to reach 1 million units.[31]

U.S. Smartphone Market Shipments by Operating System		
3rd Quarter 2010, Units in millions		
OS Vendor	Units	% share
Android (Google open system)	9.1	43.6
Apple (iPhone)	5.5	26.2
RIM (BlackBerry)	5.1	24.2
Microsoft	0.6	3.0
Others	0.6	3.0
Total	20.9	100.0

Source: Canalys estimates, Canalys 2010.

1. The chapter discusses three perspectives of competitive advantage. If Microsoft is successful in claiming a significant share of the burgeoning smartphone market, will the economic, accounting, or shareholder perspective be affected first? Which firm's performance would be the most affected by this type of market shift?

2. What *qualitative* elements are important for these firms? How would you rate Google and Microsoft on these aspects?

Take-Away Concepts

This chapter demonstrated three traditional approaches for measuring firm performance and competitive advantage and two conceptual frameworks designed to provide a more holistic perspective on firm performance.

LO 5-1 Describe and evaluate economic value creation when measuring competitive advantage.

>> Three components are critical to evaluating any good or service: value (V), price (P), and cost (C). In economics, cost includes opportunity cost.

>> Economic value created is the difference between a buyer's willingness to pay for a good or service and the firm's cost to produce it ($V - C$).

>> A firm has a competitive advantage when it is able to create more economic value than its rivals.

>> To measure firm-level competitive advantage, we estimate the economic value created for all products and services offered by the firm.

LO 5-2 Describe and evaluate accounting profitability when measuring competitive advantage.

>> To measure accounting profitability, we use standard metrics derived from publicly available accounting data.

>> Commonly used profitability metrics in strategic management are return on assets (ROA), return on equity (ROE), return on invested capital (ROIC), and return on revenue (ROR).

>> All accounting data are historical and thus backward-looking. They do not consider off–balance sheet items such as an innovation competency. They focus mainly on tangible assets, which are no longer the most important.

LO 5-3 Describe and evaluate shareholder value creation when measuring competitive advantage.

>> The measure of competitive advantage that matters from the shareholders' perspective is the return on (risk) capital.

>> Investors are primarily interested in total return to shareholders, which includes stock price appreciation plus dividends received over a specific period.

>> Total return to shareholders is an external performance metric; it indicates how the market views all available information about a firm's past, current state, and expected future performance.

>> Stock prices can be highly volatile, which makes it difficult to assess firm performance. Overall macroeconomic factors have a direct bearing on stock prices. Also, stock prices frequently reflect the psychological mood of the investors, which can at times be irrational.

LO 5-4 Describe and evaluate the balanced-scorecard approach for assessing competitive advantage.

>> The balanced-scorecard approach provides a more integrative view of competitive advantage.

>> Its goal is to harness multiple internal and external performance dimensions to balance financial and strategic goals.

>> Managers develop strategic objectives for the balanced scorecard by answering four key questions:

1. How do customers view us?
2. How do we create value?
3. What core competencies do we need?
4. How do shareholders view us?

LO 5-5 Describe and evaluate the triple-bottom-line framework when assessing competitive advantage.

>> Sustainable strategy refers to a firm's ability to maintain its performance in the economic, social, and ecological context—called the triple bottom line.

LO 5-6 Compare and contrast different approaches to measuring competitive advantage, and derive managerial implications.

>> Both quantitative and qualitative criteria matter when assessing the effectiveness of a firm's strategy.

>> Competitive advantage is best measured by criteria that reflect performance of the company overall; the goal of strategic management is to integrate and align each functional-level activity to obtain superior performance at the company level.

>> Any performance metric must be interpreted relative to competitors and the industry average.

Key Terms

Balanced scorecard *(p. 124)*
Consumer surplus *(p. 115)*
Economic value created *(p. 115)*
Opportunity costs *(p. 116)*
Profit (or producer surplus) *(p. 115)*

Risk capital *(p. 121)*
Total return to shareholders *(p. 121)*
Triple bottom line *(p. 128)*
Value *(p. 115)*

Discussion Questions

1. Domino's Pizza was 50 years old in 2010. Visit the company's business-related website (www.dominos-biz.com) and read the company profile under the "Investors" tab. Does the firm focus on the economic, accounting, or shareholder perspective in describing its competitive advantage in the profile?

2. Shareholder perspective is perhaps the most widely employed measure of competitive advantage for publicly traded firms. What are some of the disadvantages of using shareholder value as the sole point of view for defining competitive advantage?

3. Interface, Inc., is discussed in Strategy Highlight 5.1. It may seem unusual for a business-to-business (B2B) carpet company to be using a triple-bottom-line approach for its strategy. What other industries do you think could productively use this approach? How would it change customers' perceptions if it did?

Ethical/Social Issues

1. You work as a supervisor in a manufacturing firm. The company has implemented a balanced-scorecard performance-appraisal system and a financial bonus for exceeding goals. A major customer order for 1,000 units needs to ship to a destination across the country by the end of the quarter, which is two days away from its close. This shipment, if it goes well, will have a major impact on both your customer-satisfaction goals and your financial goals.

   With 990 units built, a machine breaks down. It will take two days to get the parts and repair the machine. You realize there is an opportunity to load the finished units on a truck tomorrow with paperwork for the completed order of 1,000 units. You can have an employee fly out with the 10 remaining parts and meet the truck at the destination city once the machinery has been repaired. The 10 units can be added to the pallet and delivered as a complete shipment of 1,000 pieces, matching the customer's order and your paperwork. What do you do?

2. The chapter mentions that accounting data do not consider off–balance sheet items. A retailer that owns its stores will list the value of that property as an asset, for example, while a firm that leases its stores will not. What are some of the accounting and shareholder advantages of leasing compared to owning retail locations?

3. How does this issue play out when comparing brick-and-mortar stores to online businesses (e.g., Best Buy versus Amazon; Barnes & Noble versus Amazon; Blockerbuster versus Netflix)? What conclusions do you draw?

Small Group Exercises

SMALL GROUP EXERCISE 1

As discussed in the chapter, a balanced scorecard views the performance of an organization through four lenses: customer, innovation and learning, internal business, and financial. According to surveys from Bain & Company (a consulting firm), in recent years about 60 percent of firms in both public and private sectors have used a balanced scorecard for performance measures. (See www.thepalladiumgroup.com for examples.)

With your group, create a balanced scorecard for the business school at your university. You might start by looking at your school's web page for a mission or vision statement. Then divide up the four perspectives among the team members to develop some key elements for each one. It may be helpful to remember the four key balanced-scorecard questions from the chapter:

1. How do customers view us? (Hint: First discuss the following: Who are the customers? The students? The companies that hire students? Others?)

2. How do we create value?

3. What core competencies do we need?

4. How do shareholders view us? (For public universities, the shareholders are the taxpayers who invest their taxes into the university. For private universities, the shareholders are the people or organizations that endow the university.)

SMALL GROUP EXERCISE 2

In the electronics retail industry, Circuit City filed for bankruptcy in the spring of 2009, but Best Buy continues on. (See ChapterCase 4, page 85) Financial data for Best Buy and Circuit City are provided in the table on the next page.

Using the financial ratios presented in Table 1 in the "How to Conduct a Case Analysis" module (at the end of the book, p. 390):

1. Calculate some of the key profitability, activity, leverage, liquidity, and market ratios for Best Buy and Circuit City.

2. Can you find signs of performance differentials between these two firms that may have indicated problems at Circuit City in 2007?

Key Financial Data for Best Buy and Circuit City

In Millions of US$ (except for per share items)	Best Buy Y/E Mar. 2008	Best Buy Y/E Mar. 2007	Circuit City Y/E Mar. 2008	Circuit City Y/E Mar. 2007
Total revenue	40,023.00	35,934.00	11,743.69	12,429.75
Cost of revenue, total	30,477.00	27,165.00	9,318.17	9,501.44
Gross profit	9,546.00	8,769.00	2,425.52	2,928.32
Selling/general/admin. expenses, total	7,385.00	6,770.00	2,770.10	2,841.62
Total operating expense	37,862.00	33,935.00	12,097.27	12,409.43
Operating income	2,161.00	1,999.00	−353.58	20.33
Income before tax	2,228.00	2,130.00	−353.58	20.33
Income after tax	1,413.00	1,378.00	−321.35	−10.18
Net income	1,407.00	1,377.00	−319.9	−8.28
Diluted weighted average shares	452.9	496.2	165.13	170.45
Dividends per share – common stock	0.46	0.36	0.16	0.12
Diluted normalized EPS	3.12	2.79	−1.69	0.83
Cash and equivalents	1,438.00	1,205.00	296.06	141.14
Short-term investments	64	2,588.00	1.37	598.34
Cash and short-term investments	1,502.00	3,793.00	297.42	739.48
Accounts receivable – trade, net	549	548	330.6	382.56
Total receivables, net	549	548	488.71	425.28
Total inventory	4,708.00	4,028.00	1,573.56	1,636.51
Total current assets	7,342.00	9,081.00	2,439.72	2,883.51
Property/plant/equipment, total – gross	5,608.00	4,904.00	2,485.60	2,221.33
Accumulated depreciation, total	−2,302.00	−1,966.00	−1,448.28	−1,300.30
Goodwill, net	1,088.00	919	118.03	121.77
Intangibles, net	102	81	18.4	19.29
Long-term investments	605	318	–	–
Other long-term assets, total	315	233	132.46	61.69
Total assets	12,758.00	13,570.00	3,745.93	4,007.28
Accounts payable	4,297.00	3,934.00	912.09	922.21
Accrued expenses	1,348.00	1,322.00	317.51	380.22
Other current liabilities, total	935	985	364.5	404.44
Total current liabilities	6,769.00	6,301.00	1,605.69	1,714.03
Total long-term debt	627	590	57.05	50.49
Total debt	816	650	68.63	57.65
Other liabilities, total	838	443	544.43	451.52
Total liabilities	8,274.00	7,369.00	2,242.76	2,216.04
Common stock, total	41	48	84.43	85.34
Additional paid-in capital	8	430	319.57	344.14
Retained earnings (accumulated deficit)	3,933.00	5,507.00	981.11	1,336.32
Total equity	4,484.00	6,201.00	1,503.17	1,791.24
Total liabilities and shareholders' equity	12,758.00	13,570.00	3,745.93	4,007.28
Total common shares outstanding	410.58	480.65	168.86	170.69

Strategy Term Project

MODULE 5: COMPETITIVE ADVANTAGE PERSPECTIVES

1. Based on information in the annual reports or published on the firm's website, summarize what the firm views as the reasons for its successes (either past or expected in the future). Search for both quantitative and qualitative success factors provided in the report.

2. Does the firm seem most focused on the economic, accounting, or shareholder perspective of its competitive advantage? Give quotes or information from these sources to support your view.

3. Many firms are now including annual corporate social responsibility (CSR) reports on their websites. See whether your firm does so. If it does not, are there other indications of a triple-bottom-line approach, including social and ecological elements, in the firm's strategies?

*my*Strategy

HOW MUCH IS AN MBA WORTH TO YOU?

The *my*Strategy box at the end of Chapter 2 asked how much you would be willing to pay for the job you want—for a job that reflects your values. Here, we look at a different issue relating to worth: How much is an MBA worth over the course of your career?

Alongside the traditional two-year full-time MBA program, many business schools also offer evening MBAs and executive MBAs. Let's assume you know you want to pursue an advanced degree, and you need to decide which program format is better for you (or you want to evaluate the choice you already made). You've narrowed your options to either (1) a two-year full-time MBA program, or (2) an executive MBA program at the same institution that is 18 months long with classes every other weekend. Let's also assume the price for tuition, books, and fees is $30,000 for the full-time program and $90,000 for the executive MBA program.

Which MBA program should you choose? Consider in your analysis the value, price, and cost concepts discussed in this chapter. Pay special attention to opportunity costs attached to different MBA program options.

Endnotes

1. This debate takes place in the following discourses, among others: Schmalensee, R. (1985), "Do markets differ much?" *American Economic Review* 75: 341–351; Rumelt, R. P. (1991), "How much does industry matter?" *Strategic Management Journal* 12: 167–185; Rumelt, R. P. (2003), "What in the world is competitive advantage?" *Policy Working Paper 2003-105*, UCLA; Porter, M. E. (1985), *Competitive Advantage: Creating and Sustaining Superior Performance* (New York: Free Press); McGahan, A. M., and M. E. Porter (1997), "How much does industry matter, really?" *Strategic Management Journal* 18: 15–30; McGahan A. M., and M. E. Porter (2002), "What do we know about variance in accounting profitability?" *Management Science* 48: 834–851; Hawawini, G., V. Subramanian, and P. Verdin (2003), "Is performance driven by industry-or firm-specific factors? A new look at the evidence," *Strategic Management Journal* 24: 1–16; McNamara, G., F. Aime, and P. Vaaler (2005), "Is performance driven by industry- or firm-specific factors? A reply to Hawawini, Subramanian, and Verdin," *Strategic Management Journal* 26: 1075–1081; Hawawini, G., V. Subramanian, and P. Verdin (2005), "Is performance driven by industry-or firm-specific factors? A new look at the evidence: A response to McNamara, Aime, and Vaaler," *Strategic Management Journal* 26: 1083–1086; and Misangyi, V. F., H. Elms, T. Greckhamer, and J. A. Lepine (2006), "A new perspective on a fundamental debate: A multi-level approach to industry, corporate, and business unit effects," *Strategic Management Journal* 27: 571–590.

2. Rumelt, R. P. (2003), "What in the world is competitive advantage?"

3. For a discussion see: McGahan, A. M., and M. E. Porter (2002), "What do

we know about variance in accounting profitability?"

4. "The term 'generally accepted accounting principles' has a specific meaning for accountants and auditors. The AICPA Code of Professional Conduct prohibits members from expressing an opinion or stating affirmatively that financial statements or other financial data 'present fairly . . . in conformity with generally accepted accounting principles,' if such information contains any departures from accounting principles promulgated by a body designated by the AICPA Council to establish such principles." Source: www.fasb.gov.

5. All listed companies on U.S. stock exchanges must file periodic reports with the SEC, which in turn makes them publicly available at their website, http://www.sec.gov/edgar.shtml. These reports are a treasure trove for your strategy term project, case analyses, and other tasks.

6. Hamel, G., and C. K. Prahalad (1994), *Competing for the Future* (Boston, MA: Harvard Business School Press).

7. Baruch, L. (2001), *Intangibles: Management, Measurement, and Reporting* (Washington, DC: Brookings Institution Press).

8. Friedman, M. (2002), *Capitalism and Freedom,* 40th anniversary edition (Chicago, IL: University of Chicago Press).

9. Fama, E. (1970), "Efficient capital markets: A review of theory and empirical work," *Journal of Finance* 25: 383–417; Beechy, M., D. Gruen, and J. Vickrey (2000), "The efficient market hypothesis:" A survey Research Discussion Paper, Federal Reserve Bank of Australia.

10. Alexander, J. (2007), *Performance Dashboards and Analysis for Value Creation* (Hoboken, NJ: Wiley-Interscience).

11. In its 2010 annual report, Microsoft provides the following comparison: Over a five-year period (June 2005–June 2010), $100 invested in (1) Microsoft stock would have grown to $100.77; in (2) the S&P 500, it would have been worth $96.09; in (3) the NASDAQ index, composed primarily of computer-related companies, it would have grown to $119.38. While outperforming the wider market, Microsoft significantly underperformed when compared to the broader computer industry. Source: Microsoft 2010 Annual Report, www.microsoft.com/investor/reports/ar10/10k_dl_dow.html.

12. This section draws on: Christensen, C. M, and M. E. Raynor (2003), *The Innovator's Solution: Creating and Sustaining Successful Growth* (Boston, MA: Harvard Business School Press).

13. Speech given by Alan Greenspan on December 5, 1996, at the American Enterprise Institute.

14. "Irrational gloom," *The Economist,* October 11, 2002.

15. Kaplan, R. S., and D. P. Norton (1992), "The balanced scorecard: Measures that drive performance," *Harvard Business Review,* January–February: 71–79.

16. Ibid.

17. Govindarajan, V., and J. B. Lang (2002), *3M Corporation,* case study, Tuck School of Business at Dartmouth.

18. Rothaermel, F. T., and A. M. Hess (2010), "Innovation strategies combined," *MIT Sloan Management Review,* Spring: 12–15.

19. Huston, L., and N. Sakkab (2006), "Connect & Develop: Inside Procter & Gamble's new model for innovation," *Harvard Business Review,* March: 58–66.

20. Clarke, R. (2009), "Failure: The secret to success," at http://dreams.honda.com/#/video_fa; and see also: Prahalad, C. K., and G. Hamel (1990), "The core competence of the corporation," *Harvard Business Review,* May–June.

21. Kaplan, R. S. (1993), "Implementing the balanced scorecard at FMC Corporation: An interview with Larry D. Brady," *Harvard Business Review,* September–October: 143–147.

22. Norreklit, H. (2000), "The balance on the balanced scorecard — a critical analysis of some of its assumptions," *Management Accounting Research* 11: 65–88; Jensen, M. C. (2002), "Value Maximization, Stakeholder Theory, and the Corporate Objective Function," in *Unfolding Stakeholder Thinking* Andriof, J., et al. (eds.), (Sheffield, UK: Greenleaf Publishing).

23. Lawrie, G., and I. Cobbold (2002), "Development of the 3rd generation balanced scorecard: Evolution of the balanced scorecard into an effective strategic performance management tool," 2GC Working Paper, 2GC Limited, Albany House, Market Street, Maidenhead, Berkshire, SL6 8BE UK.

24. Kaplan, R. S., and D. P. Norton (1992), "The balanced scorecard: Measures that drive performance"; Kaplan, R. S., and D. P. Norton (2007), "Using the balanced scorecard as a strategic management system," *Harvard Business Review,* July–August.

25. "After the leak. The gusher in the gulf may soon be sealed. BP's woes will be harder to cap," *The Economist,* July 22, 2010; and "BP's spill costs look manageable 8 months later," *Associated Press,* December 29, 2010.

26. Anderson, R. C. (2009), *Confessions of a Radical Industrialist: Profits, People, Purpose—Doing Business by Respecting the Earth* (New York: St. Martin's Press).

27. Norman, W., and C. MacDonald (2004), "Getting to the bottom of 'triple bottom line reads: line,'" *Business Ethics Quarterly* 14: 243–262.

28. Collins, J. C., and J. I. Porras (1994), *Built to Last: Successful Habits of Visionary Companies* (New York: HarperBusiness), p. 93.

29. Anderson, R. C. (2009), *Confessions of a Radical Industrialist,* p. 5; TED talk, "Ray Anderson on the business logic of sustainability," www.ted.com; and Perkins, J. (2009), *Hoodwinked: An Economic Hit Man Reveals Why the World Financial Markets Imploded—and What We Need to Do to Remake Them* (New York: Crown Business), p. 107.

30. Bilton, N. (2010), "The race to dominate the smartphone market," *The New York Times,* November 1, 2010.

31. Hardy, E. (2011), "Microsoft has sold more than two million Windows Phone 7 devices," January 27, 2011, www.brighthand.com.

Analysis: Getting Started
1. What Is Strategy and Why Is It Important?
2. The Strategic Management Process

External and Internal Analysis
3. External Analysis: Industry Structure, Competitive Forces, and Strategic Groups
4. Internal Analysis: Resources, Capabilities, and Activities
5. Competitive Advantage and Firm Performance

Implementation
11. Organizational Design: Structure, Culture, and Control
12. Corporate Governance, Business Ethics, and Strategic Leadership

GAINING & SUSTAINING COMPETITIVE ADVANTAGE

Formulation: Corporate Strategy
8. Corporate Strategy: Vertical Integration and Diversification
9. Corporate Strategy: Acquisitions, Alliances, and Networks
10. Global Strategy: Competing Around the World

PART 2

Formulation: Business Strategy
6. Business Strategy: Differentiation, Cost Leadership, and Integration
7. Business Strategy: Innovation and Strategic Entrepreneurship

PART 2

PART 2
Strategy Formulation

CHAPTER 6

Business Strategy: Differentiation, Cost Leadership, and Integration

LEARNING OBJECTIVES
After studying this chapter, you should be able to:

LO 6-1   Define business-level strategy and describe how it determines a firm's strategic position.

LO 6-2   Examine the relationship between value drivers and differentiation strategy.

LO 6-3   Examine the relationship between cost drivers and cost-leadership strategy.

LO 6-4   Assess the benefits and risks of cost-leadership and differentiation business strategies vis-à-vis the five forces that shape competition.

LO 6-5   Explain why it is difficult to succeed at an integration strategy.

LO 6-6   Evaluate value and cost drivers that may allow a firm to pursue an integration strategy.

LO 6-7   Describe and evaluate the dynamics of competitive positioning.

Trimming Fat at Whole Foods Market

WHEN FOUR YOUNG ENTREPRENEURS opened a small natural-foods store in Austin, Texas, in 1980, they never imagined it would one day turn into an international supermarket chain with stores in the United States, Canada, and the United Kingdom. Thirty years later, with the acquisition of a close competitor, Wild Oats, Whole Foods now has over 300 stores, employs some 60,000 people, and earned $10 billion in revenue in 2010. Its mission is to offer the finest natural and organic foods available, maintain the highest quality standards in the grocery industry, and remain firmly committed to sustainable agriculture. Clearly, the customers the company wanted to serve were ready for Whole Foods!

Whole Foods is a high-end grocery store. In addition to natural and organic foods, it also offers a wide variety of prepared foods and luxury food items, such as $400 bottles of wine. The decision to sell high-ticket items incurs higher costs for the company because such products require more expensive in-store displays and more highly skilled workers, and many fresh items require high turnover. In order to delight its customers with a superior shopping experience, Whole Foods has developed an innovative human resource program, which focuses on happy employees, continuing education, and self-directed teams. Whole Foods has been included in *Fortune*'s list of the "Best Companies to Work For" every year

of its existence. Whole Foods is also active in a number of social causes, donating 5 percent of its net profits to charities every year.

Given its unique strategic position as an upscale grocer offering natural, organic, and luxury food items, Whole Foods enjoyed a competitive advantage during the economic boom through early 2008. But as consumers became more budget conscious during the recession of 2008–2009, the company's financial performance deteriorated. Competitive intensity also increased markedly because basically every supermarket chain now offers organic food.

To revitalize Whole Foods, co-founder and CEO John Mackey decided to "trim fat" on two fronts: First, the supermarket chain refocused on its mission to offer wholesome and healthy food options. In Mackey's words, Whole Foods had been selling "a bunch of junk," including candy. Mackey is passionate about helping U.S. consumers overcome obesity in order to help reduce heart disease and diabetes. Given that, the new strategic intent at Whole Foods is to become the champion of healthy living not only by offering natural and organic food choices, but also by educating consumers with its new Healthy Eating initiative. Whole Foods Market now has "Take Action Centers" in every story to educate customers on many food-related topics like genetic engineering, organic foods, pesticides, and sustainable agriculture.

Second, Whole Foods will trim fat by reducing costs. For example, it has expanded its private-label product line by 5 percent; it now includes over 2,300 products at lower prices. Moreover, to attract more customers who buy groceries for an entire family or group, Whole Foods now offers volume discounts to compete with Costco, the largest membership club chain in the U.S. To offer its private-label line and volume-discount packages, Whole Foods needs to rely more on low-cost suppliers and enhance its logistics system to cover larger geographic areas more efficiently. It remains to be seen if Whole Foods can increase the value gap by improving its differentiated appeal that allows it to command premium prices, while keeping its cost structure in check at the same time.[1]

After reading the chapter, you will find more about this case, with related questions, on page 163.

▲ **THE WHOLE FOODS STORY** raises a number of interesting issues that we will address in this chapter. At the business level, Whole Foods differentiates itself from competitors by offering top-quality foods obtained through sustainable agriculture. This strategy implies that Whole Foods focuses on increasing the perceived value created for customers, which allows it to charge a premium price. This strategy proved successful initially. Over time, though, in response to both changing external and internal factors, the strategy needed to be fine-tuned to fit the changing environment. Whole Foods needed to take a fresh look at reinvigorating its business-level strategy in order to better serve its particular market and strengthen its competitive position.

The first strategic initiative featured in the ChapterCase—becoming the champion of healthy living—therefore aims at further enhancing its differentiated appeal. Whole Foods needs to staff its education centers with higher-qualified personnel than found in other grocery stores, but this in turn drives up its cost structure. To reduce pressure on the profit margin, Whole Foods's CEO John Mackey knows that he must control the company's cost structure, which is higher than that of other grocers and has been rising. Whole Foods Market also is attempting to improve its logistics capabilities in order to offer private-label and large packages at a profit. The expectation is that the strategic initiatives featured in the ChapterCase will enhance Whole Foods's strategic profile, and thus help it regain its competitive advantage.

This chapter, the first in Part 2 on strategy formulation, takes a close look at business-level strategy and how to compete for advantage.

BUSINESS-LEVEL STRATEGY: HOW TO COMPETE FOR ADVANTAGE

>> **LO 6-1**
Define business-level strategy and describe how it determines a firm's strategic position.

Business-level strategy details the actions managers take in their quest for competitive advantage when competing in a single product market.[2] It may involve a single product or a group of very similar products that use the same channel. It concerns the broad question, "How should we compete?" To formulate an appropriate business-level strategy, managers must answer the "who-what-why-and-how" questions of competition:

- *Who*—which customer segments—will we serve?
- *What* customer needs, wishes, and desires will we satisfy?
- *Why* do we want to satisfy them?
- *How* will we satisfy our customers' needs?[3]

To formulate an effective business strategy, managers need to keep in mind that a firm's competitive advantage is determined jointly by industry characteristics and firm characteristics (see Exhibit 6.1). The more attractive an industry is, the more profitable it is. As discussed in Chapter 3 industry attractiveness can be assessed using the structure-conduct-performance (SCP) framework and the five forces model plus the availability of

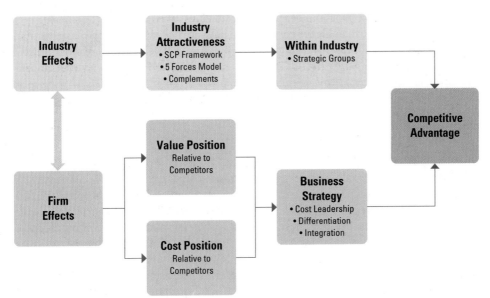

EXHIBIT 6.1

Industry and Firm
Effects Jointly
Determine Competitive
Advantage

complements. Managers need to be certain that the business strategy is aligned with the five forces that shape competition. They can evaluate performance differences among clusters of firms in the same industry by conducting a strategic-group analysis. The concepts introduced in Chapter 4 allow us to look inside firms and explain why they differ based on their resources, capabilities, and activities.

At the firm level, performance is determined by value and cost positions relative to competitors. Whole Foods, as the leading supermarket chain of natural and organic foods, has a strong value position in comparison to its competitors. On the other hand, its relative cost position is weaker due to its higher cost structure, thereby reducing its ability to compete solely on price.

Strategic Position

We noted (in Chapter 5) that a firm's competitive advantage is based on the difference between the *perceived value* a firm is able to create for consumers (V), captured by how much consumers are willing to pay for a product or service, and the total cost (C) the firm incurs to create that value. The greater the economic value created ($V - C$), the greater the firm's competitive advantage. Therefore, to answer the business-level strategy question of how to compete, managers have two primary competitive levers at their disposal: value (V) and cost (C).

A firm's business-level strategy determines its strategic position—its strategic profile based on value creation and cost—in a specific product market. A firm stakes out a valuable and unique position that allows it to meet customer needs while creating as large a gap as possible between the value the firm's product creates and the cost required to produce it. Higher value tends to require higher cost. Thus, to achieve a desired strategic position, managers must make strategic trade-offs—situations that require choosing

---

business-level strategy The actions managers take in their quest for competitive advantage when competing in a single product market.

strategic position A firm's strategic profile based on value creation and cost. The goal is to create as large a gap as possible between the value the firm's product or service creates and the cost required to produce it ($V - C$).

strategic trade-offs Situations that require choosing between a cost or value position, necessary because higher value tends to require higher cost.

between a cost or value position. Managers must address the tension between value creation (which tends to lead to higher cost) and the pressure to keep cost in check so as not to erode the firm's economic value creation. (The difference between value creation and cost is sometimes called the *value gap.*) A business strategy is more likely to lead to a competitive advantage if it allows firms to either *perform similar activities differently,* or *perform different activities* than their rivals that result in creating more value or offering similar products or services at lower cost.[4]

Generic Business Strategies

There are two fundamentally different generic business strategies—*differentiation* and *cost leadership.* A differentiation strategy seeks to create higher value for customers than the value that competitors create, by delivering products or services with unique features while keeping cost at the same or similar levels. A cost-leadership strategy, in contrast, seeks to create the same or similar value for customers by delivering products or services at a lower cost than competitors, enabling the firm to offer lower prices to its customers.

These two strategies are called *generic strategies* because they can be used by any organization—manufacturing or service, large or small, for-profit or not-for-profit, public or private, U.S. or non-U.S.—in the quest for competitive advantage, independent of industry context. Differentiation and cost leadership require distinct strategic positions in order to increase a firm's chances to gain and sustain a competitive advantage.[5] Because value creation and cost tend to be positively correlated, there exist important trade-offs between value creation and low cost.

Different generic strategies can lead to competitive advantage, even in the *same industry.* For example, Rolex and Timex both compete in the market for wristwatches, yet they follow different business strategies. Rolex follows a differentiation strategy: It creates a higher value for its watches by making higher-quality timepieces with unique features that last a lifetime and that bestow a perception of prestige and status upon their owners. Customers are willing to pay a premium for these attributes. Timex, in contrast, follows a cost-leadership strategy: It uses lower cost inputs and efficiently produces a wristwatch of acceptable quality, highlights reliability and accuracy, and prices its timepieces at the low end of the market. The issue is not to compare Rolex and Timex directly—they compete in different market segments of the wristwatch industry. Both can achieve a competitive advantage using diametrically opposed business strategies. Rather, the idea is to compare Rolex's strategic position with the next-best differentiator (e.g., Ebel), and Timex's strategic position with the next-best low-cost producer (e.g., Swatch).

When considering different business strategies, managers also must define the scope of competition—whether to pursue a specific, narrow part of the market or go after the broader market.[6] In the preceding example, Rolex focuses on a small market segment: affluent consumers who want to present a certain image. Timex offers watches for many different segments of the mass market.

Now we can combine the dimensions describing a firm's strategic position (*differentiation vs. cost*) with the scope of competition (*narrow vs. broad*). As shown in Exhibit 6.2, by doing so we get the two major generic (or broad) business strategies (*cost leadership* and *differentiation*), shown as the top two boxes in the matrix, and what are termed the *focused* version of each (shown as the bottom two boxes in the matrix). The focused versions of the strategies—focused cost-leadership strategy and focused differentiation strategy—are essentially the same as the broad generic strategies *except* that the competitive scope is narrower. The manufacturing company BIC pursues a focused cost-leadership strategy, offering disposable pens and cigarette lighters at a very low price (often free promotional give-aways by companies), while La Fraicheur pursues a focused differentiation strategy, offering exquisite luxury wine coolers priced at up to 100,000 euros a piece.

The automobile industry provides an example of the *scope of competition.* Alfred P. Sloan, long-time president and CEO of GM, defined the carmaker's mission as providing *a car for every purse and purpose.* GM was one of the first to implement a multidivisional structure in order to separate the brands into divisions, allowing each brand to create its unique strategic position within the broad automotive market. The position varies even with a brand. For example, the current Chevy product lineup ranges from the low-cost-positioned Aveo, starting at a price of about $12,000, to the highly differentiated Cadillac Escalade SUV priced at roughly $70,000.

Tesla Motors, maker of electric cars, offers a highly differentiated product and pursues only a small market segment. It pursues a *focused differentiation strategy.* Currently, Tesla focuses on well-heeled, environmentally conscious consumers. It offers its Roadster for a base price of about $110,000, and in 2012 is planning to launch the Model S—a four-door sedan. With only those two products, the company does not plan to sell more than 20,000 vehicles a year,[7] equal to less than 0.20 percent U.S. market share of auto sales. Tesla Motors is pursuing a focused-differentiation strategy, focusing on a narrow market segment of customers who are willing to pay a premium price.

EXHIBIT 6.2

Strategic Position and Competitive Scope: Generic Business Strategies

Source: Adapted from M. E. Porter (1980), *Competitive Strategy. Techniques for Analyzing Industries and Competitors* (New York: Free Press).

DIFFERENTIATION STRATEGY: UNDERSTANDING VALUE DRIVERS

The goal of a generic differentiation strategy is to add unique features that will increase the perceived value of goods and services in the minds of the consumers so they are willing to pay a higher price. Ideally, a firm following a differentiation strategy aims to achieve in the minds of consumers a level of value creation that its competitors cannot easily match. The focus of competition in a differentiation strategy tends to be on unique product features, service, and new product launches, or on marketing and promotion rather than price. For example, the carpet company Interface is a leader in sustainability and offers innovative products such as its Cool Carpet, the world's first carbon-neutral floor covering.

>> **LO 6-2**
Examine the relationship between value drivers and differentiation strategy.

differentiation strategy Generic business strategy that seeks to create higher value for customers than the value that competitors create, by delivering products or services with unique features while keeping the firm's cost structure at the same or similar levels.

cost-leadership strategy Generic business strategy that seeks to create the

same or similar value for customers by delivering products or services at a lower cost than competitors, enabling the firm to offer lower prices to its customers.

scope of competition The size—narrow or broad—of the market in which a firm chooses to compete.

focused cost-leadership strategy Same as the cost-leadership strategy except with a narrow focus on a niche market

focused differentiation strategy Same as the differentiation strategy except with a narrow focus on a niche market.

Interface's customers reward it with a willingness to pay a higher price for its environmentally friendly products.[8]

A company that uses a differentiation strategy can achieve a competitive advantage as long as its economic value created $(V - C)$ is greater than that of its competitors. Panel (a) in Exhibit 6.3 shows that firm B, a differentiator, achieves a competitive advantage over firm A. Firm B not only offers greater value than firm A, but also achieves *cost parity* (meaning it has the same costs as firm A). However, even if firm B fails to achieve cost parity (which is often the case since higher value tends to go along with higher costs in terms of higher-quality raw materials, research and development, employee training to provide superior customer service, and so on), it can still gain a competitive advantage if its economic value creation exceeds that of its competitors. This situation is depicted in Panel (b) of Exhibit 6.3. In both situations, firm B's economic value creation, $(V - C)_B$, is greater than that of firm A $(V - C)_A$. Firm B, therefore, achieves a competitive advantage because it can charge a premium price, reflecting its higher value creation.

Although increased value creation is a defining feature of a differentiation strategy, managers must also control cost. If cost rises too much as the firm creates more value, the value gap shrinks, negating any differentiation advantage. Rising costs have lowered Starbucks's profitability in recent years, for example. To combat a squeeze on margins, Starbucks's managers are now applying lean manufacturing techniques to streamline processes and lower the firm's cost structure.[9]

Although a differentiation strategy is generally associated with premium pricing, managers have an important second pricing option. When a firm is able to offer a differentiated product or service and can control its costs at the same time, it is able to gain market share from other firms by charging a similar price but offering more perceived value. By leveraging its differentiated appeal of superior customer service and quality in delivery, for example, Marriott offers a line of different hotels, such as its flagship Marriott full-service business hotel equipped to host large conferences, Residence Inn for extended stay, Marriott Courtyard for business travelers, and Marriott Fairfield Inn for inexpensive leisure and family travel.[10] Although these hotels are roughly comparable to competitors in price, they generally offer a higher perceived value. This difference between price and value allows Marriott to gain market share and post superior performance.

EXHIBIT 6.3

Differentiation Strategy: Achieving Competitive Advantage

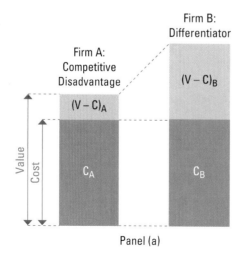

Panel (a)

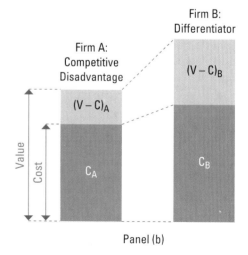

Panel (b)

Value Drivers

Managers can adjust a number of different levers to improve a firm's strategic position. These levers either increase perceived value or decrease costs. Here, we will study the most salient *value drivers* that managers have at their disposal.[11] They are:

- Product features
- Customer service
- Customization
- Complements

These value drivers are related to a firm's expertise in and organization of different internal value chain activities (a concept first introduced in Chapter 4). Although these are the most important value drivers, no such list can be complete. Applying the concepts introduced in this chapter should allow managers to identify other important value and cost drivers unique to their business.

When attempting to increase the perceived value of the firm's product or service offerings, managers must remember that the different value drivers contribute to competitive advantage *only if* their increase in value creation (ΔV) exceeds the increase in costs (ΔC). The condition of $\Delta V > \Delta C$ must be fulfilled if a differentiation strategy is to strengthen a firm's strategic position and thus enhance its competitive advantage.

PRODUCT FEATURES. One of the obvious but most important levers that managers can adjust are the product features and attributes, thereby increasing the perceived value of the product or service offering. For example, a BMW M3 comes with many more performance features than a Honda Accord. Adding unique product features allows firms to turn commodity products into differentiated products that command a premium price. By following its *philosophy of making products that are easy to use for the widest spectrum of possible users,*[12] OXO differentiates its kitchen utensils through its patent-protected ergonomically designed soft black rubber grips.

CUSTOMER SERVICE. Managers can increase the perceived value of their firms' product or service offerings by focusing on customer service and responsiveness. For example, the online retailer Zappos earned a reputation for superior customer service by offering free shipping both ways: to the customer and for returns.[13] Zappos's managers didn't view this as an additional expense but rather as part of their marketing budget. There seemed to be a good return on investment as word spread through the online shopping community. Competitors took notice, too: In the summer of 2009, Amazon bought Zappos for over $1 billion.[14]

The hotel industry provides a second example of superior customer service. Following its credo, "We are Ladies and Gentlemen serving Ladies and Gentlemen," the Ritz-Carlton has become one of the world's leaders in providing a personalized customer experience based on sophisticated analysis of data gathered about each guest, including past choices. It offers personalized customer service that few hotel chains can match.

L. L. Bean was founded in 1912 to sell the waterproof "Maine Hunting Shoe"®—a unique product that came with a guarantee of 100 percent satisfaction. The company built its business on superior customer service and customer satisfaction. Today, L. L. Bean's policy of "Shipped for Free. Guaranteed to Last." continues to focus on these strengths.

To excel at customer service, managers must be able to identify unmet customer needs and find ways to satisfy them or exceed customer expectations. As discussed in Strategy Highlight 6.1 (next page), the creation of Toyota's luxury brand Lexus illustrates how superior customer service can increase perceived product value.

Toyota: From "Perfect Recall" to "Recall Nightmare"

When Toyota launched its Lexus brand in 1989, it faced a steep uphill battle. The luxury car segment was dominated by Mercedes-Benz, which combined high performance with style and cutting-edge engineering. Other strong players in the luxury car segment included BMW and Cadillac.

Lexus needed a perfect launch of its new line of luxury vehicles to stand a chance against the strong competitors in the market. Yet its LS400 line required a recall a little more than a year after launch. Lexus's initial quality problems could have spelled an early doom for the new brand, whose slogan is "The Relentless Pursuit of Perfection." To address this serious threat, the brand's managers decided to go the extra mile. Rather than broadly announcing the recall in the media as is customary, it called each owner individually and advised bringing the car in for the recommended repair. When owners picked up their cars after the repair, they found their Lexus had been detailed and the gas tank filled. If owners lived far from a Lexus dealership, the company flew mechanics to the customer's location. In less than three weeks, Lexus was able to resolve the recall problems on all its 8,000 LS400 vehicles sold in the United States. The media dubbed Lexus's effort "a perfect recall."

By exceeding customer expectations, Lexus managers turned a serious threat into an opportunity and established the brand's reputation for superior customer service. Lexus's response was especially well received because customers who buy a brand-new and unknown luxury brand tend to be opinion leaders. They influence other consumers by sharing their product evaluation through word of mouth (or today, by viral messaging online). Only two years after its launch, Lexus was ranked first on vehicle quality and customer satisfaction by J.D. Power & Associates, a leading information-services firm. In the same year (1991), Lexus became the top-selling luxury brand in the United States. It has been one of the top-selling brands ever since.

However, after being a leader in quality for almost 20 years, Toyota faced the largest recall in automotive history in early 2010 when it called back more than eight million vehicles due to an alleged faulty accelerator pedal and alleged problems with the onboard electronics system. Rather than a nimble and brash new entry in the U.S. automotive market, Toyota was now the largest car manufacturer in the world. To defend its reputation as a quality leader it again needed to exhibit superior customer responsiveness. But satisfying more than eight million customers was much more challenging than pleasing the 8,000 original Lexus customers.[15]

CUSTOMIZATION. Customization allows firms to go beyond merely adding differentiating features to tailoring products and services for specific customers. Advances in manufacturing and information technology have even made feasible mass customization—the manufacture of a large variety of customized products or services done at a relatively low unit cost.[16] Customization and low cost were once opposing goals—you could have one or the other, but not both. Today, some companies are able to conquer this trade-off by using the Internet. You can design your own T-shirts at threadless.com or create customized sneakers at nike.com. BMW allows you to design your customized vehicle online and then follow the manufacturing progress in real time.

COMPLEMENTS. When studying industry attractiveness in Chapter 3, we identified the availability of complements as an important force determining the profit potential of an industry. Complements add value to a product or service when they are consumed in tandem. Finding complements, therefore, is an important task for managers in their quest to enhance the value of their offerings.

The introduction of AT&T U-verse is a recent example of managers leveraging complements to increase the perceived value of a service offering.[17] AT&T's U-verse service bundles high-speed Internet access, phone, and TV services. Service bundles can be further

mass customization The manufacture of a large variety of customized products or services at relatively low unit cost.

enhanced by DVR capabilities that allow users to pause live TV, to record up to four live TV shows at once, and to access video on demand. A DVR by itself is not very valuable, but included as a "free" add-on to subscribers, it turns into a complement that significantly enhances the perceived value of the service bundle. Leveraging complementary products allowed AT&T to break into the highly competitive television services market, significantly enhancing the value of its service offerings.

By choosing the differentiation strategy as the strategic position for a product, managers focus their attention on adding value to the product through its unique features that respond to customer preferences, customer service during and after the sale, or an effective marketing campaign that communicates the value of the product's features to the target market. While this positioning involves increased costs (for example, higher-quality inputs or innovative research and development activities), customers will be willing to pay a premium price for the product or service that satisfies their needs and preferences. In the next section, we will discuss how managers formulate a cost leadership strategy.

COST-LEADERSHIP STRATEGY: UNDERSTANDING COST DRIVERS

The goal of a cost-leadership strategy is to reduce the firm's cost below that of its competitors. The *cost leader,* as the name implies, focuses its attention and resources on reducing the cost at which it is able to offer a product or service (and still make a profit in the long term). The cost leader optimizes all of its value chain activities to achieve a low-cost position. Although staking out the lowest-cost position in the industry is the overriding strategic objective, a cost leader still needs to offer products and services of acceptable value.

A cost leader can achieve a competitive advantage as long as its economic value created $(V - C)$ is greater than that of its competitors. Panel (a) in Exhibit 6.4 shows that firm B, a cost leader, achieves a competitive advantage over firm A because firm B not only has lower cost than firm A, but also achieves *differentiation parity* (meaning it creates the same value as firm A). Thus, firm B's economic value creation, $(V - C)_B$, is greater than that of firm A $(V - C)_A$. As an example, GM and Korean car manufacturer Hyundai offer some models that compete directly with one another, yet Hyundai's cars tend be produced at lower cost but provide a similar value proposition.

What if firm B fails to create differentiation parity? Such parity is often hard to achieve since value creation tends to go along with higher costs, and firm B's strategy is aimed at lower costs. Firm B can still gain a competitive advantage as long as its economic value

>> **LO 6-3**
Examine the relationship between cost drivers and cost-leadership strategy.

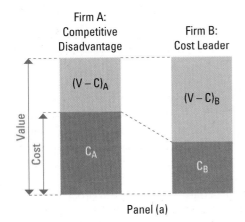

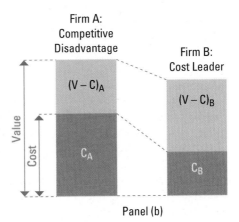

EXHIBIT 6.4

Cost-Leadership Strategy: Achieving Competitive Advantage

Ryanair: Lower Cost than the Low-Cost Leader!

Southwest Airlines is a classic example of a company pursuing a cost-leadership strategy.[18] Ryanair is pursuing a similar strategy in Europe. Headquartered in Dublin, Ireland, Ryanair proudly calls itself "the nastiest airline in the world" because of its relentless effort to drive down costs. In fact, Ryanair is the lowest-cost airline in the world. It flies some 200 Boeing 737 aircraft over more than 850 routes across Europe and North Africa, dozens of them priced as low as $8.

How can this be possible? Ryanair is the epitome of a no-frills airline: the seats don't recline, they have no seat-back pockets (safety cards are printed on the back of the seat in front of you), life jackets are in the overhead compartment, and the older planes have no window shades. These choices lower aircraft-purchase costs or allow faster cleaning and turnaround. Ryanair has explored other ideas to further reduce costs, such as removing two toilets to add six more seats, charging for the use of toilets, charging a premium for overweight passengers, having passengers carry their luggage to and from the airplane, and so on.

Although Ryanair's tickets are cheap, "extras" such as pillows, blankets, and a bottle of water require an additional fee. It costs $8 to check in online, but if you forget to do so, Ryanair will happily check you in at the airport for $65. Your first checked bag costs $15, the second $30. Ryanair offers many other amenities, and its website has been described as a bazaar: You can book a hotel room, rent a car, get a credit card, buy insurance, and even gamble. In flight, attendants sell merchandise such as digital cameras ($137.50) and MP3 players ($165). If you want to contact Ryanair, you can't via the website or e-mail; instead, you must use a premium-rate phone line. It is estimated that more than 20 percent of Ryanair's revenues flow from such ancillary services, unusual for an airline.

Ryanair is the epitome of unbundling air travel into its many components. Traditionally, air travel was sold at one price, which included "free" checking of bags as well as meals served on board. However, the extremely price-conscious traveler who can plan ahead to avoid the surcharges can still fly cheaply across Europe.[19]

creation exceeds that of its competitors. This situation is depicted in Panel (b) of Exhibit 6.4: even with lower value (no differentiation parity) but lower cost, firm B's economic value creation, $(V - C)_B$, still is greater than that of firm A $(V - C)_A$. For example, as the low-cost leader, Walmart was able to take market share from Kmart, which filed for bankruptcy in 2002. In the early 2000s, Dell dominated Apple, Compaq, Gateway, HP, and others in the computer industry by utilizing a low-cost strategy.

In both situations in Exhibit 6.4, firm B's economic value creation is greater than that of firm A. Firm B achieves a competitive advantage in both cases. Either it can charge similar prices as its competitors and benefit from a greater profit margin per unit, or it can charge lower prices than its competition and gain higher profits from higher volume. Both variations of a cost-leadership strategy can result in competitive advantage.

While companies successful at cost leadership must excel at controlling costs, this doesn't mean they can neglect value creation. Hyundai signals the quality of its cars with a 10-year, 100,000-mile warranty, the most comprehensive in the industry. Walmart offers products of acceptable quality, including many brand-name products. Within the airline industry, Strategy Highlight 6.2 shows how Ryanair has been able to devise and implement a cost-leadership strategy.

Cost Drivers

The most important *cost drivers* that managers can manipulate to keep their costs low are:

- Cost of input factors
- Economies of scale
- Learning-curve effects
- Experience-curve effects

However, this list is only a starting point; managers may consider other cost drivers, depending on the unique situation.

COST OF INPUT FACTORS. One of the most basic advantages a firm can have over its rivals is access to lower-cost input factors such as raw materials, capital, labor, and IT services. The South African company De Beers has long held a very strong position in the market for diamonds because it tightly controls the supply of raw materials. The aluminum producer Alcoa has access to lower-cost bauxite mines in the United

States, which supply a key ingredient for aluminum. GE, through its GE Capital division, has a lower cost of capital than other industrial conglomerates such as Siemens, Philips, or ABB. To lower labor costs for some types of tasks, some U.S. companies decide to outsource jobs to India, known for its low-cost call centers, data processing and accounting services, and medical-image reading.[20]

ECONOMIES OF SCALE. Larger firms might be in a position to reap *economies of scale,* decreases in cost per unit as output increases. This relationship between unit cost and output is depicted in the first (left-hand) part of Exhibit 6.5: Cost per unit falls as output increases up to point Q_1. A firm whose output is closer to Q_1 has a cost advantage over other firms with less output. In this sense, bigger is better.

EXHIBIT 6.5

Economies of Scale, Minimum Efficient Scale (MES), and Diseconomies of Scale

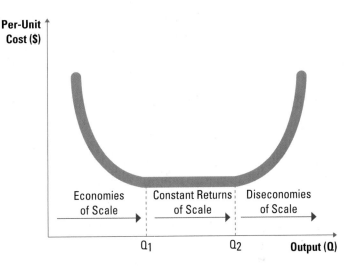

In the airframe-manufacturing industry, for example, reaping economies of scale and learning are critical for cost-competitiveness. Thus, Boeing chose not to compete with Airbus in the market for superjumbo jets; rather, it chose to focus on a smaller, fuel-efficient airplane (the 787 Dreamliner, priced at roughly $155 million) that allows for long-distance point-to-point connections. Each market segment is large enough to allow for significant scale and learning effects for only one manufacturer. Boeing can expect to reap significant economies of scale and learning. By early 2010, it had received almost 900 orders for the Dreamliner, a record number for any airplane.[21] At the same time, Airbus had delivered 26 A380 super jumbos (sticker price, $335 million), with a total of 202 orders on its books.[22]

What causes per-unit cost to drop as output increases (up to point Q_1)? Economies of scale allow firms to:

- Spread their fixed costs over a larger output.
- Employ specialized systems and equipment.
- Take advantage of certain physical properties.

Spreading Fixed Costs over Larger Output. Larger output allows firms to spread their fixed costs over more units. For example, between 2007 and 2009, Microsoft spent approximately $25 billion on R&D, a significant portion of it on its new Windows 7 operating system.[23] This R&D expense was a fixed cost Microsoft had to incur before a single copy of Windows 7 was sold. However, once the initial version of the new software was completed, the marginal cost of each additional copy was basically zero, especially for copies sold in digital form online. Given that Microsoft dominates the operating system market for personal computers with more than 90 percent market share, it expects to sell several hundred million copies of Windows 7, thereby spreading its huge fixed cost of development over a large output. Microsoft's large installed base of Windows operating systems throughout the world provides it with competitive advantage, because it can leverage its economies of scale to drive down the per-unit cost for each additional copy of Windows 7.

economies of scale Decreases in cost per unit as output increases.

Employing Specialized Systems and Equipment. Larger output also allows firms to invest in more specialized systems and equipment such as enterprise resource planning (ERP) software or manufacturing robots. To be cost-competitive in today's market, for example, industry experts believe a car manufacturer must produce at least five million vehicles per year.[24] GM introduced the Chevy Volt in late 2010, the first plug-in hybrid vehicle that is estimated to get 230 mpg fuel efficiency. It is priced at about $40,000, almost twice as expensive as a Toyota Prius that has been on the market longer and presumably has more scale efficiencies. Yet GM is counting on selling the Chevy Volt in large numbers so that economies of scale will kick in and drive down its production costs, and, therefore, lower the price to the end consumer.[25]

Taking Advantage of Certain Physical Properties. Economies of scale also occur because of certain physical properties. One such property is known in engineering as the *cube-square rule:* The volume of a body such as a pipe or a tank increases disproportionately more than its surface. This same principle makes big box retail stores such as Walmart, Target, and the French retailer Carrefour cheaper to build and run. They can also stock much more merchandise and handle inventory more efficiently. These and other scale benefits combine to explain the rise of superstores that are often 200,000 square feet or more. Other retailers that have leveraged the superstore concept to emerge as category killers are Toys R Us, Home Depot, Barnes and Noble, and Best Buy. Their huge size makes it difficult for department stores or small retailers to compete on cost and selection.

Look again at Exhibit 6.5. The output range between Q_1 and Q_2 in the figure is considered the minimum efficient scale (MES) in order to be cost-competitive. Between Q_1 and Q_2, the returns to scale are constant. It is the output range needed to bring the cost per unit down as much as possible, allowing a firm to stake out the lowest-cost position achievable through economies of scale. If the firm's output range is less than Q_1 or more than Q_2, the firm is at a cost disadvantage. For example, chipmaker AMD cannot muster the scale in production that Intel enjoys and thus is not able to drive down its cost as much. This puts AMD at a competitive disadvantage.

The concept of minimum efficient scale applies not only to production processes but also to managerial tasks such as how to organize work. Due to investments in specialized technology and equipment (e.g. electric arc furnaces), Nucor is able to reach MES with much smaller batches of steel than larger, fully vertically integrated steel companies using older technology. Nucor's optimal plant size is about 500 people, which is much smaller than at larger integrated steel makers like U.S. Steel (which often employs thousands of workers per plant).[26] Of course, minimum efficient scale depends on the specific industry: The average per-unit cost curve, depicted conceptually in Exhibit 6.5, is a reflection of the underlying production function, which is determined by technology and other input factors.

Benefits to scale cannot go on indefinitely, though. Bigger is not always better; in fact, sometimes bigger is worse. Beyond Q_2 in Exhibit 6.5, firms experience diseconomies of scale—increases in cost as output increases. Why? As firms get too big, the complexity of managing and coordinating raises the cost, negating any benefits to scale. Large firms tend to become overly bureaucratic, with too many layers of hierarchy, and thus grow inflexible and slow in decision making. To avoid problems associated with diseconomies of scale, Gore Associates, maker of Gore-Tex fabric, Glide dental floss, and many other innovative products, breaks up its company into smaller units. Managers at Gore Associates found that employing about 150 people per plant allows them to avoid diseconomies of scale. Gore's Ben Hen states: "We put 150 parking spaces in the lot, and when people start parking on the grass, we know it's time to build a new plant."[27]

minimum efficient scale (MES) Output range needed to bring down the cost per unit as much as possible, allowing a firm to stake out the lowest-cost position that is achievable through economies of scale.

diseconomies of scale Increases in cost per unit when output increases.

Finally, there are also physical limitations to scale. Airbus is pushing the envelope with its A380 aircraft, which can hold more than 850 passengers and fly up to 8,200 miles (enough to travel non-stop from Boston to Hong Kong at about 600 mph). The goal, of course, is to drive down the cost of the average seat-mile flown (CASM, a standard cost metric in the airline industry). It remains to be seen whether the A380 superjumbo will enable airlines to reach minimum efficient scale or will simply be too large to be efficient. For example, boarding and embarking procedures must be streamlined in order to accommodate more than 850 people in a timely and safe manner. Many airports around the world will need to be retrofitted with longer and wider runways to allow the superjumbo to take off and land.

Scale economies are critical to driving down a firm's cost and thus strengthening a cost-leadership position. Although managers need to increase output to operate at a minimum efficient scale (between Q_1 and Q_2 in Exhibit 6.5), they also need to be watchful not to drive scale beyond Q_2, where they would encounter diseconomies. Monitoring the firm's cost structure closely over different output ranges allows managers to fine-tune operations and benefit from economies of scale.

LEARNING CURVE. Learning by doing can also drive down cost. As individuals and teams engage repeatedly in an activity, whether writing computer code, developing new medicines, or building submarines, they learn from their cumulative experience.[28] In the business world, *learning curves* were first documented in aircraft manufacturing as the United States ramped up production in the 1930s, prior to its entry into World War II.[29] Every time production was doubled, the per-unit cost dropped by a predictable and constant rate (approximately 20 percent).[30] This important relationship is captured in Exhibit 6.6, where different colors denote different levels of learning curves: 90 percent (purple), 80 percent (green), and 70 percent (blue). As learning occurs, you move down the learning curve. The steeper the learning curve, the more learning takes place. For example, a 90 percent learn-

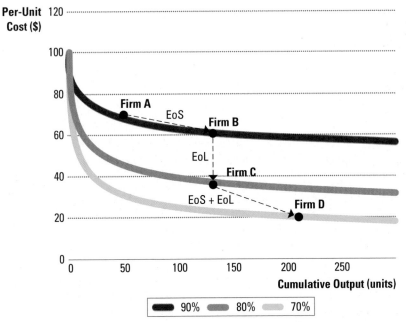

EXHIBIT 6.6

Gaining Competitive Advantage Through Leveraging Learning and Experience Curve Effects

EoS = Economies of Scale
EoL = Economies of Learning

ing curve indicates that per-unit cost drops 10 percent every time output is doubled. A 70 percent learning curve indicates a 30 percent drop every time output is doubled.

It is not surprising that a learning curve was first observed in aircraft manufacturing. An aircraft is an extremely complex industrial product; a modern commercial aircraft can contain more than one million different parts, compared with a few thousand for a car. The more complex the production process, the more learning effects we can expect. As cumulative output increases, managers learn how to optimize the process and workers improve their performance through repetition. Learning curves are a robust phenomenon that has been observed in many industries, not only in manufacturing processes like building airplanes, cars, ships, and semiconductors, but also in alliance management, pizza franchising, and health care.[31] For example, physicians who perform only a small number of cardiac surgeries per year can have a patient mortality rate five times higher than physicians who perform the same surgery more frequently.[32]

There are some important differences between economies of scale and learning effects.[33] In some production processes (e.g., a simple one-step process in the manufacture of steel rods), effects from economies of scale can be quite significant, while learning effects are minimal. In contrast, in some professions (brain surgery or the practice of estate law), learning effects can be substantial, while economies of scale are minimal. Managers need to understand the difference in order to calibrate their business-level strategy. For example, if a firm's cost advantage is due to economies of scale, a manager should be less concerned about employee turnover (and thus a potential loss in learning) and more concerned with drops in production runs. In contrast, if the firm's low-cost position is based on complex learning, managers should be much more concerned if a key employee (e.g., a star analyst at an investment bank or a star researcher at a pharmaceutical company) was to leave.

EXPERIENCE CURVE. The concept of an *experience curve* attempts to capture both economies of scale and learning effects.[34] In this perspective, economies of scale allow movement down a *given* learning curve based on current production technology. By moving further down a given learning curve than competitors, a firm can gain a competitive advantage. For example, Exhibit 6.6 shows that firm B is further down the purple (90 percent) learning curve than firm A. Firm B leverages economies of scale to gain an advantage over firm A.

As we know, however, technology and production processes do not stay constant. If firm C is able to implement a new production process (such as lean manufacturing), it initiates an entirely new and steeper learning curve. In Exhibit 6.6, firm C is able to gain a competitive advantage over both firms A and B through economies of learning by jumping down to the green (80 percent) learning curve, reflecting the new and lower-cost production process introduced. However, combining both economies of scale and learning effects, firm D is breaking away from firm C, gaining a competitive advantage. By capturing both economies of scale and learning effects, firm D is able to implement a cost-leadership strategy and enjoy a competitive advantage over firms A, B, and C. Taken together, learning by doing allows a firm to lower its per-unit costs by moving down a given learning curve, while leveraging experience based on economies of scale *and* learning allows the firm to leapfrog to a steeper learning curve, thereby further driving down its per-unit costs.

By choosing the cost leadership strategy, managers must focus their attention on lowering the overall costs of producing the product or service while maintaining an acceptable level of quality that will serve the needs of the customer. Cost leaders appeal to the price-conscious buyer, whose main criterion is the price of the product or service. By attending to the reduction of costs in each functional area (or value activity), managers aim to be the low-cost provider with the ability to offer the lowest price in the market. As successful cost leaders like Walmart illustrate, the low-cost producer with high volume can be a very profitable business.

BUSINESS-LEVEL STRATEGY AND THE FIVE FORCES: BENEFITS AND RISKS

The five forces model introduced in Chapter 3 helps managers assess the forces—threat of entry, power of suppliers, power of buyers, threat of substitutes, and rivalry among existing competitors—that make some industries more attractive than others. With this understanding of industry dynamics, managers use one of the generic business-level strategies to protect themselves against the forces that drive down profitability.[35] The business-level strategies introduced in this chapter allow firms to carve out strong strategic positions that enhance the likelihood of gaining and sustaining competitive advantage. Exhibit 6.7 details the relationship between competitive positioning and the five forces. In particular, it highlights the benefits and risks of cost-leadership and differentiation business strategies, which we discuss next.

>> **LO 6-4**
Assess the benefits and risks of cost leadership and differentiation business strategies vis-à-vis the five forces that shape competition.

EXHIBIT 6.7

Competitive Positioning and the Five Forces: Benefits and Risks of Cost-Leadership and Differentiation Business Strategies

Competitive Force	Cost Leadership		Differentiation	
	Benefits	**Risks**	**Benefits**	**Risks**
Threat of entry	• Protection against entry due to economies of scale	• Erosion of margins • Replacement	• Protection against entry due to intangible resources such as a reputation for innovation, quality, or customer service	• Erosion of margins • Replacement
Power of suppliers	• Protection against increase in input prices, which can be absorbed	• Erosion of margins	• Protection against increase in input prices, which can be passed on to customers	• Erosion of margins
Power of buyers	• Protection against decrease in sales prices, which can be absorbed	• Erosion of margins	• Protection against decrease in sales prices, because well-differentiated products or services are not perfect substitutes	• Erosion of margins
Threat of substitutes	• Protection against substitute products through further lowering of prices	• Replacement, especially when faced with innovation	• Protection against substitute products due to differential appeal	• Replacement, especially when faced with innovation
Rivalry among existing competitors	• Protection against price wars because lowest-cost firm will win	• Focus of competition shifts to non-price attributes • Lowering costs to drive value creation below acceptable threshold	• Protection against competitors if product or service has enough differential appeal to command premium price	• Focus of competition shifts to price • Increasing differentiation of product features that do not create value but raise costs • Increasing differentiation to raise costs above acceptable threshold

Source: Based on M. E. Porter, "The five competitive forces that shape strategy," *Harvard Business Review,* January 2008; and M. E. Porter (1980), *Competitive Strategy: Techniques for Analyzing Industries and Competitors* (New York: Free Press).

Benefits and Risks of the Cost-Leadership Strategy

A cost-leadership strategy is defined by obtaining the lowest-cost position in the industry while offering acceptable value. The cost leader, therefore, is protected from other competitors because of having the lowest cost. If a price war ensues, the low-cost leader will be the last firm standing; all other firms will be driven out as margins evaporate. Since reaping economies of scale is critical to reaching a low-cost position, the cost leader is likely to have a large market share, which in turn reduces the threat of entry.

A cost leader is also fairly well isolated from threats of powerful suppliers to increase input prices, because it is more able to absorb price increases through accepting lower profit margins. Likewise, a cost leader can absorb price reductions more easily when demanded by powerful buyers. Should substitutes emerge, the low-cost leader can try to fend them off by further lowering its prices to reinstall relative value with the substitute. For example, Walmart tends to be fairly isolated from these threats. Walmart's cost structure combined with its large volume allows it to work with suppliers in keeping prices low, to the extent that suppliers are often the party who experiences a profit margin squeeze.

Although a cost-leadership strategy provides some protection against the five forces, it also carries some risks. If a new entrant with new and relevant expertise enters the market, the low-cost leader's margins may erode due to loss in market share while it attempts to learn new capabilities. For example, Walmart faces challenges to its cost leadership: Target (which until 2000 was the Dayton-Hudson Company) has had success due to its superior merchandising capabilities. The Dollar Store has drawn customers who prefer a smaller format than the big box of Walmart. The risk of replacement is particularly pertinent if a potent substitute emerges due to an innovation. Powerful suppliers and buyers may be able to reduce margins so much that the low-cost leader could have difficulty covering the cost of capital, and thus lose the potential for a competitive advantage.

The low-cost leader also needs to stay vigilant to keep its cost the lowest in the industry. Over time, competitors can beat the cost leader by implementing the same business strategy, but more effectively. While keeping its cost the lowest in the industry is imperative, the cost leader must not forget that it needs to create an acceptable level of value. If continuously lowering costs leads to a value proposition that falls below an acceptable threshold, the low-cost leader's market share will evaporate. Finally, the low-cost leader faces significant difficulties when the focus of competition shifts from price to non-price attributes.

Target has been able to compete with Walmart by building equivalent skills in efficient logistics expertise, thus achieving cost parity. At the same time, Target outdoes Walmart in product selection, merchandising, and store layout so that its stores offer a higher-quality shopping experience for the customer, thus creating higher value.

Benefits and Risks of the Differentiation Strategy

A differentiation strategy is defined by finding a strategic position that creates higher perceived value while controlling costs. The successful differentiator is able to stake out a unique strategic position, where it can benefit from imperfect competition (as discussed in Chapter 3), and thus command a premium price. Such a position reduces rivalry among competitors.

A successful differentiation strategy is likely to be based on unique or specialized features of the product, on an effective marketing campaign, or on intangible resources such as a reputation for innovation, quality, and customer service. A rival would need to improve the product features as well as build a similar or more effective reputation in order to gain market share. Thus, the threat of entry is reduced: Competitors will find such intangible advantages time-consuming and costly, and maybe impossible, to imitate. If the source of the differential appeal is intangible rather than tangible (e.g., reputation rather than observable product and service features), a differentiator is even more likely to sustain its advantage.

Moreover, if the differentiator is able to create a significant difference between perceived value and current market prices, the differentiator will not be so threatened by increases in input prices due to powerful suppliers. Although an increase in input factors could erode margins, a differentiator is likely able to pass on price increases to its customers as long as its value creation exceeds the price charged. Since a successful differentiator creates perceived value in the minds of consumers and builds customer loyalty, powerful buyers demanding price decreases are unlikely to emerge. A strong differentiated position also reduces the threat of substitutes, because the unique features of the product have been created to appeal to customer preferences, keeping them loyal to the product. For example, Apple has built strong differentiated appeal for its products. As Apple creates new customer needs (even if customers are initially unaware of the need), it launches new products. Users of an iPhone are loyal to the product and unlikely to switch to a rival's offering.

The viability of a differentiation strategy is severely undermined when the focus of competition shifts to price rather than value-creating features. This can happen when products become commoditized (the original IBM personal computer) and an acceptable standard of quality has emerged across rival firms (IBM clones). A differentiator also needs to be careful not to overshoot its differentiated appeal by adding product features that raise costs but not the perceived value in the minds of consumers. Finally, a differentiator needs to be vigilant that its costs of providing uniqueness do not rise above the customer's willingness to pay.

It is important to note that none of the business-level strategies depicted in Exhibit 6.2 is inherently superior. The success of each is context-dependent and relies on two factors:

- How well the strategy leverages the firm's internal strengths while mitigating its weaknesses; and
- How well it helps the firm exploit external opportunities while avoiding external threats.

There is no single correct generic strategy for a specific industry. The deciding factor is that the chosen business strategy provides a strong position that attempts to maximize economic value creation and is effectively implemented.

INTEGRATION STRATEGY: COMBINING COST LEADERSHIP AND DIFFERENTIATION

Competitive conditions in an industry may require firms to develop skills in lowering costs as well as adding uniqueness—particularly in globalized industries. For example, success may require lowering costs in order to compete with firms in countries with lower labor costs and may require adding special features to respond to local customer preferences in individual country markets. Since either increasing perceived value or lowering production costs can increase a firm's competitive advantage, it is tempting to conclude that managers should be focusing on *both efforts*. To accomplish this, they would need to integrate two different strategic positions: differentiation and low cost.[36] As we will show, managers should not pursue this strategy unless competitive conditions require this position, because it is a complex strategy to execute due to the conflicting requirements of each generic strategy.

>> **LO 6-5**
Explain why it is difficult to succeed at an integration strategy.

Integration Strategy at the Business Level

A successful integration strategy requires that trade-offs between differentiation and low cost are reconciled. This is often difficult because differentiation and low cost are distinct

integration strategy
Business-level strategy that successfully combines differentiation and cost leadership activities.

strategic positions that require the firm to effectively manage internal value chain activities that are fundamentally different from one another. For example, a cost leader would focus research and development on process technologies in order to improve efficiency, but a differentiator would focus research and development on product technologies in order to add uniqueness. If successful, an integration strategy allows a firm to offer a differentiated product or service at low cost.

The startup Leopard Cycles, founded in 2004, shows how to address the necessary trade-offs inherent in an integration strategy. A customized road-race bicycle like those ridden by professionals such as Lance Armstrong, Alberto Contador, or Meredith Miller was once an expensive proposition that could cost up to $20,000.[37] Combining the latest flexible-manufacturing techniques with Internet-enabled technologies, Leopard Cycles offers mass-customized race bicycles built with advanced materials such as carbon fiber. Leopard Cycles describes how it addresses the trade-off between value and cost as follows: "Being the low-cost producer is mutually exclusive with exotic materials; however we're a firm believer that you don't have to be the most expensive to be the best."[38] This position implies that an integration of low cost and product differentiation enables companies to increase the perceived value of their products, while keeping the cost increase in check. Leopard Cycles prices its customized road-race bikes between $1,500 and $2,500, only about 15 percent of what one would have paid for such a specialized bicycle just a few years before.

Being successful at an integration strategy doesn't imply that the firm must be the highest value creator *and* the lowest-cost producer in its respective industry. Whether an integration strategy can lead to competitive advantage, however, depends on the *difference* between value creation (V) and cost (C), and thus on the magnitude of economic value created ($V - C$). The goal of an integration strategy is to have a larger economic value created than that of your competitors. This is what Avon has accomplished in the cosmetics industry. Exhibit 6.8 compares the value and cost positions of three cosmetics companies: L'Oreal, Avon, and Revlon. Each of these companies has succeeded in carving out a well-defined strategic position within the cosmetics world: L'Oreal is a differentiator; Revlon is a cost leader; Avon is an integrator.

EXHIBIT 6.8

Avon's Attempt at Achieving Competitive Advantage by Pursuing an Integration Strategy

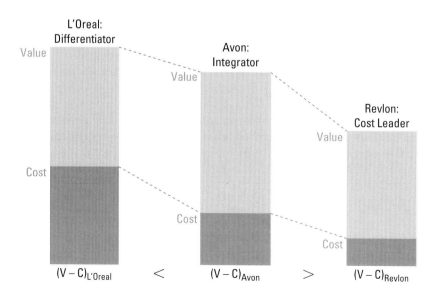

Avon has been able to raise the perceived value of its products while lowering its production costs. Under the leadership of its CEO, Andrea Jung, it began to pursue an integration strategy in 2002 by investing over $100 million in R&D and building a new research facility.[39] Avon's R&D investments were intended to increase the perceived value of its products, by developing cosmetics that look good *and* are good for the skin. In the same year, she began to lower Avon's cost structure by investing more than $50 million into optimizing its supply chain.[40] Avon's shift from a differentiation strategy to an integration strategy seems to be successful: Its profits rose 180 percent from 2002 ($3.9 billion) to 2010 ($10.9 billion). The key point is that Avon has achieved the highest economic value by following an integration strategy [in Exhibit 6.8, $(V - C)_{L'Oreal} < (V - C)_{Avon} > (V - C)_{Revlon}$]. When successful, investments in differentiation and low cost are not substitutes but are complements, providing important spill-over effects.

Although quite difficult to execute, a successfully implemented integration strategy allows firms two pricing options: First, the firm can charge a higher price than the cost leader, reflecting its higher value creation and thus generating greater profit margins. Second, the firm can lower its price below that of the differentiator (because of its lower cost structure); it thus can gain market share and make up the loss in margin through increased sales. An integration strategy is difficult to implement, though. It requires the reconciliation of fundamentally different strategic positions—differentiation and low cost—which in turn require distinct internal value chain activities (see Chapter 4) that allow the firm to increase value *and* lower cost at the same time.

Value and Cost Drivers of Integration Strategy

For an integration strategy to succeed, managers must resolve trade-offs between the two generic strategic positions—low cost and differentiation. Some possible levers they can use to overcome these challenges include quality, economies of scope, innovation, and the firm's structure, culture, and routines. These are critical: They allow managers to simultaneously *increase* perceived value and *lower* cost. Although we discuss each of these value and cost drivers individually, they are *interdependent*. For example, innovations like lean manufacturing contribute to better quality and customer service, which reinforce one another and thus enhance the brand of a product or service.

>> LO 6-6
Evaluate value and cost drivers that may allow a firm to pursue an integration strategy.

QUALITY. The quality of a product denotes its durability and reliability. Quality not only can increase a product's perceived value, but also can lower its cost. Through techniques like total quality management, companies design and build products with quality in mind, while increasing their differentiated appeal. By building in better quality, companies lower the cost of both production and after-sale service requirements. Thus, quality is a two-pronged activity: It raises economic value creation $(V - C)$ by simultaneously increasing V and lowering C.

ECONOMIES OF SCOPE. We saw that economies of scale allow a firm to lower its per-unit cost as its output increases. The concept economies of scope describes the savings that come from producing two (or more) outputs at less cost than producing each output individually, even though using the same resources and technology. Starbucks, for example, is already set up to boil purified water for its hot coffee beverages; thus, it reaps economies of scope when it offers tea in addition to coffee. As a result, Starbucks lowers its cost structure by sharing its production assets over multiple outputs, while increasing its menu and thus its differentiated appeal.

economies of scope Savings that come from producing two (or more) outputs at less cost than producing each output individually, despite using the same resources and technology.

INNOVATION. Broadly defined, *innovation* describes any new product and process, or any modification of existing ones.[41] Innovation is frequently required to resolve existing trade-offs when companies pursue an integration strategy. As we saw earlier, Leopard Cycles leveraged the innovation of flexible manufacturing systems to create customized road-race bicycles of high quality at low cost. This innovation enabled managers to solve the trade-off between customization and cost, and also to increase the quality of the product, further enhancing its differentiated appeal.

Similarly, international furniture retailer IKEA orchestrates different internal value chain activities to reconcile the tension between differentiation and cost leadership in order to carve out a unique strategic position. In particular, IKEA uses innovation in furniture design, engineering, and store design to solve the trade-offs between value creation and production cost. Josephine Rydberg-Dumont, President of IKEA Sweden, highlights how difficult resolving this trade-off is: "Designing beautiful-but-expensive products is easy. Designing beautiful products that are inexpensive and functional is a huge challenge."[42] IKEA leverages its deep design and engineering expertise to offer furniture that is stylish and functional and that can be easily assembled by the consumer. IKEA also focuses on lowering cost by displaying its products in a warehouse-like setting, thus reducing inventory cost. Customers serve themselves, and then transport the furniture to their homes in IKEA's signature flat-packs for assembly. In this way, IKEA is able to pursue an integration strategy, leveraging innovation to increase the perceived value of its products, while simultaneously lowering its cost.

Given its importance in a firm's quest for competitive advantage, we'll discuss innovation as a business strategy in depth in Chapter 7.

STRUCTURE, CULTURE, AND ROUTINES. A firm's structure, culture, and routines are critical when pursuing an integration strategy. The challenge that managers face is to structure their organizations so that they both control cost *and* allow for creativity that can lay the basis for differentiation. Doing the two together is hard to accomplish. Achieving a low-cost position requires an organizational structure that relies on strict budget controls, while differentiation requires an organizational structure that allows creativity and customer responsiveness to thrive, which typically necessitates looser organizational structures and controls.

The goal for managers who want to pursue an integration strategy should be to build an ambidextrous organization, one that enables managers to balance and harness different activities in trade-off situations.[43] Here, the trade-offs to be addressed involve the simultaneous pursuit of low cost and differentiation strategies. Notable management practices that companies use to resolve this trade-off include flexible and lean manufacturing systems, total quality management, just-in-time inventory management, and Six Sigma.[44] Other management techniques that allow firms to reconcile cost and value pressures are the use of teams in the production process and decentralized decision making at the level of the individual customer.

Ambidexterity describes a firm's ability to address trade-offs not only at one point but also over time. It encourages managers to balance *exploitation* (applying current knowledge to enhance firm performance in the short term) with *exploration* (searching for new knowledge that may enhance a firm's future performance).[45] For example, while Intel focuses on maximizing sales from its *current* cutting-edge microprocessors, it also has several different teams with different time horizons working on *future* generations of microprocessors.[46] In ambidextrous organizations, managers constantly analyze their existing business processes and routines, looking for ways to change them in order to resolve trade-offs across internal value chain activities and time.[47] Given the importance of

ambidextrous organization An organization able to balance and harness different activities in trade-off situations.

a firm's structure, culture, and routines to gaining and sustaining competitive advantage, we dedicate Part 3 of this book, Strategy Implementation, to discussing this important topic in detail.

Although appealing in a theoretical sense, an integration strategy is actually quite difficult to translate into reality. The reason is that differentiation and cost leadership are distinct strategic positions that require important trade-offs.[48] Many firms that attempt to pursue an integration strategy fail because they end up being *stuck in the middle:* They succeed at neither a differentiation nor a cost-leadership strategy. In a world of strategic trade-offs, increasing value and lowering cost have opposite effects. Improved product features, customer services, and customization all result in higher cost, while offering a no-frills product reduces perceived value. Thus, it happens quite often that a firm can't do both but must choose to be *either* a differentiator *or* a cost leader.

When a firm is unsuccessful in pursuing an integration strategy and ends up stuck in the middle, the result is a competitive *disadvantage.* For example, the DaimlerChrysler merger was motivated by the integration of the differentiation advantage based on Daimler's engineering prowess and the low-cost manufacturing expertise of Chrysler. The resulting cars were a disaster. They were neither differentiated nor low cost. Daimler lost some $35 billion in the ill-fated merger.

We now have finished our discussion of value and cost drivers and how they are used to formulate and implement business-level strategies—differentiation, cost leadership, and integration. Exhibit 6.9 provides a summary of these drivers and their effects. In particular, the exhibit highlights drivers that uniquely affect either value creation or low cost (used for

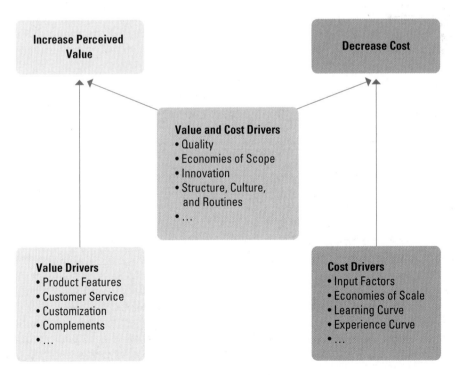

EXHIBIT 6.9

Value and Cost Drivers

differentiation *or* cost leadership strategies) and drivers that simultaneously increase value while lowering cost (used for integration strategies).

Integration Strategy at the Corporate Level

In Chapter 1, we noted that it is helpful to break down strategy formulation into three distinct levels: corporate, business, and functional (see again Exhibit 1.3). Up to this point in this chapter, we have addressed what managers can do at both the business and functional levels to enhance the chances that an integration strategy will succeed. Another option is to reconcile the trade-offs that arise from pursuing an integration strategy at the corporate level. Corporate-level strategy concerns the overall competitiveness of a multibusiness company, sometimes called a conglomerate. In particular, corporate-level strategy concerns decisions about which industries a company should compete in and which types of business-level strategies each unit ought to pursue to maximize overall shareholder value. Conglomerates and other companies may decide to coordinate an integration strategy at the corporate, rather than the business, level.

The Tata Group of India provides an example. A widely diversified multinational conglomerate, headquartered in Mumbai, India, it is active in industries ranging from tea, to hospitality, steel, IT, communications, power, and automobiles.[49] In June 2008, Tata Motors attracted attention in the automotive world when it bought Jaguar and Land Rover from Ford for $2.3 billion. With this purchase, Tata hopes to leverage the prestige Jaguar and Land Rover brands to offer differentiated products.

In the spring of 2009, the Indian Tata Motors attracted even more attention when it unveiled its Tata Nano car. The Nano is the lowest-priced car in the world. It accommodates passengers just over six feet tall, goes from zero to 60 mph in 30 seconds, and gets 67 mpg, beating the Toyota Prius for fuel consumption. The Tata Nano, clearly a no-frills car, exemplifies a focused low-cost strategy. The rear hatch can't be opened, it doesn't have a radio or glove compartment, and its top speed is a little over 60 mph. Nonetheless, at about 50 percent cheaper than the next-lowest-cost car, the Tata Nano is likely to find tens of millions of customers in the fast-growing Indian and Chinese markets. (However, keep this in mind about any cost-leadership strategy: If the product or service does not provide acceptable value, it will not matter how low the price is. Although the Tata Nano is arguably the lowest-priced car in the world, if its reliability, performance, and safety features are unacceptable to customers, the car likely will not sell at company expectations.)

The Tata Group is attempting to carve out different strategic positions in its different divisions. The luxury division of Tata Motors, with the Jaguar and Land Rover brands, is pursuing a *focused* differentiation strategy; the Nano car division is pursuing a *focused* cost-leadership strategy. Although their respective strategic profiles are basically the opposite of one another (differentiation vs. low-cost), both business-level strategies are aimed at a *specific* segment of the market. Jaguar and Land Rover are both considered luxury brands in their respective categories, while the Nano is clearly a low(est)-cost offering, focused on a very specific market niche. Indeed, the Nano focuses on *non-consumption*.[50] Buyers of the Nano will not replace other vehicles, but will be first-time car buyers moving up from bicycles and mopeds. By offering the Nano, Tata is able to bring millions of new car buyers into the market and thus increase the size of the automobile market. Taken together, Tata's corporate strategy seems to be attempting to integrate different strategic positions, pursued by different strategic business units, each with its own profit and loss responsibility.[51] We will study corporate strategy in detail in Chapters 8 and 9.

conglomerate
An organization that combines two or more business units, often active in different industries, under one overarching corporation.

THE DYNAMICS OF COMPETITIVE POSITIONING

Strategic positions, moreover, are not fixed, but can—and need to—change over time as the environment changes. For example, eBay, the successful pioneer in online auctions, decided to retreat from competing in online retailing.[52] Although the company will continue to compete in the online-marketplace for used and overstocked goods, it will no longer compete in the retail market for *new* goods. This strategic shift allows eBay to avoid competing head-on with the online retail giant Amazon, which has morphed into a full-fledged online shopping mall. To further increase the focus on its core business, eBay sold its Skype Internet phone business to a group of private investors.[53] With these strategic moves, eBay returned to its core competency as the web's leading auction house, reaffirming a focused differentiation strategy.

>> **LO 6-7**
Describe and evaluate the dynamics of competitive positioning.

Companies that successfully implement one of the generic business strategies (differentiation or cost leadership) are more likely to attain competitive advantage. To do so, companies seek to reach the so-called productivity frontier, which is the value-cost relationship that captures the result of performing best practices at any given time.[54] Firms that exhibit effectiveness and efficiency reach the productivity frontier; others are left behind. Moreover, the productivity frontier represents possible strategic positions the firm can take relating to value creation and low cost. A firm's business strategy determines which strategic position it aspires to along the productivity frontier.

To illustrate this concept, let's look at the competitive dynamics in the mobile devices industry (including portable computers, phones, and other handheld devices) by highlighting the different competitive positions of Apple, HP, and Dell over time. At a given time, the horizontal axis in Exhibit 6.10 indicates best practice in cost leadership, and the vertical axis indicates best practice in differentiation.[55] Combining both cost leadership and differentiation, the company that seeks an integration strategy stakes out a position in the center part in the best-practice frontier (somewhere between the axes). The dashed line shows the productivity frontier in 2005. Both Apple and Dell had carved out strong strategic positions—Apple as differentiator and Dell as cost leader—and as a consequence, both

productivity frontier
Relationship that captures the result of performing best practices at any given time; the function is convex (bowed outward) to capture the trade-off between value creation and production cost.

enjoyed superior performance. Both were able to move to the productivity frontier because their strategic positions were clearly formulated and well-executed. In contrast, HP was "stuck in the middle" in 2005; when compared with Apple and Dell respectively, it could offer neither value-creating differentiation nor low cost. HP had acquired Compaq in 2002 for $25 billion. This merger, which created the world's largest computer PC manufacturer, was intended to stake out a strategic position as integrator, providing "high-tech at low cost." By 2005, however, HP was not able to reconcile the cost-differentiation trade-off, and thus was unable to reach the productivity frontier. HP's board replaced CEO Carly

EXHIBIT 6.10

The Dynamics of Competitive Positioning: Apple, HP, and Dell

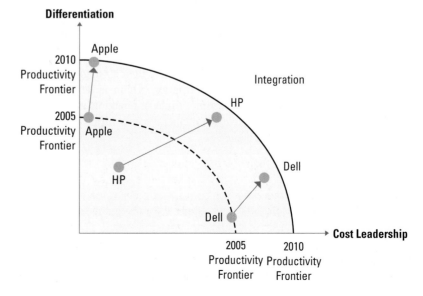

Fiorina with Mark Hurd (who in turn was replaced by Leo Apotheker in 2010, who in turn was replaced by Meg Whitman in 2011; see ChapterCase 12).

Fast-forward to 2010 . . . There, the competitive dynamics look quite different. Continued product and process innovations as well as improvements in functional strategies (e.g., more-efficient supply chain management and more-effective marketing—think of Apple's reinvented retail outlets) further pushed out the productivity frontier, now indicated by the solid line. Under Steve Jobs's leadership, Apple's successful innovations (iPhone, iTunes, iPad, iBookstore) and operational effectiveness allow the firm to maintain a strong strategic position as a differentiator, and thus sustain its competitive advantage.

On the other hand, by 2010 Dell's strategic position as cost leader appeared no longer as valuable as in the early 2000s, because one of the key competitive success factors in 2010 became product differentiation. Thus, Dell was attempting to change its strategic position, moving from its extreme cost-leadership strategy toward more differentiation. In 2007, founder Michael Dell returned from retirement to take over as CEO. In 2008, Dell hired an industrial designer from Nike to come up with colorful futuristic designs for its product offerings.[56] In 2009, Dell purchased Perot Systems, an IT service provider, for $3.9 billion to further enhance its differential appeal and to better compete with HP, which acquired EDS, another IT service provider, for $13 billion in 2008.[57] Yet, Dell is learning first-hand that reconciling the trade-offs inherent in pursuing low cost and differentiation simultaneously is non-trivial. As Exhibit 6.10 shows, although Dell is moving toward the differentiation axis, it had not reached the productivity frontier in 2010, and thus was experiencing a competitive disadvantage.

Under the leadership of CEO Mark Hurd, HP made significant progress toward reducing cost, by trimming its work force by about 10 percent, while also increasing the differential appeal of its product and service offerings. This performance allowed HP to move closer toward the productivity frontier, and to stake out a more clearly defined strategic position as an integrator. ⌕

In summary, strategic positioning is critical to gaining competitive advantage. Well-formulated and implemented generic business strategies (i.e., low cost *or* differentiation) enhance the firm's chances of obtaining superior performance. In some instances, a few exceptional firms might be able to reconcile the significant trade-offs between increasing value and lowering production cost by pursuing both business strategies simultaneously. These integration strategies tend to be successful only if a firm is able to rely on an innovation that allows it to reconcile the trade-offs mentioned (such as Toyota in the 1980s and 1990s with its lean-manufacturing approach, before that approach diffused widely).

Given the dynamics of competitive positioning, firms cannot stand still but must constantly refine and improve their strategic position over time. The goal is to not fall behind the productivity frontier, which is defined by the theoretically possible best practice at any given time. Since innovation is such an essential part of business strategy and competitive advantage, we now turn to discussing innovation in much more detail in the next chapter.

CHAPTERCASE 6 | *Consider This . . .*

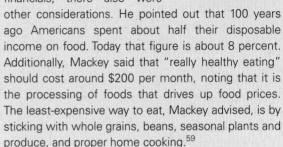

WHOLE FOODS continues to seek ways to differentiate itself from the competition. As the ChapterCase noted, the firm spends 5 percent of its net profits on a variety of charities, and it also provides opportunities for patrons to contribute to such causes.

In September 2010, Whole Foods enhanced a "back-to-school" project it started in 2009. It set a goal to put 300 salad bars in public schools within a 50-miles radius of any Whole Foods store. The firm solicited contributions from customers for this cause. In February 2011, Whole Foods announced the fund-raising had surpassed the original $750,000 goal. With over $1.4 million in collections, the company expanded the program to more than 500 elementary, middle, and high schools across the United States. Whole Foods is also expanding its in-store educational efforts with "wellness clubs" in some stores in the summer of 2011. These dedicated areas of the store give customers a chance to learn first-hand about healthy cooking and eating.[58]

In an interview on the impact of the recent recession, CEO John Mackey noted that while there was some impact on the firm's financials, there also were other considerations. He pointed out that 100 years ago Americans spent about half their disposable income on food. Today that figure is about 8 percent. Additionally, Mackey said that "really healthy eating" should cost around $200 per month, noting that it is the processing of foods that drives up food prices. The least-expensive way to eat, Mackey advised, is by sticking with whole grains, beans, seasonal plants and produce, and proper home cooking.[59]

1. What value drivers is Whole Foods using to remain differentiated in the face of Walmart and other competitors now selling organic foods? (Looking back at Exhibit 6.9 may be useful.)

2. Given the discussion in the ChapterCase about Whole Foods trimming its cost structure, does the firm risk being "stuck in the middle"? Why or why not?

3. What other methods could Whole Foods use to successfully drive its business strategy?

Take-Away Concepts

This chapter discussed two generic business-level strategies (*differentiation* and *cost-leadership*), some factors that companies can use to drive those strategies, and *integration strategy*, the attempt to find a competitive advantage by reconciling the trade-offs between the two generic business strategies, as summarized by the following learning objectives and related take-away concepts.

LO 6-1 Define business-level strategy and describe how it determines a firm's strategic position.

>> Business-level strategy determines a firm's strategic position in its quest for competitive advantage when competing in a single industry or product market.

>> Strategic positioning requires that managers address strategic trade-offs that arise between value and cost, because higher value tends to go along with higher cost.

>> Differentiation and cost leadership are distinct strategic positions.

>> Besides selecting an appropriate strategic position, managers must also define the scope of competition—whether to pursue a specific market niche or go after the broader market.

LO 6-2 Examine the relationship between value drivers and differentiation strategy.

>> The goal of a differentiation strategy is to increase the perceived value of goods and services so that customers will pay a higher price for additional features.

>> In a differentiation strategy, the focus of competition is on non-price attributes.

>> Some of the unique value drivers managers can manipulate are product features, customer service, customization, and complements.

>> Value drivers contribute to competitive advantage only if their increase in value creation (ΔV) exceeds the increase in costs (ΔC).

LO 6-3 Examine the relationship between cost drivers and cost-leadership strategy.

>> The goal of a cost-leadership strategy is to reduce the firm's cost below that of its competitors.

>> In a cost-leadership strategy, the focus of competition is on lowest-possible price, while offering acceptable value.

>> Some of the unique cost drivers that managers can manipulate are the cost of input factors, economies of scale, and learning and experience curve effects.

>> No matter how low the price, if there is no acceptable value proposition, the product or service will not sell.

LO 6-4 Assess the benefits and risks of cost leadership and differentiation business strategies vis-à-vis the five forces that shape competition.

>> The five forces model helps managers use generic business strategies to protect themselves against the industry forces that drive down profitability.

>> Differentiation and cost-leadership strategies allow firms to carve out strong strategic positions, not only to protect themselves against the five forces, but also to benefit from them in their quest for competitive advantage.

>> Exhibit 6.7 lists benefits and risks of each business strategy.

LO 6-5 Explain why it is difficult to succeed at an integration strategy.

>> A successful integration strategy requires that trade-offs between differentiation and low cost be reconciled.

>> Integration strategy often is difficult because the two distinct strategic positions require internal value chain activities that are fundamentally different from one another.

>> When firms fail to resolve strategic trade-offs between differentiation and cost, they end up being stuck in the middle. They then succeed at neither strategy, leading to a competitive disadvantage.

LO 6-6 Evaluate value and cost drivers that may allow a firm to pursue an integration strategy.

>> To address the trade-offs between differentiation and cost leadership at the business level, managers may leverage quality, economies of scope, innovation, and the firm's structure, culture, and routines.

>> The trade-offs between differentiation and low cost can either be addressed at the business level or at the corporate level.

LO 6-7 Describe and evaluate the dynamics of competitive positioning.

>> Strategic positions need to change over time as the environment changes.

>> Best practices determine the productivity frontier at any given time.

>> Reaching the productivity frontier enhances the likelihood of obtaining a competitive advantage.

>> Not reaching the productivity frontier implies competitive disadvantage if other firms *are* positioned at the productivity frontier.

Key Terms

Ambidextrous organization (p. 158)

Business-level strategy (p. 140)

Conglomerate (p. 160)

Cost-leadership strategy (p. 142)

Differentiation strategy (p. 142)

Diseconomies of scale (p. 150)

Economies of scale (p. 149)

Economies of scope (p. 157)

Focused cost-leadership strategy (p. 142)

Focused differentiation strategy (p. 142)

Integration strategy (p. 155)

Mass customization (p. 146)

Minimum efficient scale (MES) (p. 150)

Productivity frontier (p. 161)

Scope of competition (p. 142)

Strategic position (p. 141)

Strategic trade-offs (p. 141)

Discussion Questions

1. What are some drawbacks and risks to a broad generic business strategy? To a focused strategy?

2. How do economies of scale and economies of scope differ?

3. How can a firm attempting to have an integrated business-level strategy manage to avoid being "stuck in the middle"?

4. In Chapter 4, we discussed the internal value chain activities a firm can perform in its business model (see Exhibit 4.6). The value chain priorities can be quite different for firms taking different business strategies. Create examples of value chains for three firms: one using cost leadership, another using differentiation, and a third using an integration business-level strategy.

Ethical/Social Issues

1. Suppose Procter & Gamble (P&G) learns that a relatively new startup company Method (www.methodhome.com) is gaining market share with a new laundry detergent in West Coast markets. In response, P&G lowers the price of its Tide detergent from $15 to $9 for a 32-load bottle only in markets where Method's product is for sale. The goal of this "loss leader" price drop is to encourage Method to leave the laundry detergent market. Is this an ethical business practice? Why or why not?

2. A company such as Intel has a complex design and manufacturing process. This should lead Intel management to be concerned with the learning curves of employees. What practices would foster or hinder the hiring, training, and retention of key employees?

Small Group Exercises

SMALL GROUP EXERCISE 1

Ryanair (see Strategy Highlight 6.2) is noted as a firm that can make a profit on an $8 ticket by imposing numerous fees and surcharges.

1. Generally an ethical business practice is to disclose fees to potential customers to permit effective cost comparisons. Log onto www.ryanair.com and determine if Ryanair has transparent disclosure of these fees.

2. If you were a competitor in the European market, such as Aer Lingus or Lufthansa, how would you compete against Ryanair knowing your cost structure would not allow price parity?

SMALL GROUP EXERCISE 2

1. In the next column is a list of prominent firms. Place each firm you know (or research online) in one of the five categories of generic business-level strategies—broad cost-leadership, focused cost-leadership, broad differentiation, focused differentiation, and integration. Explain your choices.

2. What are some common features for firms you have placed within each category?

Ann Taylor	McKinsey & Co.
BIC	Nike
Big Lots	Patek Philippe
Black & Decker	Porsche
Clif Bar	Rhapsody
Coca-Cola	Rolls-Royce
Dollar Stores	Ryanair
Google	Samuel Adams
Goya Foods	Singapore Airlines
Greyhound Lines	Target
Kia Motors	Toyota
Lands' End	Vanguard
Liberty Mutual	Victoria's Secret
Louis Vuitton	WellPoint
Martin Guitars	Zara

Strategy Term Project

MODULE 6: BUSINESS STRATEGY

In this module, we will look at the business model your selected company uses and analyze its business-level strategy to see if it is appropriate for the strategic position. If your firm is a large multibusiness entity, you will need to choose one of the major businesses (strategic business unit, or SBU) of the firm for this analysis. In prior chapters, we collected information about this firm's external environment and some of its internal competitive advantages. Using this information and any other you have gathered, address the following questions.

1. Does your selected business have differentiated products or services? If so, what is the basis for this differentiation from the competition?

2. Does your firm have a cost-leadership position in this business? If so, can you identify which cost drivers it uses effectively to hold this position?

3. What is your firm's approach to the market? If it segments the market, identify the scope of competition it is using.

4. Using the answers to the preceding questions, identify which generic business strategies your firm is employing. Is the firm leveraging the appropriate value and cost drivers for the business strategy you identified? Explain why or why not.

5. As noted in the chapter, each business strategy is context-dependent. What do you see as positives and negatives with the selected business strategy of your firm in its competitive situation?

6. In Chapter 3, we identified strategic groups in the industry relevant to your firm. Review the firms listed in the same strategic group as your selected firm. See if there is a similarity with the generic business strategy used by each. In most strategic groups, there will be market and some strategy similarities across the firms.

7. What suggestions do you have to improve the firm's business strategy and strategic position?

*my*Strategy

DIFFERENT VALUE AND COST DRIVERS— WHAT DETERMINES *YOUR* BUYING DECISIONS?

Differentiation positioning versus low-cost strategies can be particularly pronounced in the retailing sector. As noted in the ChapterCase, Whole Foods is a differentiated grocery store that is finding it necessary to respond to low-cost leaders, such as Walmart, that have entered the organic food market. Additionally, Whole Foods must contend with a possibly shrinking market segment of customers who will pay extra for organic foods in an economic downturn. Some customers who might enjoy going to Whole Foods are finding they get more for their money at a traditional grocer such as Publix or Safeway.

What role does the awareness of a firm's strategy have on your buying decisions? Will you select (or stay away from) certain brands due to their position on global warming or certain social causes? Or are price and availability the real drivers of your purchasing dollars?

What if you needed to buy a pair of casual shoes? You have budgeted $60 for this purchase. You are in a local store and you have found two pairs of shoes you like. They are both $55. One is made by a company whose shoes you have purchased before, and you found the shoes durable and comfortable. The other pair is made by a newer company; you've never owned their products but a friend of yours told you a bit about the company before class a few weeks ago. (He also had been shopping for shoes.) The following is a brief write-up on each company. Which shoes do you buy?

1. G.H. Bass was founded in 1876 in Wilton, Maine, and over its storied history has largely maintained a differentiated position of high quality and comfortable casual shoes. The Bass Weejun loafer was introduced in the U.S. in 1936 and has continued to propel the firm as one of America's top-selling shoe brands. They also retail in Europe, Asia, and South America.

2. TOMS shoes was launched in 2006 in Venice, California, with a canvas shoe design adapted from Argentina, the alpargata. The shoes are sold via the company's website www.tomsshoes.com and also through a limited number of retail stores in the U.S., Europe, parts of Asia, and South America. From the start, TOMS has included a social aspect to the firm. For every pair of shoes purchased, TOMS sends one free pair to a child who can't afford to buy shoes. The firm also sponsors "shoe drops" and will sometimes have celebrity participants in the free-shoe-distribution events. In September 2010, the company's "One for One" program surpassed one million pairs of shoes provided to children in need.[60]

Endnotes

1. This ChapterCase is based on: "Frank talk from Whole Foods' John Mackey," *The Wall Street Journal,* August 4, 2009; "As sales slip, Whole Foods tries to push health," *The Wall Street Journal,* August 5, 2009; and "The conscience of a capitalist," *The Wall Street Journal,* October 3, 2009, www.wholefoodsmarket.com.

2. This discussion is based on: Porter, M. E. (1980), *Competitive Strategy: Techniques for Analyzing Industries and Competitors* (New York: Free Press); Porter, M. E. (1985), *Competitive Advantage: Creating and Sustaining Superior Performance* (New York: Free Press); Porter, M. E. (1996), "What is strategy?" *Harvard Business Review,* November–December; and Porter, M. E. (2008), "The five competitive forces that shape strategy," *Harvard Business Review,* January.

3. These questions are based on: Abell, D. F. (1980), *Defining the Business: The Starting Point of Strategic Planning* (Englewood Cliffs, NJ: Prentice-Hall); Porter, M. E. (1996), "What is strategy?"; and Priem, R. (2007), "A consumer perspective on value creation," *Academy of Management Review* 32: 219–235.

4. Porter, M. E. (1996), "What is strategy?"

5. The discussion of generic business strategies is based on: Porter, M. E. (1980), *Competitive Strategy: Techniques for Analyzing Industries and Competitors*; Porter, M. E. (1985), *Competitive Advantage: Creating and Sustaining Superior Performance*; Porter, M. E. (1996), "What is strategy?"; and Porter, M. E. (2008), "The

five competitive forces that shape strategy."

6. To decide if and how to divide up the market, you can apply the market segmentation techniques you have acquired in your marketing and micro-economics classes.

7. Elon Musk in "Uber Entrepreneur: An Evening with Elon Musk," Churchill Club, Mountain View, CA, April 7, 2009 (available at ForaTV: http://fora .tv/2009/04/07/Uber_Entrepreneur_ An_Evening_with_Elon_Musk).

8. Anderson, R. C., and R. White (2009), *Confessions of a Radical Industrialist: Profits, People, Purpose— Doing Business by Respecting the Earth* (New York: St. Martin's Press).

9. "Latest Starbucks buzzword: 'Lean' Japanese techniques," *The Wall Street Journal,* August 4, 2009.

10. Christensen, C. M., and M. E. Raynor (2003), *The Innovator's Solution: Creating and Sustaining Successful Growth* (Boston, MA: Harvard Business School Press).

11. The interested reader is referred to the strategy, marketing, and economics literatures. A good start in the strategy literature is the classic work of M. E. Porter: Porter, M. E. (1980), *Competitive Strategy: Techniques for Analyzing Industries and Competitors*; Porter, M. E. (1985), *Competitive Advantage: Creating and Sustaining Superior Performance*; and Porter, M. E. (2008), "The five competitive forces that shape strategy."

12. www.oxo.com/about.jsp.

13. "Amazon opens wallet, buys Zappos," *The Wall Street Journal,* July 23, 2009.

14. Hsieh, T. (2010), *Delivering Happiness: A Path to Profits, Passion, and Purpose* (New York: Business Plus).

15. This strategy highlight is based on: Gladwell, M. (2000), *The Tipping Point: How Little Things Can Make a Big Difference* (New York: Little, Brown and Company); Liker, J. (2003), *The Toyota Way* (Burr Ridge, IL: McGraw-Hill); Dawson, C. (2004), *Lexus: The Relentless Pursuit* (Hoboken, NJ: Wiley); Collins, J. (2009), *How the Mighty Fall and Why Some Companies Never Give In* (New York: HarperCollins); "Toyota recall spreads to Europe, China," *The Wall Street Journal,* January 28, 2010; "Car maker's fixes may not solve issue," *The Wall Street Journal,* February 24, 2010; and "Recall dims Japan's export outlook," *The Wall Street Journal,* February 24, 2010.

16. Davis, S. M. (1987), *Future Perfect* (Reading, MA: Addison-Wesley).

17. www.att.com/u-verse/.

18. See a discussion of Southwest Airlines's business activities in Chapter 5.

19. This strategy highlight is based on: Anderson, C. (2009), *Free: The Future of a Radical Price* (New York: Hyperion); "Walmart with wings," *BusinessWeek,* November 27, 2006; "Snarling all the way to the bank," *The Economist,* August 23, 2007; and "Ryanair's O'Leary: The duke of discomfort," *Bloomberg Businessweek,* September 2, 2010, www.ryanair.com.

20. Friedman, T. (2005), *The World is Flat: A Brief History of the Twenty-First*

Century (New York: Farrar, Strauss and Giroux).

21. "Boeing looks beyond Dreamliner's first flight," *The Wall Street Journal,* December 15, 2009, www.boeing.com.

22. www.airbus.com/en/aircraftfamilies/a380/home/.

23. Kevin Turner, COO Microsoft. Keynote Speech at Microsoft's Worldwide Partner Conference, New Orleans, July 15, 2009.

24. "Fiat nears stake in Chrysler that could lead to takeover," *The Wall Street Journal,* January 20, 2009.

25. "GM hopes Volt juices its future," *The Wall Street Journal,* August 12, 2009.

26. "Nucor's new plant project still on hold," *Associated Press,* July 23, 2009, www.nucor.com.

27. Gladwell, M. (2002), *The Tipping Point: How Little Things Can Make a Big Difference* (New York: Back Bay Books) p. 185.

28. Levitt, B., and J. G. March (1988), "Organizational learning," in Scott, W. R. (ed.), *Annual Review of Sociology* 14: 319–340 (Greenwich, CT: JAI Press).

29. For insightful reviews and syntheses on the learning curve literature, see: Yelle, L. E. (1979), "The learning curve: Historical review and comprehensive survey," *Decision Sciences* 10: 302–308; and Argote, L., and G. Todorova (2007), "Organizational learning: Review and future directions," in Hodgkinson, G. P., and J. K. Ford (eds.), *International Review of Industrial and Organizational Psychology* 22: 193–234 (New York: Wiley).

30. Wright, T. P. (1936). "Factors affecting the cost of airplanes," *Journal of Aeronautical Sciences* 3: 122–128.

31. This discussion is based on: Darr, E. D., L. Argote, and D. Epple (1995), "The acquisition, transfer and depreciation of knowledge in service organizations: Productivity in franchises," *Management Science* 42: 1750–1762; King, A. W., and A. L. Ranft (2001), "Capturing knowledge and knowing through improvisation: What managers can learn from the thoracic surgery board certification process," *Journal of Management* 27: 255–277; Zollo, M., J. J. Reuer, and H. Singh (2002), "Interorganizational routines

and performance in strategic alliances," *Organization Science* 13: 701–713; Hoang, H., and F. T. Rothaermel (2005), "The effect of general and partner-specific alliance experience on joint R&D project performance," *Academy of Management Journal* 48: 332–345; Rothaermel, F. T., and D. L. Deeds (2006), "Alliance type, alliance experience, and alliance management capability in high-technology ventures," *Journal of Business Venturing* 21: 429–460; Pisano, G. P., R. M. Bohmer, and A. C. Edmondson (2001), "Organizational differences in rates of learning: Evidence from the adoption of minimally invasive cardiac surgery," *Management Science* 47: 752–768; Edmondson, A. C., R. M. Bohmer, and G. P. Pisano (2001), "Disrupted routines: Team learning and new technology implementation in hospitals," *Administrative Science Quarterly* 46: 685–716; Thompson, P. (2001), "How much did the liberty shipbuilders learn? New evidence from an old case study," *Journal of Political Economy* 109: 103–137; and Gulati, R., D. Lavie, and H. Singh (2009), "The nature of partnering experience and the gain from alliances," *Strategic Management Journal* 30: 1213–1233.

32. Ramanarayanan, S. (2008), "Does practice make perfect: An empirical analysis of learning-by-doing in cardiac surgery." Available at SSRN: http://ssrn.com/abstract=1129350.

33. Technically speaking, learning effects occur over time as output is accumulated, while economies of scale are captured at one point in time when output is increased. Although learning peters out at some point (as shown in Exhibit 6.10 as learning curves flatten out), there are no diseconomies to learning (as shown in Exhibit 6.8 past output Q_2).

34. Boston Consulting Group (1972), *Perspectives on Experience* (Boston, MA: Boston Consulting Group).

35. This discussion is based on: Porter, M. E. (1979), "How competitive forces shape strategy," *Harvard Business Review,* March–April: 137–145; Porter, M. E. (1980), *Competitive Strategy. Techniques for Analyzing Industries and Competitors;* and Porter, M. E. (2008), "The five competitive forces that shape strategy."

36. This discussion is based on: Hill, C.W.L. (1988), "Differentiation versus low cost or differentiation and low cost: A contingency framework," *Academy of Management Review* 13: 401–412; and Miller, A., and G. G. Dess (1993), "Assessing Porter's model in terms of its generalizability, accuracy, and simplicity," *Journal of Management Studies* 30: 553–585.

37. "Would you spend $14,000 for this bike? Techies drive demand for custom models," *The Boston Globe,* April 23, 2006.

38. www.leopardcycles.com/about.php.

39. "Avon to spruce up its R&D budget with $100 million and new facility," *The Wall Street Journal,* May 23, 2002.

40. "Avon plans to realign European manufacturing to meet accelerating demand and reduce costs," *Associated Press,* April 12, 2002.

41. This discussion is based on: Afuah, A. (2009), *Strategic Innovation. New Game Strategies for Competitive Advantage* (New York: Routledge); Hill, C.W.L., and F. T. Rothaermel (2003), "The performance of incumbent firms in the face of radical technological innovation," *Academy of Management Review* 28: 257–274; Rothaermel, F. T., and A. Hess, "Finding an innovation strategy that works," *The Wall Street Journal,* August 17, 2009; and Rothaermel, F. T., and A. Hess (2010), "Innovation strategies combined," *MIT Sloan Management Review,* Spring: 12–15.

42. "IKEA: How the Swedish retailer became a global cult brand," *BusinessWeek,* November 14, 2005.

43. This discussion is based on: O'Reilly, C. A., III, and M. L. Tushman (2007), "Ambidexterity as dynamic capability: Resolving the innovator's dilemma," *Research in Organizational Behavior* 28: 1–60; Raisch, S., and J. Birkinshaw (2008), "Organizational ambidexterity: Antecedents, outcomes, and moderators," *Journal of Management* 34: 375–409; and Rothaermel, F. T., and M. T. Alexandre (2009), "Ambidexterity in technology sourcing: The moderating role of absorptive capacity," *Organization Science* 20: 759–780.

44. Hamel, G. (2006), "The why, what, and how of management innovation," *Harvard Business Review,* February.

45. March, J. G. (1991), "Exploration and exploitation in organizational learning," *Organization Science* 2: 319–340; and Levinthal, D. A., and J. G. March (1993), "The myopia of learning," *Strategic Management Journal* 14: 95–112.

46. Author's interviews with Intel managers and engineers.

47. Brown, S. L., and K. M. Eisenhardt (1997), "The art of continuous change: Linking complexity theory and time-paced evolution in relentlessly shifting organizations," *Administrative Science Quarterly* 42: 1–34; and O'Reilly, C. A., B. Harreld, and M. Tushman (2009), "Organizational ambidexterity: IBM and emerging business opportunities," *California Management Review* 51: 75–99.

48. This discussion is based on: Porter, M. E. (1980), *Competitive Strategy*; and Porter, M. E. (1996), "What is strategy?"

49. This example is based on: "No small achievement," *The Economist,* March 26, 2009; "The new people's car," *The Economist,* March 26, 2009; and "Tata takes charge," *The Economist,* August 20, 2009.

50. Christensen, C. M., and M. E. Raynor (2003), *The Innovator's Solution: Creating and Sustaining Successful Growth* (Boston, MA: Harvard Business School Press).

51. Tushman, M., W. K. Smith, R. C. Wood, G. Westerman, and C. O. O'Reilly (2010), "Organizational designs and innovation streams," *Industrial and Corporate Change* 19: 1331–1366.

52. "eBay retreats in web retailing," *The Wall Street Journal,* March 12, 2009.

53. "eBay sells Skype to investor group," *The Wall Street Journal,* September 1, 2009.

54. Porter, M. E. (1996), "What is strategy?"

55. The shape of the productivity frontier is concave to indicate the trade-offs between low cost and differentiation.

56. "Taking the dull out of Dell," *BusinessWeek,* November 3, 2008.

57. "Dell to buy Perot in catch-up deal," *The Wall Street Journal,* September 22, 2009.

58. Material for this case discussion is from: "More than 500 schools awarded grants for salad bars," Whole Foods Market Press Release, February 1, 2011, www.wholefoodsmarket.com/backtoschool/; and "ECO:nomics: Whole Foods CEO says eating healthy costs less," WSJ Video, March 3, 2011.

59. "ECO:nomics: Whole Foods CEO says eating healthy costs less."

60. This section is based on: https://bassshoes.harborghb.com/bass-shoes-history; Jennifer Irwin, "The lowly alpargata steps forward," *The New York Times*, January 17, 2007; and www.tomsshoes.com.

CHAPTER 7

Business Strategy: Innovation and Strategic Entrepreneurship

LEARNING OBJECTIVES

After studying this chapter, you will be able to:

LO 7-1 Define innovation and describe its role in the competitive process.

LO 7-2 Describe the competitive implications of different stages in the industry life cycle.

LO 7-3 Apply strategic management concepts to entrepreneurship and innovation.

LO 7-4 Evaluate different types of innovation and derive their strategic implications.

LO 7-5 Describe the long-tail concept and derive strategic implications.

LO 7-6 Evaluate discontinuities and describe the dynamics of paradigm changes.

LO 7-7 Identify the process leading to hypercompetition, and explain why competitive advantage can often be sustained through continuous innovation.

From Encyclopedia Britannica to Encarta to Wikipedia

HAILING BACK TO the 18th-century Scottish Enlightenment, the *Encyclopedia Britannica* was once the gold standard for authoritative reference works, delving into more than 65,000 topics with articles by some 4,000 scholarly contributors, including many by Nobel Laureates. The beautiful leather-bound, multivolume set made a nice decorative item in many literate homes.

In the early 1990s, when total sales for encyclopedias were over $1.2 billion annually, *Encyclopedia Britannica* was the undisputed market leader, holding more than 50 percent market share and earning some $650 million in revenues. Not surprisingly, its superior differentiated appeal was highly correlated with cost, reflected in its steep sticker price of up to $2,000.

Innovation changed all that. Banking on the widespread diffusion of the personal computer, Microsoft launched its electronic encyclopedia Encarta in 1993 at a price of $99. Although some viewed it as merely a CD-version of the lower-cost and lower-quality *Funk & Wagnall's Encyclopedia,* sold in supermarkets, Encarta still took a big bite out of Britannica's market.

Within only three years, the market for printed encyclopedias had shrunk by half, and Britannica's revenues along with it, while Microsoft sold over $100 million worth of Encarta CDs.

In 2001, Internet entrepreneur Jimmy Wales launched Wikipedia, the free online multilanguage encyclopedia. In Hawaiian, *wiki* means quick, referring to the instant do-it-yourself editing capabilities of the site. Wikipedia now has 18 million articles in 281 languages, including over 3.6 million items in English.

Since it is open source, any person, expert or novice, can contribute content and edit pages using the handy "edit this page" button. Thousands of Wikipedians across the world have done so.

Although Wikipedia's volume of English entries is almost 40 times greater than that of Britannica, the site is not as error-prone as you might think. Wikipedia relies on the "wisdom of the crowds," which assumes "the many" often know more than the expert. A peer-reviewed study by *Nature* of 42 science topics found four errors in Wikipedia and three in Britannica. Such errors can be corrected more or less in real time on Wikipedia, whereas Britannica must wait until its next printing.

Because Wikipedia was able to significantly increase value creation and drive costs to zero, there is little future for printed or CD-based encyclopedias. Today, Wikipedia is one of the most-visited websites in the world.[1]

After reading the chapter, you will find more about this case, with related questions, on page 193.

▲ **INNOVATION IS** a powerful driver in the competitive process. With introduction of its CD-based Encarta, Microsoft destroyed about half the value created by Britannica. In turn, Wikipedia used the Internet to destroy Encarta's business, which Microsoft shut down in 2009. At the same time, Wikipedia created substantial value for consumers because it shifted value creation and capture away from Britannica's and Microsoft's proprietary business models for encyclopedias to an open-source model powered by user-generated content. Innovation enables firms to redefine the marketplace in their favor and achieve growth.[2] As a key aspect of business strategy formulation, innovation and the related topic of strategic entrepreneurship are the focus of this chapter.

COMPETITION DRIVEN BY INNOVATION

>> LO 7-1
Define innovation and describe its role in the competitive process.

Invention describes the discovery of any new product, process, or idea, or the modification and recombination of existing ones; innovation concerns the *commercialization* thereof.[3] For example, the Wright brothers invented the airplane, which was commercialized by Boeing and others. As shown in Exhibit 7.1, an innovation needs to be novel, useful, and successfully implemented in order to help firms gain and sustain a competitive advantage.

The successful commercialization of a new product or service allows a firm to extract temporary monopoly profits. Initially, for example, Apple faced no direct competition to its iPhone. Its smartphone innovation reshaped the mobile phone industry structure in its favor, resulting in a competitive advantage. To sustain a competitive advantage, however, a firm must continuously innovate—that is, it must produce a string of successful new products or services over time. In this spirit, not only has Apple introduced the improved iPhone 4, it also has launched the iPad, a multimedia tablet computer, in early 2010 with the intent to drive convergence in computing, telecommunications, and media content. The iPad is also positioned to challenge Amazon's Kindle, the market leader in e-book readers. Continuous innovation is the engine behind many other successful companies, such as 3M, GE, Google, HP, Intel, P&G, and Sony.

innovation The commercialization of any new product, process, or idea, or the modification and recombination of existing ones. To drive growth, innovation also needs to be useful and successfully implemented.

Competition is a process driven by the "perennial gale of creative destruction," in the words of economist Joseph Schumpeter.[4] The continuous waves of leadership changes in the encyclopedia business, detailed in the ChapterCase, demonstrate the potency of innovation as a competitive weapon: It can simultaneously create and destroy value. Firms must be able to innovate while also fending off competitors' innovations. A successful strategy requires both an effective offense and a hard-to-crack defense.

Many firms have dominated an early wave of innovation only to be destroyed by the next wave. Examples include:

- *The move from typewriters to computers:* Wang Laboratories, a computer company that led the market for word-processing machines, destroyed typewriter companies like Smith Corona and Underwood. It then was undone by computer makers like IBM and Compaq. Today, IBM has exited the personal computer market, selling its PC division to the Chinese technology company Lenovo, and Compaq has been acquired by HP.

- *The explosion of television-viewing options:* The traditional television networks (ABC, CBS, and NBC) have been struggling to maintain viewers and advertising

EXHIBIT 7.1

Innovation: A Novel and Useful Idea that Is Successfully Implemented

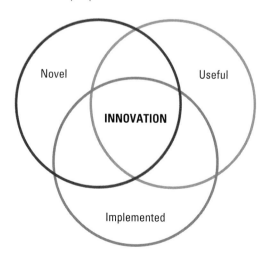

revenues as cable and satellite providers have offered innovative programming. Those same cable and satellite providers are trying hard to hold on to viewers as more and more people gravitate toward customized content online. To exploit such opportunities, Google acquired YouTube in 2006 for $1.65 billion, and Comcast, the largest cable operator in the U.S., purchased a majority stake in NBC Universal in 2009 valued at close to $14 billion.[5] Comcast's acquisition helps it integrate delivery services and content, with the goal of establishing itself as a new player in the media industry.

■ *The trend toward drugs designed for individual patients:* Established pharmaceutical companies like Merck and Pfizer brought major new drugs to market within the past decade, using a chemical-based drug discovery and development paradigm. These same companies are struggling to maintain their dominance as relative newcomers like Amgen and Genentech are leveraging advances in genomics, genetic engineering, and biotechnology to produce drugs that are better targeted to treat diseases and that eventually can be designed for individual patients.

We now turn to a discussion of how the role of innovation in driving competitive behavior changes throughout the evolution of an industry.

INNOVATION AND THE INDUSTRY LIFE CYCLE

Innovations frequently lead to the birth of new industries. Innovative advances in IT and logistics facilitated the creation of the overnight express delivery industry by FedEx and big-box retailing by Walmart. The Internet set online retailing in motion, with new companies such as Amazon and eBay taking the lead, and revolutionized the advertising industry through Yahoo and Google. Currently, advances in nanotechnology promise to revolutionize many different industries, ranging from medical diagnostics and surgery to lighter and stronger airplane components.[6]

Industries tend to follow a predictable industry life cycle: As an industry evolves over time, we can identify four distinct stages: *introduction, growth, maturity,* and *decline.* Exhibit 7.2 depicts a typical industry life cycle, with corresponding consumer-adoption categories.[7]

>> **LO 7-2**
Describe the competitive implications of different stages in the industry life cycle.

industry life cycle
The four different stages—introduction, growth, maturity, and decline—that occur in the evolution of an industry over time.

EXHIBIT 7.2

The Industry Life Cycle and Consumer-Adoption Categories

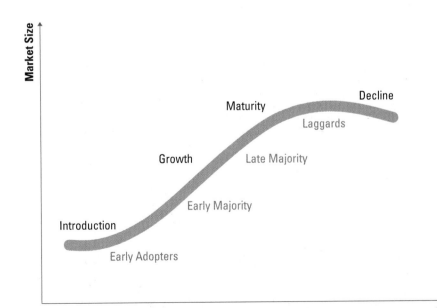

The number and size of competitors change as the industry life cycle unfolds. Likewise, different types of consumers enter the market at each stage. Thus, both the supply and demand sides of the market change as the industry ages. Each stage of the industry life cycle requires different competencies in order for the firm to perform well and satisfy that stage's unique customer group. In this chapter, we illustrate how the type of innovation changes at each stage of the life cycle as well as how innovation can initiate and drive a new life cycle. Be aware, too, that other factors such as fads in fashion, changes in demographics, or de-regulation, can affect the dynamics behind industry life cycles.

Introduction Stage

When an individual or company launches a successful innovation, a new industry may emerge. In this introductory stage, the innovator's core competency is R&D, necessary to creating a new product category that will attract customers. This is a capital-intensive process, in which the innovator is investing in designing a unique product, trying new ideas to attract customers, and producing small quantities—all of which contribute to a high price when the product is launched. Initial market growth is slow: Only *early adopters* are willing to pay a premium price to have the latest gadget. They frequently tolerate technological imperfections and like to tinker with the products. For example, the GRiD Compass was introduced as a laptop for early adopters in the early 1980s. By today's standards, it was not only heavy (almost three times the weight of today's laptops), but also expensive, costing about $18,000 in today's dollars. The performance of a new product also tends to be inferior in some respects. For example, not only were early laptops almost too heavy to carry around, their computing power and display capabilities were only a fraction of those available in a desktop computer.

In this introductory stage, when barriers to entry tend to be high, generally only a few innovators are active in the market. They emphasize unique product features and performance rather than price. When introduced in the spring of 2010, for example, Apple's iPad was priced at $499 for 16GB of storage space and $829 for 64GB with a 3G Wi-Fi connection.[8] Despite those hefty prices, early adopters eagerly lined up.

While there are some benefits to being early in the market, such as building a reputation for innovation, innovators also encounter some first-mover disadvantages. They must educate potential customers about the product's intended benefits, find distribution channels and complementary assets, and continue to perfect the fledgling product. While a core competency in R&D is necessary to create or enter an industry in the introductory stage, some competency in marketing also is helpful in achieving market acceptance. Competition can be intense, and early winners are well-positioned to stake out a strong position for the future. For example, though they have attracted challengers, the innovators in the personal computer industry, such as Intel and Microsoft, are still holding on to their lead some 30 years later.

The strategic objective during the introductory stage is to achieve market acceptance and seed future growth. One way to accomplish these objectives is to leverage network effects,[9] the positive effect that one user of a product or service has on the value of that product for other users. Network effects occur when the value of a product or service increases, often exponentially, with the number of users. If successful, network effects propel the industry to the next stage of the life cycle, the growth stage (which we discuss next). In the early days of the Internet, for instance, only a small network of scientists had access to e-mail. Today, e-mail is a ubiquitous communications tool with more than a billion users, and thus is much more valuable to users. Strategy Highlight 7.1 describes how Apple leveraged the network effects generated by countless complementary software applications (apps) to achieve dominance in the smartphone market.

network effects
The positive effect (externality) that one user of a product or service has on the value of that product for other users.

STRATEGY HIGHLIGHT 7.1

Apple Leverages Network Effects to Propel Growth

Apple launched its enormously successful iPhone in the summer of 2007. A year later, it followed up with the Apple App Store, which boasts that, for almost anything you might need, "there's an app for that." *Apps* are software programs developed to provide mobile users with small and inexpensive business and personal services wherever they may be. They allow iPhone (and now iPad) users to access their business contacts via LinkedIn, check their packages via FedEx, get the latest news on CNN, or engage in customer relations management using Salesforce. You can access Facebook to check on your friends and play social games such as FarmVille, where some 85 million players earn virtual currency by plowing fields and raising and trading livestock. Although the software programs are tiny, the industry is quite large. It is estimated to grow to over $4 billion by 2012, producing successful startups like Zynga (the maker of FarmVille) along the way.

Even more important is the effect apps have on the value of an iPhone. Arguably, the explosive growth of the iPhone is due to the fact that the Apple App Store offers a huge selection of apps to its users. (An estimated 300,000 apps were downloaded more than 10 billion times as of spring 2011.) In contrast, RIM (the maker of the BlackBerry), Nokia, and Microsoft are all playing catch-up. The availability of apps, in turn, leads to network effects that increase the value of the iPhone for its users. Exhibit 7.3 shows how. Increased value creation, as we know from Chapter 6, is positively related to demand, which in turn increases the installed base of Apple iPhones. This in turn incentivizes software developers to write more apps, positively reinforcing the virtuous cycle. Making apps widely available helped Apple stake out a strong position in the smartphone industry. Moreover, all the apps, as well as purchases from the iTunes library and the newly created iBook store, are transferable from the iPhone to the iPad. Taken together, positive network efforts are likely to increase demand for the iPad as well.[10]

EXHIBIT 7.3

Leveraging Network Economics: Apple's iPhone

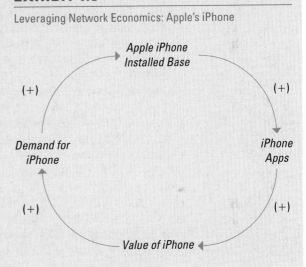

Growth Stage

Market growth accelerates in the second (the growth) stage of the industry life cycle. After the initial innovation has gained market acceptance, demand increases rapidly as first-time buyers rush to enter the market, convinced by the proof-of-concept demonstrated by early adopters in the introductory stage. The new group of buyers, called the *early majority,* is at the leading edge of a large customer wave. The early majority also sees the benefit that can be gained from adopting a new product or service.

As the size of the early majority expands, a standard (or *dominant design*) signals the market's agreement on a common set of engineering features and design choices.[11] An agreed-upon standard, such as the IBM PC, ensures that all components of the system work well together, regardless of who developed them. It also helps legitimize the new technology by reducing uncertainty and confusion. Thus, a standard or dominant design tends to capture a larger market share and can persist for a long time. The Wintel standard marked the beginning of exponential growth in the personal computer industry; it now holds about 90 percent of market share.

standard An agreed-upon solution about a common set of engineering features and design choices; also known as *dominant design.*

A more recent example is the high-definition format war to supersede standard DVDs and CDs. Blu-ray, backed by an association of electronics companies including Sony, Panasonic, Philips, LG, Hitachi, and Samsung, bested the HD-DVD format backed by Toshiba. Some argue that Sony's PlayStation 3 acted as a catalyst for adopting the Blu-ray format. A tipping point in favor of the Blu-ray format was reached when Warner Bros. decided to release discs only in Blu-ray format beginning in the summer of 2008. Within weeks, leading retailers such as Walmart, Best Buy, and the now-defunct Circuit City began carrying DVDs in Blu-ray format, and did not stock as large a selection in the HD-DVD format; Netflix and Blockbuster began renting Blu-ray DVDs predominantly. As a consequence, thousands of titles are now available on high-definition Blu-ray discs. The competitive implications are tremendous: Industry agreement on the format has opened a new market for both Blu-ray disc players and titles. Barriers to entry fell as technological uncertainties were overcome, and many new and established firms rushed to participate in the growth opportunity.

The high-def format war was fought in the marketplace. However, government bodies or industry associations can also set standards by making top-down decisions. The European Union determined in the 1980s that GSM (Global System for Mobile Communications) should be the standard for cell phones in Europe. The United States relied instead on a market-based approach, and CDMA (code division multiple access), a proprietary standard developed by Qualcomm, emerged as an early leader. While North American manufacturers and service providers such as AT&T, Verizon, Motorola, and others were fighting a format war, Scandinavian companies such as Nokia and Ericsson faced no such uncertainty, and they leveraged their early lead into market dominance. Today, about 80 percent of the global mobile market uses the GSM standard.

Since demand is strong during the growth phase, both efficient and inefficient firms thrive; the rising tide lifts all boats. Moreover, prices begin to fall as standard business processes are put in place and firms begin to reap economies of scale and learning. Distribution channels are thus expanded, and complementary assets become widely available.[12]

Though the emergence of a dominant design fosters the development of complementary assets, Strategy Highlight 7.2 shows that firms sometimes choose *not to support* certain new standards or applications.

After a standard or dominant design is established in an industry, the basis of competition tends to move away from product innovations toward process innovations.[13] Product innovations, as the name suggests, are embodied in new products—the jet airplane, electric vehicle, MP3 player, and netbook. On the other hand, process innovations are new ways to produce existing products or to deliver existing services. Process innovations are made possible through advances such as the Internet, lean manufacturing, Six Sigma, biotechnology, nanotechnology, and so on. The biotech startup Genentech, for example, was the first firm to use genetic engineering to discover and develop new medicines such as human insulin and human growth hormones.

As captured in Exhibit 7.4 (page 178), *product* innovation is the most important competitive weapon when initiating a new industry life cycle; at that point (typically, at the introduction stage), the level of process innovation at first is low. This pecking order, however, reverses over time. Eventually (usually in the growth stage), an industry standard emerges (indicated by the blue dashed line in the figure). At that point, most of the technological and commercial uncertainties about the new product are gone. After the market accepts a radical product innovation, and a standard for the new technology has emerged, *process* innovation rapidly becomes more important than product innovation. As market demand increases, economies of scale kick in: Firms establish and optimize standard business processes through applications of lean manufacturing, Six Sigma, and so on. As a consequence, product improvements become incremental, while the level of process innovation rises.

product innovations
New products, such as the jet airplane, electric vehicle, MP3 player, and netbook.

process innovations
New ways to produce existing products or deliver existing services.

Some Standards Die Hard: QWERTY vs. DSK

The QWERTY keyboard, named for the sequence of the first six letters on the upper-left row, was introduced in the 1870s as a way to *slow* typists in order to avoid jamming the type bars in mechanical typewriters. While generally considered an inefficient arrangement of the most frequently used letters, the QWERTY keyboard remains the standard today, but not for lack of alternatives.

In the 1930s, August Dvorak, a professor of education at the University of Washington, designed and patented an alternative keyboard intended to *speed up* typing. Professor Dvorak placed the most frequently used letters, such as vowels, in the center row where the typist's fingers rest, and he moved less commonly used letters to the first and third keyboard rows. This design, the Dvorak

Simplified Keyboard or DSK, minimizes the typist's finger reach and thus increases typing speed and accuracy. But given the sunk cost people had invested in learning the QWERTY keyboard, the DSK did not catch on.

Today, however, every personal computer comes with an optional DSK setting that requires only a minor software modification. Even though most people have never heard about it, the DSK has a passionate core of devotees. They were quite surprised to learn that when smartphones with virtual keyboards, like the iPhone and the BlackBerry Storm, and the media tablet iPad were introduced, they came only with the traditional QWERTY keyboard layout. A software developer created an iPhone app to allow users to add the Dvorak layout. But since it is not an "approved Apple App," users must hack into their systems to install the unofficial program. (Caution: Such "jail breaking" voids the iPhone's warranty.) This example shows how hard it can be to overthrow entrenched standards, even when they are inferior and the cost of alternative options is quite low.[14]

The Dvorak keyboard locates the most frequently used letters in the center row, to increase typing speed.

At the end of a life cycle (in the decline stage), the level of process innovation reaches its maximum, while the level of incremental product innovation reaches its minimum, as Exhibit 7.4 shows. This dynamic interplay between product and process innovation starts anew with the emergence of the next radical innovation that opens up a new industry.

The core competencies for competitive advantage in the growth stage tend to shift toward manufacturing and marketing capabilities, with an R&D emphasis on process innovation in order to improve efficiency. Since market demand is robust in this stage and more competitors have entered the market, there tends to be more strategic variety: Some competitors will continue to follow a *differentiation* strategy, emphasizing unique features, product functionality, and reliability. Other firms may conclude that lower prices are a potent competitive weapon and thus employ a *cost-leadership strategy*. Many firms in the

EXHIBIT 7.4

Product and Process
Innovation and the
Emergence of an
Industry Standard

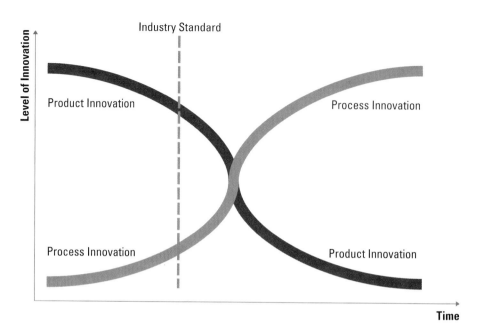

growth stage conclude that lower price is a key success factor; to bring more consumers into the market, prices have to come down. When Apple released the iPad 2 in spring 2011, prices for the original iPad dropped significantly. Access to efficient and large-scale manufacturing (such as those offered by Foxconn in China) and effective supply-chain capabilities are key success factors when market demand increases rapidly.

The key objective for firms during the growth phase is to stake out a strong strategic position not easily imitated by rivals. In the fast-growing shapewear industry, startup company Spanx has staked out a strong position. In 1998, Florida State University graduate Sara Blakely decided to cut the feet off her pantyhose to enhance her looks when wearing pants.[15] Soon after she obtained a patent for her bodyshaping undergarments, and Spanx began production and retailing of its shapewear in 2000. Sales grew exponentially after Blakely appeared on the *Oprah Winfrey Show.* By 2008, Spanx had grown to 75 employees and sold an estimated 5.4 million Spanx "power panties," with sales exceeding $750 million. The shapewear industry's explosive growth has attracted several other players: Flexees by Maidenform, Body Wrap, and Miraclesuit, to name a few. They are all attempting to carve out positions in the new industry.

Maturity Stage

As an industry moves into the mature stage, growth comes from buyers called the *late majority* entering the market. The purchasing power of the early majority subsides. Their demand was satisfied in the growth stage, and they are now making only replacement or repeat purchases. Given the large market size achieved from the growth stage, any additional market demand in the maturity stage is limited. This limited market demand in turn increases competitive intensity within the industry. Firms begin to compete directly against one another for market share, rather than trying to capture a share of an increasing pie.

The winners in this increasingly competitive environment are generally firms that stake a strong position as cost leaders. Key success factors are the manufacturing and process engineering capabilities to drive costs down. Assuming an acceptable value proposition, price is the dominant competitive weapon in the mature stage; product features and performance requirements are now well established. A few firms may be able to implement an integration strategy, combining differentiation and low cost, but given the intensity of competition, many weaker firms are forced to exit. Generally, the larger firms with economies of scale are the ones that survive as the industry consolidates and excess capacity is removed. The industry structure morphs into an oligopoly, in which only a few large firms remain. In the airline industry, for example, the large number of bankruptcies, as well as recent mega-mergers such as those of Delta and Northwest and of United and Continental, are a consequence of low growth in a mature market characterized by significant excess capacity.

Decline Stage

Changes in the external environment often take industries from maturity to decline. In this final stage of the industry life cycle, the size of the market contracts as demand falls. *Laggards*—customers who adopt a new product only if it is absolutely necessary, such as first-time cell phone adopters today—are the last consumer segment to come into the market. Their demand is far too small to compensate for reduced demand from the early and late majority, who are moving on to different products and services. Excess industry capacity in the declining stage puts strong pressure on prices and can increase competitive intensity, especially if the industry has high exit barriers. At this stage, managers generally have four strategic options: *exit, harvest, maintain,* or *consolidate.*[16]

In pursuing a *harvest strategy,* the firm reduces investments in product support and allocates only a minimum of human and other resources. While several companies such as IBM, Brother, Olivetti, and Nakajima still offer typewriters, they don't invest much in future innovation. Instead, they are maximizing cash flow from their existing typewriter product line. Philip Morris, on the other hand, is following a *maintain strategy* with its Marlboro brand, continuing to support marketing efforts at a given level despite the fact that U.S. cigarette consumption has been declining.

Although market size shrinks in a declining industry, some firms may choose to *consolidate* the industry by buying rivals (those who choose to exit). This allows the consolidating firm to stake out a strong position—possibly approaching monopolistic market power, although in a declining industry.[17] For example, although the computing industry has moved to distributed computing, where the Internet is powered by thousands of server farms made up of computers, routers, and switches, IBM still holds a dominant position in mainframe computers, on which banks and insurance companies rely because they are reliable and secure. As of 2009, IBM was selling about $3.5 billion worth of mainframes a year. The surprising fact is that although mainframe revenues make up only about 3.5 percent of IBM's overall revenues, each dollar spent on mainframes works like a multiplier because it pulls in additional dollars from lucrative service and maintenance contracts. One research firm estimates that even today 40 percent of IBM's profits are directly or indirectly related to mainframes.[18]

Exhibit 7.5 (next page) summarizes the features of the industry life cycle at each stage. A word of caution is in order, however: Although the industry life cycle is a useful framework to guide strategic choice, industries do not *have to evolve* through these stages. Motorola initiated an ill-fated satellite-based telephone system, Iridium, which was soon displaced by cell phones that rely on earth-based networks of radio towers. Thus the global satellite telephone industry never moved beyond the introductory stage of the industry life cycle.

Moreover, innovations can emerge at any stage of the industry life cycle, which in turn can initiate a new cycle. Industries can also be rejuvenated, often in the declining stage.

EXHIBIT 7.5

Features of the Industry Life Cycle

	Life Cycle Stages			
	Introduction	**Growth**	**Maturity**	**Decline**
Core Competency	R&D, some marketing	R&D, some manufacturing, marketing	Manufacturing, process engineering, marketing	Manufacturing, process engineering, marketing, service
Type of Buyers	Early adopters	Early majority	Late majority	Laggards
Market Growth	Slow	High	None to moderate	Negative
Price	High	Falling	Low	Low to high
Market Size	Small	Larger	Largest	Small to moderate
Number of Competitors	Few, if any	Many	Moderate, but large	Few, if any
Mode of Competition	Non-price Competition	Non-price competition	Price	Price or non-price competition
Business-level Strategy	Differentiation	Differentiation	Cost-leadership, or integration strategy	Cost-leadership, differentiation, or integration strategy
Strategic Objective	Achieving market acceptance	Staking out a strong strategic position	Maintaining strong strategic position	Exit, harvest, maintain, or consolidate

Although the old-line steel industry relying on fully integrated mills has been in decline for a long time, mini steel mills started a new industry life cycle by using the electric-arc furnace, a process innovation that enabled the newcomers to produce high-quality steel in small batches at low prices. Although the industry life cycle is a useful tool, it does not explain everything about changes in industries. Some industries may never go through the entire life cycle, while others are continually renewed through innovation. Entrepreneurs are the agents that introduce change into the system.

STRATEGIC ENTREPRENEURSHIP

Entrepreneurship describes the process by which people undertake economic risk to innovate—to create new products, processes, and sometimes new organizations.[19] If successful, entrepreneurship not only drives the competitive process, it also creates value for the individual entrepreneurs and society at large. *Entrepreneurs* innovate by commercializing ideas and inventions. Joseph Schumpeter argued that innovating is at least as difficult and demanding as inventing.[20] Entrepreneurs are, therefore, the change agents who make the process of creative destruction happen. They seek out or create new business opportunities and then assemble the resources necessary to exploit them.[21] These new businesses create employment opportunities and value for society.

Although many new ventures fail, many achieve success, and some achieve spectacular success. Examples of the latter are:

entrepreneurship
The process by which people undertake economic risk to innovate—to create new products, processes, and sometimes new organizations.

■   Jeff Bezos is the founder of Amazon.com, today the world's largest online retailer. The stepson of a Cuban immigrant, Bezos graduated from Princeton and then worked as a financial analyst on Wall Street. In 1994, after reading that the Internet was growing by

2,000 percent a month, he set out to leverage the Internet as a new distribution channel. Listing products that could be sold online, he finally settled on books, because that retail market was fairly fragmented, with huge inefficiencies in its distribution system. Perhaps even more important, books represent a perfect commodity, because they are identical regardless of where a consumer buys them.

- Oprah Winfrey, best-known for her self-titled TV talk show, is also founder and CEO of Harpo Productions, a multimedia company. Some of Harpo's well-known products include *The Oprah Winfrey Show, Dr. Phil, The Rachael Ray Show, The Dr. Oz Show, Oprah.com, O, The Oprah Magazine,* and *O at Home.* In January 2011, she launched a new cable-TV channel jointly with Discovery Communications: *OWN, The Oprah Winfrey Network.*[22] A graduate of Tennessee State University, Oprah used her entrepreneurial talents to rise from poverty and an abusive childhood to become one of the most successful entrepreneurs in the multimedia business, with a net worth of over $2 billion.[23] In 2011, Oprah Winfrey ended her all-time record-setting talk show to devote her entrepreneurial talents to *OWN*.

- Jeff Hawkins, a serial entrepreneur, was one of the first to understand that external opportunities were pointing toward mobile computing. In the early 1990s, despite the high-profile failure of Apple's Newton, Hawkins clearly envisioned a future in which everyone would own a "personal computer that fits in their pocket."[24] This device would be the person's primary computer and would be accessed much more frequently than a laptop or desktop. His analysis of the external environment told Hawkins this was inevitable, and he believed mobile computing would happen faster if better devices were available. He went on to invent the PalmPilot, a handheld computer, and founded Palm Computing in 1992. Later, Hawkins continued to innovate by introducing the Treo, one of the first smartphones (a mobile phone offering PC-like capabilities), and founded Handspring in 1998.

Note that beyond starting new businesses, entrepreneurs are *change agents* who transform innovation into reality. Apple Inc. is known as one of the world's most innovative companies, and its co-founder Steve Jobs is credited with Apple's most important breakthrough innovations. Steve Jobs also founded Pixar, one of the most successful film studios of all time. Leveraging 3D computer animation, Pixar has created blockbuster hits such as *Toy Story 1, 2,* and *3, A Bug's Life, Monsters Inc., Finding Nemo,* and *The Incredibles,* among others. Steve Jobs is clearly an entrepreneur extraordinaire, and has effected continuous innovation in his quest to create value through new products or services.

Strategic entrepreneurship describes the pursuit of innovation using tools and concepts from strategic management.[25] We can leverage innovation for competitive advantage by applying a strategic management lens to entrepreneurship. The fundamental question of strategic entrepreneurship, therefore, is how to combine entrepreneurial actions that create new opportunities or exploit existing ones with strategic actions we take in the pursuit of competitive advantage.[26] Procter & Gamble's continued innovation in detergents is an example of strategic entrepreneurship, because P&G managers leverage strategic analysis, formulation, and implementation when deciding which new type of detergent to research, when to launch it, and how to implement the necessary organizational changes. Each new release is an innovation, and thus an act of entrepreneurship planned and executed using strategic management concepts.

To further explore strategic entrepreneurship, we now turn to a discussion of the different types of innovation that may be pursued, as well as the strategic implications of each type.

strategic entrepreneurship
The pursuit of innovation using the tools and concepts available in strategic management.

EXHIBIT 7.6

Types of Innovation: Combining Markets and Technologies

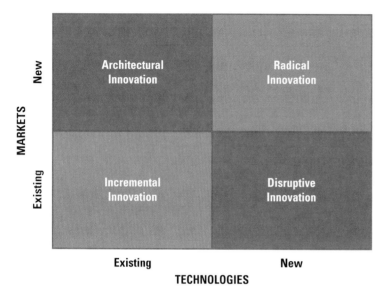

TYPES OF INNOVATION

The better we understand different types of innovation, the more accurately we can assess their strategic implications. We need to know, in particular, along which dimensions we should assess innovations.

One insightful way to categorize innovations is to measure their degree of newness in terms of *technology* and *markets*.[27] Here, *technology* refers to the methods and materials used to achieve a commercial objective.[28] For example, Apple integrates different types of technologies (hardware, software, microprocessors, the Internet, and so on) to produce and deliver an array of mobile devices and services (e.g., iBookstore). We also want to understand the *market* for an innovation—e.g., whether an innovation is introduced into a new or

an existing market—because an idea or invention turns into an innovation only when it is successfully commercialized.[29] Measuring an innovation along the technology and market dimensions gives us the framework depicted in Exhibit 7.6. Along the horizontal axis, we ask whether the innovation builds on existing technologies or creates a new one. On the vertical axis, we ask whether the innovation is targeted toward existing or new markets. Four types of innovations emerge: incremental, radical, architectural, and disruptive innovations.

Incremental and Radical Innovations

Although radical breakthroughs such as MP3 players and magnetic resonance imaging (MRI) radiology capture most of our attention, the vast majority of innovations are actually incremental ones. An incremental innovation squarely builds on the firm's established knowledge base and steadily improves the product or service it offers.[30] It targets existing markets using existing technology. Strategy Highlight 7.3 describes how Gillette leverages incremental innovation to gain and sustain a competitive advantage.

The Gillette example shows how radical innovation created a competitive advantage that the company sustained by follow-up incremental innovation. Such an outcome is not a foregone conclusion, though. In some instances, the innovator is outcompeted by second movers that quickly introduce a very similar incremental innovation to continuously improve their own offering. For example, although CNN was the pioneer in 24-hour cable news, today it is only the third most popular choice in this category, having been surpassed by Fox News and MSNBC.[31]

On the other hand, radical innovation draws on novel methods or materials, is derived either from an entirely different knowledge base or from recombination of the firm's existing knowledge base with a new stream of knowledge, or targets new markets by using new technologies.[32] Well-known examples of radical innovations include the introduction of the mass-produced automobile (the Ford Model T), the X-ray, the airplane, and more recently biotechnology breakthroughs such as genetic engineering and the decoding of the human genome.

incremental innovation An innovation that squarely builds on the firm's established knowledge base, steadily improves the product or service it offers, and targets existing markets by using existing technology.

radical innovation An innovation that draws on novel methods or materials, is derived from either an entirely different knowledge base or from the recombination of the firm's existing knowledge base with a new stream of knowledge, or targets new markets by using new technologies.

Many firms get their start by successfully commercializing radical innovations, some of which, like the airplane, even give birth to new industries. Although the British firm de Havilland first commercialized the jet-powered passenger airplane, Boeing was the company that rode this radical innovation to industry dominance. More recently, Boeing's leadership has been challenged by Airbus, and today each company has approximately half the market. This stalemate is now being contested by aircraft manufacturers such as Bombardier of Canada and Embraer of Brazil who are moving up-market by building larger luxury jets that are competing with some of the smaller airplane models offered by Boeing and Airbus.[33]

Once firms have achieved market acceptance of a breakthrough innovation, they tend to follow up with incremental rather than radical innovations. Over time, these companies morph into industry incumbents. Future radical innovations are generally introduced by new entrepreneurial ventures. Why is this so? Let's look at the reasons, which are economic, organizational, and strategic.[34]

ECONOMIC REASONS FOR INCREMENTAL INNOVATION. Economists highlight the role of *incentives* in strategic choice. Once an innovator has become an established incumbent firm (such as Google has today), it has strong incentives to defend its strategic position and market power. An emphasis on incremental innovations strengthens the incumbent firm's position and thus maintains high entry barriers. As a result, the incumbent firm uses incremental innovation to extend the time it can extract profits based on a favorable industry structure (see the discussion in Chapter 3). Any potential radical innovation threatens the incumbent firm's dominant position.

The incentives for entrepreneurial ventures, however, are just the opposite. Successfully commercializing a radical innovation is frequently the only option to enter an industry protected by high entry barriers. One of the first biotech firms, Amgen, used newly discovered drugs based on genetic engineering to overcome entry barriers to the pharmaceutical industry, in which incumbents had enjoyed notoriously high profits for several decades. Because of differential economic incentives, incumbents push forward with incremental innovations, while new entrants focus on radical innovations.

ORGANIZATIONAL REASONS FOR INCREMENTAL INNOVATION. From an organizational perspective, as firms become established and grow, they rely more heavily on formalized business processes and structures. In some cases, the firm may experience inertia, so that changes to the status quo may be resisted. Incumbent firms, therefore, tend to favor incremental innovations that reinforce the existing organizational structure and power distribution while avoiding radical innovation that could disturb the existing power distribution (e.g., between different functional areas, such as R&D and marketing). New entrants, however, do not have formal organizational structures and processes, giving them more freedom to launch an initial breakthrough.

From King Gillette to King of Incremental Innovation

In 1903, entrepreneur Mr. King C. Gillette invented and began selling the safety razor with a disposable blade. This radical innovation launched the Gillette company (now a brand of Procter & Gamble). To sustain its competitive advantage, Gillette not only made sure that its razors were inexpensive and widely available (thus introducing the "razor and razor blade" business model),[35] but also continually improved its razor blades. In a classic example of incremental innovation, Gillette kept adding an additional blade with each new version of its razor until the number had gone from one to six![36] Though this innovation strategy seems predictable, it worked: Gillette's top-selling razor today, the Fusion, holds about 45 percent market share and brings in annual revenues of more than $1 billion. Moreover, with each new razor introduction, Gillette is able to push up its per-unit cartridge price. A four-pack of razors for the new Fusion Proglide retailed for $17.99 when introduced in 2010.[37]

STRATEGIC REASONS FOR INCREMENTAL INNOVATION. A final reason incumbent firms tend to be a source of incremental rather than radical innovations is that they become embedded in a network of suppliers, buyers, complementors, and so on.[38] They no longer make independent decisions but must consider the ramifications on other parties in their value network. Continuous incremental innovations reinforce this network and keep all its members happy, while radical innovations disrupt it. Again, new entrants don't have to worry about preexisting value networks, since they will be building theirs around the radical innovation they are bringing to a new market.

Architectural and Disruptive Innovations

FedEx's architectural innovation built upon the hub-and-spoke system (first introduced by Delta in its Atlanta hub) to create the express-delivery industry.

Firms can also innovate by leveraging *existing technologies* into *new markets*. Doing so generally requires them to reconfigure the components of a technology, meaning they alter the overall "architecture" of the product.[39] An architectural innovation, therefore, is a new product in which known components, based on existing technologies, are reconfigured in a novel way to create new markets.

For example, in the 1980s Xerox was the most dominant copier company worldwide.[40] It produced high-volume, high-quality copying machines that it leased to its customers through a service agreement. While these machines were ideal for the high end of the market, Xerox ignored small and medium-sized businesses. By applying an architectural innovation, the Japanese entry Canon was able to redesign the copier so that it didn't need professional service—reliability was built directly into the machine, and the user could replace parts such as the cartridge. This allowed Canon to apply the "razor and razor blade" business model, charging relatively low prices for its copiers but higher prices for cartridges. What Xerox had not envisioned was the possibility that the components of the copying machine could be put together in a different way that was more user-friendly.

Finally, a disruptive innovation leverages *new technologies* to attack *existing markets*. It invades an existing market from the bottom up, as shown in Exhibit 7.7.[41] The dashed blue lines represent different market segments, from segment 1 at the low end to segment 4 at the high end. As first demonstrated by Professor Clayton Christensen of the Harvard Business School, the dynamic process of disruptive innovation begins when a startup firm introduces a new product based on a new technology to meet existing customer needs. To be a disruptive force, however, this new product or technology has to have additional characteristics: It begins as a low-cost solution to an existing problem. Initially, its performance is inferior to the existing technology, but its rate of technological improvement over time is faster than the rate of performance increases required by different market segments. In Exhibit 7.7, the purple path captures the new technology's trajectory, or rate of improvement over time.

The following examples illustrate disruptive innovations:

- Japanese carmakers successfully followed a strategy of disruptive innovation by first introducing small fuel-efficient cars, and then leveraging their low-cost and high-quality advantages into high-end luxury segments, captured by brands such as Lexus, Infiniti, and Acura.

- Digital photography improved enough over time to provide higher-definition pictures. As a result, it has been able to replace film photography, even in most professional applications.

architectural innovation A new product in which known components, based on existing technologies, are reconfigured in a novel way to attack new markets.

disruptive innovation An innovation that leverages new technologies to attack existing markets from the bottom up.

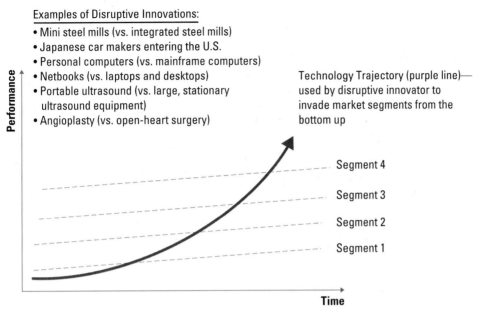

Examples of Disruptive Innovations:
- Mini steel mills (vs. integrated steel mills)
- Japanese car makers entering the U.S.
- Personal computers (vs. mainframe computers)
- Netbooks (vs. laptops and desktops)
- Portable ultrasound (vs. large, stationary ultrasound equipment)
- Angioplasty (vs. open-heart surgery)

Technology Trajectory (purple line)— used by disruptive innovator to invade market segments from the bottom up

Performance

Segment 4
Segment 3
Segment 2
Segment 1

Time

EXHIBIT 7.7

Disruptive Innovation Invading Different Market Segments from the Bottom Up

- Data storage products advanced from the floppy disk to the hard disk to the CD, then to the ZIP drive, and now to flash drives. Each new memory device invaded the market from the bottom up and performance improved over time.

- Mini computers disrupted mainframe computers; desktop computers disrupted mini computers; laptops disrupted desktop computers; now netbooks under $200 are disrupting laptops.

- Throughout the 1990s, Swatch's low-cost, fun watches disrupted watches that were like expensive jewelry. Today, timekeeping functions of smartphones are replacing wristwatches altogether.

One factor favoring the success of disruptive innovation is that it relies on stealth attack: It invades the market from the bottom up, by first capturing the low end. Many times, incumbent firms fail to defend (and sometimes are even happy to cede) the low end of the market, because it is frequently a low-margin business. The emergence of electric arc furnaces, for example, was a disruptive innovation that allowed so-called mini-mills like Nucor and Chaparral to produce steel in small batches and at lower cost compared with fully integrated steel mills such as U.S. Steel or Bethlehem Steel. Initially, though, the quality of steel produced by mini-mills was poor and could compete only in the lowest tier of the market: steel used to reinforce construction concrete (rebar steel). Once the mini-mills entered segment 1 of the steel market, the integrated mills could no longer be cost-competitive given their high fixed cost; the incumbents happily ceded segment 1 of the market to the new entrants because it was a low-margin business to begin with. However, invading segment 1 of a market creates a beachhead for a new technology, which the new entrant uses to gain more market expertise, build economies of scale, lower cost, and further improve quality. The new entrant is then able to leverage its disruptive technology to continue to invade the existing firm's territory from the bottom up, following the purple trajectory in Exhibit 7.7, one market segment at a time.

Google, for example, is using its new operating system, Chrome OS, as a beachhead to invade Microsoft's stronghold.[42] Chrome OS is optimized to run on netbooks, the

STRATEGY HIGHLIGHT 7.4

GE's Reverse Innovation: Disrupt Yourself!

GE Healthcare is a leader in diagnostic devices. Realizing that the likelihood of disruptive innovation increases over time, GE now uses reverse innovation to disrupt itself. A high-end ultrasound machine found in cutting-edge research hospitals in the United States or Europe costs $230,000. There is no market for these high-end, high-price products in developing countries. Given their large populations, however, there *is* a strong medical need for ultrasound devices.

In 2002, a local GE team in China, through a bottom-up strategic initiative, developed an inexpensive, portable ultrasound device, combining laptop technology with a probe and sophisticated imaging software. This lightweight device (11 pounds) was first used in rural China. In the spring of 2009, GE unveiled the new medical device under the name Venue 40 in the United States, at a price of less than $30,000. There was high demand from many American general practitioners, who could not otherwise afford the quarter of a million dollars needed to procure a high-end machine (that weighed about 400 pounds). In the fall of 2009, GE's chairman and CEO Jeff Immelt unveiled the Vscan, an even smaller device that looks like a cross between an early iPod and a flip phone. The Vscan is expected to cost only about $12,000. GE views it as the "stethoscope of the 21st century," which a primary care doctor can hang around her neck when visiting patients.[45]

fastest-growing segment in computing. To appeal to users who spend most of their time on the web accessing e-mail and other online applications, for instance, it is designed to start up in a few seconds. Moreover, Google provides Chrome OS free of charge.[43] In contrast to Microsoft's proprietary Windows operating system, Chrome OS is open-source software, freely accessible to anyone for further development and refinement. In this sense, Google is leveraging crowdsourcing in its new product development, just as Threadless uses crowdsourcing to design and market T-shirts and Wikipedia uses the wisdom of the crowds to collectively edit encyclopedia entries.

Another factor favoring the success of disruptive innovation is that incumbent firms often are slow to change. Incumbent firms that listen closely to their current customers will respond by continuing to invest in the existing technology and in incremental changes to the existing products. When a newer technology matures and proves to be a better solution, those same customers will switch over. At that time, however, the incumbent firm does not yet have a competitive product ready that is based on the disruptive technology. Although customer-oriented mission statements are more likely to guard against firm obsolescence than product-oriented ones (see Chapter 2), they are no guarantee that a firm can hold out in the face of disruptive innovation. One of the counterintuitive findings that Clayton Christensen unearthed in his studies is that it can hurt incumbents to listen only to their existing customers.

Although these examples show that disruptive innovations are a serious threat for incumbent firms, some have devised strategic initiatives to counter them. A first option is to invest in staying ahead of the competition. Apple continuously innovates—Steve Jobs has always believed that he knows what customers need even before they realize it. Apple is famous for not soliciting customer feedback or studying markets. A second approach is to guard against disruptive innovation by protecting the low end of the market (segment 1 in Exhibit 7.7) by introducing low-cost innovations to preempt stealth competitors. Intel introduced the Celeron chip, a stripped-down, budget version of its Pentium chip, in 1998. More recently, Intel followed up with the Atom chip, a new processor that is inexpensive and consumes little battery power, to power low-cost netbooks.[44]

A third way to guard against disruptive innovations is to use reverse innovation, rather than wait for others to do it to you. In *reverse innovation* a firm develops products specifically for emerging markets such as China and India, and then introduces these innovations into developed markets such as the United States or the European Union. Strategy Highlight 7.4 describes how GE Healthcare invented and commercialized a disruptive innovation in China that is now making a big splash in the United States.

The Internet as Disruptive Force: The Long Tail

The Internet enables digitization and, as a consequence, acts as an especially disruptive force.[46] Everything that can go digital will—creating some losers and some winners. We are all familiar with the impact that the digitization of music, books, and movies has had on brick-and-mortar sellers. Web applications like TurboTax and LegalZoom are replacing professional tax accountants and attorneys. Online gaming is the fastest-growing segment in the $55 billion video game industry.[47] Online digitization is thus both a threat and an opportunity.

>> **LO 7-5**
Describe the long-tail concept and derive strategic implications.

These observations and their strategic implications have been explained by Chris Anderson, editor-in-chief of *Wired*. The "long tail" phenomenon[48] is that 80 percent of offerings in a category are *not* big hits (see Exhibit 7.8). It turns out that 80 percent of sales in a given product category (such as movies, books, and songs) come from "blockbusters" in the "short head" of the distribution curve, which represents only 20 percent of the offerings in a category. This phenomenon is captured by the *Pareto principle,* also known as the *80-20 rule,* which says that roughly 80 percent of effects come from 20 percent of the causes.

The *short head* represents the mainstream, where all the blockbusters, bestsellers, and hits are to be found. These products tend to appeal to the largest segment of the market with homogenous tastes. In the physical world of brick-and-mortar retail stores, these product selections are often the only choice on display, because there are significant costs to carrying broader inventory to meet a wider variety of consumer needs.

The disruptive force of the Internet provides an opportunity to online retailers to benefit from marketing the long tail, which is the remaining 80 percent. Online retailers can "sell less of more" by taking advantage of low-cost virtual shelf space, which is basically unlimited. The Internet, combined with sophisticated search engines and inventory-management software, allows firms to drive down transaction costs to match individual consumer demand with supply. As shown by the dotted line in Exhibit 7.8, the combined effects of these advances in technology make it possible to increase the number of units

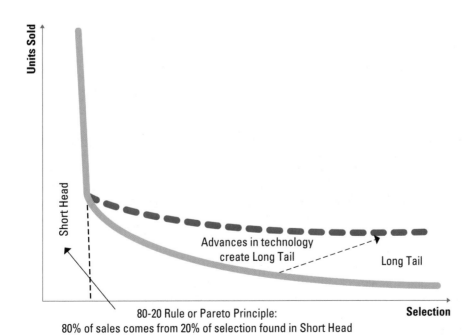

EXHIBIT 7.8

The Short Head and the Long Tail

Source: Adapted from C. Anderson (2006), *The Long Tail: Why the Future of Business Is Selling Less of More* (New York: Hyperion).

sold—that is, create the long tail. The long tail business model is one in which companies can obtain a large part of their revenues by selling a small number of units from among almost unlimited choices.

The long tail allows online retailers to overcome the problem of thin markets, in which transactions are likely not to take place because there are only a few buyers and a few sellers and they have difficulty finding each other. We can look at eBay as an example of an online retailer with an innovative approach to retailing, enabling buyers and sellers to meet online to exchange any good, no matter how exotic, at no cost to the buyer. Google also benefits from the long tail, because it is able to match even small advertisers with their target demographics.

The long tail captures the bottom of the iceberg, the non-obvious choices. By leveraging sophisticated IT systems, online retailers like Rhapsody, Netflix, and Amazon are now able to aggregate these choices (see Exhibit 7.9). Even Walmart, the world's largest retailer,

EXHIBIT 7.9

The Long-Tail Consequences: Selling Less of More

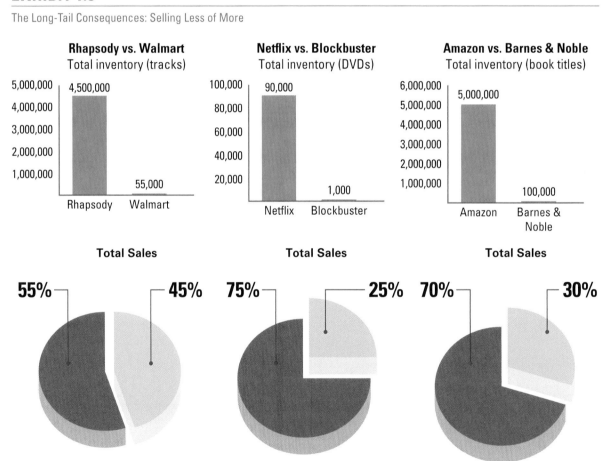

Source: Adapted and updated from C. Anderson (2006), *The Long Tail: Why the Future of Business Is Selling Less of More* (New York: Hyperion), p. 23.

carries only about 55,000 music tracks. In contrast, Rhapsody's inventory contains 4.5 million tracks. The average Blockbuster store carries about 1,000 DVD titles; Netflix carries about 90,000. The typical Barnes & Noble superstore holds some 100,000 book titles; on Amazon you can find 5 million. All in all, the leading online retailers carry an inventory 50 to 90 times larger than those of their largest brick-and-mortar competitors. Between 25 and 45 percent of all revenues for Rhapsody, Netflix, and Amazon come from the long tail, or products not available in offline retail stores.

The Internet as a disruptive innovation enables companies to solve important strategic trade-offs. It lowers the costs of shelf space, inventory, and distribution to near zero and enables firms to aggregate non-hits and match unique consumer preferences to supply. While the early experiences of media and entertainment industries illustrate the long-tail business model, it is expected that the model can be used to build a business in any product or service that can be digitized.

DISCONTINUITIES: PERIODS OF PARADIGM CHANGE

Innovation is a powerful force with potentially lethal consequences for incumbent firms. Startups like Skype are riding the wave of new technology—voice over Internet Protocol or VoIP—to offer *free* long-distance phone calls to anyone in the world. Just a decade ago, you would have paid several dollars *a minute* if you wanted to call overseas from the United States. Today, all you need is a computer or mobile phone with an Internet connection. Although this new technology is clearly an opportunity for Skype, it is a threat for traditional telephone companies the world over, and indeed it is creating major industry upheaval. Yet, Skype is still struggling to reach broader demographics and to identify a business model that allows it to earn revenue from this innovation. In 2011, Microsoft acquired Skype for $8.5 billion, providing Microsoft with a globally used Internet service of high brand recognition.[49]

>> **LO 7-6**
Evaluate discontinuities and describe the dynamics of paradigm changes.

Discontinuities are periods of time in which the underlying technological standard changes. As we have seen, VoIP is challenging the traditional landline technology. Earlier discontinuities include, among others, the move from:

■ Propeller airplanes to supersonic jets

■ Film-based to digital cameras

■ Branch-based brick-and-motor banking to online banking (and the same for stock brokerage)

■ Large (tube-based) computer and TV screens to high-definition flat-panel displays

■ The vinyl record player to the cassette tape to the CD, and then to digital MP3 players like the iPod

Discontinuities can lead to a paradigm shift, a situation in which a new technology revolutionizes an existing industry and eventually establishes itself as the new standard.

---

long tail Business model in which companies can obtain a large part of their revenues by selling a small number of units from among almost unlimited choices.

thin markets A situation in which transactions are likely not to take place because there are only a few buyers and sellers, who have difficulty finding each other.

discontinuities Periods of time in which the underlying technological standard changes.

paradigm shift A situation in which a new technology revolutionizes an existing industry and eventually establishes itself as the new standard.

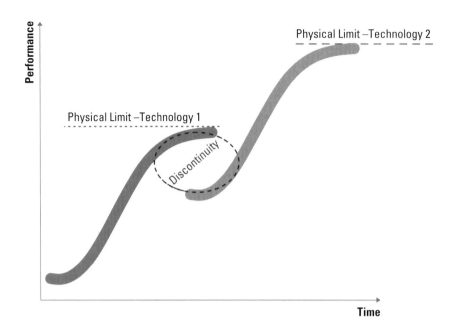

Exhibit 7.10, which plots the performance of a given technology against time, shows this transition. Each technology S-curve represents a different technology. Here, the blue one is the older incumbent technology, and the green one is the newer technology.

Given the potentially devastating effects of innovation on incumbent firms, one of the key questions managers need to answer is, "Can you predict *when* innovation leads to a discontinuity in an industry?" Although the future is unknowable, Richard Foster, formerly Senior Partner at McKinsey & Company, developed a predictive framework to address this important question. By studying the rate of improvement of many different types of technologies over time, ranging from heart replacement surgery to sailing ships, pocket watches, and chemicals, Foster found that technologies follow a predictable technology S-curve, improving in performance over time as a consequence of continued R&D effort. The take-off is slow because each new technology faces major science, engineering, and business challenges. Once these have been solved, exponential improvements set in. One key factor Foster discovered, however, is that each technology eventually reaches a physical limit due to laws of nature. For example, silicon-based computing is reaching a physical limit because we cannot place an infinite number of transistors on a tiny silicon chip. The dashed line in Exhibit 7.10 indicates the physical limit of technology 1.

The probability of a discontinuity increases as technology 1 approaches its physical limit. After 100 years of using internal combustion engines for cars and trucks, we can see the internal-combustion paradigm reaching a physical limit for several reasons, including the fact that fossil fuels are finite and there is an environmental need to lower the level of CO_2 emissions. Not surprisingly, as the rate of improvement in a given technology slows down, R&D investments in alternative solutions increase. At the onset of a discontinuity, however, the next dominant technology is far from clear, because a swarm of new technologies enters the fray.

The emergence of a number of new options requires that incumbent firms place some strategic bets on emerging technologies. Former Intel CEO Andy Grove compared a discontinuity to a situation in which a firm must pay a large entry fee to enter a casino. This fee represents the continued R&D expenditure the firm needs to create

absorptive capacity
A firm's ability to understand, evaluate, and integrate external technology developments.

hypercompetition
A situation in which competitive intensity has increased and periods of competitive advantage have shortened, especially in newer, technology-based industries, making any competitive advantage a string of short-lived advantages.

absorptive capacity—its ability to understand external technology developments, evaluate them, and integrate them into current products or create new ones.[50] By keeping many options open, the firm also avoids technological lock-out.[51] Inside the casino, so to speak, games of chance are being played at many different tables, each representing a new technology. Companies must pick which tables to play and how much to gamble.

Currently, in the car industry, different technologies are being put forth as potential alternatives to gasoline, including electric, hybrid (a cross between gasoline and electric), hydrogen, biofuels, solar, steam, and even exotic alternatives like algae. One technology will eventually emerge as the new paradigm, but during the discontinuity, the winner is far from clear. (MiniCase 7, page 375, describes the current battle for the next dominant technology in the car industry.)

When new technologies emerge, however, old ones do not simply disappear.[52] Rather, performance of the old technologies may improve, even significantly, in the face of apparently superior competition. When angioplasty was first introduced to open blocked arteries with minimal invasive heart surgery, we might have expected that the performance outcomes for patients still needing open-heart (coronary artery bypass) surgery would decline because the patients who were not eligible for angioplasty and thus still needed open-heart bypass surgery would be the sicker ones. With the overall patient pool receiving open-heart surgery now being much sicker, one would have expected a higher mortality rate. The empirical data, however, showed a *lower* mortality rate for open-heart patients. Why? Cardiothoracic surgeons were now focusing on just one specific patient group, which in turn enhanced their learning effects (see Chapter 6). Operating on more of the same type of cases allowed them to move down the learning curve more quickly and thus achieve better outcomes than before the introduction of angioplasty.

Taken together, most industries experience discontinuities over time. Discontinuities have significant implications for the competitive dynamics in an industry, creating opportunities as well as threats. Generally, discontinuities favor new entrants; they enjoy the "attacker's advantage" as Richard Foster put it.[53] In contrast, incumbent firms are often—but not always—impaired in their response. As a consequence, discontinuities frequently lead to changes in industry leadership, and thus affect which firms enjoy a competitive advantage.

HYPERCOMPETITION

The accelerated pace of innovation has had a significant impact on the nature of competitive advantage. Coining the term hypercompetition, Professor Rich D'Aveni of Dartmouth College argues that competitive intensity has increased and that periods of competitive advantage have shortened, especially in newer, technology-based industries.[54] As a consequence, no single strategy can sustain competitive advantage over time. Rather, any competitive advantage must be a string of short-lived advantages, achieved through a constant escalation of competition in price, quality, timing and know-how, capital commitments, and supply chain management.[55]

The phenomenon of hypercompetition is depicted in Exhibit 7.11 (next page). Here, the innovator launches a radical innovation and is able to exploit its competitive advantage over a given time period (Competitive Advantage 1). To further sustain its competitive advantage and keep new entrants out of the market, however, the innovator must follow up on its initial radical innovation before its advantage expires fully. The firm must cannibalize its own competitive advantage with a follow-up incremental innovation (Competitive Advantage 2) to preempt any potential rivals. The process continues with several subsequent incremental innovations. Each of these incremental innovations is shown as smaller

GAINING & SUSTAINING COMPETITIVE ADVANTAGE

>> LO 7-7
Identify the process leading to hypercompetition, and explain why competitive advantage can often be sustained through continuous innovation.

EXHIBIT 7.11

Hypercompetition Driven by Continuous Innovation

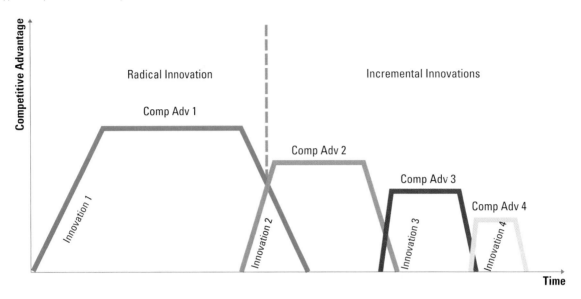

and of shorter duration than the previous one, illustrating the increased speed with which competitive advantage is lost.

As an example, Intel was successful in extending its superior performance when introducing the microprocessor embedded in the IBM PC by using continued innovation to drive the x86 chip architecture relentlessly forward: 286, 386, Pentium, Pentium II, Pentium III, Pentium 4, Pentium D, Pentium Dual Core, and so on. This process cannot go on forever, however (as shown in Exhibit 7.10), since technologies will approach their physical limits. Currently, the line widths on Intel's advanced processors is 45 nm.[56] As the number of transistors on a single chip increases, the generated heat cannot be managed satisfactorily. As silicon-based computing is reaching diminishing returns, new computing technologies will emerge.

As Exhibit 7.11 illustrates, the duration and magnitude of each subsequent competitive advantage are both smaller than for the preceding advantage. This reduction implies that a firm cannot indefinitely sustain a competitive advantage based on continuous incremental innovation. Nor can other firms gain advantages based on incremental innovation. At some point, a radical innovation is needed to start this process anew.

Professor Michael Porter, however, argues that hypercompetition is not inevitable. Rather, he says, it is a self-inflicted wound caused by a lack of distinct strategic positioning, as discussed in the last chapter.[57] Porter argues that hypercompetition is the result of firms *imitating* one another rather than attempting to be *different from* one another. Thus, firms begin to copy successful strategic initiatives of the industry leaders. This might allow these firms to excel at operational effectiveness (i.e., best in-class practices) but they will fail at strategic positioning. As a result, firms become much more competitive, but also more similar—leading to hypercompetition, where no advantage can be sustained (similar to the perfect competitive industry structure discussed in Chapter 3).

In this and the previous chapter, we discussed how firms can use business-level strategy—differentiation, cost leadership, integration, and innovation—to gain and sustain competitive advantage. We now turn our attention to corporate-level strategy to help us understand how executives make decisions about where to compete (in terms of industries, value chains, and geography) and how to create synergies among different business units. A thorough understanding of business and corporate strategy is necessary to formulate and sustain a winning strategy.

CHAPTERCASE 7 | *Consider This . . .*

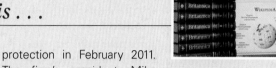

WIKIPEDIA, AS DISCUSSED in ChapterCase 7, leverages specific capabilities enabled by innovations of the Internet. Beyond the technical challenges of web interfaces, servers, and bandwidth for delivery is a sometimes-overlooked capability: the Wikipedians themselves. Over 14 million people have registered accounts to contribute edits to Wikipedia. More than 300,000 users provide edits to the website at least once a month. These volunteers build the content for the site, using a creative commons license that ensures free access to any of the more than 80 million unique visitors each *month* (as of January 2011).[58] This crowdsourcing and its legal underpinnings are successful only as long as individuals are willing to spend their own time contributing to the site for no pay or other extrinsic benefits. The ability to attract and utilize legions of interested individuals is vital to the success of Wikipedia both today and into the future.

While the death of Encarta was not a major blow for Microsoft as a whole, the same cannot be said for the effect that online shopping and e-books had for Borders Group Inc. Borders filed for bankruptcy protection in February 2011. The firm's president, Mike Edwards, said Borders is closing 200 superstores and some other properties. Borders owed nearly $200 million to publishers at the time of its Chapter 11 filing.[59] There is little doubt that a major culprit of this bankruptcy for Borders is its slow recognition of the impact of online and e-book sales on its business. Borders used Amazon for all of its online business until opening its own website (Borders.com) in 2008. Additionally, the Borders e-reader (from Kobo) was not on the market until June 2010.[60] In comparison, the Amazon Kindle launched in November 2007, and Barnes & Noble launched the Nook in November 2009.

1. How can Wikipedia maintain and grow its ability to harness the crowdsourcing of its "Wikipedians" to maintain high-quality (and quickly updated) content?

2. How has the "long tail" affected both Wikipedia and Borders Group?

3. What type of innovations should each of these two companies use to gain or sustain a competitive advantage?

Take-Away Concepts

This chapter discussed various aspects of innovation and strategic entrepreneurship as a business-level strategy, as summarized by the following learning objectives and related take-away concepts.

LO 7-1 Define innovation and describe its role in the competitive process.

>> Continuous innovation is the engine behind successful companies.

>> Innovation is a potent competitive weapon; it enables firms to redefine the marketplace in their favor and achieve much-needed growth.

>> The successful commercialization of a new product or service allows a firm to extract temporary monopoly profits.

LO 7-2 Describe the competitive implications of different stages in the industry life cycle.

>> Innovations frequently lead to the birth of new industries.

>> Industries generally follow a predictable industry life cycle, with four distinct stages: introduction, growth, maturity, and decline.

>> Different life-cycle stages have different consumer adoption rates and different competitive implications (see Exhibit 7.4).

LO 7-3 Apply strategic management concepts to entrepreneurship and innovation.

>> Strategic entrepreneurship focuses on generating integrated insights pertaining to innovation and change using the concepts available in strategic management.

LO 7-4 Evaluate different types of innovation and derive their strategic implications.

>> Four types of innovation emerge when applying the existing versus new dimensions of technology and markets: incremental, radical, architectural, and disruptive innovations.

LO 7-5 Describe the long-tail concept and derive strategic implications.

>> The Internet is a strongly disruptive force that digitizes any industry that can be digitized.

>> The long tail describes a business model in which companies can obtain a significant part of their revenues by selling a small number of units from among almost unlimited choices.

LO 7-6 Evaluate discontinuities and describe the dynamics of paradigm changes.

>> Discontinuities can lead to a paradigm shift, in which a new technology revolutionizes an existing industry and eventually establishes itself as the new standard.

>> Technologies follow a predictable technology S-curve, improving in performance over time as a consequence of continued R&D effort.

>> The probability of a discontinuity increases when a given technology approaches its physical limit.

LO 7-7 Identify the process leading to hypercompetition and explain why competitive advantage can be sustained through continuous innovation.

>> Competitive intensity has increased and periods of competitive advantage have shortened, especially in newer, technology-based industries.

>> No single strategy can sustain competitive advantage over time.

>> Any competitive advantage must be a string of short-lived advantages. This is achieved through a constant escalation of competition in the areas of price, quality, timing and know-how, capital commitments, and supply-chain management.

>> Hypercompetition can result from a lack of strategic positioning.

Key Terms

Absorptive capacity *(p. 191)*	Incremental innovation *(p. 182)*	Process innovations *(p. 176)*
Architectural innovation *(p. 184)*	Innovation *(p. 172)*	Product innovations *(p. 176)*
Discontinuities *(p. 189)*	Industry life cycle *(p. 173)*	Radical innovation *(p. 182)*
Disruptive innovation *(p. 184)*	Long tail *(p. 188)*	Standard *(p. 175)*
Entrepreneurship *(p. 180)*	Network effects *(p. 174)*	Strategic entrepreneurship *(p. 181)*
Hypercompetition *(p. 191)*	Paradigm shift *(p. 189)*	Thin markets *(p. 188)*

Discussion Questions

1. Assume you work for a small firm that developed a better and faster operating system for netbooks than Microsoft Windows. What strategy might the firm use to unseat Windows in this market?

2. How does the industry life cycle affect business strategy? Detail your answer based on each stage: introduction, growth, maturity, and decline.

3. Describe a firm you think has been highly innovative. Which of the four types of innovation—radical, incremental, disruptive, or architectural—did it use? Did the firm use different types over time?

4. Why are standards important in many industries? As standards get adapted and become dominant, how does this process influence the competitive nature of the industry?

Ethical/Social Issues

1. You are a co-founder of a startup firm making electronic sensors. After a year of sales your business is not growing rapidly, but you have some steady customers keeping the business afloat. A major supplier has informed you it can no longer supply your firm because it is moving to serve large customers only, and your volume does not qualify. Though you have no current orders to support an increased commitment to this supplier, you do have a new version of your sensor coming out that you hope will increase the purchase volume by over 75 percent and qualify you for continued supply. This supplier is important to your plans. What do you do?

2. Making innovations successful often relies on being the first to commercialize a technology. What are some practices a firm could use to enhance its first-mover advantage? Does the stage of the industry life cycle affect the available practices? Are there long-term consequences for the firm from these practices?

Small Group Exercises

SMALL GROUP EXERCISE 1

Your group works for Warner Music Group (www.wmg.com), a large music record label whose sales are declining largely due to piracy. Your supervisor assigns you the task of developing a strategy for improving this situation.

1. What are the key issues you must grapple with to improve the position of Warner Music Group (WMG)?

2. In what phase of the life cycle is the record-label industry?

3. How does this life-cycle phase affect the types of innovation that should be considered to help WMG be successful?

SMALL GROUP EXERCISE 2

Strategy Highlight 7.4 outlines GE's development of the Vscan, which will likely cannibalize the sales of its existing ultrasound machines. Part of the difficult decision to reverse-innovate is the prospect of losing not just sales revenue but also jobs. In 2010, GE Healthcare employed over 45,000 people. Assume 10,000 jobs strongly connected to supporting GE's high-end imaging systems are in imminent jeopardy if sales of the systems drop off. Put yourself in the role of GE Healthcare managers.

1. Pull together a memo of talking points for the managers of the new Vscan that may put many other men and women at GE out of work.

2. How do you explain the societal benefits of lower-cost medical scanning equipment yet address real job security concerns among the employees?

Strategy Term Project

MODULE 7: INNOVATION STRATEGY

In this section, you will study the environment of the firm you have selected for the strategy term project and the firm's susceptibility to technological disruptions from new entrants.

1. Where is your firm's industry on the life cycle as shown in Exhibit 7.2?

2. What is the dominant technological design of the industry in which your firm is primarily located?

3. Did this dominant technology develop quickly or more slowly? Can you identify what influenced the speed of diffusion?

4. Where is the dominant technology on the S-curve in your focal industry? What alternative technologies could present a paradigm shift as shown in Exhibit 7.10?

5. What is the role of standards in the focal industry?

6. From a marketing perspective, what attributes describe the current major customer segment for your firm?

7. Are intellectual property rights important for your firm? Can you find what strategies the firm is implementing to protect its proprietary position?

*my*Strategy

DO YOU WANT TO BE AN ENTREPRENEUR?

About 75 percent of Stanford MBAs plan to start their own business upon graduation. Moreover, economic downturns appear to be the best time to start a company. Many of today's *Fortune-100* and high-tech success stories were launched in economic downturns. The global depression of 1873–1895 witnessed the founding of today's industry giants like AT&T, GE, Hershey's, Gillette, Johnson & Johnson, Abbott, Lilly, Merck, and Bristol-Myers. Similarly, Hewlett-Packard (HP), Texas Instruments, and United Technologies got their starts during the Great Depression of 1929–1939 in the United States.

The success story of Silicon Valley began with the founding of HP in Palo Alto, California. This cluster of high-tech innovators, venture capitalists, and entrepreneurs took off during a time when the stock market had crashed by some 90 percent and almost one in three U.S. workers were unemployed. Apple, Microsoft, LexisNexis, FedEx, and Genentech began their corporate lives during the oil price shocks and subsequent recession in the mid-1970s. During the early 1980s, inflation raged and mortgage rates were over 20 percent. Still, during this period entrepreneurs founded Amgen, CNN, MTV, E*Trade, AOL, Adobe, and Autodesk.[61]

1. Why do you think recessions are a good time to start a business? Wouldn't that seem counterintuitive?

2. Thinking about today's business climate, would you say that now is a good time to start a business? Why or why not?

3. If you were to start a business, what type of business would you want to start, and why? What idea would you be commercializing?

4. Does it matter *where* (in terms of geography) you start your business? Why or why not?

5. Explain how your startup could gain and sustain a competitive advantage.

Endnotes

1. This ChapterCase is based on: Surowiecki, J. (2004), *The Wisdom of Crowds* (New York: Bantam Dell); "Internet encyclopedias go head-to-head," *Nature,* December 15, 2005; Anderson, C. (2006), *The Long Tail. Why the Future of Business Is Selling Less of More* (New York: Hyperion); Anderson, C. (2009), *Free. The Future of a Radical Price* (New York: Hyperion); "Wikipedia's old-fashioned revolution," *The Wall Street Journal,* April 6, 2009; www.encyclopediacenter.com; www.alexa.com/topsites; and http://en.wikipedia.org/wiki/Jimmy_Wales; http://en.wikipedia.org/wiki/Wikipedia.

2. Rothaermel, F. T., and A. Hess (2010), "Innovation strategies combined," *MIT Sloan Management Review,* Spring: 12–15.

3. Schumpeter, J. A. (1942), *Capitalism, Socialism, and Democracy* (New York: Harper & Row). For an updated and insightful discussion, see Foster, R., and S. Kaplan (2001), *Creative Destruction: Why Companies that Are Built to Last Underperform the Market—and How to Successfully Transform Them* (New York: Currency/Doubleday).

4. Schumpeter, J. A. (1942), *Capitalism, Socialism, and Democracy*; Foster, R., and S. Kaplan (2001), *Creative Destruction: Why Companies that Are Built to Last Underperform the Market—and How to Successfully Transform Them.*

5. "Comcast, GE strike deal; Vivendi to sell NBC stake," *The Wall Street Journal,* December 4, 2009.

6. This discussion is based on: Rothaermel, F. T., and M. Thursby (2007), "The nanotech vs. the biotech revolution: Sources of incumbent productivity in research," *Research Policy* 36: 832–849; and Woolley, J. (2010), "Technology Emergence through Entrepreneurship across Multiple Industries," *Strategic Entrepreneurship Journal* 4: 1–21.

7. Moore, G. A. (2002), *Crossing the Chasm* (New York: HarperCollins).

8. www.apple.com/ipad/pricing/.

9. This discussion is based on: Arthur, W. B. (1989), "Competing technologies, increasing returns, and lock-in by

historical events," *Economics Journal* 99: 116–131; Hill, C. W. L. (1997), Establishing a standard: Competitive strategy and winner take all industries, *Academy of Management Executive* 11: 7–25; and Shapiro, C., and H. R. Varian (1998), *Information Rules. A Strategic Guide the Network Economy* (Boston, MA: Harvard Business School Press).

10. This Strategy Highlight is based on: "Inside the app economy," *BusinessWeek,* October 22, 2009, www.apple.com/iphone/apps-for-iphone/.

11. This discussion is based on: Utterback, J. M. (1994), *Mastering the Dynamics of Innovation* (Boston, MA: Harvard Business School Press); Anderson, P., and M. Tushman (1990), "Technological discontinuities and dominant designs: A cyclical model of technological change," *Administrative Science Quarterly* 35: 604–634; and Schilling, M. A. (1998), "Technological lockout: An integrative model of the economic and strategic factors driving technology success and failure," *Academy of Management Review* 23: 267–284.

12. This discussion is based on: Teece, D. J. (1986), "Profiting from technological innovation: Implications for integration, collaboration, licensing and public policy," *Research Policy* 15: 285–305; and Ceccagnoli, M., and F. T. Rothaermel (2008), "Appropriating the returns to innovation," *Advances in Study of Entrepreneurship, Innovation, and Economic Growth* 18: 11–34.

13. Abernathy, W. J., and J. M. Utterback (1978), "Patterns of innovation in technology," *Technology Review* 80: 40–47; Benner, M., and M. A. Tushman (2003), "Exploitation, exploration, and process management: The productivity dilemma revisited," *Academy of Management Review* 28: 238–256.

14. This Strategy Highlight is based on: Cassingham, R. R. (1986), *Dvorak Keyboard: The Ergonomically Designed Keyboard, Now an American Standard* (Calgary, Alberta: Freelance Communications); Arthur, W. B. (1989), "Competing technologies, increasing returns, and lock-in by historical events," *Economics Journal* 99: 116–131; and "Smart keyboard seem dumb to people

of their type," *The Wall Street Journal,* September 28, 2009.

15. The history of Spanx is documented at www.spanx.com.

16. Harrigan, K. R. (1980), *Strategies for Declining Businesses* (Lexington, MA: Heath).

17. Ibid.

18. "Back in fashion," *The Economist,* January 14, 2010.

19. Schramm, C. J. (2006), *The Entrepreneurial Imperative,* (New York: HarperCollins). Dr. Carl Schramm is president of the Kauffman Foundation, the world's leading foundation for entrepreneurship.

20. Schumpeter, J. A. (1942), *Capitalism, Socialism, and Democracy*; Foster, R., and S. Kaplan (2001), *Creative Destruction: Why Companies that Are Built to Last Underperform the Market—and How to Successfully Transform Them.*

21. Shane, S., and S. Venkataraman (2000), "The promise of entrepreneurship as a field of research," *Academy of Management Review* 25: 217–226; Alvarez, S., and J. B. Barney (2007), "Discovery and creation: Alternative theories of entrepreneurial action," *Strategic Entrepreneurship Journal* 1: 11–26.

22. "Oprah Winfrey to end her program in 2011," *The Wall Street Journal,* November 19, 2009.

23. *Forbes Special Edition: "Billionaires,"* March 29, 2010.

24. Hawkins, J. (2009), "Inside the mind of a reluctant entrepreneur," *Presentation at the Stanford's Entrepreneurial Thought Leader Series,* May 13, 2009.

25. Hitt, M. A., R. D. Ireland, S. M. Camp, and D. L. Sexton (2002), "Strategic entrepreneurship: Integrating entrepreneurial and strategic management perspectives," in Hitt, M. A., R. D. Ireland, S. M. Camp, and D. L. Sexton (eds.), *Strategic Entrepreneurship: Creating a New Mindset* (Oxford, UK: Blackwell Publishing); Rothaermel, F. T. (2008), "Strategic management and strategic entrepreneurship," *Presentation at the Strategic Management Society Annual International Conference,* Cologne, Germany, October 12.

26. Ibid; Bingham, C. B., K. M. Eisenhardt, and N. R., Furr (2007), "What makes a process a capability? Heuristics, strategy, and effective capture of opportunities," *Strategic Entrepreneurship Journal* 1: 27–47.

27. Shuen, A. (2008), *Web 2.0: A Strategy Guide* (Sebastopol, CA: O'Reilly Media); Thursby, J., and M. Thursby (2006), *Here or There? A Survey in Factors of Multinational R&D Location* (Washington, DC: National Academies Press).

28. Byers, T. H., R. C. Dorf, and A. J. Nelson (2011), *Technology Entrepreneurship: From Idea to Enterprise* (Burr Ridge, IL: McGraw-Hill).

29. This discussion is based on: Schumpeter, J. A. (1942), *Capitalism, Socialism, and Democracy;* Freeman, C., and L. Soete (1997), *The Economics of Industrial Innovation* (Cambridge, MA: MIT Press); and Foster, R., and S. Kaplan (2001), *Creative Destruction: Why Companies that Are Built to Last Underperform the Market—and How to Successful Transform Them.*

30. The discussion of incremental and radical innovations is based on Hill, C. W. L., and F. T. Rothaermel (2003), "The performance of incumbent firms in the face of radical technological innovation," *Academy of Management Review* 28: 257–274.

31. "Pioneering CNN rates behind Fox News, MSNBC," *NBC Washington,* March 30, 2009.

32. Hill, C. W. L., and F. T. Rothaermel (2003), "The performance of incumbent firms in the face of radical technological innovation," *Academy of Management Review* 28: 257–274.

33. "The challengers. A new breed of multinational company has emerged," *The Economist,* January 10, 2008.

34. This discussion is based on Hill, C. W. L., and F. T. Rothaermel (2003), "The performance of incumbent firms in the face of radical technological innovation."

35. Gillette took off when it decided to "give away" its razors (sell them at or below cost, or give them away outright) and make money on selling expensive razors. This business model is now found in many situations: "give away" the printer, and make money on cartridges; "give away" the video game console to make money off the games; "give away" the cell phone to make money with a two-year service plan; "give away" the coffeemakers to make money from expensive coffee sachets. For a more in-depth discussion, see Anderson, C. (2009), *Free: The Future of a Radical Price.*

36. The razor model chronology includes Trac II, Atra, Sensor, Sensor Excel, Sensor 3, Mach 3, Mach 3 Venus, Mach 3 Turbo, Mach 3 Turbo Venus Divine, Fusion, and others.

37. This Strategy Highlight is based on: Anderson, C. (2009), *Free: The Future of a Radical Price;* and "P&G razor launches in recession's shadow," *The Wall Street Journal,* February 12, 2010.

38. Brandenburger, A. M., and B. J. Nalebuff (1996), *Co-opetition* (New York: Currency Doubleday); and Christensen, C. M., and J. L. Bower (1996), "Customer power, strategic investment, and the failure of leading firms," *Strategic Management Journal* 17: 197–218.

39. Henderson, R., and K. B. Clark (1990), "Architectural innovation: The reconfiguration of existing technologies and the failure of established firms," *Administrative Science Quarterly* 35: 9–30.

40. This example is drawn from: Chesbrough, H. (2003), *Open Innovation. The New Imperative for Creating and Profiting from Technology,* (Boston, MA: Harvard Business School Press).

41. The discussion of disruptive innovation is based on: Christensen, C. M. (1997), *The Innovator's Dilemma: When New Technologies Cause Great Firms to Fail* (Boston, MA: Harvard Business School Press); and Christensen, C. M., and M. E. Raynor (2003), *The Innovator's Solution: Creating and Sustaining Successful Growth* (Boston, MA: Harvard Business School Press).

42. "Introducing the Google Chrome OS," *The Official Google Blog,* July 7, 2009, http://googleblog.blogspot.com/2009/07/introducing-google-chrome-os.html.

43. See discussion on Business Models in Chapter 1. See also: Anderson, C. (2009), *Free: The Future of a Radical Price.*

44. The new processor is not only inexpensive but also consumes little battery power. Moreover, it marks a departure from the Wintel (Windows and Intel) alliance, because Microsoft did not have a suitable operating system ready for the low-end netbook market. Many of these computers are using free software such as Google's Android operating system and Google Docs for applications.

45. This Strategy Highlight is based on: Immelt, J. R., V. Govindarajan, and C. Timble (2009), "How GE is disrupting itself," *Harvard Business Review,* October; Author's interviews with Michael Poteran of GE Healthcare (10/30/09 and 11/04/09); and "Vscan handheld ultrasound: GE unveils 'stethoscope of the 21st century,'" *Huffington Post,* October 20, 2009.

46. This section is based on: Anderson, C. (2006), *The Long Tail. Why the Future of Business Is Selling Less of More;* and Anderson, C. (2009), *Free. The Future of a Radical Price.*

47. "A giant sucking sound," *The Economist,* November 5, 2009.

48. Anderson, C. (2006), *The Long Tail. Why the Future of Business Is Selling Less of More.*

49. "Microsoft near deal to acquire Skype," *The Wall Street Journal*, May 10, 2011.

50. This discussion is based on: Cohen, W. M., and D. A. Levinthal (1990), "Absorptive capacity: A new perspective on learning and innovation," *Administrative Science Quarterly* 35: 128–152; and Rothaermel, F. T., and M. T. Alexandre (2009), "Ambidexterity in technology sourcing: The moderating role of absorptive capacity," *Organization Science* 20: 759–780.

51. Schilling, M. A. (1998), "Technological lockout: An integrative model of the economic and strategic factors driving technology success and failure," *Academy of Management Review* 23: 267–284.

52. This discussion is based on: Snow, D. (2008), "Beware of old technologies' last gasps," *Harvard Business Review,* January. See also "The Henry Ford of Heart Surgery," *The Wall Street Journal,* November 25, 2009.

53. Foster, R. N. (1986), *Innovation: The Attacker's Advantage* (New York: Summit Books).

54. This discussion is based on: D'Aveni, R. A. (1994), *Hypercompetition. Managing the Dynamics of Strategic Maneuvering* (New York: Free Press).

55. Although the notion of hypercompetition is intuitively appealing, there is an ongoing debate in the literature whether the empirical data indeed confirms it. For recent contributions, see: Gimeno, J., and C. Y. Woo (1996), "Hypercompetition in a multimarket environment: The role of strategic similarity and multimarket contact in competitive de-escalation," *Organization Science* 7: 322–341; Makadok, R. (1998), "Can first-mover and early-mover advantages be sustained in an industry with low barriers to entry/imitation?" *Strategic Management Journal* 19: 683–696; McNamara, G., P. M. Vaaler, and C. Devers (2003), "Same as it ever was: The search for evidence of increasing hypercompetition, *Strategic Management Journal* 24: 261–278; Thomas, L. G. (1996), "The two faces of competition: Dynamic resourcefulness and the hypercompetitive shift," *Organization Science* 7: 221–242; Vaaler, P., and G. McNamara (2009), "Are technology-intensive industries more dynamically competitive? No and yes," *Organization Science* 20: in press; Thomas, L. G., and R. A. D'Aveni (2009), "The changing nature of competition in the US manufacturing sector, 1950 to 2002," *Strategic Organization* 7: 387–431; Wiggins, R.W., and T. W. Ruefli (2002), "Sustained competitive advantage: Temporal dynamics and the incidence and persistence of superior economic performance," *Organization Science* 13: 82–105; and Wiggins, R. W., and T. W. Ruefli (2005), "Schumpeter's ghost: Is hypercompetition making the best of times shorter?" *Strategic Management Journal* 26: 887–911.

56. nm = nanometer = 1 billionth of a meter.

57. Porter, M. E. (1996), "What is strategy?" *Harvard Business Review,* November–December.

58. Data from Wikipedia, www.wikipedia.org/wiki/wikipedia:about.

59. "For Borders, a scramble to be lean," *The Wall Street Journal,* March 14, 2011.

60. "Borders and the 20-20 hindsight phenomenon," *Forbes,* March 12, 2011.

61. This *my*Strategy example is based on: "14 big businesses that started in a recession," www.insidecrm.com, November 11, 2008; "Full-time MBA Programs: Stanford University," *BusinessWeek,* November 13, 2008; "Start-ups that thrive in a recession," *The Wall Street Journal,* February 4, 2009; and "Why great companies get started in the downturns," www.vcconfidential.com, February 24, 2009.

CHAPTER 8

Corporate Strategy: Vertical Integration and Diversification

LEARNING OBJECTIVES

After studying this chapter, you should be able to:

LO 8-1 Define corporate-level strategy, and describe the three dimensions along which it is assessed.

LO 8-2 Describe and evaluate different options firms have to organize economic activity.

LO 8-3 Describe the two types of vertical integration along the industry value chain: backward and forward vertical integration.

LO 8-4 Identify and evaluate benefits and risks of vertical integration.

LO 8-5 Describe and examine alternatives to vertical integration.

LO 8-6 Describe and evaluate different types of corporate diversification.

LO 8-7 Apply the core competence–market matrix to derive different diversification strategies.

LO 8-8 Explain when a diversification strategy creates a competitive advantage, and when it does not.

Refocusing GE: A Future of Clean-Tech and Health Care?

JEFFREY IMMELT WAS appointed chairman and CEO of General Electric (GE) on September 7, 2001. Since then, the external environment has experienced continuous and dramatic change: first, the social and economic effects of the 9/11 terrorist attacks, followed later by the 2008–2009 financial meltdown. Although GE is a diversified conglomerate that spans many industries and markets, the recession in 2001 and the even deeper recession of 2008–2009 hit the company especially hard. One reason is the financial hit that GE Capital took, since more than half of GE's profits came from that unit. In a critical 17 months, GE's share price fell 84 percent, from $42.12 (on October 2, 2007) to $6.66 (on March 5, 2009), equating to a loss in shareholder value of $378 billion. Between 2008 and 2010, GE significantly underperformed the Dow Jones Industrial Index. To compound matters, GE also lost its AAA credit rating, and the company had to ask for a $15 billion liquidity injection from famed investor Warren Buffett.

The need for change was clear to Immelt. In 2009, GE's five business units (Technology Infrastructure, Energy Infrastructure, Capital Finance, Consumer and Industrial, and NBC Universal) brought in $157 billion in annual revenues. More than 50 percent of those revenues came from outside the United States, and GE employed more than 300,000 people in over 100 countries. Immelt decided to refocus

GE's portfolio of businesses to reduce its exposure to capital markets and to achieve reliable and sustainable future growth by leveraging its core competencies in industrial engineering. GE sold a majority stake in NBC Universal to Comcast, the largest U.S. cable operator, and also put its century-old appliance unit up for sale. GE had identified the green economy and, more recently, health care as major future-growth industries. To capitalize on these opportunities, GE launched two strategic initiatives: *ecomagination* and *healthymagination*.

Ecomagination is GE's clean-tech strategic initiative, launched in 2005 and renewed in 2010 by adding another $10 billion in investments. As Immelt explains, its strategic intent is "to focus our unique energy, technology, manufacturing, and infrastructure capabilities to develop tomorrow's solutions such as solar energy, hybrid locomotives, fuel cells, lower-emission aircraft engines, lighter and stronger materials, efficient lighting, and water purification technology."[1] GE's stated goal is, by 2012, to reduce global greenhouse gas emissions by 1 percent and GE's total water consumption by 20 percent (from a 2006 baseline). Since 2005, GE has invested billions in clean-tech R&D. The ecomagination initiative generates roughly $25 billion in annual revenues for GE.

Healthymagination, launched in 2009, is GE's newest strategic initiative. Its goal is to increase the quality of and access to health care while lowering its cost. Investing $6 billion by 2015, GE's strategic intent is to reduce the cost of health care by 15 percent, increase access to essential health care services worldwide by 15 percent, reach a minimum of 100 million people a year, and improve health care quality by 15 percent by streamlining health care procedures, processes, and standards.[2]

After reading the chapter, you will find more about this case, with related questions, on page 226.

▲ **AS A MULTIBUSINESS** enterprise, GE has been changing its corporate strategy by moving away from slow-growing businesses (appliances and entertainment) and turning to future-growth industries such as clean-tech and health care. More importantly, Jeffrey Immelt reduced GE's exposure to the financial markets by trimming the GE Capital unit. Although GE Capital produced roughly half of GE's profits (based on one-third of its revenues), it made GE more vulnerable to changes in the macro environment, as became painfully apparent in the 2008–2009 financial crisis. These changes in GE's strategy demonstrate that firms must decide in which industries and global markets to compete, and that these choices are likely to change over time. Answers to these important questions are captured in a firm's *corporate-level strategy,* which we cover in the next three chapters.

In this chapter, we define corporate-level strategy and then look at two fundamental corporate-level strategy topics: vertical integration and diversification. We address horizontal integration by studying acquisitions, strategic alliances, and networks in Chapter 9, before turning our attention to global strategy in Chapter 10.

WHAT IS CORPORATE-LEVEL STRATEGY?

>> **LO 8-1**
Define corporate-level strategy, and describe the three dimensions along which it is assessed.

In Chapters 6 and 7, we saw that *business-level strategy* concerns the quest for gaining and sustaining competitive advantage in a *single product market* (how to compete). Corporate-level strategy involves the decisions that senior management makes and the actions it takes in the quest for competitive advantage in several industries and markets simultaneously (where to compete). When formulating corporate strategy, managers must clarify the firm's focus on specific product and geographic markets. Although many managers have input in this important decision-making process, the responsibility for corporate strategy ultimately rests with the CEO. We noted in ChapterCase 8, for example, Jeffrey Immelt's attempt to refocus GE on future-growth industries through the *ecomagination* and *healthymagination* strategic initiatives. In his 2010 letter to shareholders, Mr. Immelt confirmed GE's back-to-its-roots corporate strategy: "As we grew, financial services became too big and added too much volatility. GE must be an industrial company first. We have increased our investment in industrial growth."[3]

As discussed in Chapter 6, the two generic business strategies that firms can pursue in their quest for competitive advantage are to: increase differentiation (while containing cost) *or* lower costs (while maintaining differentiation). If trade-offs can be reconciled, some firms might be able to pursue an integration strategy by increasing differentiation *and* lowering costs. To gain and sustain competitive advantage, therefore, any corporate strategy must align with and strengthen a firm's business strategy, whether it is differentiation, cost leadership, or an integration strategy.

Corporate strategy concerns the scope of the firm,[4] which determines the boundaries of the firm along three dimensions: industry value chain, products and services, and geography (regional, national, or global markets). To determine these boundaries, executives must decide:

- In what stages of the *industry value chain* (the transformation of raw materials into finished goods and services along distinct vertical stages) to participate. This decision determines the firm's *vertical integration.*

- What *range of products and services* the firm should offer. This decision determines the firm's *horizontal integration,* or *diversification.*

- Where in the world to compete. This decision determines the firm's *global strat*egy.

These are the fundamental corporate-level strategic decisions. Exhibit 8.1 depicts the horizontal, vertical, and geographic dimensions along which corporate strategy is assessed. The three dimensions create a space in which corporate executives most position the company for competitive advantage.

The underlying strategic management concepts that will guide our discussion of the vertical, horizontal, and geographic scope of the firm are *economies of scale and scope,* and *transaction costs.*

As discussed in Chapter 6, *economies of scale* occur when a firm's average cost per unit decreases as its output increases. Anheuser-Busch InBev, the largest global brewer (producer of brands such as Budweiser, Bud Light, Stella Artois, and Beck's), reaps significant economies of scale. Given its size, it is able to spread its fixed costs over the millions of gallons of beer it brews each year, in addition to the significant buyer power its large market share affords. Larger market share, therefore, often leads to lower costs. *Economies of scope,* in turn, are the savings that come from producing two (or more) outputs or providing different services at less cost than producing each individually, though using the same resources and technology. Leveraging its online retailing expertise, for example, Amazon benefits from economies of scope: By leveraging its core competency in superior IT systems, it can offer a large range of different product and service categories at a lower cost than it would take to offer each product line individually. This leveraging explains why Amazon offers not only a wide array of goods online but also cloud computing services. (By spreading its fixed cost over many different product and service lines, Amazon also benefits from economies of scale.)

The second underlying strategic management concept that will guide our discussion is *transaction costs,* which are all costs associated with an economic exchange. We begin our study of corporate strategy by drawing on transaction cost economics to explain the choices firms make concerning their scope. This strategic management framework enables managers to answer the question of whether it is cost-effective for their firm to grow its scope by taking on greater ownership of the *production* of needed inputs or of the *channels* by which it distributes its outputs (vertical integration). Later, we will explore managerial decisions relating to diversification, which directly affect the horizontal dimension (the firm's scope of products and services) in multi-industry competition. We take up horizontal integration in more detail in the next chapter. Although we touch upon a firm's geographic scope in this chapter, we study it in more depth in Chapter 10, which is devoted to global strategy.

EXHIBIT 8.1

The Three Dimensions of Corporate-Level Strategy: Vertical Integration, Horizontal Integration, and Geographic Scope

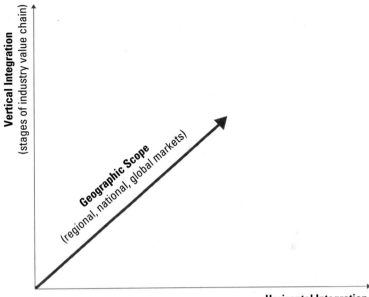

corporate-level strategy The decisions that senior management makes and the actions it takes in the quest for competitive advantage in several industries and markets simultaneously; addresses *where to compete.*

scope of the firm The boundaries of the firm along three dimensions: industry value chain, products and services, and geography (regional, national, or global markets).

TRANSACTION COST ECONOMICS AND THE SCOPE OF THE FIRM

>> **LO 8-2**
Describe and evaluate different options firms have to organize economic activity.

Determining the scope of the firm so that it is more likely to gain and sustain a competitive advantage is the critical challenge in corporate-level strategy.[5] A theoretical framework in strategic management called transaction cost economics explains and predicts the scope of the firm, which is central to formulating a corporate-level strategy. Insights gained from transaction cost economics help managers decide what activities to do in-house versus what services and products to obtain from the external market. The key insight of transaction cost economics is that different *institutional arrangements*—markets versus firms—have different costs attached.

To start, we need to identify transaction costs: these are all costs associated with an economic exchange, whether it takes place within the boundaries of a firm or in markets.[6] When companies transact in the open market, they incur the costs of searching for an economic agent (a firm or an individual) with whom to contract, negotiating, monitoring, and enforcing the contract.

Transaction costs can occur within the firm as well. Considered administrative costs, they include costs pertaining to organizing an economic exchange within a hierarchy—for example, the costs of recruiting and retaining employees, paying salaries and benefits, setting up a shop floor, providing office space and computers, and organizing, monitoring, and supervising work. Administrative costs also include costs associated with coordinating economic activity between different business units of the same corporation (such as transfer pricing for input factors) and between business units and corporate headquarters (including important decisions pertaining to resource allocation, among others). Administrative costs tend to increase with organizational size and complexity.

Firms vs. Markets: Make or Buy?

Transaction cost economics allows us to explain which activities a firm should pursue in-house ("make") versus which goods and services to obtain externally ("buy"). These decisions help determine the scope of the firm. In some cases, costs of using the market (such as search costs, negotiating and drafting contracts, monitoring work, and enforcing contracts when necessary) may be higher than integrating the activity within a single firm and coordinating it through an organizational hierarchy. When the costs of pursuing an activity in-house are less than the costs of transacting for that activity in the market ($C_{in\text{-}house} < C_{market}$), then the firm should *vertically integrate* by owning production of the needed inputs or the channels for the distribution of outputs. In other words, when *firms* are more efficient in organizing economic activity than are *markets,* which rely on contracts among (many) independent actors, firms should vertically integrate.[7]

For example, rather than contracting in the open market for individual pieces of software code, Microsoft hires programmers to write code in-house. Owning these software-development capabilities is valuable to the firm because its costs (salaries and benefits to in-house computer programmers) are less than what they would be in the open market. More importantly, Microsoft benefits from economies of scope in software development resources and capabilities, since skills acquired in writing software code for its Windows operating system are transferable to other Microsoft applications like Word or Excel. Indeed, Microsoft's programmers have a considerable advantage over outside developers. Due to their familiarity with the proprietary source code for Windows 7, Microsoft's newest operating system (which contains millions of lines of software code), they are able to produce applications that run seamlessly and reliably on computers that use Windows 7. Since many leading software firms rely on proprietary software code and algorithms, using the open market to transact for individual pieces of software would be prohibitively expensive. Also the software firms would need to disclose to outside developers a source of their competitive advantage, thus negating their value-creation potential.

Firms and markets, as different institutional arrangements for organizing economic activity, have their own distinct advantages and disadvantages, summarized in Exhibit 8.2. Advantages of firms include making command-and-control decisions, by fiat along hierarchical lines of authority; coordinating highly complex tasks to allow for specialized division of labor; and creating a community of knowledge. Disadvantages of organizing economic activity within firms include administrative costs and low-powered incentives, such as hourly wages and salaries (which often are less attractive motivators than the entrepreneurial opportunities and rewards that can be obtained in the open market), and the principal–agent problem.

EXHIBIT 8.2

Organizing Economic Activity: Firm vs. Markets

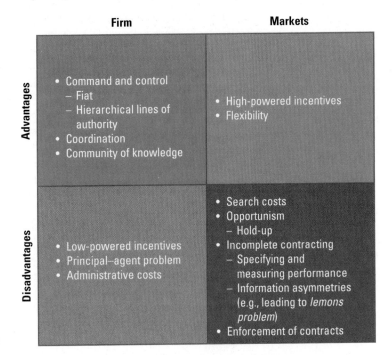

Another disadvantage of organizing economic activity within firms, as opposed to within markets, is the principal–agent problem that can arise when an agent (such as a manager), performing activities on behalf of the principal (the owner) of the firm, pursues his or her own interests.[8] Indeed, the separation of ownership and control is one of the hallmarks of a publicly traded company, and so some degree of the principal–agent problem is almost inevitable.[9] The problem arises when the agents, acting on behalf of the principals, pursue their own interests such as job security and managerial perks (e.g., corporate jets and golf outings). These interests conflict with the principals' goals—in particular, creating shareholder value. One potential way to overcome the principal–agent problem is to make managers owners through stock options. We will revisit the principal–agent problem, with related ideas, in Chapters 11 and 12.

Compared to firms, markets provide high-powered incentives. Rather than work as a salaried engineer for an existing firm, for example, an individual can start a new venture offering specialized software. One of the most high-powered incentives of the open market is to take a new venture through an initial public offering (IPO), or be acquired by an existing firm. In these so-called *liquidity events,* a successful entrepreneur can make potentially enough money to provide financial security for life.[10] Moreover, transacting in markets

---

transaction cost economics
A theoretical framework in strategic management to explain and predict the scope of the firm, which is central to formulating a corporate-level strategy that is more likely to lead to competitive advantage.

transaction costs All costs associated with an economic exchange, whether within a firm or in markets.

administrative costs All costs pertaining to organizing an economic exchange within a hierarchy, including recruiting and

retaining employees, paying salaries and benefits, and setting up a business.

principal–agent problem
Situation in which an agent performing activities on behalf of a principal pursues his or her own interests.

enables those who wish to purchase goods to compare prices and services among many different providers, and thus increases transparency and flexibility.

On a very fundamental level, perhaps the biggest disadvantage of transacting in markets, rather than owning the various production and distribution activities within the firm itself, entails non-trivial *search costs*. In particular, firms face search costs when they must scour the market to find suppliers from among the many firms competing to offer similar products and services. Even more difficult can be the search to find suppliers when the specific products and services needed are not offered at all by firms currently in the market.

Transacting in the market has several other notable disadvantages. First, it runs the risk of opportunism by other parties. *Opportunism* is behavior characterized by seeking self-interest with guile (which we'll discuss in more detail later). In addition, there is the problem of *incomplete contracting*. Although market transactions are based on implicit and explicit contracts, all contracts are incomplete to some extent, since not all future contingencies can be anticipated at the time of contracting. It is also difficult to specify expectations (e.g., What stipulates "acceptable quality" in a graphic design project?) or to measure performance and outcomes (e.g., What does "excess wear and tear" mean when returning a leased car?).

Frequently, sellers have better information about products and services than buyers, which in turn creates information asymmetries, situations in which one party is more informed than another, mostly due to the possession of private information. When firms transact in the market, such unequal information can lead to a *lemons problem.* Information asymmetries can result in the crowding out of desirable goods and services by inferior ones. Nobel Laureate George Akerlof first described this situation using the market for used cars as an example.[11] Assume only two types of cars are sold: good cars and bad cars (lemons). Good cars are worth $8,000 and bad ones are worth $4,000. Moreover, only the seller knows whether a car is good or is a lemon. Assuming the market supply is split equally between good and bad cars, the probability of buying a lemon is 50 percent. Buyers are aware of the general possibility of buying a lemon and thus would like to hedge against it. Therefore, they split the difference and offer $6,000 for a used car. This discounting strategy has the perverse effect of crowding out all the good cars because the sellers perceive their value to be above $6,000. Assuming that to be the case, all used cars offered for sale will be lemons.

As illustrated by the lemons example, information asymmetries in markets can lead to perverse effects. Applying this insight to the market for collaborative R&D projects in biotechnology, empirical research supports the lemons hypothesis.[12] In particular, the researchers suggest that biotechnology startups have a tendency to develop the most-promising R&D projects internally, while, at the same, they offer inferior R&D projects ("lemons") to large pharmaceutical companies for joint development through strategic alliances.

Finally, it often is difficult, costly, and time-consuming to *enforce legal contracts.*[13] Not only does litigation absorb a significant amount of managerial resources and attention, it can easily amount to several million dollars in legal fees. Legal exposure, therefore, is one of the major hazards in using markets rather than integrating an activity within a firm's hierarchy.

Also, note that the *resource-based view of the firm* (introduced in Chapter 4) provides an alternative perspective on the make-or-buy decision. Rather than being determined by transaction costs, a firm's boundaries are delineated by its knowledge bases and competencies.[14] Activities that draw on what the firm knows how to do well (e.g., Honda's core competency in small, highly reliable engines, or Google's core competency in developing proprietary search algorithms) should be done in-house, while non-core activities can be outsourced. In this perspective, the internally held knowledge determines a firm's boundaries.

information asymmetries Situations in which one party is more informed than another, mostly due to the possession of private information.

Alternatives on the Make-or-Buy Continuum

The "make" and "buy" choices *anchor each end of a continuum* from markets to firms, as depicted in Exhibit 8.3. Several alternative hybrid arrangements are in fact available between these two extremes.[15] Moving from transacting in the market ("buy") to full integration ("make"), alternatives include short-term contracts as well as various forms of strategic alliances (long-term contracts, equity alliances, and joint ventures) and parent–subsidiary relationships.

SHORT-TERM CONTRACTS. When engaging in *short-term contracting,* a firm sends out *requests for proposals (RFPs)* to several companies, which initiates competitive bidding for contracts to be awarded with a short duration, generally less than one year. The benefit to this approach lies in the fact that it allows a somewhat longer planning period than individual market transactions. Moreover, the buying firm can often demand lower prices due to the competitive bidding process. The drawback, however, is that firms responding to the RFP have no incentive to make any transaction-specific investments (e.g., new machinery to improve product quality) due to the short duration of the contract. Since short-term contracts are unlikely to be of strategic significance, they are not subsumed under the term *strategic alliances,* but rather are considered to be *mere contractual arrangements.*

STRATEGIC ALLIANCES. As we move toward greater integration on the make-or-buy continuum, the next organizational forms are strategic alliances. In a broad sense, *strategic alliances* are voluntary arrangements between firms that involve the sharing of knowledge, resources, and capabilities with the intent of developing processes, products, or services together.[16] Alliances have become a ubiquitous phenomenon, especially in high-tech industries. Moreover, strategic alliances can facilitate investments in transaction-specific assets without encountering the administrative costs involved in owning firms in various stages of the industry value chain.

Strategic alliances is an umbrella term that denotes different hybrid organizational forms—among them, long-term contracts, equity alliances, and joint ventures. Given their prevalence in today's competitive landscape, as a key vehicle to execute a firm's corporate strategy, we take a quick look at strategic alliances here and then study them in more depth in Chapter 9.

Long-Term Contracts. We noted that firms in short-term contracts have no incentive to make transaction-specific investments. *Long-term contracts,* which work much like short-term

EXHIBIT 8.3

Alternatives along the Make-or-Buy Continuum

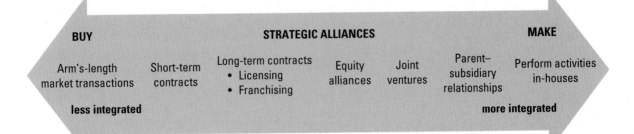

Toyota Locks Up Lithium for Car Batteries

Global demand for lithium-ion batteries to propel cars is estimated to grow almost a hundred-fold, to $25 billion in 2014, up from a mere $278 million in 2009. However, this type of battery requires large amounts of high-quality lithium, which is difficult and costly to extract. Given the specific geological conditions, the company mining the lithium must deploy specialized equipment.

Toyota Motor Corporation was interested in securing a long-term supply of lithium to power its growing fleet of hybrid vehicles. It approached Orocobre, which holds the exploration rights to a large salt-lake area in northwestern Argentina. Although lithium is found in several rock formations across the globe, large quantities can be extracted in a cost-effective manner only below the surfaces of salt flats. However, initial investments in specialized equipment worth several hundred million dollars are required even to understand the *quality* of the deposits. If the findings are positive, more investments would be needed to exploit them commercially.

Should Orocobre make the investment in the specialized equipment? What if the lithium is not of the quality expected, or a new technology emerges that is superior to lithium-ion batteries? Toyota would then have an incentive to walk away from the deal. To negate this concern, Toyota took an equity stake worth an estimated $100 to $120 million in this project.[17]

contracts but with a duration generally greater than one year, help overcome this drawback. Long-term contracts help facilitate transaction-specific investments. Licensing, for example, is a form of long-term contracting in the manufacturing sector that enables firms to commercialize intellectual property (such as a patent). The first biotechnology drug to reach the market, Humulin (human insulin), was developed by Genentech and commercialized by Eli Lilly based on a licensing agreement.

In service industries, franchising is an example of long-term contracting. In these arrangements, a franchisor (such as McDonald's, Burger King, 7-Eleven, H&R Block, or Subway) grants a franchisee (usually an entrepreneur owning no more than a few outlets) the right to use the franchisor's trademark and business processes to offer goods and services that carry the franchisor's brand name. Besides providing the capital to finance the expansion of the chain, the franchisee generally pays an up-front (buy-in) lump sum to the franchisor plus a percentage of revenues.

Long-term contracting, however, also has drawbacks. As mentioned earlier, all contracts are incomplete to some extent. Incomplete contracts open the door for opportunism by one of the contractual parties due to diverging motivations and incentives.

Equity Alliances. Yet another form of strategic alliance is an *equity alliance*—a partnership in which at least one partner takes partial ownership in the other partner. A partner purchases an ownership share by buying stock (making an equity investment). The taking of equity tends to signal greater commitment to the partnership.

Strategy Highlight 8.1 describes an equity alliance between Toyota and Orocobre Ltd., an Australian mineral-resource company, to make specialized investments for the exploration and mining of lithium, a critical input for lithium-ion batteries used in hybrid and electric vehicles.

In the Strategy Highlight, if Toyota were merely to transact for the lithium in the market—by simply signing a contract with Orocobre that it would purchase any lithium it mined—Toyota could walk away from the exploratory project undertaken by Orocobre if the results were not what it had expected, or if the forecasted demand for lithium-ion batteries did not materialize. In a contractual arrangement, one transaction partner could attempt to *hold up* the other, by demanding lower prices or threatening to walk away from the agreement altogether (with whatever financial penalties might be included in the contract). To assuage Orocobre's concerns, Toyota made a credible commitment— a long-term strategic decision that is both difficult and costly to reverse. Alternatively, Toyota could have bought Orocobre outright. This would have been, however, a much more costly and riskier strategic move.

Joint Ventures. In a joint venture, which is another special form of strategic alliance, two or more partners create and jointly own a new organization. Since the partners contribute equity to a joint venture, they make a long-term commitment, which in turn facilitates transaction-specific investments. Dow Corning, owned jointly by Dow Chemical and Corning, is an example of a joint venture. Dow Corning, which focuses on silicone-based technology, employs roughly 10,000 people and has $5 billion in annual revenues.[18] This example shows that some joint ventures can be Fortune 500 companies in their own right. Hulu, which offers web-based streaming video of TV shows and movies, is also a joint venture. It is owned by NBC Universal, Fox Entertainment Group, and ABC Inc. We will further discuss joint ventures in Chapter 9.

PARENT–SUBSIDIARY RELATIONSHIP. The *parent–subsidiary relationship* describes the most-integrated alternative to performing an activity within one's own corporate family. The corporate parent owns the subsidiary and can direct it via command and control. Transaction costs that arise are frequently due to political turf battles, which may include (among other areas) the capital budgeting process and transfer prices. For example, although GM owns its European carmakers Opel and Vauxhall, it had problems bringing some of their know-how and design of small fuel-efficient cars back into the U.S. This particular parent–subsidiary relationship was burdened by political problems because managers in Detroit did not respect the engineering behind the small, fuel-efficient cars that Opel and Vauxhall made. They thus were not interested in using European know-how for the U.S. market (and didn't want to pay much or anything for it). Moreover, Detroit was tired of subsidizing the losses of Opel and Vauxhall, and felt that its European subsidiaries were manipulating the capital budgeting process.[19] In turn, the Opel and Vauxhall subsidiaries felt resentment toward their parent company: GM had initially planned to sell them as part of its bankruptcy restructuring whereas they, instead, hoped to be spun out as independent companies.[20]

Having fully considered transactions cost economics and the scope of the firm to lay a strong theoretical foundation, we now turn our attention to the firm's scope along the vertical industry value chain.

VERTICAL INTEGRATION ALONG THE INDUSTRY VALUE CHAIN

The first key question when formulating corporate-level strategy is: In what stages of the industry value chain should the firm participate? Deciding whether to make (within the firm) or buy (in the market from other firms) the various activities in the industry value chain involves the concept of vertical integration. Vertical integration is the firm's ownership of its production of needed inputs or of the channels by which it distributes its outputs. In particular, vertical integration can be measured by a firm's value added: What percentage of a firm's sales is generated within the firm's boundaries?[21] The degree of vertical integration tends to correspond to the number of industry value-chain stages in which it directly participates.

---

licensing A form of long-term contracting in the manufacturing sector that enables firms to commercialize intellectual property.

franchising A long-term contract in which a franchisor grants a franchisee the right to use the franchisor's trademark and business processes to offer goods and services that carry the franchisor's brand name; the franchisee in turn pays an up-front buy-in lump sum and a percentage of revenues.

credible commitment A long-term strategic decision that is both difficult and costly to reverse.

joint venture Organizational form in which two or more partners create and jointly own a new organization.

vertical integration The firm's ownership of its production of needed inputs or of the channels by which it distributes its outputs.

EXHIBIT 8.4

Backward and Forward Vertical Integration along an Industry Value Chain

UPSTREAM INDUSTRIES

BACKWARD VERTICAL INTEGRATION

DOWNSTREAM INDUSTRIES

FORWARD VERTICAL INTEGRATION

Stage 1
- Raw Materials

Stage 2
- Components
- Intermediate Goods

Stage 3
- Final Assembly
- Manufacturing

Stage 4
- Marketing
- Sales

Stage 5
- After-Sales Service and Support

Exhibit 8.4 depicts a generic industry value chain. Industry value chains are also called *vertical value chains,* because they depict the transformation of raw materials into finished goods and services along distinct vertical stages. Each stage of the vertical value chain typically represents a distinct *industry* in which a number of different firms are competing.

In Chapter 4, we introduced the concept of the firm-level internal value chain. That internal value chain depicts the activities the firm engages in to transform inputs into outputs, with activities ranging from basic R&D to customer service. Internal, firm-level value chains are also called *horizontal value chains.* Thus, there are two intersecting value chains: the *industry value chain* running *vertically* from upstream to downstream, and the *firm-level value chain* running *horizontally.*[22] In this chapter on corporate-level strategy, the one of interest is the vertical, industry value chain.

To understand the concept of vertical integration along the different stages of the industry value chain more fully, let's take your cell phone as an example. This ubiquitous device is the result of a globally coordinated industry value chain of different products and services. The raw materials to make your cell phone, such as chemicals, ceramics, metals, oil (for plastic), and so on, are commodities. In each of these commodity businesses are different companies, such as DuPont (U.S.), BASF (Germany), Kyocera (Japan), and ExxonMobil (U.S.). Intermediate goods and components such as integrated circuits, displays, touch screens, cameras, and batteries are provided by firms such as Jabil Circuit (U.S.), Intel (U.S.), LG Display (Korea), Altek (Taiwan), and BYD (China). Original equipment manufacturing firms (OEMs) such as Flextronics (Singapore) or Foxconn (China) typically assemble cell phones under contract for consumer electronics and telecommunications companies like Ericsson (Sweden), Motorola (U.S.), Nokia (Finland), RIM (Canada), and so on. If you look closely at an iPhone, for example, you'll notice that it says "Designed by Apple in California. Assembled in China." Finally, to get wireless data and voice service, you pick a service provider such as AT&T, Sprint, or Verizon. All of these companies—from the raw-materials suppliers to the service providers—comprise the global industry value chain that, as a whole, delivers you a working cell phone. Determined by their corporate strategy, each firm decides where in the industry value chain to participate, and thus the vertical scope of the firm.

industry value chain Depiction of the transformation of raw materials into finished goods and services along distinct vertical stages, each of which typically represents a distinct *industry* in which a number of different firms are competing.

>> LO 8-3
Describe the two types of vertical integration along the industry value chain: backward and forward vertical integration.

Types of Vertical Integration

Along the industry value chain, there are varying degrees of vertical integration. Weyerhaeuser, one of the world's largest paper and pulp companies, is *fully vertically integrated:* all activities are conducted within the boundaries of the firm. As an example, Weyerhaeuser owns forests, grows and cuts its timber, mills it, manufactures a variety of different paper and construction products, and distributes them to retail outlets and other large customers. Weyerhaeuser's value added is 100 percent. Weyerhaeuser, therefore, competes in a number of different industries and faces different competitors in each.

On the other end of the spectrum are firms that are more or less *vertically disintegrated*. These are firms that focus on only one or a limited few stages of the industry value chain. For instance, Zara, a Spanish clothing and accessory designer, is vertically disintegrated to a large extent in the upstream industry stages. Zara runs a hyper-efficient global logistics operation that allows it to produce fashion trends faster than any competitor.[23] Zara designs new fashion trends and then outsources most of its manufacturing to Asia and the Middle East, even though some of the more high-end fashions are produced in Spain closer to its headquarters. While other international competitors take months to bring new designs to market, Zara designs, manufactures, and gets products to market in about four weeks. Zara captures significant value from orchestrating its network of suppliers, buyers, and other business partners. Designing fashionable clothing and accessories in fast cycles is a competency that obeys the VRIO principles (discussed in Chapter 4), and thus can lay the foundation for competitive advantage. (Zara does own some retail outlets, so it is not fully vertically disintegrated along the entire industry value chain.)

Be aware that *not all industry value-chain stages are equally profitable.* Zara, for instance, designs fashions but has others produce and ship the products. Similarly, Apple captures significant value by designing mobile devices through integration of hardware and software in novel ways, but it outsources the manufacturing of its device to generic OEMs. The logic behind these decisions can be explained by applying the structure-conduct-performance (SCP) model (introduced in Chapter 3) and the VRIO model. In the cell phone manufacturing industry structure, the many small OEMs are almost completely interchangeable and are thus exposed to the perils of perfect competition. On the other hand, Apple's competencies in innovation, system integration, and marketing, are valuable, rare, and unique (non-imitable) resources, and Apple is organized to capture most of the value it creates. In terms of industry structure, Apple's continued innovation through new introductions of products and services provides it with temporary competitive advantage. Even so, competitors are not sitting idle.

To compete with Apple's iPhone, Google launched the Nexus One (in 2010), a smartphone that used Google's Android open-source operating system. Google, at its heart a software company, chose to have HTC of Taiwan manufacture the product's hardware.[24] Exhibit 8.5 displays part of the value chain for smartphones. In this figure, note HTC's transformation from a no-name manufacturer (for example, of Google's Nexus One) to a significant player in the design, manufacture, and sales of smartphones. It now offers a lineup of

EXHIBIT 8.5

HTC's Backward and Forward Integration along the Industry Value Chain in the Smartphone Industry

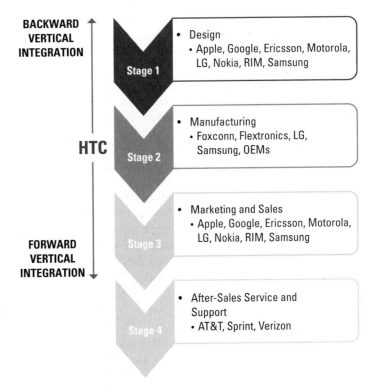

BACKWARD VERTICAL INTEGRATION

Stage 1
- Design
  - Apple, Google, Ericsson, Motorola, LG, Nokia, RIM, Samsung

HTC

Stage 2
- Manufacturing
  - Foxconn, Flextronics, LG, Samsung, OEMs

Stage 3
- Marketing and Sales
  - Apple, Google, Ericsson, Motorola, LG, Nokia, RIM, Samsung

FORWARD VERTICAL INTEGRATION

Stage 4
- After-Sales Service and Support
  - AT&T, Sprint, Verizon

smartphones under the HTC label.[25] Over time, HTC was able to upgrade its capabilities from merely manufacturing smartphones to also designing products.[26] In doing so, HTC engaged in backward vertical integration—moving ownership of activities upstream to the originating (inputs) point of the value chain. Moreover, by moving downstream into sales and increasing its branding activities, HTC has also engaged in forward vertical integration—moving ownership of activities closer to the end (customer) point of the value chain. HTC is benefitting from economies of scope through participating in different stages of the industry value chain. For instance, it now is able to share competencies in product design, manufacturing, and sales, while at the same time attempting to reduce transaction costs.

Benefits and Risks of Vertical Integration

>> **LO 8-4**
Identify and evaluate benefits and risks of vertical integration.

To decide the degree and type of vertical integration to pursue, managers need to understand the possible benefits and risks of vertical integration.

BENEFITS OF VERTICAL INTEGRATION. Vertical integration, either backward or forward, can have a number of benefits, including:[27]

- Securing critical supplies
- Lowering costs
- Improving quality
- Facilitating scheduling and planning
- Facilitating investments in specialized assets

As noted earlier, HTC started as an OEM for brand-name mobile device companies such as Motorola, Nokia, and others. It backwardly integrated into smartphone design by acquiring One & Co., a San Francisco–based design firm.[28] The acquisition allowed HTC to secure scarce design talent and capabilities that it leveraged into the design of smartphones with superior quality and features built in, thus enhancing the differentiated appeal of its products. Moreover, HTC can now design phones that leverage its low-cost manufacturing capabilities.

Likewise, forward integration into distribution and sales allows companies to more effectively plan for and respond to changes in demand. HTC's forward integration into sales enables it to offer its products directly to wireless providers such as AT&T, Sprint, and Verizon. HTC even offers unlocked phones directly to the end consumer via its website. Thus, HTC is now in a much better position to respond if, for example, demand for its latest phone should suddenly pick up.

There appear to be cyclical trends to vertical integration over time. A decade ago, vertical integration seemed to fall out of favor as firms focused on their core activities while outsourcing the non-core ones. More recently, however, some companies seem to be more inclined to vertically integrate, as shown in Strategy Highlight 8.2.[29]

Vertical integration allows firms to increase operational efficiencies through improved coordination and fine-tuning of adjacent value chain activities. Keeping the downstream value-chain activities independent worked well for PepsiCo and Coca-Cola during the 1980s and 1990s, when consumption of soda beverages was on the rise. However, independent bottlers are cost-effective only when doing large-volume business of a few, limited product offerings. With Pepsi's and Coke's more diversified portfolio of noncarbonated and healthier drinks, the costs of outsourcing bottling and distribution to independent bottlers increased significantly. (Some of the independent bottlers even lack the equipment to produce the niche drinks now in demand.) In addition, the independent bottlers' direct store-delivery system adds significant costs. To overcome this problem, the soft drink giants had begun to deliver some of their niche products (such as Pepsi's Gatorade and SoBe Lifewater and Coke's Powerade and Glacéau) directly to warehouse retailers like Sam's Club and Costco.

Given the increase of costs using the market, the forward integration of Pepsi and Coca-Cola is in line with predictions derived from transaction cost economics. Controlling the delivery part of the value chain also enhances the soft drink giants' bargaining power when negotiating product price, placement, and promotion. Looking at Porter's five forces model, Pepsi and Coke are reducing the bargaining power of buyers and thus shifting the industry structure in their favor. End consumers are likely to benefit from Coke's and Pepsi's forward integration in the form of lower prices and a wider variety of niche drinks. Taken together, vertical integration can increase differentiation and reduce costs, thus strengthening a firm's strategic position as the gap between value creation and costs widens.

Vertical integration along the industry value chain can also facilitate *investments in specialized assets.* What does this mean? Specialized assets have significantly more value in their intended use than in their next-best use (i.e., they have high opportunity cost).[31] They can come in several forms:[32]

- *Site specificity.* Assets are required to be co-located, such as the equipment necessary for mining bauxite and aluminum smelting.
- *Physical-asset specificity.* Assets whose physical and engineering properties are designed to satisfy a particular customer, such as bottling machinery for Coca-Cola and PepsiCo. Since the bottles have different (even trademarked) shapes, they require unique molds.
- *Human-asset specificity.* Investments made in human capital to acquire unique knowledge and skills, such as mastering the routines and procedures of a specific organization, which are not transferable to a different employer.

Why do investments in specialized assets tend to incur high opportunity costs? Making the specialized investment opens up the threat of *opportunism* by one of the partners. Opportunism is defined as self-interest seeking with guile.[33] Backward vertical integration

---

STRATEGY HIGHLIGHT 8.2

Back to the Future: PepsiCo's Forward Integration

In 2009, PepsiCo forwardly integrated by buying its bottlers in order to obtain more control over its quality, pricing, distribution, and in-store display. This $7.8 billion purchase reversed a 1999 decision in which PepsiCo spun out its bottlers to focus on marketing. According to CEO Indra Nooyi, Pepsi's plans (stated in 2009) were to broaden its menu of offerings to include a slew of new noncarbonated beverages like flavored water enhanced with vitamins and fruit juices. With an integrated value chain, Ms. Nooyi hoped to improve decision making and enhance flexibility to bring innovative products to market faster, while reducing costs by more than $400 million.

Due to the strategic interdependence of companies in an oligopoly (as studied in Chapter 3), it came as no surprise when only a few months later, in early 2010, Pepsi's archrival Coca-Cola responded with its own forward integration move, when it purchased its bottlers for $12.2 billion. Coca-Cola also indicated that more control of manufacturing and distribution were the key drivers behind this deal. Moreover, Coca-Cola pegged the expected cost savings at $350 million. Like PepsiCo, Coca-Cola's forward integration also represented a major departure from its decade-old business model with large independent bottlers and distributors.[30]

---

backward vertical integration Changes in an industry value chain that involve moving ownership of activities upstream to the originating (inputs) point of the value chain.

forward vertical integration Changes in an industry value chain that involve moving ownership of activities closer to the end (customer) point of the value chain.

specialized assets Assets that have significantly more value in their intended use than in their next-best use (high opportunity cost); they come in three types: site specificity, physical asset specificity, and human asset specificity.

is often undertaken to overcome the threat of opportunism and in securing key raw materials. For example, steelmaker Nucor recently bought SHV North America, providing Nucor with global sourcing of scrap materials for its innovative technology using electric-arc furnaces.[34]

RISKS OF VERTICAL INTEGRATION. Depending on the situation, vertical integration has several risks, including:[35]

- Increasing costs
- Reducing quality
- Reducing flexibility
- Increasing the potential for legal repercussions

A higher degree of vertical integration can lead to increasing costs for a number of reasons. In-house suppliers tend to have higher cost structures because they are not exposed to market competition. Knowing there will always be a buyer for their products reduces their incentives to lower costs. In contrast, suppliers in the open market, because they serve a much larger market, can achieve economies of scale that elude in-house suppliers. Organizational complexity increases with higher levels of vertical integration, thereby increasing administrative costs such as determining the appropriate transfer prices between an in-house supplier and buyer. Administrative costs arise from the coordination of multiple divisions, political maneuvering for resources, consumption of company perks, or simply from employees slacking off.

The knowledge that there will always be a buyer for their products not only reduces the incentives of in-house suppliers to lower costs; it also can reduce the incentive to increase quality or come up with innovative new products. Moreover, given their larger scale and exposure to more customers, external suppliers often can reap higher learning and experience effects and so develop unique capabilities or quality improvements.

A higher degree of vertical integration can also reduce a firm's strategic flexibility, especially when faced with changes in the external environment such as fluctuations in demand and technological change.[36] For instance, when technological process innovations enabled significant improvements in steel-making, mills like U.S. Steel and Bethlehem Steel were tied to their fully integrated business models and unable to switch technologies, leading to the bankruptcy of many integrated steel mills. Non-vertically integrated mini-mills such as Nucor and Chaparral, on the other hand, invested in the new steel-making process and grew their business by taking market share away from the less flexible integrated producers.[37]

U.S. regulators like the Federal Trade Commission (FTC) and the Justice Department (DOJ) tend to allow vertical integration, arguing that it generally makes firms more efficient and lowers costs, which in turn can benefit customers. However, due to monopoly concerns, vertical integration has not gone unchallenged.[38] The FTC, for example, carefully reviewed PepsiCo's plan to reintegrate its two largest bottlers, which gives the firm full control of about 80 percent of its North American distribution. Before engaging in vertical integration, therefore, managers need to be aware that this corporate strategy can increase the potential for legal repercussions.

>> **LO 8-5**
Describe and examine alternatives to vertical integration.

Alternatives to Vertical Integration

Ideally, one would like to find alternatives to vertical integration that provide similar benefits without the accompanying risks. Are there such alternatives?

TAPER INTEGRATION. One alternative to vertical integration is taper integration. It is a way of orchestrating value activities in which a firm is backwardly integrated but it also relies on outside-market firms for some of its supplies, and/or is forwardly integrated but also relies on outside-market firms for some if its distribution.[39] Exhibit 8.6 illustrates the concept of taper integration along the vertical industry value chain. Here, the firm sources intermediate goods and components from in-house suppliers as well as from outside suppliers. In a similar fashion, a firm sells its products through company-owned retail outlets and through independent retailers. Both Apple and Nike, for example, use taper integration: They own retail outlets but also use other retailers, both brick-and-mortar and online.

Taper integration has several benefits.[40] It exposes in-house suppliers and distributors to market competition, so that performance comparisons are possible. Rather than hollowing out its competencies by relying too much on outsourcing, taper integration allows a firm to retain its competencies in manufacturing and retailing.[41] Moreover, taper integration also enhances a firm's flexibility. For example, when adjusting to fluctuations in demand, a firm could cut back on the finished goods it delivers to external retailers while continuing to stock its own stores. Finally, when using taper integration, firms can combine internal and external knowledge, possibly paving the path for innovation. Based on a study of 3,500 product introductions in the computer industry, researchers have provided empirical evidence that taper integration can be beneficial.[42] Firms that pursued taper integration achieved superior performance in both innovation and financial performance when compared with firms that focused more on vertical integration or strategic outsourcing.

EXHIBIT 8.6

Taper Integration along the Industry Value Chain

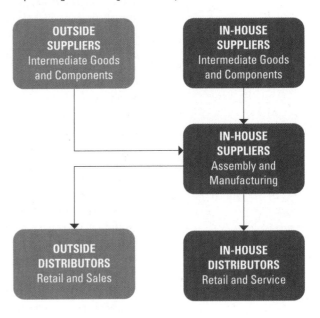

STRATEGIC OUTSOURCING.   Another alternative to vertical integration is strategic outsourcing, which involves moving one or more internal value chain activities outside the firm's boundaries to other firms in the industry value chain. A firm that engages in strategic outsourcing reduces its level of vertical integration. Rather than developing their own human resource management systems, for instance, most firms outsource these non-core activities to companies like PeopleSoft (owned by Oracle), EDS (owned by HP), or Perot Systems (owned by Dell), who can leverage their deep competencies and produce scale effects.

In the popular media and everyday conversation, you may hear the term "outsourcing" used to mean sending jobs out of the country. Actually, when outsourced activities take place outside the home country, the correct term is *off-shoring* (or *off-shore outsourcing*). By whatever name, it is a *huge* phenomenon. For example, Infosys, one of the world's largest technology companies and provider of IT services to many Fortune 100 companies, is located in Bangalore, India. The global off-shoring market is estimated to be $1.4 trillion, and is expected to grow at a compound annual growth rate of 15 percent. Banking and financial services, IT, and health care are the most active sectors in such off-shore outsourcing.[43] More recently, U.S. law firms began to send low-end legal work, such as drafting standard contracts and background research, off-shore to India.[44]

taper integration
A way of orchestrating value activities in which a firm is backwardly integrated but also relies on outside market firms for some of its supplies, and/or is forwardly integrated but also relies on outside-market firms for some of its distribution.

strategic outsourcing
Moving one or more internal value chain activities outside the firm's boundaries to other firms in the industry value chain.

CORPORATE DIVERSIFICATION: EXPANDING BEYOND A SINGLE MARKET

Early in the chapter, we listed three questions related to corporate-level strategy and, in particular, the scope of the firm. The second of those questions relates to the firm's *degree of diversification:* What range of products and services should the firm offer? In particular, why do some companies compete in a single product market, while others compete in several different product markets? Coca-Cola, for example, focuses on soft drinks and thus on a *single* product market. Its archrival PepsiCo competes directly with Coca-Cola by selling a wide variety of soft drinks and other beverages, and also offering chips (Lay's, Doritos, and Cheetos) as well as Quaker Oats products (oatmeal and granola bars).

Similarly, why do some companies compete beyond their national borders, while others prefer to focus on the domestic market? Kentucky Fried Chicken (KFC), the world's largest quick-service chicken restaurant chain, operates more than 5,200 outlets in the U.S., and more than 15,000 outlets internationally in 109 countries.[45] It is particularly popular in China. In 2010, KFC had annual revenues of $12 billion. On the other hand, Chick-fil-A with $3.5 billion in revenues (in 2010) and more than 1,500 outlets competes only domestically at this time.

Answers to questions about the number of markets to compete in and where to compete relate to the broad topic of diversification—increasing the variety of products or markets in which to compete. A *non-diversified company* focuses on a single market, whereas a *diversified company* competes in several different markets simultaneously.[46]

There are various general diversification strategies:

■ A firm that is active in several different product markets is pursuing a product diversification strategy.

■ A firm that is active in several different countries is pursuing a geographic diversification strategy.

■ A company that pursues *both* a product *and* a geographic diversification strategy simultaneously follows a product–market diversification strategy.

Because shareholders expect continuous growth from public companies, managers frequently turn to product and geographic diversification to achieve it. It is therefore not surprising that the vast majority of the Fortune 500 companies are diversified to some degree. However, achieving performance gains through diversification is not guaranteed. Some forms of diversification are more likely to lead to performance improvements than others. We now discuss which diversification types are more likely to increase value creation, and why.

Types of Corporate Diversification

>> **LO 8-6**
Describe and evaluate different types of corporate diversification.

To understand the types and degrees of corporate diversification, Richard Rumelt of UCLA developed a helpful classification scheme, depicted in Exhibit 8.7. A *single-business firm* derives 95 percent or more of its revenues from one business. Although Google is active in many different businesses, it obtains more than 95 percent of its revenues ($24 billion in 2009) from online advertising.[47] A *dominant-business firm* derives between 70–95 percent of its revenues from a single business, but it pursues at least one other business activity. Although Microsoft is primarily a software company, it also offers computer hardware products such as the Xbox 360 game console, which contributed close to 8 percent of Microsoft's $59 billion revenues in 2009.[48]

A firm follows a related diversification strategy when it derives less than 70 percent of its revenues from a single business activity but obtains revenues from other lines of

Type of Diversification	Revenues from Primary Activity	Sample Firms	
Single Business	> 95%	Coca-Cola, DeBeers, Google	
Dominant Business	70–90%	Harley-Davidson, Microsoft, Nestlé	
Related Diversification			
1) Related-Constrained	< 70%	ExxonMobil, Johnson & Johnson	
2) Related-Linked	< 70%	Amazon, Disney	
Unrelated Diversification	< 70%	Berkshire Hathaway, GE, Tata Group	

EXHIBIT 8.7

Different Types of Diversification

Source: Adapted from R. P. Rumelt (1974), *Strategy, Structure, and Economic Performance* (Boston, MA: Harvard Business School Press).

business linked to the primary business activity. The rationale behind related diversification is to benefit from economies of scale and scope: These multibusiness firms can pool and share resources as well as leverage competencies across different business lines. Strategy Highlight 8.3 (next page) describes Exxon's strategic move toward related diversification.

We can further identify two types of related diversification strategy: related-constrained and related-linked. When executives consider business opportunities only where they can leverage their existing competencies and resources, the firm is using *related-constrained diversification*. The choices of alternative business activities are limited—constrained—by the fact that they need to be related through common resources, capabilities, and activities. ExxonMobil's diversification move into natural gas is an example of related-constrained diversification.

If executives consider new business activities that share only a limited number of linkages, the firm is using *related-linked diversification*. For example, Disney follows a related-linked diversification strategy. It is active in a wide array of business activities, from cable and

---

diversification An increase in the variety of products or markets in which to compete.

product diversification strategy Corporate strategy in which a firm is active in several different product markets.

geographic diversification strategy Corporate strategy in which a firm is active in several different countries.

product–market diversification strategy Corporate strategy in which a firm is active in several different product markets and several different countries.

related diversification strategy Corporate strategy in which a firm derives less than 70 percent of its revenues from a single business activity but obtains revenues from other lines of business that are linked to the primary business activity.

ExxonMobil Diversifies into Natural Gas

In 2008, ExxonMobil reported the highest profits ever recorded by any company, with a net income of over $45 billion on revenues of about $475 billion. To illustrate the magnitude of ExxonMobil's profitability, it earned more than $1,426 in profit for every second of 2008!

Although ExxonMobil's financial performance is impressive, within its portfolio of current operations, the overwhelming majority of its profits come from petroleum-based products. Given the current political and regulatory sentiments and the global movement toward cleaner energy sources, if ExxonMobil fails to supplement its core business (based on petroleum-based energy sources) with greener energy sources, the company will likely not be able to sustain its superior performance over time.

To avoid this fate, ExxonMobil initiated a major strategic thrust into clean energy by focusing on natural gas, a low-carbon alternative to petroleum. This strategic move is an example of horizontal integration. In 2009, ExxonMobil bought XTO Energy, a natural gas company, for $31 billion. XTO Energy is known for its ability to extract natural gas from unconventional places such as shale rock, where huge deposits have been found recently in the United States. ExxonMobil hopes to leverage its core competency in the exploration and commercialization of petroleum energy sources into natural gas. Roughly 85 percent of the world's energy demand today is met by fossil fuels, including petroleum, coal, and natural gas. ExxonMobil is taking the lead among the energy giants by producing nearly equal numbers of barrels of crude oil and natural gas, making it the world's largest producer of natural gas. The company believes that roughly 50 percent of the world's energy for the next 50 years will continue to come from fossil fuels, but that its diversification into natural gas, the cleanest of the fossil fuels in terms of greenhouse gas emissions, will pay off.[49]

network television stations and movies to amusement parks, cruises, and retailing, which share some common resources, capabilities, and activities. Similarly, Amazon.com began business by selling only one product: books. Over time it expanded into CDs, and over time leveraged its online retailing capabilities into a wide array of product offerings. Today, as the world's largest online retailer, and given the need to build huge data centers to service its peak holiday demand, Amazon decided to leverage spare capacity into cloud computing, offering Internet-based computing services, again benefiting from economies of scope (and scale).[50]

Finally, a firm follows an *unrelated diversification strategy* when less than 70 percent of its revenues come from a single business and there are few, if any, linkages among its businesses. GE, for example, is following an unrelated diversification strategy. Linkages between household appliances, TV shows, jet engines, ultrasound machines, and wind turbines are not readily apparent. It should come as no surprise that each of GE's divisions has its own CEO and is managed as a standalone business with profit-and-loss responsibility. The Indian Tata Group is even more diversified.[51] Its product offering includes cars (Jaguar, Land Rover, and Nano), chemicals, steel, consulting, software, coffee, tea, and luxury hotel resorts. Some of its strategic business units are giants in their own right. The Tata group includes Asia's largest software company (TCS) and India's largest steelmaker. It also owns the renowned Taj Hotels & Resorts.

Some research evidence suggests that an unrelated diversification strategy can be advantageous.[52] This arrangement helps firms gain and sustain competitive advantage because it allows the conglomerate to overcome institutional weaknesses in emerging economies, such as lack of capital markets and well-defined legal systems and property rights. Companies like GE, Berkshire Hathaway, the South Korean LG chaebol, and the Tata group are all considered *conglomerates* due to their unrelated diversification strategy.

Leveraging Core Competencies for Corporate Diversification

In Chapter 4, when looking inside the firm, we introduced the idea that competitive advantage can be based on core competencies. Core competencies are unique skills and strengths that allow firms to increase the perceived value of their product and service offerings and/or lower the cost to produce them.[53] Examples of core competencies are:

- Walmart's ability to effectively orchestrate a globally distributed supply chain at low cost
- Apple's ability to integrate hardware and software into products that provide a superior user experience
- Infosys's ability to provide high-quality information technology services at low cost through leveraging its global delivery model (i.e., taking work to the location where it makes the best economic sense based on the available talent and the least amount of acceptable risk)

>> **LO 8-7**
Apply the core competence–market matrix to derive different diversification strategies.

To survive and prosper, companies need to grow. This mantra holds especially true for publicly owned companies, because they create shareholder value through profitable growth. Managers respond to this relentless growth imperative by leveraging their existing core competencies to find future growth opportunities. Strategy consultants Gary Hamel and C. K. Prahalad advanced the *core competence–market matrix,* depicted in Exhibit 8.8, as a way to guide managerial decisions in regards to diversification strategies. The first task for managers is to identify their existing core competencies and understand the firm's current market situation. When applying an existing or new dimension to core competencies and markets, four quadrants emerge, each with distinct strategic implications.

The lower-left quadrant combines existing core competencies with existing markets. Here, managers must come up with ideas of how to leverage existing core competencies to improve the firm's current market position. In 2010, Bank of America was the largest bank in the United States (measured by deposits) and had at least one customer in 50 percent of U.S. households.[54] Just 20 years earlier Bank of America had been North Carolina National Bank (NCNB), a regional bank in North Carolina. One of NCNB's unique core competencies was acquisitions. It bought smaller banks to supplement its organic growth throughout the 1970s and 80s, and from 1989 to 1992, NCNB purchased over 200 regional community and thrift banks, to further improve its market position. It then turned its core competency to national banks, with a goal of becoming the first nationwide bank. Known as NationsBank in the 1990s, it purchased Barnett Bank, BankSouth, FleetBank, LaSalle, CountryWide Mortgages, and its namesake Bank of America. This example illustrates how

unrelated diversification strategy Corporate strategy in which a firm derives less than 70 percent of its revenues from a single business activity and there are few, if any, linkages among its businesses.

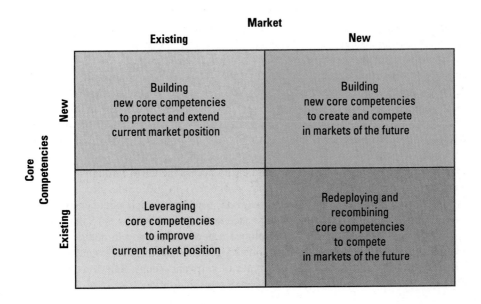

EXHIBIT 8.8

The Core Competence–Market Matrix

Source: Adapted from G. Hamel and C. K. Prahalad (1994), *Competing for the Future* (Boston, MA: Harvard Business School Press).

NationsBank, rebranded as Bank of America since 1998, honed and deployed its core competency of acquiring and integrating other commercial banks and dramatically grew its scope to emerge as one of the leading banks in the United States. (By the way, we will study the topic of acquisitions in more detail in Chapter 9.)

The lower-right quadrant of Figure 8.8 combines existing core competencies with new market opportunities. Here, managers must strategize about how to redeploy and recombine existing core competencies to compete in future markets. At the height of the financial crisis in the fall of 2008, Bank of America bought the investment bank Merrill Lynch for $50 billion.[55] Although many problems ensued for Bank of America following the Merrill Lynch acquisition, it is now the bank's investment and wealth management division. Bank of America's corporate managers leveraged an existing competency (acquiring and integrating) into a new market (investment and wealth management). The combined entity is now leveraging economies of scope through cross-selling when, for example, consumer banking makes customer referrals for investment bankers to follow up.[56]

The upper-left quadrant combines new core competencies with existing market opportunities. Here, managers must come up with strategic initiatives to build new core competencies to protect and extend the company's current market position. For example, in the early 1990s, Gatorade dominated the market for sports drinks, a segment in which it had been the original innovator. (Some 25 years earlier, medical researchers at the University of Florida had created the drink to enhance the performance of the Gators, the university's football team. Stokley-Van Camp commercialized and marketed the drink, and eventually sold it to Quaker Oats.) PepsiCo brought Gatorade into its lineup of soft drinks when it acquired Quaker Oats in 2001. By comparison, Coca-Cola had existing core competencies in marketing, bottling, and distributing soft drinks, but had never attempted to compete in the sports-drink market. Over a 10-year R&D effort, Coca-Cola developed competencies in the development and marketing of their own sports drink, Powerade, which launched in 1990. As of 2009, Powerade held about 20 percent of the sports drink market, making it a viable competitor to Gatorade, which still holds about 75 percent of the market.[57]

Finally, the upper-right quadrant combines new core competencies with new market opportunities. Hamel and Prahalad call this combination "mega opportunities"—those that hold significant future-growth opportunities. At the same time, it is likely the most challenging diversification strategy because it requires building new core competencies to create and compete in future markets. Salesforce.com is a company that employs this strategy well.[58] In recent years, Salesforce experienced tremendous growth, the bulk of it coming from the firm's existing core competency in delivering customer relationship management (CRM) software to its clients. Salesforce's product distinguished itself from the competition by providing software as a service via cloud computing: Clients did not need to install software or manage any servers, but could easily access the CRM through a web browser (a business model called *software as a service,* or *SaaS*). In 2007, Salesforce recognized an emerging market for *platform as a service* (*PaaS*) offerings, which would enable clients to build their own software solutions that are accessed the same way as the Salesforce CRM. Seizing the opportunity, Salesforce developed a new competency in delivering software development and deployment tools that allowed its customers to either extend their existing CRM offering or build completely new types of software. Today, Salesforce's Force.com offering is one of the leading providers of PaaS tools and services.

diversification discount Situation in which the stock price of highly diversified firms is valued at less than the sum of their individual business units.

diversification premium Situation in which the stock price of related-diversification firms is valued at greater than the sum of their individual business units.

Taken together, the core competence–market matrix provides guidance to executives on how to diversify in order to achieve continued growth. Once managers have a clear understanding of their firm's core competencies, they have four options to formulate corporate strategy: (1) leverage existing core competencies to improve current market position; (2) build new core competencies to protect and extend current market position; (3) redeploy and recombine existing core competencies to compete in markets of the future; and (4) build new core competencies to create and compete in markets of the future.

Corporate Diversification

GAINING & SUSTAINING COMPETITIVE ADVANTAGE

Corporate managers pursue diversification to gain and sustain competitive advantage. But does corporate diversification indeed lead to superior performance? To answer this question, we can evaluate the performance of diversified companies. The critical question to ask when doing so is whether the individual businesses are worth more under the company's management than if each were managed individually.

Research shows that the diversification-performance relationship is a function of the underlying type of diversification. A cumulative body of research indicates an inverted U-shaped relationship between the type of diversification and overall firm performance, as depicted in Exhibit 8.9.[59] High and low levels of diversification are generally associated with lower overall performance, while moderate levels of diversification are associated with higher firm performance. This implies that companies that focus on a single business, as well as companies that pursue unrelated diversification, often fail to achieve additional value creation. Firms that compete in single markets could potentially benefit from economies of scope by leveraging their core competencies into adjacent markets.

>> **LO 8-8**
Explain when a diversification strategy creates a competitive advantage, and when it does not.

Firms that pursue unrelated diversification are often unable to create additional value, and thus experience a diversification discount in the stock market: the stock price of such highly diversified firms is valued at less than the sum of their individual business units.[60] In contrast, companies that pursue related diversification are more likely to improve their performance, and thus create a diversification premium: the stock price of related-diversification firms is valued at greater than the sum of their individual business units.[61]

Why is this so? At the most basic level, a corporate diversification strategy enhances firm performance when its value creation is greater than the costs it incurs. Exhibit 8.10 (next page) lists the sources of value creation and costs for different corporate strategies, for vertical integration as well as related and unrelated diversification. For diversification to enhance firm performance, it must do at least one of the following:

- Provide economies of scale, and thus reduce costs.
- Exploit economies of scope, and thus increase value.
- Reduce costs *and* increase value.

EXHIBIT 8.9

The Diversification-Performance Relationship

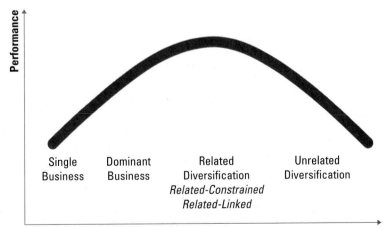

Source: Adapted from L. E. Palich, L. B. Cardinal, and C. C. Miller (2000), "Curvilinearity in the diversification-performance linkage: An examination of over three decades of research," *Strategic Management Journal* 21: 155–174.

EXHIBIT 8.10

Vertical Integration and Diversification: Sources of Value Creation and Costs

Corporate Strategy	Sources of Value Creation (*V*)	Sources of Costs (*C*)
Vertical Integration	• Securing critical supplies • Lowering costs • Improving quality • Facilitating scheduling and planning • Facilitating investments in specialized assets	• Increasing costs • Reducing quality • Reducing flexibility • Increasing potential for legal repercussions
Related Diversification	• Economies of scope • Economies of scale • Restructuring • Internal capital markets	• Coordination costs • Influence costs
Unrelated Diversification	• Restructuring • Internal capital markets	• Influence costs

We discussed these drivers of competitive advantage—economies of scale, economies of scope, and increase in value and reduction of costs—in depth in Chapter 6 in relation to business strategy. In addition to these criteria, executives can enhance performance using a diversification strategy by:

- Restructuring
- Using internal capital markets

RESTRUCTURING. *Restructuring* describes the process of reorganizing and divesting business units and activities to refocus a company in order to leverage its core competencies more fully. ChapterCase 8 highlighted the restructuring that has taken place at GE to leverage its core competency in management processes and industrial engineering. The Belgium-based Anheuser-Busch InBev recently sold Busch Entertainment, its theme park unit that owns SeaWorld and Busch Gardens, to a group of private investors for roughly $3 billion. This strategic move allows InBev to focus more fully on its core business and to pay for its 2008 acquisition of Anheuser-Busch, which cost $52 billion.[62]

Corporate-level executives can restructure the portfolio of their firm's businesses, much like an investor can change a portfolio of stocks. One helpful tool to guide corporate portfolio planning is the Boston Consulting Group (BCG) growth-share matrix, shown in Exhibit 8.11.[63] This matrix locates the firm's individual SBUs in two dimensions: relative market share (horizontal axis) and speed of market growth (vertical axis). The firm plots its SBUs into one of four categories in the matrix (dog, cash cow, star, and question mark), and each category warrants a different investment strategy.

SBUs identified as *dogs* are relatively easy to identify: They are the low-performing businesses. Dogs hold a small market share in a low-growth market; they have low and unstable earnings, combined with neutral or negative cash flows. The strategic recommendations are either to divest (sell) the business or to *harvest* it (stop investing in the business and squeeze out as much cash flow as possible before shutting it down or selling it).

Cash cows, in contrast, are SBUs that compete in a low-growth market but hold considerable market share. Their earnings and cash flows are high and stable. The strategic recommendation is to invest enough into cash cows to hold their current position, and to avoid having them turn into dogs (as indicated by the arrow).

Boston Consulting Group (BCG) growth-share matrix A corporate planning tool in which the corporation is viewed as a portfolio of business units, which are represented graphically along relative market share (horizontal axis) and speed of market growth (vertical axis). SBUs are plotted into four categories (dog, cash cow, star, and question mark), each of which warrants a different investment strategy.

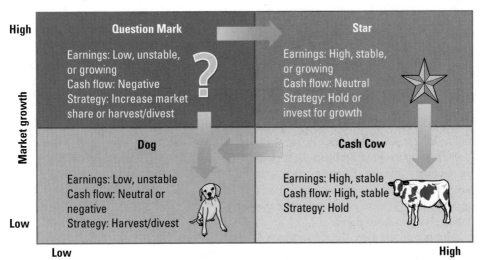

EXHIBIT 8.11

Restructuring the
Corporate Portfolio:
The Boston Consulting
Group Growth-Share
Matrix

A corporation's *star* SBUs hold a high market share in a fast-growing market. Their earnings are high and either stable or growing. The recommendation for the corporate strategist is to invest sufficient resources to hold the star's position or even increase investments for future growth. As indicated by the arrow, stars may turn into cash cows as the market in which the SBU is situated slows down due to reaching maturity.

Finally, some SBUs are *question marks:* It is not clear whether they will turn into dogs or stars. Their earnings are low and unstable, but they might be growing. The cash flow, however, is negative. Ideally, corporate executives want to invest in question marks to increase their relative market share so they turn into stars. If market conditions change, however, or the overall market growth slows down, then a question-mark SBU is likely to turn into a dog. In this case, executives would want to harvest the cash flow or divest the SBU.

INTERNAL CAPITAL MARKETS. *Internal capital markets* can be a source of value creation in a diversification strategy if the conglomerate's headquarters does a more efficient job of allocating capital through its budgeting process than what could be achieved in external capital markets. Based on private information, corporate-level managers are in a position to discover which of their strategic business units will provide the highest return to invested capital. In addition, internal capital markets may allow the company to access capital at a lower cost. Until recently, GE Capital brought in close to $70 billion in annual revenues, and generated more than half of GE's profits.[64] In combination with GE's triple-A debt rating, having access to such a large finance arm allowed GE to benefit from a lower cost of capital, which in turn was a source of value creation in itself. In 2009, GE lost its AAA debt rating and is now in the process of downsizing its finance unit. The lower debt rating and the smaller finance unit are likely to result in a higher cost of capital, and thus a potential loss in value creation through internal capital markets.

The strategy of related diversification (either related-constrained or related-linked) is more likely to enhance corporate performance than either a single or dominant level of diversification or an unrelated level of diversification. The reason is that the sources of value creation include not only restructuring, but more fundamentally, the potential benefits of economies of scope and scale. To create additional value, however, the benefits from these sources of incremental value creation must outweigh their costs. A related-diversification strategy entails two additional types of costs: coordination and influence costs. *Coordination costs* are a function of the number, size, and types of businesses that are linked to one another. *Influence costs* occur due to political maneuvering by managers to influence capital and resource allocation and the resulting inefficiencies stemming from suboptimal allocation of scarce resources.[65] In summary, related diversification is more likely to generate incremental value than unrelated diversification. 🔍

Although diversification can create shareholder value in theory, it is often difficult to realize in practice.[66] Why then do we see so much diversification taking place? One answer is the principal–agent problem discussed earlier, in which the interests of managers and shareholders diverge. Diversification generally leads to larger entities and thus bestows more power, prestige, and pay on corporate executives.[67] In Chapters 11 and 12, we study organizational structure and corporate governance to understand how to align interests of managers and shareholders.

Another reason why we see so much diversification is that interdependent competitors in oligopolistic industry structures are forced to engage in diversification in response to moves by direct rivals. Based on research conducted on competitive dynamics,[68] following ExxonMobil's acquisition of XTO Energy to move into the natural-gas sector, other oil majors also acquired natural-gas companies in response. In January 2010, the French energy company Total acquired an equity stake in Chesapeake Energy, the second largest producer of natural gas in the U.S.[69]

Some researchers suggest that *bandwagon effects* occur—firms copying moves of industry rivals.[70] A bandwagon effect can be observed, for example, in the recent related-diversification moves in the computer industry, in which hardware companies have moved into the software and services sector and vice versa:[71]

- IBM transformed itself from a hardware company into a global-services company (see Strategy Highlight 4.2). To further strengthen its strategic position in IT services, IBM acquired PricewaterhouseCoopers Consulting in 2002 for $3.5 billion and divested its low-margin PC business to the Chinese technology company Lenovo in 2005.

- In 2008, computer maker HP bought EDS, an IT services company, for more than $13 billion.

- In 2009, Oracle, a leader in enterprise software, acquired Sun Microsystems, a hardware company, for $7.4 billion.

- So as not to miss out on the apparent business opportunities available by combining computer hardware and software and services, Dell purchased Perot Systems for close to $4 billion in the fall of 2009.

- At about the same time, document-technology company Xerox bought ACS, an IT services company for $6.4 billion.

Such integration between hardware and software leads to industry convergence and brings with it a new set of competitors.

Taken together, the relationship between diversification strategy and competitive advantage depends on the *type of diversification.* There exists an inverted U-shaped relationship between the level of diversification and performance improvements. On average, related diversification (either related-constrained or related-linked) is most likely to lead to superior performance because it taps into multiple sources of value creation (economies of scale and scope, restructuring). To achieve a net positive effect on firm performance, however, related diversification must overcome additional sources of costs such as coordination and influence costs.

CORPORATE STRATEGY: COMBINING VERTICAL INTEGRATION AND DIVERSIFICATION

We are now in a position to combine vertical integration and diversification to understand a firm's corporate strategy in a more holistic fashion. A firm's overall corporate strategy concerns both its level of integration along the vertical value chain and its level of diversification.

As an example, take the computer-technology company Oracle, which earned $23 billion in revenues in 2009. Exhibit 8.12 depicts Oracle's corporate strategy along the vertical value chain and levels of diversification. Oracle's core competency lies in enterprise software (see center of figure). Oracle engaged in related diversification through backward vertical integration into computer hardware by acquiring Sun Microsystems, and forward vertical integration into human resource management systems (HRMS) and customer relations management (CRM) software by acquiring PeopleSoft. In its corporate strategy, moreover, Oracle pursues related as well as unrelated diversification. It leveraged its core competency into intellectual property (IP) management for media and entertainment businesses by its acquisition of Sophoi. Finally, Oracle pursued unrelated diversification into online identity theft and fraud protection through its acquisition of Bharosa. It is also noteworthy that through organic growth, Oracle executed its corporate strategy along the vertical value chain and on diversification through acquisitions. It now has over 40 subsidiaries, some of them quite large, such as BEA Systems.

In summary, executives determine the scope of the firm in such a fashion as to enhance the firm's ability to gain and sustain a competitive advantage. To delineate the boundaries of the firm, executives must formulate corporate-level strategy along three important dimensions (look back at Exhibit 8.1): vertical integration, horizontal integration, and global scope. As the examples in this chapter have indicated, executives implement corporate strategy through a variety of vehicles—acquisitions, alliances, and networks. Given their importance, we study these vehicles of corporate strategy in detail in the next chapter.

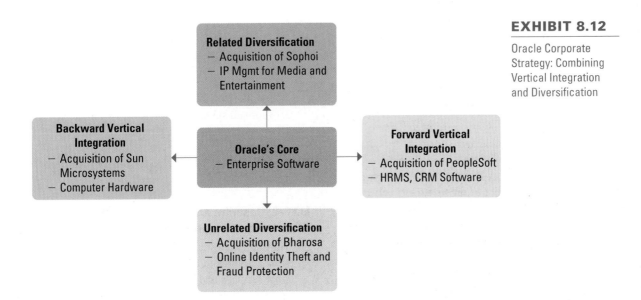

EXHIBIT 8.12

Oracle Corporate Strategy: Combining Vertical Integration and Diversification

CHAPTERCASE 8 | *Consider This . . .*

A **S DISCUSSED IN** the ChapterCase, General Electric has been refocusing its businesses through aggressive corporate divestitures (i.e., NBC Universal) and restructuring (GE Capital). Yet it is also making new investments: In 2010, GE produced $20 billion in revenue from businesses the firm was not in only a decade earlier. GE has also been increasing its global footprint. International sales have soared from 19 percent of sales in 1980, to 34 percent in 2000, to nearly 55 percent in 2010.[72]

Chairman and CEO Jeffrey Immelt believes that tackling big problems on a global scale is a strength of conglomerates such as GE. An example of a large-scale problem is the fact that according to the United Nations, in 2010 nearly one-fourth of the world's population lived without access to reliable power. In one of the fastest-growing economies in the world, India, the electrical coverage rate in 2008 was 65 percent. India has set a goal to provide electricity to all its citizens using a combination of national-scale power systems for the major cities and smaller "micro grids" for rural areas. India and other rapidly developing nations are seeking to replicate a "leap frog" approach in energy similar to that used in telecommunications. Instead of investing in vast quantities of landline communications wires, India built extensive mobile capabilities for communication needs. In energy, this means using software enabled "smart grid" electrical systems and smaller-scale but numerous renewable generation (such as wind, solar, and biomass) locations across the country. The Indian government is also encouraging smaller investments in order to improve the efficiency of existing fossil-fuel–based generators.[73] When completed, this energy infrastructure is likely to be more economical and robust than most systems in the "more developed" Western economies.

1. Where do *ecomagination and healthymagination* fit on the core competence–market matrix for GE? (See Exhibit 8.8.)

2. Take either the energy or health care industry and draw the industry value chain. What areas of potential vertical integration should GE consider?

3. What related diversification would you suggest for GE in reference to its focus for the future?

4. How do GE's corporate-level strategic initiatives of energy, health care, and globalization reinforce each other? How might they generate conflicts in the company?

Take-Away Concepts

This chapter defined corporate-level strategy and then looked at two fundamental corporate-level strategy topics, vertical integration and diversification, as summarized by the following learning objectives and related take-away concepts.

LO 8-1 Define corporate-level strategy, and describe the three dimensions along which it is assessed.

>> While business strategy addresses "how to compete," corporate strategy addresses "where to compete."

>> Corporate strategy concerns the scope of the firm along three dimensions: (1) vertical integration (along the industry value chain); (2) horizontal integration (diversification); and (3) geographic scope (global strategy).

>> To gain and sustain competitive advantage, any corporate strategy must support and strengthen a firm's strategic position regardless of whether it is a differentiation, cost leadership, or integration strategy.

LO 8-2 Describe and evaluate different options firms have to organize economic activity.

>> Transaction cost economics help managers decide what activities to do in-house ("make") versus what services and products to obtain from the external market ("buy").

>> When the costs to pursue an activity in-house are less than the costs of transacting in the market ($C_{in\text{-}house} < C_{market}$), then the firm should vertically integrate.

>> In the resource-based view of the firm, a firm's boundaries are delineated by its knowledge bases and competencies.

>> Moving from less integrated to more fully integrated forms of transacting, alternatives include: short-term contracts, strategic alliances (including long-term contracts, equity alliances, and joint ventures), and parent–subsidiary relationships.

LO 8-3 Describe the two types of vertical integration along the industry value chain: backward and forward vertical integration.

>> Vertical integration denotes a firm's value added—what percentage of a firm's sales is generated by the firm within its boundaries.

>> Industry value chains (vertical value chains) depict the transformation of raw materials into finished goods and services. Each stage typically represents a distinct industry in which a number of different firms are competing.

>> Backward vertical integration involves moving ownership of activities upstream nearer to the originating (inputs) point of the industry value chain.

>> Forward vertical integration involves moving ownership of activities closer to the end (customer) point of the value chain.

LO 8-4 Identify and evaluate benefits and risks of vertical integration.

>> Benefits of vertical integration include: securing critical supplies, lowering costs, improving quality, facilitating scheduling and planning, and facilitating investments in specialized assets.

>> Risks of vertical integration include: increasing costs, reducing quality, reducing flexibility, and increasing the potential for legal repercussions.

>> Vertical integration contributes to competitive advantage if the incremental value created is greater than the incremental costs of the specific corporate-level strategy.

LO 8-5 Describe and examine alternatives to vertical integration.

>> Taper integration is a strategy in which a firm is backwardly integrated but also relies on outside-market firms for some of its supplies, and/or is forwardly integrated but also relies on outside-market firms for some if its distribution.

>> Strategic outsourcing involves moving one or more value chain activities outside the firm's boundaries to other firms in the industry value chain. Off-shoring is the outsourcing of activities outside the home country.

LO 8-6 Describe and evaluate different types of corporate diversification.

>> A single-business firm derives 95 percent or more of its revenues from one business.

>> A dominant-business firm derives between 70 and 95 percent of its revenues from a single business, but pursues at least one other business activity.

>> A firm follows a related diversification strategy when it derives less than 70 percent of its revenues from a single business activity, but obtains revenues from other lines of business that are linked to the primary business activity. Choices within a related diversification strategy can be related-constrained or related-linked.

>> A firm follows an unrelated diversification strategy when less than 70 percent of its revenues come from a single business, and there are few, if any, linkages among its businesses.

LO 8-7 Apply the core competence–market matrix to derive different diversification strategies.

>> When applying an existing/new dimension to core competencies and markets, four quadrants emerge, as depicted in Exhibit 8.8.

>> The lower-left quadrant combines existing core competencies with existing markets. Here, managers need to come up with ideas of how to leverage existing core competencies to improve their current market position.

>> The lower-right quadrant combines existing core competencies with new market opportunities. Here, managers need to think about

how to redeploy and recombine existing core competencies to compete in future markets.

>> The upper-left quadrant combines new core competencies with existing market opportunities. Here, managers must come up with strategic initiatives of how to build new core competencies to protect and extend the firm's current market position.

>> The upper-right quadrant combines new core competencies with new market opportunities. This is likely the most challenging diversification strategy because it requires building new core competencies to create and compete in future markets.

LO 8-8 Explain when a diversification strategy creates a competitive advantage, and when it does not.

>> The diversification-performance relationship is a function of the underlying type of diversification.

>> The relationship between the type of diversification and overall firm performance takes on the shape of an inverted U (see Exhibit 8.9.).

>> In the BCG matrix, the corporation is viewed as a portfolio of businesses, much like a portfolio of stocks in finance (see Exhibit 8.11). The individual SBUs are evaluated according to relative market share and speed of market growth, and plotted into one of four categories (dog, cash cow, star, and question mark. Each category warrants a different investment strategy.

>> Both low levels and high levels of diversification are generally associated with lower overall performance, while moderate levels of diversification are associated with higher firm performance.

Key Terms

Administrative costs *(p. 204)*

Backward vertical integration *(p. 212)*

Boston Consulting Group (BCG) growth-share matrix *(p. 222)*

Corporate-level strategy (corporate strategy) *(p. 202)*

Credible commitment *(p. 208)*

Diversification *(p. 216)*

Diversification discount *(p. 221)*

Diversification premium *(p. 221)*

Forward vertical integration *(p. 212)*

Franchising *(p. 208)*

Geographic diversification strategy *(p. 216)*

Industry value chain *(p. 210)*

Information asymmetries *(p. 206)*

Joint venture *(p. 209)*

Licensing *(p. 208)*

Principal–agent problem *(p. 205)*

Product diversification strategy *(p. 216)*

Product–market diversification strategy *(p. 216)*

Related diversification strategy *(p. 216)*

Scope of the firm *(p. 202)*

Specialized assets *(p. 213)*

Strategic outsourcing *(p. 215)*

Taper integration *(p. 215)*

Transaction cost economics *(p. 204)*

Transaction costs *(p. 204)*

Unrelated diversification strategy *(p. 218)*

Vertical integration *(p. 209)*

Discussion Questions

1. When Walmart decided to incorporate grocery stores into some locations and created "supercenters," was this a business-level strategy of differentiation or a corporate-level strategy of diversification? Why? Explain your answer.

2. How can related diversification create a competitive advantage for the firm?

3. Franchising is widely used in the casual dining and fast-food industry, yet Starbucks is quite successful with a large number of company-owned stores. How do you explain this difference? Is Starbucks bucking the bandwagon effect, or is something else going on?

Ethical/Social Issues

1. The chapter notes that many firms choose to outsource their human resource management systems. If a firm has a core value of respecting its employees and rewarding top performance with training, raises, and promotions, does outsourcing HR management show a lack of commitment by the firm?

2. Nike is a large and successful firm in the design of athletic shoes. It could easily decide to forward-integrate to manufacture the shoes it designs. Therefore, the firm has a credible threat over its current manufacturers. If Nike has no intention of actually entering the manufacturing arena, is its supply chain management team being ethical with the current manufacturers if the team mentions this credible threat numerous times in annual pricing negotiations? Why or why not?

Small Group Exercises

SMALL GROUP EXERCISE 1

Agriculture is one of the largest and oldest industries in the world. In the U.S. and many other countries, farmers often struggle to turn a profit given the variances of weather and commodity prices. Some working farms are turning to tourism as an additional and complementary revenue source. A study from the U.S. Census of Agriculture in 2007 found nearly 25,000 farms providing some level of agri-tourism and recreation services. (There were 2.2 million farms in the census, almost triple the number from 2002.) In 2010, the Department of Agriculture announced a new grant program aimed at providing public access to private farms for such purposes. Small farms worldwide are participating in this trend by offering "pick your own" crops in season as well as small bed-and-breakfast experiences.

Perhaps one of the most successful large companies leading this marriage of industries is a dairy farm in Indiana: Fair Oaks Farms. Fair Oaks Farms is home to 30,000 cows and produces enough milk to feed 8 million people. It also hosts nearly 500,000 tourists each year, who come to see the hands-on adventure center and the working milking operations. (A video of the operation is available at www.youtube.com/watch?v=JJRy82i8e5Q.) Such ingenious business diversification can have many benefits to the agricultural industry.[74]

1. What other industrial or commercial industries could benefit from such potential tourist or recreational revenues?

2. In your group, list other industry combinations that you have seen to be successful.

SMALL GROUP EXERCISE 2

Target and Walmart are significant rivals in the retailing industry. Though Walmart is the world's largest company (2010 sales of $420 billion), Target had been growing faster than Walmart until the 2008 recession. From 2003 to 2007, same-store sales at Target grew an average of 4.6 percent, while Walmart's comparable growth was 2.9 percent.

However, in 2008 Target's same-store sales fell 2.6 percent, while Walmart's rose 3.3 percent. What drove this difference? Product mix seems to be a large factor. Target devotes less than 20 percent of its space to consumables such as health and beauty products and food. Walmart, by contrast, has 45 percent of its shelf space for consumables, with groceries being a major component. Though an obvious answer for Target is to continue following Walmart into groceries, consider that the average net profit of the grocery industry was less than 1.4 percent from 2002 to 2008. As a team, assume you've been called in to consult with Target on the problem.[75]

1. What should Target do to get back on a growth track?

2. Is Target's problem strategy or execution?

3. What action plan would you recommend?

Strategy Term Project

MODULE 8: VERTICAL INTEGRATION

In this section, you will study the boundaries of the firm you have selected for your strategy project in reference to the vertical value chain activities of its industry.

1. Draw out the vertical value chain for your firm's industry. List the major firms in each important activity along the chain (see Exhibits 8.4 and 8.5 as examples). Note that a firm's name may appear multiple times in the value chain. This indicates some level of vertical integration by the firm. If your firm is in many different industries (e.g., GE), then choose the dominant industry or the one that intrigues you the most and use only that one for this analysis.

2. Is your firm highly vertically integrated? If yes, does it also employ taper integration?

3. Are any of the vertical value chain operations off-shored? If so, list some of the pros and cons of having this part of the value chain outside the home country.

4. Use the preceding vertical value chain to identify the corporate strategy of the firm. In other words, where within the industry has the firm chosen to compete? Based on where it competes, describe what you now see as its corporate strategy.

5. In Module 2, you were asked to identify the mission and major goals for your selected company. Go back to that information now and compare the mission and goals to what you have found as the corporate strategy. Are the mission, goal, and corporate strategy in alignment? Do you see any holes or conflicts among these three elements? Can you relate the performance of the firm to this finding in any way? (If all three are consistent, is this a well-performing unit?) If there is a conflict between the corporate strategy and the mission, does this lack of alignment contribute to performance problems? Why or why not?

*my*Strategy

HOW DIVERSIFIED ARE YOU?

When someone asks a manager about diversification, quite often the questioner is referring to the manager's overall portfolio or savings and retirement investments. While that is an important financial consideration, here we are asking you to think about diversification a bit differently.

Corporations diversify by investing time and resources into new areas of business. As individuals, each of us makes choices about how to spend our time and energies. Typically, we could divide our time between school, work, family, sleep, and play. During high-stress work projects, we likely devote more of our time to work; when studying for final exams or a professional board exam (like the CPA exam), we probably spend more time and effort in the "student learning" mode. This manner of dividing our time can be thought of as "personal diversification." Just as companies can invest in related or unrelated activities, we make similar choices. While we attend college, we may choose to engage in social and leisure activities with campus colleagues, or we may focus on classwork at school and spend our "play time" with an entirely separate set of people.

Using Exhibit 8.7 as a guide, list each of your major activity areas. Think of each of these as a business. (If you are literally "all work and no play," you are a single-business type of personal diversification.) Instead of revenues, estimate the percentage of *time* you spend per week in each activity. (Most people will be diversified, though some may be dominant perhaps in school or work.) To assess your degree of *relatedness* and *unrelatedness,* consider the subject matter and community involved with each activity. For example, if you are studying ballet and working as an accountant, those would be largely unrelated activities (unless you are an accountant for a ballet company!).

1. What conclusions do you derive based on your personal diversification strategy?

2. Do you need to make adjustments to your portfolio of activities? Explain the reasons for your answer.

Endnotes

1. Jeffrey Immelt, quoted in "Ecomagination: Inside GE's Power Play," by J. Makower, May 8, 2005, www.worldchanging.com/archives/002669.html.

2. This ChapterCase is based on: "A slipping crown," *The Economist,* March 13, 2009; "Comcast, GE strike deal; Vivendi to sell NBC stake," *The Wall Street Journal,* December 4, 2009; "Ecomagination: Inside GE's power play," *Worldchanging,* May 8, 2005; "GE: How clean (and not-so-clean) tech drives Ecomagination," *The Wall Street Journal,* May 27, 2009; "GE launches 'Healthymagination'; will commit $6 billion to enable better health focusing on cost, access and quality," GE press release, May 7, 2009; "GE may shed storied appliance unit," *The Wall Street Journal,* May 15, 2008; "GE's chief declines $12 million bonus amid crisis," *The Wall Street Journal,* February 19, 2009; GE Annual Reports (various years); www.ge.com; and www.wolframalpha.com.

3. 2010 Letter to Shareholders in 2009 GE Annual Report.

4. Collis, D. J. (1995), "The scope of the corporation," *Harvard Business School Note,* 9-795-139.

5. The literature on transaction cost economics is rich and expanding. For important theoretical and empirical contributions, see: Folta, T. B. (1998), "Governance and uncertainty: The trade-off between administrative control and commitment," *Strategic Management Journal* 19: 1007–1028; Klein, B., R. Crawford, and A. Alchian (1978), "Vertical integration, appropriable rents, and the competitive contracting process," *Journal of Law and Economics* 21: 297–326; Leiblein, M. J., and D. J. Miller (2003), "An empirical examination of transformation-and firm-level influences on the vertical boundaries of the firm," *Strategic Management Journal* 24: 839–859; Leiblein, M. J., J. J. Reuer, and F. Dalsace (2002), "Do make or buy decisions matter? The influence of organizational governance on technological performance," *Strategic Management Journal* 23: 817–833; Mahoney, J. (1992), "The choice of organizational form: Vertical financial ownership versus other methods of vertical integration," *Strategic Management Journal* 13: 559–584; Mahoney, J. T. (2005), *Economic Foundations of Strategy* (Thousand Oaks, CA: Sage); Williamson, O. E. (1975), *Markets and Hierarchies,* (New York: Free Press); Williamson, O. E. (1981), "The economics of organization: The transaction cost approach," *American Journal of Sociology* 87: 548–577; and Williamson, O. E. (1985), *The Economic Institutions of Capitalism* (New York: Free Press).

6. This draws on: Mahoney, J. T. (2005), *Economic Foundations of Strategy* (Thousand Oaks, CA: Sage); Williamson, O. E. (1975), *Markets and Hierarchies* (New York: Free Press); Williamson, O. E. (1981), "The economics of organization: The transaction cost approach," *American Journal of Sociology* 87: 548–577; Williamson, O. E. (1985), *The Economic Institutions of Capitalism* (New York: Free Press); and Hart, O., and O. Moore (1990), "Property rights and the nature of the firm," *Journal of Political Economy* 98: 1119–1158.

7. Highlighting the relevance of research on transaction costs, both Ronald Coase (1991) and Oliver Williamson (2009), who further developed and refined Coase's initial insight, were each awarded a Nobel Prize in economics.

8. This is based on: Berle, A., and G. Means (1932), *The Modern Corporation & Private Property* (New York: Macmillan); Jensen, M., and W. Meckling (1976), "Theory of the firm: Managerial behavior, agency costs and ownership structure," *Journal of Financial Economics* 3: 305–360; and Fama, E. (1980), "Agency problems and the theory of the firm," *Journal of Political Economy* 88: 375–390.

9. Berle, A., and G. Means (1932), *The Modern Corporation & Private Property.*

10. This discussion draws on: Zenger, T. R., and W. S. Hesterly (1997), "The disaggregation of corporations: Selective intervention, high-powered incentives, and molecular units," *Organization Science* 8: 209–222; and Zenger, T. R., and S. G. Lazzarini (2004), "Compensating for innovation: Do small firms offer high-powered incentives that lure talent and motivate effort," *Managerial and Decision Economics* 25: 329–345.

11. This discussion draws on: Akerlof, G. A. (1970), "The market for lemons: Quality uncertainty and the market mechanism," *Quarterly Journal of Economics* 94: 488–500.

12. Pisano, G. P. (1997), "R&D performance, collaborative arrangements, and the market-for-know-how: A test of the 'lemons' hypothesis in biotechnology," *Working Paper No. 97-105,* Harvard Business School; Lerner J., Merges, R. P. (1998), "The control of technology alliances: An empirical analysis of the biotechnology industry," *Journal of Industrial Economics* 46: 125–156; Rothaermel, F. T., and D. L. Deeds (2004), "Exploration and exploitation alliances in biotechnology: A system of new product development," *Strategic Management Journal* 25: 201–221.

13. Somaya, D. (2003), "Strategic determinants of decisions not to settle patent litigation" *Strategic Management Journal* 24: 17–38.

14. Kogut, B., and U. Zander (1992), "Knowledge of the firm, combinative capabilities, and the replication of technology," *Organization Science* 3: 383–397; O'Connor, G. C., and M. Rice (2001), "Opportunity recognition and breakthrough innovation in large firms," *California Management Review* 43: 95–116; O'Connor, G.C, and R. W. Veryzer (2001), "The nature of market visioning for technology-based radical innovation," *Journal of Product Innovation Management* 18: 231–24.

15. This discussion draws on: Williamson, O. E. (1991), "Comparative economic organization: The analysis of discrete structural alternatives," *Administrative Science Quarterly* 36: 269–296.

16. This is based on: Gulati, R. (1998), "Alliances and networks," *Strategic Management Journal* 19: 293–317; Ireland, R. D., M. A. Hitt, and D. Vaidyanath (2002), "Alliance management as a source of competitive advantage," *Journal of Management* 28: 413–446; Hoang, H., and F. T. Rothaermel (2005), "The effect of

general and partner-specific alliance experience on joint R&D project performance," *Academy of Management Journal* 48: 332–345; and Lavie, D. (2006), "The competitive advantage of interconnected firms: An extension of the resource-based view," *Academy of Management Review* 31: 638–658.

17. This strategy highlight is based on "Toyota sets pact on lithium," *The Wall Street Journal,* January 20, 2010.

18. www.dowcorning.com.

19. "Rising from the ashes in Detroit," *The Economist,* August 19, 2010.

20. "Small cars, big question," *The Economist,* January 21, 2010.

21. Tucker, I., and R. P. Wilder (1977), "Trends in vertical integration in the U.S. manufacturing sector," *Journal of Industrial Economics,* 26: 81–97; Harrigan, K. R. (1984), "Formulating vertical integration strategies," *Academy of Management Review* 9: 638–652; Harrigan, K. R. (1986), "Matching vertical integration strategies to competitive conditions," *Strategic Management Journal* 7: 535–555; Rothaermel, F. T., M. A. Hitt, and L. A. Jobe (2006), "Balancing vertical integration and strategic outsourcing: Effects on product portfolios, new product success, and firm performance," *Strategic Management Journal* 27: 1033–1056.

22. Besanko, D., D. Dranove, M. Shanley, and S. Schaefer (2010), *Economics of Strategy,* 5th ed. (Hoboken, NJ: John Wiley & Sons).

23. "Global stretch: When will Zara hit its limits?" *The Economist,* March 10, 2011.

24. "The lowdown on teardowns," *The Economist,* January 21, 2010.

25. "HTC clones Nexus One, launches 3 new phones," *Wired.com,* February 16, 2010.

26. www.htc.com.

27. Harrigan, K. R. (1984), "Formulating vertical integration strategies," *Academy of Management Review* 9: 638–652; Harrigan, K. R. (1986), "Matching vertical integration strategies to competitive conditions," *Strategic Management Journal* 7: 535–555.

28. "HTC clones Nexus One, launches 3 new phones," *Wired.com,* February 16, 2010.

29. "Companies more prone to go vertical," *The Wall Street Journal,* December 1, 2009.

30. This Strategy Highlight is based on: "Pepsi bids $6 billion for largest bottlers, posts flat profit," *The Wall Street Journal,* April 20, 2009; "PepsiCo buys bottlers for $7.8 billion," The Wall Str*eet Journal,* August 5, 2009; "Companies more prone to go vertical," *The Wall Street Journal,* December 1, 2009; and "Coca-Cola strikes deal with bottler," *The Wall Street Journal,* February 25, 2010.

31. Williamson, O. E. (1975), *Markets and Hierarchies* (New York: Free Press); Williamson, O. E. (1981), "The economics of organization: The transaction cost approach," American Journal of Sociology 87: 548–577; Williamson, O. E. (1985), *The Economic Institutions of Capitalism* (New York: Free Press); Poppo, L., and T. Zenger (1998), "Testing alternative theories of the firm: Transaction cost, knowledge based, and measurement explanations for make or buy decisions in information services," *Strategic Management Journal* 19: 853–878.

32. Williamson, O. E. (1975), *Markets and Hierarchies* (New York: Free Press); Williamson, O. E. (1981), "The economics of organization: The transaction cost approach," *American Journal of Sociology* 87: 548–577; Williamson, O. E. (1985), *The Economic Institutions of Capitalism* (New York: Free Press).

33. Williamson, O. E. (1975), *Markets and Hierarchies* (New York: Free Press).

34. "Companies more prone to go vertical," *The Wall Street Journal,* December 1, 2009.

35. Harrigan, K. R. (1984), "Formulating vertical integration strategies," *Academy of Management Review* 9: 638–652; Harrigan, K. R. (1986), "Matching vertical integration strategies to competitive conditions," *Strategic Management Journal* 7: 535–555; Afuah, A. (2001), "Dynamic boundaries of the firm: Are firms better off being vertically integrated in the face of a technological change?" *Academy of Management Journal* 44: 1211–1228; Rothaermel, F. T., M. A. Hitt, and L. A. Jobe (2006), "Balancing vertical integration and strategic outsourcing: Effects on product portfolios, new product success, and firm performance," *Strategic Management Journal* 27: 1033–1056.

36. Afuah A. (2001), "Dynamic boundaries of the firm: are firms better off being vertically integrated in the face of a technological change?"

37. Ghemawat, P. (1993), "Commitment to a process innovation: Nucor, USX, and thin slab casting," *Journal of Economics and Management Strategy* 2: 133–161; Christensen, C. M., and M. E. Raynor (2003), *The Innovator's Solution: Creating and Sustaining Successful Growth* (Boston, MA: Harvard Business School Press).

38. "Companies more prone to go vertical," *The Wall Street Journal,* December 1, 2009.

39. Harrigan, K. R. (1984), "Formulating vertical integration strategies," *Academy of Management Review* 9: 638–652.

40. This is based on: Harrigan, K. R. (1984), "Formulating vertical integration strategies"; and Harrigan, K. R. (1986), "Matching vertical integration strategies to competitive conditions," *Strategic Management Journal* 7: 535–555.

41. This is based on the following: Prahalad and Hamel argued that a firm that outsources too many activities risks hollowing out ("unlearning") their core competencies because the firm no longer participates in key adjacent value chain activities. A similar argument has been made by Teece (1986); Prahalad, C. K., and G. Hamel (1990), "The core competence of the corporation," *Harvard Business Review,* May–June; and Teece, D. J. (1986), "Profiting from technological innovation: Implications for integration, collaboration, licensing and public policy," *Research Policy* 15: 285–305.

42. Rothaermel, F. T., M. A. Hitt, and L. A. Jobe (2006), "Balancing vertical integration and strategic outsourcing: Effects on product portfolios, new product success, and firm performance," *Strategic Management Journal* 27: 1033–1056.

43. "Global outsourcing market to be worth $1,430bn by 2009," *Computer Business Review,* August 2007.

44. "Passage to India," *The Economist,* June 26, 2010.

45. www.kfc.com/about/.

46. This section is based on: Rumelt, R. P. (1974), *Strategy, Structure, and*

Economic Performance (Boston, MA: Harvard Business School Press); Montgomery, C. A. (1985), "Product-market diversification and market power," *Academy of Management Review* 28: 789–798.

47. This is based on: Google Annual Reports; "Radio tunes out Google in rare miss for Web titan," *The Wall Street Journal,* May 12, 2009.

48. Microsoft 2009 Annual Report.

49. This strategy highlight is based on: ExxonMobil, Annual Reports; "Oil's decline slow Exxon, Chevron Profit Growth," *The Wall Street Journal,* January 30, 2009; "The greening of ExxonMobil," *Forbes,* August 24, 2009; Friedman, T. L. (2008), *Hot, Flat, and Crowded. Why We Need a Green Revolution—And How It Can Renew America* (New York: Farrar, Straus and Giroux); "Exxon to acquire XTO Energy in $31 billion stock deal," *The Wall Street Journal,* December 14, 2009; and "ExxonMobil buys XTO Energy," *The Economist,* December 17, 2009.

50. "Rebooting their systems," *The Economist,* March 10, 2011.

51. "The Tata group," *The Economist,* March 3, 2011.

52. This is based on: Peng, M. W., and P. S. Heath (1996), "The growth of the firm in planned economies in transitions: Institutions, organizations, and strategic choice," *Academy of Management Review* 21: 492–528; Peng, M. W. (2000), *Business Strategies in Transition Economies* (Thousand Oaks, CA: Sage); and Peng, M. W. (2005), "What determines the scope of the firm over time? A focus on institutional relatedness," *Academy of Management Review,* 30: 622–633.

53. Prahalad, C. K., and G. Hamel (1990), "The core competence of the corporation."

54. This discussion is based on: Burt, C., and F. T. Rothaermel (2013), "Bank of America and the New Financial Landscape," case study, in Rothaermel, F.T., *Strategic Management* (Burr Ridge IL: McGraw-Hill).

55. Bank of America had long coveted Merrill Lynch, a premier investment bank. Severely weakened by the global financial crisis, Merrill Lynch became a takeover target, and Bank of America made a bid. In the process, Bank of America learned that Merrill Lynch's exposure to subprime mortgages and other exotic financial instruments was much larger than previously disclosed. Other problems included Merrill Lynch's payments of multimillion-dollar bonuses to many employees, despite the investment bank's having lost billions of dollars (in 2008). After learning this new information, Bank of America (under its then-CEO Ken Lewis) attempted to withdraw from the Merrill Lynch takeover. The Federal Reserve Bank, under the leadership of its chairman, Ben Bernanke, insisted that Bank of America fulfill the agreement, noting that the takeover was part of a grand strategy to save the financial system from collapse. Once Bank of America shareholders learned that CEO Ken Lewis had not disclosed the problems at Merrill Lynch, they first stripped him of his chairmanship of the board of directors, and later fired him as CEO. For a detailed and insightful discussion on the Merrill Lynch takeover by Bank of America, see Lowenstein, R. (2010), *The End of Wall Street* (New York: Penguin Press).

56. "Bank of America and Merrill Lynch," *The Economist,* April 14, 2010.

57. "PepsiCo says Gatorade makeover on track," *The Wall Street Journal,* July 23, 2009.

58. This is based on: "Oracle vs. sales-force.com," Harvard Business School case study, 9-705-440; and "How to innovate in a downturn," *The Wall Street Journal,* March 18, 2009.

59. Palich, L. E., L. B. Cardinal, and C. C., Miller (2000), "Curvilinearity in the diversification-performance linkage: An examination of over three decades of research," *Strategic Management Journal* 21: 155–174.

60. This is based on: Lang, L.H.P., and R. M. Stulz (1994), "Tobin's *q,* corporate diversification, and firm performance," *Journal of Political Economy* 102: 1248–1280; Martin, J. D., and A. Sayrak (2003), "Corporate diversification and shareholder value: A survey of recent literature," *Journal of Corporate Finance* 9: 37–57; and Rajan, R., H. Servaes, and L. Zingales (2000), "The cost of diversity: The diversification discount and inefficient investment," *Journal of Finance* 55: 35–80.

61. Villalonga, B. (2004), "Diversification discount or premium? New evidence from the business information tracking series," *Journal of Finance* 59: 479–506.

62. This section is based on: "U.S. clears InBev to buy Anheuser," *The Wall Street Journal,* November 15, 2008; and "Blackstone nears deal," *The Wall Street Journal,* October 5, 2009.

63. This section is based on: Boston Consulting Group (1970), *The Product Portfolio* (Boston, MA); and Shay, J. P., and F. T. Rothaermel (1999), "Dynamic competitive strategy: Towards a multi-perspective conceptual framework," *Long Range Planning* 32: 559–572.

64. GE Annual Reports.

65. Milgrom, P., and J. Roberts (1990), "Bargaining costs, influence costs, and the organization of economic activity," in Alt, J., and K. Shepsle (eds.), *Perspectives on Positive Political Economy* (Cambridge, UK: Cambridge University Press).

66. Porter, M. E. (1987), "From competitive advantage to corporate strategy," *Harvard Business Review,* May–June: 43–59.

67. This discussion is based on: Finkelstein, S., and D. C. Hambrick (1989), "Chief executive compensation: A study of the intersection of markets and political processes," *Strategic Management Journal* 10: 121–134; and Lambert, R. A., D. F. Larcker, and K. Weigelt (1991), "How sensitive is executive compensation to organizational size?" *Strategic Management Journal* 12: 395–402.

68. This discussion is based on: Chen, M. J. (1996), "Competitor analysis and interfirm rivalry: Toward a theoretical integration," *Academy of Management Review* 21: 100–134; Ferrier, W. J., K. G. Smith, and C. M. Grimm (1999), "The role of competitive action in market share erosion and industry dethronement: A study of industry leaders and challengers," *Academy of Management Journal* 42: 372–388; and Ferrier, W. J. (2001), "Navigating the competitive landscape: The drivers and consequences of competitive aggressiveness," *Academy of Management Journal* 44: 858–877.

69. "Chesapeake Energy corporation provides quarterly operational update," *The Wall Street Journal,* May 3, 2010.

70. This discussion is based on: Bikchandani, S., D. Hirshleifer, and I. Welch (1999), "Theory of fads, fashion, custom, and cultural change as informational cascades," *Journal of Political Economy* 100: 992–1026; Abrahamson, E. (1996), "Management fashion," *Academy of Management Review* 21: 254–285; and Surowiecki, J. (2004), *The Wisdom of Crowds. Why the Many Are Smarter than the Few and How Collective Wisdom Shapes Business,* *Economies, Societies, and Nations* (New York: Doubleday).

71. This discussion is based on: "Dell to buy Perot Systems for $3.9 billion," *The Wall Street Journal,* September 21, 2009; "Dell to buy Perot Systems in catch-up deal," *The Wall Street Journal,* September 22, 2009; and "Xerox buys ACS," *The Economist,* October 1, 2009.

72. 2010 General Electric Annual Report: shareholder letter dated February 25, 2011.

73. Heintzelman, D. (2010), "India's path to renewable power," *Bloomberg Businessweek*, Viewpoint Column, May 27. (Mr. Heintzelman is president & CEO of GE Energy Services.)

74. This Small Group Exercise is based on: The Rural Community Building website produced by the American Farm Bureau Federation; *America's Heartland* "Episode 311"; and Fair Oaks Farms Dairy (www.fofarms.com).

75. This Small Group Exercise is based on: Gregory, S. (2009), "Walmart vs. Target: No contest in the recession," *Time,* March 14; and Food Marketing Institute Annual Financial Report, December 2008.

CHAPTER 9

Corporate Strategy: Acquisitions, Alliances, and Networks

LEARNING OBJECTIVES

After studying this chapter, you should be able to:

LO 9-1   Differentiate between mergers and acquisitions, and explain why firms would use either as a vehicle for corporate strategy.

LO 9-2   Define horizontal integration and evaluate the advantages and disadvantages of this corporate-level strategy.

LO 9-3   Evaluate whether mergers and acquisitions lead to competitive advantage.

LO 9-4   Define strategic alliances, and explain why they are important corporate strategy vehicles and why firms enter into them.

LO 9-5   Describe three alliance governance mechanisms and evaluate their pros and cons.

LO 9-6   Describe the three phases of alliance management, and explain how an alliance management capability can lead to a competitive advantage.

LO 9-7   Define strategic networks and evaluate the advantages and disadvantages of different network positions.

Facebook: From Dorm Room to Dominant Social Network

FACEBOOK WAS FOUNDED in a dorm room at Harvard in 2004 by 19-year-old Mark Zuckerberg and three college pals. What began as a hobby to let Ivy leaguers socialize online is now the world's largest social networking site, with more than 500 million users and estimated revenues of $2 billion in 2010. After Google, Facebook is the second most popular website worldwide. Zuckerberg sees online social networking as the "most powerful and transformative social change" in recent history.[1] Indeed, it's made him the world's youngest billionaire.

Before Facebook became a global phenomenon, it had to overcome the first-mover advantage held by MySpace. Launched in 2003, MySpace was an early leader in social networking. Its success attracted the attention of News Corp. and other media outlets. News Corp. acquired MySpace for $580 million in 2005. As a subsidiary of a publicly owned company, MySpace's revenues and profitability became more pressing issues after the acquisition. MySpace's business model shifted from accumulating more users to growing revenues and profits, by focusing on a few ad-heavy markets such as the U.S., UK, Germany, France, and Japan. MySpace was hit hard by the global economic downturn that began in 2008. A year later, it had laid off 45 percent of its staff.

Facebook, on the other hand, remained a private company. Among its other investors, Microsoft purchased a $240 million equity stake in 2007, and a Russian investment group added $200 million in 2009. Facebook's managers thus had less pressure to produce bottom-line results than did MySpace. This allowed the company to pursue a different business model: more users first, profits later. While MySpace concentrated on a few developed markets, Facebook pursued a truly global strategy. Facebook encouraged 300,000 users worldwide to help translate the website into more than 70 languages. Today, more than 70 percent of its users are outside the United States. In 2008, Facebook displaced MySpace as the most popular social networking site (see Exhibit 9.1, next page).

As a way to increase its online influence, Facebook also introduced features to draw wider-ranging social graphs (pictures of networks) of its user base. For example, other websites can install a "Like" or "Recommend" button which Facebook users can click to signal their activity on a specific website. Facebook users can announce to their social network when they buy a pair of shoes on Zappos.com, trade stocks on Zecco.com, or review a restaurant on Zagat.com. Mark Zuckerberg describes this innovation as "the most transformative thing we have ever done for the Web."[2]

However, it is not all smooth sailing for Facebook. The company has repeatedly come under attack for allegedly insufficient protection of users' privacy. Moreover, to maintain its elaborate technology platform and to fund future growth, the company will need to figure out a sustainable business model.[3]

After reading the chapter, you will find more about this case, with related questions, on page 257.

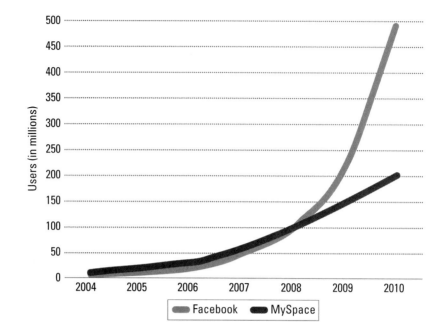

▲ **A NETWORK'S VALUE** rises exponentially with the number of its members. With more than 500 million users, Facebook benefits from network effects (a concept introduced in Chapter 7): It attracts the world's top software developers to create apps (such as FarmVille), an important complementary service. These apps in turn make Facebook more attractive for new users, further increasing its membership. The more people are on Facebook, the more valuable it is to be a member of its online community. As its users share more freely and take their networks of friends with them wherever else they may go on the web, the better Facebook is able to learn about the likes and dislikes of its users and thus serve up more customized online advertising.[4] With revenues approaching $30 billion (in 2010), Google has already proved that online advertising is a highly profitable business. Online social networking may turn out to be a winner-take-all market, and Facebook is clearly playing to win.

Firms, like individuals, often form ties such as alliances to share information and pursue common interests. Organizations also join networks, such as the innovation system orchestrated by InnoCentive, in order to get access to a diverse pool of knowledge and resources to advance strategic objectives that they couldn't pursue in isolation. In addition to internal organic growth, firms have several critical strategic options to pursue common interests, enhance competitiveness, and increase revenues: acquisitions, alliances, and networks. We devote this chapter to the study of these fundamental vehicles through which to implement corporate strategy.

INTEGRATING COMPANIES: MERGERS AND ACQUISITIONS

>> **LO 9-1**
Differentiate between
mergers and acquisitions,
and explain why firms
would use either as a
vehicle for corporate
strategy.

A traditional and popular vehicle for executing corporate strategy is mergers and acquisitions (M&A). Thousands of mergers and acquisitions occur each year, with a cumulative value in the trillions of dollars.[5] Although people sometimes use the terms as synonymous, and usually in tandem, mergers and acquisitions are, by definition, distinct from each other. A merger describes the joining of two independent companies to form *a combined entity*. An acquisition describes the purchase or takeover of one company by another. Mergers tend to be friendly; in mergers the target firm would like to be acquired. Disney's acquisition of Pixar, for example, was a friendly one, in which both management teams believed that joining the two companies was a good idea. Acquisitions can be friendly or unfriendly. When a target firm does not want to be acquired, the acquisition is considered a hostile takeover. British telecom company Vodafone's acquisition of Germany-based Mannesmann, a diversified conglomerate with holdings in telephony and Internet services, at an estimated value of $150 billion, was a hostile one.

In defining mergers and acquisitions, size can matter as well. The combining of two firms of comparable size is often described as a merger (even though it might in fact be an acquisition). For example, the integration of Daimler and Chrysler was pitched as a merger, though in reality Daimler acquired Chrysler (and later sold it). In contrast, when large, incumbent firms such as the Tata Group, Cisco Systems, or GE buy up startup companies, the transaction is generally described as an acquisition. An example is HP's relatively inexpensive $1.2 billion acquisition of Palm, a pioneer in personal digital assistants (PDAs),[6] which HP hopes will provide a stronger position in the fast-growing smartphone and tablet-computer markets. The distinction between mergers and acquisitions, however, is a bit blurry, and many observers simply use the umbrella term M&A.

Horizontal Integration: Merging with Competitors

In contrast with vertical integration, which concerns the number of activities a firm participates in up and down the industry value chain (as discussed in Chapter 8), horizontal integration is the process of acquiring and merging with competitors. Horizontal integration is a type of corporate strategy that can improve a firm's strategic position in a single industry. An industry-wide trend toward horizontal integration leads to industry consolidation. In the computer industry, for example, HP acquired Compaq in 2002. The pharmaceutical industry has also seen considerable consolidation, with Pfizer merging with Wyeth, and Merck and Schering-Plough merging in 2009. In the event-promotion business, the only remaining segment in the music industry in which revenues are increasing, Live Nation acquired Ticketmaster in 2010. In March 2011, AT&T agreed to buy T-Mobile USA from Deutsche Telekom AG for $39 billion in cash and stock. This deal—if approved by regulators—would consolidate the industry by combining the No. 2 and No. 4 U.S. wireless phone carriers.

There are four main benefits to a horizontal integration strategy:

- Reduction in competitive intensity
- Lower costs
- Increased differentiation
- Access to new markets and distribution channels

---

merger The joining of two independent companies to form a combined entity.

acquisition The purchase or takeover of one company by another; can be friendly or unfriendly.

hostile takeover Acquisition in which the target company does not wish to be acquired.

horizontal integration The process of acquiring and merging with competitors, leading to industry consolidation.

EXHIBIT 9.2

Sources of Value
Creation and Costs in
Horizontal Integration

Corporate Strategy	Sources of Value Creation (*V*)	Sources of Costs (*C*)
Horizontal Integration	• Reduction in competitive intensity • Lower costs • Increased differentiation • Access to new markets and distribution channels	• Integration failure • Reduced flexibility • Increased potential for legal repercussions

Exhibit 9.2 previews the sources of value creation and costs in horizontal integration, which we discuss next.

>> **LO 9-2**
Define horizontal integration and evaluate the advantages and disadvantages of this corporate-level strategy.

REDUCTION IN COMPETITIVE INTENSITY. Looking through the lens of the structure-conduct-performance (SCP) model (introduced in Chapter 3), horizontal integration changes the underlying industry structure in favor of the surviving firms. Excess capacity is taken out of the market, and competition decreases as a consequence of horizontal integration (assuming no new entrants). As a whole, the industry structure becomes more consolidated and thus potentially more profitable. If the surviving firms find themselves in an oligopolistic industry structure and their focus is on non-price competition (e.g., R&D spending, customer service, or advertising) the industry can indeed be quite profitable, and rivalry decreases among existing firms. Recent horizontal integration in the U.S. airline industry, for example, provided several benefits to the surviving carriers. By reducing excess capacity, the mergers between Delta and Northwest Airlines (in 2008), United Airlines and Continental (in 2010), and Southwest and AirTran (in 2010) lowered competitive intensity in the industry overall.

Horizontal integration, therefore, can favorably affect several of Porter's five forces for the surviving firms: strengthening bargaining power vis-à-vis suppliers and buyers, reducing the threat of entry, and reducing rivalry among existing firms. Because of the potential to reduce competitive intensity in an industry, government authorities such as the FTC and/or the European Commission usually must approve any large horizontal integration activity. For example, the FTC did not approve the proposed merger between Staples and Office Depot, arguing that the remaining industry would have only two competitors (the other one being Office Max). Staples and Office Depot argued that the market for office supplies needed to be defined more broadly to include large retailers such as Walmart and Target. The U.S. courts sided with the FTC, which argued that the prices for end consumers would be significantly higher if the market had only two category killers.[7]

LOWER COSTS. Research provides empirical evidence that firms use horizontal integration to lower costs through economies of scale, and thus enhance their economic value creation and in turn their performance.[8] In industries that have high fixed costs, achieving economies of scale through large output is critical in lowering costs. The dominant pharmaceutical companies like Pfizer, Roche, and Novartis, for example, maintain large sales forces ("detail people") who call on doctors and hospitals to promote their products. These specialized sales forces often number 10,000 or more, and thus are a significant fixed cost to the firms, even though part of their compensation is based on commissions.

Food Fight: Kraft's Hostile Takeover of Cadbury

In 2010, Kraft Foods bought its UK-based competitor Cadbury PLC for close to $20 billion in a hostile takeover. The combined Kraft–Cadbury entity is projected to have annual sales of over $50 billion and a 15 percent worldwide market share. Unlike the more diversified food-products company Kraft, Cadbury is focused solely on candy and gum. Hailing back to 1824, Cadbury established itself in markets across the globe, in concert with the British Empire.

Kraft was strongly attracted to Cadbury due to its advantageous position in countries such as India, Egypt, and Thailand and in fast-growing markets in Latin America. Cadbury holds 70 percent of the market share for chocolate in India, with more than 1 billion people. Children there specifically ask for "Cadbury chocolate" instead of just plain "chocolate." It is difficult for outsiders like Kraft to break into emerging economies because Cadbury has perfected its distribution system to meet the needs of millions of small, independent vendors. To secure a strong strategic position in these fast-growing emerging markets, therefore, Kraft felt that horizontal integration with Cadbury was critical. Still, Kraft faces formidable competitors in global markets, including Nestlé and Mars (which is especially strong in China where its famous Snickers bar was the official chocolate of the 2008 Olympic Games in Beijing).

In the U.S. market, the Cadbury acquisition will allow Kraft to access convenience stores, a new distribution channel for the company, and one that is growing fast and tends to have high profit margins. To achieve a stronger strategic position in the domestic market, however, Kraft will have to compete with The Hershey Company, the largest U.S. chocolate manufacturer. This battle will likely be intense because Hershey's main strategic focus is on the domestic market, with less than 10 percent of its revenues coming from international operations. With the U.S. population growing slowly and becoming more health conscious,[10] Hershey will need to re-evaluate its corporate strategy soon.

Maintaining such a large and sophisticated sales force (many with MBAs) is costly if the firm has only a few drugs it can show the doctor. As a rule of thumb, if a pharma company does not possess a blockbuster drug that brings in more than $1 billion in annual revenues, it cannot maintain its own sales force.[9] When existing firms like Pfizer and Wyeth merge, they join their drug pipelines and portfolios of existing drugs. Moreover, they are able to reduce their sales forces and lower the overall cost of distribution.

INCREASED DIFFERENTIATION. Horizontal integration through M&A can help firms strengthen their competitive positions by increasing the differentiation of their product and service offerings. In particular, horizontal integration can do this by filling gaps in a firm's product offering, allowing the combined entity to offer a complete suite of products and services. To enhance its differentiated appeal, Oracle acquired PeopleSoft for $10 billion in 2005. This horizontal integration joined the world's leading enterprise software company (Oracle), whose core competency is in database management systems, with a market leader in human resource management systems (PeopleSoft). This move allowed Oracle to offer its customers a complete suite of enterprise software systems to optimize their entire vertical and horizontal value chains.

ACCESS TO NEW MARKETS AND DISTRIBUTION CHANNELS. Horizontal integration can also help firms gain access to new markets and distribution channels. Strategy Highlight 9.1 discusses Kraft's acquisition of Cadbury to tap into new distribution channels in both the U.S. and fast-growing international markets.

Mergers and Acquisitions

Do mergers and acquisitions create competitive advantage? Despite their popularity, the answer, surprisingly, is that in most cases they do not. In fact, the M&A performance track

GAINING & SUSTAINING COMPETITIVE ADVANTAGE

record is rather abysmal. Most mergers destroy shareholder value because the anticipated synergies never materialize.[11] If there is any value creation, it generally accrues to the shareholders of the firm that was taken over (the acquiree), because acquirers often pay a premium when buying the target company.[12]

Exhibit 9.3 depicts recent M&As with record shareholder value destruction. The green bar shows how much the acquirer paid for the target firm; the beige line shows the amount of shareholder value that was destroyed after the merger. Take as an example the ill-fated AOL Time Warner merger in 2000. AOL acquired Time Warner for $164 billion, merging an Internet-access service provider with an old-line content company, and creating the first new media company of the 21st century. Since the hoped-for synergies never materialized, and due to the culture clash between a traditional media company and an Internet venture, the merger destroyed an estimated $91 billion in shareholder value, putting the total bill for this corporate-level move at over $255 billion. Similarly, Vodafone's hostile takeover of Mannesmann destroyed even more shareholder value (an estimated total of $287 billion).

Given that M&As, on average, destroy rather than create shareholder value, why do we see so many mergers? Reasons include:

- The desire to overcome competitive disadvantage
- Superior acquisition and integration capability
- Principal–agent problems

DESIRE TO OVERCOME COMPETITIVE DISADVANTAGE. In some instances, mergers are not motivated by gaining competitive advantage, but by overcoming a competitive disadvantage. For example, to compete more successfully with Nike, the worldwide leader in sport shoes and apparel, Adidas (#2) acquired Reebok (#3) for $3.8 billion in 2006. This acquisition allowed the now-larger Adidas group to benefit from economies of scale and scope that were unachievable when Adidas and Reebok operated independently. Overcoming its competitive disadvantage against Nike in turn strengthened Adidas's competitive position. Indeed, overcoming a competitive disadvantage may put an organization on the road to gaining a competitive advantage.

EXHIBIT 9.3

Value Destruction in M&A: The Worst Offenders

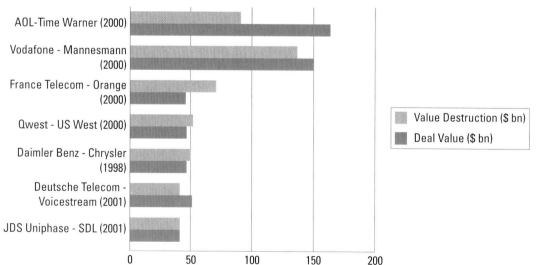

Source: Author's depiction of data obtained from C. S. Tullett (2006), "The world's worst M&A deals," *Here is the City News,* April 16, 2006. Calculation of value destruction based on the total equity value of the acquiring company, in excess of what would have occurred had it just performed in line with the market (up to three years post-merger).

SUPERIOR ACQUISITION AND INTEGRATION CAPABILITY. Acquisition and integration capabilities are not equally distributed across firms. Although there is strong evidence that M&As, *on average,* destroy rather than create shareholder value, it does not exclude the possibility that *some* firms are consistently able to identify, acquire, and integrate target companies to strengthen their competitive positions. Since it is valuable, rare, and difficult to imitate, a superior acquisition and integration capability, together with past experience, can lead to competitive advantage.

Cisco Systems, a networking and telecommunications company, is one such firm with an exemplary acquisitions record.[13] To position itself more strongly coming out of the 2001 stock market crash, Cisco embarked on an acquisitions-led growth strategy in which it acquired more than 130 technology companies.[14] Through this process, it diversified from computer networking routers to local area networking switching, Voice over IP (Internet telephony), and home networks. While Cisco acquired mainly smaller technology companies, it also acquired several larger firms including Linksys, Scientific Atlanta, and WebEx, now each multibillion-dollar businesses in their own right. Cisco buys successful companies, provides them with important complementary assets, and then lets them continue to be successful more or less on their own. Because of this superior integration template, which was refined by moving down the experience curve, Cisco kept the management of the larger firms it acquired and managed the relationships more like strategic alliances (discussed later in the chapter) than acquisitions.[15]

PRINCIPAL–AGENT PROBLEMS. When discussing diversification in the last chapter, we noted that some firms diversify through acquisitions due to principal–agent problems.[16] Managers, as agents, are supposed to act in the best interest of the principals, the shareholders. However, managers may have incentives to grow their firms through acquisitions—not for anticipated shareholder value appreciation, but to build a larger empire, which is positively correlated with prestige, power, and pay. Besides providing higher compensation and more corporate perks, a larger organization may also provide more job security, especially if the company pursues unrelated diversification.

A related problem is **managerial hubris,** a form of self-delusion in which managers convince themselves of their superior skills in the face of clear evidence to the contrary.[17] Managerial hubris comes in two forms. First, managers of the acquiring company convince themselves that they can manage the business of the target company more effectively, and thus can create additional shareholder value. This justification is often used for an unrelated diversification strategy. Second, although most top-level managers are aware that the vast majority of acquisitions destroys rather than creates shareholder value, they see themselves as the exceptions to the rule. Managerial hubris has led to many ill-fated deals, destroying billions of dollars. For example, Quaker Oats Company acquired Snapple because its managers thought that Snapple was another Gatorade, which was a standalone company that could be easily integrated.[18] In contrast, Snapple relied on a decentralized network of independent distributors and retailers who did not want Snapple to be taken over and who made it difficult and costly for Quaker Oats Company to integrate Snapple. The acquisition failed—and Quaker Oats was eventually taken over itself, by PepsiCo. Similarly, when Sony bought Columbia Pictures, its managers attempted to secure complementary products such as a movie library for its hardware, but failed to create synergies from the profoundly different types of businesses. 🔍

> **managerial hubris**
> A form of self-delusion, in which managers convince themselves of their superior skills in the face of clear evidence to the contrary.

Because mergers and acquisitions do not necessarily lead to the growth that firms expect, what other corporate strategies are there that might do so? We'll look next at strategic alliances.

STRATEGIC ALLIANCES: CAUSES AND CONSEQUENCES OF PARTNERING

strategic alliance
A voluntary arrangement between firms that involves the sharing of knowledge, resources, and capabilities with the intent of developing processes, products, or services to lead to competitive advantage.

relational view of competitive advantage Strategic management framework that proposes that critical resources and capabilities frequently are embedded in strategic alliances that span firm boundaries.

Strategic alliances are voluntary arrangements between firms that involve the sharing of knowledge, resources, and capabilities with the intent of developing processes, products, or services.[19] Firms enter many types of alliances, from small contracts that have no bearing on a firm's competitiveness to multibillion-dollar joint ventures that can make or break the company. An alliance, therefore, qualifies as *strategic* only if it has the potential to affect a firm's competitive advantage. A strategic alliance has the potential to help a firm gain and sustain a competitive advantage when it joins together resources and knowledge in a combination that obeys the VRIO principles (introduced in Chapter 4).[20]

Some researchers suggest that the locus of competitive advantage is often not found within the individual firm but within strategic partnerships. According to this relational view of competitive advantage, critical resources and capabilities frequently are embedded in strategic alliances that span firm boundaries. Applying the VRIO framework introduced in Chapter 4, we know that the basis for competitive advantage is formed when strategic alliances create resource combinations that are valuable, rare, and difficult to imitate, and the alliances are organized appropriately to allow for value capture. In support of this perspective, over 80 percent of Fortune 1000 CEOs indicated in a recent survey that more than one quarter of their firm's revenues were derived from strategic alliances.[21]

Through a strategic alliance with DreamWorks Animation SKG, HP created the Halo Collaboration Studio, which makes virtual communication possible around the globe.[22] Halo's conferencing technology gives participants the vivid sense that they are in the same room. The conference rooms match, down to the last detail, giving participants the impression that they are sitting together at the same table. DreamWorks produced the computer-animated movie *Shrek 2* using this new technology for its meetings. People with different creative skills—script writers, computer animators, directors—though dispersed geographically, were able to participate as if in the same room, even seeing the work on each other's laptops. Use of the technology enabled faster decision making, enhanced productivity, reduced (or even eliminated) travel time and expense, and increased job satisfaction. Neither HP nor DreamWorks would have been able to produce this technology breakthrough alone,

EXHIBIT 9.4

Number of R&D Alliances

Source: Data drawn from the MERIT-CATI database; courtesy of Professor John Hagedoorn. For a detailed description of the MERIT-CATI database, see: J. Hagedoorn (2002), "Inter-firm R&D partnerships: An overview of major trends and patterns since 1960," *Research Policy* 31: 477–492.

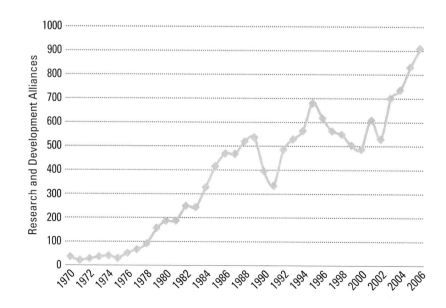

but moving into the videoconferencing arena together via a strategic alliance allowed both partners to pursue related diversification. Moreover, HP's alliance with DreamWorks Animation SKG enabled HP to compete head on with Cisco's high-end videoconferencing solution, TelePresence.[23]

The use of strategic alliances as a vehicle for corporate strategy has exploded since the 1980s, with thousands forming each year. Exhibit 9.4 depicts the number of alliances formed for R&D purposes since 1970. Such strategic alliances are attractive because they enable firms to achieve goals faster and at lower costs than going it alone. Globalization has also contributed to an increase in cross-border strategic alliances.

Why Do Firms Enter Strategic Alliances?

To affect a firm's competitive advantage, an alliance must promise a positive effect on the firm's economic value creation through increasing value and/or lowering costs (see discussion in Chapter 5). This logic is reflected in the common reasons why firms enter alliances:[24] They do so to:

- Strengthen competitive position
- Enter new markets
- Hedge against uncertainty
- Access critical complementary assets
- Learn new capabilities

STRENGTHEN COMPETITIVE POSITION. Firms can use strategic alliances to change the industry structure in their favor.[25] Firms frequently use strategic alliances when competing in so-called battles for industry standards (see discussion in Chapter 7). Or they may also initiate these alliances by themselves to challenge market leaders and thus change the underlying market structure. Strategy Highlight 9.2 shows how Apple orchestrated a web of strategic alliances with publishing houses to challenge Amazon's early lead in the delivery of e-content.

ENTER NEW MARKETS. Firms may use strategic alliances to enter new markets, either in terms of geography or products and services.[26] In some instances, governments (such as Saudi Arabia or China) require that foreign firms have a local joint venture partner before doing business in their countries. These

Strategic Alliances to Challenge Amazon

In 2007, Amazon established its Kindle device as the dominant e-reader by offering content (e-books, newspapers, and magazines) for instant download at heavily discounted prices. Kindle users paid $9.99 for e-books, including new releases and *The New York Times*'s best sellers. Amazon lost money on each e-book sold, because it had to pay publishers between $12.99 and $14.99 per e-book. Still, it was able to leverage this pricing strategy to establish Kindle as the dominant e-reader in the market.

Selling below cost is the same pricing strategy Amazon had used successfully when it first established itself as the leading e-tailer in sales of printed books. Amazon's e-book pricing strategy, however, did not sit well with content providers. They did not want to set an expectation in consumers' minds that all e-books should be priced at $9.99. Also, anchoring the e-book prices clearly would have negative repercussions for the sale of printed books, which are priced higher.

Apple crafted a different e-book business model. To attack Amazon's stronghold, Apple orchestrated a web of strategic alliances with major publishing houses such as HarperCollins, Macmillan, McGraw-Hill, and Simon & Schuster prior to launching its iPad product. To incentivize the publishers, Apple offered to let the content providers set the sales prices directly for the end consumers. These alliances aided Apple in populating its iBookstore with much needed content.

The publishers liked this deal. They retained pricing power over e-books, which allowed them to break the customer expectation that e-books should be priced at $9.99. Their alliances with Apple gave the publishers much needed leverage in negotiations with Amazon. Applying industry structural analysis, the bargaining power of suppliers—in this case, the content providers—increased from Amazon's perspective. In fact, book publishers even threatened to withhold or delay book titles if Amazon would not change its pricing structure. As a result, Amazon reluctantly changed its e-book pricing strategy and now charges between $12.99 and $14.99 for some new releases.

cross-border strategic alliances have both benefits and risks. While the foreign firm can benefit from local expertise and contacts, it is exposed to the risk that some of its proprietary know-how may be appropriated by the foreign partner. We will address such issues in the next chapter when studying global strategy.

In ChapterCase 1, we saw that Microsoft, though the leader in PC-based software, has been struggling for years to gain a foothold in the online search and advertising market. As personal computing moves more and more into the cloud, and PC-based software can be replaced by free online offerings such as Google Docs, it is critical for Microsoft to establish future revenue streams. The new cloud computing market, in which money is made from the accompanying online advertising, is expected to reach over $30 billion by 2014.[27]

Although Yahoo's co-founder and then-CEO Jerry Yang rebuffed Microsoft's $48 billion acquisition bid for Yahoo in the summer of 2008, Microsoft was able to get a much better deal through a subsequent strategic alliance. In early 2009, Yahoo appointed Carol Bartz as its new CEO, and she almost immediately rekindled negotiations with Microsoft's CEO Steve Ballmer, who suggested a strategic alliance between the two companies. Yahoo and Microsoft formed a partnership through which Yahoo's searches are powered by Microsoft's search engine, Bing. In return, Yahoo gets a portion of the revenues from the search ads sold on its sites. With its technology now powering some 30 percent of all online searches, Microsoft is able to fine-tune Bing. Thus, Microsoft can strengthen its competitive position against Google's dominance in online search and advertisement.[28] In the end, this strategic alliance was a low-cost alternative to an acquisition for Microsoft. But why did Yahoo agree to the deal? It entered this alliance because it had not generated the cash flow necessary to continuously update its own search technology.

HEDGE AGAINST UNCERTAINTY. In dynamic markets, strategic alliances allow firms to limit their exposure to uncertainty in the market.[29] For instance, in the wake of the biotechnology revolution, incumbent pharmaceutical firms such as Pfizer, Novartis, and Roche entered into hundreds of strategic alliances with biotech startups.[30] These alliances allowed the big pharma firms to make small-scale investments in many of the new biotechnology ventures that were poised to disrupt existing market economics. In some sense, the pharma companies were taking real options in these biotechnology experiments, providing them with the right but not the obligation to make further investments when new drugs were introduced from the biotech companies. Once the new drugs were a known quantity, the uncertainty was removed, and the incumbent firms could react accordingly.

For example, in 1990 the Swiss pharma company Roche initially invested $2.1 billion in an equity alliance to purchase a controlling interest (>50 percent) in the biotech startup Genentech. In 2009, after witnessing the success of Genentech's drug discovery and development projects in subsequent years, Roche spent $47 billion to purchase the remaining minority interest in Genentech, making it a wholly owned subsidiary.[31] Taking a wait-and-see approach by entering strategic alliances allows incumbent firms to buy time and wait for the uncertainty surrounding the market and technology to fade. Many firms in fast-moving markets appear to subscribe to this rationale. Besides biotechnology, it has also been documented in nanotechnology, semiconductors, and other dynamic markets.[32]

ACCESS CRITICAL COMPLEMENTARY ASSETS. The successful commercialization of a new product or service often requires complementary assets such as marketing, manufacturing, and after-sale service.[33] In particular, new firms are in need of complementary assets to complete the value chain from upstream innovation to downstream commercialization. Building downstream complementary assets such as marketing and regulatory expertise or a sales force is often prohibitively expensive and time-consuming, and thus frequently

Pixar and Disney: From Alliance to Acquisition

Pixar started out as a computer hardware company producing high-end graphic display systems. One of its customers was Disney. To demonstrate the graphic display systems' capabilities and thus increase sales, Pixar produced short, computer-animated movies. In the beginning, though, despite being sophisticated, Pixar's computer hardware was not selling well, and the new venture was hemorrhaging money. In rode Steve Jobs to the rescue. Shortly after being ousted from Apple in 1986, Jobs bought the struggling hardware company for $5 million and founded Pixar Animation Studios, investing another $5 million into the company.

To finance and distribute its newly created computer-animated movies, Pixar entered a strategic alliance with Disney. Disney's distribution network and its stellar reputation in animated movies were critical complementary assets that Pixar needed to commercialize its new type of films. In turn, Disney was able to rejuvenate its floundering product lineup, retaining the rights to the newly created Pixar characters and to any sequels.

Pixar became successful beyond imagination as it rolled out one blockbuster after another: *Toy Story* (*1, 2,* and *3*), *A Bug's Life, Monsters, Inc., Finding Nemo,* and *The Incredibles,* grossing several billion dollars. Given Pixar's huge success and Disney's abysmal performance with its own releases during this time, the bargaining power in the alliance shifted dramatically. Renegotiations of the Pixar–Disney alliance broke down altogether in 2004, reportedly because of personality conflicts between Steve Jobs and Disney Chairman/CEO Michael Eisner. After Eisner left Disney in the fall of 2005, Disney acquired Pixar for $7.4 billion, a deal that made Steve Jobs the largest shareholder of Disney.

The early Pixar–Disney alliance not only served as a vehicle to match the two entities' complementary assets, but also led eventually to the acquisition of Pixar by Disney. The alliance gave Disney an inside perspective on Pixar's valuable core competencies in the creation of computer-animated features. In 2009, driven by poor performance in its internal movie creation efforts,[34] Disney also added *Spiderman, Iron Man, The Incredible Hulk,* and *Captain America* to its lineup of characters by acquiring Marvel Entertainment for $4 billion.

not an option for new ventures. Strategic alliances allow firms to match complementary skills and resources to complete the value chain. Moreover, licensing agreements of this sort allow the partners to benefit from a division of labor, allowing each to efficiently focus on its core expertise. Strategy Highlight 9.3 shows how fledgling startup Pixar found itself in dire straits in the early 1990s, and how an alliance with Disney rescued the computer-animated movie studio.

LEARN NEW CAPABILITIES. Firms enter strategic alliances because they are motivated by the desire to learn new capabilities from their partners.[35] When the collaborating firms are also competitors, *co-opetition* ensues (introduced in Chapter 1).[36] Such co-opetition can lead to learning races in strategic alliances,[37] a situation in which both partners are motivated to form an alliance for learning, but the rate at which the firms learn may vary. The firm that learns faster and thus accomplishes its goal more quickly has an incentive to exit the alliance or, at a minimum, to reduce its knowledge sharing. Since the cooperating firms are also competitors, learning races can have a positive effect on the winning firm's competitive position vis-à-vis its alliance partner.

NUMMI (New United Motor Manufacturing, Inc.) was the first joint venture in the U.S. automobile industry, formed between GM and Toyota in 1984. Recall from Chapter 8 that joint ventures are a special type of a strategic alliance in which two partner firms create a third, jointly owned entity. In the NUMMI joint venture, each partner was motivated to learn new capabilities: GM entered the strategic alliance to learn the lean manufacturing

learning races Situations in which both partners in a strategic alliance are motivated to form an alliance for learning, but the rate at which the firms learn may vary; the firm that accomplishes its goal more quickly has an incentive to exit the alliance or reduce its knowledge sharing.

system pioneered by Toyota in order to produce high-quality, fuel-efficient cars at a profit. Toyota entered the alliance to learn how to implement its lean manufacturing program with an American work force. NUMMI was a test-run for Toyota before building fully owned *greenfield plants* (new manufacturing facilities) in Alabama, Indiana, Kentucky, Texas, and West Virginia. In this 25-year history, GM and Toyota built some 7 million high-quality cars at the NUMMI plant. In fact, NUMMI was transformed from worst performer (under GM ownership prior to the joint venture) to GM's highest-quality plant in the U.S. In the end, as part of GM's bankruptcy reorganization during 2009–2010, it pulled out of the NUMMI joint venture.

The joint venture between GM and Toyota can be seen as a learning race. Who won? Researchers argue that Toyota was faster in accomplishing its alliance goal—learning how to manage U.S. labor—because of its limited scope.[38] Toyota had already perfected lean manufacturing; all it needed to do was to train U.S. workers in the method and transfer this knowledge to its subsidiary plants in the U.S. On the other hand, GM had to learn a completely new production system. GM was successful in transferring lean manufacturing to its newly created Saturn brand (which was discontinued in 2010 as part of GM's reorganization), but it had a hard time implementing lean manufacturing in its *existing* plants. These factors suggest that Toyota won the learning race with GM, which in turn helped Toyota gain and sustain a competitive advantage over GM in the U.S. market.

Also, note that different motivations for forming alliances are not necessarily independent and can be intertwined. For example, firms that collaborate to access critical complementary assets may also want to learn from one another to subsequently pursue vertical integration. In sum, alliance formation is frequently motivated by leveraging economies of scale, scope, specialization, and learning.

Governing Strategic Alliances

>> **LO 9-5**
Describe three alliance governance mechanisms and evaluate their pros and cons.

In Chapter 8, we showed that strategic alliances lie in the middle of the buy-vs.-make continuum (see Exhibit 8.3). Alliances can be governed by the following mechanisms: (1) contractual agreements for *non-equity alliances,* (2) *equity alliances,* and (3) *joint ventures.*[39] Exhibit 9.5 provides an overview of the key characteristics of the three alliance types, including their advantages and disadvantages.

NON-EQUITY ALLIANCES. The most common type of alliance is a non-equity alliance, which is based on contracts between firms. The most frequent forms of non-equity alliances are *supply agreements, distribution agreements,* and *licensing agreements.* As suggested by their names, these contractual agreements are vertical strategic alliances, connecting different parts of the industry value chain. In a non-equity alliance, firms tend to share explicit knowledge—knowledge that can be codified. Patents, user manuals, fact sheets, and scientific publications are all ways to capture explicit knowledge, which concerns the notion of *knowing about* a certain process or product.

Licensing agreements are contractual alliances in which the participants regularly exchange codified knowledge. In 1978, biotech firm Genentech licensed its newly developed drug Humulin (human insulin) to the pharmaceutical firm Eli Lilly for manufacturing, facilitating approval by the Food and Drug Administration (FDA), and distribution. This partnership was an example of a vertical strategic alliance: one partner (Genentech) was positioned upstream in the industry value chain (focusing on R&D), while the other partner (Eli Lilly) was positioned downstream (focusing on manufacturing and distribution). This type of vertical arrangement is often described as a "hand-off" from the upstream partner to the downstream partner, and is possible because the underlying knowledge is largely

non-equity alliance Partnership based on contracts between firms. The most frequent forms are *supply agreements, distribution agreements,* and *licensing agreements.*

explicit knowledge Knowledge that can be codified (e.g., information, facts, instructions, recipes); concerns *knowing about* a process or product.

EXHIBIT 9.5

Key Characteristics of Different Alliance Types

Alliance Type	Governance Mechanism	Frequency	Type of Knowledge Exchanged	Pros	Cons	Examples
Non-equity (supply, licensing, and distribution agreements)	Contract	Most common	Explicit	• Flexible • Fast • Easy to initiate and terminate	• Weak tie • Lack of trust and commitment	• Genentech–Lilly (exclusive) licensing agreement for Humulin • Microsoft–IBM (non-exclusive) licensing agreement for MS-DOS
Equity (purchase of an equity stake or corporate venture capital, CVC investment)	Equity investment	Less common than non-equity alliances, but more common than joint ventures	Explicit; exchange of tacit knowledge possible	• Stronger tie • Trust and commitment can emerge • Window into new technology (option value)	• Less flexible • Slower • Can entail significant investments	• Renault–Nissan alliance based on cross equity holdings, with Renault owning 44.4% in Nissan; and Nissan owning 15% in Renault • Roche's equity investment in Genentech (prior to full integration)
Joint venture (JV)	Creation of new entity by two or more parent firms	Least common	Both tacit and explicit knowledge exchanged	• Strongest tie • Trust and commitment likely to emerge • May be required by institutional setting	• Can entail long negotiations and significant investments • Long-term solution • JV managers have double reporting lines (2 bosses)	• Hulu, JV owned by NBC, Fox, and ABC • Dow Corning, JV owned by Dow Chemical and Corning

explicit and can be easily codified. When Humulin reached the market in 1982, it was the first approved genetically engineered human therapeutic worldwide.[40] Subsequently, Humulin became a billion-dollar blockbuster drug.

Because of their contractual nature, non-equity alliances are flexible and easy to initiate (and terminate). However, because they can be temporary in nature, they also sometimes produce weak ties between the alliance partners, which can result in a lack of trust and commitment.

EQUITY ALLIANCES. In an equity alliance, at least one partner takes partial ownership in the other partner. Equity alliances are less common than contractual, non-equity alliances because they often require larger investments. Because they are based on partial ownership rather than contracts, equity alliances are used to signal stronger commitments. Moreover, equity alliances allow for the sharing of tacit knowledge—knowledge that cannot be codified.[41] Tacit knowledge concerns the *knowing how* to do a certain task. It can be acquired only through actively participating in the process. In an equity alliance, therefore, the partners frequently exchange personnel to make the acquisition of tacit knowledge possible.

Toyota is using an equity alliance with Tesla Motors, a designer and developer of electric cars, to learn new knowledge and gain a window into new technology. In spring 2010, Toyota made a $50 million equity investment in the California startup company. Tesla has two cars in its lineup: a $109K roadster and a $50K family sedan. It has manufactured and sold about 1,500 roadsters and plans to build 20,000 of its sedans in 2012, to be manufactured at the New United Motor Manufacturing (NUMMI) auto plant in Fremont, California, which Tesla Motors bought from Toyota. Tesla's CEO Elon Musk stated, "the Tesla factory effectively leverages an ideal combination of hardcore Silicon Valley engineering talent, traditional automotive engineering talent and the proven Toyota production system."[42] Toyota, which plans to sell all-electric cars in the U.S. by 2012, hopes to infuse its company with Tesla's entrepreneurial spirit. Toyota President Akio Toyoda commented that "by partnering with Tesla, my hope is that all Toyota employees will recall that 'venture business spirit' and take on the challenges of the future."[43] Mr. Toyoda hopes that a transfer of tacit knowledge will take place, in which Tesla's entrepreneurial spirit reinvigorates Toyota.[44]

Another governance mechanism that falls under the broad rubric of equity alliances is corporate venture capital (CVC) investments, which are equity investments by established firms in entrepreneurial ventures.[45] The value of CVC investments is estimated to be in the double-digit billion-dollar range each year. Larger firms frequently have dedicated CVC units, such as Dow Venture Capital, Siemens Venture Capital, Kaiser Permanente Ventures, and Johnson & Johnson Development Corporation. Rather than hoping primarily for financial gains, as do traditional venture capitalists, CVC investments create real options in terms of gaining access to new, and potentially disruptive, technologies.[46] Research indicates that CVC investments have a positive impact on value creation for the investing firm, especially in high-tech industries such as semiconductors, computing, and the medical-device sector.[47]

Equity alliances tend to produce stronger ties and greater trust between partners than non-equity alliances do. They also offer a window into new technology that, like a real option, can be exercised if successful, or abandoned if not promising. The downside of equity alliances is the amount of investment that can be involved, as well as a possible lack of flexibility and speed in putting together the partnership.

JOINT VENTURES. A joint venture (JV) is a standalone organization created and jointly owned by two or more parent companies (as discussed in Chapter 8). For example, Hulu (a video-on-demand service) is jointly owned by NBC, ABC, and Fox. Since partners contribute equity to a joint venture, they are making a long-term commitment. Exchange of

equity alliance
Partnership in which at least one partner takes partial ownership in the other partner.

tacit knowledge
Knowledge that cannot be codified; concerns *knowing how* to do a certain task and can be acquired only through active participation in that task.

corporate venture capital (CVC)
Equity investments by established firms in entrepreneurial ventures; CVC falls under the broader rubric of equity alliances.

joint venture A standalone organization created and jointly owned by two or more parent companies.

both explicit and tacit knowledge through interaction of personnel is typical. Equity alliances and joint ventures are frequently stepping stones toward full integration of the partner firms either through a merger or an acquisition. Essentially, they are often used as a "try before you buy" strategic option.[48] Joint ventures are also frequently used to enter foreign markets where the host country requires such a partnership to gain access to the market in exchange for advanced technology and know-how. In terms of frequency, joint ventures are the least common of the three types of strategic alliances.

The advantages of joint ventures are the strong ties, trust, and commitment that can result between the partners. However, they can entail long negotiations and significant investments. If the alliance doesn't work out as expected, undoing the JV can take some time and involve considerable cost. A further risk is that knowledge shared with the new partner could be misappropriated by opportunistic behavior. Finally, any rewards from the collaboration must be shared between the partners.

Alliance Management Capability

Strategic alliances create a paradox for managers. Although alliances appear to be necessary to compete in many industries, between 30 and 70 percent of all strategic alliances do not deliver the expected benefits, and thus are considered failures by at least one alliance partner.[49] Given the high failure (or at least, disappointment) rate, effective alliance management is critical to gaining and sustaining a competitive advantage, especially in high-technology industries.[50]

Alliance management capability is a firm's ability to effectively manage three alliance-related tasks concurrently, often across a portfolio of many different alliances (see Exhibit 9.6):[51]

- Partner selection and alliance formation
- Alliance design and governance
- Post-formation alliance management

PARTNER SELECTION AND ALLIANCE FORMATION. When making the business case for an alliance, the expected benefits of the alliance must exceed its costs. When one or more of the five reasons for alliance formation are present—to strengthen competitive position, enter new markets, hedge against uncertainty, access critical complementary resources, or learn new capabilities—the firm must select the best possible alliance partner. Research has identified partner compatibility and partner commitment as necessary conditions for successful alliance formation.[52] *Partner compatibility* captures aspects of cultural fit between different firms. *Partner commitment* concerns the willingness to make available necessary resources and to accept short-term sacrifices to ensure long-term rewards.

ALLIANCE DESIGN AND GOVERNANCE. Once two or more firms agree to pursue an alliance, managers must then design the alliance and choose an appropriate governance

>> **LO 9-6**
Describe the three phases of alliance management, and explain how an alliance management capability can lead to a competitive advantage.

alliance management capability A firm's ability to effectively manage three alliance-related tasks concurrently: (1) partner selection and alliance formation, (2) alliance design and governance, and (3) post-formation alliance management.

EXHIBIT 9.6

Alliance Management Capability

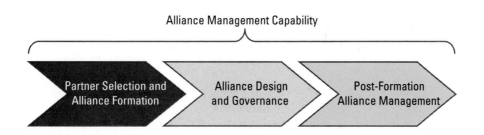

Alliance Management Capability

Partner Selection and Alliance Formation → Alliance Design and Governance → Post-Formation Alliance Management

mechanism from among the three options: non-equity contractual agreement, equity alliances, or joint venture. For example, in a study of over 640 alliances, researchers found that the joining of specialized complementary assets increases the likelihood that the alliance is governed hierarchically. This effect is stronger in the presence of uncertainties concerning the alliance partner as well as the envisioned tasks.[53]

In addition to the formal governance mechanisms, *inter-organizational trust* is a critical dimension of alliance success.[54] Because all contracts are necessarily incomplete, trust between the alliance partners plays an important role for effective post-formation alliance management. Effective governance, therefore, can be accomplished only by skillfully combining formal and informal mechanisms.

POST-FORMATION ALLIANCE MANAGEMENT. The third phase in a firm's alliance management capability concerns the ongoing management of the alliance. To be a source of competitive advantage, the partnership needs to create resource combinations that obey the VRIO criteria. As shown in Exhibit 9.7, this can be most likely accomplished if the alliance partners make relation-specific investments, establish knowledge-sharing routines, and build interfirm trust.[55]

Hewlett-Packard, for example, is known as having made relation-specific investments to create long-term partnerships with several smaller technology firms co-located in Silicon Valley.[56] HP's strategy of forming a dense network of alliances with smaller firms contrasts sharply with Digital Equipment Corporation's (DEC) strategy of "going it alone." HP's network of alliances provided a competitive advantage over DEC, which was characterized as having a "more insular organizational structure and corporate mindset."[57] Not surprisingly, DEC went defunct in 1998 and HP acquired some of its assets. Finally, firms that are able to establish effective knowledge-sharing routines with its suppliers and buyers, as does 3M, tend to be more innovative.[58]

Trust is a critical aspect of any alliance. Interfirm trust entails the expectation that each alliance partner will behave in good faith and develop norms of reciprocity and fairness.[59] Such trust helps to ensure that the relationship survives and thereby increases the

EXHIBIT 9.7

How to Make Alliances Work

Source: Adapted from J. H. Dyer and H. Singh (1998), "The relational view: Cooperative strategy and the sources of interorganizational advantage," *Academy of Management Review* 23: 660–679.

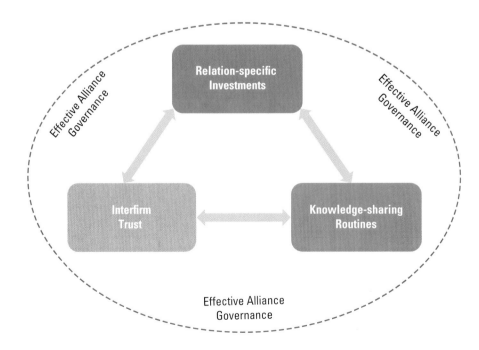

possibility of meeting the intended goals of the alliance. Interfirm trust is also important for fast decision making.[60] Indeed, several firms such as Eli Lilly, HP, Procter & Gamble, and IBM compete to obtain trustworthy reputations in order to become the alliance "partner of choice" for small technology ventures, universities, and individual inventors.

Indeed, the systematic differences in firms' alliance-management capability can be a source of competitive advantage.[61] But how do firms go about building alliance-management capability? The answer is to build capability through repeated experiences over time. In support, several empirical studies have shown that firms move down the learning curve and become better at managing alliances through repeated alliance exposure.[62]

The "learning-by-doing" approach has value for small ventures in which a few key people coordinate most of the firms' activities.[63] However, there are clearly limitations for larger companies. Firms such as ABB, GE, Philips, or Siemens are engaged in hundreds of alliances simultaneously. In fact, if alliances are not managed from a portfolio perspective at the corporate level, serious negative repercussions can emerge.[64] Groupe Danone, a large French food conglomerate, lost its leading position in the highly lucrative and fast-growing Chinese market because its local alliance partner, Hangzhou Wahaha Group, terminated their long-standing alliance.[65] Wahaha accused different Danone business units of subsequently setting up partnerships with other Chinese firms that were a direct competitive threat to Wahaha. This example makes it clear that although alliances are important vehicles by which to pursue business-level strategy, they are best managed at the corporate level.

To accomplish effective alliance management, researchers suggest that firms create a *dedicated alliance function,*[66] led by a vice president or director of alliance management and endowed with its own resources and support staff. The dedicated alliance function should be given the tasks of coordinating all alliance-related activity in the entire organization, taking a corporate-level perspective. It should serve as a repository of prior experience and be responsible for creating processes and structures to teach and leverage that experience and related knowledge throughout the rest of the organization across all levels. Empirical research shows that firms with a dedicated alliance function are able to create value from their alliances above and beyond what could be expected based on experience alone.[67]

Pharmaceutical company Eli Lilly is an acknowledged leader in alliance management.[68] Lilly's Office of Alliance Management, led by a director and endowed with several managers, manages its far-flung alliance activity across all hierarchical levels and around the globe. Lilly's process prescribes that each alliance is managed by a three-person team: an alliance champion, alliance leader, and alliance manager. The *alliance champion* is a senior, corporate-level executive responsible for high-level support and oversight. This senior manager is also responsible for making sure that the alliance fits within the firm's existing alliance porfolio and corporate-level strategy. The *alliance leader* has the technical expertise and knowledge needed for the specific technical area and is responsible for the day-to-day management of the alliance. The *alliance manager,* positioned within the Office of Alliance Management, serves as an alliance process resource and business integrator between the two alliance partners, and provides alliance training and development, as well as diagnostic tools.

Some companies are also able to leverage the relational capabilities obtained through managing alliance portfolios into a successful acquisition strategy.[69] As detailed earlier, Eli Lilly has an entire department at the corporate level devoted to managing its alliance portfolio. Following up on an earlier 50/50 joint venture formed with Icos (maker of the $1 billion-plus erectile-dysfunction drug Cialis), Lilly acquired Icos in 2007. More recently (in 2008), Eli Lilly outmaneuvered Bristol-Myers Squibb to acquire biotech venture ImClone for $6.5 billion. ImClone discovered and developed the cancer-fighting drug

Erbitux, also a $1 billion blockbuster in terms of annual sales. The acquisition of these two smaller biotech ventures allowed Lilly to fill its empty drug pipeline.[70]

Strategy researchers, therefore, have suggested that corporate-level managers should not only coordinate the firm's portfolio of alliances, but also leverage their relationships to successfully engage in mergers and acquisitions.[71] That is, rather than focusing on developing an alliance-management capability in isolation, firms should develop a *relational capability* that allows for the successful management of both strategic alliances *and* mergers and acquisitions.

STRATEGIC NETWORKS

>> **LO 9-7**
Define strategic networks and evaluate the advantages and disadvantages of different network positions.

When several firms form alliances to pursue a common purpose, they build a strategic network. A strategic network is a social structure composed of multiple organizations (called *network nodes*) and the links among the nodes (called *network ties*). Strategic networks emerge as companies add more and more partners over time to an existing alliance.[72] Pursuing a *network strategy*—that is, forming strategic networks—enables firms to achieve goals they cannot or would not want to accomplish alone or with more traditional two-company alliances.

Consider the Star Alliance, the first global airline network. It includes such well-known carriers as Air Canada, Air China, Continental Airlines, Lufthansa, Singapore Airlines,

and United Airlines, and provides customers worldwide access to more than 21,000 daily flights to 1,100 destinations in 181 countries.[73] Through code sharing, the Star Alliance allows for seamless travel among more than 25 international airlines—a goal that the individual airlines could not accomplish on their own. Indeed, some scholars argue that in many industries it is not single firms that compete against one another but rather entire networks.[74] In the airline industry, the Star Alliance contends with two other prominent strategic networks: SkyTeam (composed of Air France, Delta, KLM, and Korean Air, among others) and Oneworld (formed by American Airlines, British Airways, Cathay Pacific, Japan Airlines, and others).

Strategic networks provide advantages but also can constrain individual members. Once a firm becomes part of a network, managers need to think about how their company's strategy affects, and is affected by, the network. Strategy Highlight 9.4 shows how membership in the European telecommunications network Unisource had negative consequences for some of its smaller member firms.

Analyzing Strategic Networks

Analysis of strategic networks enables us to understand the benefits and costs accrued by individual firms embedded in a network.[75] Not all network relationships are equally beneficial, and not all network positions provide the same advantages. One important distinction concerns the quality of the tie, in particular, the distinction between strong and weak ties.[76] *Strong ties* are characterized by trusting relationships established through frequent, face-to-face interactions between managers over time, and may even include friendships across different firms. They may contain an equity-sharing element such as an R&D joint venture. Strong ties are beneficial to the transfer of tacit knowledge and for rapid decision making. In contrast, *weak ties* are characterized by infrequent and shallower interactions. They tend

strategic network
A social structure composed of multiple organizations (*network nodes*) and the links among the nodes (*network ties*).

STRATEGY HIGHLIGHT 9.4

When Strategic Networks Become Dysfunctional

Prior to deregulation of the European telecommunications market in the 1990s, telecom providers were nationally owned, and telecom service offerings were more or less limited to their respective home countries. Despite their monopoly positions, many telecom providers lost money and needed taxpayer subsidies. The EU's deregulation of the telecom market put tremendous pressure on telecom firms in smaller countries.

To compete more effectively with larger rivals like Deutsche Telekom and France Télécom and to offer a larger service area, Swedish telecom firm Telia and Dutch telecom firm KPN formed a joint venture, Unisource. As business customers demanded global coverage and more sophisticated data and voice services, other telecom providers joined the alliance. In this period (the 1990s), breakthroughs such as the rise of the Internet and wireless telephony provided huge opportunities but also posed significant threats in terms of regulatory and technology changes in the external environment.

From the original two-partner joint venture, the Unisource alliance morphed into a global strategic network in less than a decade, encompassing about 25 telecom companies (including AT&T) in 11 countries on 4 continents. Many of the managers, especially the ones who led smaller firms, quickly learned that they were no longer able to influence the network. Instead, they were dominated by it and severely restricted in their firms' strategic flexibility. Problems arose for a number of reasons. Some network members made significant investments early on that would reap benefits only much later. Other network members behaved opportunistically, adopting a free-rider approach. When AT&T joined the network to enhance its European presence and allow Unisource members to provide services in the U.S., it became clear that AT&T, with its enormous size, would dominate the network.

In the end, for some firms, the costs of being part of Unisource outweighed the benefits. Some of the smaller firms decided to exit the network. Unisource hastily invited new telecom providers to join out of fear of losing telecommunications coverage in certain key geographic areas, but these newcomers were less committed to the overall network strategy and preferred to pursue their own strategic advantages. As a result, the once-flourishing telecom network turned dysfunctional. Unisource collapsed within a few short months of the membership shuffle.[77]

to be governed by contractual arrangements. Weak ties usually allow for the transfer of explicit knowledge only. Given the different resource requirements in terms of managerial time and attention, firms typically maintain a larger number of weak ties than strong ties.

To understand the different positions of individual firms in strategic networks, it is helpful to graph all the nodes in the network and their ties. Exhibit 9.8 (see next page) depicts a hypothetical strategic network; the purple nodes are firms and the blue connections are the ties between them. When we look at it this way, a couple of observations jump out. Firm A is centrally located in a cluster of six firms (indicated by the dotted oval); it has the highest degree centrality of all the firms in the network—the number of direct ties a firm has in a network, out of the possible direct ties (in this case, $n = 7$); the more direct ties, the more centrally located the firm is. Firm A not only is highly visible and prominent in this cluster, but also has access to many channels of information. Moreover, the cluster of firms around firm A exhibits a high degree of *closure,* meaning that most of the firms are connected to one another. Interfirm networks in Silicon Valley, for example, are characterized by a high degree of closure.[78] A high degree of closure implies that most firms know each other, which facilitates trust,[79] and which in turn lowers transaction costs and improves efficiency and firm performance. Since research has shown that high degree centrality improves firm performance, firm A is well positioned within this cluster.[80]

degree centrality
The number of direct ties a firm has in a network, out of the possible direct ties; the more direct ties, the more centrally located the firm is.

EXHIBIT 9.8

Firms Embedded in
Strategic Networks

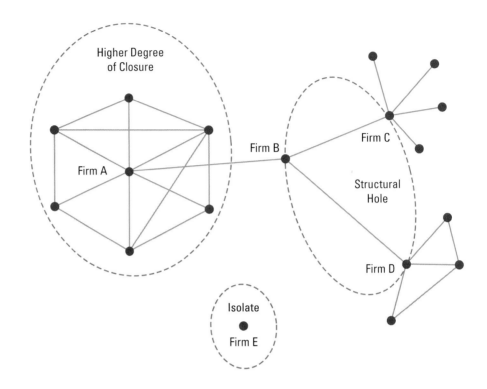

Firm B occupies a powerful position in this network because it acts as a *knowledge broker* between three subnetworks formed around firm A, firm C, and firm D. In this role, firm B bridges and connects the three clusters making up the network. In particular, firm B spans several structural holes—spaces where two organizations are connected to the same organization, but are not connected to each other. In Exhibit 9.8, one of the structural holes is highlighted in the dotted oval. Here, firms C and D are connected to firm B, but not to one another. Generally, firms that bridge structural holes gain information and control benefits over the nonconnected firms.[81] Firm B has access to a diverse set of information emanating from the subnetworks of firms A, C, and D, allowing it to gain access to timely information and to obtain referrals. Moreover, occupying a structural hole gives firm B power because it can play firm C off against firm D, and vice versa.

A knowledge broker is a powerful position to occupy within a network. Researchers have shown that continuous innovation is based on a firm's ability to broker, connect, and recombine different strands of knowledge.[82] A position as a knowledge broker allows a firm to find novel solutions to thorny problems because it often has access to diverse knowledge, and can link that information to implement solutions in the form of new products or processes. The design consultancy IDEO, famous for creating Apple's first computer mouse and Whole Foods's shopping cart, strategically positions itself as a knowledge broker in different design, technology, and market-domain networks to achieve continuous innovation.[83]

In contrast to knowledge brokers, some firms are considered *isolates,* meaning they are not connected to any other firm in the network. In Exhibit 9.8, for example, firm E is an isolate. Because it cannot benefit from any advantages from the resources within the network, its position is weak. Indeed, firm E is likely to have a competitive disadvantage, given the strong empirical evidence that interfirm cooperation and openness have a positive effect on continued innovation and superior firm performance.[84, 85]

structural holes
Spaces where two organizations are connected to the same organization, but are not connected to one another. Firms that bridge structural holes (*brokers*) gain information and control benefits over the nonconnected firms.

The network in Exhibit 9.8 as a whole is characterized by the small-world phenomenon.[86] The small-world phenomenon occurs when a network exhibits local clusters, each with high degree centrality. Here, there are local clusters around firm A, firm C, and firm D, connected by bridging ties A–B, B–C, and B–D. In a small-world network, the path length between any two nodes in the network is short, meaning any firm can reach any other firm in the network through a small number of connections. Many small-world networks have been observed. When plotting the thousands of technology alliances worldwide, for example, a small-world network emerges, with two main components (electronics-based industries, and chemical- and medical-based industries) that are connected by few brokers.[87] The Internet is also a small-world network, because clusters of local network servers are connected by a few bridging ties, increasing the speed of global communication and data transfer. Small-world networks further enhance the value of broker positions like the one held by firm B.

Strategic networks are powerful vehicles to execute business and corporate-level strategy. Managers need to be aware of the potential benefits to be had from networks, but also of potential downsides. In addition, not all network positions are created equal. Thus, in addition to managing a firm's alliance portfolio, strategists also need to understand that its alliances embed the firm in different networks. They must manage network participation in such a way as to carve out an advantageous position that will provide benefits that could not be had otherwise.

We now have concluded our discussion of corporate strategy. Acquisitions, alliances, and networks are key vehicles to execute corporate strategy, each with its distinct advantages and disadvantages. It is also clear from this chapter that mergers and acquisitions, strategic alliances, and networks are a global phenomenon. In fact, the strategic networks in the airline and telecommunications industries discussed in this chapter were formed with the intent of providing global reach, which of course provides additional challenges as well as opportunities. In the next chapter, we discuss strategy in a global world.

> **small-world phenomenon** Situation in which a network exhibits local clusters, each with high degree centrality.

CHAPTERCASE 9 | *Consider This . . .*

IN CHAPTERCASE 9, we explored Facebook's growth into a dominant social network, and the chapter also noted the importance to the success of Facebook of complements such as software apps like FarmVille. These apps help drive users to return frequently to Facebook for updates on these social games. Zynga, founded in July 2007, is the world's largest provider of social games (including FarmVille). As of March 2011, Zynga had over 250 million active users playing its games at least monthly. In May 2010, Facebook and Zynga signed a five-year "strategic relationship" agreement that, among other things, increased the use of Facebook credits on Zynga's games.

Zynga, however, has broader ambitions than being the biggest app-provider to Facebook. By early 2011, Zynga games were available on eight different game portals including iPhone, Android, and MSN Games. Zynga purchased six firms in 2010 to fulfill the expected demand of such large and growing marketplace relationships. These acquisitions brought new content material to the Zynga platform (e.g., "Words with Friends" and "Rock Legends"). Additionally, Zynga used acquisitions to expand globally (purchasing Unoh Inc. in Tokyo and XPD in Beijing) and to build its internal growth, as it launched its first international office in Bangalore,

India, in February 2010. Finally, Zynga struck a deal in 2010 for its first retail promotion: The world's largest convenience store retail chain, 7-Eleven, branded items such as Slurpees with designs from the FarmVille, Mafia Wars, and YoVille games, offering redemption codes for in-game rewards. For Zynga, 2010 was quite a year—filled with acquisitions, alliances, and network building![88]

1. Based on ChapterCase 9 (p. 237), what do you see as some of the main differences between MySpace and Facebook? How did their business models differ? What were the strategic implications of these differences?

2. App-developers like Zynga have been credited with much of the reason for the rapid growth of both Facebook and various brands of smartphones. Yet managing eight or more delivery outlets can be difficult for new (and often small) firms, like Zynga, to coordinate. What suggestions do you have for how these young firms might handle these relationships successfully?

3. Go to www.zynga.com/about/news.php and look at the most recent press announcements from Zynga. Is the firm using more acquisitions or alliances in building its business? What seems to be the primary reason for this activity?

4. Given Zynga's recent activities in network building, what do you see as advantages and disadvantages of Zynga's network strategy?

Take-Away Concepts

This chapter discussed three mechanisms of corporate-level strategy (acquisitions, alliances, and networks), as summarized by the following learning objectives and related take-away concepts.

LO 9-1 Differentiate between mergers and acquisitions and explain why firms would use either as a vehicle for corporate strategy.

>> A merger describes the joining of two independent companies to form a combined entity.

>> An acquisition describes the purchase or (hostile) takeover of one company by another.

>> The distinction between mergers and acquisitions (M&A) can be blurry. Many observers simply use the umbrella term M&A to describe horizontal integration.

>> Firms can use M&A activity for competitive advantage when they possess a superior relational capability, which is often built on superior alliance management capability.

LO 9-2 Define horizontal integration and evaluate the advantages and disadvantages of this corporate-level strategy.

>> Horizontal integration is the process of acquiring and merging with competitors, leading to industry consolidation.

>> As a corporate strategy, firms use horizontal integration to: (1) reduce competitive intensity, (2) lower costs, (3) increase differentiation, and (4) access new markets and distribution channels.

LO 9-3 Evaluate whether mergers and acquisitions lead to competitive advantage.

>> Most mergers and acquisitions destroy shareholder value because anticipated synergies never materialize.

>> If there is any value creation in M&As, it generally accrues to the shareholders of the firm that is taken over (the acquiree), because acquirers often pay a premium when buying the target company.

>> M&As are a popular corporate-level strategy for three reasons: (1) the desire to overcome competitive disadvantage, (2) the quest for superior acquisition and integration capability, and (3) because of principal–agent problems.

LO 9-4 Define strategic alliances and explain why they are important corporate strategy vehicles, and why firms enter into them.

>> Strategic alliances have the goal of sharing knowledge, resources, and capabilities in order to develop processes, products, or services.

alliance formation, (2) alliance design and governance, and (3) post-formation alliance management.

>> Firms build a superior alliance management capability through "learning-by-doing" and by establishing a dedicated alliance function.

LO 9-7 Define strategic networks and evaluate the advantages and disadvantages of different network positions.

>> A strategic network is an alliance of several firms to pursue a common purpose. It is a social structure of multiple organizations (network nodes) and the links among the nodes (network ties).

>> A firm with a high degree centrality in a strategic network is connected to many other firms, provides social capital to the central firm, and is trusted in the closely connected network cluster (firm A in Exhibit 9.8).

>> A network broker firm connects different network clusters (firm B in Exhibit 9.8). The broker often spans structural holes, which strengthens its position, especially in a small-world network.

>> A firm not connected to any other firm in a network is an isolate (firm E in Exhibit 9.8). Given its lack of connections, an isolate frequently is at a competitive disadvantage.

Acquisition *(p. 238)*

Alliance management capability *(p. 251)*

Corporate venture capital (CVC) *(p. 250)*

Degree centrality *(p. 255)*

Equity alliance *(p. 250)*

Explicit knowledge *(p. 248)*

Horizontal integration *(p. 239)*

Hostile takeover *(p. 239)*

Joint venture *(p. 250)*

Learning races *(p. 247)*

Managerial hubris *(p. 243)*

Merger *(p. 238)*

Non-equity alliance *(p. 248)*

Relational view of competitive advantage *(p. 244)*

Small-world phenomenon *(p. 257)*

Strategic alliance *(p. 244)*

Strategic network *(p. 254)*

Structural hole *(p. 256)*

Tacit knowledge *(p. 250)*

Discussion Questions

1. Horizontal integration has benefits to the firms involved. Consider the consolidation in the event-promotion business when Live Nation bought Ticketmaster in 2010. List some specific advantages of this acquisition for Live Nation. Do you see any downside to the merger?

2. The chapter identifies three governing mechanisms for strategic alliances (non-equity, equity, and joint venture). Provide the benefits for each of these mechanisms.

3. The alliance purpose can affect which governance structure is optimal. Compare a pharmaceutical R&D alliance with a prescription-drug marketing agreement, and recommend a governing mechanism for each. Provide reasons for your selections.

4. Alliances are often used to pursue business-level goals but they may be managed at the corporate level. Explain why this portfolio approach to alliance management would make sense.

5. Describe the difference between a strong tie and a weak tie in a network. How are weak ties sometimes more useful to the firm/individual?

Ethical/Social Issues

1. If mergers and acquisitions quite often end up providing a competitive disadvantage, why do so many of them take place? Given the poor track record, is the continuing M&A activity a result of principal–agent problems and managerial hubris? Are there other reasons?

2. Alliances and acquisitions can sometimes lead to less access or higher prices for consumers. Comcast is buying NBC Universal (from GE). When one content provider and the Internet access provider are the same, will this lead to some content being favored over others on the Internet? For example, will Comcast want to send Universal movies (which it owns) with faster download capabilities than it sends a Harry Potter movie from Warner Brothers (which it doesn't own)? (If so, this would violate a "net-neutrality" policy that has generally been honored—that all information on the Internet is treated equally as far as speed and cost per size of content.)[89]

2. When a firm builds a strategic network of alliances, there is often concern about the fair treatment of all the firms in the network. What are some ways an alliance management organization could mitigate concerns about equitable treatment within the network of firms?

Small Group Exercises

SMALL GROUP EXERCISE 1

In this chapter, we studied the idea of horizontal integration. One industry currently going through a wave of consolidation of competitors is the commercial airline industry. Assume Southwest Airlines has just changed CEOs. The new CEO vows to make Southwest the largest airline company in the United States and plans to buy another airline to increase Southwest's scale. Southwest reported cash reserves in excess of $3 billion dollars at the end of 2009, so it is in a healthy financial position for an acquisition. The chart at the top of the next page shows some relevant comparisons of major U.S. airlines ($ in millions).

Consider overall size and existing complementary airline routes as major factors in selecting an appropriate partner for Southwest. You can find route maps on the websites of all major airlines, or go to a site such as www.airlineroutemaps.com/USA/index.shtml to compare several airlines on one web page. You may also want to refer back to Exhibit 3.7 for the strategic groups map of the U.S. airline industry. As a team, review this financial and routing data and make a recommendation to the new leadership of Southwest for its best potential partner.

SMALL GROUP EXERCISE 2

The global public relations and communications firm Burson-Marsteller studied the 100 largest companies in the 2009 *Fortune* list and found that 79 percent of them use Twitter, Facebook, YouTube, or corporate blogs to communicate with customers and other

Category	Alaska	JetBlue	US Airways	Southwest
Operating revenues	$2,718	$3,286	$8,106	$10,350
Operating expenses	$2,460	$3,007	$7,804	$10,088
Operating income	$258	$279	$302	$262
Net income	$122	$58	($205)	$99
Employees	8,912	10,583	31,340	34,874
Airplanes	115	151	349	537
Total passenger miles	18,362	25,955	57,889	74,457
Load factor	79.30%	79.7%	81.9%	76.0%

Source: 2009 data compiled by Robert Herbst at www.airlinefinancials.com.

stakeholders. Two-thirds of the Fortune 100 have at least one Twitter account (the most popular platform); 54 percent have at least one Facebook fan page; 50 percent have at least one YouTube channel; and 33 percent have at least one corporate blog. A fifth (20 percent) of the companies use all four social media platforms.

The firm also broke its findings down by region (North America, Europe, Asia-Pacific and Latin America) and network. Geographically, social networks like Twitter and Facebook are mostly West-oriented. Asia-Pacific companies don't use them as much, instead preferring corporate blogs. When Asia-Pacific companies do use Twitter or Facebook, it's usually to engage consumers in Europe and North America.[90]

In your group, select three firms and research their social media web presence.

1. Do the firms seem to do a good job of managing their web identity?

3. What differences do you find among the three firms?

Strategy Term Project

MODULE 9: STRATEGIC ALLIANCE AND M&A STRATEGY

In this section, you will study your selected firm's use of acquisitions and alliances to grow or change its business.

1. Has your firm participated in any mergers or acquisitions in the past three years? What was the nature of these actions? Did they result in a consolidation of competitors?

2. Research what strategic alliances your firm has entered in the past three years. If there are several of these, choose the three you identify as the most important for further analysis. Based on company press releases and business journal reports for each alliance, what do you find to be the main reason the firm entered these alliances?

3. Do you think each of the three alliances achieves the original intent, and therefore is successful? Why or why not?

4. Does your firm have an identifiable alliance-management organization? Can you find any evidence that this organization improves the likelihood of success for these alliances? What responsibilities does this alliance-management organization have in your firm?

5. Go to LinkedIn (www.linkedin.com) and see what executive officers or groups your firm may have set up on the professional networking site. Next, look to see if the firm has a "fan page" on Facebook. Is there also a "detractors page" for your firm? How would you assess your firm's use of web networks and social media for its business?

*my*Strategy

WHAT IS YOUR NETWORK STRATEGY?

Most of us participate in one or more popular social networks online such as Facebook, MySpace, or LinkedIn. While many of us spend countless hours in these social networks, you may not have given a lot of thought to your network strategy.

Social networks describe the relationships or ties between individuals linked to one another. An important element of social networks is the *different strengths of ties* between individuals. Some ties between two people in a network may be very strong (e.g., "soul mates" or "best friends"), while others are weak (mere acquaintances—"I talk to her briefly in my yoga class"). As a member of a social network, you have access to social capital, which is derived from the connections within and between social networks. It is a function of whom you know, and what advantages you can create through those connections. *Social capital* is an important concept in business.

Some Facebook users claim to have 2,000 or more "friends." With larger networks, one expects to have greater social capital, right? Though this seems obvious, academic research suggests that humans have the brain capacity to maintain a functional network of only about 150 people. This so-called *Dunbar number* was derived by extrapolating from the brain sizes and social networks of primates.

Far fetched? Not necessarily. You may have a lot more than 150 friends on Facebook, but researchers call that number the *social core* of any network. Why is this the case? Even though it takes only a split second to accept a new friend request on Facebook, friendships still need to be "groomed." To develop a meaningful relationship, you need to spend some time with this new friend, even in cyberspace. Recent data from Facebook provides support for the concept of a social core, as the average number of a user's friends is 120, with women having more friends than men. However, the number of friends a Facebook user frequently interacts with is a lot smaller, and tends to be stable over time. The more frequent the exchanges among friends, the smaller the inner core. For example, on average, men leave comments for 17 friends and communicate with 10, while women leave comments for 26 friends and communicate with 16.

Social networking sites allow users to broadcast their lives and to passively keep track of more people, and thus to enlarge their social networks, even though many of those ties tend to be weak. It may come as a surprise, however, to learn that research shows new opportunities such as job offers tend to come from weak ties, because it is these weak ties that allow you to access non-redundant and novel information. This phenomenon is called *strength of weak ties*. So, in thinking about how to leverage your social capital more fully as part of your network strategy, rather than always communicating with the same people, it may pay off for you to invest a bit more time grooming your weak ties.[91]

1. Draw up a list of up to 12 people at your university with whom you regularly communicate (in person, electronically, or both). Draw your network (place names or initials next to each node), and connect every node where people you communicate with also talk to one another (i.e., indicate friends of friends). Can you identify strong and weak ties in your network?

2. What is the *degree of closure* in your network? The density of your network reflects the degree of closure. Network density can be calculated in three simple steps.

   Step 1: Create a simple matrix in which you list the names of the people in your network on both the horizontal and vertical axis. (This can be easily done in an Excel spreadsheet.) Then put an X in each box, indicating who knows whom in your network. Each X corresponds to a social tie in your network. Count the total number of X's in your matrix. Let's assume X = 8.

   Step 2: If your network contains 12 people (including yourself), N = 12. The maximum network density is calculated by the following formula: $[N \times (N - 1)] / 2$. If your network size is 12, then your maximum network density is $[12 \times (12 - 1)] / 2 = 66$. This is the maximum number of ties in your network when everybody knows everybody.

   Step 3: To calculate your actual network density, divide X by N: Network density = (X/N). In the example with 8 ties in a network of 12 people, the network density is 0.67. The closer this number is to 1, the denser the network.

3. Network density is bound by 0 and 1. Is a network density that approaches 1 the most beneficial? Why or why not? Think about weak ties, which can also be indirect connections.

4. Compare your network to that of your group members (2–4 people in your class). Do you find any commonalities in your networks? Who has the greatest social capital, and why? What can you do to "optimize" your network structure?

5. Can you draw the joint network of your study group?

6. In this joint (study group) network, can you identify different network positions such as those discussed in the chapter: centrally located person(s) and broker(s), or a person who connects different

clusters? Can you identify people with high and low social capital? Are there any dense clusters in this network? Would that indicate the existence of cliques? Is it a small-world network? What other implications can you draw?

Endnotes

1. "Facebook CEO in no rush to 'friend' Wall Street," *The Wall Street Journal,* March 3, 2010.

2. "Facebook wants to know more than just who your friends are," *The Wall Street Journal,* April 22, 2010.

3. This ChapterCase is based on: "Facebook's land grab in the face of a downturn," *Bloomberg Businessweek,* November 20, 2008; "A special report on social networking," *The Economist,* January 30, 2010; "Facebook CEO in no rush to 'friend' Wall Street," *The Wall Street Journal*; "The world's billionaires," *Forbes,* March 10, 2010; "Facebook wants to know more than just who your friends are," *The Wall Street Journal*; "Facebook's Washington problem," *Bloomberg Businessweek,* May 13, 2010; "Lives of others," *The Economist,* May 20, 2010; www.comscore.com; www.facebook.com; and www.myspace.com.

4. "Lives of others," *The Economist,* May 20, 2010.

5. Hitt, M. A., R. D. Ireland, and J. S. Harrison (2001), "Mergers and acquisitions: A value creating or value destroying strategy?" in, Hitt, M. A. R. E. Freeman, and J. S. Harrison, *Handbook of Strategic Management* (Oxford, UK: Blackwell-Wiley): 384–408.

6. "HP gambles on ailing Palm," *The Wall Street Journal,* April 29, 2010.

7. Allen, W. B., N. A. Doherty, K. Weigelt, and E. Mansfield (2005), *Managerial Economics,* 6th ed. (New York: Norton); and Breshnahan, T., and P. Reiss (1991), "Entry and competition in concentrated markets," *Journal of Political Economy* 99: 997–1009.

8. Brush, T. H. (1996), "Predicted change in operational synergy and post-acquisition performance of acquired

businesses," *Strategic Management Journal* 17: 1–24.

9. Tebbutt, T. (2010), "An insider's perspective of the pharmaceutical industry," presentation in "Competing in the Health Sciences," Georgia Institute of Technology, January 29. Mr. Tebbutt is former President of UCB Pharma.

10. This Strategy Highlight is based on: "Cadbury rejects Kraft's $16.73 billion bid," *The Wall Street Journal,* September 7, 2009; "Food fight," *The Economist,* November 5, 2009; "Cadbury accepts fresh Kraft offer," *The Wall Street Journal,* January 19, 2010; "Kraft wins a reluctant Cadbury with help of clock, hedge funds," *The Wall Street Journal,* January 20, 2010; the author's personal communication with Dr. Narayanan Jayaraman, Georgia Institute of Technology; and The Hershey Company, 2008 Annual Report.

11. Capron, L. (1999), "The long-term performance of horizontal acquisitions," *Strategic Management Journal* 20: 987–1018; Capron, L., and J. C. Shen (2007), "Acquisitions of private vs. public firms: Private information, target selection, and acquirer returns," *Strategic Management Journal* 28: 891–911.

12. Jensen, M. C., and R. S. Ruback (1983), "The market for corporate control: The scientific evidence," *Journal of Financial Economics* 11: 5–50.

13. Dyer, J. H., P. Kale, and H. Singh (2004), "When to ally and when to acquire," *Harvard Business Review,* July–August; Mayer, D., and M. Kenney (2004), "Ecosystems and acquisition management: Understanding Cisco's strategy," *Industry and Innovation* 11: 299–326.

14. "Silicon Valley survivor," *The Wall Street Journal,* July 28, 2009.

15. Kale, P., H. Singh, and A. P. Raman (2009), "Don't integrate your acquisitions, partner with them," *Harvard Business Review,* December.

16. This discussion is based on: Finkelstein, S., and D. C. Hambrick (1989), "Chief executive compensation: A study of the intersection of markets and political processes, *Strategic Management Journal* 10: 121–134; Lambert, R. A., D. F. Larcker, and K. Weigelt (1991), "How sensitive is executive compensation to organizational size?" *Strategic Management Journal* 12: 395–402; and Finkelstein, S. (2003), *Why Smart Executives Fail, and What You Can Learn from Their Mistakes* (New York: Portfolio).

17. This discussion is based on: Finkelstein, S. (2003), *Why Smart Executives Fail, and What You Can Learn from Their Mistakes*; and Finkelstein, S., J. Whitehead, and A. Campbell (2009), *Think Again: Why Good Leaders Make Bad Decisions and How to Keep It from Happening to You* (Boston, MA: Harvard Business School Press).

18. The examples are drawn from: Finkelstein, S. (2003), *Why Smart Executives Fail, And What You Can Learn from Their Mistakes;* and Finkelstein, S., J. Whitehead, and A. Campbell (2009), *Think Again: Why Good Leaders Make Bad Decisions and How to Keep It from Happening to You.*

19. Gulati, R. (1998), "Alliances and networks," *Strategic Management Journal* 19: 293–317.

20. This discussion draws on: Dyer, J. H., and H. Singh (1998), "The relational view: Cooperative strategy and the sources of interorganizational advantage," *Academy of Management Review* 23: 660–679.

21. Kale, P., and H. Singh (2009), "Managing strategic alliances: What do we know now, and where do we go from here?" *Academy of Management Perspectives* 23: 45–62.

22. The author participated in the HP demo; and "HP unveils Halo collaboration studio: Life-like communication leaps across geographic boundaries," HP Press Release, December 12, 2005.

23. "Bank of America taps Cisco for TelePresence," *InformationWeek,* March 30, 2010.

24. For a review of the alliance literature, see: Gulati, R. (1998), "Alliances and networks," *Strategic Management Journal* 19: 293–317; Dyer, J. H., and H. Singh (1998), "The relational view: Cooperative strategy and the sources of interorganizational advantage," *Academy of Management Review* 23: 660–679; Inkpen, A. (2001), "Strategic alliances," in Hitt, M. A., R. E. Freeman, and J. S. Harrison, *Handbook of Strategic Management;* Ireland, R. D., M. A. Hitt, and D. Vaidyanath (2002), "Alliance management as a source of competitive advantage," *Journal of Management* 28: 413–446; Lavie, D. (2006), "The competitive advantage of interconnected firms: An extension of the resource-based view," *Academy of Management Review* 31: 638–658; Kale, P., and H. Singh (2009), "Managing strategic alliances: What do we know now, and where do we go from here?" *Academy of Management Perspectives* 23: 45–62.

25. Kogut, B. (1991), "Joint ventures and the option to expand and acquire," *Management Science* 37: 19–34.

26. Markides, C. C., and P. J. Williamsen (1994), "Related diversification, core competences, and performance," *Strategic Management Journal* 15: 149–165 (Summer Special Issue); Kale, P., and H. Singh (2009), "Managing strategic alliances: What do we know now, and where do we go from here?" *Academy of Management Perspectives* 23: 45–62.

27. "Microsoft, Yahoo tout ad alliance," *The Wall Street Journal,* July 30, 2009.

28. Ibid.

29. Tripsas, M. (1997), "Unraveling the process of creative destruction: Complementary assets and incumbent survival in the typesetter industry,"

Strategic Management Journal 18: 119–142.

30. Rothaermel, F. T. (2001), "Incumbent's advantage through exploiting complementary assets via interfirm cooperation," *Strategic Management Journal* 22: 687–699. Rothaermel, F. T. (2001), "Complementary assets, strategic alliances, and the incumbent's advantage: An empirical study of industry and firm effects in the biopharmaceutical industry," *Research Policy* 30: 1235–1251; Hill, C. W. L., and F. T. Rothaermel (2003), "The performance of incumbent firms in the face of radical technological innovation," *Academy of Management Review* 28: 257–274; Rothaermel, F. T., and C. W. L. Hill (2005), "Technological discontinuities and complementary assets: A longitudinal study of industry and firm performance," *Organization Science* 16: 52–70.

31. Arthaud-Day, M. L., F. T. Rothaermel, and W. Zhang (2013), "Genentech: After the Acquisition by Roche," case study, in, Rothaermel, F. T. *Strategic Management* (Burr Ridge, IL: McGraw-Hill).

32. Jiang, L., J. Tan, and M. Thursby (2011), "Incumbent firm invention in emerging fields: Evidence from the semiconductor industry," *Strategic Management Journal,*; Rothaermel, F. T., and M. Thursby (2007), "The nanotech vs. the biotech revolution: Sources of incumbent productivity in research," *Research Policy* 36: 832–849.

33. This discussion is based on: Teece, D. J. (1986), "Profiting from technological innovation: Implications for integration, collaboration, licensing and public policy," *Research Policy* 15: 285–305; Tripsas, M. (1997), "Unraveling the process of creative destruction: Complementary assets and incumbent survival in the typesetter industry"; Rothaermel, F. T. (2001), "Incumbent's advantage through exploiting complementary assets via interfirm cooperation," *Strategic Management Journal* 22 (6–7): 687–699; Ceccagnoli, M., and F. T. Rothaermel (2008), "Appropriating the returns to innovation," *Advances in Study of Entrepreneurship, Innovation, and Economic Growth* 18: 11–34; Rothaermel, F. T., and W. Boeker (2008), "Old technology meets new

technology: Complementarities, similarities, and alliance formation," *Strategic Management Journal* 29 (1): 47–77; and Hess, A. M., and F. T. Rothaermel (2011), "When are assets complementary? Star scientists, strategic alliances and innovation in the pharmaceutical industry," *Strategic Management Journal* 32: 895–909.

34. This Strategy Highlight is based on: Paik, K. (2007), *To Infinity and Beyond!: The Story of Pixar Animation Studies* (New York: Chronicle Books); and "Marvel superheroes join the Disney family," *The Wall Street Journal,* August 31, 2009.

35. Mowery, D. C., J. E. Oxley, and B. S. Silverman (1996), "Strategic alliances and interfirm knowledge transfer," *Strategic Management Journal* 17: 77–91 (Winter Special Issue).

36. Brandenburger, A. M., and B. J. Nalebuff (1996), *Co-opetition* (New York: Currency Doubleday); Gnyawali, D., and B. Park (2011), "Co-opetition between Giants: Collaboration with competitors for technological innovation," *Research Policy,*; Gnyawali, D., J. He, and R. Madhaven (2008), "Co-opetition: Promises and challenges," in Wankel, C. (ed.), *21st Century Management: A Reference Handbook* (Thousand Oaks, CA: Sage): 386–398.

37. This discussion is based on: Hamel, G., Y. Doz, and C. K. Prahalad (1989), "Collaborate with your competitors— and win," *Harvard Business Review* (January–February): 190–196; Hamel, G. (1991), "Competition for competence and interpartner learning within international alliances," *Strategic Management Journal* 12: 83–103 (Summer Special Issue); Khanna, T., R. Gulati, and N. Nohria (1998), "The dynamics of learning alliances: Competition, cooperation, and relative scope," *Strategic Management Journal* 19: 193–210; Larsson, R., L. Bengtsson, K. Henriksson, and J. Sparks (1998), "The interorganizational learning dilemma: Collective knowledge development in strategic alliances," *Organization Science* 9: 285–305; and Kale, P., and H. Perlmutter (2000), "Learning and protection of proprietary assets in strategic alliances: Building relational capital," *Strategic Management Journal* 21: 217–237.

38. Nti, K. O., and R. Kumar (2000), "Differential learning in alliances," in, Faulkner, D., and M. de Rond (eds.), *Cooperative Strategy. Economic, Business, and Organizational Issues* (Oxford, UK: University Press): 119–134. For an opposing viewpoint, see: Inkpen, A. C. (2008), "Knowledge transfer and international joint ventures: The case of NUMMI and General Motors," *Strategic Management Journal* 29: 447–453.

39. This discussion is based on: Gulati, R. (1998), "Alliances and networks," *Strategic Management Journal* 19: 293–317; Ireland, R. D., Hitt, M. A. and Vaidyanath D. (2002), "Alliance management as a source of competitive advantage," *Journal of Management* 28: 413–446; Hoang, H., and F. T. Rothaermel (2005), "The effect of general and partner-specific alliance experience on joint R&D project performance," *Academy of Management Journal* 48: 332–345; and Lavie, D. (2006), "The competitive advantage of interconnected firms: An extension of the resource-based view," *Academy of Management Review* 31: 638–658.

40. This is based on: Pisano, G. P., and Mang P. (1993), "Collaborative product development and the market for know-how: Strategies and structures in the biotechnology industry," in Rosenbloom, R. and R. Burgelman (eds.), *Research on Technological Innovation, Management, and Policy* (Greenwich, CT: J.A.I. Press) 109–136; and Hoang, H., and F. T. Rothaermel (2010), "Leveraging internal and external experience: Exploration, exploitation, and R&D project performance," *Strategic Management Journal* 31 (7): 734–758.

41. The distinction of explicit and tacit knowledge goes back to the seminal work by Polanyi, M. (1966), *The Tacit Dimension* (Chicago, IL: University of Chicago Press). For more recent treatments, see: Spender, J.-C. (1996), "Managing knowledge as the basis of a dynamic theory of the firm," *Strategic Management Journal* 17: 45–62 (Winter Special Issue); Spender, J.-C., and R. M. Grant (1996), "Knowledge and the firm," *Strategic Management Journal* 17: 5–9 (Winter Special Issue); and Crossan, M. M., H. W. Lane, R. E. White (1999), "An organizational learning framework: From intuition to institution," *Academy of Management Review* 24: 522–537.

42. "Toyota and Tesla partnering to make electric cars," *The Wall Street Journal*, May 21, 2010.

43. Ibid.

44. Ibid.

45. For an insightful treatment of CVC investments see: Dushnitsky, G., and M. J. Lenox (2005a), "When do incumbent firms learn from entrepreneurial ventures? Corporate venture capital and investing firm innovation rates," *Research Policy* 34: 615–639; Dushnitsky, G., and M. J. Lenox (2005b), "When do firms undertake R&D by investing in new ventures?" *Strategic Management Journal* 26: 947–965; Dushnitsky, G., and M. J. Lenox (2006), "When does corporate venture capital investment create value?" *Journal of Business Venturing* 21: 753–772; and Wadhwa, A., and S. Kotha (2006), "Knowledge creation through external venturing: Evidence from the telecommunications equipment manufacturing industry," *Academy of Management Journal* 49: 1–17.

46. Benson, D., and R. H. Ziedonis (2009), "Corporate venture capital as a window on new technology for the performance of corporate investors when acquiring startups," *Organization Science* 20: 329–351.

47. Dushnitsky, G., and M. J. Lenox (2006), "When does corporate venture capital investment create value?" *Journal of Business Venturing* 21: 753–772.

48. Higgins, M. J., and D. Rodriguez (2006), "The outsourcing of R&D through acquisition in the pharmaceutical industry," *Journal of Financial Economics* 80: 351–383; Benson, D., and R. H. Ziedonis (2009), "Corporate venture capital as a window on new technology for the performance of corporate investors when acquiring startups," *Organization Science* 20: 329–351.

49. Reuer, J. J., M. Zollo, and H. Singh (2002), "Post-formation dynamics in strategic alliances," *Strategic Management Journal* 23: 135–151.

50. This discussion is based on: Dyer, J. H., and H. Singh (1998), "The relational view: Cooperative strategy and the sources of interorganizational advantage," *Academy of Management Review* 23: 660–679; Ireland, R. D., M. A. Hitt, and D. Vaidyanath (2002), "Alliance management as a source of competitive advantage," *Journal of Management* 28: 413–446; and Lavie, D. (2006), "The competitive advantage of interconnected firms: An extension of the resource-based view," *Academy of Management Review* 31: 638–658.

51. For an insightful discussion of alliance management capability and alliance portfolios, see: Rothaermel, F. T., and D. L. Deeds (2006), "Alliance type, alliance experience, and alliance management capability in high-technology ventures," *Journal of Business Venturing* 21: 429–460; Hoffmann, W. (2007), "Strategies for managing a portfolio of alliances," *Strategic Management Journal* 28: 827–856; Schreiner, M., P. Kale, and D. Corsten (2009), "What really is alliance management capability and how does it impact alliance outcomes and success?" *Strategic Management Journal* 30: 1395–1419; Ozcan, P., and K. M. Eisenhardt (2009), "Origin of alliance portfolios: Entrepreneurs, network strategies, and firm performance," *Academy of Management Journal* 52: 246–279; and Schilke, O., and A. Goerzten (2010), "Alliance management capability: An investigation of the construct and its measurement," *Journal of Management* 36: 1192–1219.

52. Kale, P., and H. Singh (2009), "Managing strategic alliances: What do we know now, and where do we go from here?" *Academy of Management Perspectives* 23: 45–62.

53. Santoro, M. D., and J. P. McGill (2005), "The effect of uncertainty and asset co-specialization on governance in biotechnology alliances," *Strategic Management Journal* 26: 1261–1269.

54. This is based on: Gulati, R. (1995), "Does familiarity breed trust? The implications of repeated ties for contractual choice in alliances," *Academy of Management Journal* 38: 85–112; and Poppo, L., and T. Zenger (2002), "Do formal contracts and relational governance function as substitutes or complements?" *Strategic Management Journal* 23: 707–725.

55. Dyer, J. H., and H. Singh (1998), "The relational view: Cooperative strategy and the sources of interorganizational advantage," *Academy of Management Review* 23: 660–679.

56. Saxenian, A. (1994), *Regional Advantage* (Cambridge, MA: Harvard University Press).

57. Ibid., 134.

58. von Hippel, E. (1988), *The Sources of Innovation* (Oxford, UK: Oxford University Press).

59. Zaheer, A., B. McEvily, and V. Perrone (1998), "Does trust matter? Exploring the effects of interorganizational and interpersonal trust on performance," *Organization Science* 8: 141–159.

60. Covey, S. M. R. (2008), *The Speed of Trust: The One Thing That Changes Everything* (New York: Free Press).

61. Dyer, J.H., and H. Singh (1998), "The relational view: Cooperative strategy and the sources of interorganizational advantage," *Academy of Management Review* 23: 660–679; Ireland, R. D., M. A. Hitt, and D. Vaidyanath (2002), "Alliance management as a source of competitive advantage," *Journal of Management* 28: 413–446; Lavie, D. (2006), "The competitive advantage of interconnected firms: An extension of the resource-based view," *Academy of Management Review* 31: 638–658.

62. This is based on: Anand, B., and T. Khanna (2000), "Do firms learn to create value?" *Strategic Management Journal* 21: 295–315; Sampson, R. (2005), "Experience effects and collaborative returns in R&D alliances," *Strategic Management Journal* 26: 1009–1031; Hoang, H., and F. T. Rothaermel (2005), "The effect of general and partner-specific alliance experience on joint R&D project performance," *Academy of Management Journal* 48: 332–345; and Rothaermel, F. T., and D. L. Deeds (2006), "Alliance type, alliance experience, and alliance management capability in high-technology ventures," *Journal of Business Venturing* 21: 429–460.

63. Rothaermel, F. T., and D. L. Deeds (2006), "Alliance type, alliance experience, and alliance management capability in high-technology ventures," *Journal of Business Venturing* 21: 429–460.

64. Hoffmann, W. (2007), "Strategies for managing a portfolio of alliances," *Strategic Management Journal* 28: 827–856.

65. Wassmer, U., P. Dussage, and M. Planellas (2010), "How to manage

alliances better than one at a time," *MIT Sloan Management Review,* Spring: 77–84.

66. Dyer, J. H., P. Kale, and H. Singh (2001), "How to make strategic alliances work," *MIT Sloan Management Review,* Summer: 37–43.

67. Kale, P., J. H. Dyer, and H. Singh (2002), "Alliance capability, stock market response, and long-term alliance success: The role of the alliance function," *Strategic Management Journal* 23: 747–767.

68. Gueth A., N. Sims, and R. Harrison (2001), "Managing alliances at Lilly," *In Vivo: The Business & Medicine Report* (June): 1–9; Rothaermel, F. T., and D. L. Deeds (2006), "Alliance type, alliance experience, and alliance management capability in high-technology ventures," *Journal of Business Venturing* 21: 429–46.

69. Dyer, J.H., Kale, P., Singh, H. (2004), "When to ally and when to acquire," *Harvard Business Review,* July-August.

70. Rothaermel, F. T., and A. Hess (2010), "Innovation strategies combined," *MIT Sloan Management Review,* Spring: 12–15.

71. Dyer, J. H., Kale, P., Singh, H. (2004), "When to ally and when to acquire," *Harvard Business Review,* July–August.

72. Gulati, R., and M. Gargiulo (1999), "Where do interorganizational networks come from?" *American Journal of Sociology* 104: 1439–1493.

73. www.staralliance.com/en/about/.

74. This is based on: Gomes-Casseres, B. (1994), "Group versus group: How alliance networks compete," *Harvard Business Review,* July–August; and Nohria, N., and C. Garcia-Pont (1991), "Global strategic linkages and industry structure," *Strategic Management Journal* 12: 105–124.

75. This discussion is based on: Burt, R. S. (1992), *Structural Holes* (Cambridge, MA: Harvard University Press); Coleman, J. S. (1990), *Foundations of Social Theory* (Cambridge, MA: Harvard University Press); Granovetter, M. (1973), "The strength of weak ties," *American Journal of Sociology* 78: 1360–1380; Gulati, R. (1998), "Alliances and networks," *Strategic Management Journal*

19: 293–317; Wasserman, S., and K. Faust (1994), *Social Network Analysis: Methods and Applications* (Cambridge, UK: Cambridge University Press); Zaheer, A., R. Gözübüyük, and H. Milanov (2010), "It's in the connections: The network perspective in interorganizational research," *Academy of Management Perspectives* 24: 62–77.

76. Granovetter, M. (1973), "The strength of weak ties," *American Journal of Sociology* 78: 1360–1380.

77. This Strategy Highlight is based on: Lechner, C., F. T. Rothaermel, and S. Agung (2007), "The emergence, evolution, and dissolution of a network system: A complexity perspective," *Academy of Management Annual Meeting,* Philadelphia, PA, August 6.

78. Saxenian, A. (1994), *Regional Advantage* (Cambridge, MA: Harvard University Press).

79. Coleman, J. S. (1990), *Foundations of Social Theory* (Cambridge, MA: Harvard University Press).

80. This is based on: Baum, J.A.C., T. Calabrese, and B. S. Silverman (2000), "Don't go it alone: Alliance network composition and startups' performance in Canadian biotechnology," *Strategic Management Journal* 21: 267–294; Rothaermel, F. T. (2001), "Incumbent's advantage through exploiting complementary assets via interfirm cooperation," *Strategic Management Journal* 22: 687–699; Shan, W., G. Walker, and B. Kogut (1994), "Interfirm cooperation and startup innovation in the biotechnology industry," *Strategic Management Journal* 15: 387–394; Tsai, W. (2001), "Knowledge transfer in intraorganizational networks: Effects of network position and absorptive capacity on business unit innovation and performance," *Academy of Management Journal* 44: 996–1004; Tsai, W. (2002), "Social structure of 'coopetition' within a multi-unit organization: Coordination, competition, and intraorganizational knowledge sharing," *Organization Science* 13: 179–190;

81. Burt, R. S. (1992), *Structural Holes* (Cambridge, MA: Harvard University Press).

82. Hargadorn, A. B. (1998), "Firms as knowledge brokers: Lessons in pursuing continuous innovation," *California Management Review* 40: 209–227.

83. Ibid.

84. This is based on: Chesbrough, H. W. (2003), *Open Innovation: The New Imperative for Creating and Profiting from Technology* (Boston, MA: Harvard Business School Press); Chesbrough, H. W., and M. M. Appleyard (2007), "Open innovation and strategy," *California Management Review* 50: 57–76.

85. Although the cluster around firm A shows a high degree of closure, in the overall network depicted in Exhibit 9.8 there aren't that many connections among all the purple dots representing individual firms. We can calculate the network's degree of closure. A network's maximum density is calculated by the formula: $[N \times (N - 1)] / 2$, where N is the number of firms. With 17 firms in the network, the maximum network density here is 136 possible ties. However, since there are only 25 ties in the network, its actual network density or degree of closure is $(25 / 136) = 0.18$. Since network density is bound by 0 (no connections) and 1 (all firms are connected to one another), we conclude that this network is quite sparse.

86. This is based on: Watts, D. J. (1999), *Small Worlds: The Dynamics of Networks between Order and Randomness* (Princeton, NJ: Princeton University Press); Watts, D. J. (2003), *Six Degrees: The Science of a Connected Age* (New York: Norton).

87. Schilling, M. A. (2009), "The global technology collaboration network: Structure, trends, and implications," Working Paper, New York University.

88. The ChapterCase 9 extension is based on: Zynga.com Press Room, various press releases (www.zynga.com/about/news.php); "Zach Gottlieb, Zynga: Redefining the 'Game of Life,'" *Wired,* June 14, 2010; "7-Eleven to celebrate store-opening milestone," *PRNewswire,* February 25, 2011; and David Dorf, "5 ways to grab customers on Facebook," *Harvard Business Review,* March 2, 2011.

89. Data sourced from "The FCC's crusade to keep the Internet free," *Bloomberg Businessweek,* August 16, 2010.

90. Data from "Global Social Media Check Up" by Burson-Marsteller PR firm, 2010.

91. This *my*Strategy section is based on: Granovetter, M. (1973), "The strength of weak ties," *American Journal of Sociology* 78: 1360–1380; and "Primates on Facebook," *The Economist,* February 26, 2009.

CHAPTER 10

Global Strategy:
Competing Around the World

LEARNING OBJECTIVES
After studying this chapter, you should be able to:

LO 10-1 Define globalization, multinational enterprise (MNE), foreign direct investment (FDI), and global strategy.

LO 10-2 Explain why companies compete abroad and evaluate advantages and disadvantages.

LO 10-3 Explain which countries MNEs target for FDI, and how they enter foreign markets.

LO 10-4 Describe the characteristics of and critically evaluate the four different strategies MNEs can pursue when competing globally.

LO 10-5 Explain why certain industries are more competitive in specific nations than in others.

LO 10-6 Evaluate the relationship between location in a regional cluster and firm-level competitive advantage.

CHAPTER CASE 10

Hollywood Goes Global

HOLLYWOOD MOVIES HAVE always been a quintessentially American product. Globalization, however, has changed the economics of the movie industry. Foreign ticket sales for Hollywood blockbusters made up 50 percent of worldwide totals in 2000; by 2010, they had jumped to nearly 70 percent. Of the total $32 billion that Hollywood movies grossed in 2010, a whopping $22 billion came from outside the United States! Today, largely due to the collapse of DVD sales, Hollywood would be unable to continue producing high-budget movies without foreign revenues, and foreign sales can make or break the success of newly released big budget movies.

Look at Exhibit 10.1 (next page), which depicts the lifetime revenues (domestic and foreign) of recent Hollywood blockbuster movies. *Avatar* is the highest-grossing movie to date, with over $2.7 billion since its release in 2009. It may surprise you to learn that non-U.S. box office sales account for almost 75 percent of that number. *Avatar* was hugely popular in Asia, especially in China, where the government gave permission to increase the number of movie theaters showing the film from 5,000 to 35,000. Another of James Cameron's

popular films, *Titanic*, grossed almost 70 percent of its $1.8 billion in overseas markets.

Given the increasing importance of non-U.S. box-office sales, especially in the BRIC countries, Hollywood studios are changing their business models. Rob Moore, Vice Chairman of Paramount Pictures, explains: "We need to make movies that have the ability to break out internationally. That's the only way to make the economic puzzle of film production work today."[1] As a result, studios are adapting scripts to appeal to global audiences, casting foreign actors in leading roles, and pulling the plug on projects that seem too U.S.-centric. For example, the film *G.I. Joe: The Rise of Cobra* prominently featured South Korean movie star Byung-hun Lee and South African actor Arnold Vosloo. On the other hand, Disney's *Wedding Banned*, a romantic comedy about a divorced couple trying to prevent their daughter from getting married, was axed in the advanced production stage despite several marquee stars (Robin Williams, Anna Faris, and Diane Keaton) because of perceptions that it would not succeed outside of the American market. Globalization also puts pressure on the pay of Hollywood stars. Given the importance of international audiences and the availability of foreign stars and movies, the days are over when stars like Tom Hanks, Eddie Murphy, and Julia Roberts can demand 20 percent royalties on total tickets sales.[2]

After reading the chapter, you will find more about this case, with related questions, on page 291.

EXHIBIT 10.1

Lifetime Revenues of Hollywood Blockbuster Movies, in $ million (release year in parentheses)

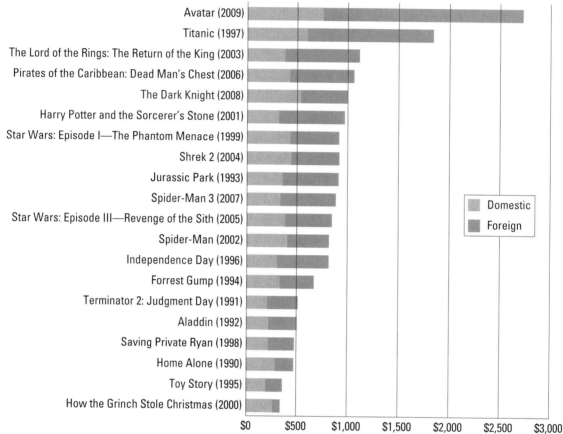

Top Movie Sales Ranking (in $million)

Source: Adapted from "Plot change: Foreign forces transform Hollywood films," *The Wall Street Journal,* August 2, 2010.

▲ **HOLLYWOOD HAS** always obtained some of its revenues from international sales, but it is now a truly global enterprise, with the vast majority of revenues coming from outside the United States. Moreover, the huge opportunities in the global movie market have also attracted new entrants. Besides wanting to cater to international audiences, Hollywood film studios are also feeling squeezed by low-cost foreign competition. For example, Bollywood, the Indian movie industry, creates its own productions and brings in low-cost but high-impact actors such as Freida Pinto and Dev Patel, who played the lead roles in the mega-success *Slumdog Millionaire. Slumdog*'s budget was merely $14 million, but the movie grossed almost $400 million and won eight Oscars. By comparison, Hollywood's budget for *Home Alone,* a similar success in terms of revenues, was nearly five times as large.

The shift in revenue sources away from the U.S. market and opportunities for future growth in emerging economies are changing the global strategy of many U.S. firms, not just Hollywood moviemakers. We noted in earlier chapters that GE and IBM are now truly global enterprises, obtaining the majority of their revenues from outside their home market. Once-unassailable U.S. firms now encounter formidable foreign competitors such as Brazil's Embraer (aerospace), China's Haier (home appliances) and Lenovo (PCs), India's

ArcelorMittal (steel), Infosys (IT services) and Reliance Group (conglomerate), Mexico's Cemex (cement), Russia's Gazprom (energy), South Korea's LG and Samsung (both in electronics and appliances), and Sweden's IKEA (home furnishings), to name just a few. This chapter is about how firms gain and sustain competitive advantage in a global world.

The competitive playing field is becoming increasingly global, as the ChapterCase about the movie industry indicates. This globalization provides significant opportunities for individuals, companies, and countries. Indeed, you can probably see the increase in globalization on your own campus. The number of students enrolled at universities outside their native countries tripled between 1980 (about one million students) to 2010 (three million students).[3] The country of choice for foreign students remains the United States, with some 600,000 enrolled per year, followed by the UK with some 360,000 foreign university students. The $40 billion higher-education industry is only one example of a global market. Taken together, the world's marketplace—made up of some 200 countries—is a staggering $60 trillion in gross domestic product (GDP), of which the U.S. market is $14 trillion, or about 23 percent.[4]

Chapter 8 looked at two dimensions of the corporate-strategy space (see Exhibit 8.1, page 203): managing the degree of vertical integration, and deciding which products and services to offer (horizontal integration and diversification). The question of how to compete effectively around the world is the third dimension of corporate strategy. We begin our study of global strategy by defining globalization before we discuss its strategic implications for competitive advantage.

WHAT IS GLOBALIZATION?

Globalization is a process of closer integration and exchange between different countries and peoples worldwide, made possible by falling trade and investment barriers, tremendous advances in telecommunications, and drastic reductions in transportation costs.[5] Combined, these factors reduce the costs of doing business around the world, opening the doors to a much larger market than any one home country. Consequently, the world's market economies are becoming more integrated and interdependent.

>> **LO 10-1**
Define globalization, multinational enterprise (MNE), foreign direct investment (FDI), and global strategy.

Globalization has led to significant increases in living standards in many economies around the world. Germany and Japan, countries that were basically destroyed after World War II, turned into industrial powerhouses, fueled by export-led growth. More recently, the Asian Tigers—Hong Kong, Singapore, South Korea, and Taiwan—turned themselves from underdeveloped countries into advanced economies, enjoying some of the world's highest standards of living. Today, the BRIC countries (Brazil, Russia, India, and China), with more than 40 percent of the world's population and producing roughly half of the world's economic growth over the last decade, are growing at a much faster clip than the developed industrial economies, and thus offer significant business opportunities.[6]

The engine behind globalization is the multinational enterprise (MNE)—a company that deploys resources and capabilities in the procurement, production, and distribution of goods and services in at least two countries. By making investments in value-chain activities abroad, MNEs thus engage in foreign direct investment (FDI).[7] For example, in order to avoid voluntary import restrictions, to take advantage of business-friendly conditions

---

globalization Process of closer integration and exchange between different countries and peoples worldwide, made possible by falling trade and investment barriers, advances in telecommunications, and reductions in transportation costs.

multinational enterprise (MNE) A company that deploys resources and capabilities in the procurement, production, and distribution of goods and services in at least two countries.

foreign direct investment (FDI) A firm's investments in value-chain activities abroad.

(low taxes, low labor cost, lower cost of living, and other incentives provided by host states) in the southern United States, and to be closer to customers in North America, the German carmaker Volkswagen recently invested $1 billion in its Chattanooga, Tennessee, plant.[8] MNEs need an effective global strategy that enables them to gain and sustain a competitive advantage when competing against other foreign and domestic companies around the world.[9]

Well-known U.S. multinational enterprises include Boeing, Caterpillar, CNN, Coca-Cola, GE, John Deere, Exxon Mobil, IBM, P&G, and Walmart. According to a 2010 research report,[10] U.S. MNEs have a disproportionally positive impact on the U.S. economy. They make up less than 1 percent of the number of total U.S. companies, but they:

- Account for 11 percent of private-sector employment growth since 1990.
- Employ 19 percent of the work force.
- Pay 25 percent of the wages.
- Account for 31 percent of the U.S. gross domestic product (GDP).
- Make up 74 percent of private-sector R&D spending.

As they attempt to take advantage of opportunities in the global economy, U.S. MNEs seem to decouple more and more from their home country. Their headquarters may still be in the United States, and they are listed on U.S. stock exchanges (e.g., NYSE or NASDAQ), but their future growth is expected to come more and more from emerging economies. In preparation, companies like GM, HP, IBM, and Microsoft are adding employees overseas while reducing domestic employment.[11]

This trend indeed raises the interesting question, "What defines a U.S. company?" If it's the address of the headquarters, then IBM, GE, and others are U.S. companies—despite the fact that a majority of their employees work outside the United States. On the other hand, non-U.S. companies such as carmakers from Japan (Toyota, Honda, and Nissan) and South Korea (Hyundai and Kia) and several engineering companies (Siemens from Germany, and ABB, a Swiss-Swedish MNE) all have made significant investments in the United States and created a large number of well-paying jobs.

As a business student, you have several reasons to be interested in MNEs. Not only can these companies provide interesting work assignments in different locations throughout the world, but they also frequently offer the highest-paying jobs for college graduates. Even if you don't want to work for an MNE, chances are that the organization you will be working for will do business with one, so it's important to understand how they compete around the globe.

Strategy Highlight 10.1 provides a brief overview of three distinct stages of globalization, each stage of which reflects a different global strategy pursued by MNEs headquartered in the United States.

GOING GLOBAL: WHY?

Clearly, the decision to pursue a global strategy comes from the firm's assessment that doing so will enhance its competitive advantage and that the benefits of globalization will exceed the costs. Here we consider both the advantages and disadvantages of "going global."

Advantages of Expanding Internationally

Why do firms expand internationally? The main reasons firms expand abroad are to:

- Gain access to a larger market
- Gain access to low-cost input factors
- Develop new competencies

Stages of Globalization

Since the beginning of the twentieth century, globalization has proceeded through three notable stages.

GLOBALIZATION 1.0: 1900–1941. Globalization 1.0 took place from about 1900 through the early years of World War II. In that period, basically all the important business functions were located in the home country. Typically, only sales and distribution operations took place overseas—essentially exporting goods to other markets. In some instances, firms procured raw materials from overseas. Strategy formulation and implementation as well as knowledge flows followed a one-way path—from domestic headquarters to international outposts. This time period saw the blossoming of the idea of MNEs, but ended with the U.S. entry into World War II.

GLOBALIZATION 2.0: 1945–2000. With the end of World War II came a new focus on growing business—not only to meet the needs that went unfulfilled during the war years but also to reconstruct the damage from the war. From 1945 to the end of the 20th century, in the Globalization 2.0 stage, MNEs began to create smaller, self-contained copies of themselves, with all business functions intact, in a few key countries (notably, Western European countries, Japan, and Australia).

This strategy required significant amounts of foreign direct investment. Although it was costly to duplicate business functions in overseas outposts, doing so allowed for greater local responsiveness to country-specific circumstances. While the corporate headquarters back in the U.S. set overarching strategic goals and allocated resources through the capital budgeting process, local mini-MNE replicas had considerable leeway in day-to-day operations. Knowledge flow back to U.S. headquarters, however, remained limited in most instances.

GLOBALIZATION 3.0: 21ST CENTURY. We are now in the Globalization 3.0 stage. MNEs that had been at the vanguard of globalization have now become global-collaboration networks (see Exhibit 10.2). Such companies now freely locate business functions anywhere in the world based on an optimal mix of costs, capabilities, and PESTEL factors. Huge investments in fiber-optic cable networks around the world have effectively reduced communication distances, enabling companies to operate 24/7, 365 days a year. When an engineer in Minneapolis, Minnesota, leaves for the evening, an engineer in Mumbai, India, begins her workday. In the Globalization 3.0 stage, the MNE's strategic objective changes. The MNE reorganizes from a multinational company with self-contained operations in a few selected countries to a more seamless global enterprise with centers of expertise. Each of these centers of expertise is a hub within a global network for delivering products and services. Consulting companies, for example, can now tap into a worldwide network of experts in real time, rather than relying on the limited number of employees in their local offices.[12]

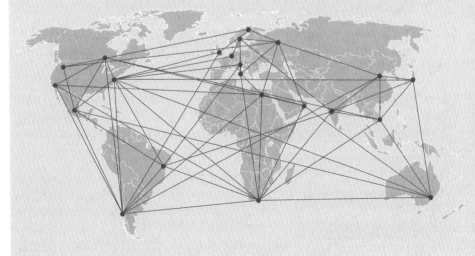

EXHIBIT 10.2

Globalization 3.0: 21st Century

Based on an optimal mix of costs, skills, and PESTEL factors, MNEs are global-collaboration networks that perform business functions throughout the world.

Source: Adapted from IBM (2009), *A Decade of Generating Higher Value at IBM*, IBM report, www.ibm .com.

GAIN ACCESS TO A LARGER MARKET. Becoming an MNE provides significant opportunities for U.S. companies, given the huge economies of scale and scope that can be reaped by participating in a much larger and more diverse market. At the same time, some countries with relatively weak domestic demand, such as China, Germany, and Japan, focus on export-led economic growth, which in turn drives many of their domestic businesses to become MNEs.

Even though the United States (with approximately 310 million people and a GDP of $14 trillion) is still the single largest economy in the world, many U.S. companies earn a significant amount of their revenues internationally. Exhibit 10.3 shows international sales as a percentage of total sales in 2010 for selected U.S. MNEs. Leading the pack, Intel obtained 80 percent of its total revenues ($44 billion) from international sales, followed by Caterpillar (67 percent, $43 billion), IBM (63 percent, $100 billion), Apple (57 percent, $87 billion), GE (53 percent, $150 billion), Boeing (42 percent, $65 billion), and Starbucks (30 percent, $11 billion). In 2010, Walmart earned about a quarter of its total sales outside the U.S. and is growing its global business at a double-digit rate. With annual sales at over $400 billion, this equates to more than $100 billion a year in global sales—a spot that would put Walmart's global unit, if it were a standalone enterprise, in the Fortune 20. Despite these impressive numbers, though, Walmart has been struggling in some major foreign markets, such as South Korea and Japan, and even exited Germany altogether (as we discuss later in the chapter).

GM once held more than 50 percent of the U.S. auto market and was the undisputed leader in global car sales between 1931 and 2008. In its heyday, GM employed 350,000 U.S. workers and was an American icon. Today, with a dismal domestic performance, GM's future will likely depend on its performance in China and other emerging economies, as Strategy Highlight 10.2 discusses.

For companies based in smaller economies, becoming an MNE may be necessary to achieve growth or to gain and sustain competitive advantage. Examples include Acer (Taiwan), Casella Wines (Australia), Nestlé (Switzerland), Nokia (Finland), Philips (Netherlands), Samsung (South Korea), and Zara (Spain). Unless companies in smaller economies "go global," their domestic markets are often too small for them to reach significant economies of scale to compete effectively against other MNEs.

EXHIBIT 10.3

International Sales as a Percentage of Total Sales in 2010 for Selected U.S. MNEs

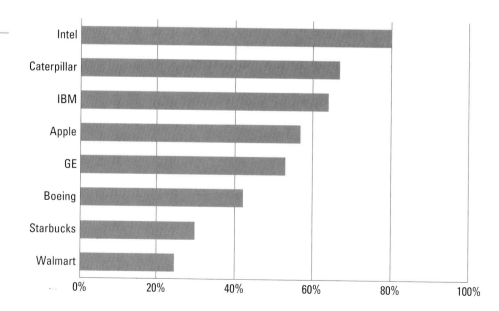

In the digital age, some MNEs are even *born global*—their founders start them with the intent of running global operations. Internet-based companies such as Amazon, eBay, Google, and LinkedIn by nature have a global presence. Indeed, Facebook, with over 600 million members around the globe, would—if it were a country—be the third most populous country worldwide after China (1.4 billion) and India (1.2 billion).[14] To better customize their websites to suit local preferences and cultures, these companies still tend to establish offices and maintain computer servers in different countries.[15] (See, for example, www.amazon.cn for China, www.amazon.de for Germany, and www.amazon.fr for France.)

Brick-and-mortar firms also can be born global. Logitech, the maker of personal peripherals such as computer mice, presentation "clickers," and video game controllers, started in Switzerland but established offices right away in Silicon Valley, California.[16] (Its two founders, one Swiss and the other Italian, each held master's degrees from Stanford University.) Pursuing a global strategy right from the start allowed Logitech to tap into the innovation expertise contained in Silicon Valley.[17] In 2010, Logitech had sales of $2 billion, with offices throughout the Americas, Asia, and Europe. Underlying Logitech's innovation competence is a network of best-in-class skills around the globe. Moreover, Logitech can organize work continuously as its teams in different locations around the globe can work 24/7.

GAIN ACCESS TO LOW-COST INPUT FACTORS.

Access to cheap raw materials such as lumber, iron ore, oil, and coal was a key driver behind Globalization 1.0 and 2.0. During Globalization 3.0, firms have expanded globally to benefit from lower labor costs in manufacturing and services. India reigns supreme in business process outsourcing (BPO), due not only to low-cost labor but also to an abundance of well-educated, English-speaking young people. Infosys and Wipro are the two most famous Indian IT service companies. Taken together, these companies employ close to 250,000 people and provide services to many of the Global Fortune 500. Many MNEs have close business ties with Indian IT firms. Some, like IBM, are engaged in foreign direct investment through equity alliances or building their own IT and customer-service centers in India. More than a quarter of Accenture's work force, a consultancy specializing in technology and outsourcing, is now in Bangalore, India.[18]

STRATEGY HIGHLIGHT 10.2

Does GM's Future Lie in China?

With a population of 1.4 billion and currently only one vehicle per 100 people—compared with a vehicle density of 94 per 100 in the U.S.—China offers tremendous growth opportunities for the automotive industry. Since China joined the World Trade Organization (WTO) in 2001, its domestic auto market has been growing at double digits annually and has now overtaken the U.S. as the largest in the world.

GM entered China in 1997 through a joint venture with Shanghai Automotive Industrial Corp (SAIC). Today, the Chinese market already accounts for 25 percent of GM's total revenues. Moreover, GM's China operation has been cost-competitive from day one. The company operates about the same number of assembly plants in China as in the U.S., but sells more vehicles while employing about half the number of employees. Chinese workers cost the firm only a fraction of what U.S. workers cost, and GM is not weighed down by additional health care and pension obligations.

GM's Buick brand is considered a luxury vehicle in China. However, GM's future may lie in the Wuling Sunshine, a small, boxy, purely functional vehicle that is currently the best-selling model in China. Priced between $5,000 and $10,000 (depending on what options the customer chooses), GM sold about 600,000 in 2009. The Wuling Sunshine may help GM further penetrate the Chinese market; it also may be an introductory car for other emerging markets, such as India. GM's low-cost strategy with this vehicle has been so successful that the firm is planning to expand the Wuling product line and offer the Wuling entry-level vehicle globally. GM already sells the Wuling Sunshine in Brazil under the Buick nameplate.

GM is betting its future on China and other emerging economies in Asia, Latin America, and the Middle East as it reinvents itself to become a lean and low-cost manufacturer of profitable small cars. To back up its strategic intent, GM has quadrupled its engineering and design personnel in China and is investing a quarter-billion dollars to build a cutting-edge R&D center on its Shanghai campus, home of its international headquarters. With car markets in the U.S. and Europe plagued by declining demand and over-capacity, GM's future may not be decided in Detroit, but in Shanghai.[13]

Likewise, China has emerged as a manufacturing powerhouse due to low labor costs and an efficient infrastructure. An American manufacturing worker costs about 20 times more in wages alone than a similarly skilled worker in China.[19] A significant cost differential exists not only for low-skilled labor, but for high-skilled labor as well. A Chinese engineer trained at Purdue University, for example, works for only a quarter of the salary in his native country compared with an engineer working in the U.S.[20] Of course, this wage disparity also reflects the difference in the two countries' cost of living.

DEVELOP NEW COMPETENCIES. Some MNEs now also pursue a global strategy in order to develop new competencies.[21] These companies are making foreign direct investments to be part of *communities of learning,* which are often contained in regional clusters.[22] AstraZeneca, a Swiss-based pharmaceutical company, relocated its research facility to Cambridge, Massachusetts, to be part of the Boston biotech cluster, in hopes of developing new R&D competencies in biotechnology.[23] Cisco is investing more than $1 billion to create an Asian headquarters in Bangalore, in order to be right in the middle of India's top IT location.[24] Unilever's new-concept center is located in downtown Shanghai, China, attracting hundreds of eager volunteers to test the firm's latest product innovations onsite, while Unilever researchers monitor consumer reactions. In these examples, AstraZeneca, Cisco, and Unilever all reap location economies—benefits from locating value-chain activities in optimal geographies for a specific activity, wherever that may be.[25]

location economies Benefits from locating value-chain activities in the world's optimal geographies for a specific activity, wherever that may be.

Many MNEs now are replacing the one-way innovation flow from Western economies to developing markets with a *polycentric innovation strategy*—a strategy in which MNEs now draw on multiple, equally important innovation hubs throughout the world (characteristic of Globalization 3.0; see Exhibit 10.2). GE Global Research, for example, orchestrates a "network of excellence" with facilities in Niskayuna, NY (USA), Bangalore (India), Shanghai (China), and Munich (Germany). Indeed, emerging economies are becoming hotbeds for low-cost innovations that find their way back to developed markets. In Bangalore, GE researchers developed the Mac 400, a handheld electrocardiogram (ECG).[26] The device is small, portable, and runs on batteries. While a conventional ECG costs $2,000, this handheld version costs $800 and enables doctors to do an ECG test at a cost of only $1 per patient. The Mac 400 is now making its entry as a disruptive innovation into the U.S. and other Western markets, with anticipated widespread use in the offices of general practitioners and emergency ambulances.

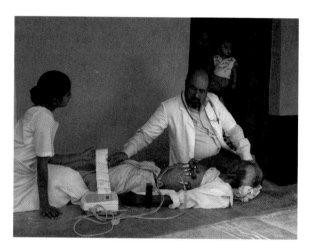

The GE Mac 400 device is small, portable, and enables doctors to do an ECG test in non-hospital settings and at low cost. It is now making its entry as a disruptive innovation in Western markets.

Disadvantages of Expanding Internationally

liability of foreignness Additional costs of doing business in an unfamiliar cultural and economic environment, and of coordinating across geographic distances.

In international expansion, firms also face some risks. In addition to the marginal costs of adding new operations, MNEs doing business abroad also must overcome the liability of foreignness. This liability consists of the additional costs of doing business in an unfamiliar cultural and economic environment, and of coordinating across geographic distances.[27] Despite such costs, many firms find that the benefits of doing business abroad outweigh the costs.

There have also been some unfortunate side-effects of the MNEs' search for low-cost labor. Low wages, long hours, and poor working and living conditions contributed to a spate of suicides at Foxconn, in China.[28] The Taiwanese company, which employs more than 800,000 people, manufactures electronics, computers, and game consoles for Apple, Dell, HP, LG, Microsoft, Nintendo, Nokia, Sony, and other well-known clients. Similarly, the Japanese carmaker Honda faced labor unrest at some of its plants in China over wage issues and working conditions.[29]

China's labor costs are steadily rising in tandem with an improved standard of living, especially in the coastal regions, where wages have risen 50 percent since 2005.[30] Some MNEs have boosted wages an extra 30 percent following the recent unrest. Many now offer bonuses to blue-collar workers and are taking other measures to avoid sweatshop allegations that have plagued companies like Nike and Levi Strauss in the past. Rising wages, fewer workers due to the effects of China's one-child-per-family policy, and appreciation of the Chinese currency now combine to lessen the country's advantage in low-cost manufacturing.[31]

Economic development has two consequences for MNEs. First, rising wages (and other costs) are likely to negate any benefits of access to low-cost input factors. Second, as the standard of living rises in emerging economies, MNEs are hoping that increased purchasing power will enable workers to purchase the products they used to make for export only.[32] This shift is in alignment with the Chinese government's economic policy, which wants to see a move from "Made in China" to "Designed in China," to capture more of the value added.[33] Also, constantly on the lookout for lower-cost alternatives in a "race-to-the-bottom," MNEs are now looking to invest in countries like Vietnam and Cambodia.

Finally, the issue of protecting intellectual property in foreign markets also looms large. The software, movie, and music industries have long lamented large-scale copyright infringements in many foreign markets. In addition, when required to partner with a foreign host firm, companies may find their intellectual property being siphoned off. Japanese and European engineering companies entered China, for example, to participate in building the world's largest network of high-speed trains worth billions of dollars.[34] Companies such as Kawasaki Heavy Industries (Japan), Siemens (Germany), and Alstom (France) were joint-venture partners with domestic Chinese companies. These firms now allege that the Chinese partners built on the Japanese and European partners' advanced technology to create their own, next-generation high-speed trains. To make matters worse, they also claim that the Chinese companies now compete *against them* in other lucrative foreign markets, such as Saudi Arabia and Brazil, with trains of equal or better capabilities but at much lower prices. This example highlights the *intellectual property exposure* that firms can face when expanding overseas.

GOING GLOBAL: WHERE AND HOW?

After discussing why companies expand internationally, we now turn our attention to the question of which countries firms choose to enter, and how they do so.

>> **LO 10-3**
Explain which countries MNEs target for FDI, and how they enter foreign markets.

Which Countries Do MNEs Enter?

As we have seen, the primary drivers behind firms engaging in FDI are to gain access to larger markets and low-cost input factors and to develop new competencies. Often, several countries and locations will work. Ireland and Portugal, for example, have similar cost structures, and both provide access to the 500 million customers in the European Union. In such cases, how does an MNE decide? When more than one country makes an attractive investment target (in terms of market size, cost of input factors, or the ability to develop competencies), *additional* factors influence the decision of *where* to invest. Two country-level factors play an important role:

- National institutions
- National culture

NATIONAL INSTITUTIONS. First, MNEs consider whether countries in which they may invest have strong legal and ethical pillars as well as well-functioning economic institutions such as capital markets and an independent central bank. Such institutions, both formal and informal, reduce uncertainty, and thus reduce transaction costs.[35] *Formal institutions* are the political and legal factors that can be analyzed according to the PESTEL framework (introduced in Chapter 3). Many European countries, for example, have more stringent environmental and data-privacy regulations than the U.S. or Asian countries. *Informal institutions* comprise the social factors of the PESTEL framework such as norms, customs, culture, and ethics. For example, although managers in many Latin countries expect their administrative assistants to serve coffee during business meetings or even run personal errands such as picking up dry cleaning, these activities are generally not part of an admin's job description in the United States (due to a different understanding about what would be considered discrimination or use of company resources for personal business).[36] Informal rules and norms are closely intertwined with a country's national culture. Institutions set the formal and informal rules of the game by which managers must play in their pursuit of competitive advantage.[37]

NATIONAL CULTURE. Dutch researcher Geert Hofstede studied what he termed national culture, the collective mental and emotional "programming of the mind" that differentiates human groups.[38] Although there is no one-size-fits-all culture that accurately describes any nation, Hofstede's work provides a useful tool to guide FDI decisions. Based on data analysis from more than 100,000 individuals from many different countries, four dimensions of culture emerged: power distance, individualism, masculinity–femininity, and uncertainty avoidance.[39] Hofstede's data analysis yielded scores for the different countries, for each dimension, on a range of zero to 100, with 100 as the high end. (More recently, Hofstede added a fifth cultural dimension: *long-term orientation*. The available data on that fifth dimension is not, at this point, as comprehensive as for the four original dimensions.)

Power-Distance. The power-distance dimension of national culture focuses on how a society deals with inequality among people in terms of physical and intellectual capabilities and how those methods translate into power distributions within organizations. High power-distance cultures, like the Philippines (94/100, with 100 = high), tend to allow inequalities among people to translate into inequalities in opportunity, power, status, and wealth. Low power-distance cultures, like Austria (11/100), on the other hand, tend to intervene to create a more equal distribution among people within organizations and society at large.

Individualism. The individualism dimension of national culture focuses on the relationship between individuals in a society, particularly in regard to the relationship between individual and collective pursuits. In highly individualistic cultures, like the U.S. (91/100), individual freedom and achievements are highly valued. As a result, individuals are only tied loosely to one another within society. In less-individualistic cultures, like Venezuela (12/100), the collective good is emphasized over the individual, and members of society are strongly tied to one another throughout their lifetimes by virtue of birth into groups like extended families.

Masculinity–Femininity. The masculinity–femininity dimension of national culture focuses on the relationship between genders and its relation to an individual's role at work and in society. In more "masculine" cultures, like Japan (95/100), gender roles tend to be clearly defined and sharply differentiated. In "masculine" cultures, values like competitiveness, assertiveness, and exercise of power are considered cultural ideals, and men are expected to behave accordingly. In more "feminine" cultures, like Sweden (5/100), values like cooperation, humility, and harmony are guiding cultural principles. The masculinity–femininity dimension uncovered in Hofstede's research is undoubtedly evolving over time, and values and behaviors are converging to some extent.

Uncertainty-Avoidance. The uncertainty-avoidance dimension of national culture focuses on societal differences in tolerance toward ambiguity and uncertainty. In particular, it highlights the extent to which members of a certain culture feel anxious when faced with uncertain or unknown situations. Members of high uncertainty-avoidance cultures, like Russia (95/100), value clear rules and regulations as well as clearly structured career patterns, lifetime employment, and retirement benefits. Members of low uncertainty-avoidance cultures, like Singapore (8/100), have greater tolerance toward ambiguity and thus exhibit less emotional resistance to change and a greater willingness to take risks.

When Starbucks entered the Chinese market in 2000, it sought to decrease the liability of foreignness by handing out keychains, to help new customers learn how to order. Layered cylinders on the mini coffee cup represent drink options—caffeinated or not, number of espresso shots, type of syrup, and so on. The customer spins the choices into the desired position and hands the keychain to the barista.

Hofstede's national-culture research becomes even more useful for managers by combining the four distinct dimensions of culture into an aggregate measure for each country. MNEs then can compare the national-culture measures for any two country pairings to inform their entry decisions.[40] The difference between scores indicates cultural distance, the cultural disparity between the internationally expanding firm's home country and its targeted host country. A firm's decision to enter certain international markets is influenced by cultural differences, and a greater cultural distance can increase the cost and uncertainty of conducting business abroad. In short, greater cultural distance increases the liability of foreignness. If we calculate the cultural distance from the U.S. to various countries, for example, we find that some countries are culturally very close to the U.S. (e.g., Australia with an overall cultural distance score of 0.02), while others are culturally quite distant (e.g., Russia with an overall cultural distance score of 4.42). As can be expected, English-speaking countries such as Canada (0.12), Ireland (0.35), New Zealand (0.26), and the UK (0.09) all exhibit a low cultural distance to the United States. Since culture is embedded in language, it comes as no surprise that cultural and linguistic differences are highly correlated. This implies that companies from Spanish-speaking countries often conduct FDI in other Spanish-speaking countries, and so on.

Although Hofstede's work made a significant contribution to the understanding of national cultures, it is not without drawbacks. One shortcoming of Hofstede's work is that

---

national culture The collective mental and emotional "programming of the mind" that differentiates human groups.

power-distance dimension Dimension of culture that focuses on how a society deals with inequality among people in terms of physical and intellectual capabilities, and how those methods translate into power distributions within organizations.

individualism dimension Dimension of culture that focuses on the relationship between individuals in a society, particularly the relationship between individual and collective pursuits.

masculinity–femininity dimension Dimension of culture that focuses on the relationship between genders and its relation to an individual's role at work and in society.

uncertainty-avoidance dimension Dimension of culture that focuses on societal differences in tolerance toward ambiguity and uncertainty.

cultural distance Cultural disparity between an internationally expanding firm's home country and its targeted host country.

although the sample was large, all individuals worked for IBM, a U.S. MNE. This can introduce a selection bias because IBM does not recruit randomly among the population. Another caveat is that Hofstede's data is a few decades old, and national cultures may have changed over time. Some argue that with the widespread use of modern telecommunications (e.g., Internet and mobile phones), cultures and values have converged to some extent.[41]

COMBINING NATIONAL INSTITUTIONS AND NATIONAL CULTURE. Taken together, both national institutions and national culture are important factors for MNEs to consider when deciding which countries to enter. As an example, beginning in the 1980s, several U.S. high-tech companies were eager to make investments in the European Union to access its large and affluent consumer market. Ireland was the preferred choice for many U.S. MNEs for the country's low cultural distance from the U.S., as well as for institutional reasons.[42] In particular, many MNEs chose Ireland as the premier location for FDI into Europe because it has one of the world's lowest corporate tax rates. Exhibit 10.4 shows that Ireland's corporate tax rate is a mere 12.5 percent compared with 33.3 percent in France. Incidentally, at 40 percent, the United States has one of the highest corporate tax rates in the world.

Because of its attractive institutional framework and low cultural distance, Ireland received roughly one-quarter of all U.S. FDI into the EU.[43] The chipmaker Intel invested some $5 billion just west of Dublin to build the largest and most advanced chipmaking facility in the world. HP is one of the biggest employers in the western part of Ireland. Apple located its European software development and support center in Ireland. Likewise, Dell has made significant investments in Ireland. More recently, the consulting firm Accenture moved its location of incorporation to Ireland, citing Ireland's economic, political, and legal strengths.[44] A significant amount of the $1.2 trillion in 2009 FDI focused on BRIC countries, with China and Brazil leading the pack.[45]

How Do MNEs Enter Foreign Markets?

Assuming an MNE has decided why and where to enter a foreign market, the remaining decision is *how* to do so. Exhibit 10.5 displays the different options managers have when

EXHIBIT 10.4

Corporate Tax Rates in Different European Countries and U.S.

Source: Author's depiction of data from "Switzerland's states compete on tax cuts," *The Wall Street Journal*, February 2, 2010. Switzerland is not part of the EU, but due to bilateral agreements with many EU members, FDI into Switzerland also provides preferred access to the EU market.

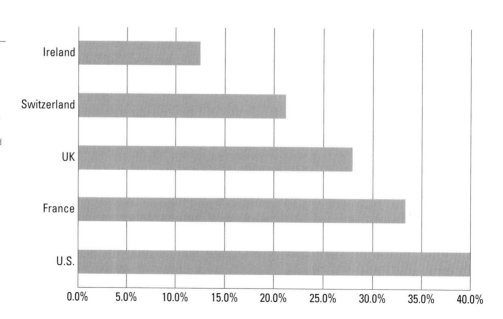

EXHIBIT 10.5

Modes of Foreign-Market Entry along the Investment and Control Continuum

entering foreign markets, along with the required investments necessary and the control they can exert.

Exporting—producing goods in one country to sell in another—is one of the oldest forms of internationalization (part of Globalization 1.0). It is often used to test whether a foreign market is ready for a firm's products. When studying vertical integration and diversification (in Chapter 8), we discussed in detail different forms along the make-or-buy continuum. As discussed in Chapter 9, acquisitions and strategic alliances (including licensing, franchising, and joint ventures) are popular vehicles for entry into foreign markets. Since we discussed these organizational arrangements in detail in previous chapters, we therefore keep this section on foreign-entry modes brief.

The framework illustrated in Exhibit 10.5, moving from left to right, has been suggested as a *stage model* of sequential commitment to a foreign market over time.[46] Though it does not apply to globally born Internet companies, it is relevant for manufacturing companies that are just now expanding into global operations. In some instances, companies are required by the host country to form joint ventures in order to conduct business there, while some MNEs prefer *greenfield operations* (building new plants and facilities from scratch), as did Motorola when it entered China in the 1990s.[47]

STRATEGY AROUND THE WORLD: COST REDUCTIONS VS. LOCAL RESPONSIVENESS

When discussing business strategy (in Chapter 6), we noted that an effective integration strategy must resolve the inherent trade-offs between cost and differentiation. In much the same fashion, MNEs face two opposing forces when competing around the globe: *cost reductions* versus *local responsiveness*.

One of the core drivers for globalization is to expand firms' total market, in order to achieve economies of scale and drive down costs. For many business executives, the move toward globalization was based on the globalization hypothesis, advanced by Professor Theodore Levitt, which states that consumer needs and preferences throughout the world are converging and thus becoming increasingly homogenous.[48] Levitt wrote (in 1983): "Nothing confirms [the globalization hypothesis] as much as the success of McDonald's from Champs-Élysées to Ginza, of Coca-Cola in Bahrain and Pepsi-Cola in Moscow, and of rock music, Greek salad, Hollywood movies, Revlon cosmetics, Sony televisions, and Levi jeans everywhere."[49] In support of the globalization hypothesis, Toyota is selling its hybrid Prius vehicle successfully in more than 70 countries. Most vehicles today are built on global platforms and modified (sometimes only cosmetically) to meet local tastes and standards.

The strategic foundations of the globalization hypothesis are based primarily on cost reduction. One key competitive weapon is lower price, and MNEs attempt to reap significant

>> **LO 10-4**
Describe the characteristics of and critically evaluate the four different strategies that MNEs can pursue when competing globally.

globalization hypothesis
Assumption that consumer needs and preferences throughout the world are converging and thus becoming increasingly homogenous.

EXHIBIT 10.6

The Integration-Responsiveness Framework: Global Strategy Positions and Representative MNEs

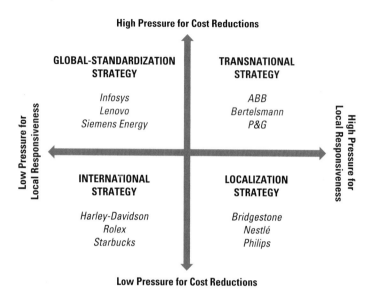

cost reductions by leveraging economies of scale and by managing global supply chains to access the lowest-cost input factors.

While there seems to be some convergence of consumer preferences across the globe, national differences remain, due to distinct institutions and cultures. For example, in the 1990s, Ford Motor Company followed this one-size-fits-all strategy by offering a more or less identical car throughout the world (the Ford Mondeo, sold as Ford Contour and Mercury Mystique in North America). Ford learned the hard way (lack of sales) that consumer preferences were not converging sufficiently to allow it to ignore regional differences.[50] In some instances, MNEs therefore experience pressure for *local responsiveness*—the need to tailor product and service offerings to fit local consumer preferences and host-country requirements. McDonald's, for example, uses mutton instead of beef in India and offers a teriyaki burger in Japan—though its basic business model of offering fast food remains the same the world over. Local responsiveness generally entails higher cost, and sometimes even outweighs cost advantages from economies of scale and lower-cost input factors.

Given the two opposing pressures of cost reductions versus local responsiveness, scholars have advanced the *integration-responsiveness framework,* shown in Exhibit 10.6.[51] This framework juxtaposes the opposing pressures for cost reductions and local responsiveness, to derive four different strategies to gain and sustain competitive advantage when competing globally. The four strategies are international strategy, localization strategy, global-standardization strategy, and transnational strategy, which we will discuss in the following sections.[52] At the end of that discussion (on page 286), Exhibit 10.7 summarizes each global strategy.

International Strategy

An *international strategy* is essentially a strategy in which a company sells the same products or services in both domestic and foreign markets. It enables MNEs to leverage their home-based core competencies in foreign markets. An international strategy is one of the oldest types of global strategies (Globalization 1.0) and is frequently the first step companies take when beginning to conduct business abroad. As shown in the integration-responsiveness framework, it is advantageous when the MNE faces low pressures for both local responsiveness and cost reductions.

An international strategy is often used successfully by MNEs with relatively large domestic markets and strong reputations and brand names. These MNEs, capitalizing on the fact that foreign customers want to buy the original product, tend to use differentiation as their preferred business strategy. For example, bikers in Poland like their Harley-Davidson motorcycles to roar just like the ones ridden by the Hells Angels in the United States. Similarly, a Brazilian entrepreneur importing machine tools from Germany expects superior engineering and quality. An international strategy tends to rely on exporting or the licensing of products and franchising of services to reap economies of scale.

A strength of the international strategy—its limited local responsiveness—is also a weakness in many industries. For example, when an MNE sells its products in foreign markets with little or no change, it leaves itself open to expropriation of intellectual property (IP). Looking at the MNE's products and services, pirates can reverse-engineer the products to discover the intellectual property embedded in them. In Thailand, for example, a flourishing market for knockoff luxury sports cars (e.g., Ferraris, Lamborghinis, and Porsches) has recently sprung up.[53] Besides the risk of exposing IP, MNEs following an international strategy are highly affected by exchange rate fluctuations. Given increasing globalization, however, fewer and fewer markets correspond to this situation—low pressures for local responsiveness and cost reductions—that gives rise to the international strategy.

Localization Strategy

MNEs pursuing a localization strategy attempt to maximize local responsiveness, hoping that local consumers will perceive them to be domestic companies. (For this reason, the localization strategy is sometimes called a *multi-domestic strategy*.) This strategy arises out of the combination of high pressure for local responsiveness and low pressure for cost reductions. MNEs frequently use a localization strategy when entering host countries with large and/or idiosyncratic domestic markets, such as Japan or Saudi Arabia. This is one of the main strategies MNEs pursued in the Globalization 2.0 stage.

A localization strategy is common in the consumer products and food industries. For example, Swiss-based Nestlé, the largest food company in the world (with revenues of $100 billion in 2010) is well known for customizing its product offerings to suit local preferences, tastes, and requirements. Given the strong brand names and core competencies in R&D and quality in the consumer products and food industries, it is not surprising that these MNEs generally pursue a differentiation strategy at the business level. An MNE following a localization strategy, in contrast with an international strategy, faces reduced exchange-rate exposure because the majority of the value creation takes place in the host country business units, which tend to span all functions.

On the downside, a localization strategy is costly and inefficient, because it requires the duplication of key business functions across multiple countries. Each country unit tends to be highly autonomous, and the MNE is unable to reap economies of scale or learning across regions. The risk of IP appropriation increases when companies follow a localization strategy. Besides exposing codified knowledge embedded in products, as is the case

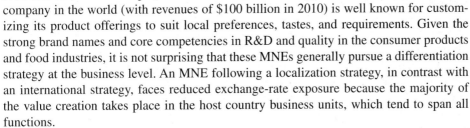

local responsiveness The need to tailor product and service offerings to fit local consumer preferences and host-country requirements; generally entails higher cost.

integration-responsiveness framework Strategy framework that juxtaposes the pressures an MNE faces for cost reductions and local responsiveness to derive four different strategies to gain and sustain competitive advantage when

competing globally: international strategy, localization strategy, global-standardization strategy, and transnational strategy.

international strategy Strategy that involves leveraging home-based core competencies by selling the same products or services in both domestic and foreign markets; advantageous when the MNE faces low pressures for both local responsiveness and cost reductions.

localization strategy Strategy pursued by MNEs that attempts to maximize local responsiveness, with the intent that local consumers will perceive them to be domestic companies; strategy arises out of the combination of high pressure for local responsiveness and low pressure for cost reductions; also called a *multi-domestic strategy*.

with an international strategy, a localization strategy also requires exposing tacit knowledge because products are manufactured locally. Tacit knowledge that is at risk of appropriation may include, for example, the process of how to create consumer products of higher perceived quality.

Global-Standardization Strategy

MNEs following a global-standardization strategy attempt to reap significant economies of scale and location economies by pursuing a global division of labor based on wherever best-of-class capabilities reside at the lowest cost. The global-standardization strategy arises out of the combination of high pressure for cost reductions and low pressure for local responsiveness. MNEs who use this strategy are often organized as networks (Globalization 3.0). This allows them to strive for the lowest cost position possible. Their business-level strategy tends to be cost leadership. Because there is little or no differentiation or local responsiveness, price becomes the main competitive weapon.

MNEs that manufacture commodity products (such as computer hardware) or offer services (such as business process outsourcing) generally pursue a global-standardization strategy. Lenovo, the Chinese computer manufacturer, is now the maker of the ThinkPad line of laptops which it acquired from IBM in 2005. To keep track of the latest developments in computing, Lenovo's research centers are located in Beijing and Shanghai in China, in Raleigh, North Carolina (in the Research Triangle Park), and in Japan.[54] To benefit from low-cost labor and to be close to its main markets in order to reduce shipping costs, Lenovo's manufacturing facilities are in Mexico, India, and China. The company describes the benefits of its global-standardization strategy insightfully: "Lenovo organizes its worldwide operations with the view that a truly global company must be able to quickly capitalize on new ideas and opportunities from anywhere. By forgoing a traditional headquarters model and focusing on centers of excellence around the world, Lenovo makes the maximum use of its resources to create the best products in the most efficient and effective way possible."[55]

One of the advantages of the global-standardization strategy—obtaining the lowest cost point possible by minimizing local adaptations—is also one of its key weaknesses. Strategy Highlight 10.3 describes how pursuing a global-standardization strategy spelled trouble for Walmart's efforts in Germany.

Transnational Strategy

MNEs pursuing a transnational strategy attempt to combine the benefits of a localization strategy (high local-responsiveness) with those of a global-standardization strategy (lowest cost position attainable). (The transnational strategy is also sometimes called *glocalization*.)[56] This strategy arises out of the combination of high pressure for local responsiveness and high pressure for cost reductions. A transnational strategy is generally used by MNEs that pursue an integration strategy at the business level by attempting to reconcile product and/or service differentiations at low cost.

Besides harnessing economies of scale and location, a transnational strategy also aims to benefit from global learning. MNEs typically implement a transnational strategy through a global matrix structure. That structure combines economies of scale along specific product divisions with economies of learning attainable in specific geographic regions. The idea is that best practices, ideas, and innovations will be diffused throughout the world, regardless of their origination. The managers' mantra is to think globally, but act locally.

global-standardization strategy Strategy attempting to reap significant economies of scale and location economies by pursuing a global division of labor based on wherever best-of-class capabilities reside at the lowest cost.

transnational strategy Strategy that attempts to combine the benefits of a localization strategy (high local-responsiveness) with those of a global-standardization strategy (lowest cost position attainable); sometimes called *glocalization*.

STRATEGY HIGHLIGHT 10.3

Walmart Retreats from Germany

In late 1997, facing a saturated U.S. market, Walmart entered Germany, then the third-largest economy in the world (behind the U.S. and Japan). At that time, the retailer was already active in six foreign countries, with some 500 stores outside the United States. Given the high pressure for cost reductions in the retail industry and Walmart's superior strategic position as the dominant cost leader in the U.S., executives decided to pursue a global-standardization strategy in Germany. In 2006, however, Walmart exited Germany, after losing billions of dollars. This massive failure came as a shock to a company that was used to success. What went wrong?

To enter Germany, Walmart acquired the 21-store Wertkauf chain and 74 hypermarkets from German retailer Spar Handels AG. Next, Walmart attempted to implement its U.S. personnel policies and procedures: the Walmart cheer, a door greeter, every associate within 10 feet of a customer smiling and offering help, bagging groceries at the checkout, video surveillance, a prohibition against dating co-workers, and so on. German employees, however, simply refused to accept these policies. There were no door greeters in the German Walmart stores. The front-line employees behaved as gruffly and rudely as they do in other retail outlets in Germany. It also didn't help that the first Walmart boss in Germany didn't speak German, and decreed that English would be the official in-house language.

Significant cultural differences aside, one of the biggest problems Walmart faced in Germany was that, lacking its usual economies of scale and efficient distribution centers, it couldn't get its costs down far enough to successfully implement its trademark cost-leadership strategy. Higher required wages and restrictive labor laws further drove up costs. As a result, the prices at Walmart in Germany weren't "always low" as the company slogan suggested, but fell in the medium range. Germany was already home to retail discount powerhouses such as Aldi and Lidl, with thousands of outlets offering higher convenience combined with lower prices. Walmart was unable to be cost-competitive against such tough domestic competition. It also faced Metro, a dominant large-box retailer, who upon entering Germany immediately initiated a price war against Walmart. In the end, a defeated Walmart sold its stores to—guess who?—Metro![57]

Although a transnational strategy is quite appealing, it is rather difficult to implement due to the organizational complexities involved. The matrix organization also is costly, because high local-responsiveness typically requires that key business functions are frequently duplicated in each host country, leading to higher costs. (We'll discuss organizational structure in more depth in the next chapter.) Further compounding the organizational complexities is the challenge of finding managers who can dexterously work across cultures in the ways required by a transnational strategy.

The German multimedia conglomerate Bertelsmann attempts to follow a transnational strategy. In 2010, Bertelsmann's revenues were 16 billion euros; it employed 104,000 people, with two-thirds of that force outside its home country. In particular, Bertelsmann operates in 63 countries throughout the world, and owns many regional leaders in their specific product categories, including Random House Publishing in the U.S. and RTL Group, Europe's second largest TV, radio, and production company (after the BBC). Bertelsmann operates its over 500 regional media divisions as more or less autonomous profit and loss centers; global learning and human resource strategies for executives are coordinated at the network level.[58]

As a summary, Exhibit 10.7 (next page) provides a detailed description of each of the four global strategies in the integration-responsiveness framework.

EXHIBIT 10.7

International, Localization, Global-Standardization, and Transnational Strategies: Characteristics, Benefits, and Risks

	Characteristics	Benefits	Risks

International Strategy	• Often the first step in internationalizing.
	• Used by MNEs with relatively large domestic markets (e.g., MNEs from U.S., Germany, Japan).
	• Well-suited for high-end products (such as machine tools) and luxury goods that can be shipped across the globe.
	• Products and services tend to have strong brands.
	• Main competitive strategy tends to be *differentiation* since exporting, licensing, and franchising add additional costs.
		• Leveraging core competence.
		• Economies of scale.
		• Low-cost implementation through:
		  • Exporting or licensing (for products)
		  • Franchising (for services)
		  • Licensing (for trademarks)
			• No or limited local responsiveness.
			• Highly affected by exchange rate fluctuations.
			• IP embedded in product or service could be expropriated.

Localization (Multi-Domestic) Strategy	• Used by MNEs to compete in host countries with large and/or lucrative but idiosyncratic domestic markets (e.g., Germany, Japan, Saudi Arabia). • Often used in consumer products and food industries. • Main competitive strategy is *differentiation*. • MNE wants to be perceived as local company.	• Highest-possible local responsiveness. • Reduced exchange-rate exposure.	• Duplication of key business functions in multiple countries leads to high cost of implementation. • Little or no economies of scale. • Little or no learning across different regions. • Higher risk of IP expropriation
Global-Standardization Strategy	• Used by MNEs that are offering standardized products and services (e.g., computer hardware or business process outsourcing). • Main competitive strategy is *price*.	• Location economies: global division of labor based on wherever best-of-class capabilities reside at lowest cost. • Economies of scale.	• No local responsiveness. • Little or no product differentiation. • Some exchange-rate exposure. • "Race to the bottom" as wages increase. • Some risk of IP expropriation.
Transnational (Glocalization) Strategy	• Used by MNEs that pursue an *integration* strategy at the business level by simultaneously focusing on product differentiation and low cost. • Mantra: Think globally, act locally.	• Attempts to combine benefits of localization and standardization strategies simultaneously by creating a global matrix structure. • Economies of scale, location, and learning.	• Global matrix structure is costly and difficult to implement, leading to high failure rate. • Some exchange-rate exposure. • Higher risk of IP expropriation.

NATIONAL COMPETITIVE ADVANTAGE: WORLD LEADERSHIP IN SPECIFIC INDUSTRIES

>> LO 10-5
Explain why certain industries are more competitive in specific nations than in others.

Globalization, the prevalence of the Internet and other advances in communications technology, and transportation logistics can lead us to believe that firm location is becoming increasingly less important.[59] Because firms can now, more than ever, source inputs globally, many believe that location must be diminishing in importance as an explanation of firm-level competitive advantage. This popular idea is called the death-of-distance hypothesis.[60] In his bestseller *The World Is Flat,* Thomas Friedman expressed a similar idea.[61]

Despite an increasingly globalized world, however, it turns out that high-performing firms in certain industries *are* concentrated in specific countries.[62] For example, the leading biotechnology, software, and Internet companies are headquartered in the United States. Some of the world's best computer manufacturers are in China and Taiwan. Many of the leading consumer electronics companies are in South Korea and Japan. The top mining companies are in Australia. The leading business process outsourcing (BPO) companies are in India. Some of the best engineering and car companies are in Germany. The world's top fashion designers are in Italy. The best wineries are in France. The list goes on. While globalization lowers the barriers to trade and investments and increases human capital mobility, one key question remains: *Why are certain industries more competitive in some countries than in others?* This question goes to the heart of the issue of national competitive advantage, a consideration of world leadership in specific industries. That issue, in turn, has a direct effect on firm-level competitive advantage.

death-of-distance hypothesis Assumption that geographic location alone should not lead to firm-level competitive advantage because firms are now, more than ever, able to source inputs globally.

national competitive advantage World leadership in specific industries.

Porter's National Competitive Advantage Framework

Michael Porter advanced a framework (see Exhibit 10.8) consisting of four interrelated factors to explain national competitive advantage:

- Factor conditions
- Demand conditions
- Competitive intensity in a focal industry
- Related and supporting industries/complementors

FACTOR CONDITIONS. *Factor conditions* describe a country's endowments in terms of natural, human, and other resources. Interestingly, natural resources are often not needed to generate world-leading companies, since competitive advantage is often based on human capital and know-how. Several of the world's most resource-rich countries (such as Afghanistan,[63] Iran, Iraq, Russia, Saudi Arabia, and Venezuela) are

EXHIBIT 10.8

Porter's Diamond of National Competitive Advantage

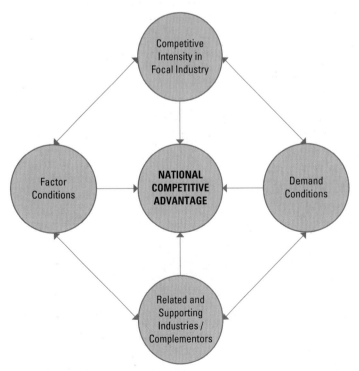

Source: Adapted from M. E. Porter (1990), "The competitive advantage of nations," *Harvard Business Review,* March–April: 78.

not home to any of the world's leading companies, even though some (though not all) do have in place institutional frameworks allowing them to be a productive member of world commerce. In contrast, countries that lack natural resources (e.g., Denmark, Finland, Israel, Japan, Singapore, South Korea, Switzerland, Taiwan, and the Netherlands) often develop world-class human capital to compensate.[64] Other important factor conditions include capital markets, a supportive institutional framework, research universities, and public infrastructure (airports, roads, schools, health care system), among others.

DEMAND CONDITIONS. *Demand conditions* are the specific characteristics of demand in a firm's domestic market. A home market made up of sophisticated customers who hold companies to a high standard of value creation and cost containment contributes to national competitive advantage. Moreover, demanding customers may also clue firms in to the latest developments in specific fields and may push firms to move research from basic findings to commercial applications for the marketplace.

For example, due to dense urban living conditions, hot and humid summers, and high energy costs, it is not surprising that Japanese customers demand small, quiet, and energy-efficient air conditioners. In contrast to the Japanese, Finns have a sparse population living in a more remote countryside. A lack of land lines for telephone service has resulted in Finnish demand for high-quality wireless services, combined with reliable handsets and long battery life that can be operated in remote areas with often hostile environments. Cell phones have long been a necessity for survival in rural areas of Finland. This situation enabled Nokia to become an early leader in cell phones.[65]

COMPETITIVE INTENSITY IN A FOCAL INDUSTRY. Companies that face a highly competitive environment at home tend to outperform global competitors that lack such intense domestic competition. Fierce domestic competition in Germany, for example, combined with demanding customers and the no-speed-limit Autobahn make a tough environment for any car company. Success requires top-notch engineering of chassis and engines as well as keeping costs and fuel consumption ($9-per-gallon gas prices) in check. This extremely tough home environment amply prepared German car companies such as Volkswagen (which also owns Audi and now Porsche), BMW, and Daimler for global competition.

RELATED AND SUPPORTING INDUSTRIES/COMPLEMENTORS. Leadership in related and supporting industries can also foster world-class competitors in downstream industries. The availability of top-notch complementors (firms that provide a good or service that leads customers to value the focal firm's offering more when the two are combined) further strengthens national competitive advantage. Switzerland, for example, leveraged its early lead in industrial chemicals into pharmaceuticals. A sophisticated health care service industry sprang up alongside as an important complementor, to provide further stimulus for growth and continuous improvement and innovation.

The effects of sophisticated customers and highly competitive industries ripple through the industry value chain to create top-notch suppliers and complementors. Toyota's global success in the 1990s and early 2000s was based to a large extent on a network of world-class suppliers in Japan.[66] This tightly knit network allowed for fast two-way knowledge sharing—this in turn improved Toyota's quality and lowered its cost, which it leveraged into a successful integration strategy at the business level.

It is also interesting to note that by 2010, Toyota's supplier advantage had disappeared.[67] It was unable to solve the trade-off between drastically increasing its volume while maintaining superior quality. Toyota's rapid growth to becoming the world's leader in volume required quickly bringing on new suppliers outside of Japan, and quality standards couldn't be maintained. Part of the problem lies in path dependence (discussed in Chapter 4), as Chinese and other suppliers could not be found quickly enough, nor could most foreign suppliers build at the required quality levels fast enough. The cultural distance between Japan and China exacerbated these problems. Combined, these factors explain the quality problems Toyota experienced recently, and serve to highlight the importance of related and supporting industries to national competitive advantage.

REGIONAL CLUSTERS

GAINING & SUSTAINING COMPETITIVE ADVANTAGE

Although the death-of-distance hypothesis seems intuitive, a closer look at the economic geography at the beginning of the 21st century raises some doubts. Not only are the leading firms in specific industries located in a small number of specific countries, they also tend to be co-located in regional clusters. A regional cluster is a group of interconnected companies and institutions in a specific industry, located near each other geographically and otherwise linked by common characteristics.[68]

If globalization and drastic advancements in technology indeed reduce the importance of firm location, what accounts for the thriving clusters of computer technology firms in Silicon Valley, medical device firms in the Chicago area, and biotechnology firms in Boston? This is not only a U.S. phenomenon, it holds worldwide. Known for their engineering prowess, car companies such as Daimler, BMW, Audi, and Porsche are clustered in southern Germany. High-performance Formula One racecars are designed and crafted in England's Motor Sport Valley, near London. Many fashion-related companies (clothing, shoes, and accessories) are located in northern Italy. Singapore is a well-known cluster for semiconductor materials. India's leading BPO firms are in Bangalore. Critical masses of world-class firms are clearly apparent in these regional clusters. Here, we put under the strategy microscope the question of whether regional clusters contribute to firm-level competitive advantage.

>> **LO 10-6**
Evaluate the relationship between location in a regional cluster and firm-level competitive advantage.

The academic literature provides evidence for a positive link between firm location in a regional cluster and competitive advantage.[69] In fact, it is surprising to learn that in light of globalization and the emergence of the Internet, firm location has actually become *more* important. Porter captures this phenomenon succinctly: "Paradoxically, the enduring competitive advantages in a global economy lie increasingly in local things—knowledge, relationships, and motivation that distant rivals cannot match."[70]

Let's look at one regional cluster in more depth: the Research Triangle Park (RTP) in North Carolina (depicted in Exhibit 10.9, next page), bounded by the cities of Chapel Hill, Durham, and Raleigh.[71] Several important cluster ingredients are readily apparent: top-notch research universities (The University of North Carolina at Chapel Hill, Duke University, and North Carolina State University); well-known MNEs (BASF, Bayer, Cisco Systems, Ericsson, and IBM, among others); good interstate highway connections; and an international airport. The RTP has one of the highest concentrations of PhDs worldwide, and it continues to attract the brightest students, researchers, and knowledge workers from around the world.

The Research Triangle contains two distinct clusters, a biopharma cluster and a communications-technology cluster. These two clusters are anchored by both U.S. and foreign MNEs. Indeed, MNEs have operations in roughly 80 percent of all research clusters around the world. The RTP alone provides some 40,000 well-paying jobs, with about 80 percent of them working for MNEs. Researchers estimate that each job in the RTP creates an additional 2.5 jobs in North Carolina, for a total of 140,000 jobs. The RTP's resident firms gain and sustain a competitive advantage based on innovation: they have generated more than 5,000 patents and well-known service and product breakthroughs such as UPC bar code, Astroturf, and 3-D ultrasound.

regional cluster A group of interconnected companies and institutions in a specific industry, located near each other geographically and also linked by common characteristics.

EXHIBIT 10.9

Mapping a Regional Cluster: Research Triangle Park, North Carolina

Source: Adapted from McKinsey Global Institute (2010), *Growth and Competitiveness in the United States: The Role of Its Multinational Companies* (London), p. 13.

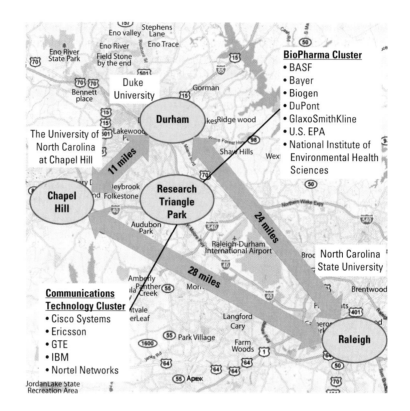

As this peek at the RTP indicates, being located in a cluster has many associated benefits: Firms located in clusters frequently benefit from knowledge spillovers provided by research universities and other firms in the vicinity. Knowledge spillovers are positive externalities that are regionally constrained.[72] A university or firm engaging in basic and applied research generates knowledge spillovers when employees, for example, share research ideas and their latest findings through informal social interactions (e.g., at a bar or their children's soccer games).

Moreover, regional clusters provide high labor mobility, because people can change jobs without moving. A software engineer can easily spend his/her entire life in the Silicon Valley and work for many different companies over the course of a career. Geographic proximity and close interactions among cluster firms, over time, contribute to the development of trust and enhance interorganizational exchange. Clusters provide more flexibility than vertical integrated hierarchies or networks of formalized alliances because firms within clusters are generally linked through informal ties.[73]

Finally, firms in a cluster often have privileged access to venture capital (VC) firms, which tend to co-locate near premier research universities in order to evaluate and fund commercially viable research.[74] This benefit is particularly critical for new-venture creation because VCs provide not only capital but also strategic and technical assistance. That assistance often takes the form of a monitoring role on the new venture's board of directors. Leading venture capital firms such as Kleiner Perkins Caufield & Byers (KPCB) in Silicon

knowledge spillover
A type of positive externality that is regionally constrained.

Valley tend to actively recruit managers, lawyers, suppliers, and customers for its portfolio companies. Because relationships between venture capitalists and their portfolio companies tend to be deep and extensive, venture capitalists generally prefer to fund ventures that are located nearby, mostly within the regional cluster. KPCB, for example, provided early-stage funding for Electronic Arts, Google, Genentech, Genomic Health, Intuit, Sun Microsystems, and VeriSign—all located in Silicon Valley.

In sum, there is strong empirical evidence that being located in a regional cluster can have a positive effect on firm competitive advantage, not only domestically, but also globally. The RTP example provides support for the paradox that, in a globalized world, the basis for firm-level competitive advantage is often local. 🔍

This concludes our discussion of global strategy. Moreover, we have now completed our study of the first two pillars of the AFI framework—Strategy Analysis (Chapters 1–5) and Strategy Formulation (Chapters 6–10). Next, we turn to the third pillar of the AFI framework— Strategy Implementation. In Chapter 11, we'll study what managers can do to implement their carefully crafted strategies successfully and how to avoid failure. In Chapter 12, we study corporate governance, business ethics, and strategic leadership.

CHAPTERCASE 10 | *Consider This . . .*

THE CHAPTERCASE discussed the surprisingly large percentage of foreign revenues garnered by the Hollywood film industry (nearly 70 percent). This number is especially large given several constraints that U.S. films have when selling internationally. First, there are numerous piracy concerns. Even in the European Union (EU), where countries like Britain and France fine consumers of pirated content, other countries such as Spain have long been havens for distribution of illegal movies and music. In February 2011, Spain passed a new law to provide better protection of copyrighted material, but enforcement may be difficult in a country where nearly 50 percent of all Internet users admit to illegally downloading copyrighted content (twice the EU average rate).[75]

China is infamous for its rampant business in illegal materials. In 2010, a Chinese government report found that the market for pirated DVDs was $6 billion. As a comparison, the *total* box-office revenues in China in

2010 were $1.5 billion.[76] One reason is that ticket prices for movies in China are steep, and are considered luxury entertainment that few can afford. Another reason that "black-market" sales in China are so high is that legitimate sales often are not allowed. China allows only about 20 new non-Chinese movies into its theaters each year. Additionally, it has strict licensing rules on the sale of home-entertainment goods. Chinese censors are not likely to approve the sale of official DVDs for movies such as *Black Swan* and *The Social Network*. As a result there is often no legitimate product competing with the bootlegged offerings available via DVD and the Internet in China.[77]

Movie studios are moving to simultaneous worldwide releases of expected blockbusters in part to try to cut down on the revenues lost to piracy. International growth is expected to continue and take increasing shares of Hollywood film revenues, especially in the face of falling U.S. DVD sales. China is reportedly building new cinema screens at a rate of three per *day* in 2011. Yet growth in China (and elsewhere) is not as profitable as traditional releases in the United States. For example, film distributors typically earn 50 to 55 percent of box-office revenues in America. The average in many other countries is closer to 40 percent (the rest goes to the cinema owner). But in China, a typical Hollywood film distributor gets only 15 percent of the box office ticket revenue.[78]

1. Given the forces on the Hollywood movie industry, is it likely we will see a decrease in the production of regional- and U.S.-centered movies, or will small independent movie producers pick up a higher share of the domestic U.S. market? Please explain.

2. What alternatives could movie producers develop to help combat the piracy of first-run movies and follow-on DVD and Internet releases?

3. How would you prioritize which nations to expand distribution into if you were working for a major Hollywood movie studio?

Take-Away Concepts

This chapter discussed the roles of MNEs for economic growth; the stages of globalization; why, where, and how companies go global; four strategies MNEs use to navigate between cost reductions and local responsiveness; national competitive advantage; and whether regional clusters can lead to competitive advantage, as summarized by the following learning objectives and related take-away concepts.

LO 10-1 Define globalization, multinational enterprise (MNE), foreign direct investment (FDI), and global strategy.

>> Globalization involves closer integration and exchange between different countries and peoples worldwide, made possible by factors such as falling trade and investment barriers, advances in telecommunications, and reductions in transportation costs.

>> A multinational enterprise (MNE) deploys resources and capabilities to procure, produce, and distribute goods and services in at least two countries.

>> Foreign direct investment (FDI) denotes a firm's investments in value-chain activities abroad.

LO 10-2 Explain why companies compete abroad and evaluate advantages and disadvantages.

>> Firms compete internationally to gain access to a larger market, gain access to low-cost input factors, and develop new competencies.

>> To compete successfully abroad, firms must overcome the liability of foreignness.

>> As local wages and costs of living increase, a low-cost location advantage evaporates. (On the upside, this can turn producers into consumers.)

>> Constant pressures to reduce cost lead to a "race-to-the-bottom" where MNEs chase the lowest cost locations.

LO 10-3 Explain which countries MNEs target for FDI, and how they enter foreign markets.

>> When an MNE has to decide between countries in which to invest, two additional country-level factors come into play: national institutions and national culture.

>> Managers have the following strategy vehicles for entering foreign markets (on a continuum from low to high investment needs and control): exporting, strategic alliances (licensing for products, franchising for services), joint venture, and subsidiary (acquisition or greenfield).

LO 10-4 Describe the characteristics of and critically evaluate the four different strategies that MNEs can pursue when competing globally.

>> To navigate between the competing pressures of cost reductions and local responsiveness, MNEs have four strategies: international, localization, global-standardization, and transnational.

>> An international strategy leverages home-based core competencies into foreign markets, primarily through exports. It is useful when the MNE faces low pressures for both local responsiveness and cost reductions.

>> A localization strategy attempts to maximize local responsiveness in the face of low pressure for cost reductions. It is costly and inefficient because it requires the duplication of key business functions in multiple countries.

>> A global-standardization strategy seeks to reap economies of scale and location by pursuing a global division of labor based on wherever best-of-class capabilities reside at the lowest cost. It involves little or no local responsiveness.

>> A transnational strategy attempts to combine the high local responsiveness of a localization strategy with the lowest-cost position attainable from a global-standardization strategy. It also aims to benefit from global learning. Although appealing, it is difficult to implement due to the organizational complexities involved.

>> Exhibit 10.7 summarizes the characteristics, benefits, and risks of the four global competition strategies.

LO 10-5 Explain why certain industries are more competitive in specific nations than in others.

>> National competitive advantage, or world leadership in specific industries, is created rather than inherited.

>> Four interrelated factors explain national competitive advantage: (1) factor conditions, (2) demand conditions, (3) competitive intensity in a focal industry, and (4) related and supporting industries/complementors.

LO 10-6 Evaluate the relationship between location in a regional cluster and firm-level competitive advantage.

>> Even in a globalized world, the basis for competitive advantage is often local.

>> Strong empirical evidence suggests that being located in a regional cluster can have a positive effect on firm-level competitive advantage, both domestically and globally.

Key Terms

Cultural distance *(p. 279)*

Death-of-distance hypothesis *(p. 287)*

Foreign direct investment (FDI) *(p. 271)*

Global-standardization strategy *(p. 284)*

Global strategy *(p. 272)*

Globalization *(p. 271)*

Globalization hypothesis *(p. 281)*

Individualism *(p. 278)*

Integration-responsiveness framework *(p. 282)*

International strategy *(p. 282)*

Knowledge spillover *(p. 290)*

Liability of foreignness *(p. 276)*

Local responsiveness *(p. 282)*

Localization strategy *(p. 283)*

Location economies *(p. 276)*

Masculinity–femininity dimension *(p. 279)*

Multinational enterprise (MNE) *(p. 271)*

National competitive advantage *(p. 287)*

National culture *(p. 278)*

Power-distance dimension *(p. 278)*

Regional cluster *(p. 289)*

Transnational strategy *(p. 284)*

Uncertainty-avoidance dimension *(p. 279)*

Discussion Questions

1. Multinational enterprises (MNEs) have an impact far beyond their firm boundaries. Assume you are working for a small firm that supplies a product or service to an MNE. How might your relationship change as the MNE moves from Globalization 2.0 to Globalization 3.0 operations?

2. Think about the last movie you saw in a movie theater. What aspects of the movie had international components in it (e.g., the plot line, locations, cast, and so on)? Are there more international elements included than compared to your favorite movie from a decade ago?

3. "Licensing patented technology to a foreign competitor is likely to reduce or eliminate the firm's competitive advantage." True or false? Write a paragraph discussing this statement.

4. Consider the city/region in which your university is located. Given the discussions in the chapter about location economies, what characteristics are unusual about your location? Do you have nearby industrial regional clusters? Access to abundant (or cheap) raw materials of some sort? University research of interest to local firms?

Ethical/Social Issues

1. The chapter notes a "race-to-the-bottom" approach that MNEs may use as they search for lower cost options. Discuss the trade-offs between the positive effects of raising the standard of living in some of the world's poorest countries with the drawbacks of moving jobs established in one country to another country.

2. The chapter notes that some firms are started in countries with relatively small populations (and thus small domestic markets), such as Taiwan, Australia, and Finland. In these cases, the firms often rapidly expand internationally to reach a large enough market for economies of scale. However, some large countries (such as Brazil, China, and Japan) have economic incentives (and sometimes mandates) for firms to export their products. There are cases where such mandates result in products available internationally but not to the local population (except perhaps through a "black-market" or unofficial distribution channel). Is this closed domestic market an ethical issue for the firm? Is it an ethical issue for the government? Why or why not?

Small Group Exercises

SMALL GROUP EXERCISE 1

The text mentions that Accenture is one firm (among many others) that has shifted its location of incorporation to Ireland. The corporate officers are still based in the United States, and the stock is traded on the NYSE. The firm stated the move was largely beneficial for corporate taxes.[79] Given the chapter discussion of "what defines a U.S. company," answer the following questions.

1. Does it matter where the firm is incorporated?

2. Are there any social or ethical arguments that the firm should be incorporated where its "home base" is located?

3. Is incorporation based on cost/quality trade-offs required to maximize shareholder wealth (thus by inference, firms that do *not* move incorporation are *reducing* the returns to their shareholders)? Please discuss.

SMALL GROUP EXERCISE 2

In this exercise, we want to apply the four types of global strategy. Imagine your group works for Clif Bar (www.clifbar.com). The firm makes nutritious, all-natural food and drinks for sport and healthy snacking. In 2010, Clif Bar was a privately held company with over 200 employees and a large majority of its sales in the United States. As of 2010, even its online sales were restricted to U.S. customers only. The firm has some distribution set up in Canada (since 1996) and the United Kingdom (since 2007). Review its website for more information about the firm and its products. Referring to the material on pages 281–286 of this chapter (including Exhibit 10.6), answer the following questions.

1. Where does this firm fall on the integration-responsiveness framework?

2. What entrance strategy should the firm employ in expanding the business to new countries?

3. Does your answer change if you find out Clif Bar is planning to expand into (a) Mexico, (b) India, or (c) Germany?

Strategy Term Project

MODULE 10: GLOBAL STRATEGY

In this section, you will study your firm's global strategy or a strategy it should pursue globally.

If your firm is already engaged in international activities, answer the following questions:

1. Is your company varying its product or service to adapt to differences in countries? Is the marketing approach different among the nations involved? Should it be?

2. Is your firm working internationally to access larger markets? To gain low-cost input factors? To develop new competencies? Is its approach in all three areas appropriate?

3. Which of the four global strategies is the firm using? Is this the best strategy for it to use? Why or why not? (Exhibit 10.7 provides a summary of the four global strategies.)

If your firm is not *now engaged internationally,* answer the following questions:

1. Would your firm's product or service need to be modified or marketed differently if it expanded beyond the home country?

2. Does your firm have the potential to access larger markets by expanding internationally? Does it have the possibility of lowering input factors with such expansion? Please explain why or why not.

3. If your firm decided to expand internationally, where does the firm reside on the integration-responsiveness framework? (Refer to Exhibit 10.6 if needed.) What does this result say about the best global strategy for your firm to use for international expansion?

*my*Strategy

SHOULD THERE BE MORE H1-B VISAS?

As the U.S. unemployment rate soared to 10 percent in 2010, H1-B visas (temporary work permits for skilled human capital) emerged as a political hot-button issue. Since 1990, Congress has allowed 65,000 H1-B visas each year, plus 20,000 for foreign students with a graduate degree from U.S. universities. This regulation was implemented partly in response to lobbying from computer technology companies like Microsoft, IBM, and Intel. H1-B visas are generally granted to foreign nationals who often have advanced degrees that are difficult to find among U.S. workers (e.g., in engineering or computer science).

The demand for H1-B visas, however, far outstrips supply by almost 10 to 1, with approximately 600,000 applications annually. In 2008, Infosys received 4,559 H1-B visas, followed by Wipro (2,678), and Satyam (1,197). Given their world-class excellence in business process outsourcing, it is not surprising that all of these are Indian IT companies. The consulting firm Accenture is also among the largest contingent for H1-B visas, with 731. Half of the engineers working for Google in its Mountain View, California, headquarters were born overseas.

Industry titans like Bill Gates (co-founder of Microsoft), Craig Barrett (former chairman of Intel), and John Lechleiter (CEO of Eli Lilly) are adamant about the need for more H1-B visas to stay competitive. (Said Mr. Barrett, "We should staple a green card to every U.S. diploma given to foreign students.")[80]

Those who have an opposing view see H1-B visas as reducing American jobs. U.S. Senator Charles Grassley (R-Iowa), for example, has suggested that when jobs are cut, foreigners should be laid off first, regardless of merit.

Senator Grassley's request contrasts with research showing that U.S. tech companies add five workers for each H1-B visa they receive. Another research study coming out of Duke and Harvard found that a majority of the high-tech companies started in Silicon Valley had founders born overseas. Some of the more famous foreign-born founders include Andy Grove (Hungarian-born former CEO of Intel and one of its earliest employees), Jerry Yang (Taiwanese-born co-founder of Yahoo), Sergey Brin (Russian-born co-founder of Google), and Tony Tsieh (founder of LinkExchange and CEO at Zappos.com, born to Taiwanese immigrants).[81]

1. Is the U.S. chasing away foreigners who may start their own companies that create jobs and wealth? Or are H1-B visa holders taking away jobs from U.S. citizens?

2. What skills and capabilities do you need to acquire and hone so that you can take advantage of opportunities afforded in a more global labor market?

Endnotes

1. "Plot change: Foreign forces transform Hollywood films," *The Wall Street Journal,* August 2, 2010.

2. This ChapterCase is based on: "Plot change: Foreign forces transform Hollywood films," *The Wall Street Journal;* "Hollywood squeezes stars' pay in slump," *The Wall Street Journal,* April 2, 2009; "News Corporation," *The Economist,* February 26, 2009; and "Slumdog Millionaire wins eight Oscars," *The Wall Street Journal,* February 23, 2009.

3. "Foreign university students," *The Economist,* August 7, 2010.

4. World Bank (2010), *World Development Indicators,* July 1.

5. Stiglitz, J. (2002), *Globalization and Its Discontents* (New York: Norton).

6. "BRICs, emerging markets and the world economy," *The Economist,* June 18, 2009.

7. Caves, R. (1996), *Multinational Enterprise and Economic Analysis* (New York: Cambridge University Press); and Dunning, J. (1993), *Multinational Enterprises and the Global Economy* (Reading, MA: Addison-Wesley).

8. "GM's latest nemesis: VW," *The Wall Street Journal,* August 4, 2010.

9. Following Peng (2010: 18), we define global strategy as a "strategy of firms around the globe—essentially various firms' theories about how to compete successfully." This stands in contrast to a narrower alternative use of the term "global strategy," which implies a global cost leadership strategy in standardized products. We follow Peng to denote this type of strategy as *standardization strategy* (Peng, 2010: 20); Peng, M. W. (2010), *Global Strategy,* 2nd ed. (Mason, OH: Cengage).

10. McKinsey Global Institute (2010), *Growth and Competitiveness in the United States: The Role of Its Multinational Companies* (London).

11. "IBM to cut U.S. jobs, expand in India," *The Wall Street Journal,* March 26, 2009.

12. This Strategy Highlight draws on: Friedman, T. L. (2005), *The World Is Flat: A Brief History of the Twenty-first Century* (New York: Farrar, Straus, and Giroux). Although we follow Friedman (2005) in using the terminology Globalization 1.0, Globalization 2.0, and Globalization 3.0, the time frame of the three different stages and the description thereof differs from Friedman (2005); and IBM (2009), *A Decade of Generating Higher Value at IBM,* IBM report, www.ibm.com.

13. This Strategy Highlight is based on: "Can China save GM?" *Forbes,* May 10, 2010; and Tao, Q. (2009), "Competition in the Chinese automobile industry," in M. Peng, *Global Strategy,* 2nd ed. (Mason, OH: South-Western Cengage), pp. 419–425.

14. "Social networks and statehood," *The Economist,* July 22, 2010.

15. Kotha, S., V. Rindova, and F. T. Rothaermel (2001), "Assets and actions: Firm-specific factors in the internationalization of U.S. Internet firms," *Journal of International Business Studies* 32: 769–791.

16. www.logitech.com.

17. Saxenian, A. (1994), *Regional Advantage* (Cambridge, MA: Harvard University Press); and Rothaermel, F. T., and D. Ku (2008), "Intercluster innovation differentials: The role of research universities," *IEEE Transactions on Engineering Management* 55: 9–22.

18. "A special report on innovation in emerging markets," *The Economist,* April 15, 2010.

19. "The rising power of the Chinese worker," *The Economist,* July 29, 2010.

20. Friedman, T. L. (2005), *The World Is Flat: A Brief History of the Twenty-first Century.*

21. Chang, S. J. (1995), "International expansion strategy of Japanese firms: Capability building through sequential entry," *Academy of Management Journal* 38: 383–407; Vermeulen, F., and H. G. Barkema (1998), "International expansion through start-up or acquisition: A learning perspective," *Academy of Management Journal* 41: 7–26; Vermeulen, F., and H. G. Barkema (2002), "Pace, rhythm, and scope: Process dependence in building a profitable multinational corporation," *Strategic Management Journal* 23: 637–653.

22. Brown, J. S., and P. Duguid (1991), "Organizational learning and communities-of-practice: Toward a unified view of working, learning, and innovation," *Organization Science* 2: 40–57.

23. Owen-Smith, J., and W. W. Powell (2004), "Knowledge networks as channels and conduits: The effects of spillovers in the Boston biotech community," *Organization Science* 15: 5–21.

24. Examples drawn from: "A special report on innovation in emerging markets," *The Economist,* April 15, 2010.

25. Dunning, J. H., and S. M. Lundan (2008), *Multinational Enterprises and the Global Economy,* 2nd ed. (Northampton, MA: Edward Elgar).

26. "A special report on innovation in emerging markets," *The Economist,* April 15, 2010.

27. Zaheer, S. (1995), "Overcoming the liability of foreignness," *Academy of Management Journal* 38: 341–363.

28. "The Foxconn suicides," *The Wall Street Journal,* May 27, 2010.

29. "Firms boost pay for Chinese," *The Wall Street Journal,* June 13, 2010.

30. "Supply chain for iPhone highlights costs in China," *The New York Times,* July 5, 2010.

31. Ibid.

32. "The rising power of the Chinese worker," *The Economist,* July 29, 2010.

33. This is based on: Friedman, T. L. (2005), *The World Is Flat: A Brief History of the Twenty-first Century;* "Supply chain for iPhone highlights costs in China," *The New York Times,* July 5, 2010; and "The rising power of the Chinese worker," *The Economist,* July 29, 2010.

34. This example is drawn from: "Train makers rail against China's high-speed designs," *The Wall Street Journal,* November 17, 2010.

35. This is based on: Williamson, O. E. (1975), *Markets and Hierarchies* (New York: Free Press); Williamson, O. E. (1981), "The economics of organization: The transaction cost approach," *American Journal of Sociology* 87: 548–577; and Williamson, O. E. (1985), *The Economic Institutions of Capitalism* (New York: Free Press).

36. Author's interview with a VP of Citibank in a Latin American country.

37. This is based on: North, D. (1990), *Institutions, Institutional Change, and Economic Performance* (New York: Norton); and Peng, M. W. (2003), "Institutional transitions and strategic choices," *Academy of Management Review* 28: 275–296.

38. Hofstede, G. H. (1984), *Culture's Consequences: International Differences in Work-Related Values* (Beverly Hills, CA: Sage), p. 21.

39. The description of Hofstede's four cultural dimensions is drawn from: Rothaermel, F. T., S. Kotha, and H. K. Steensma (2006), "International market entry by U.S. Internet firms: An empirical analysis of country risk, national culture, and market size," *Journal of Management* 32: 56–82.

40. This is based on: Kogut, B., and H. Singh (1988), "The effect of national culture on the choice of entry mode," *Journal of International Business Studies* 19: 411–432; Rothaermel, F. T., S. Kotha, and H. K. Steensma (2006), "International market entry by U.S. Internet firms: An empirical analysis of country risk, national culture, and market size"; Cultural distance from the United States, for example, is calculated as follows: $CD_j = \sum_{i=1}^{4} \{(I_{ij} - I_{iu})^2/V_i\}/4$, where I_{ij} stands for the index for the ith cultural dimension and jth country, V_i is the variance of the index of ith dimension, u indicates the United States, and CD_j is the cultural distance difference of the jth country from the United States.

41. Cairncross, F. (1997), *The Death of Distance: How the Communications Revolution Will Change Our Lives* (Boston, MA: Harvard Business School Press).

42. This is based on: O Riain, S. (2000), "The flexible developmental state: Globalization, information technology and the 'Celtic Tiger,'" *Politics and Society* 28: 157–193; and "A survey of Ireland," *The Economist,* October 14, 2004.

43. Examples drawn from: "A survey of Ireland," *The Economist.*

44. Today, some argue that Ireland's low corporate tax rate contributed to its financial difficulties in the wake of the global financial crisis; see "Tax torment," *The Economist,* March 17, 2011.

45. UNCTAD (2010), "Global FDI flows will exceed $1.2 trillion in 2010," *United Nations Conference on Trade and Development Report,* www.unctad.org.

46. Johanson, J., and J. Vahlne (1977), "The internationalization process of the firm," *Journal of International Business Studies* 4: 20–29.

47. Fuller, A. W., and F. T. Rothaermel (2008), "The Interplay between capability development and strategy formation: Motorola's entry into China," Working Paper, Georgia Institute of Technology.

48. Levitt, T. (1983), "The globalization of markets," *Harvard Business Review,* May–June: 92–102.

49. Ibid., 93.

50. Mol, M. (2002). Ford Mondeo: A Model T world car? In: Tan, F. B. (Ed.), Cases on Global IT Applications and Management: Successes and Pitfalls, pp. 69-89.

51. Prahalad, C. K., and Y. L. Doz (1987), *The Multinational Mission* (New York: Free Press); and Roth, K., and A. J. Morrison (1990), "An empirical analysis of the integration-responsiveness framework in global industries," *Journal of International Business Studies* 21: 541–564.

52. Bartlett, C. A., S. Ghoshal, and P. W. Beamish (2007), *Transnational Management: Text, Cases and Readings in Cross-border Management,* 5th ed. (Burr Ridge, IL: McGraw-Hill).

53. "Ditch the knock-off watch, get the knock-off car," *The Wall Street Journal Video,* August 8, 2010.

54. www.lenovo.com/lenovo/US/en/locations.html.

55. Ibid.

56. This is based on: Bartlett, C. A., S. Ghoshal, and P. W. Beamish (2007), *Transnational Management: Text, Cases and Readings in Cross-border Management;* and Friedman, T. L. (2005), *The World Is Flat: A Brief History of the Twenty-first Century.*

57. This strategy highlight is based on: Knorr, A., and A. Arndt (2003), "Why did Wal-Mart fail in Germany?" in A. Knorr, A. Lemper, A. Sell, and K. Wohlmuth (eds.), *Materialien des Wissenschaftsschwerpunktes "Globalisierung der Weltwirtschaft,"* Vol. 24 (IWIM—Institute for

World Economics and International Management, Universität Bremen, Germany); the author's onsite observations at Walmart stores in Germany; and "Hair-shirt economics: Getting Germans to open their wallets is hard," *The Economist,* July 8, 2010. For a recent discussion of Walmart's global efforts, see: "After early errors, Wal-Mart thinks locally to act globally," *The Wall Street Journal,* August 14, 2009.

58. Mueller, H.-E. (2001), "Developing global human resource strategies," Paper presented at the European International Business Academy, Paris, December 13–15; Mueller, H.-E. (2001), "Wie Global Player den Kampf um Talente führen," *Harvard Business Manager* 6: 16–25.

59. This section draws on: Rothaermel, F. T., and D. Ku (2008), "Intercluster innovation differentials: The role of research universities," *IEEE Transactions on Engineering Management* 55: 9–22.

60. This is based on: Buckley, P. J., and P. N. Ghauri (2004), "Globalisation, economic geography and the strategy of multinational enterprises," *Journal of International Business Studies* 35: 81–98; and Cairncross, F. (1997), *The Death of Distance: How The Communications Revolution Will Change Our Lives* (Boston, MA: Harvard Business School Press). For a counterpoint, see: Ghemawat, P. (2007), *Redefining Global Strategy: Crossing Borders in a World Where Differences Still Matter* (Boston, MA: Harvard Business School Press).

61. Friedman, T. L. (2005), *The World Is Flat: A Brief History of the Twenty-first Century.*

62. This section is based on: Porter, M. E. (1990), "The competitive advantage of nations," *Harvard Business Review,* March–April: 73–91; and Porter, M. E. (1990), *The Competitive Advantage of Nations* (New York: Free Press).

63. "U.S. identifies vast mineral riches in Afghanistan," *The New York Times,* June 13, 2010.

64. For an insightful recent discussion, see: Breznitz, D. (2007), *Innovation and the State: Political Choice and Strategies for Growth in Israel, Taiwan, and Ireland* (New Haven, CT: Yale University Press).

65. More recently, however, Nokia has lost some of its leadership to Apple, RIM of Canada, and Samsung of South Korea.

66. Dyer, J. H., and K. Nobeoka (2000), "Creating and managing a high-performance knowledge-sharing network: The Toyota case," *Strategic Management Journal* 21: 345–367.

67. This discussion is based on: "Toyota slips up," *The Economist,* December 10, 2009; "Toyota: Losing its shine," *The Economist,* December 10, 2009; "Toyota heir faces crises at the wheel," *The Wall Street Journal,* January 27, 2010; "Toyota's troubles deepen," *The Economist,* February 4, 2010; "The humbling of Toyota," *Bloomberg Businessweek,* March 11, 2010; and "Inside Toyota, executives trade blame over debacle," *The Wall Street Journal,* April 13, 2010.

68. Porter, M. E. (1998), "Clusters and the new economics of competition," *Harvard Business Review,* November–December: 77–90.

69. For a review, see: Jenkins, M., and S. Tallman (2010), "The shifting geography of competitive advantage: Clusters, networks and firms," *Journal of Economic Geography* 10: 599–618; Porter, M. E. (1988), "Clusters and competition: New agendas for companies, governments, and institutions," in Porter, M. E. (ed.), *On Competition* (Boston: Harvard Business School Press); Porter, M. E. (1990), *The Competitive Advantage of Nations* (New York: Free Press); Porter, M. E. (1998), "Clusters and the new economics of competition," *Harvard Business Review,* November–December: 77–90; Rothaermel, F. T., and D. Ku (2008), "Intercluster innovation differentials: The role of research universities," *IEEE Transactions on Engineering Management* 55: 9–22; and Tallman, S., M. Jenkins, N. Henry, and S. Pinch (2004), "Knowledge, clusters and competitive advantage," *Academy of Management Review* 29: 258–271.

70. Porter, M. E. (1990), *The Competitive Advantage of Nations* (New York: Free Press), p. 77.

71. McKinsey Global Institute (2010), *Growth and Competitiveness in the United States: The Role of its Multinational Companies.*

72. For a review, see: Agarwal, R., D. B. Audretsch, and M. B. Sarkar (2007), "The process of creative construction: Knowledge spillovers, entrepreneurship, and economic growth," *Strategic Entrepreneurship Journal* 1: 263–286; Audretsch, D. B., and M. P. Feldman (1996), "R&D spillovers and the

geography of innovation and production," *American Economic Review* 86: 630–640; Audretsch, D. B., and E. E. Lehmann (2005), "Mansfield's missing link: The impact of knowledge spillovers on firm growth," *Journal of Technology Transfer* 30: 207–210; Audretsch, D. B., E. E. Lehmann, and S. Warning (2005), "University spillovers and new firm location," *Research Policy* 34: 1113–1122; Audretsch, D. B., and P. E. Stephan (1996), "Company–scientist locational links: The case of biotechnology," *American Economic Review* 86: 641–652; Rothaermel, F. T., and M. Thursby (2005), "University-incubator firm knowledge flows: Assessing their impact on incubator firm performance," *Research Policy* 34: 305–320; and Rothaermel, F. T., and M. Thursby (2005), "Incubator firm failure or graduation? The role of university linkages," *Research Policy* 34: 1076–1090.

73. Saxenian, A. (1994), *Regional Advantage* (Cambridge, MA: Harvard University Press).

74. Gompers, P. A., and J. Lerner (2001), *The Money of Invention: How Venture Capital Creates New Wealth* (Boston, MA: Harvard Business School Press).

75. "Ending the open season on artists," *The Economist,* February 17, 2011.

76. Levin, D., and J. Horn (2011), "DVD pirates running rampant in China," *Los Angeles Times,* March, 22.

77. Ibid.

78. "Bigger abroad," *The Economist,* February 17, 2011.

79. "Accenture Is Seeking to Change Tax Locales," *The Wall Street Journal,* May 27, 2009.

80. Barrett, C. (2009), "We need an immigration stimulus," *The Wall Street Journal,* April 27.

81. This *my*Strategy is based on: "U.S. tech companies add five workers for each H-1B visa they seek," *InformationWeek,* March 10, 2008; "Still coming to America," *The Wall Street Journal,* March 27, 2009; "Work-visa numbers get squishy—and get played," *The Wall Street Journal,* March 31, 2009; "Tech recruiting clashes with immigration rules," *The New York Times,* April 11, 2009; "We need an immigration stimulus," *The Wall Street Journal,* April 27, 2009; and a collection of many articles pertaining to this topic found at http://wadhwa.com/.

Analysis: Getting Started
1. What Is Strategy and Why Is It Important?
2. The Strategic Management Process

External and Internal Analysis
3. External Analysis: Industry Structure, Competitive Forces, and Strategic Groups
4. Internal Analysis: Resources, Capabilities, and Activities
5. Competitive Advantage and Firm Performance

GAINING & SUSTAINING COMPETITIVE ADVANTAGE

PART 3

Implementation
11. Organizational Design: Structure, Culture, and Control
12. Corporate Governance, Business Ethics, and Strategic Leadership

Formulation: Corporate Strategy
8. Corporate Strategy: Vertical Integration and Diversification
9. Corporate Strategy: Acquisitions, Alliances, and Networks
10. Global Strategy: Competing Around the World

Formulation: Business Strategy
6. Business Strategy: Differentiation, Cost Leadership, and Integration
7. Business Strategy: Innovation and Strategic Entrepreneurship

PART 3
Strategy Implementation

CHAPTER 11

Organizational Design:
Structure, Culture, and Control

LEARNING OBJECTIVES
After studying this chapter, you should be able to:

LO 11-1   Define organizational design and list its three components.

LO 11-2   Explain how organizational inertia can lead established firms to failure.

LO 11-3   Define organizational structure and describe its four elements.

LO 11-4   Compare and contrast mechanistic versus organic organizations.

LO 11-5   Describe different organizational structures and match them with appropriate strategies.

LO 11-6   Describe the elements of organizational culture, and explain where organizational cultures can come from and how they can be changed.

LO 11-7   Compare and contrast different strategic control and reward systems.

CHAPTERCASE 11

Zappos: An Organization Designed to Deliver Happiness

DELIVERING HAPPINESS is the title of *The New York Times* bestseller by Tony Hsieh, CEO of Zappos, the online shoe and clothing store (www.zappos.com). Delivering happiness is also Zappos's mission. To make its customers, employees, and shareholders happy, Tony Hsieh (pronounced "shay") and other Zappos leaders designed a unique organization.

To live up to its mission, Zappos decided that exceptional customer service should be its core competency. They put several policies and procedures in place to "deliver WOW through service"—the first of its 10 core values (see Exhibit 11.1 on the next page). For example, shipments to and from customers within the U.S. are free of charge, allowing customers to order several pairs of shoes and send back (within a liberal 365 days) those that don't fit or are no longer wanted. Repeat customers are automatically upgraded to complimentary express shipping. One of the most important lessons Hsieh learned is, "never outsource your core competency!"[1] Customer service, therefore, is done exclusively in-house. Perhaps even more importantly, Zappos does not provide a script or measure customer-service reps' call times. Rather, the company leaves it up to the individual "Customer Loyalty Team" member to deliver exceptional customer service: "We want our reps to let their true

personalities shine during each phone call so that they can develop a personal emotional connection with the customer."[2] (In fact, one customer-service phone call lasted almost six hours!) The same trust in the customer-service reps applies to e-mail communication. Zappos's official communication policy is to "be real and use your best judgment."[3]

As Zappos grew, its managers realized that it was critical to explicitly define a set of core values from which to develop the company's culture, brand, and strategy. It wanted to make sure that, in a time of fast growth, all employees understood the same set of values and expected behaviors. Zappos's list of 10 core values was crafted through a bottom-up initiative, in which all employees were invited to participate. Zappos also restructured its performance-evaluation system, to give these values "teeth": The firm rewards employees who apply the values well in their day-to-day decision making. In this way, Zappos's managers directly connected the informal cultural control system to the formal reward system. CEO Tony Hsieh states, "Ideally, we want all 10 core values to be reflected in everything we do, including how we interact with each other, how we interact with our customers, and how we interact with our vendors and business partners. . . . Our core values should always be the framework from which we make all of our decisions."[4]

When establishing customer service as a core competency, one of the hardest decisions Tony Hsieh made was to pull the plug on drop-shipment orders (orders for which Zappos would be the intermediary, relaying orders to particular shoe vendors who then ship directly to the customer). Such orders were very profitable (Zappos would not have to stock all the shoes) and were appealing because the fledgling startup was still losing money. The problem was two-fold. The vendors were slower than Zappos in filling orders. In addition, they did not accomplish the reliability metric that Zappos wanted for exceptional service: 95 percent accuracy was simply not good enough! Instead, Zappos decided to forgo drop shipments and instead built a larger warehouse to stock a full inventory. This move enabled the firm to achieve close to 100 percent accuracy in its shipments, many of which were overnight.

In addition to making customers happy, Zappos also works to keep its own employees happy. Although it now employs over 1,500 people, Zappos's organizational structure is extremely flat. Once an employee has mastered a job, he or she is rotated to a different job, often horizontally. This system allows Zappos to create a large pool of trained talent, and makes it easier to promote from within. In keeping with another of its core values, "create fun and a little weirdness," the Las Vegas–based startup offers employees "free" lunches, employer-paid health care benefits, a designated nap room, concierge service, an onsite life coach who is also a chiropractor, a library of books on happiness (along with other bestsellers), onsite seminars on personal growth, and fun events such as pajama parties at work. In 2011, Zappos was ranked #6 in *Fortune*'s "100 Best Companies to Work For" list (the highest ranking for a relatively young firm).

Finally, Zappos has also made its shareholders happy. In 2009, Amazon acquired the startup in a deal valued at $1.2 billion. Although now a subsidiary of Amazon, Zappos continues to operate as an independent brand.[5]

After reading the chapter, you will find more about this case, with related questions, on page 324.

▲ **ZAPPOS'S CEO** Tony Hsieh and other managers thought long and hard about what type of structure, culture, and processes to put in place that would support the firm's strategic goals. They proactively designed an organization that enabled them to implement its differentiation strategy effectively. Zappos's managers further refined their organizational design through trial-and-error, being transparent, and soliciting bottom-up feedback, while making the tough strategic decisions of what not to do.

ChapterCase 11 brings us to the final piece of the AFI framework: strategy implementation. Strategy implementation concerns the organization, coordination, and integration of how work gets done. It is key to gaining and sustaining competitive advantage. Although the discussion of strategy formulation (what to do) is distinct from strategy implementation (how to do it), formulation and implementation must be part of an interdependent, reciprocal process in order to ensure continued success. That need for interdependence is why the AFI

strategy implementation
The part of the strategic management process that concerns the organization, coordination, and integration of how work gets done. It is key to gaining and sustaining competitive advantage.

EXHIBIT 11.1

Zappos's 10 Core Values

Source: Hsieh, T. (2010), *Delivering Happiness: A Path to Profits, Passion, and Purpose* (New York: Business Plus), pp. 157–160.

1. Deliver WOW through service.
2. Embrace and drive change.
3. Create fun and a little weirdness.
4. Be adventurous, creative, and open-minded.
5. Pursue growth and learning.
6. Build open and honest relationships with communication.
7. Build a positive team and family spirit.
8. Do more with less.
9. Be passionate and determined.
10. Be humble.

framework is illustrated as a circle, rather than a linear diagram. The design of an organization, the matching of strategy and structure, and its control and reward systems determine whether an organization that has chosen an effective strategy will thrive or wither away.

In this chapter, we study the three key levers that managers have at their disposal when *designing their organizations for competitive advantage:* structure, culture, and control. We begin our discussion with organizational structure. We discuss not only different types of organizational structures, but also why and how they need to change over time as successful firms grow in size and complexity. We highlight the critical need to match strategy and structure, and then dive into corporate culture. An organization's culture can either support or hinder its quest for competitive advantage.[6] Finally, we study strategic control systems, which allow managers to receive feedback on how well a firm's strategy is being implemented.

Managers employ these three levers—structure, culture, and control—to coordinate work and motivate employees across different levels, functions, and geographies. How successful they are in this endeavor determines whether they are able to translate their chosen business, corporate, and global strategies into strategic actions and business models, and ultimately whether the firm is able to gain and sustain a competitive advantage.

HOW TO ORGANIZE FOR COMPETITIVE ADVANTAGE

Organizational design is the process of creating, implementing, monitoring, and modifying the structure, processes, and procedures of an organization. The key components of organizational design are structure, culture, and control. The goal is to design an organization that allows managers to effectively translate their chosen strategy into a realized one. Simply formulating an effective strategy, however, is a necessary but not sufficient condition for gaining and sustaining competitive advantage. Some might argue that strategy execution is more important.[7] Often, managers do a good job of analyzing the firm's internal and external environments to formulate a promising business, corporate, and global strategy, but then fail to implement the chosen strategy successfully. That is why some scholars refer to implementation as the "graveyard of strategy."[8]

>> **LO 11-1**
Define organizational design and list its three components.

Not surprisingly, the inability to implement strategy effectively is the number-one reason boards of directors fire CEOs.[9] Strategy Highlight 11.1 (next page) shows the result of Yahoo's co-founder and CEO Jerry Yang's failure to make the necessary changes to the Internet firm's organizational structure.

Since strategy implementation transforms theory into strategic actions and business models, it often requires changes within the organization. However, strategy implementation often fails because managers are unable to make the necessary changes due to its effects on resource allocation and power distribution within an organization.[10]

organizational design
The process of creating, implementing, monitoring, and modifying the structure, processes, and procedures of an organization.

As demonstrated by business historian Alfred Chandler in his seminal book *Strategy and Structure*, organizational structure must follow strategy in order for firms to achieve superior performance: "Structure can be defined as the design of organization through which the enterprise is administered... the thesis deduced [from studying the administrative history of DuPont, GM, Sears Roebuck, and Standard Oil from the early to mid-1900s] is that *structure follows strategy*."[11] This tenet implies that to implement a strategy successfully, organizational design must be flexible enough to accommodate the formulated strategy and future growth and expansion.

>> **LO 11-2**
Explain how organizational inertia can lead established firms to failure.

Organizational Inertia and the Failure of Established Firms

In reality, however, a firm's strategy often follows its structure.[12] This reversal implies that some managers consider only strategies that do not change existing organizational

Draw Me Yahoo's Org Chart

In the fall of 2008, Yahoo's co-founder and CEO Jerry Yang was ousted precisely because he failed to implement necessary strategic changes after Yahoo lost its competitive advantage.[13] In the two years leading up to his exit, Yahoo had lost more than 75 percent of its market value. Mr. Yang was described as someone who preferred consensus among his managers to making tough strategic decisions needed to change Yahoo's structure. That preference, though, led to bickering and infighting.

Carol Bartz, who replaced Jerry Yang as CEO, recalls saying, "Well, Jerry, why don't you draw me an org chart. . . . Why don't you show me who on this org would make the big decision—the big search decision. So he started drawing arrows. And it was like a Dilbert cartoon. It was very odd. I said, you need management here. I couldn't figure out who was in charge of anything, and he didn't explain that part very well."[14] One of the first things Ms. Bartz did, therefore, was to change Yahoo's organizational structure both to decentralize decision making and to increase the accountability of individual employees. In addition, she clarified the lines of authority. With its new organizational design in place, Ms. Bartz hopes Yahoo's rate of innovation will increase to improve its competitiveness.[15]

structures; they do not want to confront the inertia that often exists in established organizations.[16] *Inertia,* a firm's resistance to change in the status quo, can set the stage for the firm's subsequent failure. Successful firms often plant the seed of subsequent failure: They optimize their organizational structure to the current situation. That tightly coupled system can break apart when internal or external pressures occur.

Exhibit 11.2 shows how success in the current environment can lead to a firm's downfall in the future, when the tightly coupled system of strategy and structure experiences internal or external shifts.[17] First, the managers achieve a mastery of, and fit with, the firm's current environment. Second, the firm often defines and measures success by financial metrics, with a focus on short-term performance. (See the discussion of metrics in Chapter 5.) Third, the firm puts in place metrics and systems to accommodate and manage increasing firm size due to continued success. Finally, as a result of a tightly coupled (albeit successful) system, organizational inertia sets in—and with it, resistance to change.

Such a tightly coupled system is prone to break apart when external and internal shifts put pressure on the system.[18] In Exhibit 11.2, the blue arrows show the firm's tightly coupled organizational design. The gray arrows indicate pressures emanating from internal shifts (such as accelerated growth, a change in business model, entry into new markets, a change in the top management team, or mergers and acquisitions). The purple arrows indicate external pressures, which can stem from any of the PESTEL forces (political, economic, sociocultural, technological, ecological, and legal, as discussed in Chapter 3). Strong external or internal pressure can break apart the current system, which may lead to firm failure.

The Key Elements of Organizational Structure

Some of the key decisions managers must make when designing effective organizations pertain to the firm's organizational structure. That structure determines how the work efforts of individuals and teams are orchestrated and how resources are distributed. In particular, an organizational structure defines how jobs and tasks are divided and integrated, delineates the reporting relationships up and down the hierarchy, defines formal communication channels, and prescribes how individuals and teams coordinate their work efforts. The key building blocks of an organizational structure are *specialization, formalization, centralization,* and *hierarchy.*

Specialization describes the degree to which a task is divided into separate jobs—that is, the *division of labor.* Larger firms, such as Fortune 100 companies, tend to have a high

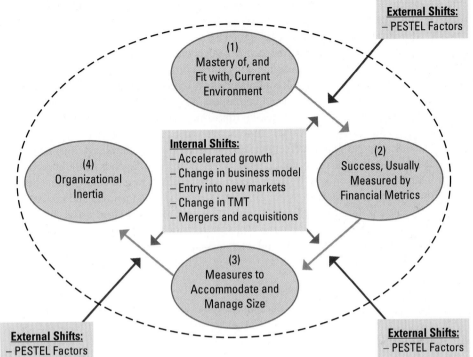

EXHIBIT 11.2

Organizational Inertia and the Failure of Established Firms When External or Internal Environments Shift

degree of specialization; smaller entrepreneurial ventures tend to have a low degree of specialization. For example, an accountant for a large firm may specialize in only one area (e.g., internal audit), whereas an accountant in a small firm needs to be more of a generalist and take on many different things (e.g., not only internal auditing, but also payroll, accounts receivable, financial planning, and taxes). Specialization requires a trade-off between breadth versus depth of knowledge. While a high degree of the division of labor increases productivity, it can also have unintended side-effects such as reduced employee job satisfaction due to repetition of tasks.

Formalization captures the extent to which employee behavior is controlled by explicit and codified rules and procedures. Formalized structures are characterized by detailed written rules and policies of what to do in specific situations. These are often codified in employee handbooks. McDonald's, for example, uses detailed standard operating procedures throughout the world to ensure consistent quality and service. Airlines also rely on a high degree of formalization to instruct pilots on how to fly their airplanes. Formalization, therefore, should not necessarily be considered bad; often it is necessary to achieve consistent and predictable results. Yet a high degree of formalization *can* slow decision making, reduce creativity and innovation, and hinder customer service.[19] Most customer service reps in call centers, for example, follow a detailed script. This is especially true when call centers are outsourced to overseas locations. (As you recall, Zappos deliberately avoided

---

organizational structure A key building block of organizational design that determines how the work efforts of individuals and teams are orchestrated and how resources are distributed.

specialization An element of organizational structure that describes the degree to which a task is divided into separate jobs (i.e., the division of labor).

formalization An element of organizational structure that captures the extent to which employee behavior is controlled by explicit and codified rules and procedures.

this approach when it made customer service its core competency.) W. L. Gore uses an extremely *informal* organizational structure to foster employee satisfaction, retention, and creativity, as discussed in Strategy Highlight 11.2.

Centralization refers to the degree to which decision making is concentrated at the top of the organization. Centralized decision making often correlates with slow response time and reduced customer satisfaction. In decentralized organizations, decisions are made and problems solved by empowered lower-level employees who are closer to the sources of issues. Different strategic management processes (discussed in Chapter 2) match with different degrees of centralization. Top-down strategic planning takes place in highly centralized organizations, whereas planned emergence is found in more decentralized organizations.

Whether centralization or decentralization is more effective depends on the specific situation. During the Gulf oil spill in 2010, BP's response was slow and cumbersome because all of the important decisions were initially made in its UK headquarters and not onsite. In this case, centralization reduced response time and led to a prolonged crisis. In contrast, the FBI and the CIA were faulted in the 9/11 Commission Report for *not being centralized enough.*[22] The report concluded that although each agency had different types of evidence

centralization
An element of organizational structure that refers to the degree to which decision making is concentrated at the top of the organization.

W. L. Gore & Associates: Informality and Innovation

W. L. Gore & Associates is the inventor of path-breaking new products such as breathable Gore-Tex fabrics, Glide dental floss, and Elixir guitar strings. Bill Gore, a former long-time employee of chemical giant DuPont, founded the company with the vision to create an organization "devoted to innovation, a company where imagination and initiative would flourish, where chronically curious engineers would be free to invent, invest, and succeed."[20] When founding the company in 1958, Bill Gore articulated four core values that still guide the company and its associates to this day:

1. Fairness to each other and everyone with whom the firm does business
2. Freedom to encourage, help, and allow other associates to grow in knowledge skill, and scope of responsibility
3. The ability to make one's own commitments and keep them
4. Consultation with other associates before undertaking actions that could cause serious damage to the reputation of the company ("blowing a hole below the waterline")

W. L. Gore & Associates is organized in an informal and decentralized manner: It has no formal job titles, job descriptions, chains of command, formal communication channels, written rules or standard operating procedures. Face-to-face communication is preferred over e-mail. There is no organizational chart. In what is called a *lattice* or *boundaryless* organizational form, everyone is empowered and encouraged to speak to anyone else in the organization. People who work at Gore are called "associates," rather than employees, indicating professional expertise and status. Gore associates organize themselves in project-based teams that are led by sponsors, not bosses. Associates invite other team members based on their expertise and interests in a more or less ad hoc fashion. Peer control in these multidisciplinary teams further enhances associate productivity. Group members evaluate each other's performance annually, and these evaluations determine each associate's level of compensation. Moreover, all associates at W. L. Gore are also shareholders of the company, and thus are part owners sharing in profits and losses.

Gore's freewheeling and informal culture has been linked to greater employee satisfaction and retention, higher personal initiative and creativity, and innovation at the firm level. Although W. L. Gore's organizational structure may look like something you might find in a small, high-tech startup company, in 2010 the firm had 9,000 employees and $2.5 billion in revenues, making Gore one of the largest privately held companies in the United States. In the same year, Gore was #13 in *Fortune*'s "100 Best Companies to Work For" list, and has been included in every edition of that prestigious ranking.[21]

that a terrorist strike in the U.S. was imminent, their decentralization made them unable to put together the pieces to prevent the 9/11 attacks.

Hierarchy determines the formal, position-based reporting lines and thus stipulates *who reports to whom*. Let's assume two firms of roughly equal size: Firm A and Firm B. If many levels of hierarchy exist between the front-line employee and the CEO in Firm A, it has a *tall structure*. In contrast, if there are few levels of hierarchy in Firm B, it has a *flat structure*.

The number of levels of hierarchy, in turn, determines the managers' span of control— how many employees directly report to a manager. In tall organizational structures (Firm A), the span of control is narrow. In flat structures (Firm B), the span of control is wide, meaning one manager supervises many employees. In recent years, firms have de-layered by reducing the headcount (often middle managers), making themselves flatter and thus more nimble. This in turn, however, puts more pressure on the remaining managers who have to supervise and monitor more direct reports due to an increased span of control.[23] Recent research suggests that managers are most effective at an intermediate point where the span of control is not too narrow or too wide.[24]

Assembling the Pieces: Mechanistic vs. Organic Organizations

Several of the building blocks of organizational structure frequently show up together, creating distinct organizational forms—organic and mechanistic organizations.[25]

Zappos and W. L. Gore are both examples of organic organizations. Such organizations have a low degree of specialization and formalization, a flat organizational structure, and decentralized decision making.[26] Organic structures tend to be correlated with the following: a fluid and flexible information flow among employees in both horizontal and vertical directions; faster decision making; and higher employee motivation, retention, satisfaction, and creativity. Organic organizations also typically exhibit a higher rate of entrepreneurial behaviors and innovation. Organic structures allow firms to foster R&D and/or marketing, for example, as a core competency. Thus, firms that pursue a differentiation strategy at the business level frequently employ an organic structure. Exhibit 11.3 (next page) highlights the key features of organic organizations.

Due to significant advances in information technology, organic organizations frequently use *virtual teams*. In these teams, geographically dispersed team members are able to collaborate through electronic communications such as e-mail, instant messaging, intranets, and teleconferencing.[27] Given time differences, virtual teams often organize work flow so that projects can be pushed forward 24 hours a day, seven days a week. Use of virtual work and collaboration technologies has enabled companies to be more nimble and to employ flatter and more decentralized organizational structures. Research data show that the largest 30 companies by market capitalization utilized networked digital technologies to double their employee productivity within a decade, despite more than doubling their number of employees. In the decades prior to the widespread use of computer-mediated work, employee productivity remained more or less flat.[28]

>> **LO 11-4**
Compare and contrast mechanistic versus organic organizations.

---

hierarchy An element of organizational structure that determines the formal, position-based reporting lines and thus stipulates who reports to whom.

span of control The number of employees who directly report to a manager.

organic organization Organizational form characterized by a low degree of specialization and formalization, a flat organizational structure, and decentralized decision making.

EXHIBIT 11.3

Mechanistic vs. Organic Organizations: The Building Blocks of Organizational Structure

	Mechanistic Organizations	**Organic Organizations**
Specialization	• High degree of specialization • Rigid division of labor • Employees focus on narrowly defined tasks	• Low degree of specialization • Flexible division of labor • Employees focus on "bigger picture"
Formalization	• Intimate familiarity with rules, policies, and processes necessary • Deep expertise in narrowly defined domain required • Task-specific knowledge valued	• Clear understanding of organization's core competencies and strategic intent • Domain expertise in different areas • Generalized knowledge of how to accomplish strategic goals valued
Centralization	• Decision power centralized at top • Vertical (top-down) communication	• Distributed decision making • Vertical (top-down and bottom-up) as well as horizontal communication
Hierarchy	• Tall structures • Low span of control • Clear lines of authority • Command and control	• Flat structures • High span of control • Horizontal as well as two-way vertical communication • Mutual adjustment
Business Strategy	• Cost-leadership strategy • Example: McDonald's	• Differentiation strategy • Examples: W. L. Gore, Zappos

Mechanistic organizations are characterized by a high degree of specialization and formalization, and a tall hierarchy that relies on centralized decision making. The fast food chain McDonald's fits this description quite well. Each step of every job (such as deep-frying fries) is documented in minute detail (e.g., what kind of vat, the quantity of oil, how many fries, what temperature, how long, and so on). Decision power is centralized at the top of the organization: McDonald's headquarters provides detailed instructions to each of its franchisees so that they provide comparable quality and service across the board (although with some local menu variations). Communication and authority lines are top-down and well defined. To ensure standardized operating procedures and consistent food quality throughout the world, McDonald's operates Hamburger University, a state-of-the-art teaching facility in a Chicago suburb, where 50 full-time instructors teach courses in chemistry, food preparation, and marketing. In 2010, McDonald's opened a second Hamburger University campus in Shanghai, China. Mechanistic structures allow for standardization and economies of scale, and thus often are used when the firm pursues a cost-leadership strategy at the business level (again, see Exhibit 11.3).

---

mechanistic organization
Organizational form characterized by a high degree of specialization and formalization, and a tall hierarchy that relies on centralized decision making.

simple structure
Organizational structure in which the founders tend to make all the important strategic decisions as well as run the day-to-day operations.

functional structure
Organizational structure that groups employees into distinct functional areas based on domain expertise.

Although at first glance organic organizations may appear to be more attractive than mechanistic ones, their relative effectiveness depends on context. McDonald's, with its over 31,000 restaurants across the globe, would not be successful with an organic structure. By the same token, a mechanistic structure would not allow Zappos or W. L. Gore to develop and hone their respective core competencies in customer service and product innovation.

The key point is this: *To gain and sustain competitive advantage, not only must structure follow strategy, but also the chosen organizational form must match the firm's business strategy.* We will expand further on the required strategy-structure relationship in the next section.

MATCHING STRATEGY AND STRUCTURE

The important and interdependent relationship between strategy and structure directly impacts a firm's performance. Moreover, the relationship is dynamic—changing over time in a predictable pattern as firms grow in size and complexity. Successful new ventures generally grow first by increasing sales, then by obtaining larger geographic reach, and finally by diversifying through vertical integration and entering into related and unrelated businesses.[29] Different stages in a firm's growth require different organizational structures. This important evolutionary pattern is depicted in Exhibit 11.4. As we will discuss next, organizational structures range from simple to functional to multidivisional to matrix.

>> **LO 11-5**
Describe different organizational structures and match them with appropriate strategies.

Simple Structure

A simple structure generally is used by small firms with low organizational complexity. In such firms, the founders tend to make all the important strategic decisions and run the day-to-day operations. Examples include entrepreneurial ventures (such as W. L. Gore in 1958, when the company operated out of Bill Gore's basement) and professional service firms (such as smaller advertising, consulting, accounting, and law firms, as well as family-owned businesses). Simple structures are flat hierarchies operated in a decentralized fashion. They exhibit a low degree of formalization and specialization. Typically, no professional management structures nor sophisticated systems are in place, often leading to an overload for the founder and/or CEO when the firms experience growth.

Functional Structure

As sales increase, firms generally adopt a functional structure, which groups employees into distinct functional areas based on domain expertise. These functional areas often correspond to distinct stages in the company value chain such as R&D, engineering and manufacturing, and marketing and sales, as well as supporting areas such as human resources, finance, and accounting. Exhibit 11.5 (next page) shows a functional structure, with the lines indicating reporting and authority relationships. The department head of each functional area reports to the CEO, who coordinates and integrates

EXHIBIT 11.4

Changing Organizational Structures and Increasing Complexity as Firms Grow

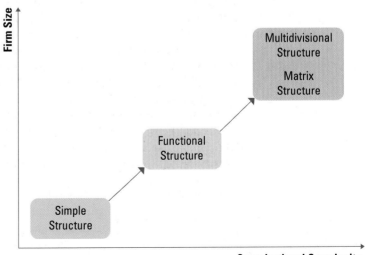

EXHIBIT 11.5

Typical Functional
Structure

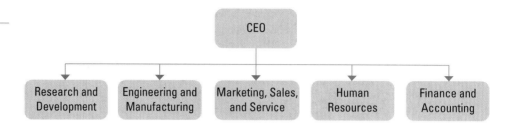

the work of each function. A business school student generally majors in one of these functional areas such as finance, accounting, IT, marketing, operations, or human resources, and is then recruited into a corresponding functional group.

Looking back to the W. L. Gore example, two years after its founding the company received a large manufacturing order for high-tech cable that it could not meet with its ad hoc basement operation. At that point, W. L. Gore reorganized itself into a functional structure. A simple structure does not provide the effective division, coordination, and integration of work required to accommodate future growth.

A functional structure allows for a higher degree of specialization and thus deeper domain expertise than a simple structure. Higher specialization also allows for a greater division of labor, which is linked to higher productivity.[30] While work in a functional structure tends to be specialized, it is centrally coordinated by the CEO (see Exhibit 11.5). A functional structure allows for an efficient top-down and bottom-up communication chain between the CEO and the functional departments, and thus relies on a relatively flat structure.

USE WITH VARIOUS BUSINESS STRATEGIES. A functional structure is recommended when a firm has a fairly narrow focus in terms of product/service offerings (i.e., low level of diversification) combined with a small geographic footprint. It matches well, therefore, with the different *business-level* strategies discussed in Chapter 6: cost-leadership, differentiation, and integration. Although a functional structure is the preferred method for implementing business strategy, *different variations and contexts require careful modifications in each case.* Exhibit 11.6 presents a detailed match between different business strategies and their corresponding functional structures.

The goal of a *cost-leadership strategy* is to create a competitive advantage by reducing the firm's cost below that of competitors while offering acceptable value. The cost leader sells a no-frills, standardized product or service to the mainstream customer. To effectively implement a cost-leadership strategy, therefore, managers must create a functional structure that contains the organizational elements of a *mechanistic structure*—one that is centralized, with well-defined lines of authority up and down the hierarchy. Using a functional structure allows the cost leader to focus on and constantly upgrade necessary core competencies in manufacturing and logistics. Moreover, the cost leader needs to create incentives to foster process innovation in order to drive down cost. Finally, since the firm services the average customer, and thus targets the largest market segment possible, it should focus on leveraging economies of scale to further drive down costs.

The goal of a *differentiation strategy* is to create a competitive advantage by offering products or services at a higher perceived value, while controlling costs. The differentiator, therefore, sells a non-standardized product or service to specific market segments in which customers are willing to pay a higher price. To effectively implement a differentiation strategy, managers rely on a functional structure that resembles an *organic organization.* In

Business-Level Strategy	Structure
Cost leadership	Functional
	• Mechanistic organization
	• Centralized
	• Command and control
	• Core competencies in efficient manufacturing and logistics
	• Process innovation to drive down cost
	• Focus on economies of scale
Differentiation	Functional
	• Organic organization
	• Decentralized
	• Flexibility and mutual adjustment
	• Core competencies in R&D, innovation, and marketing
	• Product innovation
	• Focus on economies of scope
Integration	Functional
	• Ambidextrous organization
	• Balancing centralization with decentralization
	• Multiple core competencies along the value chain required: R&D, manufacturing, logistics, marketing, etc.
	• Process and product innovations
	• Focus on economies of scale and scope

EXHIBIT 11.6

Matching Business-Level Strategy and Structure

particular, decision making tends to be decentralized to foster and incentivize continuous innovation and creativity as well as flexibility and mutual adjustment across areas. Using a functional structure with an organic organization allows the differentiator to focus on and constantly upgrade necessary core competencies in R&D, innovation, and marketing. Finally, the functional structure should be set up to allow the firm to reap economies of scope from its core competencies, such as by leveraging its brand name across different products or its technology across different devices.

A successful *integration strategy* requires reconciliation of the trade-offs between differentiation and low cost. To effectively implement an integration strategy, the firm must be both efficient and flexible. For example, the integrator must balance centralization (to control costs) with decentralization (to foster creativity and innovation). Managers must, therefore, attempt to combine the advantages of the functional-structure variations used for cost leadership and differentiation while mitigating their disadvantages. Moreover, the integrator needs to develop several distinct core competencies to both drive up perceived value and lower cost. It must further focus on both product and process innovations in an attempt to reap economies of scale and scope. All of these challenges make it clear that although an integration strategy is attractive at first glance, it is quite difficult to implement given the range of important trade-offs that must be addressed.

As mentioned in Chapter 6, managers can implement an integration strategy by building an *ambidextrous* organization, which attempts to balance and harness different activities in trade-off situations.[31] One example is the attempt to balance *exploitation* (applying current knowledge to enhance firm performance in the short term) with *exploration* (searching for new knowledge that may enhance future performance).[32] To transform a functional structure into an ambidextrous organization, the CEO (or a team of top executives) must personally take responsibility for the integration and coordination across different functional areas. In a recent study of 13 business units that produced 22 innovations over time, researchers found that ambidextrous organizations were most effective in executing continuous innovation.[33] Strategy Highlight 11.3 shows how *USA Today* used an ambidextrous organizational design to successfully reintegrate its independent online unit.

DRAWBACKS. While certainly attractive, the functional strategy is not without significant drawbacks. One is that, although the functional strategy facilitates rich and extensive communication between members of the *same* department, it frequently lacks effective communication channels *across* departments. (Notice in Exhibit 11.5 the lack of links between different functions.) The lack of linkage between functions is the reason, for example, why R&D managers often do not communicate directly with marketing managers. In an

---

STRATEGY HIGHLIGHT 11.3

USA Today: Leveraging Ambidextrous Organizational Design

The newspaper *USA Today,* published by Gannett Company, has one of the widest print circulations in the United States (close to 2 million). Though highly profitable, in the mid-1990s the newspaper faced the emerging threat of online news media, which is mostly free for the end user. Gannett decided to create a competing online offering— *USA Today.com.* It set up the new unit more or less independently from the namesake newspaper. The online news unit hired staff from the outside, and its first general manager put in place an organizational structure with fundamentally different roles and incentives, and a different culture. Physically separated from the print newspaper, *USA Today.com* resembled an online startup company in the media business more than a traditional newspaper outlet. *USA Today.com*'s culture was that of a new high-tech venture, whereas the print media *USA Today* had a more conservative corporate culture. Roughly 80 percent of the online news originated from sources other than the print version.

Although *USA Today.com* successfully attracted readers and advertising dollars, Gannett starved the fledgling startup by draining resources. As a result, *USA Today.com* lost some key editorial talent because it could not provide competitive compensation packages. To solve this problem, *USA Today.com*'s general manager pushed for even greater independence and for profit-and-loss responsibility. That decision further isolated the startup from the print-news unit.

By 2000, Gannett decided it was time to integrate *USA Today.com* with the newspaper, to create synergies between the two news outfits. It no longer made sense to duplicate all editorial functions and to create content separately. Given the strained relationship and large cultural differences between the print newspaper and the online business, however, this seemed a daunting task.

The newly appointed general manager of *USA Today.com* decided to put in place an ambidextrous organizational structure: the online unit remained somewhat independent but important functions were integrated at the top through joint editorial meetings and senior management teams. To support this integration, the president of *USA Today* shifted compensation incentives for both senior teams to accomplish *joint* goals rather than to focus solely on their business unit performance. General managers of each unit implemented further integration through weekly meetings of lower-level editorial staff. The general managers of each unit, therefore, were the key integrating linchpins between formerly independent business units, allowing for synergies to emerge.[34]

ambidextrous organization, a top-level manager such as the CEO must take on the necessary coordination and integration work.

To overcome the lack of cross-departmental collaboration in a functional structure, a firm can set up *cross-functional teams.* In these temporary teams, members come from different functional areas to work together on a specific project or product, usually from start to completion. Each team member has two supervisors to report to: the team leader and the respective functional department head. As we saw in Strategy Highlight 11.2, W. L. Gore employs cross-functional teams successfully.

A second critical drawback of the functional structure is that it cannot effectively address a higher level of diversification, which often stems from further growth.[35] This is the stage at which firms find it effective to evolve and adopt a multidivisional or matrix structure, both of which we will discuss next.

Multidivisional Structure

Over time, as a firm diversifies into different product lines and geographies, it implements a multidivisional or a matrix structure (as shown in Exhibit 11.4). The multidivisional structure (or M-form) consists of several distinct strategic business units (SBUs), each with its own profit-and-loss (P&L) responsibility. Each SBU is operated more or less independently from one another, and each is led by a CEO (or equivalent general manager) who is responsible for the unit's business strategy and its day-to-day operations. The CEOs of each division in turn report to the corporate office, which is led by the company's highest-ranking executive (titles vary and include president or CEO for the entire corporation). Since most large firms are diversified to some extent across different product lines and geographies, the M-form is a widely adopted organizational structure.

For example, Zappos is an SBU under Amazon, which employs a multidivisional structure. Also, W. L. Gore uses a multidivisional structure to administer its differentiation and related diversification strategies. It has four product divisions (electronic products, industrial products, medical products, and fabrics division) with manufacturing facilities in the U.S., China, Germany, Japan, Scotland, and business activities in 30 countries across the globe.[36]

A typical M-form is shown in Exhibit 11.7 (next page). In this example, the company has four SBUs, each led by a CEO. Corporations may use SBUs to organize around different businesses and product lines or around different geographic regions. Each SBU represents a self-contained business with its *own* hierarchy and organizational structure. In Exhibit 11.7, SBU 2 is organized using a functional structure, while SBU 4 is organized using a matrix structure. The CEO of each SBU must determine which organizational structure is most appropriate to implement the SBU's business strategy.

A firm's corporate office is supported by company-wide staff functions such as human resources, finance, and corporate R&D. These staff functions support all of the company's SBUs, but are centralized at corporate headquarters to benefit from economies of scale and to avoid duplication within each SBU. Since most of the larger enterprises are publicly held stock companies, the president reports to a board of directors who represents the interests of the shareholders (indicated by the dotted line in Exhibit 11.7).

The president, with help from corporate headquarters staff, monitors the performance of each SBU and determines how to allocate resources across units.[37] Corporate headquarters adds value by functioning as an internal capital market. The goal is to be more efficient at allocating capital through its budgeting process than what could be achieved in external capital markets. This can be especially effective if the corporation overall can access capital at a lower cost than competitors due to a favorable (AAA) debt rating. Corporate

multidivisional structure (M-form) Organizational structure that consists of several distinct strategic business units (SBUs), each with its own profit-and-loss (P&L) responsibility.

EXHIBIT 11.7

Typical Multidivisional
(M-Form) Structure
(Note SBU 2 uses a
functional structure
and SBU 4 uses a
matrix structure)

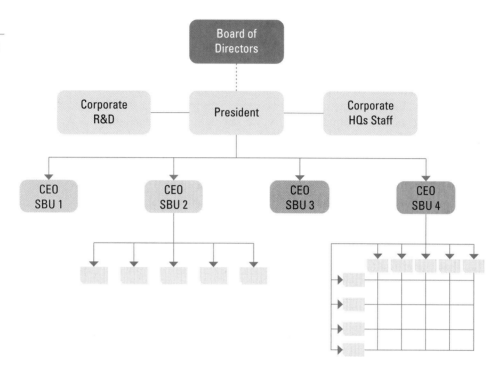

headquarters can also add value through restructuring the company's portfolio of SBUs by selling low-performing businesses and adding promising businesses through acquisitions.

General Electric (GE), featured in ChapterCase 8, has five divisions organized around different businesses. Given that GE follows an unrelated diversification strategy, it makes sense to separate its different business activities; light bulbs, *NBC Dateline,* jet engines, electrocardiograms, and nuclear reactors have little in common. Moreover, GE has sold several low-performing businesses in mature industries and acquired new businesses in promising industries such as health care and energy.

USE WITH VARIOUS CORPORATE STRATEGIES. To achieve an optimal match between strategy and structure, different *corporate-level* strategies require different organizational structures. In Chapter 8, we identified four types of corporate diversification (see Exhibit 8.7): single business, dominant business, related diversification, and unrelated diversification. Each is defined by the percentage of revenues obtained from the firm's primary activity. Firms that follow a single-business or dominant-business strategy at the corporate level gain at least 70 percent of their revenues from their primary activity; they generally employ a functional structure. For firms that pursue either related or unrelated diversification, the M-form is the preferred organizational structure. Exhibit 11.8 matches different corporate-level strategies and their corresponding organizational structures.

Managers using the M-form organizational structure to support a *related-diversification* strategy should ideally concentrate decision making at the top of the organization. Doing so allows a high level of integration. It also enables corporate headquarters to help leverage and transfer across different SBUs core competencies that form the basis for a related diversification. *Co-opetition* among the SBUs is both inevitable and necessary. They compete with one another for resources such as capital and managerial talent, but they also need to cooperate to share competencies.

Corporate-Level Strategy	Structure
Single business	Functional structure
Dominant business	Functional structure
Related diversification	Cooperative multidivisional (M-form)
	• Centralized decision making
	• High level of integration at corporate headquarters
	• Co-opetition among SBUs
	◦ Competition for resources
	◦ Cooperation in competency sharing
Unrelated diversification	Competitive multidivisional (M-form)
	• Decentralized decision making
	• Low level of integration at corporate headquarters
	• Competition among SBUs for resources

EXHIBIT 11.8

Matching Corporate-Level Strategy and Structure

In contrast, managers using the M-form structures to support an *unrelated-diversification* strategy should decentralize decision making. Doing so allows general managers to respond to specific circumstances, and leads to a low level of integration at corporate headquarters. Since each SBU is evaluated as a standalone profit-and-loss center, SBUs end up in *competition* with each other. A high-performing SBU might be rewarded with greater capital budgets and strategic freedoms; low-performing businesses might be spun off. As explained in Chapter 8, the BCG growth-share matrix helps corporate executives when making these types of decisions.

Matrix Structure

To reap the benefits of both the M-form and the functional structure, many firms employ a mix of these two organizational forms, called a matrix structure. Exhibit 11.9 (next page) shows an example. In it, the firm is organized according to SBUs (along a horizontal axis, like in the M-form), but also has a second dimension of organizational structure (along a vertical axis). In this case, the second dimension consists of different geographic areas, each of which generally would house a full set of functional activities. The idea behind the matrix structure is to combine the benefits of the M-form (domain expertise, economies of scale, and the efficient processing of information), with those of the functional structure (responsiveness and decentralized focus).

The horizontal and vertical reporting lines between SBUs and geographic areas intersect, creating nodes in the matrix. Exhibit 11.9 highlights one employee, represented by the purple node. This employee works (in a group with other employees) in SBU 2 (the company's health care unit) for the Europe division in France. Therefore, this employee has two bosses—the CEO of the health care SBU and the general manager (GM) for the Europe division. Both supervisors in turn report to corporate headquarters, which is led by the president of the corporation (indicated in Exhibit 11.9 by the reporting lines from the SBUs and geographic units to the president).

The specific organizational configuration depicted in Exhibit 11.9 is a *global matrix structure*. Firms tend to use it to pursue a *transnational strategy,* in which the firm combines the benefits of a localization strategy (high local responsiveness) with those of a global standardization strategy (lowest cost position attainable). In a global matrix structure, the

matrix structure Organizational structure that combines the functional structure with the M-form.

EXHIBIT 11.9

Typical Matrix
Structure with
Geographic and SBU
Divisions

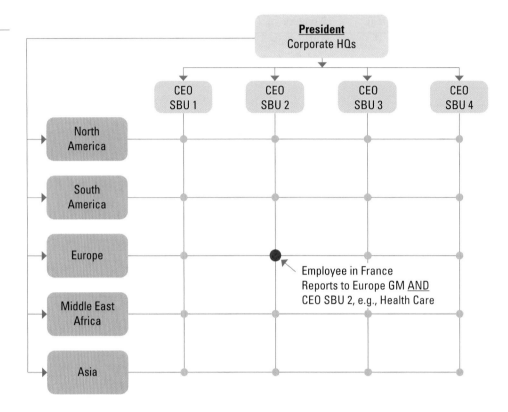

EXHIBIT 11.9

Typical Matrix Structure with Geographic and SBU Divisions

geographic divisions are charged with local responsiveness and learning. At the same time, each SBU is charged with driving down costs through economies of scale and other efficiencies. A global matrix structure also allows the firm to feed local learning back to different SBUs and thus to diffuse it throughout the organization.

The matrix structure is quite versatile, because managers can assign different groupings along the vertical and horizontal axes. A common form of the matrix structure uses different projects or products on the vertical axis, and different functional areas on the horizontal axis. In that traditional matrix structure, *cross-functional* teams work together on different projects. In contrast to the cross-functional teams discussed earlier in the W. L. Gore example, the teams in a matrix structure tend to be more permanent rather than project-based.

Though it is appealing in theory, the matrix structure does have shortcomings. It is usually difficult to implement: Implementing two layers of organizational structure creates significant organizational complexity and increases administrative costs. Also, reporting structures in a matrix are often not clear. In particular, employees can have trouble reconciling goals presented by their two (or more) supervisors. Less-clear reporting structures can undermine accountability (by creating multiple principal–agent relationships) and can thus make performance appraisals more difficult. Adding a layer of hierarchy can also slow decision making and increase bureaucratic costs.

Given the advances in computer-mediated collaboration tools, some firms have replaced the more rigid matrix structure with a *network structure*. A network structure allows the firm to connect centers of excellence whatever their global location (similar to Exhibit 10.2).[38] The firm thus benefits from *communities of practice*, which store important organizational learning and expertise. To avoid undue complexity, however, these network

Global Strategy	Structure
International	Functional
Localization (Multidomestic)	Multidivisional
	• Geographic areas
	• Decentralized decision making
Global standardization	Multidivisional
	• Product divisions
	• Centralized decision making
Transnational	Global matrix
	• Balance of centralized and decentralized decision making
	• Additional layer of hierarchy to coordinate both:
	○ Geographic areas
	○ Product divisions

EXHIBIT 11.10

Matching Global Strategy and Structure

structures need to be supported by corporate-wide procedures and policies to streamline communication, collaboration, and allocation of resources.[39]

USE WITH VARIOUS GLOBAL STRATEGIES. We already noted that a global matrix structure fits well with a transnational strategy. To complete the strategy-structure relationships in the global context, we also need to consider the international, localization, and standardization strategies discussed in Chapter 10. Exhibit 11.10 shows how different global strategies best match with different organizational structures.

In an *international strategy,* the company leverages its home-based core competency by moving into foreign markets. An international strategy is advantageous when the company faces low pressure for both local responsiveness and cost reductions. Companies pursue an international strategy through a differentiation strategy at the business level. The best match for an international strategy is a *functional* organizational structure, which allows the company to leverage its core competency most effectively. This approach is similar to matching a business-level differentiation strategy with a functional structure (discussed in detail earlier).

When a multinational enterprise (MNE) pursues a *localization strategy,* it attempts to maximize local responsiveness, in the face of low pressures for cost reductions. An appropriate match for this type of global strategy is the *multidivisional* organizational structure. That structure would enable the MNE to set up different divisions based on geographic regions (e.g., by continent). The different geographic divisions operate more or less as standalone SBUs to maximize local responsiveness. Decision making is decentralized.

When following a *global-standardization strategy,* the MNE attempts to reap significant economies of scale as well as location economies by pursuing a global division of labor based on wherever best-of-class capabilities reside at the lowest cost. Since the product offered is more or less an undifferentiated commodity, the MNE pursues a cost-leadership strategy. The optimal organizational structure match is, again, a *multidivisional* structure. Rather than focusing on geographic differences (as in the localization strategy), the focus is on driving down costs due to consolidation of activities across different geographic areas.

ORGANIZATIONAL CULTURE: VALUES, NORMS, AND ARTIFACTS

>> **LO 11-6**

Describe the elements of organizational culture, and explain where organizational cultures can come from and how they can be changed.

Organizational culture is the second key building block when designing organizations for competitive advantage. Just as people have distinct personalities, so too do organizations have unique cultures that capture "how things get done around here." Organizational culture describes the collectively shared values and norms of an organization's members.[40] *Values* define what is considered important. (See Zappos's 10 core values in Exhibit 11.1 as an example.) *Norms* define appropriate employee attitudes and behaviors. [41]

Employees learn about an organization's culture through *socialization*, a process whereby employees internalize an organization's values and norms through immersion in its day-to-day operations.[42] Successful socialization, in turn, allows employees to function productively and to take on specific roles within the organization. *Strong cultures* emerge when the company's core values are widely shared among the firm's employees and when the norms have been internalized.

Think back to the Zappos ChapterCase. The company's strong culture is a strategically relevant asset that allows it to gain and sustain a competitive advantage. In contrast, although GM also had a strong culture, it was a highly bureaucratic one in which people who showed "too much" initiative were not promoted. That strong culture at GM was a strategic *liability* because it increased organizational inertia.[43]

Although more or less invisible, corporate culture finds its expression in *artifacts*. Artifacts include elements like the design and layout of physical space (e.g., cubicles or private offices); symbols (e.g., the type of clothing worn by employees); vocabulary; what stories are told (see the Zappos example that follows); what events are celebrated and highlighted; and how they are celebrated (e.g., a formal dinner versus a company BBQ when the firm reaches its sales target).

Exhibit 11.11 depicts the elements of organizational culture—values, norms, and artifacts—in concentric circles. The most important, and least visible, one—values—is in the center. As we move outward in the figure, from values to norms to artifacts, culture becomes more observable. Understanding what organizational culture is, and how it is created, maintained, and changed, can help you be a more effective manager. A unique culture that is strategically relevant can also be the basis of a firm's competitive advantage (as discussed in the *Gaining & Sustaining Competitive Advantage* section that follows).

Where Do Organizational Cultures Come From?

Often, company founders define and shape an organization's culture, which can persist for many decades after their departure. This phenomenon is called founder imprinting.[44] Firm founders set the initial strategy, structure, and culture of an organization by transforming their vision into reality. Famous founders who have left strong imprints on their organizations include Steve Jobs (Apple), Walt Disney (Disney), Michael Dell (Dell), Sergei Brin and Larry Page (Google), Oprah Winfrey (Harpo Productions and *OWN*, the Oprah Winfrey Network), Bill Gates (Microsoft), Larry Ellison (Oracle), Ralph Lauren (Polo Ralph Lauren), Martha Stewart (Martha Stewart Living Omnimedia), and Herb Kelleher (Southwest Airlines).

EXHIBIT 11.11

The Elements of Organizational Culture: Values, Norms, and Artifacts

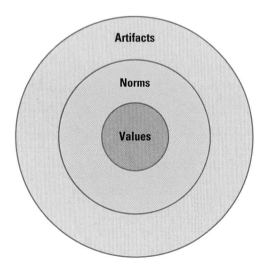

Walmart's founder Sam Walton personified the retailer's cost-leadership strategy. At one time the richest man in America, Sam Walton drove a beat-up Ford pickup truck, got $5 haircuts, went camping for vacations, and lived in a modest ranch home in Bentonville, Arkansas.[45] Home to one of the largest companies on the planet, the company's Arkansas headquarters in Bentonville was described by Thomas Friedman in his book *The World Is Flat* as follows: "[Walmart's corporate headquarters] are crammed into a reconfigured warehouse . . . a large building made of corrugated metal, I figured it was the maintenance shed."[46]

The culture that founders initially imprint is reinforced by their strong preference to recruit, retain, and promote employees who subscribe to the same values. In turn, more people with similar values are attracted to that organization.[47] As the values and norms held by the employees become more similar, the firm's corporate culture becomes stronger and more distinct.

Besides founder imprinting, however, a firm's culture can also flow from its values, especially if they are linked to the company's reward system. For example, Zappos established its unique organizational culture through explicitly stated values that are connected to its reward system (see Exhibit 11.1). To recruit people that fit with the company's values, Tony Hsieh has all new-hires go through a four-week training program. It covers such topics as company history, culture, and vision, as well as customer service.[48] New-hires also spend two weeks on the phone as customer-service reps. What's novel about Zappos's approach is that at the end of the first week, the company offers any new hire $2,000 to quit (plus pay for the time already worked). This offer stands until the end of the fourth week, when the training program is completed. Individuals who choose to stay on despite the enticing offer tend to fit well with and strengthen Zappos's distinct culture.[49]

How Does Organizational Culture Change?

An organization's culture can be one of its strongest assets, but also its greatest liability. An organization's culture can turn from a core competency into a *core rigidity* if it no longer has a good fit with the external environment.[50] For example, GM's bureaucratic culture, combined with its innovative M-form structure, was once hailed as the key to superior efficiency and management.[51] However, that culture became a liability when the external environment changed following the oil-price shocks in the 1970s and the entry of Japanese carmakers into the U.S.[52] As mentioned earlier, GM's strong culture led to organizational inertia. This resulted in a failure to adapt to changing customer preferences for more fuel-efficient cars, and prevented higher quality and more innovative designs. GM lost customers to foreign competitors, who offered these things. In such times, corporate culture may need to be changed to address a breakdown in the culture-environment relationship.

The primary avenues of culture change (often combined with changes in strategy and structure) include *bringing in new leadership* and *mergers and acquisitions (M&As)*. Leaders and top executives shape corporate culture in the way they set up an organization's structure, resource-allocation process, and reward system. As discussed in Strategy Highlight 11.1, Carol Bartz was brought in as the new Yahoo CEO to implement cultural and structural changes, in order to make the Internet services company competitive again. Strategy Highlight 11.4 (next page) describes former-CEO Carly Fiorina's attempt to change HP's organizational culture through M&A.

Organizational Culture and Competitive Advantage

Can organizational culture be the basis of a firm's (sustainable) competitive advantage? For this to occur, according to the resource-based view of the firm, the resource—in this case, organizational culture—must be valuable, rare, difficult to imitate, and the firm must

organizational culture
The collectively shared values and norms of an organization's members; a key building block of organizational design.

founder imprinting
A process by which the founder defines and shapes an organization's culture, which can persist for decades after his or her departure.

GAINING & SUSTAINING COMPETITIVE ADVANTAGE

Carly Fiorina at HP: Cultural Change via Shock Therapy

In 1999, Carly Fiorina was appointed CEO of Hewlett-Packard (HP), one of the leading U.S. technology companies. Ms. Fiorina was the first outsider to become CEO of the venerable technology company, and the first woman to lead a Fortune 20 company. The board hoped Ms. Fiorina would change HP's culture to make it more competitive, particularly in the booming Internet economy in which competitors like Cisco, Sun Microsystems, and IBM were riding high.[53]

In 2002, Ms. Fiorina engineered HP's acquisition of Compaq, for $25 billion, to pursue "high-tech at low-cost" (as discussed in Chapter 4). However, this was not the only motivation for the mega merger. An equally important but unstated reason was that Ms. Fiorina needed a shock to HP's system: She was convinced that HP had grown complacent and needed to "root out the rot that insiders tolerate or fail even to see."[54] The merger with Compaq gave Ms. Fiorina the opportunity to make some tough but necessary structural changes, including laying off some 25 percent of the work force at a place where employees were accustomed to lifetime employment. She also redesigned the organizational structure to make HP more nimble and put in a more merit-based rather than seniority-based reward system.[55]

While many believe that Carly Fiorina failed in creating the change that HP needed (the board let her go in 2005), others believe that her successor—Mark Hurd—benefited from the tough changes that Ms. Fiorina implemented.[56] (In 2010, Leo Apotheker replaced Mark Hurd in the wake of an ethics scandal, which we will discuss in the next chapter.)

be organized to capture the value created. That is, the VRIO principles must hold (see Chapter 4).[57]

Let's look at two examples of how culture affects employee behavior and ultimately firm performance:

- If you have flown with Southwest Airlines (SWA), you may have noticed that things are done a little differently there. Some argue that SWA's business strategy—being a cost leader in point-to-point air travel—is fairly simple, and that SWA's competitive advantage actually comes from its unique culture.[58] Friendly and highly energized employees work across functional and hierarchical levels. Even Southwest's pilots pitch in when needed. As a result, SWA's turn time between flights is only 15 minutes, whereas competitors frequently take two to three times as long.

- Zappos's number-one core value is to "deliver WOW through service." CEO Tony Hsieh shares the following story to illustrate this core value in action: "I was in Santa Monica, California, a few years ago at a Skechers sales conference. . . . [In the early hours of the morning], a small group of us headed up to someone's hotel room to order some food. My friend from Skechers tried to order a pepperoni pizza from the room-service menu, but was disappointed to learn that the hotel we were staying at did not deliver hot food after 11:00 p.m. We had missed the deadline by several hours. . . . A few of us cajoled her into calling Zappos to try to order a pizza. She took us up on our dare, turned on the speakerphone, and explained to the (very) patient Zappos rep that she was staying in a Santa Monica hotel and really craving a pepperoni pizza, that room service was no longer delivering hot food, and that she wanted to know if there was anything Zappos could do to help. The Zappos rep was initially a bit confused by the request, but she quickly recovered and put us on hold. She returned two minutes later, listing the five closest places in the Santo Monica area that were still open and delivering pizzas at that time."[59]

In the SWA example, the company's unique culture helps it keep costs low by turning around its planes faster, thus keeping them flying longer hours (among many other activities that lower SWA's cost structure).[60] In the Zappos example, providing a "wow" customer experience by "going the extra mile" didn't save Zappos money, but in the long run superior experience does increase the company's perceived value, and thereby its economic value creation. Indeed, Tony Hsieh makes it a point to conclude the story with the following statement: "As for my friend from Skechers? After that phone call, she's now a customer for life."[61]

Let's consider how an organization's culture can have a strong influence on employee behavior.[62] First, a positive culture motivates and energizes employees by appealing to their higher ideals. Internalizing the firm's values and norms, employees feel that they are part of a larger, meaningful community attempting to accomplish important things. When employees are intrinsically motivated this way, the firm can rely on fewer levels of hierarchy; thus close monitoring and supervision are less needed. Moreover, motivating through inspiring values allows the firms to tap employees' emotions so that they use both their heads and their hearts when making business decisions. Strong organizational cultures that are strategically relevant, therefore, align employees' behavior more fully with the organization's strategic goals. In doing so, they better coordinate work efforts, and they make cooperation more effective. They also strengthen employee commitment, engagement, and effort. Effective alignment in turn allows the organization to develop and refine its core competencies, which can form the basis for competitive advantage.

Applying the VRIO principles to the SWA and Zappos examples, we see that both cultures are valuable (lowering costs for SWA and increasing perceived value created for Zappos), rare (not many other firms, if any, have an identical culture), non-imitable (despite attempts by competitors), and organized to capture some part of the incremental economic value they create due to their unique cultures. It appears that at both SWA and Zappos, a unique organizational culture can in fact provide the basis for a (sustained) competitive advantage. These cultures, of course, need to be in sync with and in support of the respective business strategies pursued (cost leadership for SWA and differentiation for Zappos). Moreover, as the firms grow and external economic environments change, these cultures must be flexible enough to adapt.

Once it becomes clear that a firm's culture is a source of competitive advantage, some competitors will attempt to imitate that culture. Therefore, only a culture that cannot be easily copied can provide a competitive advantage. However, it can be difficult, at best, to imitate the cultures of successful firms, for two reasons: *causal ambiguity* and *social complexity.* While one can observe that a firm has a unique culture, the causal relationships among values, norms, artifacts, and the firm's performance may be hard to establish, even for people who work within the organization. For example, employees may become aware of the effect culture has on performance only after significant organizational changes occur. Moreover, organizational culture is socially complex. It encompasses not only interactions among employees across layers of hierarchy, but also the firm's outside relationships with its customers and suppliers.[63] Such a wide range of factors is difficult for any competing firm to imitate.

It is best to develop a strong and strategically relevant culture in the first few years of a firm's existence. It has been documented that the initial structure, culture, and control mechanisms set up in a new firm can be a significant predictor of later success.[64] In other empirical research, founder CEOs had a stronger positive imprinting effect than non-founder CEOs.[65] This stronger imprinting effect, in turn, resulted in higher performance of firms led by founder CEOs. In addition, consider that the vehicles of cultural change—changing leadership and growing through M&As—do not have a stellar record of success.[66] Indeed, researchers estimate that only about 20 percent of organizational change attempts are successful.[67] Thus, it is even more important to get the culture right from the beginning and then adapt it as the business evolves.

Combining theory and empirical evidence, we can see that organizational culture can help a firm gain and sustain competitive advantage *if* the culture makes a positive contribution to the firm's economic value creation and obeys the other VRIO principles. Organizational culture is an especially effective lever for new ventures due to its malleability. Firm founders, early-stage CEOs, and venture capitalists, therefore, should be proactive in attempting to create a culture that leads to or at least supports a firm's competitive advantage. 🔍

STRATEGIC CONTROL AND REWARD SYSTEMS

>> **LO 11-7**
Compare and contrast
different strategic
control and reward
systems.

Strategic control and reward systems are the third and final key building block when designing organizations for competitive advantage. Strategic control and reward systems are internal-governance mechanisms put in place to align the incentives of principals (shareholders) and agents (employees). These systems allow managers to specify goals, measure progress, and provide performance feedback. In Chapter 5, we discussed how firms can use the balanced-scorecard framework as a strategic control system. Here we discuss additional control and reward systems: organizational culture, input controls, and output controls.

As discussed earlier, *organizational culture* can be a powerful motivator. It also can be an effective control system. Norms, informal and tacit in nature, act as a social control mechanism. Steelmaker Nucor, for example, achieves organizational control through an employee's peer group: Each group member's compensation, including the foreman's, depends on the group's *overall productivity.* Peer control, therefore, exerts a powerful force on employee conformity and performance.[68] Besides soliciting expected behavior, social norms also apply *sanctions* such as sarcasm, ostracism, and ridicule (and sometimes even physical force) in the face of undesirable behavior.[69] Values and norms also provide control by helping employees address unpredictable and irregular situations and problems (common in service businesses). In contrast, rules and procedures (e.g., codified in an employee handbook) can address only circumstances that can be predicted.

Input Controls

Input controls seek to define and direct employee behavior through a set of explicit and codified rules and standard operating procedures. Firms use input controls when the goal is to define the ways and means to reach a strategic goal and to ensure a predictable outcome. They are called input controls because management designs these mechanisms so they are considered *before* employees make any business decisions; thus, they are an input into the value-creation activities.

The use of *budgets* is key to input controls. Managers set budgets before employees define and undertake the actual business activities. For example, managers decide how much money to allocate to a certain R&D project before the project begins. In diversified companies using the M-form, corporate headquarters determines the budgets for each division. Public institutions, like some universities, also operate on budgets that must be balanced each year. Their funding often depends to a large extent on state appropriations and thus fluctuates depending on the economic cycle. During recessions, budgets tend to be cut, and they expand during boom periods.

Standard operating procedures, or policies and rules, are also a frequently used mechanism when relying on input controls. In our discussion on formalization, we described how McDonald's relies on detailed operating procedures to ensure consistent quality and service worldwide. The goal is to specify the conversion process from beginning to end in great detail to guarantee standardization and minimize deviation. This is important when a company operates in different geographies and with different human capital throughout the globe but needs to deliver a standardized product or service.

Output Controls

Output controls seek to guide employee behavior by defining expected results (outputs), but leave the means to those results open to individual employees, groups, or SBUs. Firms frequently tie employee compensation and rewards to predetermined goals, such as a specific sales target or return on invested capital. When factors internal to the firm determine the relationship between effort and expected performance, outcome controls are especially effective. At the corporate level, outcome controls discourage collaboration among different strategic business units. They are therefore best applied when a firm focuses on a single line of business or pursues unrelated diversification.

These days, more and more work requires creativity and innovation, especially in highly developed economies.[70] As a consequence, so-called *results-only-work-environments* (*ROWEs*) have attracted significant attention. ROWEs are output controls that attempt to tap intrinsic (rather than extrinsic) employee motivation, which is driven by the employee's interest in and the meaning of the work itself. In contrast, extrinsic motivation is driven by external factors such as awards and higher compensation or punishments such as demotion and lay-off (the *carrot-and-stick approach*). According to a recent synthesis of the strategic human resources literature, intrinsic motivation in a task is highest when an employee has autonomy (about what to do), mastery (how to do it), and purpose (why to do it).[71]

Daniel Pink's book on motivation (*Drive: The Surprising Truth About What Motivates Us*) discusses the limits of the carrot-and-stick approach versus the motivational impact of autonomy.

Today, 3M is best known for its adhesives and other consumer and industrial products.[72] But its full name reflects its origins: 3M stands for Minnesota Mining and Manufacturing Company. Over time, 3M has relied on the ROWE framework and has morphed into a highly science-driven innovation company. At 3M, employees are encouraged to spend 15 percent of their time on projects of their *own choosing*. If any of these projects look promising, 3M provides financing through an internal venture-capital fund and other resources to further develop their commercial potential. In fact, several of 3M's flagship products, including Post-It Notes and Scotch Tape, were the results of serendipity (see Chapter 2). To foster continued innovation, moreover, 3M requires each of its divisions to derive at least 30 percent of their revenues from products introduced in the past four years.

This concludes our discussion of organizational design. As we have seen, formulating an effective strategy is a necessary but not sufficient condition for gaining and sustaining competitive advantage; strategy *execution* is at least as important for success. Successful strategy implementation requires managers to design and shape structure, culture, and control mechanisms. In doing so, they execute a firm's strategy as they put its accompanying business model into action. Strategy formulation and strategy implementation, therefore, are iterative and interdependent activities. In existing firms, strategy implementation necessitates organizational change. Managing effective organizational change requires strategic leadership that is ethical and effectively governed. We now move on to our concluding chapter, where we study corporate governance, business ethics, and strategic leadership.

---

strategic control and reward systems A key building block of organizational design; internal-governance mechanisms put in place to align the incentives of principals (shareholders) and agents (employees).

input controls Mechanisms in a strategic control and reward system that seek to define and direct employee behavior through a set of explicit and codified rules and standard operating procedures, considered prior to the value-creating activities.

output controls Mechanisms in a strategic control and reward system that seek to guide employee behavior by defining expected results (outputs), but leave the means to those results open to individual employees, groups, or SBUs.

CHAPTERCASE **11** | *Consider This . . .*

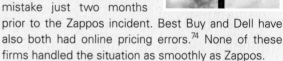

ZAPPOS WANTS TO "deliver WOW through service." We saw an example of this culture in the story of the Zappos customer service rep who provided contacts for local pizza delivery to an out-of-town guest. Though it is a memorable story, providing the pizza 411-service did not involve significant cost to the employee or the firm for delivering "WOW through service." However, at midnight on Friday, May 21, 2010, Zappos created a problem that required a significant financial cost to deliver that "WOW." Due to a programming error in its pricing engine, Zappos accidentally capped the sales price at $49.95 for all products sold on its sister site (www.6pm.com). The mistake was not discovered until 6 a.m. Zappos pulled down the site to correct the pricing problem. Once fixed, there remained a question of what to do about the products sold with the erroneous prices.

Zappos's terms and conditions clearly state that the firm is under no obligation to fulfill orders placed due to pricing mistakes. However, Zappos decided to honor every sale made in the time frame between midnight and 6 a.m.—resulting in a loss of over $1.6 million.

That's putting your money where your "WOW" is![73]

Amazon, which owns Zappos, had its own pricing mistake just two months prior to the Zappos incident. Best Buy and Dell have also both had online pricing errors.[74] None of these firms handled the situation as smoothly as Zappos.

1. What elements of an organic organization are apparent from the chapter material on Zappos? (Refer to Exhibit 11.3.)

2. How does the Zappos business strategy match its organizational structure?

3. Which strategic control and reward system discussed in the chapter would be most appropriate for Zappos?

4. Do you think Zappos's decision to honor every sale, despite its explicit business terms and conditions that would allow it not to do so, was a sound one? Why or why not?

Take-Away Concepts

In this chapter, we studied the three key levers that managers have at their disposal when designing their firms for competitive advantage—structure, culture, and control—as summarized by the following learning objectives and related take-away concepts.

LO 11-1 Define organizational design and list its three components.

>> Organizational design is the process of creating, implementing, monitoring, and modifying the structure, processes, and procedures of an organization.

>> The key components of organizational design are structure, culture, and control.

>> The goal is to design an organization that allows managers to effectively translate their chosen strategy into a realized one.

LO 11-2 Explain how organizational inertia can lead established firms to failure.

>> Organizational inertia can lead to the failure of established firms when a tightly coupled system of strategy and structure experiences internal or external shifts.

>> Firm failure happens through a dynamic, four-step process (see Exhibit 11.2).

LO 11-3 Define organizational structure and describe its four elements.

>> An organizational structure determines how firms orchestrate employees' work efforts and distribute resources. It defines how firms divide and integrate tasks, delineates the reporting relationships up and down the hierarchy, defines formal communication channels, and prescribes how employees coordinate work efforts.

>> The four building blocks of an organizational structure are specialization, formalization, centralization, and hierarchy (see Exhibit 11.3).

LO 11-4 Compare and contrast mechanistic versus organic organizations.

>> Organic organizations are characterized by a low degree of specialization and formalization, a flat organizational structure, and decentralized decision making.

>> Mechanistic organizations are described by a high degree of specialization and formalization, and a tall hierarchy that relies on centralized decision making.

>> The comparative effectiveness of mechanistic versus organic organizational forms depends on the context.

LO 11-5 Describe different organizational structures and match them with appropriate strategies.

>> To gain and sustain competitive advantage, not only must structure follow strategy, but also the chosen organizational form must match the firm's business strategy.

>> The strategy-structure relationship is dynamic, changing in a predictable pattern—from simple to functional structure, then to multidivisional (M-form) and matrix structure—as firms grow in size and complexity.

>> In a simple structure, the founder tends to make all the important strategic decisions as well as run the day-to-day operations.

>> A functional structure groups employees into distinct functional areas based on domain expertise. Its different variations are matched with different business strategies: cost-leadership, differentiation, and integration (see Exhibit 11.6).

>> The multidivisional (M-form) structure consists of several distinct SBUs, each with its own profit-and-loss responsibility. Each SBU operates more or less independently from one another, led by a CEO responsible for the business strategy of the unit and its day-to-day operations (see Exhibit 11.7).

>> The matrix structure is a mixture of two organizational forms: the M-form and the functional structure (see Exhibit 11.9).

>> Exhibits 11.8 and 11.10 show how best to match different corporate and global strategies with respective organizational structures.

LO 11-6 Describe the elements of organizational culture, and explain where organizational cultures can come from and how they can be changed.

>> Organizational culture describes the collectively shared values and norms of its members.

>> Values define what is considered important, and norms define appropriate employee attitudes and behaviors.

>> Corporate culture finds its expression in artifacts, which are observable expressions of an organization's culture.

LO 11-7 Compare and contrast different strategic control and reward systems.

>> Strategic control and reward systems are internal governance mechanisms put in place to align the incentives of principals (shareholders) and agents (employees).

>> Strategic control and reward systems allow managers to specify goals, measure progress, and provide performance feedback.

>> Besides the balanced-scorecard framework, managers can use organizational culture, input controls, and output controls as part of the firm's strategic control and reward systems.

>> Input controls define and direct employee behavior through explicit and codified rules and standard operating procedures.

>> Output controls guide employee behavior by defining expected results, but leave the means to those results open to individual employees, groups, or SBUs.

Key Terms

Centralization *(p. 306)*

Formalization *(p. 305)*

Founder imprinting *(p. 318)*

Functional structure *(p. 309)*

Hierarchy *(p. 307)*

Input controls *(p. 322)*

Matrix structure *(p. 315)*

Mechanistic organization *(p. 308)*

Multidivisional structure (M-form) *(p. 313)*

Organic organization *(p. 307)*

Organizational culture *(p. 318)*

Organizational design *(p. 303)*

Organizational structure *(p. 304)*

Output controls *(p. 322)*

Discussion Questions

1. Why is it important for an organization to have alignment between its strategy and organizational structure?

2. The chapter notes that changing organizational culture is daunting and provides examples of Yahoo, GM, and HP. What other firms have attempted to change their culture in recent years? What techniques did they use for the transition? Was it successful?

3. Strategy Highlight 11.2 discusses the informal organizational structure of W. L. Gore & Associates. Go to the firm's website (www.gore.com) and review the product scope of the firm.

    a. What commonalities across the products would likely be enhanced by flexible cross-functional teams?

    b. What would be your expectations of the type of norms found at W. L. Gore?

Ethical/Social Issues

1. As noted in Chapter 5, many public firms are under intense pressure for short-term (such as quarterly) financial improvements. How might such pressure, in combination with output controls, lead to possible unethical behaviors?

2. Strong company cultures can have many benefits, such as those described in the Zappos example.

However, sometimes a strong organizational culture is less positive. Name some examples of organizational culture leading to business failure, criminal behavior, or civil legal actions.

3. What makes some strong cultures helpful to gaining and sustaining a competitive advantage, while other strong cultures are a liability to achieving that goal?

Small Group Exercises

SMALL GROUP EXERCISE 1

Your classmates are a group of friends who have decided to open a small retail shop. The team is torn between two storefront ideas. The first idea is to open a high-end antique store selling household items used for decorations in upscale homes. Members of the team have found a location in a heavily pedestrian area near a local coffee shop. The store would have many items authenticated by a team member's uncle, who is a certified appraiser.

In discussing the plan, however, two group members suggest shifting to a drop-off store for online auctions such as eBay. In this business model, customers drop off items they want to sell, and the retail store

does all the logistics involved—listing and selling the items on eBay, and then shipping them to buyers—for a percentage of the sales price. They suggest that a quick way to get started is to become a franchisee for a group such as "I Sold It" (www.877isoldit.com).

1. What is the business strategy for each store concept?

2. How would the organizational structure be different for the concepts?

3. What would likely be cultural differences in the two store concepts?

4. How would the control and reward systems be different?

SMALL GROUP EXERCISE 2 (ETHICAL/SOCIAL ISSUES)

Employee morale can directly affect productivity in the workplace. A poll taken in January 2010 found that 50 percent of respondents (in small- and medium-sized firms) indicated employee morale was down.[75] Assume your group is brought in to a business unit, and your analysis shows a significant excess headcount in the accounting and purchasing departments. Your team is now responsible for developing a plan to lay off

25 percent of the employees in those departments. You have six months to identify whom to lay off to reduce the headcount. (If you have no personal experience with work-force reductions, use an Internet search engine and look up "successful layoffs" for some guidance.)

1. How can you downsize the departments without hurting the morale of the remaining workers?

2. What steps do you take to treat with dignity the employees forced to leave?

Strategy Term Project

MODULE 11: ORGANIZATIONAL IMPLEMENTATION PROCESSES[76]

In this module, you will study the organizational implementation processes of your selected firm. You will again rely on annual reports, news articles, and press releases for information to analyze and formulate your answers. You will identify a major strategic

change the firm should seriously consider implementing and then follow a six-step process to study the implementation impacts.

Implementation is a critical step in putting a planned action into effect. It often introduces change into the organization and can be met with strong resistance. The six stages outlined in Exhibit 11.12 can help

EXHIBIT 11.12

Implementation Framework

Implementation Stage	Key Questions to Ask in This Stage
Stage 1 People, skills, and organizational structure	• When must the strategy/strategic initiative be implemented? (How flexible is that date?) • Who is going to do it? What human skills are needed? • Do affected employees understand their roles? • Will the organization need to hire or lay off people? If so, how should we go about it? • How should the firm be organized? What structure should be implemented? Why and how?
Stage 2 Organizational culture	• What culture in the organization is required for the implementation to be successful? • If the current culture differs from the culture needed for the success of the strategy implementation, how should the firm go about changing its culture?
Stage 3 Reward system	• Is a reward structure in place to accomplish the task? • If not, what type of reward structure needs to be introduced to ensure successful strategy implementation?
Stage 4 Resource requirements	• What resources (financial and otherwise) are needed? • Are they in place? • If not, how can the firm obtain the required resources?
Stage 5 Supporting activities	• How is the implementation to be supported? • What policies, procedures, and IT support are needed? • Does the firm need external help (e.g., consulting services)? If so, what kind of services would the firm need, and why?
Stage 6 Strategic leadership	• What types of strategic leaders are required to make the change happen? • Does the firm have them in-house? • Should the firm hire some strategic leaders from outside? • How should the firm train its managers to create a pipeline of strategic leaders?

leaders and organizations determine *how* to implement a particular plan. These questions provide a framework for the strategic change. You may be able to find a prior successful strategic change the firm undertook and use this prior implementation as a guide for your suggested change.

As you progress through the six stages, reflect on what you have learned about your firm in the prior modules. In some cases, you will need to make educated guesses for the answer since you are looking at implementation from outside the organization. However, over the ten modules you have completed, you have already learned much about the firm.

Answer the following questions for your selected organization.

1. From your knowledge of the firm, identify a major strategic change the firm should seriously consider. Briefly describe what the goal of the initiative is for the organization.

2. Work your way through the six stages in Exhibit 11.12, answering as many of the questions as you can for the proposed strategic change. As you develop the project plans with specifics for each of the stages, the plan should provide flexibility, allowing for unexpected contingencies to emerge.

*my*Strategy

FOR WHAT TYPE OF ORGANIZATION ARE *YOU* BEST-SUITED?

As noted in the chapter, firms can have very distinctive cultures. Recall that Zappos has a standing offer to pay any new hire $2,000 to quit the company during the first month. Zappos makes this offer to help ensure that those who stay with the company are comfortable in its "create fun and a little weirdness" environment.

You may have taken a personality test such as Myers-Briggs or The Big Five. These tests may be useful in gauging compatibility of career and personality types. They are often available for both graduate and undergraduate students at university career-placement centers. In considering the following questions, think about your next job and your longer-term career plans.

1. Review Exhibit 11.3 and circle the organizational characteristics you find appealing. Cross out those factors you think you would not like. Do you find a trend toward either the mechanistic or organic organization?

2. Have you been in school or work situations in which your values did not align with those of your peers or colleagues? How did you handle the situation? Are there certain values or norms important enough for you to consider as you look for a new job?

3. As you consider your career after graduation, which control and rewards system discussed in the concluding section of the chapter would you find most motivating? Is this different from the controls used at some jobs you have had in the past?

Endnotes

1. Hsieh, T. (2010), *Delivering Happiness: A Path to Profits, Passion, and Purpose* (New York: Business Plus), p. 130.

2. Ibid., p. 145.

3. Ibid., p. 177.

4. Ibid., pp. 157–160.

5. This ChapterCase is based on: Hsieh, T. (2010), *Delivering Happiness: A Path to Profits, Passion, and Purpose*.

6. Barney, J. B. (1986), "Organizational culture: Can it be a source of sustained competitive advantage?" *Academy of Management Review* 11: 656–665.

7. Bossidy, L., R. Charan, and C. Burck (2002), *Execution: The Discipline of Getting Things Done* (New York: Crown Business); and Hrebiniak, L. G. (2005), *Making Strategy Work: Leading Effective Execution and Change* (Philadelphia: Wharton School Publishing).

8. Grundy, T. (1998), "Strategy implementation and project management," *International Journal of Project Management* 16: 43–50.

9. Bossidy, L., R. Charan, and C. Burck (2002), *Execution: The Discipline of Getting Things Done;* and Herold, D. M., and D. B. Fedor (2008), *Change the Way You Lead Change: Leadership Strategies that Really Work* (Palo Alto, CA: Stanford University Press).

10. Herold, D. M., and D. B. Fedor (2008), *Change the Way You Lead Change.*

11. Chandler, A. D. (1962), *Strategy and Structure: Chapters in the History of American Industrial Enterprise* (Cambridge, MA: MIT Press), p. 14 (italics added).

12. Hall, D. J., and M. A. Saias (1980), "Strategy follows structure!" *Strategic Management Journal* 1: 149–163.

13. "Yang's exit doesn't fix Yahoo," *The Wall Street Journal,* November 19, 2008.

14. "A question of management: Carol Bartz on how Yahoo's organizational structure got in the way of innovation," *The Wall Street Journal,* June 2, 2009.

15. Ibid.

16. Hill, C.W.L., and F. T. Rothaermel (2003), "The performance of incumbent firms in the face of radical technological innovation," *Academy of Management Review* 28: 257–274.

17. I gratefully acknowledge Professor Luis Martins's input on this exhibit.

18. In his insightful book, Finkelstein (2003) identifies several key transition points that put pressure on an organization and thus increase the likelihood of subsequent failure. See Finkelstein, S. (2003), *Why Smart Executives Fail: And What You Can Learn from Their Mistakes* (New York: Portfolio).

19. Fredrickson, J. W. (1986), "The strategic decision process and organizational structure," *Academy of Management Review* 11: 280–297; Eisenhardt, K. M. (1989), "Making fast strategic decisions in high-velocity environments," *Academy of Management Journal* 32: 543–576; and Wally, S., and R. J. Baum (1994), "Strategic decision speed and firm performance," *Strategic Management Journal* 24, 1107–1129.

20. Hamel, G. (2007), *The Future of Management* (Boston, MA: Harvard Business School Press), p. 84.

21. This Strategy Highlight is based on: Hamel, G. (2007), *The Future of Management;* Collins, J. (2009), *How the Mighty Fall: And Why Some Companies Never Give In* (New York: HarperCollins); and www.gore.com.

22. *The 9/11 Report. The National Commission on Terrorist Attacks Upon the United States* (2004), http://govinfo .library.unt.edu/911/report/index.htm.

23. Child, J., and R. G. McGrath (2001), "Organization unfettered: Organizational forms in the information-intensive economy," *Academy of Management Journal* 44: 1135–1148; and Huy, Q. N. (2002), "Emotional balancing of organizational continuity and radical change: The contribution of middle managers," *Administrative Science Quarterly* 47: 31–69.

24. Theobald, N. A., and S. Nicholson-Crotty (2005), "The many faces of span of control: Organizational structure across multiple goals," *Administration and Society* 36: 648–660.

25. This section draws on: Burns, T., and G. M. Stalker (1961), *The Management of Innovation* (London: Tavistock).

26. This section draws on: Burns, T., and G. M. Stalker (1961), *The Management of Innovation;* Perry-Smith, J. E., and C. E. Shalley (2003), "The social side of creativity: A static and dynamic social network perspective," *Academy of Management Review* 28: 89–106; and Shalley, C. E., and J. E. Perry-Smith (2008), "The emergence of team creative cognition: The role of diverse outside ties, sociocognitive network centrality, and team evolution," *Strategic Entrepreneurship Journal* 2: 23–41.

27. Hagel III, J., J. S. Brown, and L. Davison (2010), *The Power of Pull: How Small Moves, Smartly Made, Can Set Big Things in Motion* (Philadelphia: Basic Books); Majchrzak, A., A. Malhotra, J. Stamps, and J. Lipnack (2004), "Can absence make a team grow stronger?" *Harvard Business Review,* May: 137–144; and Malhotra, A., A. Majchrzak, A, and B. Rosen, (2007), "Leading far-flung teams," *Academy of Management Perspectives* 21: 60–70.

28. Bryan, L. L., and C. I. Joyce (2007), "Better strategy through organizational design," *The McKinsey Quarterly* 2: 21–29.

29. Chandler, A. D. (1962), *Strategy and Structure: Chapters in the History of American Industrial Enterprise.*

30. Ibid. Also, for a more recent treatise across different levels of analysis, see Ridley, M. (2010), *The Rational Optimist: How Prosperity Evolves* (New York: HarperCollins).

31. Rothaermel, F. T., and M. T. Alexandre (2009), "Ambidexterity in technology sourcing: The moderating role of absorptive capacity," *Organization Science* 20: 759–780.

32. Levinthal, D. A., and J. G. March (1993), "The myopia of learning," *Strategic Management Journal* 14: 95–112; and March, J. G. (1991), "Exploration and exploitation in organizational learning," *Organization Science* 2: 319–340.

33. Tushman, M., W. K. Smith, R. C. Wood, and G. Westerman (2010), "Organizational designs and innovation streams," *Industrial and Corporate Change* 19: 1331–1366.

34. Ibid.

35. Chandler, A. D. (1962), *Strategy and Structure: Chapters in the History of American Industrial Enterprise.*

36. www.gore.com.

37. Williamson, O. E. (1975), *Markets and Hierarchies* (Free Press: New York); and Williamson, O. E. (1985), *The Economic Institutions of Capitalism* (Free Press: New York).

38. Bryan, L. L., and C. I. Joyce (2007), "Better strategy through organizational design"; Hagel III, J., J. S. Brown, and L. Davison (2010), *The Power of Pull: How Small Moves, Smartly Made, Can Set Big Things in Motion*; Majchrzak, A., A. Malhotra, J. Stamps, and J. Lipnack (2004), "Can absence make a team grow stronger?"; Malhotra, A., A. Majchrzak, and B. Rosen (2007), "Leading far-flung teams."

39. Brown, J. S., and P. Duguid (1991), "Organizational learning and communities-of-practice: Toward a unified view of working, learning, and innovation," *Organization Science* 2: 40–57.

40. This section draws on: Barney, J. B. (1986), "Organizational culture: Can it be a source of sustained competitive advantage?"; Chatman, J. A., and S. Eunyoung Cha (2003), "Leading by leveraging culture," *California Management Review* 45: 19–34; Kerr, J., and J. W. Slocum (2005), "Managing corporate culture through reward systems," *Academy of Management Executive* 19: 130–138; O'Reilly, C.A., J. Chatman, and D. L. Caldwell (1991), "People and organizational culture: A profile comparison approach to assessing person-organization fit," *Academy of Management Journal* 34: 487–516; and Schein, E. H. (1992), *Organizational Culture and Leadership* (San Francisco: Jossey-Bass).

41. Chatman, J. A., and S. Eunyoung Cha (2003), "Leading by leveraging culture," pp. 19–34

42. Chao, G. T., A. M. O'Leary-Kelly, S. Wolf, H. J. Klein, and P. D. Gardner (1994), "Organizational socialization: Its content and consequences," *Journal of Applied Psychology* 79: 730–743.

43. Hill, C.W.L., and F. T. Rothaermel (2003), "The performance of incumbent firms in the face of radical technological innovation," *Academy of Management Review* 28: 257–274.

44. Nelson, T. (2003), "The persistence of founder influence: Management, ownership, and performance effects at initial public offering," *Strategic Management Journal* 24: 707–724.

45. A&E Biography Video (1997), *Sam Walton: Bargain Billionaire.*

46. Friedman, T. L. (2005), *The World Is Flat. A Brief History of the 21st Century* (New York: Farrar, Straus and Giroux), pp. 130–131.

47. Schneider, B., H. W. Goldstein, and D. B. Smith (1995), "The ASA framework: An update," *Personnel Psychology* 48: 747–773.

48. Hsieh, T. (2010), *Delivering Happiness. A Path to Profits, Passion, and Purpose,* p. 145.

49. Less than 1 percent of new hires take Zappos up on the $2,000 offer to quit during the training program.

50. Leonard-Barton, D. (1995), *Wellsprings of Knowledge: Building and Sustaining the Sources of Innovation* (Boston, MA: Harvard Business School Press Press).

51. Chandler, A. D. (1962), *Strategy and Structure: Chapters in the History of American Industrial Enterprise.*

52. Birkinshaw, J. (2010), *Reinventing Management. Smarter Choices for Getting Work Done* (Chichester, West Sussex, UK: Jossey-Bass).

53. Collins, J. (2009), *How the Mighty Fall: And Why Some Companies Never Give In.*

54. "All Carly, all the time," *Forbes,* December 13, 1999.

55. Author's interview with a Distinguished Technologist at HP.

56. "HP says goodbye to drama," *BusinessWeek,* September 12, 2005.

57. This section is based on: Barney, J. B. (1986), "Organizational culture: Can it be a source of sustained competitive advantage?"; Barney, J. (1991), "Firm resources and sustained competitive advantage," *Journal of Management* 17: 99–120; and Chatman, J. A., and S. Eunyoung Cha (2003), "Leading by leveraging culture," pp. 19–34.

58. Hoffer Gittel, J. (2003), *The Southwest Airlines Way* (Burr Ridge, IL: McGraw-Hill); and O'Reilly, C., and J. Pfeffer, J. (1995), "Southwest Airlines: Using human resources for competitive advantage," case study, Graduate School of Business, Stanford University.

59. Hsieh, T. (2010), *Delivering Happiness. A Path to Profits, Passion, and Purpose,* p. 146.

60. See discussion in Chapter 4 on SWA's activities supporting its cost leadership strategy. Recently, SWA has experienced problems with the fuselage of their 737 cracking prematurely. See: "Southwest's solo flight in crises," *The Wall Street Journal,* April 8, 2011.

61. Hsieh, T. (2010), *Delivering Happiness. A Path to Profits, Passion, and Purpose,* p. 146.

62. Chatman, J. A., and S. Eunyoung Cha (2003), "Leading by leveraging culture," pp. 19–34.

63. Hoffer Gittel, J. (2003), *The Southwest Airlines Way* (Burr Ridge, IL: McGraw-Hill).

64. Baron, J. N., M. T. Hannan, and M. D. Burton (2001), "Labor pains: Change in organizational models and employee turnover in young, high-tech firms," *American Journal of Sociology* 106: 960–1012; and Hannan, M. T., M. D. Burton, and J. N. Baron (1996), "Inertia and change in the early years: Employment relationships in young, high technology firms," *Industrial and Corporate Change* 5: 503–537.

65. Nelson, T. (2003), "The persistence of founder influence: Management, ownership, and performance effects at initial public offering," *Strategic Management Journal* 24: 707–724.

66. See the section "*Gaining & Sustaining Competitive Advantage*: Mergers and Acquisitions" in Chapter 9.

67. Herold, D. M., and D. B. Fedor (2008), *Change the Way You Lead Change: Leadership Strategies that Really Work.*

68. Barnes, F. C., and B. B. Tyler (2010), "Nucor in 2010," case study.

69. Roethlisberger, F. J., and W. J. Dickson (1939), *Management and the Worker* (Cambridge, MA: Harvard University Press).

70. Pink, D. H. (2009), *Drive: The Surprising Truth about What Motivates Us* (New York: Riverhead Books).

71. Ibid.

72. 3M Company (2002), *A Century of Innovation: The 3M Story* (Maplewood, MN: The 3M Company).

73. The ChapterCase 11 information is based on "Zappos screws up pricing and sells products at $1.6M below costs . . . Then honors the sales!" *Business Insider,* May 23, 2010; and "6pm.com pricing mistake," *The Zappos Family Blog,* May 21, 2010.

74. "Zappos will honor $1.6 million pricing mistake," *MSN MoneyCentral,* May 25, 2010; and "Amazon wields $25 gift certificates to pacify frustrated comic book fans," *TechCrunch.com,* March 9, 2010.

75. "Employee Morale & Engagement Survey," press release, *CheckPoint HR,* February 23, 2010.

76. Input for this module is used with the permission of Blaine Lawlor, strategic management professor, University of West Florida.

Corporate Governance, Business Ethics, and Strategic Leadership

LEARNING OBJECTIVES

After studying this chapter, you should be able to:

LO 12-1   Describe and evaluate the relationship between strategic management and the role of business in society.

LO 12-2   Conduct a stakeholder impact analysis.

LO 12-3   Critically evaluate the relationship between corporate social responsibility (CSR) and competitive advantage.

LO 12-4   Describe the role of corporate governance and evaluate different governance mechanisms.

LO 12-5   Describe and evaluate the relationship between business strategy and ethics.

LO 12-6   Describe the different roles that strategic leaders play and how to become a strategic leader.

HP's CEO Mark Hurd Resigns amid Ethics Scandal

MARK HURD WAS appointed Hewlett-Packard's CEO in the spring of 2005, following Carly Fiorina's tumultuous tenure. He had begun his business career 25 years earlier as an entry-level salesperson with NCR, a U.S. technology company best known for its bar code scanners in retail outlets and automatic teller machines (ATMs). By the time he had ascended to the role of CEO at NCR, he had earned a reputation as a low-profile, no-nonsense manager focused on flawless strategy execution. When he was appointed HP's CEO, industry analysts praised its board of directors. Moreover, investors hoped that Mr. Hurd would run an efficient and lean operation at HP, to return the company to former greatness and, above all, profitability.

Mr. Hurd did not disappoint. By all indications, he was highly successful at the helm of HP. The company became number one in desktop computer sales and increased its lead in inkjet and laser printers to more than 50 percent market share. Through significant cost-cutting and streamlining measures, Mr. Hurd turned HP into a lean operation. For example, he oversaw large-scale layoffs and a pay cut for all remaining employees as he reorganized the company. Wall Street rewarded HP shareholders with a 110 percent stock price appreciation during Mr. Hurd's tenure, outperforming the NASDAQ composite index by a wide margin.

Yet, in the summer of 2010, the HP board found itself caught "between a rock and a hard place," with no easy options in sight. Jodie Fisher, a former adult-movie actress, filed a lawsuit against Mr. Hurd, alleging sexual harassment. As an independent contractor, she worked as a hostess at HP-sponsored events. In this function, she screened attending HP customers and personally ensured that Mr. Hurd would spend time with the most important ones. With an ethics scandal looming, and despite Mr. Hurd's stellar financial results for the company, HP's board of directors forced Mr. Hurd to resign.

The HP board of directors found that Mr. Hurd had not expressly violated the company's sexual harassment policy. However, it *did* find inaccurate expense reports that he allegedly filed to conceal a "close personal relationship" with Ms. Fisher. The investigation also revealed that HP made payments to Ms. Fisher in instances where there was no legitimate business purpose. Finally, the board alleged that Mr. Hurd leaked private information to Ms. Fisher about the company's intention to acquire EDS, a large information-technology company, months prior to the actual transaction. Following his resignation, Mr. Hurd, who departed with a severance package estimated at $45 million, stated: "I realized there were instances in which I did not live up to the standards and principles of trust, respect and integrity that I have espoused at HP and which have guided me throughout my career."[1]

Reactions were mixed. Some corporate-governance scholars argued that Mr. Hurd should have been fired for cause. Others were not so sure. The most outspoken critic of the board's decision was Larry Ellison, co-founder and CEO of Oracle, who argued, "The HP board just made the worst personnel decision since the idiots on the Apple

board fired Steve Jobs many years ago. That decision nearly destroyed Apple and would have if Steve
hadn't come back and saved them."[2]

Investors seemed to agree with Mr. Ellison's
assessment: HP's market value dropped by roughly
$10 billion on the first trading day after Mr. Hurd
resigned. (As you'll see in the *Consider This . . .* section at the end of the chapter, Mr. Ellison plays a key
role in the unfolding story.)

After reading the chapter, you will find more about this case, with related questions, on page 357.

▲ **MARK HURD'S PROBLEMS** at HP illustrate how intricate and intertwined corporate
governance, business ethics, and strategic leadership issues can be. The incident demonstrates the difficult decisions that a board of directors must make when governing a public
company: Should the board force a highly successful CEO to resign when ethical shortcomings are discovered but before an investigation proves or disproves illegal behavior?
Would the board (and the company, and the stockholders) have been better served by just
reprimanding the CEO? On the other hand, would a mere reprimand communicate to the
employees and other stakeholders that performance trumps ethics? The ChapterCase also
highlights how ethical shortcomings by executives can dramatically affect firm performance.
Finally, it illustrates implications for strategic leadership: CEOs of Fortune 500 companies
are under constant public scrutiny and must adhere to the highest ethical standards; if they
do not, they cannot expect their employees to do the same. Unethical behavior can quickly
destroy the reputation of a CEO, one of the most important assets he or she possesses.

In this chapter, we wrap up our discussion of strategy implementation, and close the circle in the AFI framework, by studying three remaining areas: corporate governance, business ethics, and strategic leadership. To ensure pursuit of its intended goals, a firm must put
in place effective *corporate-governance* mechanisms to direct and control the enterprise.
Studying *business ethics* enables managers to reason about the role of business in society
and to think through complex decisions in an increasingly dynamic, interdependent, and
global marketplace. Finally, *strategic leadership* pertains to individuals' use of power and
influence to direct the activities of others when pursuing an organization's goals.[3]

To integrate our discussion on corporate governance, business ethics, and strategic leadership, we begin by taking a closer look at the intersection between strategic management
and the role of business in society. Strategic management provides a powerful toolkit for
helping firms to gain and sustain competitive advantage. The modern business organization
is one of the most powerful institutions on the planet. To be effective as a strategic manager
and leader, you must understand and appreciate the role of business in society.

STRATEGIC MANAGEMENT AND
THE ROLE OF BUSINESS IN SOCIETY

>> **LO 12-1**
Describe and evaluate
the relationship
between strategic
management and the
role of business in
society.

The public stock company is the institutional backbone of any modern, free-market economy. Exhibit 12.1 shows the levels of hierarchy in a public stock company. The state (society) grants shareholders a charter of incorporation. In turn, shareholders appoint a board
of directors to govern and oversee the firm's management. The managers in turn hire and
supervise employees to perform the actual work (producing products or providing services). The public stock company enjoys four characteristics that make it an attractive
corporate form: limited liability for investors, transferability of investor interests (i.e., the
trading of stocks), legal personality, and separation of ownership and control.[4]

In the first decade of the 21st century, however, two major events eroded the public's trust in business as an institution and free-market capitalism as an economic system.[5] The erosion began with the accounting scandals at Enron, WorldCom, Tyco, Adelphia, Global Crossing, and Arthur Andersen, which lead to bankruptcies, large-scale employment loss, and billions of dollars of shareholder value destruction. A *BusinessWeek* reporter commented wryly: "Watching executives climb the courthouse steps became a spectator sport."[6]

Then, in the fall of 2008, the global financial crisis (GFC) struck, shaking the entire free-market system to its core. Although the reasons for the GFC are quite complex and still being debated,[7] we know a few key factors. A real estate bubble had emerged, fueled by cheap credit, especially the availability of subprime mortgages. When that bubble burst, those who had unsustainable mortgages, investors holding derivative securities based on those mortgages, and the financial institutions that had sold the securities, all faced financial stress or bankruptcy. Some went under and others were sold off at fire-sale prices. Home foreclosures skyrocketed as a large number of lenders defaulted on their mortgages. House prices in the U.S. plummeted by roughly 30 percent. By November 2008, the Dow Jones Industrial Average (DJIA) had lost about half its market value. The government bailed out struggling financial institutions and businesses with a $700 billion package. As the financial tsunami moved from Wall Street to Main Street, the result was a 10 percent unemployment rate and a deep recession in the United States (and most of the world).

Although the two crises differ in their specifics, two common features emerge that are pertinent to our study of strategic management.[8] First, both crises demonstrate that managerial actions can affect the economic well-being of large numbers of people around the

EXHIBIT 12.1

The Public Stock Company: Hierarchy of Authority

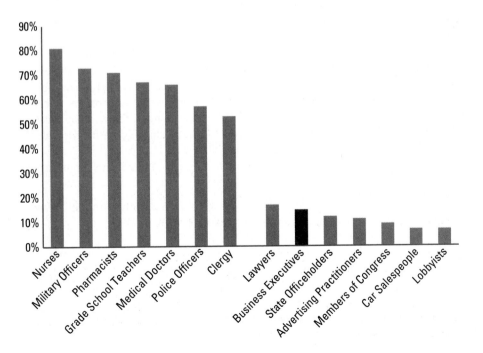

EXHIBIT 12.2

Honesty and Ethics Ranking of Different Professions

The bar chart indicates the percentage of Americans who responded to the question, "How would you rate the honesty and ethical standards of people in different fields?" with the answer "very high/high." The poll ranked 22 professions. The left part of the exhibit shows the top seven ranked professions. The right part of the exhibit shows the bottom seven professions, with business executives at 15 percent.

Source: Author's depiction of data from Gallup's 2010 "Honesty and Ethics Survey," www.gallup.com/poll/1654/honesty-ethics-professions.aspx.

globe. Effective and ethical business practices can produce significant wealth, and unethical behavior can destroy it. Respondents in a recent Gallup poll, asked to assess the honesty and ethics of different professions, ranked business executives near the bottom—just ahead of members of Congress, car salespeople, and lobbyists (see Exhibit 12.2, previous page).

The second pertinent feature is stakeholders—the large and diverse number of organizations, groups, and individuals who can affect or be affected by the actions of a firm. Managers must consider numerous stakeholders in their decisions. Doing so can be a form of corporate social responsibility (discussed more fully later in the chapter). Doing so also is important because *failure* to consider stakeholders can boomerang, and undermine corporate objectives if stakeholders' needs are not met. Borrowers, for example, who bought subprime mortgages are customers of financial institutions. When they default in large numbers, they can threaten the survival of the financial institutions (indeed, of the entire financial system). Effective stakeholder management, therefore, is necessary to ensure continued survival of the firm and to sustain any competitive advantage.[9]

Stakeholder Strategy

Stakeholder strategy has emerged as an integrative approach to connect corporate governance, business ethics, and strategic leadership, and thus to help managers think through these issues in a holistic fashion.[10] In Chapter 1, we defined *stakeholders* as individuals or groups that can affect or are affected by a firm's actions. They have a claim or interest in the firm's performance and continued survival because they make specific contributions for which they expect rewards in return. The firm has a multifaceted exchange relationship with a number of diverse internal and external stakeholders (see Exhibit 1.8, p. 19).

Stakeholder theory is a theoretical framework that is concerned with how various stakeholders create and trade value. According to this theory, the unit of analysis is the web of exchange relationships a firm has with the groups and individuals that can affect the firm or are affected by it.[11] Stakeholder theory describes "how customers, suppliers, employees, financiers (stockholders, bondholders, banks, etc.), communities and managers interact to jointly create and trade value."[12] The main thesis of stakeholder theory is that effective management of these different groups and individuals can help the firm achieve its goals and also improve its chances of gaining and sustaining competitive advantage. Indeed, a core tenet of stakeholder theory is that a single-minded focus on shareholders alone exposes a firm to undue risks that can undermine economic performance and can even threaten the very survival of the enterprise. The strategist's job, therefore, is to understand and appreciate the complex web of relationships among different stakeholders—to "manage and shape these relationships to create as much value as possible for *stakeholders* and to manage the distribution of that value."[13]

Scholars have provided several arguments as to why effective stakeholder management can benefit firm performance:[14]

- Satisfied stakeholders are more cooperative and thus more likely to reveal information that can further increase the firm's value creation or lower its costs.

---

stakeholder strategy An integrative approach to connect corporate governance, business ethics, and strategic leadership.

stakeholder theory A theoretical framework concerned with how various

stakeholders create and trade value; its main thesis is that effective management of the web of exchange relationships among stakeholders can help the firm achieve its goals and improve its chances of gaining and sustaining competitive advantage.

stakeholder impact analysis A decision tool with which managers can recognize, assess, and address the needs of different stakeholders, to allow the firm to perform optimally and act as a good corporate citizen.

- Increased trust lowers transaction costs.

- Effective management of the complex web of stakeholders can lead to greater organizational adaptability and flexibility.

- Negative outcomes can be avoided and risk exposure can be reduced, creating more predictable and stable returns.

- Firms can build strong reputations that are rewarded in the marketplace by business partners, employees, and customers. Most managers do care about public perception of the firm, as evidenced by high-profile rankings such as the "World's Most Admired Companies" published annually by *Fortune*.[15]

Stakeholder Impact Analysis

The key challenge of stakeholder management is to ensure that a firm's primary stakeholders such as shareholders and other investors achieve their objectives, while other stakeholders' needs are recognized and addressed in an ethical manner, so that they too can be satisfied. This all sounds good in theory, but how should managers go about this in practice?

>> **LO 12-2**
Conduct a stakeholder impact analysis.

Stakeholder impact analysis provides such a tool for managers. With it, they can recognize, assess, prioritize, and address the needs of different stakeholders, to allow the firm to perform optimally while at the same time acting as a good corporate citizen. In particular, managers must go through a five-step process when recognizing and addressing stakeholders' claims. In each step, managers need to pay particular attention to three important stakeholder attributes: *power, legitimacy,* and *urgency*.[16]

- A stakeholder has *power* over a company when it can get the company to do something that it would not otherwise do.

- A stakeholder has a *legitimate claim* when it is perceived to be (legally) valid or otherwise appropriate.

- A stakeholder has an *urgent claim* when it requires a company's immediate attention and response.

Exhibit 12.3 depicts the five steps in stakeholder impact analysis and the key questions to be asked. We now discuss each step in detail.

EXHIBIT 12.3

Stakeholder Impact Analysis

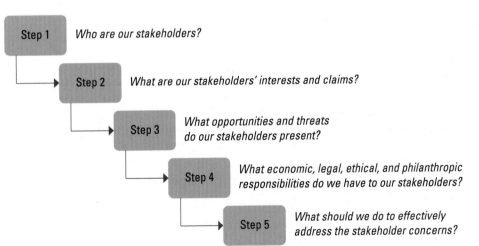

Step 1 — Who are our stakeholders?

Step 2 — What are our stakeholders' interests and claims?

Step 3 — What opportunities and threats do our stakeholders present?

Step 4 — What economic, legal, ethical, and philanthropic responsibilities do we have to our stakeholders?

Step 5 — What should we do to effectively address the stakeholder concerns?

STEP 1. In step 1, the firm asks, "Who are our stakeholders?" In Chapter 1, we identified both key internal and external stakeholders. Internal stakeholders are stockholders, employees, and board members. External stakeholders include customers, suppliers, alliance partners, creditors, unions, communities, and governments.

In the stakeholder-identification step, the firm focuses on stakeholders that currently have, or potentially can have, a material effect on a company. This prioritization identifies the most powerful stakeholders and their needs. For public-stock companies, key stakeholders are, first and foremost, the shareholders, as well as other suppliers of capital. If shareholders are not satisfied with their returns to investment, for example, they will sell the company's stock, leading to depreciation in the firm's market value. A second group of stakeholders includes customers, suppliers, and unions. Any of these groups, if their needs are not met, can materially affect the company's operations. Labor disputes, for example, can lead to strikes and thus loss of revenues and an increase in costs. Suppliers and local communities are also powerful groups of stakeholders that can materially affect the smooth operation of the firm.

STEP 2. In step 2, the firm asks, "What are our stakeholders' interests and claims?" That is, managers need to specify and assess the interests and claims of the pertinent stakeholders using the power, legitimacy, and urgency criteria introduced earlier. As the legal owners, for example, shareholders have the most legitimate claim on a company's profits. However, the separation between ownership and control has been blurring. Many companies incentivize top executives through stock options. They also turn employees into shareholders through *employee stock ownership plans* (*ESOPs*) that allow them to purchase stock at a discounted rate or use company stock as an investment vehicle for retirement savings. For example, Coca-Cola, Google, Microsoft, Southwest Airlines, Starbucks, Walmart, and Whole Foods offer ESOPs.

Even within stakeholder groups there can be significant variation in the power a stakeholder may exert on the firm. For example, managers pay much more attention to large institutional investors than to the millions of smaller, individual investors. Institutional investors have considerable sway because of the size of their assets under management (AUM): TIAA-CREF[17] has $400 billion in AUM, CalPERS[18] has $200 billion in AUM, and The Vanguard Group has $1.4 trillion AUM. Although both individual and institutional investors can claim the same legitimacy as stockholders, institutional investors have much more power over a firm: They can buy and sell a large number of shares at once, or exercise block voting rights in the corporate-governance process. These abilities make institutional investors a much more potent stakeholder. In recent years, institutional investors have become more active participants in corporate governance.

STEP 3. In step 3, the firm asks, "What opportunities and threats do our stakeholders present?" Since stakeholders have a claim on the company, opportunities and threats are two sides of the same coin. Consumer boycotts, for example, can be a credible threat to a company's behavior. For example, some consumers boycotted Nestlé products due to the firm's promotion of infant formula over breast milk in developing countries. PETA[19] called for a boycott of McDonald's due to alleged animal-rights abuses.

In the best-case scenario, managers transform such threats into opportunities. In 2001, the Dutch government blocked Sony Corp.'s entire holiday season shipment of PlayStation game systems (valued at roughly $500 million) into the European Union[20] due to a small but legally unacceptable amount of toxic cadmium discovered in one of the system's cables. This incident led to an 18-month investigation in which Sony inspected over 6,000 supplier factories around the world to track down the source of the problem. The findings allowed

Sony to redesign and develop a cutting-edge supplier management system that adheres to a stringent extended value chain responsibility.

STEP 4. In step 4, the firm asks, "What economic, legal, ethical, and philanthropic responsibilities do we have to our stakeholders?" To identify these responsibilities more effectively, scholars have advanced the notion of corporate social responsibility (CSR). This framework helps firms recognize and address the economic, legal, ethical, and philanthropic expectations that society has of the business enterprise at a given point in time.[21] CSR goes beyond the notion of encouraging businesses to "just be nice." Instead, managers need to realize that *society* grants shareholders the right and privilege to create a publicly traded stock company, and therefore the firm owes something to society.[22] Moreover, CSR provides managers with a conceptual model that more completely describes a society's expectations and thus can guide strategic decision making more effectively. In particular, CSR has four components: economic, legal, ethical, and philanthropic responsibilities.

Economic Responsibilities. The business enterprise is first and foremost an economic institution. Investors expect an adequate return for their risk capital. Consumers expect safe products and services at appropriate prices and quality. Suppliers expect to be paid in full and on time. Governments expect the firm to pay taxes and to manage natural resources such as air and water under a decent stewardship. To accomplish all this, firms must obey the law and act ethically in their quest to gain and sustain competitive advantage.

Legal Responsibilities. Laws and regulations are a society's codified ethics, as they embody notions of right and wrong. They also establish the rules of the game. For example, business as an institution can function because property rights exist and contracts can be enforced in courts of law. Managers must ensure that their firms obey all the laws and regulations, including but not limited to labor, consumer, and environmental laws.

One far-reaching piece of U.S. legislation, for example, is the Accounting Reform and Investor Protection Act of 2002 (commonly known as the Sarbanes-Oxley Act or SOX), passed in response to the accounting scandals mentioned earlier. Among different stipulations, Sarbanes-Oxley increases a CEO's and CFO's personal responsibilities for the accuracy of reported accounting data. It also strengthens the independence of accounting firms (they are no longer allowed to provide consulting services to the firms they audit) and affords stronger protection for whistleblowers.

Due to a firm's significant legal responsibilities, many companies appoint compliance officers, and some even have an office of corporate citizenship. At GE, for example, a vice president leads the office of corporate citizenship. Its compliance group "includes more than 1,000 experienced lawyers located at GE businesses throughout the world whose job is to help the company achieve its goals with unyielding integrity and compliance with the law."[23]

Ethical Responsibilities. Legal responsibilities, however, often define only the minimum acceptable standards of firm behavior. Frequently managers are called upon to go beyond what is required by law. This is because the letter of the law cannot address or anticipate all possible business situations and newly emerging concerns (such as Internet privacy or advances in genetic engineering and stem cell research).

A firm's ethical responsibilities, therefore, go beyond its legal responsibilities; they embody the full scope of expectations, norms, and values of its stakeholders. Managers are called upon to do what society deems just and fair. Starbucks, for example, developed an ethical sourcing policy to help source coffee of the highest quality, while adhering to fair trade and responsible growing practices.

> **corporate social responsibility**
> A framework that helps firms recognize and address the economic, legal, social, and philanthropic expectations that society has of the business enterprise at a given point in time.

Philanthropic Responsibilities. Philanthropic responsibilities are often subsumed under the idea of *corporate citizenship,* reflecting the notion of voluntarily giving back to society. The top three corporate donors in 2009 among the Fortune 100 companies were:

- Walmart: $288 million for education, environmental protection, and conservation, health, and hunger
- AT&T: $240 million for arts and culture, community and economic development, education, health, and the United Way
- Bank of America: $209 million for the arts and culture, community and economic development, education, and human services[24]

The pyramid in Exhibit 12.4 summarizes our discussion of corporate social responsibility.[25] It shows the four components of CSR, beginning with economic responsibilities as the foundational building block, followed by legal, ethical, and philanthropic responsibilities. Note that economic and legal responsibilities are required of companies by society and shareholders, while ethical and philanthropic responsibilities result from a society's expectations toward business. Moreover, there will always be a tension between the different CSR dimensions discussed—e.g., not everything that is legal is also ethical, and not everything that is ethical is also legal. (We'll discuss this last point in more detail when we discuss the relationship between strategy and ethics.) Rather than recommending that a corporation fulfill its responsibilities in a sequential fashion, however, the pyramid symbolizes the need for these responsibilities to be carefully balanced and pursued simultaneously. Doing so ensures not only effective strategy implementation, but also long-term competitiveness.

STEP 5. Finally, in step 5, the firm asks, "What should we do to effectively address the stakeholder concerns?" In the last step in stakeholder management, managers need to decide the appropriate course of action, given all the preceding factors. Going back to the attributes of power, legitimacy, and urgency helps to prioritize the legitimate claims and to address them based on the company's responsibilities.

For example, in the aftermath of the Gulf oil spill, BP faced thousands of claims by many small business owners in the tourism and fishing industries along the Gulf coast. These business owners were not powerful individually, nor did they have valid legal claims

EXHIBIT 12.4

The Pyramid of Corporate Social Responsibility

Source: Adapted from A. B. Carroll (1991), "The pyramid of corporate social responsibility: Toward the moral management of organizational stakeholders," *Business Horizons*, July–August: 42.

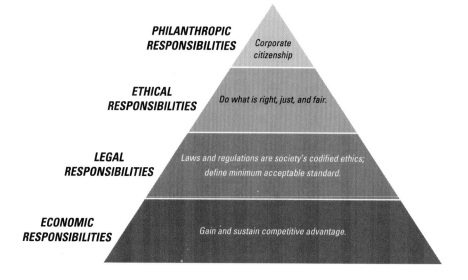

without facing protracted and expensive court proceedings. They were nonetheless very powerful as a collective organized in a potential class-action lawsuit. Moreover, their claims were legitimized by the political will of the U.S. government, which has the power to withdraw BP's business license altogether or cancel current permits and withhold future ones. Thus, the small business owners along the Gulf coast were powerful BP stakeholders with a legitimate claim that needed to be addressed quickly. In response, BP agreed to set apart $20 billion in a fund to be dispersed by a third-party mediator.

Corporate Social Responsibility

Following the two shocks to the free-market capitalist system discussed earlier, the notion of corporate social responsibility is rapidly gaining ground. Today, a firm's responsibilities must be expanded beyond an earlier perspective advocated by Nobel laureate Milton Friedman, who (in 1962) stated, "there is one and only one social responsibility of business—to use its resources and engage in activities designed to increase its profits so long as it stays within the rules of the game, which is to say, engages in open and free competition without deception or fraud."[26] However, Friedman's statement provides a useful foundation: Shareholders not only provide the necessary risk capital but are also the legal owners of public companies and thus have the most legitimate claim. Today, though, many firms seek to do more in terms of social responsibility. The question we investigate here is whether corporate social responsibility helps firms gain and sustain competitive advantage.

A recent survey measured attitudes toward business responsibility in various countries.[27] The survey asked the top 25 percent of income earners holding a university degree in various countries whether they agree with Milton Friedman's philosophy that "the *social responsibility* of business is to increase its profits." The results, displayed in Exhibit 12.5, revealed some intriguing national differences. When asked, the United Arab Emirates (UAE), a small and business-friendly country, came out on top, with 84 percent of respondents agreeing. The top five countries also included two of the four Asian Tigers[28] (South Korea and Singapore, where roughly two-thirds agree) as well as Japan and India, a rising economic power.

GAINING & SUSTAINING COMPETITIVE ADVANTAGE

>> **LO 12-3**
Critically evaluate the relationship between corporate social responsibility (CSR) and competitive advantage.

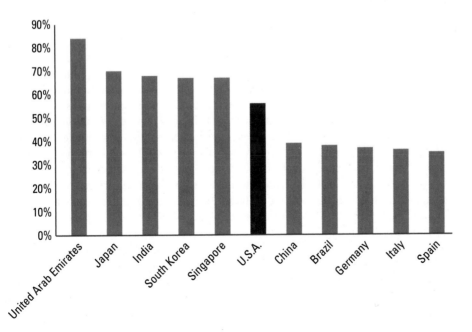

EXHIBIT 12.5

Global Survey of Attitudes Toward Business

The bar chart indicates the percentage of members of the "informed public" (defined as people who hold university degrees and are in the top 25 percent in their particular income and age groups in their respective countries) who "strongly agree/somewhat agree" with Milton Friedman's philosophy, "*The social responsibility of business is to increase its profits.*"

Source: Author's depiction of data from Edelman's (2011) Trust Barometer as included in "Milton Friedman goes on tour," *The Economist,* January 27, 2011.

Interestingly, the countries where the fewest people agreed with Friedman were China, Brazil, Germany, Italy, and Spain, where less than 40 percent of the respondents were supportive of an exclusive focus on shareholder capitalism. China and Brazil are also part of the rising BRIC powerhouses, but are found—in contrast to India—at the bottom of the ranking. Although they have achieved a high standard of living, European countries such as Germany, Italy, and Spain have always tempered the free-market system with a strong social element, leading to so-called *social market economies.* The respondents from these countries seem to be more supportive of a stakeholder-management approach to business.

The United States, often held up as the bastion of free-market capitalism, came in ninth out of 23 countries surveyed, placing roughly in the middle of the continuum. In particular, a bit more than half (56 percent) of U.S. respondents subscribed to Friedman's philosophy.

A reconciliation between the perspectives of shareholder value creation (Friedman's philosophy) and corporate social responsibility has been under way in the past few decades. Neglecting to take important stakeholders into consideration can destroy shareholder value and thus threaten the very survival of a firm.[29] Porter and Kramer suggest that managers should focus not on short-term financial performance but on *shared value*, which includes both shareholder value creation and value creation for society.[30] They argue that managers need to reestablish the important relationship between superior firm performance and social progress. They recommend that firms should focus on three things within the shared-value-creation framework:

1. Expand their customer base to bring in nonconsumers such as those at the bottom of the pyramid (discussed in Chapter 1).
2. Expand their traditional internal firm value chains to include more nontraditional partners such as *nongovernmental organizations* (NGOs). NGOs are not-for-profit organizations that pursue a particular cause in the public interest, and are independent of any governments. Habitat for Humanity and Greenpeace, for example, are NGOs.
3. Focus on creating new regional clusters (discussed in Chapter 10).

Porter and Kramer argue that these strategic actions will in turn lead to a larger pie of revenues and profits that can be distributed among a company's stakeholders.

General Electric, for example, recognizes a convergence between shareholders and stakeholders to create shared value. It states in its Governance Principles: "Both the board of directors and management recognize that the long-term interests of shareowners are advanced by responsibly addressing the concerns of other stakeholders and interested parties, including employees, recruits, customers, suppliers, GE communities, government officials and the public at large."[31] Enlightened self-interest requires a firm's leaders to consider all important stakeholders when managing an enterprise for competitive advantage.

The empirical evidence linking corporate social responsibility and firm performance is somewhat mixed. In a detailed analysis of 52 empirical studies, researchers found that CSR is likely to lead to superior firm performance in terms of financial performance and higher reputation scores.[32] In a separate study, other researchers undertook a detailed analysis of 95 empirical research studies that looked at the relationship between CSR and firms' financial performance.[33] In 80 out of the 95 studies (84 percent), the assumed *causal relationship* ("What causes what?") was that CSR would *lead to* improved financial performance, and thus potentially to competitive advantage. A little more than half of these 80 studies (53 percent) found a statistically significant positive relationship between CSR and financial performance. These studies support the notion that *firms can do well (financially) by doing good (through CSR).*

On the other hand, in a smaller set of studies, researchers assumed that firm financial performance would *predict* CSR, meaning that firms engage in CSR when they have the financial means to do so. Roughly 68 percent of these 19 studies found that superior financial performance leads to CSR. These companies *do good* when they themselves *do well*.

Taken together, although there seems to be a positive relationship between CSR and firm financial performance in the majority of the studied cases, it is not entirely clear what causes what. 🔍

CORPORATE GOVERNANCE

Corporate governance concerns the mechanisms to direct and control an enterprise in order to ensure that it pursues its strategic goals successfully and legally.[34] Corporate governance is about checks and balances; it's about asking the tough questions at the right time. The accounting scandals and the GFC were able to get so out of hand because the enterprises involved did not properly implement or effectively use corporate governance mechanisms. Similarly, a lack of regular oversight by federal agencies such as the U.S. Security and Exchange Commission (SEC) made Bernard Madoff's $65 billion Ponzi scheme possible. A whistleblower had informed the SEC that Madoff's alleged returns were mathematically impossible, but the SEC failed to follow up. Several years later, Madoff's sons reported his fraud to the authorities.[35]

Corporate governance addresses the *principal–agent problem* (introduced in Chapter 8), which can occur any time an agent performs activities on behalf of a principal.[36] In publicly traded companies, the stockholders (the principals) are the legal owners of the company, and they give the professional managers (the agents) the authority to make decisions on their behalf. The conflict arises if the agents also pursue their own personal interests, which can be at odds with the principals' goals. For their part, agents are interested in maximizing their total compensation, including benefits, job security, status, and power. Principals desire maximization of total returns to shareholders.

The risk of opportunism on behalf of agents is exacerbated by *information asymmetry:* the agents are generally better informed than the principals. Indeed, managers tend to have access to private information that outsiders, especially investors, are not privy to. Insider trading cases provide an example of egregious exploitation of information asymmetry. In the case of ImClone, a biotech company, information asymmetry led to prison terms for its CEO Samuel Waksal and business celebrity Martha Stewart, who sold ImClone stock based on insider information provided by Mr. Waksal. In another case, the hedge fund Galleon Group was engulfed in an insider trading scandal involving several publicly traded technology companies such as Google, Intel, and IBM.

Information asymmetry also can breed on-the-job consumption, perquisites, and excessive compensation. Dennis Kozlowski, former CEO of Tyco, a diversified conglomerate, used company funds for his $30 million New York City apartment (the shower curtain alone was $6,000) and for a $2 million birthday party for his second wife.[37] John Thain, former CEO of Merrill Lynch (now part of Bank of America), spent $1.2 million of company funds on redecorating his office, while he demanded cost cutting and frugality from his employees.[38] Such uses of company funds, in effect, mean that shareholders pay for those items and activities. Mr. Thain also allegedly requested a bonus in the range of $10 to $30 million in 2009 despite Merrill Lynch having lost billions of dollars and being unable to continue independently.

The principal–agent problem is a core part of agency theory, which views the firm as a *nexus of legal contracts*. Besides dealing with the relationship between shareholders and managers, its concerns also cascade down the organizational hierarchy. Employees who perform the actual operational labor are agents who work on behalf of the managers. Such

>> **LO 12-4**
Describe the role of corporate governance and evaluate different governance mechanisms.

corporate governance
A system of mechanisms to direct and control an enterprise in order to ensure that it pursues its strategic goals successfully and legally.

agency theory
A theory that views the firm as a nexus of legal contracts.

front-line employees often enjoy an informational advantage over management. They may tell their supervisor that it took longer to complete a project or serve a customer than it actually did, for example. Some employees may be tempted to use informational advantage for their own self-interest (e.g., shirking on the job by spending time on Facebook during work hours, using the company's computer and Internet connection).

The managerial implication of agency theory relates to the management functions of organization and control: The firm needs to design work tasks, incentives, and employment contracts and other control mechanisms in ways that minimize opportunism on behalf of the agents. At the same time, the activities of the agents should maximize shareholder value creation for the principals.[39] Governance mechanisms are used to reduce information asymmetry and to align incentives between principals and agents. These governance mechanisms need to be designed in such a fashion as to overcome two specific agency problems: adverse selection and moral hazard.

In principal–agent relationships, *adverse selection* describes a situation in which an agent misrepresents his or her ability to do the job. (Such misrepresentation is especially rampant during the recruiting process.) Once hired, the principal often cannot accurately assess whether the agent can do the work for which he is being paid. The problem is especially pronounced in team production, when the principal often cannot ascertain the contributions of individual team members. This in turn creates an incentive for opportunistic employees to free-ride on the efforts of others.

Moral hazard describes the difficulty of the principal to ascertain whether the agent has really put forth a best effort. In this situation, the agent is *able* to do the work, but may decide not to do so. For example, a company scientist at a biotechnology company may decide to work on his own research project (hoping to eventually start his own firm), rather than on the project that he was assigned. While working on his own research on company time, he might also use the company's laboratory and technicians. Given the complexities of basic research, it is often hard, especially for nonscientist principals, to ascertain which problem a scientist is working on.[40]

To overcome these principal–agent problems, firms put several governance mechanisms in place. We shall discuss several of them next, beginning with the board of directors.

The Board of Directors

The day-to-day business operations of a publicly traded stock company are conducted by its managers and employees, under the direction of the chief executive officer (CEO) and the oversight of the board of directors. The board of directors, the centerpiece of corporate governance, is composed of inside and outside directors.[41] The board is elected by the shareholders to represent their interests (see Exhibit 12.1). Prior to the annual shareholders' meeting, the board proposes a slate of nominees, although shareholders can also directly nominate director candidates. In general, large institutional investors support their favored candidates through their accumulated proxy votes. The board members meet several times a year to review and evaluate the company's performance and to assess its future strategic plans as well as opportunities and threats.

In addition to general strategic oversight and guidance, the board of directors has other, more specific functions, including:

- Selecting, evaluating, and compensating the CEO. The CEO reports to the board. Should the CEO lose the board's confidence, the board may fire him or her.

- Overseeing the company's CEO succession plan. Both HP and Apple have been criticized for poor succession planning. HP's board was apparently unprepared to deal with the unexpected departure of Mark Hurd.[42] Likewise, institutional shareholders criticized Apple for not (publicly) addressing CEO succession in light of Steve Jobs's repeated medical leaves.[43]

- Providing guidance to the CEO in the selection, evaluation, and compensation of other senior executives.
- Reviewing, monitoring, evaluating, and approving any significant strategic initiatives and corporate actions.
- Conducting a thorough risk assessment and proposing options to mitigate risk. The boards of directors of the financial firms at the center of the GFC were faulted for not noticing or not appreciating the risks the firms were exposed to.
- Ensuring that the firm's audited financial statements represent a true and accurate picture of the firm.
- Ensuring the firm's compliance with laws and regulations. The boards of directors of firms caught up in the accounting scandals early this century were faulted for being negligent in their company oversight and not adequately performing several of the functions listed here.

The board of directors is composed of inside and outside directors. Inside directors are generally part of the company's senior management team, such as the chief financial officer (CFO) and the chief operating officer (COO). They are appointed by shareholders to provide the board with necessary information pertaining to the company's internal workings and performance. Without this valuable inside information, the board would not be able to effectively monitor the firm. As senior executives, however, inside board members' interests tend to align with management and the CEO rather than the shareholders. Outside directors, on the other hand, are not employees of the firm. They are frequently senior executives from other firms or full-time professionals appointed to serve on several boards simultaneously. Given their independence, they are more likely to watch out for the interests of shareholders.

Board independence is critical to effectively fulfilling a board's governance responsibilities. Given that board members are directly responsible to shareholders, they have an incentive to ensure that the shareholders' interests are pursued. If not, they can experience a loss in reputation or can be removed outright. The HP board of directors experienced a significant shake-up following the Mark Hurd ethics scandal (see the *Consider This* follow-up to the ChapterCase on page 357).[44]

Strategy Highlight 12.1 (next page) takes a closer look at the composition and workings of General Electric's board of directors.

In recent years, members of boards of directors have been held more and more legally responsible for the firm's strategic actions. Shareholders may sue the board, for example, for selling the company at too low a price and for other material decisions affecting the firm's market valuations. HP's shareholders sued the board of directors claiming that disclosing details pertaining to Mark Hurd's resignation led to a significant loss in the

---

board of directors The centerpiece of corporate governance, composed of inside and outside directors, who are elected by the shareholders to represent their interests.

inside directors Board members who are generally part of the company's senior management team; appointed by shareholders to provide the board with necessary information pertaining to the company's internal workings and performance.

outside directors Board members who are not employees of the firm, but who are frequently senior executives from other firms or full-time professionals. Given their independence, they are more likely to watch out for shareholder interests.

GE's Board of Directors

In 2011, the GE board is composed of individuals from the business world (chairpersons and CEOs of Fortune 500 companies spanning a range of industries), academia (university presidents, business school professors, and deans), and politics. (For the latest listing, see www.ge.com/company/leadership/directors.html.) Including the board's chairman, there are 17 members on the board. This is considered an appropriate number of directors for a company of GE's size (roughly $230 billion in market capitalization as of spring 2011). In contrast, Apple's board of directors has only six members, while its market capitalization is about $325 billion. Indeed, Apple's board of directors has been criticized for having become too insular in recent years.[45]

At GE, 15 of the 17 board members are independent outside directors. (Mr. Penske has a material relationship with GE through his business, Penske Corporation.) GE's board has only one inside director, Jeffrey Immelt, GE's CEO, who also acts as chairman of the board. In roughly two-thirds of U.S. public firms, the CEO of the company typically also serves as chair of the board of the directors. This practice has been declining somewhat in recent years. Arguments can be made both for and against splitting the roles of CEO and chairman of the board. On the one hand, the CEO has invaluable inside information that can help in chairing the board effectively. On the other hand, the chairman may influence the board unduly through setting the meeting agendas or suggesting board appointees who are friendly toward the CEO. Given the recent crises discussed earlier, the trend toward *separation of CEO/chair duality* is likely to continue. Because one of the key roles of the board is to monitor and evaluate the CEO's performance, there is clearly a conflict of interest when the CEO actually chairs the board. In Germany, the law requires this separation, while companies in other European countries also tend to separate the two roles.

Of GE's 17 directors, 4 are women (24 percent) and 2 are ethnic minorities (12 percent). In general, women and minorities remain underrepresented on boards of directors across the U.S. (and throughout most of the world). GE's board is actually fairly diverse when compared with other Fortune 500 companies, which in 2010 averaged less than 16 percent women on their boards. Diversity in the boardroom is an asset: more diverse boards are less likely to fall victim to groupthink, a situation in which opinions coalesce around a leader without individuals critically challenging and evaluating that leader's opinions and assumptions. Cohesive, non-diverse groups are highly susceptible to groupthink, which in turn can lead to flawed decision making with potentially disastrous consequences.

To accomplish their responsibilities, boards of directors are usually organized into different committees. GE's board has four committees, each with its own chair: the audit committee, the nominating and corporate governance committee, the management development and compensation committee, and the public responsibilities committee.

GE's board of directors meets a dozen or more times annually. With increasing board accountability in recent years, boards now tend to meet more often. Moreover, many firms limit the number and type of directorships a board member may hold concurrently.[46]

company's credibility and thus a substantial drop in the firm's shareholder value.[47] To perform their strategic oversight tasks, board members apply the strategic management theories and concepts presented in this textbook, among other more specialized tools such as those originating in finance and accounting.

groupthink
A situation in which opinions coalesce around a leader without individuals critically challenging and evaluating that leader's opinions and assumptions.

Other Governance Mechanisms

While the board of directors is the central governance piece for a public stock company, several other corporate mechanisms are worth noting—*executive compensation, the market for corporate control,* and *financial statement auditors and government regulators.*

EXECUTIVE COMPENSATION. The board of directors determines executive compensation packages. To align incentives between shareholders and management, boards use equity compensation by granting stock options. These give the recipient the right to buy a company's stock at a predetermined price sometime in the future. If the company's share price rises above the negotiated strike price (which is often the "as is" price on the day when compensation is negotiated), the executive stands to reap (significant) gains.

CEO pay, in particular, has attracted significant attention in recent years. Two issues are at the forefront: (1) the absolute size of the CEO pay package compared with the pay of the average employee, and (2) the relationship between firm performance and CEO pay. The ratio of CEO to average employee pay in the U.S. is about 300 to 1, up from roughly 40 to 1 in 1980.[48] In 2010, the highest paid CEO was Gregory Maffei of Liberty Media, who took home about $87 million in direct compensation. Next on the list were Larry Ellison of Oracle ($69m), Ray Irani of Occidental Petroleum ($52m), Carol Bartz of Yahoo ($45m), and Leslie Moonves of CBS ($38m).[49]

In some instances, the pay–firm performance relationship is strong, while in others it is nonexistent or even negative.[50] When we discussed competitive advantage in Chapter 5, we noted that Liberty Media was the number-one performer in return on revenue, achieving over 60 percent (see Exhibit 5.4) and a total shareholder return of 247 percent.[51] In this case, Gregory Maffei's compensation package was closely tied to performance. In other cases, the relationship between performance and pay is less clear. Yahoo, for example, underperformed the NASDAQ 100 index by a wide margin, but CEO Carol Bartz still obtained one of the largest compensation packages. As CEO of The Home Depot, Robert Nardelli earned annual compensation packages of over $200 million, but under Nardelli's tenure (2000–2007), the company's stock remained flat, while the share price of its main competitor, Lowe's, nearly doubled.

Responding to shareholder criticism, the GE board recently revised the compensation package for Jeffrey Immelt, GE's CEO and chairman of the board.[52] The compensation package was changed to include a stronger performance-related equity component. In particular, GE's board attached strings on stock options already granted to Mr. Immelt. The revised compensation package now stipulates conditions: The stock options will vest only if GE's stock and dividend performance in its industrial businesses (energy, health care, and technology infrastructure) is equal to or better than the performance of the Standard & Poor 500 stock index. In addition, half of the options will vest only if GE achieves at least $55 billion in cash flow from operating activities between 2011 and 2014. This unusual move by GE's board of directors underscores the increasing clout of vocal shareholders, who have expressed dissatisfaction with GE's performance over the last decade. They expect that linking compensation to specific performance measures tied to GE's core competency in industrial engineering will result in improved stock performance.

Some recent experiments in behavioral economics caution that incentives that are too high-powered (e.g., outsized bonuses) may have a negative effect on job performance. That is, when the incentive level is very high, an individual may get distracted because too much attention is devoted to the outsized bonus to be enjoyed in the near future. This in turn can further increase job stress and negatively impact job performance.[53]

THE MARKET FOR CORPORATE CONTROL. The board of directors and executive compensation are *internal* corporate-governance mechanisms. The *market for corporate control* is an important *external* corporate-governance mechanism. It consists of investors who

stock options An incentive mechanism to align the interests of shareholders and managers, by giving the recipient the right to buy a company's stock at a predetermined price sometime in the future.

seek to gain control of an underperforming corporation by buying shares of its stock in the open market. To avoid such attempts, corporate managers strive to maximize shareholder value by delivering strong share-price performance or putting in place poison pills (discussed later).

Here's how the market for corporate control works: If a company is poorly managed, its performance suffers and its stock price falls as more and more investors sell their shares. Once shares fall to a low enough level, the firm may become the target of a *hostile takeover* (as discussed in Chapter 9). Besides competitors, so-called *corporate raiders* (e.g., Carl Icahn and T. Boone Pickens) or *hedge funds* (e.g., The Blackstone Group and Soros Fund Management) will buy enough shares to exert control over a company. The new owner will either replace the old management (in order to manage the company in a way so as to create more value for its shareholders) or break up the company and sell off its pieces. In either case, since a firm's existing management faces the threat of losing their jobs and their reputations as effective executives if their firms sustain a competitive disadvantage, the market for corporate control is a credible governance mechanism.

To avoid being taken over against their consent, some firms put in place *poison pills.* These are defensive provisions that kick in should a buyer reach a certain level of share ownership without top management approval. For example, a poison pill could allow existing shareholders to buy additional shares at a steep discount. Those additional shares would in turn make any takeover attempt much more expensive, and thus function as a deterrent. With the rise of the institutional investors, poison pills have become rare because they retard an effective function of equity markets.

Although poison pills are becoming rarer, the market for corporate control is alive and well, as shown in the recent hostile takeover of Cadbury by Kraft (see Strategy Highlight 9.1) or the $20 billion hostile takeover of U.S. biotech firm Genzyme by Sanofi-Aventis, a French pharmaceutical company.[54] However, the market for corporate control is a last resort because it comes with significant transaction costs. To succeed in its hostile takeover bid, for example, Sanofi-Aventis had to pay a nearly 40 percent premium above Genzyme's share price. Thus, this tactic is generally activated only when internal corporate-governance mechanisms have not functioned effectively.

AUDITORS, GOVERNMENT REGULATORS, AND INDUSTRY ANALYSTS. Auditors, government regulators, and industry analysts serve as additional external-governance mechanisms. All public companies listed on the U.S. stock exchanges must file a number of financial statements with the Security and Exchange Commission (SEC). To avoid misrepresentation of financial results, all public statements must follow generally accepted accounting principles (GAAP)[55] and are audited by certified public accountants.

The SEC is the federal agency primarily responsible for enforcing the laws and regulations pertaining to publicly traded companies in the United States. As part of its disclosure policy, the SEC makes all financial reports filed by public companies available electronically via the EDGAR database (www.secfilings.com). This database contains more than 7 million financial statements, going back several years. Industry analysts scrutinize these reports in great detail, trying to identify any financial irregularities and to assess firm performance. Given recent high-profile oversights such as the accounting scandals and fraud cases mentioned earlier, the SEC has come under pressure to step up its monitoring and enforcement.

Industry analysts often base their buy, hold, or sell recommendations on financial statements filed with the SEC and other business news published in *The Wall Street Journal, Bloomberg Businessweek, Fortune, Forbes,* and other business media such as CNBC. Researchers, however, have questioned the independence of industry analysts and credit-rating agencies that evaluate companies (such as Fitch, Moody's, and Standard & Poor's).[56]

This is because the investment banks and rating agencies frequently have lucrative business relationships with the companies they are supposed to evaluate, creating conflicts of interest. A study of over 8,000 analysts' ratings of corporate equity securities, for example, revealed that investment bankers rated their own clients more favorably.[57]

In addition, an industry has sprung up around assessing the effectiveness of corporate governance in individual firms. Research outfits such as GovernanceMetrics (http://www2.gmiratings.com/) provide independent and sophisticated corporate governance ratings. The ratings from these external watchdog organizations inform a wide range of stakeholders, including investors, insurers, auditors, regulators, and others.

Corporate-governance mechanisms play an important part in aligning the interests of principals and agents. Equally important are the "most internal of control mechanisms": *business ethics*—a topic we discuss below. First, though, we'll look at different corporate governance systems around the world.

Corporate Governance Around the World

As discussed earlier, attitudes toward business vary around the world. Due to differences in national institutions and cultures, variations of free-market economic systems have emerged.[58] State-planned (communist and socialist) systems are on the retreat worldwide (with Cuba and North Korea the primary remaining examples); most economies today have some form of free markets. The extent to which markets are "free" varies, however, from country to country: *State-directed capitalism,* practiced by China, is on one end of a continuum, and *free-market capitalism* on the other end.

The United States has historically had one of the most free-market–oriented economies. In response to the global financial crisis, though, the federal government has become a bigger player in the U.S. economy, creating new monetary and fiscal policies: large stimulus packages; low or zero interest rates; increased regulation and direct government ownership of companies such as GM and AIG; and government receivership for mortgage institutions Fannie Mae and Freddie Mac.[59] Although the capitalist system remains the dominant economic system globally, governments are important players in most free-market economies.

GERMANY. Given national differences, corporate governance also differs around the world. The EU's largest economy, Germany, has, since World War II, developed *stakeholder capitalism.* In this model of governance, workers' representatives typically occupy half the seats on a company's board of directors.[60] Companies are required to act on behalf of *all* stakeholders, and not just those owning shares in the firm. Shareholder activism is quite restrained in Germany compared with the United States or Britain, and German investors have more-limited power. As a result, the tensions between shareholder value creation and employee concerns are lower in German firms.

Another reason for less tension between shareholders and management is that the largest German firms are often debt-financed rather than equity-financed. This difference puts banks, rather than shareholders, at the center of German corporate governance. Relying on debt-financing allows German managers and employees to take a longer-term perspective. In the recent Great Recession (2008–2009), German firms generally focused more on maintaining a high level of employment

than on cutting costs by laying off workers. Many German firms instituted *Kurzarbeit*—voluntary reduction of work hours by employees, to keep them on the payroll—subsidized by the federal government.[61] This contrast can be seen in the results of a survey that asked corporate managers which is more important—saving jobs or paying dividends. In Germany, 60 percent said jobs. In the United States and Britain, 90 percent said dividends.[62]

FRANCE. France, Europe's second-largest economy in the EU, also uses a stakeholder-capitalist system. France has perhaps even more direct government involvement in company ownership and in determining strategic directions of state-owned companies. For example, the French government threatened both carmaker Renault and nuclear-energy company Areva with a loss of subsidies if they shifted manufacturing jobs and operations outside France. The French government is directly involved in important strategic decisions at the company level.

In Strategy Highlight 12.1, we mentioned that less than 16 percent of the board seats of large U.S. companies are held by women. Female participation in board membership is even lower in France, at 11 percent. To overcome underrepresentation of women on corporate boards, the French government passed a law requiring large companies to reserve at least 40 percent of the board seats for women. France thus became the second country, after Norway, to set a compulsory quota for women in the boardroom.[63] However, some of the subsequent board appointments, made to be compliant with the new law, have raised eyebrows. Dassault Aviation, a manufacturer of fighter planes and corporate jets, appointed Nicole Dassault to its board of directors.[64] Ms. Dassault is the 80-year-old wife of Serge Dassault, the company's controlling shareholder. The world's largest luxury goods company, Louis Vuitton (LVMH), appointed Bernadette Chirac, the 77-year-old wife of the former French president Jacques Chirac.[65] Some executives plan to appoint their girlfriends or their 18-year-old daughters to fill the quotas.

One thing that the appointments to fill quotas demonstrates is that many companies, both French and other multinationals, have failed to create a pipeline of female executives with the potential to become board members. It often takes decades of industry and executive experience to become an effective board member. Companies that have been more progressive in training women and providing career paths into managerial and executive ranks are more likely to gain and sustain competitive advantage. This is because their boards of directors are less likely to fall victim to groupthink.

CHINA. China, now the second-largest economy worldwide in nominal GDP (behind the United States and before Japan), uses state-directed capitalism to organize economic activity. China began implementing economic reforms in the 1980s.[66] Its move toward a more market-oriented system has accelerated since 2001, when it joined the World Trade Organization (WTO), an international body that aims to liberalize and supervise global trade.

In China, the most significant businesses are *state-owned enterprises* (*SOEs*), in which the state is the majority or sole owner. Given this ownership structure, social goals such as high levels of employment and provision of benefits (e.g., housing, health care, and so on) are seen as equally important or more important than profitability. On the downside, principal–agent problems are rampant in SOEs: Managers have no incentive to run the enterprises effectively. Nonetheless, China is putting the institutional entities in place to foster a free-market capitalist system. Examples include the Shanghai stock exchange, which lists roughly 900 publicly traded companies and has (as of spring 2011) a $2.7 trillion market capitalization.

When competing around the world, managers need to be mindful of the differences in corporate governance in the countries in which they do business. Many international companies have stumbled by not managing corporate-governance relationships appropriately within the given institutional context. China sentenced employees of Australian mining giant Rio Tinto to long prison terms on alleged bribery and industrial espionage charges.[67] In Russia, BP did not consult its existing Russian joint-venture partner TNK-BP before striking a new deal in Russia with the government-owned Rosneft, an energy company.[68] TNK-BP is an equity partnership between BP and a group of Russian investors. By failing to seek approval from TNK-BP for the deal with Rosneft, BP did not follow standard communication requirements embedded in its governance structure. In this case, the principal (BP), and not the agent (TNK-BP), acted opportunistically by taking advantage of information asymmetry. The Russian owners of TNK-BP filed a successful injunction to stop the Rosneft deal with a court in the UK. Both cases point toward the intersection of corporate governance and business ethics, which we will discuss next.

STRATEGY AND BUSINESS ETHICS

The accounting scandals and GFC have placed business ethics center stage in the public eye. Business ethics is an agreed-upon code of conduct in business, based on societal norms. Business ethics lay the foundation and provide training for "behavior that is consistent with the principles, norms, and standards of business practice that have been agreed upon by society."[69] These principles, norms, and standards of business practice differ to some degree in different cultures around the globe. But a large number of research studies have found that some notions—such as fairness, honesty, and reciprocity—are universal norms.[70] As such, many of these values have been codified into law.

>> **LO 12-5**
Describe and evaluate the relationship between business strategy and ethics.

However, law and ethics are not synonymous. This distinction is important. Many managers throughout the world subscribe to Milton Friedman's dictum that the sole responsibility of business is to make as much profit as possible while staying within the law. (Again, see Exhibit 12.5.) A note of caution is in order, though: *A manager's actions can be completely legal, but ethically questionable.* For example, consider the actions of mortgage-loan officers who—being incentivized by commissions—persuaded unsuspecting consumers to sign up for exotic mortgages, such as "option ARMs." These mortgages offer borrowers the choice to pay less than the required interest, which is then added on to the principal while the interest rate can adjust upward. Such actions may be legal, but they are unethical, especially if there are indications that the borrower might be unable to repay the mortgage once the interest rate moves up.[71]

Staying within the law, therefore, is a *minimum acceptable standard.* For this reason, many organizations have explicit *codes of conduct.* These codes go above and beyond the law in detailing how the organization expects an employee to behave and to represent the company in business dealings. Since business decisions are not made in a vacuum but are embedded within a societal context that expects ethical behavior, managers can use a number of questions to improve their decision making. When facing an ethical dilemma, a manager can ask whether the intended course of action falls within the *acceptable norms of professional behavior* as outlined in the organization's code of conduct. Moreover, the manager should imagine whether he or she would feel *comfortable explaining and defending the decision in public.* How would the media report the business decision if it were to become public? How would the company's stakeholders feel about it?

While other leading professions have accepted codes of conduct (e.g., the bar association in the practice of law and the Hippocratic oath in medicine), management has not achieved the same level of professionalism and status.[72] To regain (or gain) society's trust, some argue that management needs an accepted code of conduct,[73] which holds members to a high professional standard and imposes consequences for misconduct. An attorney, for example, can be disbarred and thus lose the right to practice law. Likewise, medical

business ethics
An agreed-upon code of conduct in business, based on societal norms.

EXHIBIT 12.6

The MBA Oath

Source: www.mbaoath.org.

As a business leader I recognize my role in society.

>> *My purpose is to lead people and manage resources to create value that no single individual can create alone.*

>> *My decisions affect the well-being of individuals inside and outside my enterprise, today and tomorrow.*

Therefore, I promise that:

>> *I will manage my enterprise with loyalty and care, and will not advance my personal interests at the expense of my enterprise or society.*

>> *I will understand and uphold, in letter and spirit, the laws and contracts governing my conduct and that of my enterprise.*

>> *I will refrain from corruption, unfair competition, or business practices harmful to society.*

>> *I will protect the human rights and dignity of all people affected by my enterprise, and I will oppose discrimination and exploitation.*

>> *I will protect the right of future generations to advance their standard of living and enjoy a healthy planet.*

>> *I will report the performance and risks of my enterprise accurately and honestly.*

>> *I will invest in developing myself and others, helping the management profession continue to advance and create sustainable and inclusive prosperity.*

In exercising my professional duties according to these principles, I recognize that my behavior must set an example of integrity, eliciting trust and esteem from those I serve. I will remain accountable to my peers and to society for my actions and for upholding these standards.

This oath I make freely, and upon my honor.

---

doctors can lose their professional accreditations if they engage in misconduct. To anchor future managers in professional values, and thus to move management closer to a truly professional status, a group of Harvard Business School students developed an MBA oath (see Exhibit 12.6). Since 2009, over 2,000 MBA students from over 500 business schools around the world have taken this voluntary pledge. The oath explicitly recognizes the role of business in society, and its responsibilities beyond shareholders. It also holds managers to a high ethical standard based on more or less universally accepted principles in order to "create value responsibly and ethically."[74] Having the highest personal integrity is of utmost importance to one's career. It takes decades to build a career, but sometimes just a few moments to destroy one.

Some people believe that unethical behavior is limited to a few "bad apples" such as Bernard Madoff and Jeffrey Skilling (of Enron).[75] The assumption here is that the vast majority of the population—and by extension, organizations—are good, and that we need only to safeguard against abuses by such bad actors. According to agency theory, it's the "bad agents" who act opportunistically and whose principals we need to be on guard against. However, research indicates otherwise.[76] While there clearly are some people with unethical or even criminal inclinations, in general one's ethical decision-making capacity depends very much on the organizational context. Research shows that if people work in organizations that expect and value ethical behavior, they are more likely to act ethically.[77] The opposite is also true. Enron's *stated* key values included respect and integrity, and its mission statement proclaimed that all business dealings should be open and fair.[78] Yet, the ethos at Enron was all about creating an inflated share price at any cost, and its employees observed and followed the behavior set by their leaders. Sometimes, it's the bad barrel that can spoil the apples!

As we can see, employees take cues from their environment on how to act. Therefore, ethical leadership is critical, and strategic leaders set the tone for the ethical climate within an organization. This is one of the reasons the HP board removed Mark Hurd, even without proof of illegal behavior or violation of the company's sexual-harassment policy. In order to foster ethical behavior in employees, top management must create an organizational structure, culture, and control system that values and encourages desired behavior. Furthermore, a company's formal and informal cultures must be aligned, and executive behavior must be in sync with the formally stated vision and values. Employees will quickly see through any duplicity. As they say, actions (by executives) speak louder than words (in vision statements). This point leads us to the important role of strategic leadership in gaining and sustaining competitive advantage in an ethical manner.

STRATEGIC LEADERSHIP

Throughout this book, we've included anecdotes of executives whose vision and actions have enabled their organizations to achieve competitive advantage. Their abilities demonstrate strategic leadership—the behaviors and styles of executives that influence others to achieve organizational goals. Strategic leadership typically resides in "executives who have overall responsibility for an organization—their characteristics, what they do, how they do it, and particularly, how they affect organizational outcomes."[79] These executives can be individuals, generally CEOs, but also can be top-management teams. The key point is that they have responsibility for the performance of the entire company or for an important strategic business unit.

> **>> LO 12-6**
> Describe the different roles that strategic leaders play and how to become a strategic leader.

Although *managerial discretion* varies across industries and time, strategic leaders do matter to firm performance.[80] Think of great business founders and their impact on the organizations they built: Steve Jobs at Apple, Michael Dell at Dell Computer, Mark Zuckerberg at Facebook, Sergei Brin and Larry Page at Google, Bill Hewlett and David Packard at HP, Bill Gates at Microsoft, Ingvar Kamprad at IKEA, Herb Kelleher at Southwest Airlines, Richard Branson at Virgin Group, and John Mackey at Whole Foods, among many others. There are also strategic leaders who have shaped and revitalized existing businesses: Steve Jobs at Pixar, Allan Mulally at Ford, Indra Nooyi at PepsiCo, Jack Welch at GE, Louis Gerstner at IBM, and Carlos Ghosn at Nissan.

At the other end of the spectrum, unfortunately, are CEOs whose decisions have led to a massive destruction of shareholder value: Charles Prince at Citigroup, Franklin Raines at Fannie Mae, Richard Wagoner at GM, Robert Nardelli at The Home Depot (and later Chrysler), Richard Fuld at Lehman Brothers, Stanley O'Neal at Merrill Lynch, Ed Zander at Motorola, Gerald Levin at Time Warner, Kerry Killinger at Washington Mutual, and so on.

Why do some leaders create great companies or manage them to greatness, while others destroy them? To answer that question, let's first consider what strategic leaders really do.

What Do Strategic Leaders Do?

To understand why some strategic leaders are more effective than others, let's take a close look of what strategic leaders actually do. In his seminal research on this subject, Henry Mintzberg shadowed CEOs minute-by-minute. He found that they do *not* remove themselves from day-to-day operations in order to devote substantial time to strategic reflection and decision making. Rather, their schedules are filled with a flurry of intense activities,

strategic leadership
The behaviors and styles of executives that influence others to achieve organizational goals.

EXHIBIT 12.7

Roles that Strategic Leaders Play

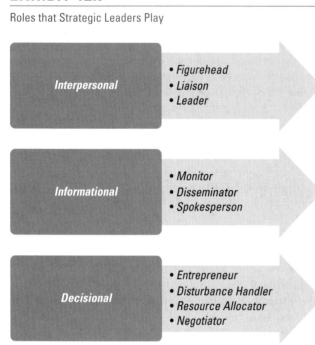

Interpersonal
- *Figurehead*
- *Liaison*
- *Leader*

Informational
- *Monitor*
- *Disseminator*
- *Spokesperson*

Decisional
- *Entrepreneur*
- *Disturbance Handler*
- *Resource Allocator*
- *Negotiator*

Source: Adapted from S. Finkelstein, D. C. Hambrick, and A. A. Cannella (2008), *Strategic leadership: Theory and Research on Executives, Top Management Teams, and Boards* (Oxford, UK: Oxford University Press), p. 18. The executive roles are based on research originally conducted by H. Mintzberg (1973), *The Nature of Managerial Work* (New York: Harper & Row).

at an unrelenting pace and with constant interruptions.[81] Other studies have found that most managers prefer oral communication: They spend most of their time "interacting—talking, cajoling, soothing, selling, listening, and nodding—with a wide array of parties inside and outside the organization."[82]

Based on his observations, Mintzberg derived a model (depicted in Exhibit 12.7) that identifies three distinct roles executives play when leading an organization: interpersonal, informational, and decisional.[83]

INTERPERSONAL ROLE. In the *interpersonal role,* the executive acts as figurehead, liaison, and leader.

- As *figurehead,* the executive appears at social functions that are often symbolic in nature such as meeting with domestic and international investors and government officials, giving interviews to CNBC, breaking ground at a new overseas facility, hosting star-performer functions for valued employees, and speaking at conferences and industry meetings.

- As *liaison,* the executive spends time building, maintaining, and developing a social network with external stakeholders to obtain valuable information and provide or call in favors.

- As *leader,* the executive fulfills more internal duties by making decisions such as selecting, training, and motivating key employees and future leaders, or reviewing and deciding upon strategic initiatives that require significant resources.

In all these roles, executives rely on interpersonal, often face-to-face, contacts.

INFORMATIONAL ROLE. In the *informational role,* the executive acts as monitor, disseminator, and spokesperson.

- As *monitor,* the executive seeks out and receives a diverse stream of often real-time information from a wide range of internal and external sources, which he or she constantly digests and evaluates. By accumulating such information about many different firm and industry aspects, the CEO serves as a kind of nerve center of the organization.

- The executive acts as *disseminator* when he or she distributes some of the stream of information *internally* to the organization. Much of the information shared is factual, based on financial data and other analysis, while some of it is based on the CEO's interpretation of events and facts.

- The *spokesperson* role occurs when the CEO distributes information *externally* to business news reporters or other stakeholders. In this case, the executive is attempting to shape and influence public opinion.

Given the ever-increasing information overload an executive experiences, much of the work in the informational role is to act as a kind of information traffic controller.

DECISIONAL ROLE. In the *decisional role,* the executive acts as entrepreneur, disturbance handler, resource allocator, and negotiator. As the name suggests, the executive's primary task here is strategic decision making.

- As *entrepreneur,* the executive scans the internal and external environments to discover new strategic initiatives. In this role, the executive also incubates and supervises current strategic initiatives.

- As *disturbance handler,* the executive acts much like an umpire in a sporting event— trying to reconcile internal and external sources of conflict, and if needed, take corrective action.

- As *resource allocator,* the executive decides what projects receive organizational resources and support. This role is directly linked to our discussion in Chapter 2 about the resource allocation process (RAP). According to one school of thought, by setting the RAP, the executive in effect formulates and implements strategy.[84]

- Finally, as *negotiator,* the executive represents the company in any major negotiation with internal and external stakeholders. The range of negotiations runs the gamut from labor contract talks with unions, to hostile-takeover discussions with competitors, to plans for entry into foreign markets with politicians.

How Do You Become an Effective and Ethical Strategic Leader?

Every board of directors and the shareholders they represent want effective strategic leadership for their company. According to the upper-echelons theory,[85] it's the top management team (at the upper echelons of an organization) that primarily determines the success or failure of an organization through the strategies they pursue. This leads us to consider the source of strategic leadership: How do you become an ethical and effective strategic leader? Is it innate? Can it be learned? The upper-echelons theory favors the idea that strong leadership is the result of both innate abilities and learning. It states that executives interpret situations through a lens of their unique perspectives, shaped by personal circumstances, values, and experiences.[86] Their leadership actions reflect characteristics of age, education, and career experiences, filtered through their personalized interpretations of the situations they face.

Given the prestige, power, and compensation of top-level executives, many aspire to be effective strategic leaders. In his bestseller *Good to Great,* strategy researcher and consultant Jim Collins identified *great companies* as those that transitioned from an average performer to achieving a sustained competitive advantage. He measured that transition as "cumulative stock returns of 6.9 times the general market in the fifteen years following their transition points."[87] Collins found patterns of leadership among the companies he studied, as pictured in the Level-5 leadership pyramid in Exhibit 12.8 (next page).[88] The pyramid is a conceptual framework that shows leadership progression through five distinct, sequential levels. Interestingly, Collins found that all companies he identified as *great* were led by Level-5 executives.

According to the Level-5 leadership pyramid, effective executives go through a natural progression of five different levels. Each level builds upon the prior one, meaning the executive can move on to the next level of leadership only when the current level has been mastered. Characteristics of the five levels are:

- The *Level-1* manager is a highly capable individual who makes productive contributions through motivation, talent, knowledge, and skills.

- The *Level-2* manager masters the skills required at Level 1, but is also a contributing team member who works effectively with others in order to achieve synergies and team objectives.

upper-echelons theory A conceptual framework that states that it's the top management team that primarily determines the success or failure of an organization through the strategies they pursue.

Level-5 leadership pyramid A conceptual framework of leadership progression with five distinct, sequential levels.

EXHIBIT 12.8

Strategic Leaders: The Level-5 Pyramid

Source: Adapted from J. Collins (2001), *Good to Great: Why Some Companies Make the Leap ... And Others Don't* (New York: HarperCollins), p. 20.

Builds enduring greatness through a combination of will power and humility. — **Level 5: Executive**

Presents compelling vision and mission to guide groups toward superior performance. Does the right things. — **Level 4: Effective Leader**

Is efficient and effective in organizing resources to accomplish stated goals and objectives. Does things right. — **Level 3: Competent Manager**

Uses high level of individual capability to work effectively with others in order to achieve team objectives. — **Level 2: Contributing Team Member**

Makes productive contributions through motivation, talent, knowledge, and skills. — **Level 1: Highly Capable Individual**

- The *Level-3* manager is a well-rounded and competent manager, a highly capable individual who is an effective team player and organizes resources effectively to achieve predetermined goals. He or she "does things right."

- At *Level 4,* the effective manager from Level 3 turns into a leader who determines what the right decisions are. The *Level-4* leader presents and effectively communicates a compelling vision and mission to guide the firm toward superior performance. He or she "does the right things."

- Finally, at *Level 5,* the manager reaches a leadership pinnacle, turning into a strategic leader. An effective strategic leader is an executive who builds enduring greatness into the organizations he or she leads.

A strategic leader who has mastered Level 5 simultaneously combines and reconciles tremendous will power and personal modesty. Such leaders, says Collins, "channel their ego needs away from themselves and into the larger goal of building a great company. It's not that Level 5 leaders have no ego or self-interest. Indeed, they are incredibly ambitious— *but their ambition is first and foremost for the institution, not themselves.*" Indeed, Jim Collins goes so far as to argue that the greatness of a strategic leader can truly be judged only if their organizations are able to sustain a competitive advantage in the years *after* the successful executive has departed from the organization.[89]

Taken together, you become an effective and ethical leader by sequentially mastering each of the five steps in the strategic leadership pyramid. Your training in college allows you to become a highly capable individual who can make productive contributions. If you take a first job immediately after your undergraduate degree, you will likely begin your corporate career in a functional area that was your focus or major in college (e.g., accounting, operations management, marketing, finance). As you move down the learning curve through group work in college and on-the-job training, you develop the ability to work effectively with others to achieve team objectives. With these skills, you move to Level-2 leadership. As responsibilities come to you, you will be able to develop and demonstrate the ability to organize resources efficiently and effectively to achieve strategic objectives. At Level 3, you have become an effective manager—someone who produces results.

Levels 4 and 5 require a stronger element of strategic leadership than the prior levels. When given the chance to work as a general manager (someone who has profit-and-loss responsibility for a unit or group), you will need Level-4 strategic leadership qualities.

At Levels 4 and 5, you will have increasingly dramatic opportunities to put to use the AFI framework you've learned from this book: You will need to be able to present a compelling vision and mission to inspire others to achieve superior performance. Doing so requires an intimate understanding not only of the inner workings of your company (Chapters 1 and 2), but also of the external environment. The internal and external analysis concepts (Chapters 3 and 4) will help you lay the foundation to formulate strategies that can improve firm performance (Chapters 5 through 7).

Having produced results at the business level, you might be tapped as the CEO of the company. At Level-5 strategic leadership, you need to reconcile a strong will and work ethic (which got you to the top) with the humility to lead a company by example. To do this effectively, you need a deep understanding of corporate-level strategy (Chapters 8 through 10) and organizational design (Chapter 11). You also will need to exhibit unfailing personal integrity (Chapter 12).

Thus, the concepts introduced in this textbook are valid for you far beyond this semester. They will become increasingly valuable as your career progresses, and you may find the need to refresh your knowledge of strategic management over time, as new opportunities come your way. The concepts and frameworks presented herein create a foundation that you can use to climb into leadership positions in whatever organization you choose to become a part of—whether it be a local nonprofit community organization or a Fortune 100 company!

CHAPTERCASE 12 | *Consider This . . .*

LARRY ELLISON, co-founder and CEO of Oracle, was one of the chief critics of Mark Hurd's ouster as HP CEO, as ChapterCase 12 noted. Mr. Ellison and Mr. Hurd are reported to be close personal friends who play tennis together frequently. Just a few weeks after Mark Hurd's resignation from HP, Oracle hired him as co-president and appointed him to the company's board of directors. Oracle's stock market value rose by roughly $10 billion after this announcement. The entire "Hurd saga" led to a stock movement of roughly $20 billion dollars (HP lost $10 billion after Mr. Hurd's ouster and Oracle gained $10 billion after hiring him) plus an undisclosed out-of-court settlement with Ms. Fisher.[90]

In November 2010, HP announced Leo Apotheker as its new CEO. The HP boardroom drama continued, however. Leo Apotheker was let go after only 11 months on the job. Mr. Apotheker, who came to HP from the German enterprise software company SAP, proposed a new corporate strategy for HP. He suggested that HP should focus on enterprise software solutions, and thus spin out its low-margin consumer hardware business. HP's consumer hardware business resulted from the legacy acquisition of Compaq and had now grown to 40 percent of HP's total revenues of $100 billion. Under Mr. Apotheker, HP also discontinued competing in the mobile device industry, most notably tablet computers—which many viewed as HP capitulating to Apple's dominance with the iPad. Moreover, as part of his new corporate strategy, Mr. Apotheker decided to buy the British software company Autonomy for more than $10 billion, which analysts saw as grossly overvalued. Mr. Apotheker was not able to convince investors of the value of this new corporate strategy; under his 11 months as CEO, HP's stock price dropped by roughly 40 percent. In September 2011, the HP board appointed Meg Whitman to be HP's new CEO. Ms. Whitman was formerly the CEO at eBay and had been appointed early in 2011 to HP's board of directors.

1. Why do you think HP lost 40 percent of its shareholder value since the summer of 2010?

2. Given HP's poor performance described in ChapterCase 12, who is to blame? The CEO or the board of directors? What recourse do shareholders have, if any?

3. Put yourself in Ms. Whitman's situation just after HP appointed her the new CEO in the fall of 2011.

What would be your strategic priorities? How would you identify them, and how would you implemented needed changes?

4. What lessons in terms of business ethics, corporate governance, and strategic leadership can be drawn from ChapterCase 12?

Take-Away Concepts

In this final chapter, we looked at stakeholder strategy, corporate governance, business ethics, and strategic leadership, as summarized by the following learning objectives and related take-away concepts.

LO 12-1 Describe and critically evaluate the relationship between strategic management and the role of business in society.

>> The public stock company is the institutional backbone of any modern free-market economy.

>> Four characteristics of the public stock company make it an attractive corporate form: limited liability for investors, transferability of investor interests (the trading of stocks), legal personality, and separation of ownership and control.

>> In the first decade of the 21st century, accounting scandals and the global financial crises eroded the public's trust in business as an institution and free-market capitalism as an economic system.

>> Effective stakeholder management is necessary to ensure the continued survival of the firm and to sustain any competitive advantage.

LO 12-2 Conduct a stakeholder impact analysis.

>> Stakeholder impact analysis considers the needs of different stakeholders, which enables the firm to perform optimally and to live up to good citizenship.

>> In a stakeholder impact analysis, managers pay particular attention to three important stakeholder attributes: power, legitimacy, and urgency.

>> Stakeholder impact analysis is a five-step process that answers the following questions:

1. Who are our stakeholders?
2. What are our stakeholders' interests and claims?
3. What opportunities and threats do our stakeholders present?
4. What economic, legal, and ethical responsibilities do we have to our stakeholders?
5. What should we do to effectively address the stakeholder concerns?

LO 12-3 Critically evaluate the relationship between corporate social responsibility (CSR) and competitive advantage.

>> A majority of empirical research studies support the notion that firms can do well (financially) by doing good (through CSR).

>> Some studies, however, found that the relationship is reversed: Superior financial performance allows firms to engage in CSR (to buy good will).

>> Although there seems to be a positive relationship between CSR and firm financial performance, it is not entirely clear what causes what.

LO 12-4 Describe the role of corporate governance and evaluate different governance mechanisms.

>> Corporate governance is about checks and balances, about asking the tough questions at the right time.

>> Corporate governance attempts to address the principal–agent problem, which describes any situation in which an agent performs activities on behalf of a principal.

>> The principal–agent problem is a core tenet in agency theory, which views the firm as a nexus of legal contracts.

>> The principal–agent problem concerns not only the relationship between owners (shareholders) and managers, but also cascades down the organizational hierarchy.

>> The risk of opportunism on behalf of agents is exacerbated by information asymmetry: Agents are generally better informed than the principals.

>> The board of directors is the centerpiece of corporate governance.

>> Other important corporate mechanisms are: executive compensation, the market for corporate control, and financial statement auditors, government regulators, and industry analysts.

LO 12-5 Describe and evaluate the relationship between business strategy and ethics.

>> The ethical pursuit of competitive advantage lays the foundation for long-term superior performance.

>> Law and ethics are not synonymous; obeying the law is the minimum that society expects of a corporation and its managers.

>> A manager's actions can be completely legal, but ethically questionable.

>> The following questions can help managers make sound ethical decisions.

1. Does the intended course of action fall within the acceptable norms of professional behavior?
2. Would the manager feel comfortable explaining and defending the decision in public?
3. How would the media report the particular business decision if it became public?
4. How would the company's stakeholders feel about it?

LO 12-6 Describe the different roles that strategic leaders play and how to become a strategic leader.

>> Strategic leaders play three different roles: interpersonal, informational, and decisional.

>> To become an effective strategic leader, a manager needs to develop a set of skills to move sequentially through five different leadership levels.

>> At Level 5, the executive is able to build enduring greatness for the company through a combination of will power and humility. At that level, ambition is primarily for the organization, rather than for the self.

Key Terms

Agency theory *(p. 343)*

Board of directors *(p. 344)*

Business ethics *(p. 351)*

Corporate governance *(p. 343)*

Corporate social responsibility (CSR) *(p. 339)*

Groupthink *(p. 346)*

Inside directors *(p. 345)*

Level-5 leadership pyramid *(p. 355)*

Outside directors *(p. 345)*

Stakeholder impact analysis *(p. 337)*

Stakeholder strategy *(p. 336)*

Stakeholder theory *(p. 336)*

Stock options *(p. 347)*

Strategic leadership *(p. 353)*

Upper-echelons theory *(p. 355)*

Discussion Questions

1. How can a firm lower the chances that key managers will pursue their own self-interest at the expense of the stockholders? At the expense of the employees?

2. The chapter notes that in 2010, in roughly two-thirds of U.S. firms, the CEO is also the chair of the board of directors. More broadly this can be viewed as an intermingling of management and ownership. Why are these two roles typically separated? Is it a positive development for so many firms to have a combined CEO and board chair?

3. In Chapter 6 (Strategy Highlight 6.1), we discussed how Toyota went from a "perfect recall" in the early days of its Lexus brand in 1989 to a "recall nightmare" of more than 8 million vehicles for accelerator problems in 2010. Some

analysts have questioned the role of Japanese corporate governance in the mishandling of the accelerator issues at Toyota.[91] These sources note Japan's governance system is geared around the company rather than the stockholders. Thus, boards are often all company insiders who bring a deep knowledge of company operations to the table. However, in Japan's rigid corporate hierarchy and emphasis on harmony, this can result in keeping bad news out of the boardroom. In 2010, Toyota's board of directors consisted of 29 men, *none* of whom were outsiders to the company.

a. How might Toyota's response to the initial accelerator concerns in 2009 have been different if the board had on it a former politician, the president of a communications firm, and the CEO of a major consumer-products company (as were on the board at Ford Motor Company in 2010)?

b. Does the *groupthink* discussion raised in Strategy Highlight 12.1 seem relevant here? Why or why not?

Ethical/Social Issues

1. Assume you work in the accounting department of a large software company. Toward the end of December, your supervisor tells you to change the dates on several executive stock option grants from March 15 to July 30. Why would she ask for this change? What should you do?

2. As noted in the chapter, CEO pay in 2010 was an incredible 300 times the average worker pay. This contrasts with historic values of between 25 and 40 times the average pay.

   a. What are the potentially negative effects of this increasing disparity in CEO pay?

   b. Do you believe that current executive pay packages are justified? Why or why not?

3. The MBA Oath (shown in Exhibit 12.6) says in part, "My decisions affect the well-being of individuals inside and outside my enterprise, today and tomorrow." This echoes what John Mackey of Whole Foods has in recent years called *conscious capitalism.*[92]

4. One example of a large firm reorienting toward this approach is PepsiCo. In the last few years, PepsiCo has been contracting directly with small farmers in impoverished areas (for example,

in Mexico). What started as a pilot project in PepsiCo's Sabritas snack food division has now spread to over 1,000 farmers providing potatoes, corn, and sunflower oil to the firm. Pepsi provides a price guarantee for farmers' crops that is higher and much more consistent than the previous system of using intermediaries. The farmers report that since they have a firm market, they are planting more crops. Output is up about 160 percent, and the farm incomes have tripled in the last three years.[93] The program has benefits for Pepsi as well. A shift to sunflower oil for its Mexican products will replace the 80,000 tons of palm oil it currently imports to Mexico from Asia and Africa, thus slashing transportation and storage costs.

   a. What are the benefits of this program for PepsiCo? What are its drawbacks?

   b. What other societal benefits could such a program have in Mexico?

   c. If you were a PepsiCo shareholder, would you support this program? Why or why not?

   d. Can you find other examples of firms employing "conscious capitalism"?

Small Group Exercises

SMALL GROUP EXERCISE 1

The section "Corporate Governance Around the World" makes clear that different countries have different systems of corporate governance, which in turn affect how firms compete for competitive advantage.

1. Discuss in your group the contrasting perspectives of "shareholder versus stakeholder" governance. What benefits and drawbacks can you find in each view?

2. Next, go online to find two sets of examples: (a) firms in the U.S. or Britain saving jobs by offering reduced hours to workers rather than having layoffs, and (b) large firms in Germany laying off employees or closing plants. What do the results of your search say about the impact of governance structure on corporate decisions?

3. Developments after the global financial crisis moved the U.S. away from being one of the most free-market economies in the world toward an economy with much more active and stronger government involvement. What implications does this shift in the political and economic environment in the United States have for large firms (such as GE or IBM) versus small firms (mom-and-pop entrepreneurs and technology startups)? How does this change the competitive landscape and the firms' strategies?

SMALL GROUP EXERCISE 2 (ETHICAL/SOCIAL ISSUES)

In the earlier Toyota discussion question, you may have noticed that all 29 board members were male.

Indeed, there is a greater percentage of women on corporate boards in Kuwait than in Japan.[94]

It is not unusual for even large corporate boards to have no women or minorities on them. In the U.S., women held 16 percent of board seats at Fortune 500 companies in 2010. In Europe, of the total number of board members in Britain, only 12 percent were women; Spain, France, and Germany all had less than 10 percent.[95] In Norway, by contrast, female members comprised 40 percent of the boards.

So how did Norway do it? In 2005, the government of Norway gave public firms two years to leap from 9 percent to 40 percent women on their boards. Is this a good idea? Spain, Italy, France, and the Netherlands must think so: Each country is considering implementing a similar quota (though generally with more than two years to implement it).

1. Discuss in your group to what extent it is a problem that women are proportionally underrepresented on corporate boards. Provide the rationale for your responses.

2. Would a regulatory quota be a good solution? Why or why not?

3. What other methods could be used to increase female and minority participation on corporate boards?

Strategy Term Project

MODULE 12: CORPORATE GOVERNANCE AND STRATEGIC LEADERSHIP

In this section, you will study the governance structure and leadership of your selected firm. This is also our concluding module, so we will have final questions for you to consider about your firm overall.

1. Find a list of the members of the board of directors for your firm. How large is the board? How many independent (non-employee) members are on the board? Are any women or minorities on the board? Is the CEO also the chair of the board?

2. Who are the largest stockholders of your firm? Is there a high degree of employee ownership of the stock?

3. In reviewing press releases and news articles about your firm over the past year, can you find examples of any actions the firm has taken that, though legal, may be ethically questionable?

4. Does the CEO of your firm show characteristics consistent with Level-5 leadership?

5. You have now completed 12 modular assignments about your selected firm. You know a lot about its mission, strategies, competitive advantage, and organization. Is this a company you would like to work for? If you had $1,000 to invest in a firm, would you invest it in the stock of this firm? Why or why not?

*my*Strategy

ARE YOU PART OF GEN-Y, OR WILL YOU MANAGE GEN-Y WORKERS?

Generation Y (born between 1980 and 2001) is entering the work force and advancing their careers now, as the Baby Boomers of their parents' generation begin to retire in large numbers. Given the smaller size of Gen Y compared to the Baby Boomers, this generation received much more individual attention from their immediate and extended families. Classes in school were much smaller than in previous generations. The parents of Gen Y members placed a premium on achievement, both academically and socially. Gen Y grew up during a time of unprecedented economic growth and prosperity, combined with an explosion in technology (including laptop computers, cell phones, the Internet, e-mail, instant messaging, and online social networks). Gen Yers are connected 24/7, and thus able to work anywhere, frequently multitasking. Due to the unique circumstances of their upbringing, they are said to be tech-savvy, family- and friends-centric, team players, achievement-oriented, but also attention-craving.[96]

Some have called Generation Y the "trophy kids," due in part to the practice of giving all Gen-Y children trophies in competitive activities, not wanting to single out winners and losers. When coaching a group of Gen-Y students for job interviews, a consultant asked them how they believe future employers view them. She gave them a clue to the answer: the letter E. Quickly, the students answered confidently: *excellent, enthusiastic,* and *energetic.* The answer the consultant was looking for was "entitled." Baby Boomers believe that Gen Y has an overblown sense of entitlement.

When they bring so many positive characteristics to the workplace, why do Baby Boomers view Gen-Y employees as entitled? Many managers are concerned that these young workers have outlandish expectations when compared with other employees: They often expect higher pay, flexible work schedules, promotions and significant raises every year, and generous vacation and personal time.[97] Managers also often find that for Gen-Y employees, the traditional annual or semi-annual performance evaluations are not considered sufficient. Instead, Gen-Y employees seek more immediate feedback, ideally daily or at least weekly. For many, feedback needs to come in the form of positive reinforcement rather than as a critique.

The generational tension seems a bit ironic, since the dissatisfied Baby Boomer managers are the same indulgent parents who raised Gen Yers. Some companies, like Google, RIM, and Sun Microsystems (Sun), have leveraged this tension into an opportunity. Google, for example, allows each employee to spend one day a week on any project of his or her own choosing, thus meeting the Gen-Y need for creativity and self-determination. Executives at RIM, the maker of the BlackBerry, have learned to motivate Gen-Y employees by sincerely respecting their contributions as colleagues rather than relying on hierarchical or position power.[98] The network-computing company Sun accommodates Gen-Yers' need for flexibility through drastically increasing work-from-home and telecommunicating arrangements, so that basically all employees now have a "floating office."

1. As you and your cohort enter the work force, do you expect to see a different set of business ethics take hold?

2. Are efforts such as the MBA Oath (discussed in this chapter) reflections of a different approach that Gen Y will take to the business environment, compared with prior generations?

3. Will you aspire to become a Level-5 strategic leader as you rise through your professional career? How would you go about moving from Level 1 to Level 5? What plan will you put in place?

Endnotes

1. "Mark Hurd neglected to follow H-P code," *The Wall Street Journal,* August 8, 2010.

2. "Oracle chief faults H.P. board for forcing Hurd out," *The New York Times,* August 9, 2010.

3. Finkelstein, S., D. C. Hambrick, and A. A. Cannella (2008), *Strategic Leadership: Theory and Research on Executives, Top Management Teams, and Boards* (Oxford, UK: Oxford University Press); and Yulk, G. (1998), *Leadership in Organizations,* 4th ed. (Englewood Cliff, NJ: Prentice-Hall).

4. Berle, A., Means, G. (1932), *The Modern Corporation & Private Property* (New York: Macmillan); and Monks, R.A.G., and N. Minow (2008),

Corporate Governance, 4th ed. (West Sussex, UK: Wiley).

5. This discussion draws on: Porter, M. E., and M. R. Kramer (2006), "Strategy and society: The link between competitive advantage and corporate social responsibility," *Harvard Business Review,* December: 80–92; Porter, M. E., and M. R. Kramer (2011), "Creating shared value: How to reinvent capitalism—and unleash innovation and growth," *Harvard Business Review,* January–February; Carroll, A. B., and A. K. Buchholtz (2012), *Business & Society. Ethics, Sustainability, and Stakeholder Management* (Mason, OH: South-Western Cengage); and Parmar, B. L., and R. E. Freeman, J. S. Harrison, A. C. Wicks, L. Purnell, and S. De Colle (2010), "Stakeholder theory: The state of the art," *Academy of Management Annals* 4: 403–445.

6. "The perp walk," *BusinessWeek,* January 13, 2003.

7. See the discussion by: Lowenstein, R. (2010), *The End of Wall Street* (New York: Penguin Press); Paulson, H. M. (2010), *On the Brink: Inside the Race to Stop the Collapse of the Global Financial System* (New York: Business Plus); and Wessel, D. (2010), *In FED We Trust: Ben Bernanke's War on the Great Panic* (New York: Crown Business).

8. Parmar, B. L., R. E. Freeman, J. S. Harrison, A. C. Wicks, L. Purnell, and S. De Colle (2010), "Stakeholder theory: The state of the art," *Academy of Management Annals* 4: 403–445.

9. Ibid.

10. To acknowledge the increasing importance of *stakeholder strategy,* the Strategic Management Society (SMS)—the leading association for academics, business executives, and consultants interested in strategic management—has recently created a *stakeholder strategy* division; see http://strategicmanagement. net/. Also see: Anderson, R. C. (2009), *Confessions of a Radical Industrialist: Profits, People, Purpose—Doing Business by Respecting the Earth* (New York: St. Martin's Press); Sisodia, R. S., D. B. Wolfe, and J. N. Sheth (2007), *Firms of Endearment: How World-Class Companies Profit from Passion and Purpose* (Upper Saddle River, NJ: Prentice-Hall Pearson); and Svendsen,

A. (1998), *The Stakeholder Strategy: Profiting from Collaborative Business Relationships* (San Francisco, CA: Berrett-Koehler).

11. This discussion is based on: Freeman, R. E. (1984), *Strategic Management: A Stakeholder Approach* (Boston, MA: Pitman); Jones, T. M. (1995), "Instrumental stakeholder theory: A synthesis of ethics and economics," *Academy of Management Review* 20: 404–437; Jones, T. M, and A. C. Wicks (1999), "Convergent stakeholder theory," *Academy of Management Review* 20: 404–437; and Parmar, B. L., R. E. Freeman, J. S. Harrison, A. C. Wicks, L. Purnell, and S. De Colle (2010), "Stakeholder theory: The state of the art," *Academy of Management Annals* 4: 403–445.

12. Parmar, B. L., R. E. Freeman, J. S. Harrison, A. C. Wicks, L. Purnell, and S. De Colle (2010), "Stakeholder theory," p. 406.

13. Ibid. Emphasis (*italics*) added.

14. Ibid., p. 416.

15. *Fortune 2010 The World Most Admired Companies,* http://money.cnn.com/magazines/fortune/mostadmired/2010/full_list/.

16. Mitchell, R. K., B. R. Agle, and D. J. Wood (1997), "Toward a theory of stakeholder identification and salience," *Academy of Management Review* 22: 853–886; and Eesley, C., and M. J. Lenox (2006), "Firm responses to secondary stakeholder action," *Strategic Management Journal* 27: 765–781.

17. TIAA-CREF is an acronym for Teachers Insurance and Annuity Association–College Retirement Equities Fund.

18. CalPERS is an acronym for California Public Employees' Retirement System.

19. People for the Ethical Treatment of Animals (PETA) is an animal rights organization.

20. This example is drawn from: Esty, D. C., and A. S. Winston (2006), *Green to Gold: How Smart Companies Use Environmental Strategy to Innovate, Create Value, and Build Competitive Advantage* (Hoboken, NJ: Wiley).

21. This discussion draws on: Carroll, A. B., and A. K. Buchholtz

(2012), *Business & Society. Ethics, Sustainability, and Stakeholder Management* (Mason, OH: South-Western Cengage); Carroll, A. B. (1991), "The pyramid of corporate social responsibility: Toward the moral management of organizational stakeholders," *Business Horizons,* July–August: 39–48; and Carroll, A. B. (1979), "A three-dimensional, conceptual model of corporate social performance," *Academy of Management Review* 4: 497–505.

22. For an insightful but critical treatment of this topic, see the 2003 Canadian documentary film *The Corporation.*

23. www.ge.com.

24. "Wal-Mart tops list of charitable cash contributors, AT&T No. 2," *USAToday.com,* August 9, 2010, www.usatoday.com/money/companies/2010-08-08-corporate-philanthropy-interactive-graphic_N.htm.

25. Carroll, A. B. (1991), "The pyramid of corporate social responsibility," pp. 39–48.

26. Friedman, M. (1962), *Capitalism and Freedom* (Chicago, IL: University of Chicago Press). Quoted in Friedman, M. (1970), "The social responsibility of business is to increase its profits," *The New York Times Magazine,* September 13.

27. "Milton Friedman goes on tour," *The Economist,* January 27, 2011.

28. The Four Asian Tigers denotes four highly developed economies in Southeast Asia (Hong Kong, Singapore, South Korea, and Taiwan).

29. Porter, M. E., and M. R. Kramer (2006), "Strategy and society: The link between competitive advantage and corporate social responsibility," *Harvard Business Review,* December: 80–92.

30. Porter, M. E., and M. R. Kramer (2011), "Creating shared value: How to reinvent capitalism—and unleash innovation and growth," *Harvard Business Review,* January–February.

31. *GE Governance Principles,* p. 1, www.ge.com.

32. Orlitzky, M., F. L. Schmidt, and S. L. Rynes (2003), "Corporate social and financial performance: A meta-analysis," *Organization Studies,* 24: 403–441.

33. Margolis, J. D., and J. P. Walsh (2001), *People and Profits? The Search for a Link between a Company's Social and Financial Performance* (Mahwah, NJ: Erlbaum).

34. Monks, R.A.G., and N. Minow (2008), *Corporate Governance,* 4th ed. (West Sussex, UK: Wiley).

35. Markopolos, H. (2010), *No One Would Listen: A True Financial Thriller* (Hoboken, NJ: Wiley).

36. Berle, A., and G. Means (1932), *The Modern Corporation & Private Property* (New York, Macmillan); Jensen, M., and W. Meckling (1976), "Theory of the firm: Managerial behavior, agency costs and ownership structure," *Journal of Financial Economics* 3: 305–360; and Fama, E. (1980), "Agency problems and the theory of the firm," *Journal of Political Economy* 88: 375–390.

37. "Top 10 crooked CEOs," *Time,* June 9, 2009.

38. "Thain ousted in clash at Bank of America," *The Wall Street Journal,* January 23, 2009.

39. Agency theory originated in finance; see Jensen, M., and W. Meckling (1976), "Theory of the firm: Managerial behavior, agency costs and ownership structure," *Journal of Financial Economics* 3: 305–360; and Fama, E. (1980), "Agency problems and the theory of the firm," *Journal of Political Economy* 88: 375–390. For an application to strategic management, see Eisenhardt, K. M. (1989), "Agency theory: An assessment and review," *Academy of Management Review* 14: 57–74; and Mahoney, J. T. (2005), *Economic Foundations of Strategy* (Thousand Oaks, CA: Sage).

40. Eisenhardt, K. M. (1989), "Agency theory: An assessment and review," *Academy of Management Review* 14: 57–74.

41. This section draws on: Monks, R.A.G., and N. Minow (2008), *Corporate Governance,* 4th ed. (West Sussex, UK: Wiley); Williamson, O. E. (1984), "Corporate governance," *Yale Law Journal* 93: 1197–1230; and Williamson, O. E. (1985), *The Economic Institutions of Capitalism* (New York: Free Press).

42. "HP looks beyond its ranks," *The Wall Street Journal,* August 9, 2010.

43. "Apple chief to take leave," *The Wall Street Journal,* January 18, 2010.

44. "HP shakes up board in scandal's wake," *The Wall Street Journal,* January 21, 2011.

45. "On Apple's board, fewer independent voices," *The Wall Street Journal,* March 24, 2010.

46. This Strategy Highlight is based on: "2010 Catalyst census: Fortune 500 women board directors," www.catalyst.org; Baliga, B. R., R. C. Moyer, and R. S. Rao (1996), "CEO duality and firm performance: What's the fuss," *Strategic Management Journal* 17: 41–53; Brickley, J. A., J. L. Coles, and G. Jarrell (1997), "Leadership structure: Separating the CEO and chairman of the board," *Journal of Corporate Finance* 3: 189–220; Daily, C. M., and D. R. Dalton (1997), "CEO and board chair roles held jointly or separately," *Academy of Management Executive* 3: 11–20; "GE governance principles," www.ge.com; Irving, J. (1972), *Victims of Groupthink. A Psychological Study of Foreign-Policy Decisions and Fiascoes,* (Boston, MA: Houghton Mifflin); Jensen, M. C. (1993), "The modern industrial revolution, exit, and the failure of internal control systems," *Journal of Corporate Finance* 48: 831–880; "On Apple's board, fewer independent voices," *The Wall Street Journal,* March 24, 2010; "Strings attached to options grant for GE's Immelt," *The Wall Street Journal,* April 20, 2011; Westphal, J. D., and E. J. Zajac (1995), "Who shall govern? CEO board power, demographic similarity and new director selection," *Administrative Science Quarterly* 40: 60–83; and Westphal, J. D., and I. Stern (2007), "Flattery will get you everywhere (especially if you are male Caucasian): How ingratiation, boardroom behavior, and demographic minority status affect additional board appointments at U.S. companies," *Academy of Management Journals* 50: 267–288.

47. "HP shareholders sue Hurd, Board over resignation," *Bloomberg Businessweek,* August 12, 2010.

48. www.faireconomy.org.

49. "Paychecks for CEOs climb," *The Wall Street Journal,* November 15, 2010.

50. Heineman, B. W. (2008), "The fatal flaw in pay for performance," *Harvard Business Review,* June; and Kaplan, S. N. (2008), "Are U.S. CEOs overpaid?" *Academy of Management Perspectives* 22: 5–20.

51. "Paychecks for CEOs climb," *The Wall Street Journal,* November 15, 2010.

52. "Strings attached to options grant for GE's Immelt," *The Wall Street Journal,* April 20, 2011.

53. Ariely, D. (2010), *The Upside of Irrationality: The Unexpected Benefits of Defying Logic at Work and at Home* (New York: HarperCollins).

54. "Sanofi wins long-sought biotech deal," *The Wall Street Journal,* February 17, 2011.

55. www.fasb.gov: "The term 'generally accepted accounting principles' has a specific meaning for accountants and auditors. The AICPA Code of Professional Conduct prohibits members from expressing an opinion or stating affirmatively that financial statements or other financial data 'present fairly . . . in conformity with generally accepted accounting principles,' if such information contains any departures from accounting principles promulgated by a body designated by the AICPA Council to establish such principles. The AICPA Council designated FASAB as the body that establishes generally accepted accounting principles (GAAP) for federal reporting entities."

56. Lowenstein, R. (2010), *The End of Wall Street* (New York: Penguin Press).

57. Hayward, M.L.A., and W. Boeker (1998), "Power and conflicts of interest in professional firms: Evidence from investment banking," *Administrative Science Quarterly* 43: 1–22.

58. Gedajlovic, E. R., and D. M. Shapiro (1998), "Management and ownership effects: Evidence from five countries," *Strategic Management Journal* 19: 533–553.

59. Lowenstein, R. (2010), *The End of Wall Street* (New York: Penguin Press).

60. Tuschke, A., and G. W. Sanders (2003), "Antecedents and consequences of corporate governance reform: The case of Germany," *Strategic Management Journal* 24: 631–649.

61. "Hoard instinct," *The Economist,* July 8, 2010.

62. "Boards behaving badly," *The Economist,* August 6, 2009.

63. "La vie en rose. French companies get serious about putting women in the boardroom," *The Economist,* May 6, 2010.

64. "Preliminary Notification To The General Meeting Of The Shareholders," Dassault Systems, May 26, 2011, www.3ds.com.

65. "Bernadette Chirac, Director, LVMH Moet Hennessy Louis Vuitton," *Bloomberg Businessweek,* http://investing.businessweek.com.

66. White, G., J. Howell, and H. Shang (1996), *In Search of Civil Society: Market Reform and Social Change in Contemporary China* (Oxford, UK: Clarendon Press); and Peng, M. W. (2003), "Outside directors and firm performance during institutional transitions," *Strategic Management Journal* 25: 453–472.

67. "China sentences Rio Tinto employees in bribe Case," *The New York Times,* March 29, 2010.

68. "BP's Russian troubles: Dudley do-wrong," *The Economist,* March 31, 2011.

69. This section draws on and the definition is from: Treviño, L. K., and K. A. Nelson (2011), *Managing Business Ethics: Straight Talk About How to Do It Right,* 5th ed. (Hoboken, NJ: Wiley).

70. Several such studies, like the "ultimatum game," are described in: Ariely, D. (2008), *Predictably Irrational: The Hidden Forces That Shape Our Decisions* (New York: HarperCollins); and Ariely, D. (2010), *The Upside of Irrationality: The Unexpected Benefits of Defying Logic at Work and at Home* (New York: HarperCollins).

71. Lowenstein, R. (2010), *The End of Wall Street* (New York: Penguin Press).

72. Khurana, R. (2007), *From Higher Aims to Hired Hands: The Social Transformation of American Business Schools and the Unfulfilled Promise of Management as a Profession* (Princeton, NJ: Princeton University Press).

73. Khurana, R., and N. Nohria (2008), "It's time to make management a true profession," *Harvard Business Review,* October: 70–77.

74. www.mbaoath.org.

75. This section draws on: Treviño, L. K., and K. A. Nelson (2011), *Managing Business Ethics.*

76. Treviño, L., and A. Youngblood (1990), "Bad apples in bad barrels: A causal analysis of ethical-decision behavior," *Journal of Applied Psychology* 75: 378–385.

77. Ibid. Also, for a superb review and discussion of this issue, see Treviño, L. K., and K. A. Nelson (2011), *Managing Business Ethics.*

78. McLean, B., and P. Elkind (2004), *The Smartest Guys in the Room: The Amazing Rise and Scandalous Fall of Enron* (New York: Portfolio).

79. Finkelstein, S., D. C. Hambrick, and A. A. Cannella (2008), *Strategic Leadership,* p. 4.

80. Hambrick, D. C., and E. Abrahamson (1995), "Assessing managerial discretion across industries: A multimethod approach," *Academy of Management Journal* 38: 1427–1441.

81. Mintzberg, H. (1973), *The Nature of Managerial Work* (New York: Harper & Row).

82. Finkelstein, S., D. C. Hambrick, and A. A. Cannella (2008), *Strategic Leadership,* p. 17.

83. This section draws on: Mintzberg, H. (1973), *The Nature of Managerial Work;* and Finkelstein, S., D. C. Hambrick, and A. A. Cannella (2008), *Strategic Leadership,* p. 17–18.

84. Bower, J. L., and C. G. Gilbert (2005), *From Resource Allocation to Strategy* (Oxford, UK: Oxford University Press).

85. Hambrick, D. C. (2007), "Upper echelons theory: An update," *Academy of Management Review* 32: 334–343; and Hambrick, D. C., and P. A. Mason (1984), "Upper echelons: The organization as a reflection of its top managers," *Academy of Management Review* 9: 193–206.

86. Ibid.

87. Collins, J. (2001), *Good to Great: Why Some Companies Make the Leap . . . And Others Don't* (New York: HarperCollins), p. 3.

88. Ibid.

89. Ibid.

90. This ChapterCase discussion is based on: "Mark Hurd neglected to follow H-P code," *The Wall Street Journal,* August 8, 2010; "Oracle chief faults HP board for forcing Hurd out," *The New York Times,* August 9, 2010; "HP shakes up board in scandal's wake," *The Wall Street Journal,* January 21, 2011; "Hewlett-Packard: Worst board ever?" *The Wall Street Journal,* September 21, 2011; "Crisis unfolds at HP over CEO," *The Wall Street Journal,* September 22, 2011; "Whitman takes charge," *The Wall Street Journal,* September 24, 2011; Collins, J. (2009), *How the Mighty Fall: And Why Some Companies Never Give In* (New York: HarperCollins); and Packard, D. (1995), *The HP Way: How Bill Hewlett And I Built Our Company* (New York: HarperCollins).

91. "Accelerating into trouble," *The Economist,* February 11, 2010; and "A recall for Toyota's corporate governance?" *Pensions & Investments,* April 5, 2010.

92. "The conscience of a capitalist," *The Wall Street Journal,* October 3, 2009.

93. "For Pepsi, a business decision with social benefit," *The New York Times,* February 21, 2011.

94. "Accelerating into trouble," *The Economist,* February 11, 2010.

95. "Skirting the issue," *The Economist,* March 11, 2010.

96. This *my*Strategy module is based on: "The 'trophy kids' go to work," *The Wall Street Journal,* October 21, 2008; and Alsop, R. (2008), *The Trophy Kids Grow Up: How the Millennial Generation Is Shaking Up the Workplace* (Hoboken, NJ: Jossey-Bass).

97. Survey by CareerBuilder.com.

98. Presentation by Robin Bienfait, CIO, RIM, March 9, 2009, Georgia Institute of Technology.

PART 4
MINICASES

MICHAEL PHELPS, nicknamed MP, won an unprecedented eight gold medals at the Beijing Summer Olympics, and while doing so set seven new world records. Eight short days in August 2008 changed Olympic history and Michael Phelps's life forever, making MP one of the greatest athletes of all time. Immediately after the event, *The Wall Street Journal* reported that Phelps would be likely to turn the eight gold medals into a cash-flow stream of more than $100 million through a variety of business activities.[1] The more obvious ones were product and service endorsements: His official sponsors included AT&T Wireless, Kellogg's, Omega, PowerBar, Rosetta Stone, Speedo, Visa, and PureSport. Other offers included the exotic and the mundane: books and movies, sculptures eternalizing his muscled torso, acrylic paintings, dog food (given Michael's love for his British bulldog, Herman), commemorative coins, tuxedos, car rims, and even bobblehead dolls.

In his youth, MP was diagnosed with attention deficit hyperactivity disorder (ADHD). Doctors prescribed swimming to help him release his energy. It worked! Between 2004 and 2008, Michael Phelps attended the University of Michigan, studying marketing and management. He had already competed quite successfully in the 2004 Athens Summer Olympics, where he won eight medals: six gold and two bronze. Right after the Athens Games, the then-19-year-old sat down with his manager, Peter Carlisle, and his long-time swim coach, Bob Bowman, to map out a detailed strategy for the next four years. The explicit goal was to win nothing less than a gold medal in each of the events in which he would compete in Beijing, thus preparing the launch pad for his superstardom.[2]

Bob Bowman was responsible for getting MP into the necessary physical shape he needed for Beijing and nurturing the mental toughness required to break Mark Spitz's 36-year record of seven gold medals won in the 1972 Munich Olympic Games. Peter Carlisle, meanwhile, conceived of a detailed strategy to launch MP as a world superstar during the Beijing Games. While MP spent six hours a day in the pool, Carlisle focused on exposing MP to the Asian market, the largest consumer market in the world, with a special emphasis on the Chinese consumer. The earliest tie-in was with a Hong Kong–based manufacturer of MP3 players and other consumer electronics, Matsunichi, with whom MP became affiliated right after the 2004 Athens Games. MP made several other visits to China during the 2005–2007 period, among them the "Visa Friendship Lanes Tour" to promote the Special Olympics.

MP's wide-ranging presence in the real world was combined with a huge exposure in the virtual world. Phelps posts and maintains his own Facebook page, with millions of "phans" whose click-through rivaled the site of President Barack Obama in popularity. MP is also a favorite of YouTube and other online blogs (e.g., Swimroom.com), garnering worldwide exposure to an extent never before achieved by an Olympian.[3] The gradual buildup of Phelps over a number of years enabled manager Peter Carlisle to launch MP as a superstar right after he won his eighth gold medal at the Beijing Games. By then, MP had become a worldwide brand.

Clearly, a successful strategy rests on leveraging unique resources and capabilities. Accordingly, some suggest that MP's success can be explained by his unique physical endowments: his long thin torso, which reduces drag; his arm span of 6 feet 7 inches (204 cm), which is disproportionate to his 6-foot-4-inch (193 cm) height; his relatively short legs for a person of his height; and his size-14 feet which work like flippers due to hypermobile ankles.[4] While MP's physical attributes are a *necessary* condition for winning, they are *not sufficient*. Many other swimmers, like the Australian Ian Thorpe (who has size-17 feet) or the German "albatross" Michael Gross (with an arm span of 7 feet or 213 cm), also brought extraordinary resource endowments to the swim meet. Yet neither of them won eight gold medals in a single Olympics.

DISCUSSION QUESTIONS

Review Chapter 1: What Is Strategy and Why Is It Important?

1. How did Michael Phelps turn into a "global brand"?

2. What does the story of Michael Phelps have to do with strategic management?

3. Following the Beijing Olympics, a photo published by a British tabloid showed Michael Phelps using a "bong," a device for smoking marijuana, at a party in South Carolina. Kellogg's withdrew Phelps's endorsement contract. What does this incident tell you about maintaining and increasing brand value over time?

4. According to a study by two economics professors at the University of California, Davis,[5] another recent example of an athlete who lost significant "brand value" is Tiger Woods, who destroyed an estimated $12 billion in stock market value of the firms sponsoring him—Accenture, Gillette, Nike, PepsiCo (Gatorade), and Electronic Arts (EA). As a manager, what lessons about celebrity endorsements can you draw from the examples of Phelps and Woods? What are some general take-aways that a strategist should keep in mind?

5. *After reading Chapter 2:* Did Michael Phelps or his team follow one of the approaches to strategy making discussed in Chapter 2? Explain your response.

Endnotes

1. "Now, Phelps chases gold on land," *The Wall Street Journal,* August 18, 2008.

2. Ibid.

3. "Michael Phelps' agent has been crafting the swimmer's image for years," *Associated Press,* September 14, 2008.

4. "Profile: Michael Phelps – A normal guy from another planet," *Telegraph,* August 15, 2008.

5. Knittel, C. R., and V. Stango (2008), "Celebrity endorsements, firm value and reputation risk: Evidence from the Tiger Woods scandal," working paper, University of California, Davis, http://faculty.gsm.ucdavis.edu/~vstango/tiger007.pdf.

ABOUT 20 MILLION U.S. MEN experience some form of male erectile dysfunction (MED), and treating the disorder with prescription drugs is a business worth more than $3 billion a year. Was this great pharmaceutical success the result of smart strategic planning? Far from it. Without serendipity, sometimes there would be no success story. Here is how two modern blockbuster drugs were discovered.

In the 1990s, researchers at Pfizer developed the compound UK-95,480 as a potential drug to treat heart disease. In their research, they focused on two things: preventing blood clots and enhancing blood flow. The drug did not achieve the desired effects in human trials, but some men in the test group reported an unexpected side-effect: prolonged erections. Pfizer's managers were quick to turn this unintended result into the blockbuster drug Viagra.

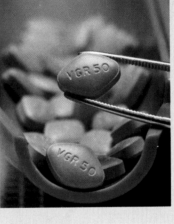

Although the old adage says lightning never strikes the same place twice, it did so in the area of MED drugs. In the mid-1990s, the biotech firm Icos was developing a new treatment for hypertension. Code named IC-351, the drug moved quickly to clinical trials because of encouraging lab results. Then unexpected things happened. First was the unusually high compliance rate of patients who took the medication required by the trial, especially males in their fifties, despite the fact that IC-351 turned out to be ineffective in treating hypertension. The second surprise was that many male patients refused to return their surplus pills. The reason: their improved sex life. Icos's IC-351 had failed to treat hypertension but succeeded at treating MED. Marketed as Cialis, it is a major competitor to Viagra, and its success led Lilly to acquire Icos for $2.3 billion in 2007.[1]

DISCUSSION QUESTIONS

Review Chapter 1: What Is Strategy and Why Is It Important?

Review Chapter 2: The Strategic Management Process.

1. Do you think "serendipity is random," as some say? Why or why not?

2. What does the "discovery" of Viagra and Cialis tell us about the strategic management process? About the role of strategic initiatives?

3. Which model of strategy process best explains the Viagra/Cialis story? Why?

4. Does the Viagra/Cialis story influence how you would design a strategic management process? Why or why not? If yes, what process would you design?

Endnotes

1. This MiniCase is based on: Mestel, R. (1999), "Sexual chemistry," *Discover*, January: 32; "Eli Lilly says Icos acquisition complete," *Reuters*, January 29, 2007; and Deeds, D. L., and F. T. Rothaermel (2003), "Honeymoons and liabilities: The relationship between alliance age and performance in R&D alliances," *Journal of Product Innovation Management* 20, no. 6: 468–484.

ACCORDING TO A STUDY by Stanford University, one-third of all U.S. consumers believe global warming is the most serious ecological issue facing the world today. More than half the respondents view this issue as extremely or very important, almost double the number just a decade ago.

The Home Depot responded to consumers' demands for more green products. On Earth Day 2007, it launched a new product label called Eco Options, using strict criteria to designate products as ecologically friendly in five ways: Sustainable Forestry, Clean Air, Water Conservation, Energy Efficient, and Healthy Home. The desire to earn an Eco Options label from The Home Depot has spurred its suppliers to innovate by offering even more ecologically friendly products, such as super low-flow toilets and energy-efficient appliances and lighting. The over 4,000 stock-keeping units (SKUs) that carry the Eco Options label brought in about $2.2 billion in sales and the brand is growing fast. The average customer's purchase basket that contains an Eco Options product was $107, compared with an overall average of $58; implying that the Eco Options label garnered an 85 percent price premium.

Competitor Lowe's was also quick to catch the green wave. Early in 2007, it began introducing organic gardening supplies, including fertilizer, soil, and insecticides that are not only ecologically friendly but also harmless for children and pets. Lowe's claims that more than 100 million people in the United States use some kind of organic lawn and garden product. It even opened new stores dedicated to ecologically friendly products such as bamboo flooring and blinds.[1]

DISCUSSION QUESTIONS

Review Chapter 3: External Analysis: Industry Structure, Competitive Forces, and Strategic Groups.

1. Apply a PESTEL analysis to the The Home Depot and Ford Motor Company. Which are the most important external forces impinging upon the companies? Are the forces the same, or are they different? Why?

2. Do you believe that The Home Depot is "catching the green wave" or merely engaging in "greenwashing" (expressing environmentalist concerns as a cover for products, policies, or activities that may not be all that green)?[2] Support your arguments.

3. Is it ethical to charge a price premium for "green-label products" even though some of them were already offered and the only change is that they now carry a "green label"? Why or why not?

4. *After reading Chapter 4:* What conclusions do you draw by applying a SWOT analysis to The Home Depot and Ford Motor Company? For which company is a stronger ecological awareness by consumers a threat, and for which one do you think it is an opportunity? Can some companies turn threats into opportunities, and if so, how?

5. *After reading Chapter 5:* Can The Home Depot's Eco Options be a significant positive contributor to firm performance as measured by:

   a. Economic value created, accounting profitability, and shareholder value?

   b. The triple bottom line?

   c. The balanced scorecard?

Endnotes

1. Author's interviews with John R. Tovar, former Regional VP, The Home Depot; "Growing number of Americans see warming as leading threat," *The Washington Post,* April 20, 2007; "More retailers go for green–The eco kind; Home Depot tags friendly products," *USA Today,* April 18, 2007; and Esty, D. C., and A. S. Winston (2009), *Green to Gold: How Smart Companies Use Environmental Strategy to Innovate, Create Value, and Build Competitive Advantage* (Hoboken, NJ: Wiley).

2. www.merriam-webster.com/dictionary/greenwashing.

INSPIRED BY ITALIAN coffee bars, Starbucks's CEO Howard Schultz set out to provide a completely new consumer experience. The trademark of any Starbucks coffeehouse is its ambience—where music and comfortable chairs and sofas encourage customers to sit and enjoy their coffee beverages. While hanging out at Starbucks, they can use the complimentary wireless hotspot or just visit with friends. The barista seems to speak a foreign language as she rattles off the offerings: Caffé Misto, Caramel Macchiato, Cinnamon Dolce Latte, Espresso Con Panna, or a Mint Mocha Chip Frappuccino, among some 30 different coffee blends. Dazzled and enchanted, customers pay $4 or more for a Venti-sized drink. Starbucks has been so successful in creating its ambience that customers keep coming back for more.

Starbucks's core competency was to create a unique consumer experience the world over. That is what customers are paying for, not for the cup of coffee or tea. The consumer experience that Starbucks created was a valuable, rare, and costly-to-imitate intangible resource. This allowed Starbucks to gain a competitive advantage.

While intangible resources are often built through learning from experience, intangible resources can atrophy through forgetting. This is what happened to Starbucks. Recently, Starbucks expanded operations by opening over 16,000 stores in some 50 countries. It also branched out into desserts, sandwiches, books, music, and other retail merchandise, straying from its core business. Trying to keep up with its explosive growth in both the number of stores and product offerings, Starbucks began to forget what made it unique. It lost the appeal that made it special, and its unique culture got diluted. For example, baristas used to grind beans throughout the day whenever a new pot of coffee had to be brewed (which was at least every eight minutes). The grinding sounds and fresh coffee aroma were trademarks of Starbucks stores. Instead, to accommodate its fast growth, many baristas began to grind all of the day's coffee beans in the morning and store them for the rest of the day.

Coming out of an eight-year retirement, Howard Schultz again took the reins as CEO and president in January 2008, attempting to re-create what had made Starbucks special. In late 2009, Starbucks introduced Via, its new instant coffee, a move that some worried might further dilute the brand. In the fall of 2010, Schultz rolled out a new guideline: Baristas would no longer multitask, making multiple drinks at the same time, but would instead focus on no more than two drinks at a time, starting a second one while finishing the first. The goal was to bring back the customer experience that built the Starbucks brand.[1]

DISCUSSION QUESTIONS

Review Chapter 4: Internal Analysis: Resources, Capabilities, and Activities.

1. How did Starbucks create its uniqueness in the first place?

2. Was Starbucks's uniqueness a VRIO resource? Did it help Starbucks gain and sustain a competitive advantage? Why or why not?

3. Why and how did Starbucks lose its uniqueness?

4. How is Starbucks attempting to re-create its uniqueness? Do you think it will be successful? Why or why not?

5. Explain Starbucks's ups and downs using (a) strategic activity systems and (b) the dynamic capabilities perspective. What implications can you draw?

6. What recommendations would you give Howard Schultz? Support your arguments.

Endnotes

1. This MiniCase is based on: Schultz, H., and D. J. Yang (1999), *Pour Your Heart Into It: How Starbucks Built a Company One Cup at a Time* (New York: Hyperion); Behar, H. (2007), *It's Not About the Coffee: Leadership Principles from a Life at Starbucks* (New York: Portfolio); "Latest Starbucks buzzword: 'Lean' Japanese techniques," *The Wall Street Journal*, August 4, 2009; and "At Starbucks, baristas told no more than two drinks," *The Wall Street Journal*, October 13, 2010, http://investor.starbucks.com.

AN INVESTMENT OF $100 in General Electric (GE) on April 22, 1981, when Jack Welch took over as chairman and CEO would have been worth $6,320 by 2000.[1] Including stock price appreciation plus dividends, GE's total shareholder return was thus 6,220 percent during this period, equating to an annual compounded growth rate of about 23 percent.

Although the sheer magnitude of GE's total returns to shareholders is impressive, to assess whether GE had a competitive advantage that produced that return, we need a benchmark. Because GE is a widely diversified conglomerate spanning financial, industrial, and media operations, one common metric for comparison is a broad stock market index like the Dow Jones Industrial Index (DJIA). The DJIA (or Dow 30) represents an average stock return, based on the stock prices of the 30 most widely held public companies in the U.S. The DJIA was established in 1896, and GE is the only company remaining from its original members.

Although the DJIA had a return of slightly over 1,000 percent between 1981 and the end of 2000, this return is dwarfed when compared with GE's more than 3,000 percent return for the same period. (See Exhibit MC5.1.) This comparison implies that GE outperformed the DJIA by a magnitude of about 3.5 during this 20-year time period.

When we apply total return to shareholders as a performance metric, GE's total return of 6,220 percent is astonishing. GE clearly enjoyed a *sustained competitive advantage* during the Jack Welch area. This feat is even more impressive for two reasons. First, the calculation was set in a way that both started at 0 percent in 1981. Second, GE is one of the 30 companies included in the DJIA, and thus it is one big reason why the DJIA performed quite well during the 1981–2000 time frame.

Jeffrey Immelt was appointed GE's CEO and chairman on September 7, 2001. The performance of GE's stock versus the DJIA during Immelt's tenure is depicted in Exhibit MC5.2.

EXHIBIT MC5.1

GE under Jack Welch: GE Stock Performance vs. DJIA, 4/1/1981–9/6/2001
Source: MSN Money.

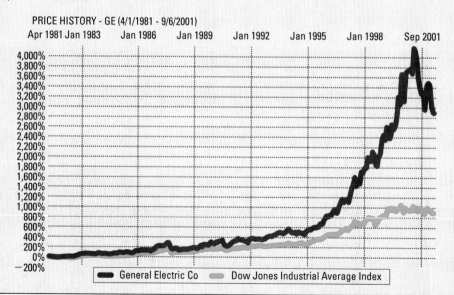

EXHIBIT MC5.2

GE under Jeffrey Immelt: GE Stock Performance vs. DJIA, 9/7/2001–1/24/2011
Source: MSN Money.

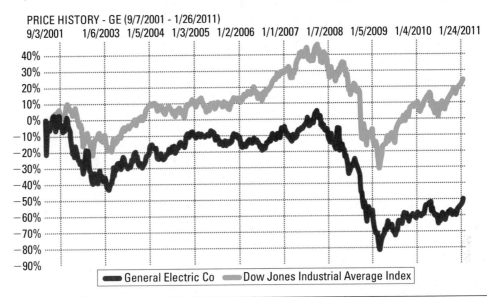

DISCUSSION QUESTIONS

Review Chapter 5: Competitive Advantage and Firm Performance.

1. Do you agree with the claim that "GE experienced a *sustained competitive advantage* under Jack Welch, while it experienced a *sustained competitive disadvantage* under Jeffrey Immelt"? Why or why not?

2. Shareholder value creation is one of the metrics discussed in Chapter 5 to assess firm performance. Do you consider this metric to be the most important one? Why or why not?

3. As discussed in Chapter 5, in what other ways could you assess firm performance and competi-tive advantage? Would that answer change your assessment of the two different time periods presented?

4. How much of the performance difference in the Welch versus Immelt time periods do you believe can be directly attributed to the respective CEO? What other factors might have played an impor-tant role in determining firm performance? (Hint: Consider especially the time period since 2001.)

Endnotes

1. "GE's Welch will be a tough act to follow; Math shows stock unlikely to repeat its rise," *The New York Times,* November 28, 2000.

JETBLUE AIRWAYS was founded by former Southwest Airlines (SWA) employee David Neeleman in 1998. Mr. Neeleman became part of SWA in 1992, when SWA acquired Morris Air, an airline he founded in 1984 at the age of 25. Morris Air was a low-fare airline that pioneered many of the activities, such as e-ticketing, that later became standard in the industry.

When Neeleman designed JetBlue, he improved upon the SWA business model to enable his new company to provide tickets at even lower costs than SWA. JetBlue reproduces many of SWA's cost-reducing activities such as flying point-to-point to directly connect city pairs. It also predominantly uses one type of airplane, the Airbus A320, to lower its maintenance costs. In addition, JetBlue flies longer distances and transports more passengers per flight than SWA, further driving down its costs. Initially, JetBlue enjoyed the lowest cost per available seat-mile in the United States.

JetBlue also attempts to enhance its differential appeal, thus driving up its perceived value. JetBlue founder Neeleman argues that the airline combines high-tech to drive down costs with "high-touch" to enhance the customer experience. Some of JetBlue's value-enhancing features include high-end 100-seat Embraer regional jets with leather seats, individual TV screens (with 20th Century Fox movies, LiveTV, Fox TV, and DirectTV programming), 100 channels of XM Satellite Radio, and free in-flight Wi-Fi capabilities (offered in partnership with BlackBerry and Yahoo), along with friendly and attentive on-board service and other amenities. (JetBlue ads invite customers to hit the in-cabin "call button.") While JetBlue offers a highly functional website for reservations and other travel-related services, some customers (about 30 percent) prefer speaking to a live agent. Rather than outsourcing its reservation system to India, JetBlue employs stay-at-home parents in the Rocky Mountain states. The company suggests this "home sourcing" is at least 30 percent more productive than outsourcing. More importantly, customers value their reservation experience much more, which the carrier believes more than makes up for the wage differential between the U.S. and India.

In early 2007, however, JetBlue's reputation for outstanding customer service ("we bring humanity back to air travel") took a major hit when several flights were delayed due to a snowstorm in which the airline kept passengers on board the aircraft, some sitting on the tarmac for up to nine hours. Many wondered whether JetBlue was losing its magic touch. In May 2007, David Neeleman left JetBlue. He founded Azul (which means "blue" in Portuguese), a Brazilian airline in 2008.[1]

DISCUSSION QUESTIONS

Review Chapter 6: Business Strategy: Differentiation, Cost Leadership, and Integration.

1. What type of generic business strategy is JetBlue pursuing: cost leadership, differentiation, or integration?

2. What challenges is JetBlue facing with its chosen business strategy? What is the cause of these challenges? How should they be addressed?

3. What do you recommend JetBlue's top management should do to improve the airline's competitiveness?

Endnotes

1. This MiniCase is based on: Neeleman, D. (2003), *Entrepreneurial Thought Leaders Lecture,* Stanford Technology Ventures Program, April 30; Friedman, T. (2005), *The World Is Flat: A Brief History of the Twenty-First Century* (New York: Farrar, Straus and Giroux); Bryce, D. J., and J. H. Dyer (2007), "Strategies to crack well-guarded markets," *Harvard Business Review,* May; "Held hostage on the tarmac: Time for a passenger bill of rights?" *The New York Times,* February 16, 2007; and "Can JetBlue weather the storm?" *Time,* February 21, 2007.

IN THE FUTURE TRANSITION away from gasoline-powered cars, Nissan's CEO Carlos Ghosn firmly believes the next technological paradigm will be electric motors. Ghosn calls hybrids a "halfway technology" and suggests they will be a temporary phenomenon at best. A number of startup companies, including Tesla Motors in the United States and BYD in China, share Ghosn's belief in this particular future scenario.

One of the biggest impediments to large-scale adoption of electric vehicles, however, is the lack of appropriate infrastructure: There are few stations on the roads where drivers can recharge their car's battery when necessary. With the mileage range of electric vehicles currently limited to 100–200 miles, a lack of recharging stations is a serious problem.

To overcome this lack of complementary assets, the California startup Better Place is building an extensive network of stations (at present, in Hawaii, Israel, Denmark, and Australia) where drivers of electric vehicles can swap their batteries. The idea is that car manufacturers will sell electric cars without the battery (dramatically lowering their price), and drivers will rent battery power by the mile from Better Place, just as they subscribe to a mobile phone service plan. If you sign up for enough miles, Better Place will even throw in the car for free, just as you get a complimentary cell phone when you sign up for a two-year service plan with your wireless provider. Moreover, drivers will not be locked into old battery technology but can take advantage of the rapid improvements battery technology is expected to make over time.

Nissan's Ghosn believes electric cars will account for 10 percent of global auto sales over the next decade. In contrast, Toyota is convinced gasoline-electric hybrids will become the next dominant technology. These different predictions have significant influence on how much money Nissan and Toyota invest in technology, and

where. Nissan plans to build one of its fully electric vehicles, the Leaf, at a plant in Smyrna, Tennessee. Toyota is expanding its R&D investments in hybrid technology. It has sold more than 2 million of its popular Prius cars since they were first introduced in 1997 and just launched a larger hybrid sedan. By 2020, Toyota plans to offer hybrid technology in all its vehicles. Eventually, the investments made by Nissan and Toyota will yield different returns, depending on which predictions (or theories of how to compete) prove more accurate.

An alternative outcome is that neither hybrids nor electric cars will become the next paradigm. To add even more uncertainty to the mix, Honda and BMW are betting on cars powered by hydrogen fuel cells. Tesla Motors is offering its roadster equipped with solar panels to provide additional power. In sum, many alternative technologies are competing to become the winner in setting a new standard for propelling cars. This situation is depicted in Exhibit MC7.1, where the new technologies represent a swarm of new entries vying for dominance. Only time will tell which technology will win this battle.[1]

EXHIBIT MC 7.1

Several Technologies Competing for Dominance

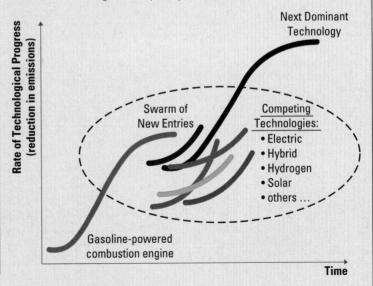

DISCUSSION QUESTIONS

Review Chapter 7: Business Strategy: Innovation and Strategic Entrepreneurship.

1. Do you believe that the internal combustion engine will lose its dominant position in the future? Why or why not? What time horizon are you looking at?

2. Which factors do you think will be most critical in setting the next industry standard for technology in car propulsion?

3. Which companies do you think are currently best positioned to influence the next industry standard in car-propulsion technology?

4. What would you recommend different competitors (e.g., Ford, GM, Toyota, Honda, and Nissan) do to influence the emerging industry standard?

Endnotes

1. This MiniCase is based on: "Bright sparks," *The Economist,* January 15, 2009; "The electric-fuel-trade acid test," *The Economist,* September 3, 2009; "At Tokyo auto show, hybrids and electrics dominate," *The New York Times,* October 21, 2009; and "Risky business at Nissan," *BusinessWeek,* November 2, 2009.

AT THE TIME OF ITS BANKRUPTCY in 2009, Circuit City was the second-largest electronics retailer in the United States, trailing only Best Buy (see ChapterCase 4). Today, however, Circuit City's core competencies—logistics and inventory management that drove down cost and allowed a focus on customer preferences in more or less real time—live on in the incarnation of CarMax, the largest used-car retailer in the U.S.[1] What's the connection here?

In the early 1990s, Circuit City executives began thinking about their core competencies more strategically. Then-CEO Richard Sharp and Senior VP Austin Ligon began brainstorming about how to leverage Circuit City's core competencies in other markets. They looked for businesses that were highly fragmented, which would allow them to leverage their retail core competency into nationwide standardization and cost savings. Both also wanted a business in which they could improve the customer's buying experience.

Sharp and Ligon zoomed in on the market for used cars. They launched CarMax in 1993, using the superstore format developed at Circuit City. Austin Ligon, CarMax's first CEO, knew they could exceed customer expectations in the used-car market because people likened the experience of buying a used car to that of having a root canal procedure. CarMax's first store opened in Richmond, Virginia, less than two miles from Circuit City's headquarters, easing the transfer of core competencies from Circuit City to CarMax.

CarMax has some unique features that many mom-and-pop used-car dealers lack. It buys any trade-in car for its Blue Book value, even if you only sell your car to CarMax but don't buy a car from CarMax. Each vehicle CarMax sells goes thorough a 125-point inspection and detailing, typically having some 12 hours of work done, prior to being displayed for sale.

CarMax also has a no-haggle pricing policy. Further, each car sold comes with a five-day no-questions-asked return policy and a 30-day warranty. All of these features make the buying experience much more predictable and pleasant.

Through centralized inventory management nationwide, a potential customer can choose from thousands of vehicles via CarMax's website at any given time. The company has been included in *Fortune*'s "100 Best Companies to Work For" every year since 2005. In 2010, CarMax was a Fortune 500 company and the largest used-car dealer in the U.S. with over 100 locations, employing 13,500 people, selling 350,000 cars, and earning revenue of more than $8 billion. Although Circuit City is now extinct, its core competencies continue to shape the retail industry—this time in the sale of used cars.[2]

DISCUSSION QUESTIONS

Review Chapter 4: Internal Analysis: Resources, Capabilities, and Activities.

Review Chapter 8: Corporate Strategy: Vertical Integration and Diversification.

1. Do you judge CarMax to be successful? Why or why not?

2. What type of diversification strategy is Circuit City's CarMax business venture?

3. Looking at the core competence–market matrix depicted in Exhibit 8.8, does Circuit City's CarMax diversification fall neatly into one of the four quadrants? Why or why not?

4. Was CarMax a good strategic move for Circuit City? Why or why not?

5. In 2002, Circuit City sold off CarMax, which trades on the NYSE under KMX. Was this a good decision by Circuit City's top management team? Why or why not?

Endnotes

1. For an in-depth treatment of how resources of extinct firms can live on and provide advantages in existing firms, see Hoetker, G., and R. Agarwal (2007), "Death hurts, but it isn't fatal: The post exit diffusion of knowledge created by innovative companies," *Academy of Management Journal* 50: 446–467.

2. This MiniCase is based on a presentation given by CarMax's first CEO, Austin Ligon, at the 2005 Strategic Management Society Conference in Orlando, Florida, October 26, 2005; and Collins, J. (2009), *How the Mighty Fall: And Why Some Companies Never Give In* (New York: HarperCollins). See also Prahalad, C. K., and G. Hamel (1990), "The core competence of the corporation," *Harvard Business Review,* May–June.

DURING MOST OF the 20th century, the closed-innovation approach was the dominant research and development (R&D) strategy for most leading industrial corporations: They tended to discover, develop, and commercialize new products internally. Although this approach was costly, it allowed firms to capture the returns to innovation.

Several factors led to a shift in the knowledge landscape from closed innovation to open innovation. They include:

- The increasing supply and mobility of skilled workers
- The exponential growth of venture capital
- The increasing availability of external options (such as spinning out new ventures) to commercialize ideas that were previously shelved
- The increasing capability of external suppliers

Together, these factors now force even the largest companies, such as AT&T, IBM, GE, and Sony, to shift their innovation strategy toward a model that blends internal with external knowledge-sourcing via licensing agreements, strategic alliances, joint ventures, and acquisitions.

In the open-innovation model, a company attempts to commercialize both its own ideas and research from other firms. It also finds external alternatives such as spin-out ventures or strategic alliances to commercialize its internally developed R&D. As Exhibit MC9.1 shows, the boundary of the firm has become porous (as represented by the dashed line in the right panel), allowing the firm to spin out some R&D projects while "sourcing in" (developing in-house) other promising projects. Exhibit MC9.2 (next page) compares and contrasts open-innovation and closed-innovation principles.

EXHIBIT MC9.1

Closed Innovation vs. Open Innovation
Source: Adapted from: H. Chesbrough (2003), "The area of open innovation," *MIT Sloan Management Review,* Spring: 35–41.

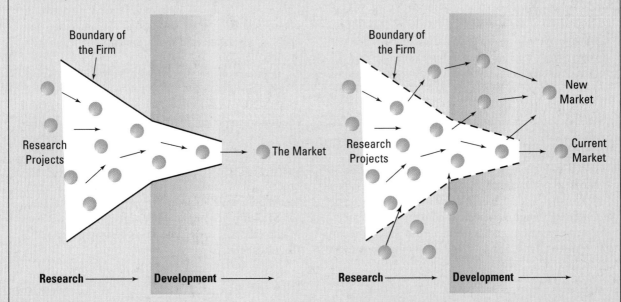

EXHIBIT MC9.2

Contrasting Principles of Closed and Open Innovation

Closed-Innovation Principles	Open-Innovation Principles
The smart people in our field work for us.	Not all the smart people work for us. We need to work with smart people inside *and* outside our company.
To profit from R&D, we must discover it, develop it, and ship it ourselves.	External R&D can create significant value; internal R&D is needed to claim (absorb) some portion of that value.
If we discover it ourselves, we will get it to market first.	We don't have to originate the research to profit from it; we can still be first if we successfully commercialize new research.
The company that gets an innovation to market first will win.	Building a better business model is often more important than getting to market first.
If we create the most and best ideas in the industry, we will win.	If we make the best use of internal and external ideas, we will win.
We should control our intellectual property (IP), so that our competitors don't profit from it.	We should profit from others' use of our IP, and we should buy others' IP whenever it advances our own business model.

Source: Adapted from H. W. Chesbrough (2003), *Open Innovation: The New Imperative for Creating and Profiting from Technology* (Boston: Harvard Business School Press).

An example of open innovation is Procter & Gamble's "Connect+Develop," or C+D (a play on research and development, or R&D). Due to the maturing of its products and markets, P&G was forced to look outside for new ideas. P&G is an $80 billion company whose investors expect it to grow 4–6 percent a year; which implies generating between $3 and $5 billion in incremental revenue annually. P&G was no longer able to generate this amount of growth through closed innovation. By 2000, P&G's closed-innovation machine had stalled, and the company lost half its market value. It needed a change in innovation strategy to drive organic growth.

P&G's Connect+Develop is a web-based interface that connects the company's internal-innovation capability with the distributed knowledge in the global community. From that external community, researchers, entrepreneurs, and consumers can submit ideas that might solve some of P&G's toughest innovation challenges. The C+D model is based on the realization that innovation was increasingly coming from small entrepreneurial ventures and even from individuals. Universities also became much more proactive in commercializing their inventions. The Internet now enables access to widely distributed knowledge from around the globe.

External collaborations fostered through the worldwide Connect+Develop network now play a role in roughly 50 percent of P&G's new products, up from about 15 percent in 2000. P&G's innovation productivity has increased, and its innovation costs have fallen. The economic benefits to an open-innovation strategy are captured in Exhibit MC9.3. Successful product innovations that resulted from P&G's open-innovation model include "Pringles meets Print" (sold for $1.5bn to Diamond Foods in 2011), Mr. Clean Magic Eraser, Swiffer Dusters, Crest SpinBrush, and Olay Regenerist.[1]

EXHIBIT MC9.3

Economic Benefits of an Open-Innovation Model

Source: Adapted from H. Chesbrough (2007), "Why companies should have open business models," *MIT Sloan Management Review,* Winter: 22–28.

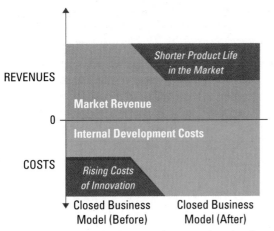

The Economic Pressure on Closed Innovation

As product life cycles become shorter and as development costs rise, the net result is that innovative companies are finding it harder to justify their investment in new products.

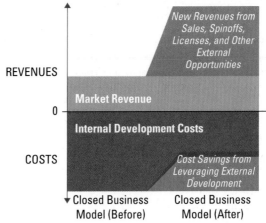

The New Business Model of Open Innovation

To offset rising development costs and shorter product life cycles, companies are experimenting with creative ways to open their business models, use external ideas and technologies in internal product development, and allow internal intellectual property to be commercialized extenally.

DISCUSSION QUESTIONS

Review Chapter 4: Internal Analysis: Resources, Capabilities, and Activities.

Review Chapter 7: Business Strategy: Innovation and Strategic Entrepreneurship.

Review Chapter 9: Corporate Strategy: Acquisitions, Alliances, and Networks.

1. Weigh the benefits and costs of closed innovation versus open innovation. What conclusions do you draw?

2. What are some of the risks of an open-innovation strategy that a company should consider before embarking on it?

3. Apply the resource-based view of the firm (discussed in Chapter 4). Do you believe P&G's Connect+Develop (C+D) open-innovation system has the potential to create a competitive advantage

for the firm? If you believe that C+D does have the potential to create a competitive advantage, do you believe it is sustainable? Why or why not?

4. Do you agree with the statement by Larry Huston and Nabil Sakkab, executives at P&G, that "Connect+Develop will become the dominant innovation model in the 21st century"?[2] Why or why not? What would its dominance do to C+D's potential to create a competitive edge for a firm?

5. *After reading Chapter 11:* Introducing the C+D innovation model requires tremendous organizational change. As Huston and Sakkab noted: "We needed to move the company's attitude from resistance to innovations 'not invented here' to enthusiasm for those 'proudly found elsewhere.' And we needed to change how we defined, and perceived, our R&D organization—from 7,500 people inside to 7,500 plus 1.5 million outside, with a permeable

boundary between them."[3] Identify some of the major obstacles a manager would encounter attempting this kind of organizational change. What recommendations would you make on how to accomplish such large-scale organizational change successfully?

Endnotes

1. This MiniCase is based on: Chesbrough, H. W. (2003), *Open Innovation: The New Imperative for Creating and Profiting from Technology* (Boston: Harvard Business School Press); Chesbrough, H. (2003), "The area of open innovation," *MIT Sloan Management Review,* Spring: 35–41; Chesbrough, H. (2007), "Why companies should have open business models," *MIT Sloan Management Review,* Winter: 22–28; Chesbrough, H. W., and M. M. Appleyard (2007), "Open innovation and strategy," *California Management Review,* Fall 50: 57–76; Huston, L., and N. Sakkab (2006), "Connect & Develop: Inside Procter & Gamble's new model for innovation," *Harvard Business Review,* March: 58–66; Rothaermel, F. T., and M. T. Alexandre (2009), "Ambidexterity in technology sourcing: The moderating role of absorptive capacity," *Organization Science,* 20: 759–780; Rothaermel, F. T., and A. M. Hess (2010), "Innovation strategies combined," *MIT Sloan Management Review,* Spring 51: 13–15; and "Diamond buys P&G's Pringles," *The Wall Street Journal,* April 6, 2011.

2. Huston, L., and N. Sakkab (2006), "Connect & Develop: Inside Procter & Gamble's new model for innovation."

3. Ibid.

THE WORLD'S MOST SUCCESSFUL global retailer, in terms of profitability, is not Walmart or the French grocery chain Carrefour, but IKEA—a home-furnishings company from Sweden. In 2010, IKEA had more than 310 stores worldwide in 38 countries, employed some 127,000 people, and earned revenues of 32 billion euros. More than 80 percent of IKEA's revenues come from Europe, with the rest from North America (16 percent) and Asia and Australia (3 percent). Although IKEA's largest market is in Germany (15 percent of total sales), its fastest-growing international markets are the United States, China, and Russia. Exhibit MC10.1 shows IKEA's growth in the number of stores and revenues worldwide since 1974. Started as a small retail outlet in 1943 by then-17-year-old Ingvar Kamprad, IKEA has become a global phenomenon.

IKEA was slow to internationalize: It took 20 years before the company expanded beyond Sweden to the neighboring country of Norway. After honing and refining its core competency of designing modern functional home furnishings at low prices, offered in a unique retail experience in its home market, IKEA followed an *international strategy,* expanding first to Europe and then beyond. Using an international strategy allowed IKEA to sell the same types of home furnishings across the globe with little adaptation (although it does make some allowances for country preferences). Because IKEA focuses on both value creation *and* low cost, it shifted more recently from an international strategy to a global-standardization strategy, in which it attempts to achieve economies of scale through managing a global supply chain. For example, since wood remains one of IKEA's main input factors, it now focuses on timber-rich Russia as a key source of supply.

Yet, IKEA faces significant challenges going forward. Finding new sources of supply to support more store openings is a challenge. Currently, IKEA can open only about 20 new stores each year because the supply chain becomes a bottleneck. Related to this issue is the fact that wood remains one of IKEA's main input factors, but the world's consumers are becoming more sensitive to the issue of deforestation

EXHIBIT MC10.1

IKEA Stores and Revenues (in billions of euros) Worldwide, 1974–2010

Source: Author's depiction of data from "The secret of IKEA's success," *The Economist,* February 24, 2011.

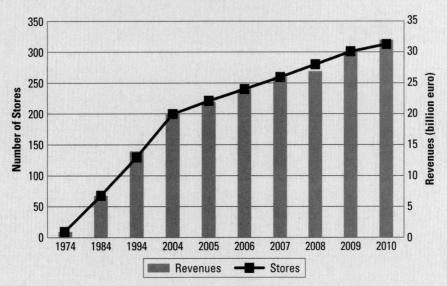

and its possible link to global warming. Thus, in the near future IKEA must find low-cost replacement materials for wood. In addition, powerful competitors have taken notice of IKEA's success. Although IKEA is growing in North America, it holds only about 5 percent of the home-furnishings market. To keep IKEA at bay, Target has recently recruited top designers and launched a wide range of low-priced furnishings. Kmart, likewise, has enrolled Martha Stewart to help with the design of its offerings of home furnishings.

Besides these external challenges, IKEA also faces significant internal ones. Although its founder Ingvar Kamprad (now in his mid-80s) no longer runs IKEA's day-to-day operations, he chairs the foundation that owns IKEA. No strategic decision is made without Mr. Kamprad's approval. Many observers compare Mr. Kamprad's influence on IKEA's culture and organization to that of the legendary Sam Walton at Walmart. Moreover, IKEA is privately held (through a complicated network of foundations and holding companies in the Netherlands, Lichtenstein, and Luxembourg); this arrangement provides benefits in terms of reducing tax exposure, but also creates constraints in accessing large sums of capital needed for rapid global expansion.[1]

DISCUSSION QUESTIONS

Review Chapter 3: External Analysis: Industry Structure, Competitive Forces, and Strategic Groups.

Review Chapter 10: Global Strategy: Competing Around the World.

1. Looking at IKEA's challenges, which ones do you think pose the greatest threat? Why?

2. How would you address the challenges you identified in Question 1?

3. Did it surprise you to learn that both a developed country (the United States) and also emerging economies (i.e., China and Russia) are the fastest-growing international markets for IKEA? Does this fact pose any challenges in the way that IKEA ought to compete across the globe? Why or why not?

4. What can IKEA do to continue to drive growth globally?

5. *After reading Chapter 12:* Assume you are hired to consult with IKEA on the topic of *business ethics* and *corporate social responsibility.* Which areas would you recommend the company be most sensitive to, and how should these be addressed?

Endnotes

1. This MiniCase is based on: "IKEA: How the Swedish retailer became a global cult brand," *BusinessWeek,* November 14, 2005; "Flat-pack accounting," *The Economist,* May 11, 2006; "Shocking tell-all book takes aim at Ikea," *Bloomberg Businessweek,* November 12, 2009; Peng, M. (2009), *Global Strategy,* 2nd ed. (Mason, OH: South-Western Cengage); and "The secret of IKEA's success," *The Economist,* February 24, 2011.

APPLE'S MARKET CAPITALIZATION in 2001 was $7 billion, while Sony's was $55 billion. Apple introduced the iPod, a portable digital music player, in October 2001 and the iTunes music store 18 months later. Through these two strategic moves Apple redefined the music industry, reinventing itself as a content-delivery mobile-device company. Signaling its renaissance, Apple changed its name from Apple Computer, Inc., to simply Apple, Inc. Many observers, however, wondered what happened to Sony—the company that created the portable-music industry by introducing the first Walkman in 1979.

Sony's strategy was to differentiate itself through the vertical integration of content and hardware, driven by its 1988 acquisition of CBS Records (later Sony Music Entertainment). This strategy contrasted sharply with Sony Music division's desire to protect its lucrative revenue-generating, copyrighted compact discs (CDs). Sony Music's engineers were aggressively combating music piracy by inhibiting the Microsoft Windows media player's ability to rip CDs and by serializing discs (assigning unique ID numbers to discs). Meanwhile Apple's engineers were developing a Digital Rights Management (DRM) system to control and restrict the transfer of copyrighted digital music. Apple's DRM succeeded, protecting the music studio's interests while creating value that enabled consumers to enjoy portable digital music.

Sony had a long history of creating electronics devices of superior quality and design. It had all the right competencies to launch a successful counterattack to compete with Apple: electronics, software, music, and computer divisions. (Sony's Electronics Division even was the battery supplier for Apple's iPod.) Cooperation among strategic business units had served Sony well in the past, leading to breakthrough innovations such as the Walkman, PlayStation, the CD, and the VAIO computer line. In this case, however, the hardware and content divisions each seemed to have its own idea of what needed to be done. Cooperation

among the Sony divisions was also hindered by the fact that their centers of operations were spread across the globe: Music operations were located in New York City and Electronics design was in Japan, inhibiting face-to-face communications and making real-time interactions more difficult.

Sony's CEO Nobuyuki Idei learned the hard way that the Music Division managers were focused on the immediate needs of their recordings competing against the consumer-driven market forces. In 2002, Idei shared his frustrations with the cultural differences between the hardware and content divisions:

> The opposite of soft alliances is hard alliances, which include mergers and acquisitions. Since purchasing the Music and Pictures businesses, more than ten years have passed, and we have experienced many cultural differences between hardware manufacturing and content businesses. . . . This experience has taught us that in certain areas where hard alliances would have taken ten years to succeed, soft alliances can be created more easily. Another advantage of soft alliances is the ability to form partnerships with many different companies. We aim to provide an open and easy-to-access environment where anybody can participate and we are willing to cooperate with companies that share our vision. Soft alliances offer many possibilities.[1]

In contrast, Apple organized a small, empowered, cross-functional team to produce the iPod in just a few months. Apple successfully outsourced and integrated many of its components and collaborated across business units. The phenomenal speed and success of the iPod and iTunes's development and seamless integration became a structural approach that Apple now applies to its successful development and launches of new products like the iPhone and iPad. By early 2011, Apple's market capitalization had increased by a factor of 44 times, to $310 billion (making it the most valuable technology company on the planet), while Sony's market value had declined by almost 40 percent, to $35 billion.[2]

DISCUSSION QUESTIONS

Review Chapter 9: Corporate Strategy: Acquisitions, Alliances, and Networks.

Review Chapter 10: Global Strategy: Competing Around the World.

Review Chapter 11: Organizational Design: Structure, Culture, and Control.

1. Why had Sony been successful in the past (e.g., with the introduction of the Walkman, PlayStation, the CD, and the VAIO computer line)?

2. What was Mr. Idei's assessment of strategic alliances vs. M&As? Do you agree or disagree? Support your assessment.

3. Why do you think Apple succeeded in the digital portable music industry, while Sony failed?

4. What could Sony have done differently to avoid failure? What lessons need to be learned?

5. What recommendations would you give Sony's CEO to help them compete against Apple?

Endnotes

1. Sony Annual Report 2002, year ended March 31, 2002, Sony Corporation, p. 9.

2. This MiniCase was prepared by Frank T. Rothaermel and Robert Redrow (of Sony Corp.). It draws on the following sources: Hansen, M. T. (2009), *Collaboration: How Leaders Avoid the Traps, Create Unity, and Reap Big Results* (Cambridge, MA: Harvard Business School Press); Sony Annual Report 2002, year ended March 31, 2002, Sony Corporation, p. 9; Sony Corporation Info, www.sony.net/SonyInfo/CorporateInfo/History/sonyhistory-e.html; and Wolframalpha, www.wolframalpha.com.

WHEN APPOINTED CEO of PepsiCo in 2006, Ms. Indra Nooyi was only the 11th woman to run a Fortune 500 company. Since then, Ms. Nooyi has been ranked in the top ten of *Forbes* magazine's list of the world's 100 most powerful women. In 2010, she topped *Fortune*'s ranking of the most powerful women in business. Today, leading a company that employs some 300,000 people worldwide, Ms. Nooyi is considered one of the most powerful business leaders globally.

A native of Chennai, India, Ms. Nooyi obtained a bachelor's degree in physics, chemistry, and mathematics from Madras Christian College, an MBA from the Indian Institute of Management, and a master's degree from Yale University. Prior to joining PepsiCo in 1994, Ms. Nooyi worked for Johnson & Johnson, Boston Consulting Group (BCG), Motorola, and ABB. For her BCG interview, right out of Yale, Ms. Nooyi wore a traditional sari. Ms. Nooyi is not the typical Fortune 500 CEO: She is well known for walking around the office barefoot and singing—a remnant from her lead role in an all-girls rock band in high school.

It should come as no surprise, therefore, that Ms. Nooyi—an executive who spends more than 50 percent of her time outside the U.S.—has been shaking up things at PepsiCo. She took the lead role in spinning off Taco Bell, Pizza Hut, and KFC in 1997. Later, she masterminded the acquisitions of Tropicana in 1998 and Quaker Oats (including Gatorade) in 2001. As CEO, Ms. Nooyi declared PepsiCo's vision as *performance with a purpose,* defined by three dimensions:

1. *Human sustainability,* which concerns the strategic intent to make PepsiCo's product portfolio healthier, to combat obesity. PepsiCo wants to make "fun foods" such as Frito-Lay and Doritos healthier (less salty and fatty), and to include healthy choices in its product portfolio (such as Quaker Oats products and Tropicana fruit juices). Ms. Nooyi is convinced that if food and beverage companies do not make their product lineups healthier to combat obesity, these companies will face the same repercussions that tobacco companies did.

2. *Environmental sustainability,* to ensure that PepsiCo's operations don't harm the natural environment. The company has initiatives such as water and energy reduction, stepping up recycling, and promoting sustainable agriculture. The goal is to transform PepsiCo into a company with a net-zero impact on the environment. Ms. Nooyi believes that young people today will not patronize a company that does not have a sustainable strategy.

3. *The whole person at work,* which attempts to create a corporate culture in which employees "not just make a living, but also have a life."[1] Ms. Nooyi argues that this allows for the unleashing of both the mental and emotional energy of every employee.

PepsiCo's vision of *performance with a purpose* acknowledges the importance of corporate social responsibility and stakeholder strategy. Ms. Nooyi is convinced that companies have a duty to society to "do better by doing better."[2] She subscribes to a triple-bottom-line approach to competitive advantage, declaring that the true profits of enterprise are not just "revenues–costs" but "revenues–costs–costs to society." Costs to society are *externalities*—such as pollution or the cost of health care to combat obesity—that companies do not bear. Ms. Nooyi argues that the time when corporations can just pass on their externalities to society is over.

Critics note, however, that although the rhetoric of *performance with a purpose* appears to be powerful, PepsiCo's financial performance so far has been disappointing. Exhibit MC12.1 (next page) shows PepsiCo's stock performance versus its archrival Coca-Cola. Since Ms. Nooyi took the helm at PepsiCo, Coca-Cola's stock has appreciated by roughly 50 percent, while PepsiCo's stock has remained flat and is merely tracking the DJIA.[3]

EXHIBIT MC12.1

Stock Performance of Pepsi vs. Coca Cola and DJIA (10/01/06–03/29/11)
Source: MSN Money.

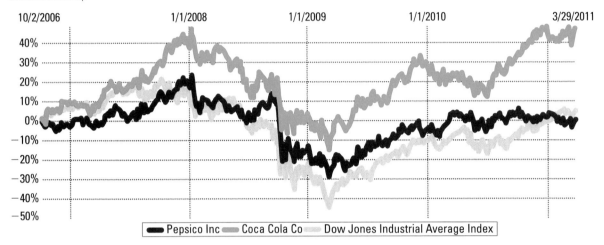

DISCUSSION QUESTIONS

Review Chapter 3: External Analysis: Industry Structure, Competitive Forces, and Strategic Groups.

Review Chapter 5: Competitive Advantage and Firm Performance.

Review Chapter 8: Corporate Strategy: Vertical Integration and Diversification.

Review Chapter 12: Corporate Governance, Business Ethics, and Strategic Leadership.

1. Apply a PESTEL framework to analyze PepsiCo's external environment. Then, conduct a SWOT analysis to see how PepsiCo is addressing the opportunities and threats present in the external environment.

2. One of the measures to assess competitive advantage (discussed in Chapter 5) is shareholder value creation. When comparing Coca-Cola and PepsiCo along this dimension, one would come to the conclusion that PepsiCo, under Ms. Nooyi's leadership, has sustained a competitive disadvantage when compared with Coca-Cola.

    a. Do you agree with this assessment? Why or why not?

    b. If you were to apply a triple-bottom-line approach to assessing competitive advantage, would you come to a different conclusion? Why or why not?

    c. If you were a board member at PepsiCo, would you be concerned? Why or why not? If you *were* concerned, what actions would you recommend?

3. As a senior executive at PepsiCo, Ms. Nooyi was the driving force behind selling PepsiCo's restaurant businesses (Taco Bell, Pizza Hut, and KFC) and acquiring Quaker Oats and Tropicana. What type of corporate-level strategic initiatives were these moves? What do you think was the rationale behind them? Using the BCG matrix, how do you assess their effectiveness?

4. What "grade" would you give Ms. Nooyi for her job performance as a strategic leader? What are her strengths and weaknesses? Where would you place Ms. Nooyi on the level-5 pyramid of strategic leadership (see Exhibit 12.8, page 356), and why? What recommendations would you give her? Support your answers.

Endnotes

1. "Conversation with Indra Nooyi Yale SOM '80," Yale University, March 3, 2010, www.youtube.com/watch?v=-msw7mJPF6A.

2. "The responsible company," *The Economist, The World in 2008.*

3. This MiniCase is based on: "PepsiCo shakes it up," *BusinessWeek,* August 14, 2006; "The Pepsi challenge," *The Economist,* August 17, 2006; "Keeping cool in hot water," *BusinessWeek,* June 11, 2007; "Pepsi gets a makeover," *The Economist,* March 25, 2010; "Indra Nooyi on Performance with Purpose 2009," PepsiCo Video, www.youtube.com/watch?v=AM-TduYdJas; "Conversation with Indra Nooyi Yale SOM '80"; and www.wolfram.alpha (use ticker symbol KO for Coca-Cola Company and PEP for PepsiCo).

PART 5
CASES

The case study is a fundamental learning tool in strategic management. We carefully wrote and chose the cases in this book to expose you to a wide variety of key concepts, industries, protagonists, and strategic problems.

In simple terms, cases tell the story of a company facing a strategic dilemma. The firms may be real or fictional in nature, and the problem may be current or one that the firm faced in the past. Although the details of the cases vary, in general they start with a description of the challenge(s) to be addressed, followed by the history of the firm up until the decision point, and then additional information to help you with your analysis. The strategic dilemma is often faced by a specific manager, who wonders what they should do. To address the strategic dilemma, you will use the AFI framework to conduct a case analysis using the tools and concepts provided in this textbook. After careful analysis, you will be able to formulate a strategic response and make recommendations about how to implement it.

Why Do We Use Cases?

Strategy is something that people learn by doing; it cannot be learned simply by reading a book or listening carefully in class. While those activities will help you become more familiar with the concepts and models used in strategic management, the only way to improve your skills in analyzing, formulating, and implementing strategy is to *practice.*

We encourage you to take advantage of the cases in this text as a "laboratory" in which to experiment with the strategic management tools you have been given, so that you can learn more about how, when, and where they might work in the "real world." Cases are valuable because they expose you to a number and variety of situations in which you can refine your strategic management skills without worrying about making mistakes. The companies in these cases will not lose profits or fire you if you miscalculate a financial ratio, misinterpret someone's intentions, or make an incorrect prediction about environmental trends.

Cases also invite you to "walk in" and explore many more kinds of companies in a wider array of industries than you will ever be able to work at in your lifetime. In this textbook alone, you will find cases about companies involved in energy infrastructure development (Siemens), medical products and services (General Electric), electronic equipment (Apple), computer networking (IBM), sustainability consulting (InterfaceRAISE), electric cars (Tesla Motors), book retailing (BetterWorld Books), and consumer products (Cola Wars), to name just a few. Your personal organizational experiences are usually much more limited, defined by the jobs held by your family members or by your own forays into the working world. Learning about companies involved in so many different types of products and services may open up new employment possibilities for you. Diversity also forces us to think about the ways in which industries (as well as people) are both similar and yet distinct, and to critically examine the degree to which lessons learned in one forum transfer to other settings (i.e., to what degree are they "generalizable"). In short, cases are a great training tool, and they are fun to study.

You will find that many of our cases are written from the perspective of the CEO or general manager responsible for strategic decision making in the organization. While you do not need to be a member of a top management team to utilize the strategic-management process, these senior leaders are usually responsible for determining strategy in most of the organizations we study. Importantly, cases allow us to put ourselves "in the shoes" of strategic leaders and invite us to view the issues from their perspective. Having responsibility for the performance of an entire organization is quite different from managing a single project team, department, or functional area. Cases can help you see the *big picture* in a way that most of us are not accustomed to in our daily, organizational lives. We recognize that most undergraduate students and even MBAs do not land immediately in the corporate boardroom. Yet having a basic understanding of the types of conversations going on in the boardroom not only increases your current value as an employee, but improves your chances of getting there someday, should you so desire.

Finally, cases help give us a *long-term* view of the firms they depict. Corporate history is immensely helpful in understanding how a firm got to its present position and why people within that organization think the way they do. Our case authors (both the author of this book and authors of cases from respected third-party sources) have spent many hours poring over historical documents and news reports in order to re-create each company's heritage for you, a luxury that most of us do not have when we are bombarded on a daily basis with homework, tests, and papers or project team meetings, deadlines, and reports. We invite you not just to learn from, but also to savor, reading each company's story.

STRATEGIC CASE ANALYSIS. The first step in analyzing a case is to *skim it for the basic facts.* As you read, jot down your notes regarding the following basic questions:

- What company or companies is the case about?
- Who are the principal actors?
- What are the key events? When and where do they happen (in other words, what is the timeline)?

Second, go back and reread the case in greater detail, this time with a focus on *defining the problem.* Which facts are relevant and why? Just as a doctor begins by interviewing the patient ("What hurts?"), you likewise gather information and then piece the clues together in order to figure out what is wrong. Your goal at this stage is to identify the "symptoms" in order to figure out which "tests" to run in order to make a definitive "diagnosis" of the main "disease." Only then can you prescribe a "treatment" with confidence that it will actually help the situation. Rushing too quickly through this stage often results in "malpractice" (that is, giving a patient with an upset stomach an antacid when she really has the flu), with effects that range from unhelpful to downright dangerous. The best way to ensure that you "do no harm" is to analyze the facts carefully, fighting the temptation to jump right to proposing a solution.

The third step, continuing the medical analogy, is to determine which analytical tools will help you to most accurately diagnose the problem(s). Doctors may choose to run blood tests or take an x-ray. In doing case analysis, we follow the steps of the *strategic-management process.* You have any and all of the following models and frameworks at your disposal:

1. Perform an **external environmental analysis** of the:
   - Macrolevel environment (PESTEL analysis)
   - Industry environment (e.g., Porter's five forces)
   - Competitive environment

2. Perform an **internal analysis** of the firm using the resource-based view:
   - What are the firm's resources, capabilities, and competencies?
   - Does the firm possess valuable, rare, costly to imitate resources, and is it organized to capture value from those resources (VRIO analysis)?
   - What is the firm's value chain?

3. Analyze the firm's current **business-level** and **corporate-level** strategies:
   - Business-level strategy (product market positioning)
   - Corporate-level strategy (diversification)
   - International strategy (geographic scope and mode of entry)
   - How are these strategies being implemented?

4. Analyze the firm's **performance:**
   - Use both financial and market-based measures.
   - How does the firm compare to its competitors as well as the industry average?
   - What trends are evident over the past three to five years?
   - Consider the perspectives of multiple stakeholders (internal and external).
   - Does the firm possess a competitive advantage? If so, can it be sustained?

CALCULATING FINANCIAL RATIOS. Financial ratio analysis is an important tool for assessing the outcomes of a firm's strategy. Although financial performance is not the only relevant outcome measure, long-term profitability is a necessary precondition for firms to remain in business and to be able to serve the needs of all of their stakeholders. Accordingly, at the end of this introductory module, we have provided a table of financial measures that can be used to assess firm performance (see Table 1, pages 396–400).

All of the following aspects of performance should be considered, because each provides a different type of information about the financial health of the firm:

- Profit ratios—how efficiently a company utilizes its resources.
- Activity ratios—how effectively a firm manages its assets.
- Leverage ratios—the degree to which a firm relies on debt versus equity (capital structure).

- Liquidity ratios—a firm's ability to pay off its short-term obligations.
- Market ratios—returns earned by shareholders who hold company stock.

MAKING THE DIAGNOSIS. With all of this information in hand, you are finally ready to *make a "diagnosis."* Describe the problem(s) or opportunity(ies) facing the firm at this point in time and/or in the near future. How are they interrelated? (For example, a runny nose, fever, stomach upset, and body aches are all indicative of the flu.) Support your conclusions with data generated from your analyses.

The following general themes may be helpful to consider as you try to pull all the pieces together into a cohesive summary:

- Are the firm's value chain (primary and support) activities mutually reinforcing?
- Do the firm's resources and capabilities fit with the demands of the external environment?
- Does the firm have a clearly defined strategy that will create a competitive advantage?
- Is the firm making good use of its strengths and taking full advantage of its opportunities?
- Does the firm have serious weaknesses or face significant threats that need to be mitigated?

Keep in mind that "problems" can be positive (how to manage increased demand) as well as negative (declining stock price) in nature. Even firms that are currently performing well need to figure out how to maintain their success in an ever-changing and highly competitive global business environment.

Formulation: Proposing Feasible Solutions

When you have the problem figured out (your diagnosis), the next step is to *propose a "treatment plan"* or solution. There are two parts to the treatment plan: the *what* and the *why*. Using our medical analogy: The *what* for a patient with the flu might be antiviral medication, rest, and lots of fluids. The *why*: antivirals attack the virus directly, shortening the duration of illness; rest enables the body to recuperate naturally; and fluids are necessary to help the body fight fever and dehydration. *The ultimate goal is to restore the patient to wellness.* Similarly, when you are doing case analysis, your task is to figure out *what* the leaders of

the company should do and *why* this is an appropriate course of action. Each part of your proposal should be justifiable based on your analyses.

One word of caution about the formulation stage: By nature, humans are predisposed to engage in "local" and "simplistic" searches for solutions to the problems they face.[1] On the one hand, this can be an efficient approach to problem solving, because relying on past experiences (what worked before) does not "waste time reinventing the wheel." The purpose of doing case analysis, however, is to *look past* the easy answers and to help us figure out not just "what works" (satisficing) but what might be the *best* answer (optimizing). In other words, do not just take the first idea that comes to your mind and run with it. Instead, write down that idea for subsequent consideration but then think about what other solutions might achieve the same (or even better) results. Some of the most successful companies engage in scenario planning, in which they develop several possible outcomes and estimate the likelihood that each will happen. If their first prediction turns out to be incorrect, then they have a "Plan B" ready and waiting to be executed.

Plan for Implementation

The final step in the AFI framework is to develop a plan for implementation. Under formulation, you came up with a proposal, tested it against alternatives, and used your research to support why it provides the best solution to the problem at hand. To demonstrate its feasibility, however, you must be able to explain *how to put it into action.* Consider the following questions:

1. *What activities need to be performed?* The value chain is a very useful tool when you need to figure out how different parts of the company are likely to be affected. What are the implications of your plan with respect to both primary activities (e.g., operations and sales/marketing/service) and support activities (e.g., human resources and infrastructure)?

2. *What is the timeline?* What steps must be taken first and why? Which ones are most critical? Which activities can proceed simultaneously, and which ones are sequential in nature? How long is your plan going to take?

3. *How are you going to finance your proposal?* Does the company have adequate cash on hand, or does it need to consider debt and/or equity financing?

How long until your proposal breaks even and pays for itself?

4. *What outcomes is your plan likely to achieve?* Provide goals that are "SMART": specific, measurable, achievable, realistic, and timely in nature. Make a case for how your plan will help the firm to achieve a strategic competitive advantage.

In-Class Discussion

Discussing your ideas in class is often the most valuable part of a case study. Your professor will moderate the class discussion, guiding the AFI process and asking probing questions when necessary. Case discussion classes are most effective and interesting when everybody comes prepared and participates in the exchange.

Actively listen to your fellow students; mutual respect is necessary in order to create an open and inviting environment in which people feel comfortable sharing their thoughts with one another. This does not mean you need to agree with what everyone else is saying, however. Everyone has unique perspectives and biases based on differences in life experiences, education and training, values, and goals. As a result, no two people will interpret the same information in exactly the same way. Be prepared to be challenged, as well as to challenge others, to consider the case from another vantage point. Conflict is natural and even beneficial as long as it is managed in constructive ways.

Throughout the discussion, you should be prepared to support your ideas based on the analyses you conducted. Even students who agree with you on the general steps to be taken may disagree on the order of importance. Alternatively, they may like your plan in principle but argue that it is not feasible for the company to accomplish. You should not be surprised if others come up with an altogether different diagnosis and prescription. For better or worse, a good idea does not stand on its own merit—you must be able to convince your peers of its value by backing it up with sound logic and support.

Things to Keep in Mind While Doing Case Analysis

While some solutions are clearly better than others, it is important to remember that there is no single, correct answer to any case. Unlike an optimization equation or accounting spreadsheet, cases cannot be reduced to a mathematical formula. Formulating and implementing strategy involves people, and working with people is inherently messy. Thus, the best way to get the maximum value from the case-analysis process is to maintain an open mind and carefully consider the strengths and weaknesses of all of the options. Strategy is an iterative process, and it is important not to rush to a premature conclusion.

For some cases, your instructor may be able to share with you what the company actually did, but that does not necessarily mean it was the best course of action. Too often students find out what happened in the "real world" and their creative juices stop flowing. Whether due to lack of information, experience, or time, companies quite often make the most expedient decision. With your access to additional data and time to conduct more detailed analyses, you may very well arrive at a different (and better) conclusion. Stand by your findings as long as you can support them with solid research data. Even Fortune 500 companies make mistakes.

Unfortunately, to their own detriment, students sometimes discount the value of cases based on fictional scenarios or set some time in the past. One significant advantage of fictional cases is that everybody has access to the same information. Not only does this "level the playing field," but it prevents you from being unduly biased by actual events, thus cutting short your own learning process. Similarly, just because a case occurred in the past does not mean it is no longer relevant. The players and technology may change over time, but many questions that businesses face are timeless in nature: how to adapt to a changing environment, the best way to compete against other firms, and whether and how to expand.

Case Limitations

As powerful a learning tool as case analysis can be, it does come with some limitations. One of the most important for you to be aware of is that case analysis relies on a process known as *inductive reasoning,* in which you study specific business cases in order to derive general principles of management. Intuitively, we rely on inductive reasoning across almost every aspect of our lives. We know that we need oxygen to survive, so we assume that all living organisms need oxygen. Similarly, if all the swans we have ever seen are white, we extrapolate this to mean that all swans are white. While such relationships are often built upon a high degree of probability, it is important to remember that they are not empirically proven. We have in fact discovered life forms (microorganisms) that rely on sulfur instead of oxygen. Likewise, just because all the swans you have seen have been white, black swans do exist.

What does this caution mean with respect to case analysis? First and foremost, do not assume that just because one company utilized a joint venture to commercialize a new innovation, another company will be successful employing the same strategy. The first company's success may not be due to the particular organizational form it selected; it might instead be a function of its competencies in managing interfirm relationships or the particularities of the external environment. Practically speaking, this is why the analysis step is so fundamental to good strategic management. Careful research helps us to figure out all of the potential contributing factors and to formulate hypotheses about which ones are most likely critical to success. Put another way, what happens at one firm does not necessarily generalize to others. However, solid analytical skills go a long way toward enabling you to make informed, educated guesses about when and where insights gained from one company have broader applications.

In addition, we have a business culture that tends to put on a pedestal high-performance firms and their leaders. Critical analysis is absolutely essential in order to discern the reasons for such firms' success. Upon closer inspection, we have sometimes found that their image is more a mirage than a direct reflection of sound business practices. Many business analysts have been taken in by the likes of Enron, WorldCom, and Bernie Madoff, only to humbly retract their praise when the company's shaky foundation crumbles. We selected many of the firms in these cases because of their unique stories and positive performance, but we would be remiss if we let students interpret their presence in this book as a whole-hearted endorsement of all of their business activities.

Finally, our business culture also places a high premium on benchmarking and best practices. Although we present you with a sample of firms that we believe are worthy of in-depth study, we would again caution you against uncritical adoption of their activities in the hope of emulating their achievements. Even when

a management practice has broad applications, strategy involves far more than merely copying the industry leader. The company that invents a best practice is already far ahead of its competitors on the learning curve, and even if other firms do catch up, the best they can usually hope for is to match (but not exceed) the original firm's success. By all means, learn as much as you can from whomever you can, but use that information to strengthen your organization's *own* strategic identity.

Frequently Asked Questions about Case Analysis

1. *Is it okay to utilize outside materials?*

Ask your professor. Some instructors utilize cases as a springboard for analysis and will want you to look up more recent financial and other data. Others may want you to base your analysis on the information from the case only, so that you are not influenced by the actions actually taken by the company.

2. *Is it okay to talk about the case with other students?*

Again, you should check with your professor, but many will strongly encourage you to meet and talk about the case with other students as part of your preparation process. The goal is not to come to a group consensus, but to test your ideas in a small group setting and revise them based on the feedback you receive.

3. *Is it okay to contact the company for more information?*

If your professor permits you to gather outside information, you may want to consider contacting the company directly. If you do so, it is imperative that you represent yourself and your school in the most professional and ethical manner possible. Explain to them that you are a student studying the firm and that you are seeking additional information, with your instructor's permission. Our experience is that some companies are quite receptive to student inquiries; others are not. You cannot know how a particular company will respond unless you try.

4. *What should I include in my case analysis report?*

Instructors generally provide their own guidelines regarding content and format, but a general outline for a case analysis report is as follows: (1) analysis of the problem; (2) proposal of one or more alternative solutions; and (3) justification for which solution you believe is best and why. The most important thing to remember is not to waste precious space repeating facts from the case. You can assume that your professor has read the case carefully. What he or she is most interested in is your analysis of the situation and your rationale for choosing a particular solution.

Endnotes

1. Cyert, R. M., and March, J. G. (2001), *A Behavioral Theory of the Firm,* 2nd ed. (Malden, MA: Blackwell Publishers Inc.).

TABLE 1

When and How to Use Financial Measures to Assess Firm Performance

Overview: We have grouped the financial performance measures into five main categories:

Table 1a: Profitability: How profitable is the company?

Table 1b: Activity: How efficient are the operations of the company?

Table 1c: Leverage: How effectively is the company financed in terms of debt and equity?

Table 1d: Liquidity: How capable is the business of meeting its short-term obligations as they fall due?

Table 1e: Market: How does the company's performance compare to other companies in the market?

Table 1a: Profitability Ratios	Formula	Characteristics
Gross margin (or EBITDA, EBIT, etc.)	(Sales − COGS) / Sales	Measures the relationship between sales and the costs to support those sales (e.g., manufacturing, procurement, advertising, payroll, etc.)
Return on assets (ROA)	Net income / Total assets	Measures the firm's efficiency in using assets to generate earnings
Return on equity (ROE)	Net income / Total stockholders' equity	Measures earnings to owners as measured by net assets
Return on invested capital (ROIC)	Net operating profit after taxes / (Total stockholders' equity + Total debt − Value of preferred stock)	Measures how effectively a company uses the capital (owned or borrowed) invested in its operations
Return on revenue (ROR)	Net income / Revenue	Measures the profit earned per dollar of revenue
Dividend payout	Common dividends / Net income	Measures the percent of earnings paid out to common stockholders
Limitations	1. Static snapshot of balance sheet.	
	2. Many important intangibles not accounted for.	
	3. Affected by accounting rules on accruals and timing. One-time non-operating income/expense.	
	4. Does not take into account cost of capital.	
	5. Affected by timing and accounting treatment of operating results.	

TABLE 1 *(continued)*

When and How to Use Financial Measures to Assess Firm Performance

Table 1b: Activity Ratios	Formula	Characteristics
Inventory turnover	COGS / Average inventory	Measures inventory management
Receivables turnover	Sales / Average accounts receivable	Measures the effectiveness of credit policies and the needed level of receivables investment for sales
Payables turnover	Sales / Average accounts payable	Measures the rate at which a firm pays its suppliers
Working capital turnover	Sales / Average working capital	Measures how much working (operating) capital is needed for sales
Fixed asset turnover	Sales / Average fixed assets	Measures the efficiency of investments in net fixed assets (property, plant, and equipment after accumulated depreciation)
Total asset turnover	Sales / Average total assets	Represents the overall (comprehensive) efficiency of assets to sales
Cash turnover	Sales / Average cash (which usually includes marketable securities)	Measures a firm's efficiency in its use of cash to generate sales
Limitations	Good measures of cash flow efficiency, but with the following limitations: 1. Limited by accounting treatment and timing (e.g., monthly/quarterly close) 2. Limitations of accrual vs. cash accounting	

TABLE 1 *(continued)*

When and How to Use Financial Measures to Assess Firm Performance

Table 1c: Leverage Ratios

Table 1c: Leverage Ratios	Formula	Characteristics
Debt to equity	Total liabilities / Total stockholders' equity	Direct comparison of debt to equity stakeholders and the most common measure of capital structure
Debt to assets	Total liabilities / Total assets	Debt as a percent of assets
Interest coverage (times interest earned)	(Net income + Interest expense + Tax expense) / Interest expense	Direct measure of the firm's ability to meet interest payments, indicating the protection provided from current operations
Long-term debt to equity	Long-term liabilities / Total stockholders' equity	A long-term perspective of debt and equity positions of stakeholders
Debt to market equity	Total liabilities at book value / Total equity at market value	Market valuation may represent a better measure of equity than book value. Most firms have a market premium relative to book value.
Bonded debt to equity	Bonded debt / Stockholders' equity	Measures a firm's leverage in terms of stockholders' equity
Debt to tangible net worth	Total liabilities / (Common equity − Intangible assets)	Measures a firm's leverage in terms of tangible (hard) assets captured in book value
Financial leverage index	Return on equity / Return on assets	Measures how well a company is using its debt

Limitations

Overall good measures of a firm's financing strategy; needs to be looked at in concert with operating results because

1. These measures can be misleading if looked at in isolation.

2. They can also be misleading if using book values as opposed to market values of debt and equity.

TABLE 1 *(continued)*

When and How to Use Financial Measures to Assess Firm Performance

Table 1d: Liquidity Ratios

Table 1d: Liquidity Ratios	Formula	Characteristics
Current	Current assets / Current liabilities	Measures short-term liquidity. Current assets are all assets that a firm can readily convert to cash to pay outstanding debts and cover liabilities without having to sell hard assets. Current liabilities are a firm's debt and other obligations that are due within a year.
Quick (acid-test)	(Cash + Marketable securities + Net receivables) / Current liabilities	Eliminates inventory from the numerator, focusing on cash, marketable securities, and receivables.
Cash	(Cash + Marketable securities) / Current liabilities	Considers only cash and marketable securities for payment of current liabilities.
Operating cash flow	Cash flow from operations / Current liabilities	Evaluates cash-related performance (as measured from the statement of cash flows) relative to current liabilities
Cash to current assets	(Cash + Marketable securities) / Current assets	Indicates the part of current assets that are among the most fungible (i.e., cash and marketable securities).
Cash position	(Cash + Marketable securities) / Total assets	Indicates the percent of total assets that are most fungible (i.e., cash).
Current liability position	Current liabilities / Total assets	Indicates what percent of total assets the firm's current liabilities represent.

Limitations

Liquidity measures are important, especially in times of economic instability, but they also need to be looked at holistically along with financing and operating measures of a firm's performance.

1. Accounting processes (e.g., monthly close) limit efficacy of these measures when you want to understand daily cash position.

2. No account taken of risk and exposure on the liability side.

TABLE 1 *(continued)*

When and How to Use Financial Measures to Assess Firm Performance

Table 1e: Market Ratios	Formula	Characteristics
Book value per share	Total stockholders' equity / Number of shares outstanding	Equity or net assets, as measured on the balance sheet
Earnings-based growth models	$P = kE / (r - g)$, where E = earnings, k = dividend payout rate, r = discount rate, and g = earnings growth rate	Valuation models that discount earnings and dividends by a discount rate adjusted for future earnings growth
Market-to-book	(Stock price × Number of shares outstanding) / Total stockholders' equity	Measures accounting-based equity
Price-earnings (PE) ratio	Stock price / EPS	Measures market premium paid for earnings and future expectations
Price-earnings growth (PEG) ratio	PE / Earnings growth rate	PE compared to earnings growth rates, a measure of PE "reasonableness"
Sales-to-market value	Sales / (Stock price × Number of shares outstanding)	A sales activity ratio based on market price
Dividend yield	Dividends per share / Stock price	Direct cash return on stock investment
Total return to shareholders	Stock price appreciation plus dividends	
Limitations	Market measures tend to be more volatile than accounting measures but also provide a good perspective on the overall health of a company when used holistically with the other measures of financial performance.	
	1. Market volatility/noise is the biggest challenge with these measures.	
	2. Understanding what is a result of a firm strategy/decision vs. the broader market is challenging.	

Note: Page numbers followed by *n* indicate material in chapter endnotes and source notes.

NAME INDEX

Note: Page numbers followed by *n* indicate material in chapter endnotes and source notes.

A

Abell, D. F., 167*n*
Abernathy, W. J., 197*n*
Abrahamson, E., 234*n*, 365*n*
Adner, R., 53*n*
Afuah, A., 81*n*, 168*n*, 232*n*
Agarwal, R., 298*n*, 378*n*
Agassi, Shai, 16
Agle, B. R., 363*n*
Agung, S., 267*n*
Aime, F., 134*n*
Akerlof, George A., 206, 231*n*
Akers, John, 103
Alchian, A., 231*n*
Alexander, J., 135*n*
Alexandre, M. T., 168*n*, 198*n*, 329*n*, 382*n*
Allen, Paul, 103
Allen, W. B., 82*n*, 263*n*
Alsop, R., 365*n*
Alvarez, S., 197*n*
Amit, R., 110*n*–111*n*
Amram, M., 53*n*
Anand, B., 266*n*
Anderson, Chris, 27*n*, 167*n*, 187, 187*n*, 188*n*, 197*n*, 198*n*
Anderson, P., 197*n*
Anderson, R. C., 81*n*, 128, 135*n*, 167*n*, 363*n*
Andrews, P., 111*n*
Apotheker, Leo, 320, 357
Appleyard, M. M., 266*n*–267*n*, 382*n*
Argote, L., 168*n*
Ariely, D., 364*n*, 365*n*
Arndt, A., 297*n*
Arthaud-Day, M., 83*n*
Arthur, W. B., 28*n*, 52*n*, 111*n*, 197*n*
Audretsch, D. B., 298*n*
Avey, Linda, 15

B

Bacon, Kevin, 39
Bain, J. S., 81*n*
Baliga, B. R., 364*n*
Ballmer, Steve, 3, 47, 103, 246
Banister, Scott, 3
Barkema, H. G., 296*n*
Barnes, F. C., 330*n*
Barney, J. B., 197*n*, 328*n*, 329*n*–330*n*
Barney, Jay, 91, 110*n*, 111*n*
Baron, J. N., 330*n*
Barrett, Craig, 295, 298*n*
Bartlett, C. A., 297*n*, 298*n*
Bartz, Carol, 246, 304, 319, 347
Baruch, L., 135*n*
Baum, J. A. C., 266*n*
Baum, R. J., 329*n*
Beamish, P. W., 297*n*, 298*n*
Beane, Billy, 4
Beechy, M., 135*n*
Behar, Howard, 44, 52*n*, 371*n*
Bengtsson, L., 264*n*
Benner, M., 197*n*
Benson, D., 265*n*
Berle, A., 231*n*, 362*n*, 364*n*
Bernanke, Ben, 233*n*

Besanko, D., 82*n*, 232*n*
Bettis, R., 81*n*
Bezos, Jeff, 94, 180–181
Bienfait, Robin, 365*n*
Bikchandani, S., 234*n*
Bilton, N., 135*n*
Bingham, C. B., 198*n*
Birkinshaw, J., 168*n*, 330*n*
Blakely, Sara, 178
Blumentritt, T., 111*n*
Boeker, W., 264*n*, 364*n*
Bohmer, R. M., 168*n*
Bossidy, L., 328*n*, 329*n*
Bower, J. L., 52*n*, 198*n*, 365*n*
Bowman, Bob, 367
Brady, Larry D., 135*n*
Brandenburger, A. M., 26*n*, 52*n*, 82*n*, 198*n*, 264*n*
Branson, Richard, 353
Breshnahan, T., 263*n*
Breznitz, D., 298*n*
Brickley, J. A., 364*n*
Brin, Sergey, 3, 6, 296, 318, 353
Brown, J. S., 297*n*, 329*n*
Brown, S. L., 52*n*, 53*n*, 169*n*
Brush, T. H., 263*n*
Bryan, L. L., 329*n*
Bryce, D. J., 374*n*
Buchholtz, A. K., 363*n*
Buckley, P. J., 298*n*
Buffett, Warren, 17, 55, 201
Burck, C., 328*n*, 329*n*
Burgelman, R. A., 52*n*, 53*n*
Burns, T., 329*n*
Burt, R. S., 266*n*
Burton, M. D., 330*n*
Byers, T. H., 198*n*

C

Cairncross, F., 27*n*, 297*n*, 298*n*
Calabrese, T., 266*n*
Caldwell, D. L., 330*n*
Cameron, James, 269
Camp, S. M., 197*n*
Campbell, A., 263*n*
Cannella, A. A., 362*n*, 365*n*
Canton, J., 27*n*
Capron, L., 263*n*
Cardinal, L. B., 221*n*, 233*n*
Carlisle, Peter, 367
Carlton, D. W., 82*n*
Carr, A., 28*n*
Carroll, A. B., 340*n*, 363*n*
Cassingham, R. R., 197*n*
Caves, R. E., 83*n*, 296*n*
Ceccagnoli, M., 111*n*, 197*n*, 264*n*
Chandler, Alfred D., 303, 329*n*, 330*n*
Chang, S. J., 296*n*
Chao, G. T., 330*n*
Charan, R., 328*n*, 329*n*
Chatman, J. A., 330*n*
Chen, M. J., 27*n*, 233*n*
Chesbrough, H. W., 111*n*, 198*n*, 266*n*–267*n*, 380*n*, 381*n*, 382*n*
Child, J., 329*n*
Chirac, Bernadette, 350
Chirac, Jacques, 350

Choudhury, N., 52*n*
Christensen, Clayton M., 26*n*, 135*n*, 167*n*, 169*n*, 184, 186, 198*n*, 232*n*
Clark, K. B., 198*n*
Clarke, Robert, 125, 135*n*
Coase, Ronald, 231*n*
Cobbold, I., 135*n*
Coff, R., 28*n*
Cohen, W. M., 198*n*
Coleman, J. S., 266*n*
Coles, J. L., 364*n*
Collins, Jim C., 51*n*, 85, 110*n*, 128, 135*n*, 167*n*, 329*n*, 330*n*, 355, 356, 356*n*, 365*n*, 378*n*
Collis, D. J., 231*n*
Cool, K., 82*n*, 102*n*, 111*n*
Corsten, D., 265*n*
Covey, S. M. R., 266*n*
Crawford, R., 231*n*
Crossan, M. M., 265*n*

D

Daily, C. M., 364*n*
Dalsace, F., 231*n*
Dalton, D. R., 364*n*
Damodaran, A., 28*n*
Darr, E. D., 168*n*
Dassault, Nicole, 350
Dassault, Serge, 350
D'Aveni, R. A., 27*n*, 191, 199*n*
Davis, S. M., 167*n*
Davison, L., 329*n*
Dawson, C., 167*n*
De Colle, S., 363*n*
Deeds, D. L., 168*n*, 231*n*, 265*n*, 266*n*, 369*n*
Deephouse, D. L., 82*n*
de Geus, A. P., 52*n*
DeHart, Jacob, 17
Dell, Michael, 318, 353
Dess, G. G., 168*n*
Devers, C., 199*n*
Dhawan, R., 28*n*
Dickson, W. J., 330*n*
Dierickx, I., 102*n*, 111*n*
Disney, Walt, 318
Dixit, A. K. S., 52*n*, 53*n*, 82*n*
Doherty, N., 82*n*, 263*n*
Dorf, David, 267*n*
Dorf, R. C., 198*n*
Doz, Y. L., 264*n*, 297*n*
Dranove, D., 82*n*, 232*n*
Drucker, P., 26*n*, 27*n*
Dudley, Bob, 60
Duguid, P., 297*n*, 329*n*
Duke, M. T., 26*n*, 42, 52*n*
Dunning, J. H., 296*n*, 297*n*
Dushnitsky, G., 265*n*
Dussage, P., 266*n*
Dvorak, August, 177
Dyer, J. H., 26*n*, 252*n*, 263*n*, 265*n*, 266*n*, 298*n*, 374*n*

E

Eberhardt, V., 51*n*–52*n*
Eckbo, Espen, 357
Edmondson, A. C., 168*n*
Edwards, Mike, 193

Note: Page numbers followed by *n* indicate material in chapter endnotes and source notes.